W9-BNG-589

The Papers of Dwight David Eisenhower

THE PAPERS OF DWIGHT DAVID EISENHOWER

THE PRESIDENCY: KEEPING THE PEACE
XIX

EDITORS

LOUIS GALAMBOS   DAUN VAN EE

EXECUTIVE EDITOR
ELIZABETH S. HUGHES

ASSOCIATE EDITORS
JANET R. BRUGGER   ROBIN D. COBLENTZ
JILL A. FRIEDMAN

ASSISTANT EDITOR
NANCY KAY BERLAGE

THE JOHNS HOPKINS UNIVERSITY PRESS
BALTIMORE AND LONDON

308.1
Ei 83c

This book has been brought to publication with the generous assistance of the National Endowment for the Humanities, the National Historical Publications and Records Commission, the Eisenhower World Affairs Institute, and the France-Merrick Foundation.

© 2001 The Johns Hopkins University Press
All rights reserved
Printed in the United States of America on acid-free paper

The Johns Hopkins University Press, 2715 North Charles Street,
Baltimore Maryland 21218-4363
www.press.jhu.edu

All illustrations in this volume are from the
Dwight D. Eisenhower Library, Abilene,
Kansas, unless indicated otherwise.

Library of Congress Cataloging-in-Publication Data

Eisenhower, Dwight D. (Dwight David), 1890–1969.
The papers of Dwight D. Eisenhower.

Vol. 6 edited by A. D. Chandler and L Galambos;
v. 7– , by L. Galambos.
Includes bibliographies and index.
Contents: v. 1–5. The war years.—[etc.]—
v. 10–11. Columbia University.—v. 12–13. NATO and the
Campaign of 1952.
1. World War, 1939–1945—United States. 2. World War,
1939–1945—Campaigns. 3. United States—Politics and
government—1953–1961. 4. Presidents—United States—
Election—1952. 5. Eisenhower, Dwight D. (Dwight David),
1890–1969. 6. Presidents—United States—Archives.
I. Chandler, Alfred Dupont, ed.   II. Galambos, Louis, ed.
III. United States. President (1953–1961 : Eisenhower)
IV. Title.
E742.5.E37   1970   973.921'092'4[B]   65-027672
ISBN 0-8018-1078-7 (v. 1–5)
ISBN 0-8018-2061-8 (v. 6–9)
ISBN 0-8018-2720-5 (v. 10–11)
ISBN 0-8018-3726-x (v. 12–13)
ISBN 0-8018-4752-4 (v. 14–17)
ISBN 0-8018-6638-3 (v. 18)
ISBN 0-8018-6684-7 (v. 19)
ISBN 0-8018-6699-5 (v. 20)
ISBN 0-8018-6718-5 (v. 21)

80.00

Published in cooperation with
The Center for the Study of Recent American History
at The Johns Hopkins University

EDITORIAL ADVISORY BOARD

William R. Brody

Alfred D. Chandler, Jr.

D. David Eisenhower II

John S. D. Eisenhower

Susan E. Eisenhower

Andrew J. Goodpaster

Steven Muller

Douglas R. Price

William C. Richardson

We dedicate these four concluding volumes of *The Papers of Dwight David Eisenhower* to the Board of Advisors of the Eisenhower Papers and to the Board of Trustees of the Johns Hopkins University, who together made it possible for us to complete this grand project.

Contents

The Papers of Dwight David Eisenhower

The Presidency: Keeping the Peace

IV

Recession and Reform

FEBRUARY 1958 TO MAY 1958

8

"To engender confidence"

To Saud ibn Abd al-Aziz   *February 1, 1958*
Secret

Your Majesty: In view of the great value which I have derived from
past opportunities to consult with you concerning developments in
the Middle East, I am taking the liberty of communicating with you
with regard to announced plans for the establishment of a union
between Egypt and Syria under the title, reportedly, of "United Arab
Republic."[1] Our information as to this development and the forces
behind it is not yet complete and indeed such information as we
have is somewhat conflicting. Nevertheless, it seems clear to us that
the proposed union could carry serious implications for other Arab
states with which we have friendly relations.[2]

However, in order for us to determine if we can assist our Arab
friends, it would be helpful to know their views and position. I understand that the Government of Iraq intends to consult with Your
Majesty's Government and with the Governments of Jordan and
Lebanon with regard to the position which might be adopted. Such
consultation, I believe, would be constructive, and I hope that Your
Majesty will be pleased to share your wise views and counsel with
these Arab states to this purpose.

The opinions of Your Majesty in this matter are of deep interest
to me, and I look forward to receiving them at your early convenience.[3]

May God have you in His safekeeping. *Your sincere friend*

[1] For background on U.S. relations with Egypt and Syria see Galambos and van Ee,
The Middle Way, no. 2147; and nos. 124 and 450 in these volumes. Syria had sought
a union with Egypt since the conclusion of a military pact between the two countries
in 1955. In November 1957 their parliaments had adopted a joint resolution supporting the principle of union, and in mid-January Egyptian President Nasser had
agreed to a merger. Egypt and Syria had announced formation of the United Arab
Republic on this same day (State, *Foreign Relations, 1958–1960,* vol. XIII, *Arab-Israeli
Dispute; United Arab Republic; North Africa* [1992], pp. 403–13).
[2] During the Baghdad Pact Ministerial Meeting, which had been held in Ankara,
Turkey, from January 27–30, various delegates had apparently expressed their concerns regarding the projected Egyptian-Syrian union. Secretary Dulles, who had attended the meeting as an observer, had told Eisenhower that the Middle East members of the pact saw the proposed merger as "an unhappy development which can
presage much trouble." No one at the conference could determine the extent of
Communist involvement, Dulles said, or whether the Communists were merely accepting Nasser's ambition to unify the Arab world under his leadership. Dulles believed that Jordan and Lebanon would feel pressure to join and that Saudi Arabia
and Iraq would be jeopardized. Only a united position among the threatened countries would allow the United States to be helpful to its Arab friends, Dulles said
(Dulles to Eisenhower, Jan. 29, 1958, AWF/D-H; Herter to Eisenhower, Jan. 30, 1958,

AWF/I: Saudi Arabia; and Telephone conversation, Eisenhower and Dulles, Feb. 1, 1958, Dulles Papers, Telephone Conversations).

As part of a plan to consolidate Arab opinion quickly, Dulles had agreed to an Iraqi request that he contact Saudi Arabia, Lebanon, and Jordan, urging their cooperation with Iraq in reaching a unified position. He suggested that Eisenhower make the approach to Saudi Arabia in a personal letter, drafted by State Department officials, to King Saud. The State Department cabled the text of Eisenhower's letter to Saud on this same day. The President and his Secretary of State agreed that any public statement regarding the merger should be withheld until they had received the monarch's views (Telephone conversations, Eisenhower and Dulles, Feb. 1, 1958; Dulles and Berry, Feb. 1, 1958; and Drafts 1 and 2, Proposed Statement, Feb. 1, 1958, all in Dulles Papers, Telephone Conversations; see also *U.S. Department of State Bulletin* 38, no. 975 [March 3, 1958], 332; and NSC meeting minutes, Feb. 7, 1958, AWF/ NSC; and Eisenhower, *Waging Peace,* pp. 262–63).

³ On February 7 King Saud would notify the United States that he would not oppose the Egyptian-Syrian merger as long as both countries freely approved, the union did not harm any other Arab state, and the objective was Arab unity (State, *Foreign Relations, 1958–1960,* vol. XIII, *Arab-Israeli Dispute; United Arab Republic; North Africa,* pp. 419–20). On February 8 Dulles would tell Eisenhower that other Arab countries, unable or unwilling to unite in a common plan, might well recognize the new republic. The United States could not justifiably withhold its recognition, he said, "without renouncing our traditional policy on Arab unity and without giving offense to the popular appeal of Arab nationalism" (Dulles to Eisenhower, Feb. 8, 1958, AWF/ D-H).

After virtually unanimous approval of the union in both Egypt and Syria, the United States would officially recognize the United Arab Republic, with Nasser as its president, on February 24. Iraq and Jordan would form their own federation, the Arab Union, on February 14 (see State, *Foreign Relations, 1958–1960,* vol. XII, *Near East Region; Iraq; Iran; Arabian Peninsula,* p. 293). For developments in Middle Eastern affairs see no. 683.

561   *EM, AWF, Administration Series*

To Arthur Frank Burns   *February 3, 1958*

Dear Arthur: I think the idea that you passed on to me from John Jewkes is excellent, especially in a theoretical sense.¹ When I read his final sentence, however, I wondered—as I often do—where all the money will come from if there isn't some rule of reason applied.²

Thank you very much for your expression of sympathy on the death of my brother Arthur. I deeply appreciate your thoughtfulness.³

With warm regard, *As ever*

¹ Former chairman of the Council of Economic Advisors, Burns had written on January 30, 1958 (AWF/A). Burns had quoted from an article entitled "The Sources of Invention," by John Jewkes, a professor of economic organization at Oxford. In the article, which would later be published in book form (see John Jewkes, *The*

Sources of Invention [London and New York, 1958]), Jewkes had argued for a society with a multiplicity of types of research agencies, such as universities, government research organizations, industrial research associations and nonprofit institutions. Since crucial discoveries could "spring up at practically any point and at any time," governments should try to "maintain the balance between the different sources of invention, to strive to prevent any one dominating to the exclusion of all others."

[2] Jewkes had said: "As contrasted with the ideal ways of organizing effort in other fields, what is needed for maximizing the flow of ideas is plenty of overlapping, healthy duplication of efforts, lots of the so-called wastes of competition and all the vigorous untidiness so foreign to the planners who like to be sure of the future."

[3] See no. 558.

562   *EM, AWF,*
                                                         Administration Series

To Alfred Maximilian Gruenther   *February 3, 1958*

Dear Al: I begin to be impressed by your mail. While I had, of course, assumed that you were writing these documents yourself—not believing anybody else could be so eloquent considering the subject— I think that there must be some other explanation.[1]

In any event, the latest one, from Mr. Walker, gave you an opportunity to set forth in interesting and lucid fashion the problem America has in this cold war business. So even if these "Letters to the Editor" have their origin in your own staff, I still approve of all the things that the answers contain.[2]

At Augusta the bridge was above average in quality; the weather was so bad as to permit one no truly expressive opinion.[3] *As ever*

[1] Gruenther's January 30 note (AWF/A) forwarded correspondence from Paul Walker in response to the request made by Eisenhower on the evening of January 28. Eisenhower had asked for another letter in support of his presidency. "But you didn't think I had one, did you?" Gruenther joked. "Well here it is, just off the top of the pile—merely one of many." Walker was the editor of the *Harrisburg* (Penn.) *Home Star*. His letter, which apparently had praised a speech Gruenther had recently made, is not in AWF.

[2] Gruenther had also included with his note his reply to Walker (AWF/A). Gruenther had written that national security consisted of "much more than military strength." Even if the United States had stationed throughout Europe all the ballistic missiles it wanted, they "would not contribute in the slightest to the amelioration of the poverty and squalor which exist in a large portion of the world," he explained. The cold war was also being fought outside Europe, and the Administration's programs supporting the Mutual Security Act and the extension of the Reciprocal Trade Agreements Act were essential in fighting the battle (see nos. 370 and 524). "The American people must understand clearly that a satisfactory solution will not be reached by military measures alone." Gruenther called on Walker and other com-

munity leaders to urge Congress to pass the Administration's program (Gruenther to Walker, Jan. 30, 1958, AWF/A, Gruenther Corr.).
[3] Eisenhower had left Washington on January 31 for three days of golf at Augusta National Golf Club.

563 *EM, AWF,*
Administration Series

To CHRISTIAN ARCHIBALD HERTER *February 3, 1958*
Confidential

Memorandum for the Under Secretary of State: Commenting on your memorandum of January twenty-nine (Subject: Official Visits in the Forepart of 1958), I note that you mention the possibility of eleven such visits. This would seem to be a reasonably good-sized invasion, and I feel would make up a fair schedule for an entire year. So I am a bit fearful of that word "Forepart."[1]

As far as your specific suggestions are concerned:

1. I feel we should not send President Coty another invitation for this particular year. I have couched our invitation to him in such warm terms, both verbally and in writing, that I think forcing upon him another invitation for 1958 would be embarrassing both for him and for me. It is possible that information has reached you that differs from mine; it is my understanding from President Coty himself that he does not see any possibility of coming to the United States during 1958.[2]

2. I suppose that we should invite either President Mirza or President Chamoun just by way of a compliment to the Mid East.[3]

3. President Ibanez' visit has, of course, already been approved.[4]

4. The visit of President Heuss has likewise been approved. The timing will be satisfactory to me.[5]

5. With respect to Prime Minister Daud and Prime Minister Nkrumah, I am quite ready to see them. In these two instances only a luncheon is indicated since I normally give a luncheon for Prime Ministers and the State Dinners are reserved for the Heads of State.[6]

6. The suggestions on page 2 are approved, provided I am in town at the time.[7]

[1] Under Secretary of State Herter wrote Eisenhower that he would subsequently receive another memorandum with recommendations for visits by Far Eastern and African heads of state during the latter part of 1958 (Jan. 29, 1958, AWF/A).

[2] For background on Eisenhower's invitations to French President René Coty see no. 520.

[3] Iskander Mirza was President of Pakistan; Camille Chamoun was President of Lebanon. Neither would visit the United States in 1958.

[4] Carlos Ibáñez del Campo, President of Chile, would cancel his scheduled visit to the United States in protest over the U.S. policy on copper importation (see State, *Foreign Relations, 1958–1960*, vol. V, *American Republics*, pp. 800–801).

[5] Herter had suggested that President Theodor Heuss of the Federal Republic of Germany visit in late May or early June. He would begin a three-day state visit on June 4 (see Heuss to Eisenhower, Feb. 15, 1958; Krekeler to Eisenhower, Feb. 22, 1958; and Eisenhower to Heuss, June 6, 7, 1958; all in AWF/I: Germany).

[6] Sardar Mohammed Daud of Afghanistan would begin a three-day official visit on June 24. For background on Ghanaian Prime Minister Kwame Nkrumah's meeting with Eisenhower on July 24 see no. 510.

[7] Herter had told Eisenhower that in addition to the official visits a number of heads of state and heads of government wished to come to Washington for brief informal visits in connection with other travel in the United States. Among those Herter included were representatives of the Scandinavian countries, who would be in the United States in connection with the Minnesota State Centennial on May 18–21, Indian Vice-President Sarvepalli Radhakrishnan, Austrian Chancellor Julius Raab, and Shah Mohammed Reza Pahlavi of Iran. Eisenhower would meet briefly with Radhakrishnan on March 19, with Raab on May 19, and with Pahlavi on June 30. None of the Scandinavian prime ministers would visit Washington. Princess Astrid of Norway and Prince Bertel of Sweden, however, would attend a private lunch with President and Mrs. Eisenhower on May 6 (see Ann Whitman memorandum, Feb. 20, 1958, AWF/D-II).

564   *EM, WHCF, Official File 3-K*

To Anna Cleave Tower   *February 4, 1958*

Dear Mrs. Tower: I appreciate your letter and especially your reference to me as a "retired General of the Army."[1] That I consider a high compliment. Never can I possibly lose my feeling of close identification with all Army people and with the Service that for most of my life was the object of my every waking moment.

I have been deeply interested in the question raised in your letter and gave it close attention when the Cordiner proposals were before me.[2] You are correct that the proposal as sent to Congress does not include a pay increase for retired personnel. The reason is that the Cordiner proposals were not devised as a pay raise but rather were intended to modernize and revamp the entire pay structure. The purpose was to attract and retain qualified personnel in the military services. At no time was the central object a pay raise. This being so, it was concluded that the use of these proposals to justify an across-the-board retired pay increase would fly in the face of the entire Cordiner approach.

Beyond question the problems you describe are worthy of the most sympathetic concern. Word has already reached me that the Congressional committees studying this subject are certain to weigh very carefully the considerations outlined above, together with all those which you raise. I suppose I don't have to tell you that such decisions as these are far from easy, but I do expect a just solution of this particular problem before the Cordiner proposals finally become law.[3]

Poor Cornelia—she seemed so unhappy during the last years of her life. I am glad that she gave you the Washington reproduction. If I am not too bold, I shall ask my secretary to send you a Lincoln reproduction as a companion piece.[4]

With thanks for your letter, and best wishes to you and your husband,[5] *Sincerely*

[1] Tower had written on January 20, 1958 (same file as document). She identified herself as "an Army Daughter and also the god-daughter of the recently deceased Mrs. Frank R. Keefer, who has so often spoken of you and your days at the Point." Mary Cornelia Terrell Keefer was the wife of Brigadier General Frank Keefer, a professor of military hygiene at West Point when Eisenhower was a cadet (see Chandler, *War Years*, no. 388). "I am writing to you," she had said, "in no political sense or even in your capacity as President, but rather, because you are a retired General of the Army, and certainly understand the military and all its facets, if anyone does."

[2] For background on the Cordiner Committee recommendations see nos. 73 and 226. Tower was upset by the Military Pay Raise bill pending in Congress (see *Public Papers of the Presidents: Eisenhower, 1958*, p. 9). Although pay raises for retired personnel had been included in the original Cordiner recommendations, the Defense Department, believing that such raises were not consistent with plans designed to "attract, retain and motivate highly qualified personnel within the active forces," had dropped the proposal (Hawkins to Goodpaster, Jan. 27, 1958, same file as document).

[3] For developments see nos. 721, 969, and 1230.

[4] Tower had written that Mrs. Keefer had given her a reproduction of Eisenhower's painting of George Washington. Tower said that she was "deeply honored" by the gift and would "treasure it" (for background see Galambos and van Ee, *The Middle Way*, no. 1617).

[5] Tower would respond on February 10 (same file as document). She would thank Eisenhower for the reproduction of his portrait of Lincoln, and for explaining the main purpose behind the Cordiner proposals. "It gives me a better understanding of the bill," she said, "and I trust Congress will act on it to the best advantage of all Service personnel."

TO FRANK RICHARDSON KENT   *February 4, 1958*
Personal

Dear Mr. Kent: Recently I learned that you have not been feeling up
to par; that, in fact, you have had to be hospitalized for the past several weeks.[1] I do hope that soon you will be able to resume your
normal routine.

I cannot claim to be one of those who have known you well, except through your writings. Indeed, I am sure that you will have no
memory of a meeting of ours of many years ago. I think that I was
a major at the time, but ever since I have retained the hope that
some day I would have the opportunity of an informal chat with you
about "shoes and ships and sealing wax—and cabbages and kings."[2]

At any rate, I wish for you a speedy return to your accustomed
health and vigor and, of course, many years of good health.[3] *Sincerely*

[1] Kent, a syndicated columnist and author, had joined the staff of the *Baltimore Sun*
in 1898 and had been managing editor from 1911–1921. His column, "The Great
Game of Politics," had been featured in some 140 newspapers since 1922. See *The
Great Game of Politics: An Effort to Present the Elementary Facts about Politics, Politicians,
and Political Machines, Candidates and Their Ways, For the Benefit of the Average Citizen*
(Garden City, N.Y., 1926). Kent's last column had appeared on January 5. The President probably had learned of Kent's illness and stay at Johns Hopkins Hospital
through Milton Eisenhower, president of The Johns Hopkins University.
[2] Eisenhower, who held the rank of major between 1924 and 1936, probably met Kent
in 1924 while stationed at Camp Meade, Maryland, where he coached the Third
Army Football Squad. Between 1927 and 1935 Eisenhower held assignments in Washington, D.C., in the offices of the Chief of Infantry, the Assistant Secretary of War,
and the Chief of Staff.
  The President was quoting Lewis Carroll's poem, "The Walrus and the Carpenter."
[3] Kent would die on April 14 (see *Baltimore Sun*, Apr. 15; and *New York Times*, Apr. 15,
17, 1958).

566   *EM, AWF, Name Series:*
                                      Disability of President Memo

TO RICHARD MILHOUS NIXON   *February 5, 1958*
Personal and secret

Dear Dick: As both of us know, there are differences of opinion as to
the exact meaning of that feature of the Constitution which provides that the Vice President will have the powers and the duties of

the President when the President is unable to discharge them. There is uncertainty expressed as to how there could be determined the degree of the President's disability that would justify transferring his powers and duties to the Vice President.[1]

An inability to discharge properly the powers and duties of the Presidency could come about in several ways. One would be disease or accident that would prevent the President from making important decisions. Such periods of inability could be prolonged but, even if only the length of hours, could require action should there be any question of real importance and urgency to be decided without delay.

Another form of inability could come about through a failure of communications between the President and the Capital at any time that he might be absent therefrom. A somewhat similar case might be an uncertainty about the whereabouts of the President, occasioned by a forced landing of the Presidential airplane.

Other types of inability could unquestionably arise.

There have been many proposals for clarifying this situation, some by law, others by Constitutional Amendment. My own opinion is that it would be difficult to write any law or an Amendment in such fashion as to take care of every contingency that might possibly occur. While the great area of uncertainty now existing could and should be drastically reduced, I am not sure that even the most carefully devised plan, objectively arrived at, could remove doubt in every instance.[2]

However, it seems to me that so far as you and I are concerned in the offices we now respectively hold, and particularly in view of our mutual confidence and friendship, we could do much to eliminate all these uncertainties by agreeing, in advance, as to the proper steps to be taken at any time when I might become unable to discharge the powers and duties of the President. Based upon my studies of the history of the Constitution and upon the advice of Constitutional authorities, I am of the opinion that this agreement would not in any way contravene the clear intention of the Constitution; on the contrary, it is rather a statement of our common intention to act completely according to the spirit of this portion of the Constitution.

Through such an agreement, we can assure that the best interests of the country would not be damaged by the doubts and indecisions that have at times existed in similar cases in the past. Moreover with this advance agreement, you could without personal or official embarrassment, make any decisions that seemed to you proper in cases where my ability to discharge my powers and duties may be in serious question.

This note, which I have been planning for some time to write, is merely to confirm, in writing, the gist of the agreement that you and I have reached between ourselves.[3]

It is simply stated:

In any instance in which I could clearly recognize my own inability to discharge the powers and duties of the Presidency I would, of course, so inform you and you would act accordingly.

With the exception of this one kind of case, you will be the individual explicitly and exclusively responsible for determining whether there is any inability of mine that makes it necessary for you to discharge the powers and duties of the Presidency, and you will decide the exact timing of the devolution of this responsibility on you. I would hope that you would consult with the Secretary of State, Governor Adams and General Heaton, and if feasible, with medical experts assembled by him, but the decision will be yours only.

I will be the one to determine if and when it is proper for me to resume the powers and duties of the Presidency.

I know, of course, that you would make any decision for taking over the presidential powers and duties only when you feel it necessary. I have no fear that you, for any fleeting or inconsequential purpose, would do so and thereby create confusion in the government. Circumstances would have to guide you, and if the imminence or occurrence of any world or domestic emergency demanded, you would have to act promptly.

There is always the possibility that, as in the cases of Garfield and Wilson, I might, without warning, become personally incapable of making a decision at the moment when it should be made.[4] The existence of this agreement recognizing your clear and exclusive responsibility for deciding upon the inability of the President to perform his duties and exercise his powers will remove any necessity or desire on the part of friends and staffs to impede the right and authority of the Vice President in reaching his decision on the matter.

There is only one final thought I would like to add. If any disability of mine should, in the judgment of any group of distinguished medical authorities that you might assemble, finally become of a permanent character, I would, of course, accept their decision and promptly resign my position. But if I were not able to do so, and the same group of consultants would so state, then you would take over not only the powers and duties but the perquisites of the Presidency, including the White House itself. In temporary cases of my "inability," we agree that you should act for the necessary period in your capacity as Vice President and, additionally, as "Acting President."[5]

With warm regard, *As ever*

[1] On Eisenhower's concern for an orderly transfer of power to the Vice-President in the case of presidential disability see nos. 58 and 107.

[2] In January the President had contemplated drafting a letter of resignation to be effective when a committee of five people of his own choosing should decide he was disabled (Ann Whitman memorandum, Jan. 3, 1958, AWF/AWD). After a discussion with Nixon, Eisenhower had asked White House aide Gerald Morgan to draft a letter, instructing him to discuss the matter with no one but the Attorney General. The letter was to state that should a disability take place, the committee could decide that the Vice-President should take over; at a later time, the committee could decide when the President was able to resume his duties. Eisenhower cited as an example, the possibility that he might be involved in an automobile accident, fall into a coma, but be perfectly able, after a time, to resume his duties. The President suggested that the committee be composed of Attorney General William Rogers, Senate Majority Leader Lyndon Johnson, Republican House Leader Joseph Martin, Jr., and Major General Leonard Heaton, the Commanding General of Walter Reed Army Hospital. Eisenhower suggested that the fifth person on the committee might be the Secretary of State, or the Surgeon General of one of the services. He added that he wanted an alternate named in case any member of the committee could not serve (see Ann Whitman memorandum, Jan. 3, 1958, AWF/AWD; see also Eisenhower, *Waging Peace*, pp. 231–35).

[3] After his advisers persuaded him that a disability committee was impractical, Eisenhower would meet with Rogers and Nixon on February 8, giving both men a copy of his letter. Word of a secret "understanding" between Eisenhower and Nixon would leak, causing Eisenhower to release to the press key portions of the letter on March 3 (see Eisenhower to Dulles, Feb. 7, 1958; Ambrose, *Nixon*, vol. I, *The Education of a Politician, 1913–1963*, pp. 451–55; see also *Public Papers of the Presidents: Eisenhower, 1958*, pp. 188–89, 198; and *New York Times*, Mar. 1, 4, 1958).

[4] Although President James Abram Garfield had been shot on July 2, 1881, he did not die until September 19 of that year. Thomas Woodrow Wilson, twenty-eighth President of the United States, suffered a stroke that had left him partially paralyzed in October 1919. The incapacitation of both men had raised serious constitutional questions concerning who should properly perform the functions of the presidency. See Allan Peskin, *Garfield* (Kent, Ohio, 1978); Woodrow Wilson, *The Papers of Woodrow Wilson*, ed. Arthur S. Link, vols. 1–69 (Princeton, N.J., 1966–94), vol. 63, *September 4–November 5, 1919* (1990), pp. 542–646; August Heckscher, *Woodrow Wilson* (New York, 1991), pp. 611–44; and Robert H. Ferrell, *Ill-Advised: Presidential Health and Public Trust* (1992), pp. 11–20. See also Eisenhower, *Waging Peace*, pp. 647–49.

[5] A bipartisan effort to deal with this problem would not be successful during 1958. The Twenty-fifth Amendment to the Constitution, regularizing procedures in the case of presidential disability, would not be ratified until 1967 (see *New York Times*, Mar. 5, 1958; see also *Congressional Quarterly Almanac*, vol. XIV, *1958*, p. 77).

567   *EM, AWF, Administration Series*

To Robert Cutler   *February 5, 1958*

Dear Bobby: It is difficult for me to think of anything that I would refuse to do that would be helpful to you personally, or that has your enthusiastic support as a public service.

But when you ask me to go on a radio program on behalf of Harvard University, you immediately place problems in my lap with other institutions, especially Columbia and Johns Hopkins.[1]

I could quite easily make an appearance supporting any project of the AAU or some such organization and would be glad to do it.[2] But to go on a program for one institution, no matter what its degree of importance, would really create some embarrassment for me.

The actual physical burden of making a tape for radio is nothing; it is only the individual character of the sponsorship that worries me. *As ever*

---

[1] Cutler, who had written on February 4 (AWF/A), held degrees from Harvard University and was vice-chairman of the overseers committee of Harvard Medical and Dental Schools. The University, he said, was campaigning nationally to raise $82.5 million from alumni, other private citizens, charitable foundations and corporations, all for the benefit of the college (as distinguished from the graduate schools). Cutler noted that the campaign reflected Eisenhower's "views of how a private educational institution should seek to increase its resources to serve the people." Cutler had attached a petition signed by Harvard University executives asking the President to record five or six sentences to be included in the nationwide broadcast. Eisenhower had been president of Columbia University from 1948–1950; his brother Milton had been president of The Johns Hopkins University since July 1956.

[2] This was the Association of American Universities. On Eisenhower's views regarding support for higher education see nos. 416 and 485.

568

To Winston Spencer Churchill
February 5, 1958

[*Dear Winston:*] Many thanks for your note.[1] Mamie and I are reserving Tuesday, the twenty-second of April, through Friday, the twenty-fifth, for your visit to the White House. We hope that Clemmie will be feeling well enough to accompany you.[2]

I believe the exhibition of your paintings opens at the Smithsonian on the evening of the twenty-fifth, and I am asking Joyce Hall if it might not be possible for you and me, together, to visit the showing privately the same day.[3] You may, of course, want to attend the formal opening, but I usually like to avoid crowds, if possible. I am, of course, holding you to your promise to give me one of the paintings; I assure you it will have *the* place of honor in the Eisenhower home.[4]

I hear that the exhibition is drawing unprecedented numbers in

Kansas City; the New York and Washington papers gave considerable space to it, which is an unusual thing for them to do for any midwestern event.[5]

Please let me know what, if any, social affairs you would like Mamie and me to hold in your honor. We want to do whatever you would like. If you prefer, we can keep your visit entirely a "family" affair.[6]

With warm regard, *As ever*

[1] On January 23 the President had invited former British Prime Minister Churchill to stay at the White House in April (see n. 3 below). Churchill had accepted on January 29 (both in AWF/I: Churchill; see also *New York Times*, Feb. 4, 8, 1958; for background see n. 3 below).

[2] Churchill, who was vacationing in Roquebrune, France, said he had forwarded Eisenhower's invitation to Lady Churchill, who was in London recuperating from "repeated doses of influenza."

[3] In March Churchill had agreed to exhibit thirty of his paintings in ten U.S. cities. Hall, president of Hallmark, Inc., had arranged the exhibition (see nos. 86 and 415).

[4] Churchill had renewed his offer to present to Eisenhower a painting of his choice (for background see no. 222).

[5] Churchill said he would never have risked "vaunting" his pictures before "a mighty nation" but for Eisenhower's encouragement. The January 22 opening of the exhibition had broken attendance records at the William Rockhill Nelson Gallery of Art in Kansas City (see Eisenhower to Franklin D. Murphy, Jan. 22; Franklin D. Murphy to Churchill, Jan. 23, Hall to Whitman, Jan. 24, Hall to Eisenhower, Jan. 24, Whitman to Hall, Jan. 28, Franklin D. Murphy to Eisenhower, Jan. 28, and Eisenhower to Franklin D. Murphy, Feb. 3, 1958, all in WHCF/PPF 833; *New York Times*, Jan. 19, 1958).

[6] As it turned out, poor health would force postponement of Churchill's visit (see undated memorandum and Churchill to Eisenhower, Apr. 8, 1958, both in AWF/I: Churchill). For developments see no. 668.

569   *EM, AWF, Name Series*

To Milton Stover Eisenhower   *February 7, 1958*

Dear Milton: Although the idea of a vacation in Wisconsin at Larry Fisher's place sounds very attractive I suspect that the thing that appeals to me about it most—the isolation—is the thing that would defeat us from accepting his hospitality next summer. I simply cannot be in a place where communications are not almost instantaneous, and I frankly feel that Mamie would not be too happy in such a setting. So, on balance, I think you better tell him that for the time being he better forget the idea. At the same time, do assure him that I am deeply appreciative of his continued thoughtfulness.[1]

With warm regard, *As ever*

[1] Milton had written on February 3 to extend an invitation from business executive Lawrence Peter Fisher to the Eisenhowers, their friends and servants. Fisher was vice president of Fisher and Company, a director of General Motors Corporation and of Continental Illinois Bank and Trust Company. Fisher owned "the greatest fishing place in Wisconsin and Michigan," Milton wrote. On the property, consisting of 25,000 acres of "native timber" and clear water lakes full of large and small mouth bass, walleyes, and trout, were a main house, a guest house, a cooking and dining cottage, a caretaker's cottage, and boats. Milton had warned of probable poor communication facilities. For background on the brothers' shared interest in fishing see no. 235.

570   *EM, AWF, Name Series: Hobbs Corr.*

To John Foster Dulles   *February 8, 1958*

Dear Foster: I am just in receipt of a letter from Major General Leland S. Hobbs, who was my West Point class mate and a very fine Division Commander in World War II.[1] I quote below that part of his letter which is not purely personal:

> "Since my retirement from the Army, I have been with this bank. My assignment in the International Division of the bank is to secure mutually profitable banking activities in countries of the Far East (specifically, Japan, Philippines, Taiwan, Korea, Thailand, Viet Nam, and Hong Kong) and most especially, at this time, obtaining *government* funds of the countries involved.
> "In making a proposed trip to those countries, it is felt that letters of introduction are essential to make sure of successful results—those letters to be from appropriate persons in your administration to their counterparts in the administration of the countries listed, and also to our Ambassador to those countries, and it is to ask your aid in securing these letters, that this note is sent to you."

Of course I am quite sure that General Hobbs is not seeking any unfair advantage for himself, but I am rather puzzled as to what I can do in the circumstances.

Without bothering yourself personally about the matter, would you ask one of your staff to give me a memorandum?[2] *As ever*

[1] Hobbs, an international banker with Colonial Trust Company in New York, had been commanding general of Fort Dix, New Jersey, before his retirement from the Army (for further background see Galambos, *Chief of Staff*, no. 547, and Galambos and van Ee, *The Middle Way*, no. 824). He had written on February 4. On this same day Eisenhower would inform Hobbs that a staff member would review the matter and advise him shortly.

[2] Acting Secretary of State Herter would notify the President on February 12 that

the State Department routinely requested "Foreign Service posts to extend appropriate courtesies, including introductions," to private American citizens. Herter offered to direct a personal request for Hobbs, and advised that he send a detailed itinerary to the State Department. With his memorandum Herter had included a "Suggested Reply to General Hobbs" (n.d.). Eisenhower would instruct Hobbs (Feb. 12) to write directly to Herter. Hobbs would thank Eisenhower on February 17. All correspondence is in AWF/N and AWF/N, Hobbs Corr.

571   *EM, AWF, Name Series*

To Joel E. Carlson   *February 10, 1958*

Dear Joel: I deeply appreciate the expressions of sympathy of Carolyn and yourself on Arthur's death. His passing leaves, as you well know, a great void in the Eisenhower family circle. I am glad that you had the opportunity to know him for the fine man that he was.[1]

My cold is still with me, but it seems to be an affliction that I share with at least half of Washington. Mamie and I have been looking forward to a vacation in Georgia starting this week, but the weather is so miserable everywhere that I am not sure whether it is worthwhile making the trip or not.[2]

With affectionate regard to you both, and many thanks for your note. *As ever*

[1] Carlson, Mrs. Eisenhower's maternal uncle and a banker from Boone, Iowa, had written on February 4 (AWF/N). Carolyn was his wife. The President's brother, Arthur, a Kansas City banker, had died on January 26 (see no. 558). Carlson had written that he had appreciated Arthur's integrity and pleasant disposition.
[2] Carlson said he hoped that the President's cold would not interfere with his plans to vacation in Thomasville, Georgia (see no. 578).

572   *EM, AWF, Administration Series*

To Raymond J. Saulnier   *February 11, 1958*

Dear Dr. Saulnier: I have read carefully your memorandum of February tenth.[1] I concur with the several actions that have been proposed by those who were present at the "Finance" meeting Monday evening and at the breakfast meeting yesterday morning. Some of the individuals were, of course, present on both occasions.[2]

One thing about which I now have some concern is that unless there is an effective and simple method of achieving coordination in all governmental efforts to bring about a prompt upswing of the economy, we might easily tend to defeat ourselves.

Since our talks have ranged all the way from hoped-for action on the part of the Federal Reserve Board through the means for expediting housing construction, urban renewal, placing of defense contracts and securing some legal authorization from the Congress, it is clear that we will operate better if some one individual can be on this kind of job full time. There is first of all the Council of Economic Advisers, the Treasury Department, Defense, Commerce, Labor, FHA, and literally a dozen others that can be helpful not only in what they do but in the way they do it. By this I mean that since the problem is as much psychological as it is material, we want to act intelligently so as to engender confidence as well as increased activity.[3]

What are your comments? *Sincerely*

[1] Saulnier's memorandum on "The Business Outlook and Its Policy Implications" is in AWF/A. He said that the current recession, which in its severity was comparable to that of 1953–1954, seemed to have accelerated "rather rapidly" in January, and that more "stimulus" was needed if a "prompt recovery" was to be achieved. Saulnier reviewed the steps taken to ease credit and the difference between the steps taken in the earlier recession and the present one. He concluded that the recession was "now far enough advanced, however, that reliance must be placed increasingly on expenditure and tax policy," and outlined steps the government should take. For background on the recession see no. 429.

[2] On the evening of Monday, February 10, Eisenhower had met at the White House with Saulnier, Treasury Secretary Robert Anderson, Federal Reserve Chairman William McChesney Martin, and White House aide Gabriel Hauge. Attending the February 11 breakfast meeting were Saulnier, Vice-President Nixon, Commerce Secretary Sinclair Weeks, Labor Secretary James Mitchell, Postmaster General Arthur Summerfield, Deputy Budget Director Maurice Stans, Press Secretary James Hagerty, and White House aides Gabriel Hauge and Wilton Persons. On February 12 Eisenhower would issue a statement on the economic situation in which he sought to alleviate public concern and to explain government plans to ameliorate the recession (see *Public Papers of the Presidents: Eisenhower, 1958*, pp. 151–52).

[3] Saulnier would respond on February 14 (AWF/A), saying that he had asked Thomas Potter Pike (A.B. Stanford 1931) to "assure coordination in our efforts to bring about a prompt upswing in the economy." Pike, a special assistant to the Secretary of Defense, had served as Assistant Secretary of Defense for Supply and Logistics from 1954–1956, and as special assistant to the President in 1956 (see also Galambos and van Ee, *The Middle Way*, no. 1344). Saulnier reassured the President that the Council of Economic Advisors would "follow these matters very closely." "I am very happy," he said, "that we have been able to get off so quickly to such a good start." For developments see no. 598.

To Sinclair Weeks   *February 13, 1958*

Dear Sinny: When I wrote to the CAB my letter of February fourth on the matter of the Trans-Pacific Renewal Case, I was under the impression that the effect would be to give me a chance to review the decision next year.[1]

It was suggested to me today that the actual effect was to transfer all jurisdiction back to the CAB. If this is the case should I, or could I, do anything that would give me the opportunity for a complete review in accordance with new facts? I think there is no reason for any very great concern because I recall that Mr. Durfee said that the Board would, in any event, review all the statistics in two years. My only concern is that we do not permit an unjustified monopoly in one of the major trans-oceanic routes when the amount of the traffic is such as to justify some competition without putting any company back on subsidies.[2]

There is no rush in answering this as I expect to be in Georgia for the next eight to ten days.[3]

With warm regard,[4] *As ever*

[1] For background see nos. 224 and 315; see also Galambos and van Ee, *The Middle Way*, nos. 1080 and 1447. On February 4 Eisenhower had written Civil Aeronautics Board Chairman James Durfee, approving the CAB's action denying the Pan American Airlines application to serve Portland and Seattle on its Great Circle Route to the Orient (see Eisenhower to Durfee, Feb. 4, 1958, and other correspondence in WHCF/OF 62). Eisenhower had added, however, that he had been impressed by the growth in traffic between North America and Asia, and he emphasized the Administration's policy to "provide competitive United States service on all international and overseas routes from all gateways," whenever the traffic justified it. He requested that the Board report back to him on the status of this traffic at a later date.

[2] On February 21, 1958, the CAB General Counsel would advise Commerce Secretary Weeks that the action taken was final, and that the President's request for 1958 traffic statistics "did not in any way serve to keep the case open" (Nash to Weeks, Feb. 21, 1958, AWF/A). Weeks would write Eisenhower (Feb. 24, 1958, AWF/A), however, that the CAB had promised in its Opinion of May 3, 1957, to "promptly move to reexamine the current route structure" should future experience indicate that either of the present routes to the Orient would generate sufficient traffic to support additional United States flag operations. If the 1958 figures showed an increase in traffic, Weeks said, "you might appropriately call upon the Board to make good on this promise."

[3] On Eisenhower's Augusta vacation see no. 578.

[4] Eisenhower sent a copy of this letter to White House Special Counsel Gerald Morgan, with a request for Morgan's opinion. There is no record of a written response from Morgan. For developments see no. 1778.

To Nikolai Aleksandrovich Bulganin   *February 15, 1958*

My dear Mr. Chairman:[1] I am in receipt of your communication of February 1. I note that it is a slightly abbreviated and moderated edition of the lengthy and rather bitter speech which Mr. Khrushchev made at Minsk on January 22.[2]

I begin to wonder, Mr. Chairman, whether we shall get anywhere by continuing to write speeches to each other? As I read your successive lengthy missives of December 10, January 8, and February 1, I cannot avoid the feeling that if our two countries are to move ahead to the establishment of better relations, we must find some ways other than mere prolongation of repetitive public debate.[3] In this connection, I have some thoughts to offer.

But first I comment briefly on your latest note.

II.

I tried in my letter to you of January 12 to put forward some new ideas. For example, I proposed strengthening the United Nations by rededication of our nations to its purposes and principles, with the accompaniment of some reduction in the use of the veto power in the Security Council.

That proposal you reject, alleging that it would give to the Security Council a power to "adopt decisions that would be binding on all States" and make it in effect a "world government". That argument is directed to a misrepresentation of my proposal. I suggested that our two nations should, as a matter of policy, avoid vetoing Security Council recommendations as to how nations might proceed toward the peaceful solution of their disputes. Surely authority to *recommend* and that only as to *procedures,* is not to impose binding decisions. Already, the General Assembly can, free of veto, recommend procedures for peaceful settlement. Would it really be catastrophic for the Security Council to exercise that same facility?

III.

Another new idea was that outer space should be perpetually dedicated to peaceful purposes. You belittle this proposal as one made to gain strategic advantages for the United States. Mr. Khrushchev in his Minsk speech said, "This means they want to prohibit that which they do not possess."

Since the record completely disproves that uncalled for statement, may we now hope between us to consider and devise cooperative international procedures to give reality to the idea of use of outer space for peace only.[4]

When the United States alone possessed atomic weapons and the Soviet Union possessed none, the United States proposed to forego its monopoly in the interest of world peace and security. We are prepared to take the same attitude now in relation to outer space. If this peaceful purpose is not realized, and the worse than useless race of weapons goes on, the world will have only the Soviet Union to blame, just as it has only the Soviet Union to blame for the fact that atomic and nuclear power are now used increasingly for weapons purposes instead of being dedicated wholly to peaceful uses as the United States proposed a decade ago.[5]

The Soviet Union refused to cooperate in tackling the problem of international control of atomic energy when that problem was in its infancy. Consequently, it has now become too late to achieve totally effective control although there can be, as we propose, a controlled cessation of further weapons testing and of the manufacture of fissionable material for weapons purposes.

But, as your Government said on May 10, 1955, a total "ban" on atomic and hydrogen weapons could not now be enforced because "the possibly would be open to a potential aggressor to accumulate stocks of atomic and hydrogen weapons for a surprise atomic attack on peace-loving states."[6]

A terrible new menace can be seen to be in the making. That menace is to be found in the use of outer space for war purposes. The time to deal with that menace is now. It would be tragic if the Soviet leaders were blind or indifferent toward this menace as they were apparently blind or indifferent to the atomic and nuclear menace at its inception a decade ago.

If there is a genuine desire on the part of the Soviet leaders to do something more than merely to talk about the menace resulting from what you described as "the production of ever newer types of weapons", let us actually do what even now would importantly reduce the scope of nuclear warfare, both in terms of checking the use of fissionable material for weapons purposes and in wholly eliminating the newest types of weapons which use outer space for human destruction.

IV.

With respect to the meeting of Heads of Government, the cumulative effect of your last three missives is to leave considerable puzzlement as to what you think another such meeting could contribute to a genuine settlement of our problems.

You have proposed, and insisted on, about ten topics which you want to have discussed at such a meeting. I, in turn, suggested some eight topics which I thought should be discussed—strengthening the United Nations, dedicating outer space to peaceful purposes, the reunification of Germany, the right of the peoples of Eastern Europe to choose the form of government under which they would live, and a number of specific proposals in the disarmament field.

I wrote that, if there were to be a top-level meeting, I would be willing to discuss your proposals in good faith if you would so discuss mine. Your answer is that I must be prepared to discuss your proposals but that as regards mine there must, you said "be unanimous agreement of all participants as to the necessity for considering such proposals". In other words, you demand the right to veto discussion of the matters I believe to be vital to peace.

I noted that Mr. Khrushchev devoted a considerable part of his Minsk speech to a discussion of conditions in Hungary, Poland, and East Germany. Does the Soviet Union claim such a proprietary interest in these lands and people that to discuss them is solely a matter of Soviet domestic concern? If not, and if these lands and people can be discussed by Soviet leaders as an international problem, why cannot we both discuss them?

If indeed a top-level conference were to apply the formula that no one is to say anything except what all the rest agree they would like to hear, we would, as I said in my last press conference, end up in the ludicrous posture of our just glaring silently at each other across the table.[7]

Perhaps the impasse to which we seem to have come can be broken by less formal and less publicized contacts through which we would continue to seek to find out whether there can be a top-level meeting which, in the words of my letter to you of January 12, 1958, "would hold good hope of advancing the cause of peace and justice in the world". Exchanges of views effected through our Ambassadors or Foreign Ministers may serve better than what Mr. Khrushchev referred to at Minsk as "polemics" between Heads of Government. The United States is accordingly consulting with some other interested nations as to the desirability of exploring, through more normal channels, the prospects of a top-level meeting which would be adequate as to subjects, and as to which preliminary exchanges would indicate good prospect of an accord. You will understand, of course, that, whatever be the preparatory procedures, these would, as far as the United States was concerned, require the participation of our Secretary of State.

V

"Polemics" will not, I fear, advance us along the path of better relations which is my nation's goal. Indeed, I deplore the constantly mounting accusations within the Soviet Union that the United States is a nation ruled by aggressive war-minded imperialists. Mr. Khrushchev's speech of January 22 is an outstanding example of such charges and indeed they are to be found in your February 1 note.

What is the explanation of such charges? They seem to fly in the face of established history.

Until the end of the First World War, war was generally accepted as a lawful means of conducting foreign policy. But after World War I showed the terrible consequences of such toleration of war, the United States took the initiative in bringing about the Pact of Paris whereby the nations of the world renounced war as an instrument of national policy.[8] An even broader renunciation of force is now found in the United Nations Charter. The United States, which initiated the concept of the international renunciation of force, has sought to adhere scrupulously to that concept.

I am really amazed now to be told by Soviet leaders, who have never even been near this country, that there are in the United States those who, in your words, "utter the dangerous call for preventive war" and conduct "unrestrained propaganda for war". If any such persons exist in the United States, I do not know of them; nor do I know of any "imperialist ruling circles" that are supposedly eager to plunge the world into war in order to make financial gains.

These allegations do not provide the real facts of American life. The real facts are the intense longing of the American people for peace; the working of the American constitutional system which assures that government shall be responsive to the peaceful will of the people; our "built-in" guarantees against the possibility of any United States Government suddenly initiating war; our national dedication to the international renunciation of force as an instrument of national policy; the decisive influence for peace of American religious, labor, intellectual and political leaders and of their organizations.

It is, of course, quite true that our people are flatly opposed to regimes which hold people against their will and which deny the principle on which our nation was founded, that governments derive their just powers from the consent of the governed and can never rightly deprive the governed of their inalienable right to life, liberty and the pursuit of happiness. Our people's rejection of many foreign and domestic aspects of Soviet methods and policies is, however, demonstrably not a moving cause to war. Otherwise we would have struck when we had atomic weapons and the Soviet Union had none; or when we had thermonuclear bombs and the Soviet Union had none.

VI.

When I contrast the actual facts of American life with such portrayals as those of Mr. Khrushchev at Minsk, and indeed of your latest communication to me, I am impressed more than ever before with the enormous difficulties besetting us in attempting to move toward better relations and with the greater necessity than ever before of doing so.

It is possible that Soviet leadership feels it necessary deliberately to misrepresent the American viewpoint. If so, one effect would be to confuse their own people and the people of those Eastern European countries under their domination, who are denied access to world information except as the Soviet leaders permit. Another effect would be to make true cooperation more difficult. Possibly also these misrepresentations constitute blind adherence to what was one of the early tenets of orthodox Communism, namely, that capitalistic societies are by their very nature warlike.

I prefer, however, to assume that these misrepresentations are not willful but result from genuine misconceptions which could be done away with.[9]

VII.

Our two nations are both now exploring and seeking to learn the truth about outer space. But is it not more important to learn the truth about each other? The ambassadorial agreement concluded between our Governments on January 27, 1958, points in this direction. It contemplates exchanges that, it is said, "will contribute significantly to the betterment of relations between the two countries, thereby contributing to a lessening of international tension".[10] I hope that we shall make full use of that agreement. But, for the most part, it deals with exchanges of technicians and specialists in various fields. Would it not be well if, in addition, leaders of thought and influential citizens within the Soviet Union should come to visit the United States, not to acquire technical knowledge but rather to learn at first hand the feeling of our people toward peace and the working of our popular institutions as they affect our conduct of foreign relations[?] Most of the Soviet citizens who exert an influence are strangers to this country with, I fear, totally false conceptions. These misconceptions I should like to see corrected in the interests of better relations. I can assure you that groups of qualified citizens of the USSR coming here for the purpose I describe would receive every facility to learn about our country and our people and the working of our political institutions.

I feel also that we need particularly to be thinking not only of the present but also of the future and of those, now young, who in a few years will be carrying heavy responsibilities that our generation will pass on to them. I think our young people should get to know more about each other. I strongly feel that the recent agreement for the exchange of 20 to 30 students a year is a small step in the right direction, but woefully inadequate.[11] I may write you further on this topic.[12]

VIII.

In the meantime, I reaffirm what has been so often said by Secretary Dulles and by myself. The American nation wants nothing more than to cooperate wholeheartedly with any Soviet Government which is genuinely dedicated to advancing, by peaceful means, the welfare of the people of the Soviet Union. It should, however, be appreciated how difficult it is to generate here the good will which the Soviet leaders claim they want, so long as there remains between our two countries the vast gulf of misunderstanding and misrepresentation that is again revealed by both speeches and written communications of Soviet leaders. If the Soviet leaders sincerely desire better relations with us, can they truly think it helpful for the Soviet Union to continue to pursue the objectives of International Communism, which include the overthrow of other governments? The Moscow Manifesto made last November by the representatives of Communist Parties from 64 nations, and the Soviet Government's official endorsement of the results of the recent Afro-Asian Conference in Cairo could not fail to raise in the minds of our people the question of the real purposes of the Soviet leaders.[13]

We shall nevertheless go on seeking such good relations. And I hope that, if there is a positive response to the concrete suggestion here made, we may perhaps do something toward ushering in a new and better era.[14] *Sincerely*

[1] Secretary Dulles and other State Department officials drafted this letter for Eisenhower after consultations with U.S. Ambassador to the Soviet Union Llewellyn E. Thompson, Jr. According to Ann Whitman, Eisenhower thought that the State Department draft was "too nasty" and consequently the President "softened it somewhat" (Ann Whitman memorandum, Feb. 7, 15, 1958, AWF/AWD; see also Memorandum of Conversation, Feb. 5, 1958, Dulles Papers, White House Memoranda Series; and Telephone conversations, Dulles and Murphy, Feb. 3, 1958; Dulles and Elbrick, Feb. 5, 1958; Dulles and Eisenhower, Feb. 9, 1958; all in Dulles Papers, Telephone Conversations; and Dulles and Eisenhower, Feb. 3, 5, 7, 1958, AWF/D). A copy of this letter as TOPOL 2833 was sent to Paris for the NATO Council on February 11 (AWF/I: Bulganin).

[2] Bulganin's letter is in AWF/I: Bulganin. Nikita Khrushchev, First Secretary of the Communist Party, had delivered his speech before the Conference of Agricultural Workers of the Byelorussian Soviet Socialist Republic. After boasting of Soviet military might and the ability to send missiles with hydrogen warheads anywhere on earth, Khrushchev had asked for an immediate summit meeting without the preliminary diplomatic negotiations Eisenhower had proposed (see State, *American Foreign Policy; Current Documents, 1958*, pp. 730–37; and AWF/I: USSR).

[3] For background on Bulganin's December and January letters and Eisenhower's response (January 12) see nos. 509 and 521.

[4] Eisenhower is probably referring to the launching of the Explorer I earth satellite on January 31 (see no. 548).

[5] On the Baruch Plan for the peaceful uses of atomic energy see Galambos, *Chief of Staff*, nos. 902, 946; and no. 192 in these volumes.

[6] The Soviet disarmament proposals are in *U.S. Department of State Bulletin* 32, no. 831 (May 30, 1955), 900–905; see also Galambos and van Ee, *The Middle Way*, nos. 1523 and 1765.

[7] See *Public Papers of the Presidents: Eisenhower, 1958*, p. 143.

[8] Eisenhower is referring to the Kellogg-Briand Pact, which was signed in August 1928; see Robert H. Ferrell, *Peace in Their Time: The Origins of the Kellogg-Briand Pact* (New Haven, Conn., 1952).

[9] State Department officials substituted this paragraph for one Eisenhower had removed. The original paragraph read: "If indeed Soviet leadership finds it necessary for internal or doctrinal reasons to adhere to theory as against fact, and willfully to poison the relations between our two great countries, with all the risks that this implies, then I fear there is little that can now be done from our side to remedy the situation." According to Ann Whitman, at the last minute the State Department had substituted this paragraph for the one Eisenhower had deleted "and told third level echelon people . . . that it had had the President's approval. I do not believe it had been so approved," she recorded. "Jim [Hagerty] had not talked to him, and I cannot find that he talked by phone to anyone at State" (Ann Whitman memorandum, Feb. 15, 1958, AWF/AWD).

[10] On the East-West exchange agreement see *U.S. Department of State Bulletin* 38, no. 973 (February 17, 1958), 243–47.

[11] The agreement had provided for the exchange of twenty students in the academic year 1958–1959 and thirty students in the following year. For more on Eisenhower's desire to expand the program see no. 552.

[12] Eisenhower would not write Bulganin on this subject. Eisenhower drafted such a letter, but Dulles, according to Ann Whitman, "was not enthusiastic" (Ann Whitman memorandum, Feb. 10, 1958, AWF/AWD). Eisenhower would, nevertheless, continue to work on this proposal (Dulles 58/3/21 #1; see also Eisenhower, *Waging Peace*, p. 411).

[13] On the Moscow Manifesto see no. 521. Five hundred delegates had attended the Afro-Asian Peoples' Solidarity Conference from December 26 to January 1. For the joint declaration issued at the close of the conference see U.S., Department of State, *American Foreign Policy; Current Documents, 1958*, pp. 1073–74.

[14] For West German Chancellor Konrad Adenauer's reaction to Eisenhower's letter see Eisenhower to Adenauer, Feb. 22, 1958, AWF/I: Adenauer; for developments see the following document.

To Harold Macmillan   *February 15, 1958*
Secret

Dear Harold: Now that you have returned from your Commonwealth tour there are two matters about which I feel I should write you.[1] I am happy that during your trip you have taken opportunities to promote our mutually held views on both these subjects.

The first of these relates to the substance of your very helpful discussions with members of the New Zealand Government as well as your public statements during your visit there. I much appreciate your kind references to me and my efforts but more especially I am pleased that you took this opportunity to exchange with members of that government certain views regarding the Far East that you and I share. I feel sure that your observations will go far toward correcting some misapprehensions.[2]

I am also glad that during your visit to Australia and more recently in your reply to Bulganin's second letter you have emphasized your belief—and mine—that unless most careful preparations precede a summit meeting such a conference would end in failure.[3]

In this regard I feel that the Soviets may have overplayed their hand especially with Khrushchev's Minsk speech and Bulganin's latest letter to me.[4] Public opinion here, as well as the attitude of some of our legislative leaders, appears to be hardening against our being rushed precipitately into a summit meeting without that insistence on preparation that would carry some hope of its success. My impression is that a similar modification of earlier attitudes may be taking place among thoughtful people elsewhere.

We shall continue to point out the need for that degree of preparatory work that will permit us to participate in a top-level meeting once we have full knowledge of what we shall talk about, how we shall treat those topics, and, to the extent of our foresight, where our discussions may lead us.

With your help I believe we shall be able to hold the line despite the efforts of the Soviet leaders to exploit those understandable hopes for peace for which even an ill-prepared summit meeting would seem to hold promise.

I believe that all our efforts should now be directed toward laying the best possible foundation on which a summit conference may be based. Preliminary conversations with the Soviets at the diplomatic level might well be initiated soon as a step toward determining those areas in which some substantial results might be achieved. Along this path I think we can proceed in sufficiently ordered manner toward a truly promising summit meeting.[5] *As ever*

[1] Macmillan had returned on February 14 from a five-week tour of six Commonwealth nations (see Macmillan, *Riding the Storm*, pp. 375–414).

[2] On January 23, in a statement made in Wellington, New Zealand, Macmillan had said that anyone who believed the propaganda about differences in U.S.-British policies was unwittingly helping the Communist cause (*New York Times*, Jan. 24, 1958). In his other public speeches Macmillan had endorsed the economic relationships between the Commonwealth countries and the United States. The ANZUS Treaty, he added, should be accepted "without cavil" (Macmillan, *Riding the Storm*, pp. 397–402; on the treaty signed in 1951 by Australia, New Zealand, and the United States for the defense of the Pacific area see Galambos, *NATO and the Campaign of 1952*, no. 1033).

[3] A summit meeting would not be fruitful, Macmillan had told Bulganin, "unless the ground has been thoroughly prepared in advance and it is clear from this preparatory work that there is broad agreement on the nature and order of the agenda and a real desire among all who participate in the meeting to make practical progress towards a settlement of the differences between us" (*Documents on International Affairs, 1957*, pp. 65–66). His letter to Bulganin, Macmillan would write, met "the American anxieties without abandoning my own position" (Macmillan, *Riding the Storm*, p. 409).

[4] See the preceding document.

[5] Macmillan would tell Eisenhower that there was "an expectation all over the world that a summit meeting should take place . . . although all sensible people accept the view that there should be proper preparation." He would suggest, as a next step, that a definite date be set, perhaps in late July or August, depending on the outcome of the preliminary meetings (Macmillan to Eisenhower, Feb. 20, 1958, same file as document). Dulles would tell Eisenhower that fixing a date before the NATO Council had had a chance to review procedural matters would be "a great mistake" even though Macmillan was "being hard-pressed by the Labor Party to move quickly in this field" (Dulles to Eisenhower, Feb. 21, 1958, AWF/D-H). For developments see no. 581.

576   *EM, AWF, International Series:*
                                                              Macmillan

To Harold Macmillan   *February 22, 1958*
Secret

Dear Harold:[1] By now you will have heard through your Embassy here in Washington of our agreement to the proposals in your message of February 16 for modifications of language in the IRBM agreement.[2]

I understand your problem on the question of manning the missiles, and we shall do our best to see to it that no statements from our side refer to the possibility of interim manning of initial IRBMs by United States personnel. There is already press speculation on this point but publication of the agreement may well reduce this, especially in view of the statement in the agreement that missiles will be manned by United Kingdom personnel.[3]

I know we are agreed that it is in our common interest to achieve the earliest possible deployment of IRBMs in the United Kingdom. Because of the time factor in training British personnel, our military believe if we are, in fact, to achieve the earliest possible deployment, it will be necessary for United States personnel to man initially the IRBM squadron scheduled for deployment to the United Kingdom this year. However, I concur with your thought that we can deal with details of this matter later in the year. I would, at the same time, point out that this question of manning is largely a technicality, since your Government and ours would have joint operational control, as they do on SAC bomber bases in the United Kingdom, regardless of whether the equipment is manned by United Kingdom or United States personnel.[4]

With warm regard, *As ever*

[1] Eisenhower, who was vacationing in Thomasville, Georgia, approved the State Department draft of this letter.

[2] For background on the development of the intermediate range ballistic missile see Galambos and van Ee, *The Middle Way*, no. 1663. In July 1956 Donald A. Quarles, then Secretary of the Air Force, had conducted preliminary discussions with British officials regarding the possibility of stationing U.S. guided missile units in the United Kingdom (State, *Foreign Relations, 1955–1957*, vol. XXVII, *Western Europe and Canada*, pp. 664–65). Eisenhower and Macmillan had discussed the proposal at their conference in Bermuda in March 1957, and on April 18 Defense Secretary Wilson had submitted the draft of an agreement to the British minister of defense (see no. 82, and State, *Foreign Relations, 1955–1957*, vol. XXVII, *Western Europe and Canada*, pp. 690–93, 700–703, 733–40, 746–47, 777–78). See also Watson, *Into The Missile Age*, pp. 167, 512–19, 542–43. For the communiqué issued after the Bermuda meeting see *U.S. Department of State Bulletin* 37, no. 928 (April 8, 1957), 561–62.

[3] Concerned that the agreement might not receive public support in Britain, Macmillan had asked Eisenhower to modify the language of the proposal to reassure the British people that the weapons would be operated by their own forces. If the missiles were installed before British personnel had been trained, and U.S. personnel had to take over in the interim, Macmillan thought that the Americans and the British could "deal with it quietly" between themselves. "If anything were to be said, either by one of our officials or of yours, in a press conference or elsewhere, about United States personnel operating the missiles to begin with, there would be hell to pay" (Macmillan to Eisenhower, Feb. 16, 1958, AWF/I: Macmillan; see also Macmillan, *Riding the Storm*, pp. 474–75). For the text of the agreement see *U.S. Department of State Bulletin* 38, no. 977 (March 17, 1958), 418–19.

[4] On the future stationing of IRBM's in other countries see no. 1189.

To Arthur Frank Burns   *February 24, 1958*

Dear Arthur: Your letter of the eighteenth didn't catch up with me until today. I appreciate your explanation of the newspaper stories.[1]

I am wondering if you could do anything publicly to set the record straight—such as a letter to TIME magazine, for example. Unfortunately, certain of our opponents have seized upon your remarks avidly; apparently the opposition has determined to concentrate its fire, recklessly in my opinion, on fanning the recession.[2]

I have just heard of the recent death of your father; you have my deepest sympathies.

With warm regard,[3] *As ever*

[1] Burns's letter is in AWF/A. Burns explained that the February 16 *New York Times* had erroneously interpreted remarks he had made to visiting alumni at Columbia University. The *Times* had suggested that Burns had criticized Eisenhower's handling of the recession and urged "prompt and massive intervention." Burns wrote that he had, in fact, made the following points: that while an upturn in the economy might occur, there was still no evidence that such an upturn was imminent; that if an upturn did not occur within several months, the government would "almost certainly" intervene, and on a large scale if necessary; and that in any case the recession would "prove to be a relatively brief and mild movement." Burns also noted that the *Times* had later run "a very constructive editorial" on his talk, repeating his emphases on the mildness of the recession and "on its unfortunate exploitation by the political opposition" (see *New York Times*, Feb. 16, 18, 1958). For background on the recession see no. 469.

[2] Burns would respond on February 28, 1958 (AWF/A), saying that he would present his views on the economics and politics of the recession during a scheduled speech in Chicago on March 22. He had concluded that "some clarification of government policy is now badly needed," and suggested that Eisenhower should state: "I both hope and expect an early upturn in the economy, as I have previously stated. Of course, no one can be certain about the precise timetable of recovery. Hence, I want to assure the American public that, in the event that definite signs of recovery should fail to appear within the next few months, I will *strongly recommend to the Congress a prompt and sizable reduction in both personal and business taxes.* I say this because I want everyone to know beyond any shadow of doubt that the government will take decisive steps, if that should become necessary, to promote recovery and to restore full prosperity" (italics in original). Such a statement, Burns said, would "greatly bolster the confidence of both consumers and businessmen," providing the "psychological basis for an early recovery."

[3] For developments see no. 604.

To George Magoffin Humphrey   *February 24, 1958*

Dear George: I have just written a separate note to Pam, but there were so many things I wanted to mention to you that I doubted would be of interest to her, I make this a separate letter.

Most importantly, of course, I want to thank you and Pam for a happy, restful, and most enjoyable ten days. I find that I relax completely at Milestone, due largely to the low-pressure atmosphere that you and Pam manage to successfully maintain.[1]

I am of course delighted that we got a chance to shoot for the final few days. At least we had a lot of fun even if the birds were wild. Incidentally, I have been somewhat at a loss to explain what could have happened to cause the difference between the way our birds acted on Saturday and the way Pete's performed.[2] Ours were so wild, as you know, that the dogs never had a real point on a covey. Pete says that his shooting was the easiest he has had all season, with the dogs behaving beautifully and with no difficulty whatsoever. Now in our case we had a piece of ground that Gordon reports as having been untouched throughout the season.[3] Consequently one would think that the birds would be tame and easy to shoot. Actually we were letting go at long shots, birds were getting up from behind us, and birds were running like deer when once we had marked them down at the end of a flight. In other words, it would have seemed that our conditions *should* have been ideal.

Anyway, it was a lot of fun and in a way I would rather have had the exciting conditions that we had rather than the more nearly perfect situation that Pete described.

Have a good trip to Europe; I shall look forward to seeing you when you return.[4]

Once again my most appreciative thanks for absorbing our menage so effortlessly and for giving us all a fine "vacation." *As ever*

---

[1] The Eisenhowers had vacationed at the Humphrey's Milestone Plantation in Thomasville, Georgia, February 13–23. For background on what Eisenhower referred to as the "annual pilgrimage" see nos. 7 and 131; and Eisenhower to Whitney, February 5, 1958, AWF/A.

[2] On February 22 the President, Humphrey, and W. Alton ("Pete") Jones had hunted quail at Greenwood, the Thomasville estate of Ambassador John Hay Whitney. Apparently, Eisenhower had lost a hunting wager with Jones (see Galambos and van Ee, *The Middle Way*, no. 1764; Humphrey and friend to Whitney, Feb. 22, 1958, AWF/A; and Eisenhower to Jones, Feb. 24, 1958, AWF/N).

[3] Gordon Simmons probably managed Whitney's estate.

[4] Humphrey and Eisenhower would meet on June 16 at the White House.

To George Edward Allen

Dear George: Now that I am back in Washington—after a taste of the desert air—I realize why you insist on staying away so long.[1]

But I am reminded more forcibly about this birthday business of yours. The only way that I can see that you continue to drop so far behind me in the count of the passing years is that you have a birthday only once every four. From this a lot of advantage can accrue, particularly for Mary. She can save her money on buying birthday presents for you. However, since I figure that you are statistically now something like fifteen years old, this possibly means to her that she still has to teach you some manners and to watch for budding romances. It may be, however, that statistics are not always as revealing as they should be accurate.

At any rate in this very confusing situation, I felicitate you once again on the successful completion of another year of your brilliant years and wish for you many happy birthdays, even if they must be four years apart.[2]

With warm regard, *As ever*

[1] The preceding day the President had accompanied Mrs. Eisenhower from Thomasville, Georgia, to Phoenix, Arizona, to Maine Chance Farm, a resort operated by the Elizabeth Arden cosmetics company. In the afternoon Eisenhower had played a full round of golf at the Paradise Valley Club before dining with the First Lady. He returned to Washington by "sleeper plane" (see the preceding document; *New York Times*, Feb. 23, 24, 1958; and Ann Whitman Diary, Feb. 24, 1958, AWF/AWD).

[2] Allen was born on February 29, 1896.

To Edward Everett Hazlett, Jr.

Dear Swede: Since I want both to send you felicitations for that nonexistent birthday of yours and to answer, at least briefly, some of the comments in your most recent letter (which I enjoyed tremendously, as I always do), I shall try to limit myself to those subjects you bring up and not go off on my usual lengthy, and I like to think philosophical, discourse.[1]

Now as to your points. Please don't concern yourself about any lack of coherence, if such there ever might be, in your letters. The important thing is that you don't tire yourself in writing them. I always like to have your thoughts, and they don't have to be in any logical order for them to be of value to me.[2]

As for my recent physical mishap, never at any time did I feel *ill*, so I don't deserve any special commendation for making the Paris trip. My only apprehension was about the formal speeches I knew I would have to make, and, to some extent, concerning the informal conferences with the various heads of government. But all in all, the experience was pleasant and I think all to the good. I especially got a kick out of my visit to my old SHAPE Headquarters.[3]

With reference to the illness itself, apparently months will be needed to complete the full cure. But the only symptom I notice now is a tendency to use the wrong word—for example, I may say "desk" when I mean "chair." But that tendency seems to be decreasing and people who haven't seen me for months say, honestly I think, that they notice a much improved condition in this ailment.

You know how I feel about the Secretary of State, both from previous letters and from the many public statements I have made. I admire tremendously his wisdom, his knowledge in the delicate and intricate field of foreign relations, and his tireless dedication to duty.[4] Apparently with strangers his personality may not always be winning, but with his friends he is charming and delightful. In addition to Mr. Dulles, Secretary Benson and Governor Adams are two individuals who have been, in my opinion, unjustly attacked.[5] They are also dedicated and completely honest men. But in this business sometimes glibness gives more surface reward than does honesty.

Speaking of personalities, the new Russian Ambassador to the United States, Mr. Mikhail Menshikov, is making quite a splash in Washington. He is extremely affable, good-looking (I am told by the ladies of my family) in the "Western sort of way" (whatever they mean by that), energetic and apparently not impressed with protocol procedures (which break with routine I admit I find refreshing). Only time will tell whether his appointment is in any way indicative of a change in official Russian policy.[6]

Oh yes, I agree completely that Bob Montgomery erred in his "stage directions" for the report to the nation immediately after the NATO Conference.[7]

Now to go back to your letter and to my health. I am trying to follow the advice of the doctors. I want to keep well and conserve my energy as much as possible for the tasks that lie ahead of me. But it is not easy since politicians have a habit of making me ill— mentally and physically! I cannot, for example, understand why any one, Democrat or Republican, would want to fan the flames of the so-called "recession" for his own political advantage at the expense of all Americans.[8] But you know as well as I do that such a thing is done daily for the cheap advantage that certain people feel they will gain personally. In the same category I put the request of some thirty Congressmen that I "fire" Benson simply because they are so avid for more governmental handouts for the farmers in their districts.[9]

Already we are in the special fever of a campaign year. If a Republican Congress could be elected it would be the neatest trick of the week. The brickbats that will be thrown at me I shall ignore, and I shall concentrate, as I have tried to do in the past, upon our national security, upon inching toward a just and durable peace for all the world, and upon sustaining the health of the American economy.

Secretary McElroy is, in my opinion, one of the best appointments that could be made. He may have started out, as you say, without too much enthusiasm for service integration, but I think he is changing his views. He has, incidentally, absorbed with unexpected rapidity the enormous complexity of the Defense Department and will, I think, make a tremendous contribution there.[10]

This whole business of inter-service rivalries has been greatly distressing to me, and to all of us. I am sure you are as sick as I am of public debates among Generals and the Secretaries of the various services.[11] You referred to the German General staff system.[12] I venture that few people really understand what happened under that so-called system. Their General Staff was *Army*.*[13] For that it was superb. But military separation in compartments was marked. Even the Ministry of War in 1914 had nothing to do with the General Staff.

I have had endless discussions in my office on the relative merits of the nuclear submarines versus nuclear aircraft carriers. I agree with you completely that the flattop is becoming obsolete and I have tried, and will continue to try, to convince the Navy big brass that their only possible use would be in a *small* war. Here you get down to an *intra* service rivalry that presents its problems, too.[14]

As for the columnist you mention, I merely say that I have not read a word of his in fifteen years. Personally I think he is a "spherical" SOB which makes him one no matter from what angle you may view him. And as for the prophecy you mention, I had not heard of it before. He *could* of course be right. But I think the good Lord will have more to do with what happens than this particular columnist.[15]

You bring up the fact that retired officers are not included in the Administration's recommendations for "cost of living" increases. These recommendations were based on the Cordiner report, which was designed to keep in the services young, able officers and *real* technicians. While the Cordiner report provided for very large increases in senior grades, the theory was that this would keep young officers in the service permanently. The general policy was to ignore all others. (This report was made, of course, when inflation was our number one domestic problem.) I think we might review the matter now, and I am assured by the experts that, in any event, the Congress will, for its own political reasons, see that retired personnel are included when the issue is finally decided.[16]

I mentioned briefly the "recession" that is worrying everyone today. We are watching the economy closely and I still believe, as I said in my last press conference, that there will be more employment opportunities by mid- or late March. But this may mark the "beginning of the end" of the recession; it will be quite a while before we reach the "end of the ending." I shall never approve a tax cut for political reasons, but there are certain economists who believe that *if the recession continues*, we may have to give serious consideration to the possibility.[17]

And a few brief points—I agree with you completely with regard to Bourguiba and I deplore the situation the French have gotten themselves, and indirectly us, into. Gaillard is inexperienced (though in this specific instance I do not believe he was to blame) but basically he seems to have some of the marks of a capable leader.[18]

Now we come to the Summit Conference. If we and our allies can first agree on the positions we will take on the various subjects that will be discussed; if the Russians will agree to a preparatory conference at a lower level; and if they will promise to abide by the agreements made at the preparatory conference—then, and only then, I am willing to meet with them. If this procedure is followed, I think we can at least hope for some success; anything else is bound to bring dismal failure.[19]

I think I have covered all your comments except the most important ones—the fine Navy football game of last year, your health, and your birthday anniversary. I was proud of Navy's team (except on one day that need not be mentioned) and I watched them on TV whenever I could.

As you know without my telling you, I am distressed about the seeming lack of progress in your physical condition and I keep hoping that the doctors will find something that will make you more comfortable. I am glad you have decided to come back to Bethesda for another go-round and I shall keep praying that the doctors there will come up with something that will help you.

And now you are about to have a birthday anniversary, an event that I suspect you regard with as much dislike and disdain as I do. But at least you have had to endure only fifteen or sixteen actual such days, while I have that imposing sixty-seven always to contemplate. But I fancy even that is little enough comfort in view of falling chests, hair and energy. At any rate you know that my prayer is that your birthday "present" for the next year will be better health.[20]

With affectionate regard to Ibby and all the best to yourself, *As ever*
P.S. Please let me know when you come to Bethesda; otherwise, I
shall have to employ my special intelligence system.

[1] Hazlett was born February 29, 1892. Eisenhower had made extensive marginal notations on his letter of January 20, 1958, labeling them "notes for reply" (AWF/N).
[2] Hazlett had apologized for not having written after Eisenhower's "slight stroke," explaining that each day he had hoped to be "up to writing you a worthwhile letter.
But it just didn't work out that way." Instead, he had at last decided to take Eisenhower's advice and write a "piecemeal letter." "There will probably be little coherence to it, but I will at least try to write a few lines whenever I am up to it," he said.
On Hazlett's health see no. 457.
[3] On Eisenhower's stroke see nos. 470 and 477. On the NATO meetings see no. 501.
On the visit to SHAPE headquarters see no. 543.
[4] Hazlett had commented that he had been pleased that during a news conference,
Eisenhower had rejected suggestions that he should replace Dulles. The President
had called the Secretary of State a "top notch man." See nos. 511 and 529.
[5] On Benson see no. 553; on Adams see nos. 393 and 553.
[6] Mikhail Alekseevich Menshikov, former Soviet minister of foreign trade and ambassador to India, had been appointed Soviet ambassador to the United States on February 10. Eisenhower would meet with Menshikov on the following day, and would describe him as "the only Russian I have ever seen smile outside of Zhukov" (Ann
Whitman memorandum, Feb. 11, 1958, AWF/AWD; see also Buchanan, Memorandum
of Conversation, Feb. 11, 1958, both in AWF/I. USSR, Telephone conversation, Dulles
and Eisenhower, Feb. 11, 1958, Dulles Papers, Telephone Conversations and AWF/D).
[7] Hazlett had criticized Robert Montgomery's staging of the President's December
23 speech on the NATO conference (see *Public Papers of the Presidents: Eisenhower,
1957*, pp. 847–49). When Eisenhower spoke, the television cameras had been focused
on him alone, Hazlett pointed out, but when Dulles spoke, the cameras had included
Eisenhower in the picture. The President had looked "decidedly ill at ease," Hazlett
said. "I think it would have been better to have you cut out at such times. It must be
difficult to know that the cameras are on you for minutes at a time when you have
nothing to do, and the whole world is watching."
[8] See no. 577.
[9] See no. 553 and *New York Times*, Feb. 22, 23, 26, 1958.
[10] Hazlett had written that he was "greatly pleased" with Eisenhower's choice of McElroy as Secretary of Defense. "McElroy seems to have got the feel of his job in short
order, and has impressed those gents on The Hill favorably. I'm afraid, though, that
you can't expect too much enthusiasm on his part as regards further tightening of
the bonds of service integration. As you undoubtedly know, he ran P-G [Proctor and
Gamble] on the theory of inter-departmental rivalries." On service integration see
nos. 401 and 549.
[11] On Eisenhower's concern over interservice rivalries see no. 390.
[12] Hazlett had expressed his "delight" that Eisenhower was taking personal interest
in the reorganization of the Defense Department. "With your firm hand at the helm,"
he said, "I feel sure I have nothing to fear about the General Staff system being imposed upon us. As you well know, the Germans failed completely to coordinate their
services in either World War." For a discussion of the German general staff see J. D.
Hittle, *The Military Staff: Its History and Development* (Harrisburg, Penn., 1961), pp. 50–
85, and Richard A. Preston, Sydney F. Wise, and Herman O. Werner, *Men In Arms:
A History of Warfare and Its Interrelationships with Western Society* (New York, 1962),
pp. 248–49, 266.
[13] Eisenhower clarified his comments with a footnote: "I am referring here to the

justly famous General Staff of 1914. Of course under Hitler there was a personal Chief of Staff that could presumably issue orders to any service. Actually Goering, as long as he was in favor, went his own way."

[14] Hazlett had said that he had heard "many outstanding things about these super-subs." "Personally," he added, "I'd rather we invested in ten nuclear submarines than one nuclear flattop—at about the same outlay. But I may be a bit biased." On intraservice rivalries see Watson, *Into the Missile Age*, pp. 40–44, 456–59.

[15] Hazlett had reported that Drew Pearson had predicted that Eisenhower would not be President by December 1958, implying that Eisenhower would have another stroke or heart attack.

[16] Hazlett had written that he was "a bit disappointed" that the Military Pay bill had not included "even a nominal 'cost of living' increase for retired officers. While his personal situation was secure, he called the move "manifestly unfair to those already retired" (for background see no. 564).

[17] Eisenhower was responding to Hazlett's concern that he might be forced into approving a tax reduction for political reasons. "Election years make things tough for you," he said. "But I also know that you'll do what you think is right, regardless of politics." See no. 577.

[18] Hazlett had asked Eisenhower how much longer the United States could tolerate the "totally irresponsible" actions of the French regarding Tunisia. He had also expressed his sympathies for Habib Bourguiba, the newly-elected Tunisian president and had asked Eisenhower if the young French Prime Minister Félix Gaillard "was dry behind the ears yet." For background on the U.S.-French conflict over supplying arms to Tunisia, U.S. relations with Bourguiba, and Eisenhower's opinion of Gaillard see no. 451.

Franco-Tunisian relations had deteriorated after France had accused the Tunisian National Guard of aiding rebels in a January 10 attack on a French patrol in Algeria. France had suspended all negotiations with Tunisia regarding military aid and, when Bourguiba refused to discuss the incident, Gaillard had recalled the French ambassador and negotiators. On February 8 a French warplane had bombed an open-air market in a Tunisian border village, killing approximately one hundred people. The attack was presumably in retaliation for the downing of a French airplane by anti-aircraft fire from the Tunisian side of the Algerian border. Eisenhower had told Secretary Dulles that France should "disavow the action and offer to pay reparations" (State, *Foreign Relations, 1958–1960*, vol. XIII, *Arab-Israeli Dispute; United Arab Republic; North Africa*, pp. 819–31; Telephone conversations, Dulles and Eisenhower, Feb. 9, 1958, Dulles Papers, Telephone Conversations and AWF/D; and Dulles and Hagerty, Feb. 10, 1958, Dulles Papers, Telephone Conversations; and Irwin M. Wall, "The United States, Algeria, and the Fall of the Fourth French Republic," *Diplomatic History* 18, no. 4 [1994], 494–95, 503–5). For developments see no. 586.

[19] Hazlett had told Eisenhower that although he had no "fixed ideas" regarding a summit conference, the President would be wasting his time unless the prospects showed "a real promise of concrete achievement." For background on the progress toward a summit conference see nos. 574 and 575.

[20] For developments see no. 622.

To Harold Macmillan   *February 26, 1958*
Secret

[*Dear Harold:*] I have your recent cable, including the suggestion that we should meet informally here in Washington. I enthusiastically concur.[1]

You indicated that if you should accept the two invitations already extended, you would be in the States between May thirty-first and June eighth. My own interest is in the latter date. If you could come back from De Pauw to be in Washington on the ninth, I would keep that day free for our meeting.[2]

I have President Heuss here on the dates June fourth to sixth inclusive, and some tentative engagements which may become quite important in the earlier part of that week.[3]

Do you think we could agree on the ninth? If you find that date satisfactory, Foster and I will make it a fixed engagement on our calendars.

If the ninth would be too late for you, I am sure that we could work out a schedule for the second.

From the reports I have received you got by splendidly with your speech of the other day. I am delighted. I hope that your presentation may cool off some of the burning, but completely unjustified, opinions that an unprepared "Summit" meeting could do the free world any good. I think we should fully expect the opposite result.[4]

On the other hand, once the NATO nations are agreed among themselves as to what our positions on various matters should be, we could fix a date for preparatory work to be initiated with the Russians.[5] We would further agree with the Soviets that when that preparatory work had received the approval of ourselves and our NATO allies, we would be ready to fix a definite date for a formal "Heads of Government" meeting. But I am quite certain that any attempt to fix a date for the latter meeting merely on the Soviet promise to perform honestly in the preparatory work would result in dismal failure.

I am looking forward to seeing you in June.[6]

With warm regard, [*As ever*]

---

[1] For background see no. 575. Macmillan had suggested that he meet Eisenhower to discuss both "tactics and strategy" regarding the proposal for a summit meeting; he proposed a date sometime between his tentative speaking engagements at The Citadel on May 31 and De Pauw University on June 8 (Macmillan to Eisenhower, Feb. 20, 1958, PREM 11/2327; and Minnich to Whitman, [Feb. 21, 1958], AWF/ D-H).

² Eisenhower also told Ann Whitman that even though it was "not his business," he preferred that Macmillan accept the De Pauw invitation rather than that extended by The Citadel (Telephone conversation, Eisenhower and Dulles, Feb. 22, 1958; and Bernau to Dulles, Feb. 22, 1958, both in Dulles Papers, Telephone Conversations).
³ On West German President Theodor Heuss's visit see no. 563.
⁴ Macmillan had told Eisenhower that in a speech to the House of Commons on February 19 he had tried to strike a balance "between robustness and conciliation" in advocating preliminary meetings before a summit conference. For more on the two-day debate in Britain on foreign affairs see Macmillan, *Riding the Storm*, pp. 470–71; on the U.S.-British positions regarding a summit meeting see no. 575.
⁵ After Eisenhower had read him the draft of this letter, Secretary Dulles told the President that preparatory work by the NATO countries had already begun. Dulles then suggested the inclusion of this sentence, to which Eisenhower agreed (Telephone conversations, Eisenhower and Dulles, Feb. 25, 1958, Dulles Papers, Telephone Conversations and AWF/D).
⁶ Macmillan would meet with Eisenhower on June 9 (see Macmillan to Eisenhower, Mar. 4, 1958, PREM 11/2327; see also no. 652). For developments regarding the summit meeting see no. 588.

582   *EM, AWF, Name Series*

To PHILIP YOUNG   *February 27, 1958*

Dear Phil: I am glad to know of your diligence, but I deplore the toll your devotion to work has taken in your letter-writing proclivities.¹ But if Ambassadors continue to write notes and spring continues to charm you (incidentally, there isn't the slightest hint of spring in Washington for which that poor old jet stream gets blamed) perhaps you can work up a little more activity on that front.

Won't you please tell the Italian Ambassador, if he is still in residence, of my very real appreciation of his note regarding the latest letter to Mr. Bulganin. I took the liberty of showing it to Foster who was, I know, equally pleased.²

I've long known your friend Staf; if he comes to Washington I shall be delighted to see him again.³

Since I live in a kind of global goldfish bowl, it seems rather futile to report to you any of my own activities. Thomasville was *cold*—and we only were able to hunt three days out of the nine we were there. I didn't get in a single game of golf due to the weather, but after a jaunt of some two thousand miles to Phoenix to take Mamie there I managed one round in warm, beautiful sunshine.⁴ Incidentally, Mamie seems to have taken a real liking to the Arizona weather, and winter vacations there might be the best answer despite the distance.

Eric Johnston put on his big bi-partisan day-long meeting in support of the mutual security program on Tuesday. It attracted a tremendous audience, but how much actual good it did in the way of Congressional votes I do not know. I made the final speech of the day. In my talk I did my best to show, once again, the vital importance I deeply feel in the success of the program. I think perhaps I feel more strongly about the rightness of the course we are proposing (and the stupidity of the opponents of the program) than, perhaps, I do about any other issue of the day.[5] Incidentally, you wouldn't like to exchange your preoccupation with crocuses (which I always thought were croci) for a few problems such as the increase in pay for federal employees, or the postal rate hassle, or tackle the gloom and doom boys on the recession issue, would you?[6] And the list doesn't end there, by any manner of means.

At any rate, all I can do is keep on trying.

Give my affectionate regard to Faith, and to young Faith, too, if she is with you.[7] And, as always, the best to yourself. *As ever*

[1] Ambassador Young had written from The Hague that his delay in correspondence supported his contention that he was "very busy" (Feb. 20, 1958, AWF/N).

[2] Young had enclosed a typewritten copy of a note written by the soon-to-be-retired Italian Ambassador to the Netherlands. Eisenhower's letter to Bulganin is no. 574. The President would meet with Secretary of State John Foster Dulles on March 1.

[3] For background on Cornelis Staf, Netherlands Defense Minister since 1951, see Galambos, *NATO and the Campaign of 1952*, no. 465.

[4] Following a vacation in Thomasville, Georgia, the Eisenhowers traveled to a resort in Phoenix, where the First Lady would remain for two weeks (see nos. 578 and 579).

[5] On January 11 the President had asked Eric A. Johnston to arrange a conference of bipartisan business and organization leaders to explore ways of increasing support for the mutual security program (see *Public Papers of the Presidents: Eisenhower, 1958*, pp. 16–17; on Johnston see no. 524). Eisenhower's address on February 25 had been broadcast nationally (see *Public Papers of the Presidents: Eisenhower, 1958*, pp. 176–85). For developments see no. 585.

[6] Young reported that the end of winter had brought a "large number of golden, butter-colored crocuses coming up in thick clumps in the oddest places." Apparently, he wrote, one of his predecessors had a "passion for golden yellow in quantity." After second thoughts about the discovery, he said jokingly, he would not report this to the State Department. For Eisenhower's views of the measure to increase federal employees' salaries see no. 328; on the postal rate hassle see no. 784; and on economic recovery see no. 572.

[7] These were Young's wife, the former Faith Adams, and their daughter.

583   *EM, AWF, DDE Diaries Series*

MEMORANDUM FOR THE RECORD   *February 28, 1958*

From time to time I have received informal recommendations from members of the automobile industry that, in order to have an equal part in collective bargaining with the UAW, there should be industry-wide bargaining on the part of the companies.[1]

Apparently all the companies except General Motors accept this view completely.

In informal conversation with Mr. Curtice, he has made arguments against the proposition. It seems to me as I listen to him that he is really more interested in General Motors' competitive position vis-a-vis the other companies than he is in the establishing of an orderly industry-wide bargaining position.[2]

I have been very careful to avoid any appearance of governmental interference into such matters and such questioning as I have done with Mr. Curtice and others has been merely for information.

Mr. Curtice took the opportunity to describe to me some of the economic consequences of the Supreme Court order requiring DuPont to divest itself of 63 million shares of General Motors stock.[3] I understand from the Attorney General that he has already submitted to the Court a plan for accomplishing the divestiture, at the same time recognizing the need for avoiding economic shocks in throwing this amount of stock suddenly upon the market. The attached memorandum briefly shows Mr. Curtice's views.[4]

Again I listened and questioned only for information, but I did acquaint the Attorney General verbally with Mr. Curtice's conviction that this divestiture will have to be accomplished very slowly and judiciously or some very bad economic effects will occur.

No action is indicated on any of these matters on my part.

[1] A memorandum dated January 10, 1958 (AWF/AWD) explained that Walter Reuther, president of the United Auto Workers, would likely make "excessive" demands on the automobile industry when contracts expired in June 1958. Reuther's tactic would be to target one of the three major companies, while letting the others continue to produce without interference. This tactic would put an "irresistible economic pressure" on the struck company, which would suffer heavy immediate financial loss and long-term damage to its competitive position due to the delay in engineering and tooling for the annual new models. On the labor side, auto union members still working at the unaffected companies would be able to provide strike benefits for idle workers. The memorandum pointed out that one method of countering the monopolistic position of the auto workers union was for industry to conduct joint bargaining, agreeing that if one company was struck to enforce contract demands, the others would immediately shut down. Although the auto companies had in the past opposed industry-wide bargaining, they were beginning to see its advantages.

[2] Harlow Herbert Curtice, president of General Motors since 1953, had been a guest at Eisenhower's February 27 stag dinner. Curtice's position on collective bargaining may have been influenced by the 1948 agreement reached between the United Auto Workers and General Motors, guaranteeing wage increases tied to a cost-of-living index in exchange for labor peace (see William Serrin, *The Company and the Union* [New York, 1973], pp. 169–76; John Barnard, *Walter Reuther and the Rise of the Auto Workers* [Boston, 1983], pp. 135–55; and David Halberstam, *The Fifties* [New York, 1993], pp. 116–30).

[3] Eisenhower was referring to the 1957 Supreme Court decision requiring that Du Pont divest itself of its twenty-three percent share of General Motors common stock. The Court's decision was the final outcome of an investigation begun in 1948 by the antitrust division of the U.S. Department of Justice into whether the Du Pont Company had conspired to acquire control of General Motors, in violation of both the Sherman and Clayton Antitrust Acts (see Charles W. Cheape, *Walter Carpenter at Du Pont and General Motors* [Baltimore, 1995], pp. 233–51; see also *New York Times,* June 4, 1957).
[4] Curtice's memorandum is not in AWF.

584   *EM, AWF,*
                                                     Administration Series

To Alfred Maximilian Gruenther   *March 1, 1958*

Dear Al: Suddenly this afternoon—somewhere between the hospital and the bridge table—I was confronted with the fact that your birthday anniversary is Monday. This note is simply to bring you my warmest felicitations.[1] (You will note, of course, how generous I am; I would not qualify my good wishes with any reference to the possible outcome of our afternoon and evening.)

At any rate, face the day with courage. You'll only be one year older and you are so young *that* couldn't possibly matter. But just wait eight or nine years!

With warm personal regard, *As ever*

[1] The President had had a tooth extracted and had undergone a complete neurological examination at Walter Reed Army Medical Center (*New York Times,* Mar. 1, 2, 1958). For background on the stroke he suffered in November 1957 see no. 477. Gruenther would celebrate his fifty-ninth birthday on March 3; Eisenhower had turned sixty-seven in October.

585   *EM, WHCF, Official File 72-F*

To Jacob Koppel Javits   *March 3, 1958*
Personal

Dear Jack: As a rule I think it is not sound policy for me to prejudge proposed legislation, especially before it has been carefully weighed by all affected Executive agencies. Yet I have some rather specific reactions to your bill, S.3301, which I would like to convey to you in confidence.[1]

In the first place, the function of the National Security Council is advisory to the President. The Council makes recommendations which assist the President in coming to his decisions as Chief Executive in the field of national security. The Council function is not unlike that of the Cabinet in other policy-making fields.[2]

In the second place, it has been my practice while President to utilize the National Security Council as a forum for the frank discussion of important issues of national security. To perform this function effectively, it is vital that only a reasonable number of persons participate in the discussions. I have observed that since the establishment by the Congress of the National Security Council in 1947, one of the main threats to its effective work has been an ever-present temptation by persons not fully familiar with its utility to increase the number of participants to unmanageable proportions.

Thirdly, the number of people who now attend weekly Council Meetings approaches the upper limit of what can contribute to a vigorous and frank exchange of views. In addition to the five statutory members of the Council (the President, the Vice President, the Secretaries of State and Defense, and the Director of Defense Mobilization), there are present, by my invitation at almost every meeting, the Secretary of the Treasury, the Director of the Budget, the Attorney General, the Chairman of the Atomic Energy Commission, the Federal Civil Defense Administrator, the Director of the United States Information Agency, and the statutory intelligence and military advisors to me and the Council (Mr. Allen Dulles and General Twining).[3] Additionally, there are in attendance certain Special Assistants having relevant duties like Mr. Cutler and Dr. Killian, two staff members, and other Executive agency heads attending on an ad hoc basis for particular items. At recent Council Meetings, the number of persons in attendance has approximated twenty.

Lastly, I am in agreement with the point of view that the President should always be free to call upon the wisdom and experience of knowledgeable people from outside of Government. A case in point is the reliance which I place on the President's Science Advisory Committee, which makes recommendations to me on national policies involving science and technology.[4] I have frequently set up special ad hoc groups to study particular problems and, through the Council, to advise me.

Experience has shown to me, however, that the most effective functioning of the Council is obtained through a regular membership made up of the heads of the Departments and agencies who have practical knowledge in the areas under consideration and who will be responsible for carrying out the policies when approved. The daily operational contacts of the Department or agency head are invaluable to recommending workable policy.

Because the President should be free to consult with those whom he feels can provide him with help, their advice should be confidential to the President and, as such, remain privileged. I deeply believe that any statutory requirement that the Council formally report each year, not only to the President but also to the Congress, would render the Council unworkable as an advisory body to the President.

Certainly, the President should have complete freedom to ask advice and counsel from individuals, whither within or without the Government. He may seek such advice and counsel from groups reporting through the Council, or, on the other hand, he may appoint a commission, the findings of which are to be reported publicly. I have used both of these procedures during the last five years.

My main point, in this quick reaction to your letter, is to say that in my judgment it would be unwise to add public members to the Council by statute and to require public reporting by the Council. This would tend to encumber the Presidency and might well result in future Presidents foregoing the use of this valuable advisory body. Such a result would be hurtful and unfortunate.[5]

With warm regards, *Sincerely*

[1] On February 19, 1958, New York Senator Jacob Javits had introduced a bill in the Senate Armed Services committee to increase the membership of the National Security Council by authorizing the appointment of four additional non-military members (*Congressional Quarterly Almanac*, vol. XIV, *1958*, p. 517). He had sent Eisenhower a copy of the bill, with a letter of explanation, on February 24 (same file as document). His action was prompted, he said, by what he believed was a "long-standing suggestion of Bernard Baruch, whom I admire and whom I know as one of your friends, that we ought to have an advisory committee of five to nine members who have had experience in government to advise the National Security Council and give it a lay public base."

[2] On the organization and functions of the NSC see Office of the Secretary of Defense, *History of the Office of the Secretary of Defense*, edited by Alfred Goldberg, 3 vols. to date (Washington, D.C., 1984–1997), vol. I, *The Formative Years, 1947–1950*, by Steven L. Reardon (1984), pp. 23–27; and Alice C. Cole, Alfred Goldberg, Samuel A. Tucker, and Rudolph A. Winnacker, eds., *The Department of Defense: Documents on Establishment and Organization, 1944–1978* (Washington, D.C., 1979), pp. 84–87.

[3] Gordon Gray was Director of the Office of Defense Mobilization. Eisenhower was referring to Treasury Secretary Robert Anderson; Budget Director Percival Brundage; Attorney General William Rogers; Atomic Energy Commission Chairman Lewis Strauss; Federal Civil Defense Administrator Leo Hoegh; United States Information Director George V. Allen.

[4] On the appointment of MIT President James R. Killian, Jr., to the newly created post of Special Assistant to the President for Science and Technology see no. 396. Cutler's title was Special Assistant to the President for National Security Affairs.

[4] See no. 396.

[5] Javits would respond to the President on March 5 (same file as document). "I deeply appreciate the unusual situation of a statutory body to advise the Chief Executive," he would write. "Naturally your wishes in a matter like this must be controlling, and I shall not bruit the matter further." No further legislative action was taken.

To John Foster Dulles   *March 3, 1958*
Personal

Dear Foster: The sentiments expressed by Ladgham, which are reported by Murphy in his cable of February 27th, coincide almost
item by item with my own views. The trick is—how do we get the
French to see a little sense?[1] *As ever*

---

[1] For background on the conflict between France and Tunisia see no. 580. A French
air attack on a Tunisian border village had prompted the Tunisian government to
announce that it would petition the U.N. Security Council to order all French troops
from Tunisian soil. Fearing that the Soviet Union would capitalize on a full discussion of the issue in the United Nations, U.S. and British officials had offered to help
negotiate a settlement. Eisenhower had told the Republican legislative leaders that
in order to keep the "flareup moderated" and to reduce pressure on Tunisia to turn
to the Soviets for help, Deputy Under Secretary of State for Political Affairs Robert
Murphy would provide his "good offices" to both Tunisia and France to aid in negotiations (State, *Foreign Relations, 1958–1960,* vol. XIII, *Arab-Israeli Dispute; United
Arab Republic; North Africa,* pp. 626–28, 823–31; *U.S. Department of State Bulletin* 38,
no. 976 [March 10, 1958], 372; Legislative Leadership meeting notes, Feb. 25, 1958,
AWF/D; and Telephone conversations, Dulles and Elbrick, Dulles and Allen Dulles,
Feb. 9, 1958; and Dulles and Wadsworth, Feb. 17, 1958, Dulles Papers, Telephone
Conversations).

Murphy had met with Tunisian Defense Secretary M. Bahi Ladgham and Foreign
Minister Sadok Mokaddem on February 26. Tunisia, Ladgham had said, wanted to
live as an independent country with close economic and cultural ties to France and
with a foreign policy oriented to the West. The Algerian problem, he said, could only
be solved through negotiations and with the cooperation of France, the United States,
the United Kingdom, Morocco, Tunisia, and the Algerian rebels. These negotiations,
Ladgham had stated, would lead to Algerian independence within the context of a
Franco-North African alliance—a relationship of great benefit to France, which was
"being bled white" (Murphy to Dulles, Feb. 27, 1958, AWF/D-H; see also Robert
Murphy, *Diplomat Among Warriors* [Garden City, N.Y., 1964], pp. 394–96).

During a discussion of Murphy's report with Dulles and Assistant Secretary of State
C. Burke Elbrick on March 1, Eisenhower had said that he thought the time had
come to ask NATO to study the whole problem "as a matter of great urgency," regardless of the effect on U.S. relations with France (Memorandum of Conversation,
Mar. 1, 1958, AWF/D; see also Telephone conversation, Dulles and Holmes, Mar. 1,
1958, Dulles Papers, Telephone Conversations).

After consulting with Elbrick, Dulles would cable this message to Murphy, then in
London, "for his highly personal information" (Dulles to Elbrick, Mar. 3, 1958, *ibid.*).
For developments see no. 600.

To Henry Allen Moe   *March 3, 1958*
Personal and confidential

Dear Dr. Moe: As a general rule I have felt that, in my present position, it was not appropriate for me to recommend any particular individual, but I do want to make an exception in the case of Dr. Hacker. I do so with the understanding that you will keep this letter entirely confidential.[1]

I have the greatest respect for Dr. Hacker's ability as a teacher of history and as a student of economic affairs, but I could not presume to judge, as you ask, the quality of his prior studies. However, based upon my observation when we were associated at Columbia, I can say that I consider his presentation of American historical themes to be extremely vivid, without dramatics or sensationalism, and to be conservative in attitude without any taint of reaction. Certainly he is scholarly and brings to his work a broad background. I consider him also competent and able in research.[2]

I hope that my comments may be helpful to you in some way, but I repeat that there must be many people better qualified to judge the importance of his prior work. I do think his present project is an interesting one and there is much evidence to support his thesis.[3]

With best wishes, *Sincerely*

[1] Moe (B.S. Hamline University 1916; B.A. Oxford 1922; B.C.L. Oxford 1923; M.D. Catholic University Chile 1957), foundation executive and secretary general of the John Simon Guggenheim Memorial Foundation, had written to Eisenhower on February 24 (same file as document). Moe had asked the President for his opinion of the work of Louis Morton Hacker, an economic historian who had listed Eisenhower as a reference on an application for a Guggenheim fellowship. Later this month Eisenhower would recommend Hacker for the presidency of the University of Nevada (see Eisenhower to Terry, Mar. 20, 1958, AWF/D).

[2] In 1949, while president of Columbia University, Eisenhower had appointed Hacker dean of Columbia University's School of General Studies. In February 1958 Hacker had resigned the position to resume teaching (see Galambos, *Columbia University*, no. 448, and *New York Times*, Feb. 4, 1958).

[3] Hacker's prospectus had outlined an economic, social, and intellectual history of the United States, 1870–1900: "The Forty Steelmasters and Their Times." Focusing on the American steel industry, Hacker wanted to rehabilitate the historical reputations of the post–Civil War industrialists, often known to liberal historians as the "Robber Barons." The "emergence of the significant industrial and mercantile enterprisers," he wrote, made the United States the "mightiest industrial nation in the world" by the turn of the century.

On April 27 Hacker would receive the fellowship (see *New York Times*, Apr. 28, 1958). Ten years later his work would be published as *The World of Andrew Carnegie: 1865–1901* (Philadelphia, 1968).

To Harold Macmillan   *March 4, 1958*
Secret

Dear Harold: I have your note of the fourth. In view of the time factor, Foster and I had a talk, after which he called Caccia into his office to explain our views. So I assume that no further reply of substance is required.[1]

As you know, I am convinced that any Summit meeting would be damaging to the free world cause unless some real agreement can be made with the Russians, one in which we can have confidence. This is why I believe so much in adequate preparation. As you point out, however, if prior agreements are going to be made on the items of the agenda, it is clear that there has to be an analysis of the substance of these items in order that joint determination of their suitability can be made.[2]

With warm regard, *As ever*

[1] For background see no. 581. On February 28 U.S. Ambassador to the Soviet Union Llewellyn E. Thompson had sent State Department officials an aide-memoire with the Soviet government's latest proposal for a summit meeting. The Soviets had agreed to U.S. and British stipulations that preparatory meetings of foreign ministers must precede a summit conference. The memorandum stated, however, that preliminary discussions should relate only to the fixing of an agenda, the determination of participants, and the date and place of the conference. Among the approved agenda items were the immediate cessation of testing, the renunciation of the use of nuclear weapons, a non-aggression treaty between the nations of NATO and those of the Warsaw Pact, and the expansion of international trade ties. The internal affairs of the Eastern European nations and the reunification of Germany were excluded from the Soviet list (Thompson to Dulles, Feb. 28, 1958, AWF/D-H; see also Howe to Goodpaster, Feb. 28, 1958, *ibid.*).

In a discussion with Secretary Dulles regarding the U.S. response to the aide-memoire, Eisenhower had said that a summit meeting was "not designed merely to be a spectacle but to conclude serious business." The substance of the meeting, not merely organizational questions, must be decided in advance (Dulles to Eisenhower, Mar. 2, 1958, *ibid.*; see also Telephone conversations, Dulles and Elbrick, Mar. 2, 1958; and Dulles and Knowland, Mar. 3, 1958, Dulles Papers, Telephone Conversations).

Although the U.S. draft reply had commended the Soviet acceptance of preliminary meetings, it disapproved limiting the meetings to organizational questions. Any summit meeting, the memorandum stated, should begin where the preceding Geneva Summit Conference had left off. The issue of German reunification was unfinished business, as was the right of Eastern European countries to choose their own governments. State Department officials subsequently cabled the U.S. response to the North Atlantic Council and to British Prime Minister Macmillan for discussion (TOPOL 3112, Mar. 1, 1958, *ibid.*; see also Telephone conversations, Dulles and Knowland, Mar. 4, 1958; Eisenhower and Dulles, and Dulles and Caccia, Mar. 5, 1958, Dulles Papers, Telephone Conversations).

"The arguments are certainly irrefutable," Macmillan had written, after receiving a copy of the U.S. response. "All the same I am wondering if it quite meets the mood in Europe." He suggested that Eisenhower tell the Soviets that in addition to determining procedure and agreeing on an agenda, the foreign ministers should decide on a priority list of subjects for discussion, without necessarily excluding other topics, should time permit. This procedure would necessitate a discussion of the substance of the items proposed, Macmillan said, and a determination of which items would receive priority (Macmillan to Eisenhower, Mar. 4, 1958, PREM 11/2327).

Discussing Macmillan's letter earlier this same day, Eisenhower had told Dulles that he would not agree to a specific date nor would he accept any agenda that did not include the reunification of Germany (Telephone conversation, Dulles and Eisenhower, Mar. 4, 1958, Dulles Papers, Telephone Conversations and AWF/D).

[2] Both Macmillan and the NATO Council would approve the final draft of the U.S. reply, which Dulles would deliver to Soviet Ambassador Menshikov on March 7 (Dulles to Eisenhower, Mar. 5, 1958; Dulles to Eisenhower, Mar. 7, 1958; and Macmillan to Dulles, Mar. 6, 1958, all in AWF/D-H; and Macmillan to Eisenhower [Mar. 6, 1958], AWF/I: Macmillan; see also *Public Papers of the Presidents: Eisenhower, 1958,* pp. 200–202; and *U.S. Department of State Bulletin* 38, no. 978 [March 24, 1958], 451–53). For developments see no. 611.

589

EM, AWF, International Series:
Macmillan

To HAROLD MACMILLAN
Cable. Confidential

March 4, 1958

Dear Harold: I understand that while both of our governments desire to retain the three-mile limit of territorial sea for security reasons and in accordance with their traditional views on freedom of the seas, both governments are agreed that some concession is necessary in order to prevent the Geneva Conference on the Law of the Sea from approving by a two-thirds majority a twelve-mile, or even broader, territorial sea.[1] The United States view that no (repeat no) concession involving recognition of a territorial sea of more than three miles can be accepted is based squarely upon the security interests of the United States and the entire free world. Accordingly, I am gravely concerned at word that your Cabinet is unable to accept a Canadian compromise proposal retaining the three-mile territorial sea, but permitting a contiguous zone of an additional nine miles in which the coastal state would have exclusive control over fishing, because of the proposal's impact upon fishing interests and communities in the UK.[2] The U.S. supports the Canadian proposal. The British alternative as we understand it is a six-mile territorial sea qualified by other nations' right of overflight of aircraft and of innocent passage of warships without notification as respects the outer three miles. My advisors are unanimous to the effect that the British alternative, even as qualified, is seriously in derogation of free world security interests. The U.S. military authorities feel strongly that they cannot accept any extension of the territorial sea beyond three miles in view of their heavy, world-wide responsibilities for the defense of the free world. This would, for example, afford Soviet submarines, in time of war, an important covered way through neutral waters that they do not now possess. It is the view of the U.S. Delegation to the Conference, shared in Washington, that any retreat from the three-mile limit, such as is involved in the British alternate proposal, will result in Conference approval of a twelve-mile territorial sea with serious damage to our security position vis-a-vis the Sino-Soviet block. The stakes are so great that, I suggest, neither of us should permit commercial considerations to control. I would be deeply appreciative if you and your Cabinet would reconsider your position on this point, if necessary, after urgent consultation between our respective military authorities.[3] *As ever*

[1] The United States had long supported international agreements regarding territorial waters, while maintaining that any proposal for expanding a country's territorial sea beyond the generally accepted three-mile limit must be consistent with the principle of freedom of the seas. Since 1930, however, a growing number of coastal nations had claimed expanded territorial waters, prompting the United Nations General Assembly to call for an international conference to examine the law of the sea. Conference participants were to consider the limits of territorial seas, the concept of freedom of the seas, the status of international fisheries, and the rights over the continental shelf.

At the beginning of the conference, which had opened in Geneva on February 24, the Soviet Union, supported by many African and Asian nations, had submitted a proposal that would allow a nation to determine the limits of its own territorial sea in any width from three to twelve miles. Trying to retain the three-mile concept, the United States had agreed to support the Canadians' proposed three-mile territorial sea limit, with a contiguous zone of nine additional miles for exclusive jurisdiction over fisheries. Freedom of the seas would continue to exist within the nine additional miles for navigation, international cables and pipelines, and air transit. For more on the preparation of the U.S. position in advance of the conference see (State, *Foreign Relations, 1955–1957*, vol. XI, *United Nations and General International Matters*, pp. 570–606; and State, *Foreign Relations, 1958–1960*, vol. II, *United Nations and General International Matters* [1991], pp. 641–51).

[2] On the preceding day Arthur H. Dean, head of the U.S. delegation to the conference, had informed State Department officials that the British Cabinet would not accept the Canadian proposal. Any exclusive fishing zone beyond the three-mile limit, the British claimed, would ruin their commercial operations off the coasts of Iceland and northern Norway (State, *Foreign Relations, 1958–1960*, vol. II, *United Nations and General International Matters*, p. 654).

[3] "We are absolutely at one with you in trying to maintain three miles as the accepted limit, for fisheries as well as for other purposes," Macmillan would reply. Although he agreed that some concessions would be necessary, he told Eisenhower that Britain could not ignore the commercial considerations. To deny British fisherman their traditional fishing grounds, Macmillan said, would cost the nation $150 million or more, would cause severe hardship in areas where other employment was difficult to find, and would affect the national balance of payments (*ibid.*, pp. 654–55). For developments see no. 609.

To Hugh Meade Alcorn   *March 4, 1958*
Personal and confidential

Dear Meade: A friend of mine had the chore of addressing five Lincoln Day Republican audiences.[1]

He was struck by the lack of young people among the groups. Of Kalamazoo he stated, "There were about four hundred and fifty people there and not more than fifty were under fifty years of age." Contrasted to this is the January twentieth dinner in Chicago. It was run by *young* people and it was attended by a large group of *young* Republicans.[2] Is there is not a lesson there?

I hear that some people—possibly tired political prophets—are painting each day darker pictures for the future of the Republican Party. I would like to see more individuals like May, Ayres, Frelinghuysen, Underwood, Galvin and Percy, to say nothing of a somewhat older group like Allott, Morton, Bush and Halleck (and all their associates I could think of who possess something of their fire and energy) start a cult of optimism and work.[3]

Incidentally, when I was a very young boy there was a five cent pulp something on the order of Dick Merriwell. Its name was "Work and Win."[4]

We know that job can be done if we can just get people placed in critical positions who will develop the necessary horse power.[5] *As ever*

---

[1] On Republican fundraising in conjunction with the Lincoln holiday see *New York Times*, February 7, 13, 1958.

[2] On Eisenhower's efforts to promote younger Republicans see Galambos and van Ee, *The Middle Way*, nos. 1782 and 1852. On Eisenhower's January 20 address to the United Republican Dinner in Chicago see nos. 539 and 554; see also *Public Papers of the Presidents: Eisenhower, 1957*, pp. 114–16, and *New York Times*, January 21, 1958.

[3] Eisenhower was referring to Edwin Hyland May, Jr. (B.A. Wesleyan University 1948) who had been elected Republican Congressman from Connecticut in 1957; Republican Congressmen William Hanes Ayres of Ohio; Peter Frelinghuysen, Jr., of New Jersey; and Cecil H. Underwood (A.M. West Virginia University 1952), who had been elected Republican governor of West Virginia in 1957. Charles Harting Percy, president of the Bell & Howell Company, was vice-chairman of the Republican National Finance Committee. Eisenhower may have been referring to Robert W. Galvin, president of Motorola, Inc. Gordon Llewellyn Allott had served as Republican Senator from Colorado since 1955; Thruston Ballard Morton, former Congressman and Assistant Secretary of State for Congressional Relations (1953–1956), had served as Republican Senator from Kentucky since 1957; Prescott Sheldon Bush had served as Republican Senator from Connecticut since 1952; Charles Abraham Halleck, former House Majority Leader (1947–1949, 1953–1955) was Republican Congressman from Indiana.

[4] Eisenhower was referring to Dick Merriwell, younger half- brother of the better known Frank Merriwell, hero of the pulp fiction adventure series by Gilbert Patten.

Work and Win was the title of an adventure weekly for children, frequently featuring the exploits of "Fred Fearnot." See John Levi Cutler, "Gilbert Patten and his Frank Merriwell Saga," *The Maine Bulletin*, 36, no. 10, University of Maine Studies, 2d ser., no. 31 (May 1934), 7–117; and Charles Bragin, *Dime Novels: Bibliography 1860–1928* (Brooklyn, N.Y., 1938).
[5] The President would meet with Alcorn on March 13, 1958. Eisenhower would at first express his opposition to campaigning for Republicans who had "publicly turned against his policies." He later relented, saying that it was hard to refuse someone like Alcorn who, over the objections of his wife, had given up a good law practice and income to aid his party (Ann Whitman memorandum, Mar. 13, 1958, AWF/AWD).

591   *EM, WHCF, Official File 105*

To Melvin Price   *March 5, 1958*

Dear Mr. Price: I have understood that since you wrote to me respecting a nuclear powered aircraft, you have kept abreast of Executive Branch deliberations on this subject through consultations with my staff and with officials of the Defense Department and Atomic Energy Commission.[1] I can now give you my decision on this program.

You mentioned two overriding objectives: first, earliest possible achievement of an operational military aircraft; second, making sure that America is the first nation to produce a nuclear powered aircraft, regardless of its utility, because of the possible world-wide significance of such an accomplishment.[2]

I find no fault with either of these objectives, but unfortunately, in present circumstances, they meet head on. If striving to be first were our shortest road to an operational military aircraft, we long ago would have pursued that course. But at the present state of the art such an effort would divert extremely scarce talent from attacking fundamental problems that must be solved before a militarily important aircraft can be produced. My conviction is that our need for the development of the high priority military aircraft overrides the first nuclear flight objective. Accordingly, I have decided that we should continue to go forward as rapidly as we effectively can with our development program, which at this stage places major emphasis on materials and reactor research, rather than to rush development of a first nuclear flight aircraft which would have little or no practical utility and would delay achievement of an effective military aircraft. We will continue, of course, to watch the developments in this field very closely and will capitalize to the greatest possible extent on such progress as is achieved.

You also stressed the need for well-defined future objectives and completion target dates.[3] The development of a nuclear propelled aircraft capable of military missions has always been the prime goal of this program. This objective is clearly understood by all engaged on the project. Because the program requires development of new materials and techniques beyond the present state of knowledge, the specifying of dates for completion of these endeavors must be somewhat arbitrary and therefore may be unrealistic.[4]

With warm regard, *Sincerely*

[1] Price, Democratic Congressman from Illinois, was chairman of the Research and Development Subcommittee of the Joint Committee on Atomic Energy. He had written the President on October 24, 1957 (same file as document), to ask for his support for the Aircraft Nuclear Propulsion (ANP) project. The Air Force had begun the project in cooperation with the AEC just after World War II. Although two separate approaches were being pursued by 1956, the problem of developing a reactor sufficiently powerful to lift an aircraft equipped with heavy shielding (used to protect the crew from radiation) had not yet been solved. Price's interest in the ANP project had been spurred by the Soviet launch of Sputnik, and by the rumor that the Soviets were about to fly their own nuclear aircraft. See Watson, *Into the Missile Age*, pp. 458–59; Hewlett and Holl, *Atoms for Peace and War*, pp. 516–18; and *Congressional Quarterly Almanac*, vol. XIV, *1958*, p. 252. See also United States Atomic Energy Commission, *Twenty-fourth Semiannual Report of the Atomic Energy Commission, July 1958* (Washington, D.C., 1958), pp. 110–12; and United States Atomic Energy Commission, *Twenty-fifth Semiannual Report of the Atomic Energy Commission, January 1959* (Washington, D.C., 1959), pp. 191–93. Price's letter had been acknowledged by Presidential Aide Bryce Harlow on October 31, 1957 (same file as document). In January 1958 Harlow would ask Presidential Scientific Advisor James Killian for a draft response to Price's October letter: "Isn't there *any* reply we can make . . . ?" (see Harlow to Killian, Jan. 13, 1958, and other correspondence and drafts in same file as document).

[2] Price had said that it was "of paramount importance to the United States to produce such an aircraft first, not only from the standpoint of national security but from the point of view of world opinion and of world confidence in American scientific capabilities."

[3] Price had criticized the nuclear aircraft program for the "lack of incentive and initiative on the part of those who have been charged with the responsibility of conducting the Program." It was, he said, "characterized by the lack of any well-defined future objective, including target dates for completion, and has not had the kind of well coordinated and centralized direction which is necessary for the successful achievement of such an extremely difficult research and development task."

[4] Eisenhower's letter to Price would be published in the *New York Times* on March 7 (see also *New York Times*, Jan. 3, 8, 28, Feb. 18, Mar. 4, 1958). Congress would again hold hearings on the ANP in 1959, but disagreements over research strategies and the value of nuclear aircraft in view of the improvements in missiles and jet aircraft would doom the project. In December 1960 the Secretary of Defense would call the project a "national disgrace," with more than a billion dollars spent and no visible results. President Kennedy would officially terminate the project on March 28, 1961 (Watson, *Into the Missile Age*, pp. 458–59).

MEMORANDUM FOR RECORD   *March 5, 1958*

Memorandum on meeting with Governor Robert Meyner of New
Jersey, March 4, 1958, from 5:00 to 6:20 P. M.[1] Only the two of us
were present.

The discussion was largely based upon friendly observations about
the international and domestic scene. Governor Meyner and I have
been friends for some years and he is quite close to two of my special friends. It was this circumstance through which I first received
his suggestion that we have a meeting.[2]

He had two suggestions, made just before the termination of our
visit.

The first suggestion was that I should invite, again, the Governors
of the several states to Washington. He thought that such meetings
have a very great value for the Governors because thereby they can
get briefings by a number of Cabinet officers and others who are
part of the Federal scene. On the other hand, he felt that the Governors could possibly be helpful in the making of worthwhile suggestions to the Federal government, particularly in the economic
field.[3]

(Incidentally, there were two men of his own party that he mentioned in terms of disparagement. They were the Governor of New
York and the Governor of Michigan.[4] He seems to think that they
are both demagogic and much more personally ambitious than their
own abilities would even remotely justify).

His second suggestion was somewhat more startling. He thought
that I had an erroneous opinion of Mr. Truman and he felt that an
hour's meeting between the two of us could do many things for the
country. He believes that a basis for such a meeting exists in the
demonstrated similarity of Mr. Truman's views and mine concerning the need for mutual security and freer trade.[5]

Governor Meyner went to some pains to say that I should try to
understand that Mr. Truman is a product of the Pendergast machine
and that his standards of conduct when he is in a political campaign
or is discussing any subject that has at any time a partisan political
tenor, are completely different from his thinking and manners at
other times.[6] He believes that Mr. Truman is most intensely concerned with the general welfare of the country and we should not
lose sight of this fact in spite of the intemperate character of his political statements.

The Governor went on to say that should there be any reason for
me to go to a Summit meeting, he thought it would be a ten strike
if Mr. Truman would go along with me.[7] He felt also that on the do-

mestic scene there would be far less division among the thinking of the rank and file of the two political parties if it could become known that Mr. Truman and I had a personal and completely private meeting. (Apparently he did not think it necessary for either of us at such a meeting to explain old misunderstandings—he simply felt that such a meeting once held would make it possible to achieve cooperation in critical times that would otherwise be impossible).

I explained to the Governor some of the reasons that I had been suspicious of Mr. Truman's motives and even his veracity. An example was his recent statement when he said that he had never suggested that I should run for the Presidency. Governor Meyner said that he would share my feelings under such circumstances, but merely stated that Mr. Truman had gotten to the point that he did not believe anything except those things which he wanted to believe. I did not argue the point in any respect, but said that it was a thought that I had kept to myself.[8]

He then said that in the event I ever felt there was validity to his suggestion, he would be pleased to act as an intermediary.

[1] For background see no. 507.

[2] Eisenhower's close friend George E. Allen had arranged this meeting.

[3] In April 1954 Eisenhower had met with the governors of the states and territories who were in Washington for the Governors' Conference. At that time he had briefed them on major problems facing the government (see Galambos and van Ee, *The Middle Way*, no. 781).

[4] Eisenhower was referring to New York Governor W. Averell Harriman and Michigan Governor G. Mennen Williams. Harriman would be defeated in his bid for reelection by Nelson Rockefeller; Williams would win reelection in 1958.

[5] For background see David McCullough, *Truman* (New York, 1992), pp. 908–14, 920–22; and Margaret Truman, *Harry S. Truman* (New York, 1974), pp. 608–9. For Eisenhower's views on mutual security and foreign aid see nos. 60 and 76.

[6] Thomas Joseph Pendergast (1872–1945), the founder of a powerful political machine in Missouri, was the political leader of Kansas City's Democrats for almost twenty-five years. On Truman's relationship with the Pendergast machine see Robert H. Ferrell, *Harry S. Truman, A Life* (Columbia, Mo., and London, 1994), pp. 93–152. See also Richard Lawrence Miller, *Truman: The Rise to Power* (New York, 1986), pp. 217–61.

[7] On plans for the summit meeting see nos. 575 and 611. On March 19 Eisenhower would suggest to Secretary of State Dulles that a prominent Democrat accompany him to the future summit meeting, and he suggested Truman as a possibility. Dulles would respond that he would prefer a Senator such as William Knowland or Lyndon Johnson to Mr. Truman (see Dulles, Memorandum of Conversation, Mar. 19, 1958, Dulles Papers, White House Memoranda Series). See also no. 703.

[8] The former President had criticized Eisenhower and the Republicans during a Democratic fundraising dinner in Washington on February 22 (see *New York Times*, Feb. 23, 1958).

To WILLIAM PIERCE ROGERS   *March 5, 1958*

Memorandum for the Attorney General: I have always taken a deep personal interest in the appointment of Federal Judges. For this reason
I should like that, before you submit a formal nomination for signature, you drop in to confer with me about the matter; if the time
element is important, you can call me on the telephone. It has been
my habit to look over such nominations very carefully before we
have committed ourselves to making them.[1]
     Many thanks.

[1] On Eisenhower's ongoing concern with the appointment of federal judges see, for
example, nos. 299 and 398; see also Galambos and van Ee, *The Middle Way*, nos. 1254
and 1365. According to Presidential Secretary Ann Whitman, Rogers had sent a judicial nomination to the White House without first discussing it with the President.
The two men would meet to talk about the issue on March 7 (Ann Whitman memorandum, Mar. 7, 1958, AWF/AWD). For further developments see nos. 1007 and 1052.

To HAROLD EDWARD STASSEN   *March 5, 1958*
Personal and confidential

Dear Harold: Recently a good Pennsylvania Republican came to me
to argue the suitability of a particular individual for the gubernatorial nomination. The man he had in mind is one that I admire, respect and like.[1]
     I informed my visitor that I had already told you that if you were
successful in the primary I would support you enthusiastically.[2] I can
say nothing more or nothing less than this to anyone else as long
as my candidate for the nomination conforms to my own standards
as to suitability. You may be sure that I shall not, in advance of the
primary, publicly or privately urge the selection of one good candidate over another.[3]
     Now a piece of news. My visitor stated that in recent weeks your
own stock had been going up rapidly in Pennsylvania. He said that
your only real weakness was a noticeable personal resentment on
the part of some of the older bosses in the state. He thought that
even in this respect you had made some advances.[4]
     Finally, he said that aside from his own candidate, he was in your
"corner."
     With warm regard, *As ever*

[1] Eisenhower was probably referring to former U.S. Steel President Benjamin Fairless. On that day the President had called Fairless in Florida to ask him to consider running for Governor of Pennsylvania (Telephone conversation, Eisenhower and Fairless, Mar. 5, 1958, AWF/D). Fairless said that while he would discuss the matter with his wife, his initial reaction was that he was too old (he was born in 1890). In a discussion of Stassen, Eisenhower said that he had a higher opinion of Stassen's abilities than did most people, but he felt that Stassen would have difficulty securing the support of the Pennsylvania Republican organization. See also Telephone conversation, Fairless and Whitman, March 6, 1958, and Graham and Whitman, March 7, 1958, AWF/D.

[2] In February 1958 Stassen had resigned his position as Special Assistant to the President for Disarmament and entered the race for governor of Pennsylvania (see Ann Whitman memorandum, Feb. 7, 1958, AWF/AWD; see also *New York Times*, Feb. 16, 1958, and nos. 182 and 191). Eisenhower had stated publicly that he believed Stassen had many traits that were "admirably fitting" for such an office and called him "a great administrator" and "an indefatigable worker" (*Public Papers of the Presidents: Eisenhower, 1958*, p. 148).

[3] On March 5, 1958, the Pennsylvania Republican organization would select Arthur T. McGonigle, a 51-year-old pretzel manufacturer, to be the organization's nominee in a three-way fight for the party's gubernatorial nomination (*New York Times*, Mar. 6, 1958).

[4] Stassen would reply on March 21 (AWF/A). He noted that it was not his intention to involve Eisenhower in the gubernatorial campaign until after the primary on May 20. However, "from May 21 on, if I am the nominee of the party, I would hope to have your strong support for the final election," he said. Stassen's program would concentrate on four points: "building up industry for more jobs; better school opportunities for youth; streamlining and modernizing the state government; and keystone leadership on the broad issues of national and international problems." Stassen would lose his bid for the Republican gubernatorial nomination; and McGonigle would be defeated in the November election (see *New York Times*, May 21, Nov. 5, 6, 1958).

595

EM, AWF,
Dulles-Herter Series

To John Foster Dulles

March 7, 1958

Dear Foster: If we are to continue this Bulganin-Eisenhower squirrel cage exercise, it seems to me that we should attempt, at the very least, such divergencies in pace and running style as may partially prevent the whole thing from becoming completely monotonous.[1]

I am not ready to suggest any completely new ideas but I am awfully weary of reading, as I do in his latest effusion, exactly the same things that he has put in his last two or three immediately preceding messages.[2] Of course I am ready to admit also that our replies are necessarily hammering away on exactly the same keys. Maybe we can merely change the timing of replies, or their tones. Possibly we can ignore some of their arguments or do anything else that may have the appearance of something new.

I am struck by the fact that when we establish troops or planes in France or any other country they become immediately "foreign bases." But when the Soviets station troops in Eastern Europe they are simply protecting the "internal rights" of the victim countries.[3]

But possibly you may have some other ideas.[4] *As ever*

---

[1] For background on the correspondence between Eisenhower and the Soviet leader see no. 574; see also Ann Whitman memorandum, Mar. 7, 1958, AWF/AWD.

[2] Bulganin had written Eisenhower again (March 3) about a summit conference (see *U.S. Department of State Bulletin* 38, no. 982 [April 21, 1958], 648–52). His earlier letters had been on December 10, 1957, January 8, and February 1, 1958.

[3] Referring to topics for consideration at the summit, Bulganin had said that the Soviet Union was prepared to discuss "the liquidation of alien military bases on foreign territories."

[4] We have no record of a response by Dulles. For more on the summit proposals and Eisenhower's reply to Bulganin's letter see nos. 611 and 619.

---

596   *EM, WHCF, Official File*
                                                             149-B-2 Oil

TO WILLIAM ALVIN MONCRIEF   *March 7, 1958*
Personal

Dear Monty:[1] Many thanks for your letter of the fifth. I was interested of course in your presentation of some of the problems of independent oil producers, as you see them.[2]

In your note you refer to what you call a "decision" of mine to implement mandatory controls. As of yet, no decision has been made. At the meeting I remarked that it appeared that such action could be necessary. But I decided nothing.[3] I must of course await the final and detailed recommendations of my special committee on crude oil imports, which was also mentioned at the meeting.[4]

With warm regard, *Sincerely*

---

[1] For background on independent oil producer Moncrief see Galambos and van Ee, *The Middle Way*, nos. 1113 and 1755.

[2] Moncrief had written on March 5, 1958 (AWF/N), following an off-the-record meeting held two days earlier at the White House. At Moncrief's suggestion, Eisenhower had met with White House aides Sherman Adams and Gerald Morgan, Treasury Secretary Anderson, Commerce Secretary Weeks, Director of the Office of Defense Mobilization Gordon Gray, and various Texas oilmen to discuss "the crisis in oil brought about by excessive and uncontrolled foreign imports" (see Moncrief to Eisenhower,

Feb. 22, 1958, same file as document, and Ann Whitman memorandum, Mar. 3, 1958, AWF/AWD, for background see no. 261). An identical letter was sent to Jake L. Hamon, an oil producer from Dallas, Texas, who had also attended the March 3 meeting (AWF/D).

[3] Moncrief had praised the President's decision to "take the necessary steps to implement mandatory controls." "It was apparent to us that you are fully aware of the threat to our security," he said, "as well as the serious impact on our economy, if the domestic oil industry is laid prostrate by a continuing and uncontrolled influx of foreign crude."

[4] Eisenhower would discuss the oil import problem at the March 7 Cabinet meeting (see Cabinet meeting minutes, Mar. 7, 1958, AWF/Cabinet). Secretary Weeks reported that the oil import situation had become more complicated because of decreased demand, the advent of new importers and certain instances of noncompliance with voluntary controls. He also noted that the Special Committee to Investigate Crude Oil Imports had not yet decided whether mandatory or voluntary controls should be imposed. Eisenhower noted that "certain producers seemed to have anticipated his decision" and asked either Secretary Anderson or Weeks to "set them straight as to the status of the matter." See Chester, *United States Oil Policy and Diplomacy*, pp. 30–34. For developments see no. 608; see also Moncrief to Eisenhower, March 28, 1958, same file as document.

597 *EM, AWF, International Series: Cortines*

To Adolfo Ruiz Cortines *March 7, 1958*

Dear Mr. President:[1] Thank you very much for your letter of February seventeenth expressing your serious concern about the possibility of an increase in United States tariffs on lead and zinc.[2] I deeply appreciate this full and friendly expression of your views, and your interest in approaching our common problems in a cooperative way.

The United States Tariff Commission has not yet completed its study of the lead and zinc case, and I know you would not want me to comment prematurely on the substance of the problem. I can assure you, however, that the interested Departments of the United States Government, and I personally, will weigh carefully the points you raise in your letter in considering this entire problem as soon as the Tariff Commission's report is presented.[3]

I take pleasure, Mr. President, in renewing to you the assurances of my highest esteem and most cordial friendship. *Sincerely*

[1] State Department officials drafted this letter to the Mexican president (see Herter to Eisenhower, Mar. 6, 1958, AWF/I: Cortines).

[2] In 1954 the U.S. Tariff Commission had recommended raising tariffs on lead and zinc to protect the domestic mining industries. In an attempt to maintain good re-

lations with the eleven lead and zinc producing countries, including Mexico, Eisenhower had rejected the commission's recommendation and asked for voluntary restraints on imports and increased stockpile purchasing. Although the government had increased its domestic purchases of both commodities, imports had increased gradually, and prices had declined. In June 1957, with Eisenhower's approval, the Interior Department had sent a proposal to Congress for a sliding scale of excise taxes on lead and zinc imports. When Congress did not act on the proposal, Eisenhower asked the Tariff Commission to investigate the lead and zinc industries (see Galambos and van Ee, *The Middle Way*, no. 1019; see also State, *Foreign Relations, 1955–1957*, vol. IX, *Foreign Economic Policy; Foreign Information Program*, pp. 264–67; *Congressional Quarterly Almanac*, vol. XIII, *1957*, pp. 654–55; Kaufman, *Trade and Aid*, pp. 118–19; and Alfred E. Eckes, Jr., *The United States and the Global Struggle for Minerals* [Austin, 1979], pp. 213–14).

President Ruiz Cortines had praised Eisenhower's 1954 decision and pointed out that Mexican exports of lead and zinc had decreased during the years immediately following the decision. The fall in prices, however, had been "a serious blow" to the Mexican mining industry (AWF/I: Cortines).

[3] On April 24 the Tariff Commission would report to Eisenhower that increased importation of lead and zinc was causing "serious injury" to domestic producers. But the commission could not agree to the need for a tariff increase. Eisenhower would tell congressional leaders that he was postponing any decision on the issue until Congress had considered the proposal for a sliding scale of import taxes (State, *American Foreign Policy; Current Documents, 1958*, pp. 1491–93, 1496). For developments see no. 774.

598   *EM, AWF, DDE Diaries Series*

TO WILLIAM FIFE KNOWLAND   *March 8, 1958*
AND JOSEPH WILLIAM MARTIN, JR.

Dear Bill:
Dear Joe: In recent press conferences I have stressed the point that in the current economic situation, certain kinds of governmental measures, including the acceleration of planned and needed public improvements, can be helpful in promoting increased growth of the economy.[1]

I have also stressed this point: the course of our huge, complex economy mainly depends upon what individual citizens do—upon their creativity, their productivity, their initiative and enterprise, and the millions of economic decisions which they freely make each day. The proper relation of government to the growth and vigor of such an economy must necessarily be to stimulate private production and employment, not to substitute public spending for private spending, nor to extend public domination over private activity.

I am concerned over the sudden upsurge of pump-priming schemes, such as the setting up of huge Federal bureaucracies of the PWA or WPA type.[2] That kind of talk evidenced lack of faith in the inherent vitality of our free economy and in the American as an individual. Schemes of that kind reflect the fallacy that economic progress is generated not by citizens wisely managing their own resources, but by the wholesale distribution of the people's money in dubious activities under Federal direction. Unsound programs of that kind would do great damage to America rather than contribute to our economic strength.[3]

My February 12 economic statement emphasized a number of important considerations:[4]

First, that current economic developments, including increased unemployment with its severe hardships for those individuals temporarily out of work, are of deep concern to us all;

Second, that the basic factors making for economic growth remain strong, justifying expectations of early economic improvement;

Third, that numerous governmental policies and programs already underway and projected will help achieve an early resumption of economic growth; and,

Fourth, that should additional governmental measures be needed, they will be taken by the Executive Branch or proposed to the Congress.

In that statement I cited a number of governmental activities currently aiding the economy. These include measures by the Federal Reserve authorities to ease credit,[5] various steps to stimulate home-building,[6] a $600 million increase in Federal aid highway expenditures next fiscal year,[7] sharply increased activity under the urban renewal program,[8] and a more than $5 billion increase in defense procurement and construction during the first six months of this calendar year over the preceding six months.[9]

A number of Administration recommendations for new legislation which could be of great help in stimulating the economy are already pending before the Congress. Again I urge the Congress to act promptly on such measures as (a) authority for additional insurance of FHA mortgages of $3 billion per year for the next five fiscal years;[10] (b) adjustment of those statutory interest rates which stifle private investment; (c) special assistance to areas of high and persistent unemployment;[11] (d) tax relief for small business;[12] (e) removal of the statutory limit on the life of the Small Business Administration and provision of new authority for loans to small business;[13] (f) a $2 billion increase in the lending authority of the Export-Import Bank;[14] and (g) a $2 billion program to modernize post office buildings and equipment.[15]

Since my February 12 statement the Administration has been developing additional orderly accelerations of programs that are genuinely needed in the public interest, have long been planned, and are already approved. I cite here some of the additional actions I have directed since February 12:

1. The Director of the Bureau of the Budget, on my instruction, has directed the executive departments and agencies to accelerate where practicable the construction of projects for which appropriated funds are available. Acceleration of civil projects alone, many of which are already in planning and engineering stages, will result in the expenditure of nearly $200 million several months earlier than previously planned. This earlier expenditure will step up such construction programs as Corps of Engineer civil works, the improvement of roads and facilities in National Parks, and the Bureau of Indian Affairs' road building and maintenance activities.

2. Additionally, certain water resource projects have been accelerated in the present fiscal year and the affected departments are submitting such amendments to the budget as are needed to continue this higher construction rate in 1959. Amendments, to be transmitted to the Congress next week, will involve increased appropriation requests as follows:

In millions

Department of Interior	
Bureau of Reclamation.	$ 46
Department of the Army	
Corps of Engineers, Rivers and	
Harbors and Flood Control.	125
Department of Agriculture	
(Watershed Protection and	
Flood Prevention Projects).	15
Total.	$ 186

In addition, an amendment to the Department of the Interior Budget will be presented to the Congress to allow an early start on small reclamation projects which were authorized by the 1956 Small Projects Act.[16]

3. The Director of the Bureau of the Budget has just released an additional $200 million to the Administrator of the Housing and Home Finance Agency. These funds will be used by the Federal National Mortgage Association to stimulate construction of homes for citizens of modest means and to implement other authorized programs. They will provide additional employment throughout the country. Should experience establish a need for more of these funds, they will be requested of the Congress.

4. In the next few days the Administration will ask the Congress to amend the Highway Act to suspend certain expenditure limitations for three years. If enacted this amendment will permit

apportionments to the States of an additional $2.2 billion of Federal funds, all of which will be placed under contract during the calendar years 1958–1961. Adoption of this amendment will permit the apportionment during each of these years of a total of $2.2 billion of Federal funds for interstate highway construction alone.[17]

5. The military departments, on my instruction, have in recent days acted to award more procurement contracts in labor surplus areas, with first priority to small business concerns in such areas. A new clause is being inserted in future contracts urging prime contractors to give preference to qualified subcontractors in labor surplus areas to the full extent permissible under existing law. The Services are also reexamining their procurements to assure that the maximum number of contracts are available to small business generally as well as to labor surplus areas.[18]

6. The Veterans Administration has acted to make private funds more readily available to veterans for acquiring home ownership under the G. I. Loan Guaranty program, and the Federal Home Loan Bank Board has launched a program to increase the availability of funds for investment in home mortgages in areas that in recent months have experienced a shortage of such funds.

7. I deeply believe that we must move promptly to meet the needs of those wage earners who have exhausted their unemployment compensation benefits under state laws and have not yet found employment. I have requested the Secretary of Labor to present to me next week a proposal which, without intruding on present state obligations and prerogatives, would extend for a brief period the duration of benefits for these unemployed workers. This would enable eligible unemployed individuals to receive weekly benefits for a longer period than is now permitted under state laws and thus enable them to continue to seek jobs with a greater measure of security. I shall shortly place such a proposal before the Congress.[19]

Finally, it should be understood that other programs and measures are under study and, as circumstances may require, will be administratively set in motion or proposed to the Congress. *Sincerely*

[1] This letter to Senate and House minority leaders Knowland and Martin was released to the press on March 8 (see *New York Times*, Mar. 9, 1958, and *Public Papers of the Presidents: Eisenhower, 1958*, pp. 208–11). A handwritten memorandum on the file copy notes that Eisenhower went over the letter "word by word;" a draft, bearing the President's extensive handwritten emendations, is in the Harlow Papers, Economy Letter.

For background on the recession see nos. 572 and 577. At his March 5, 1958, news conference Eisenhower had stated that while the economy had a way of "steering its own course" apart from the actions of the federal and state governments, there were a number of things that the government could do to ease the recession.

[2] Eisenhower was referring to the Public Works Administration (PWA), established by Franklin Roosevelt in 1933 under the National Industrial Recovery Act to reduce unemployment and increase purchasing power through the construction of highways and public buildings. Another New Deal agency, the Work Projects Administration (WPA; also called the Works Progress Administration), was created in 1935. In addition to the construction of roads, buildings and parks, the WPA employed thousands of artists, writers and actors in such cultural programs as the creation of art work for public buildings, the documentation of local life, and the organization of community theaters. The National Youth Administration (NYA), also sponsored by the WPA, helped provide part-time jobs for young people.

[3] See *New York Times*, February 8, March 2, 4, 1958; see also Saulnier, *Constructive Years*, pp. 109–11. At this point in his letter, the President deleted the following sentence from an earlier draft: "The nation must not be again subjected to the public spending philosophy that failed to remedy unemployment in its own day, was saved from its own errors only by the greater tragedy of war, and would again fail if revisited upon America now" (Harlow Papers, Economy Letter).

[4] See *New York Times*, February 13, 1958; see also *Public Papers of the Presidents: Eisenhower, 1958*, pp. 151–52.

[5] In January Federal Reserve Banks in New York and six other cities approved a cut in the discount rate from 3 percent to 2¾ percent (see *New York Times*, Jan. 22, 24, 1958); on February 19 the Federal Reserve Board had reduced the reserve requirements of its member banks, thus making more money available for loans (see *New York Times*, Feb. 20, 1958).

[6] On January 8, 1958, the Federal Housing Administration (FHA) had rescinded a regulation requiring home buyers to pay closing costs with their own cash. The agency had also instructed lenders to be more lenient in considering the income qualifications of potential home buyers (see *New York Times*, Jan. 12, Feb. 13, 1958).

[7] See *New York Times*, February 13, 1958.

[8] See *ibid.*

[9] See *New York Times*, February 6, 1958.

[10] The Senate would pass the Emergency Housing Bill, S. 3418, on March 12; the House would follow suit on March 19. Eisenhower would sign the bill on April 1. The legislation lowered down payments on house sales under the FHA housing program; increased the President's fund under which the Federal National Mortgage Association could purchase home mortgages; and extended the Veterans Administration's direct-loan and guaranteed loan programs. In an effort to encourage more capital to flow into the mortgage market, it also permitted the VA to increase the interest rate on GI mortgages and increased the funding for military housing mortgages (see *Congressional Quarterly Almanac*, vol. XIV, *1958*, pp. 229–30).

[11] By the end of April the Senate would consider legislation to offer federal aid to urban areas of chronic high unemployment and to rural areas depressed by high unemployment and low income levels (see *ibid.*, pp. 147–50). For developments see no. 784.

[12] The Small Business Tax Revision Act of 1958, incorporated in the Technical Amendments Act, would provide an estimated $260 million in tax relief for small businesses through changes in laws on depreciation write-offs, estate taxes, and earnings credits (see *Congressional Quarterly Almanac*, vol. XIV, *1958*, pp. 262–63).

[13] On July 18 Eisenhower would sign legislation converting the Small Business Administration from a temporary organization to a permanent federal agency. The law would also increase the revolving fund for business loans, increase the limits on loans, and authorize a maximum yearly interest rate (see *ibid.*, pp. 257–61).

[14] On May 8, 1958, Congress would approve a $2 billion increase in the lending authority of the Export-Import Bank (see *ibid.*, p. 60). For developments see no. 831.
[15] For background see no. 176. The White House had announced on February 11 that Eisenhower had directed Postmaster General Summerfield to present to Congress a $2 billion program for post office modernization. Summerfield's program called for a government contribution for equipment and improvements, while private investors would supply $1.5 billion to erect facilities to be occupied under lease. The government expenditure was to be financed by revenues from increased postage rates (see *New York Times*, Feb. 13, 1958; and *Congressional Quarterly Almanac*, vol. XIV, *1958*, pp. 209–11).
[16] The Small Reclamation Projects Act of 1956 authorized federal grants and fifty-year loans for approved local reclamation projects of up to $5 million, or seventy-five percent of the total costs (see *Congressional Quarterly Almanac*, vol. XII, *1956*, pp. 505–6).
[17] The Federal Aid Highway Act of 1958 was designed to add over $3 billion in new federal funds to expenditures for highway construction during fiscal years 1959-60-61. In addition to new funds, the act also suspended for two years the pay-as-you go provision of the 1950 Highway Act, permitting the expenditure of a previously authorized $400 million in FY 1959 before gasoline tax revenues had been collected (see *Congressional Quarterly Almanac*, vol. XIV, *1958*, pp. 140–45).
[18] For developments see no. 817.
[19] The Temporary Unemployment Compensation Act of 1958 would provide federal funds to states for the extension of unemployment benefits by a maximum of fifty percent. Eisenhower would sign the bill on June 4 (*Congressional Quarterly Almanac*, vol. XIV, *1958*, pp. 153–56). For developments see no. 633.

599

DIARY
Memorandum for files

Jim Black was in to see me for some twenty minutes.[1] I could not determine exactly the purpose of Mr. Black's visit with me. He did tell me something about a law suit now pending in the Supreme Court which is known as the "Memphis Case."[2] I told him that I had no interest in any law suits and did not have the time to study them. But he gave an economic twist to his presentation by saying that if the Supreme Court did not reverse the Appeal Court decision, a number of steel companies would have to cancel (and in some cases have already cancelled) contracts for making of steel pipe.

I reminded him that I had nothing to do with such cases and we would have to see what the Supreme Court said.

[1] James Cunard Black, manager of the Republic Steel Corporation in Washington, D.C., had met with Eisenhower for twenty minutes that morning (for background see Galambos, *NATO and the Campaign of 1952*, no. 478; Galambos, *Columbia University*, no. 944).

² On February 3, 1958, the Supreme Court had agreed to review the so-called "Memphis case," in which a lower federal court had ruled that unless customers agreed, rate increases filed by natural gas pipeline companies could not go into effect until the Federal Power Commission had conducted proceedings to determine their legality. The pipeline companies opposed to the ruling argued that it was unfair to make them keep charging rates that the commission might later find inadequate. Many companies feared they might go bankrupt under such a policy in times of rising prices (see *New York Times*, Feb. 4, 1958). On December 8 the Supreme Court would rule in favor of the pipeline companies, allowing gas prices to go up six months after the filing of new rate schedules, subject to later revision by the FPC (see *New York Times*, Dec. 9, 1958).

600   *EM, AWF, International Series: Tunisia*

To Habib Bourguiba   *March 10, 1958*

*Dear Mr. President:*¹ I have received through Ambassador Slim your message of February twenty-eighth setting forth your concern about the situation facing the civil population in the area along the border between Algeria and Tunisia.²

We have had somewhat conflicting reports as to the situation in this area, which I hope will not lead to consequences of the proportions which you fear.³ The United States cannot of course be indifferent to any situation which exacts a toll in lives and human misery. I continue to hope most earnestly for a peaceful and equitable solution which will respect the interests of all the parties concerned, and you may be sure that we shall continue to exert our influence to this end. Only in this way, I believe, can the real cause of suffering be removed.

As you know, the United States Government is now contributing to the relief of civilian refugees in Tunisia.⁴ I assure you that we stand ready, here as elsewhere, to continue with those efforts, and, in the light of the findings of qualified experts, to do what we can further to alleviate the suffering which causes you and us so much concern.⁵

With warm regard, *Sincerely*

¹ State Department officials drafted this letter to the Tunisian president. Eisenhower's letter incorporated suggestions from Robert Murphy, who was in London to assist negotiations designed to relieve tensions between France and Tunisia (Herter to Eisenhower, Mar. 9, 1958, AWF/I: Tunisia; see also State, *Foreign Relations, 1958–1960*, vol. XIII, *Arab-Israeli Dispute; United Arab Republic; North Africa*, p. 831; for background see no. 586).
² Monghi Slim, former Tunisian minister of state and minister of the interior, had become ambassador to the United States in September 1956. Seeking to impede

arms traffic from Tunisia into Algeria, the French were reported to have created a no man's land in Algeria along the Tunisian border (*New York Times*, Feb. 24, 1958). President Bourguiba had appealed to Eisenhower on behalf of "a defenseless civilian population" displaced by the French action. "Already, refugees, children and old people are pouring by the thousands into Tunisia," he said, "abandoning their homes and, in many cases, their families" (Bourguiba to Eisenhower [Feb. 28, 1958], AWF/ I: Tunisia).

[3] Acting Secretary Herter had told Eisenhower that the State Department had received indications from the French that the displacements might not be as great as Bourguiba had originally feared (Herter to Eisenhower, Mar. 9, 1958, AWF/I: Tunisia).

[4] For U.S. assistance to Tunisian relief projects see State, *Foreign Relations, 1958–1960*, vol. XIII, *Arab-Israeli Dispute; United Arab Republic; North Africa*, pp. 836–37.

[5] Eisenhower would also write to King Idris of Libya regarding the displacement of civilians and the President's desire to see "a just and peaceful solution to the Algerian conflict" (Eisenhower to Idris, Mar. 13, 1958, WHCF/CF: State Department).

On March 20 Secretary Dulles would tell the National Security Council that Bourguiba had approved an agreement with France, allowing neutral observers to replace French military personnel remaining at four Tunisian airfields. Future discussions would determine control over the French air base at Bizerte (NSC meeting minutes, Mar. 21, 1958, AWF/NSC; State, *Foreign Relations, 1958–1960*, vol. XIII, *Arab-Israeli Dispute; United Arab Republic; North Africa*, p. 838; and *U.S. Department of State Bulletin* 38, no. 981 [April 14, 1958], 607). For developments see no. 650.

601   *EM, AWF, Administration Series*

To JOSEPH MORRELL DODGE   *March 10, 1958*

Dear Joe: Your recommendation—plus my previous knowledge of Mr. Burnett's books—insures that I shall enjoy "Bitter Ground." Many thanks for your kindness in sending it to me.[1]

Incidentally, it seems much too long since we have seen you here in the White House. I'd like the opportunity for a chat with you; I would especially value your impressions as to the economic situation.[2]

With warm regard, *As ever*

[1] In a note that accompanied the novel (n.d., AWF/N), Dodge had said he had enjoyed it and thought that the President might "like it for R&R" [rest and recreation]. For background on Dodge's familiarity with Eisenhower's taste in books see Galambos and van Ee, *The Middle Way*, no. 1323. Eisenhower was referring to William Riley Burnett's *Bitter Ground* (New York, 1958), a novel about a gambler who seizes control of a western community.

[2] Eisenhower would meet with his former budget director on November 17, 1958, at the White House. On the 1957–1958 recession see no. 598.

To John Hay Whitney   *March 10, 1958*

Dear Jock: One of my very fine friends, Herbert Blunck, is going, with his wife, to spend a few days in Europe this spring.[1] He should arrive in Britain on the fifteenth of April (and he is staying at the Savoy).

They are both charming people and have not even suggested to me that they should call on you. But he, as General Manager of the Statler Hotel in Washington, has extended to me so many personal courtesies over a period of more than a decade that it would be some satisfaction to me if I could in any way help him and his wife to take a bit more enjoyment out of their quick tour.

With this thought in mind, I wonder if you would find it possible to receive him if Mr. Blunck should request a call upon you. I am sure there is nothing in the way of help or assistance that they need or could possibly desire, but I think that the satisfaction of a short visit to the American Ambassador in London would be an honor that they would value. I do hope I am not asking too much of you.[2]

With affectionate regard to Betsey and all the best to yourself, *As ever*

[1] Herbert Christopher Blunck had been manager of the Washington Statler Hotel since 1944. His wife was the former Janet Elizabeth Edwards.
[2] Ambassador Whitney would reply on March 18 (AWF/A) that he would welcome the Bluncks upon their arrival and invite them to the mansion in Regent's Park. "In fact," Whitney added, "if he's a golfer I'll hope to take some of his 'dollars-for-Britain.'" See also Eisenhower to Washburn, March 10, 1958, AWF/A: USIA.

603   *Jackson Papers*

To Charles Douglas Jackson   *March 11, 1958*

Dear C.D.: I like your suggestion as to a switch in presentation of the necessity for foreign aid to the Congress, and I shall see if I can't utilize it to good advantage.[1]

Meantime I have heard conflicting reports as to the arrangements Foster Dulles and Chris Herter made with you. Whatever the final details are, I'm delighted that you are going to pitch in and help. We need the lift you always bring to any subject.[2]

With warm regard, *As ever*

[1] In waging the cold war, Jackson said, the United States had "a reasonably well balanced triangular operation"—a large military budget, a huge gross national prod-

uct, and an appreciable foreign aid program. The Russian triangle, on the other hand, was heavily weighted toward the military. If some form of disarmament agreement were reached, the Soviet Union could move vast sums of money released from the military budget into the foreign aid program, resulting in "a long, tough economic-warfare competition." Jackson suggested that Eisenhower tell congressional leaders that they must be prepared to meet this kind of economic competition; the alternatives were either surrender or an accelerated arms race (Jackson to Eisenhower, Mar. 6, 1958, AWF/A).

On April 22 Eisenhower would tell the Republican legislative leaders that he believed adequate funding of the mutual security program was more important than "searching for new ways to put more money into the defense complex" (Notes on Legislative Leadership Meeting, Apr. 12, 1958, AWF/D). In a speech before the Republican National Committee on May 6 he would emphasize the relationship between foreign aid and meeting the Soviet economic challenge (*Public Papers of the Presidents: Eisenhower, 1958*, pp. 378–86). For more on Eisenhower's belief in a strong foreign aid program see no. 60.

[2] Jackson had told Eisenhower that Under Secretary of State Herter had talked to him about preparing a statement on the U.S. disarmament position. "I will go to work on this right away," he said, "and hope to have something worth demolishing within a fortnight."

The "conflicting reports" Eisenhower mentions may have referred to conversations he had had with Dulles and Sherman Adams regarding a role for Jackson in the proposed meetings of the foreign ministers. According to Dulles, Jackson had agreed to aid State Department officials in preliminary preparations for the conference. Ann Whitman had reported, however, that when Herter and Robert Cutler had discussed the subject of Jackson's assignment with Eisenhower, the President had said, "fairly disgustedly," that no one seemed to know what the job was. According to Whitman, Jackson thought the assignment was disarmament, but Dulles had "very clearly told the President it was preparatory work for [the] Summit meeting" (Telephone conversations, Eisenhower and Dulles, Dulles and Adams, Mar. 4, 1958, Dulles Papers, Telephone Conversations and AWF/D; see also Ann Whitman memorandum, Mar. 4, 1958, AWF/AWD). On discussions regarding a summit conference see no. 589.

604   *EM, AWF, Administration Series*

To Arthur Frank Burns   *March 12, 1958*
Personal

Dear Arthur: I trust that I am not getting stubborn in my attitude about logical Federal action in this business slump, but I am bound to say that I cannot help but feel that precipitate, and therefore largely unwise, action would be the worst thing that we could now do.[1] I realize that to be conservative in this situation—and flatly to say so—can well get me tagged as an unsympathetic, reactionary fossil. But my honest conviction is that the greatest service we can now do for our country is to oppose wild-eyed schemes of every kind. I am against vast and unwise public works programs (they would need some years to get truly underway) as well as the slash-bang kinds of tax cutting from which the proponents want nothing so much as immediate political advantage.[2]

Especially I believe what you have to say in your second paragraph.[3] I not only believe it, but I am thoroughly convinced that it must be one of our real guideposts as we push along with the work of stimulating an upturn in the economy. Indeed, because I may send a copy of this letter to one or two friends, I am quoting what you have to say on this particular point:

> "It (a public works program of increasing scope) would do little to check the recession this year. It would sharply increase spending next year and still later years, when our economy is likely to be feeling inflationary pressures once again. And it may raise the level of Federal spending to a point where it will become difficult to convince Congress in a later year that we need, perhaps or probably, to spend more for defense."

This morning I had a long conference with the Budget Director, Bob Anderson, Gabe Hauge and others.[4] After the conference was over the newspaper men got hold of Bob Anderson and he talked to them informally.[5] Afterward the talk was recorded and I am sending you a copy.

You will recall that in the last couple of years there was a good deal of talk about inflation.[6] But no one, except the Federal Reserve Board, did much to check it.[7] One did not then see Congress proposing anything of this kind whatever except, of course, so far as it felt it politically expedient to heed the public demand for economy. But now everybody and his brother has his own pet project to stop deflation. In fact, one bill just introduced in the House includes eighteen public works projects which have never been surveyed. No engineering studies for any of these has been approved by any agency of the Federal government.[8]

We shall continue to push on with the things that we believe are useful. One of these, of course, is the *acceleration of public works already under way*.[9] These have to be paid for in any event; acceleration of the work will cost nothing in the long run, and the additional work will be helpful now.

Administrative actions have already been taken to support home building and we have asked for legislation to push harder on this particular matter. However, some of the bills on this subject are bad.

Tax cuts *may* have to be made, and with the general proposition made in your last two letters I completely agree.[10] But how I pray that when and if such action is necessary, we may have some statesmen and economists in controlling positions, rather than demagogues.[11]

With warm regard, *As ever*

¹ For background see no. 598.

² On calls for a tax cut see, for example, *New York Times*, January 20, February 9, 1958. See also Saulnier, *Constructive Years*, pp. 111–15.

³ Burns had written on March 10, 1958 (AWF/A), saying that he feared that the Eisenhower Administration would "gradually be drawn into a public works program of increasing scope." On Democratic party pressure for public works to spur the economy see, for example, *New York Times*, February 8, 1958.

⁴ Budget Director Percival Brundage would announce his resignation on March 14, 1958. In addition to Treasury Secretary Anderson and White House Special Assistant Hauge, Eisenhower had met with Chairman of the Council of Economic Advisors Saulnier, Under Secretary of Labor James T. O'Connell, and Assistant Budget Director Maurice Stans. White House aides Wilton "Jerry" Persons, Gerald Morgan, and Press Secretary James Hagerty also attended the meeting.

⁵ Anderson had told the press that a decision on a tax cut would not be made until the course of the economy was clarified (*New York Times*, Mar. 13, 1958).

⁶ See Galambos and van Ee, *The Middle Way*, nos. 1578, 2005, and 2136.

⁷ See *ibid.*, nos. 1877 and 1957.

⁸ On March 9 congressional Democrats announced plans to introduce a $2.5 billion program to loan municipalities money to build sewer and water facilities, public libraries, transportation facilities, various public buildings and works, and fire and police protection facilities (see *New York Times*, Mar. 10, 1958).

⁹ On March 14 Eisenhower would ask Congress for $125 million in funds to permit faster work on Army Engineers civil works projects (see *New York Times*, Mar. 15, 1958). The funds would permit the restoration of the projects to their original schedule, overturning a slowdown ordered the previous year.

¹⁰ Burns had written that if it were not for politics, "it might be well to wait a while before enacting a tax reduction. But as things seem to be shaping up," he said, "I have come to the conclusion that a tax cut, to apply both to individuals and businesses, has now become desirable. A tax cut today can still be effective in checking the recession this year. It will also tend to discourage ever-larger public expenditures. Perhaps most important of all, it is a solution based on free enterprise, in contrast to the public works programs which can only serve to expand the role of government in our economy." See also no. 577.

¹¹ For developments see no. 615.

605 *EM, AWF, Dulles-Herter Series*

To John Foster Dulles *March 12, 1958*
Secret

*Dear Foster:*¹ I am quite ready to accommodate my early summer schedule to any particular period in which President Garcia might find it convenient to come to Washington, except only in the case of actual interference with another engagement that has already been set up. I will be glad to hold the dates June 16th to 18th. Or, in July, he could take either of the first two weeks, beginning Monday the 7th or Monday the 14th, for a three day visit.²

I think there is no one who would hazard a guess as to the date

771

that the Congress will adjourn, but I should think any of these I have just mentioned would be before adjournment can possibly occur.

Chris Herter tells us that your Department will take up with the Congress President Garcia's possible appearance before a joint session of Congress, and says further that an invitation to him to do so would be practically automatic.[3]

Thank you for your daily reports and for keeping me in close touch with the progress of your negotiations.[4]

With warm regard, and my prayers that your patience will outlast the preparation of the communique.[5] *As ever*

[1] State Department officials had sent this message to Secretary Dulles through the U.S. embassy in Manila, where he was attending the fourth meeting of the Southeast Asia Treaty Organization Council (see State, *Foreign Relations, 1958–1960*, vol. XV, *South and Southeast Asia* [1992], pp. 832–35; and State, *Foreign Relations, 1958–1960*, vol. XVI, *East Asia–Pacific Region; Cambodia; Laos* [1992], pp. 6–24).

[2] Carlos P. Garcia, former Vice-President and Secretary for Foreign Affairs, had become president of the Republic of the Philippines in March 1957 . Dulles had told Eisenhower that after accepting the President's invitation to visit the United States, Garcia had indicated that he wanted to come when Congress was in session. "It was apparent," Dulles said, "that he hopes to be invited to address a joint session of the Congress" (Dulles to Eisenhower, Mar. 12, 1958, AWF/D-H; see also no. 537).

[3] Garcia would visit Washington on June 17–19 and address a joint session of Congress on June 18.

[4] On the preceding day Dulles had told Eisenhower that the council had approved two U.S. proposals "of some delicacy": the establishment of contacts with NATO and the exchange of military information with such non-pact countries as Korea and Formosa. Dulles also reported that he and the British and French foreign ministers had agreed that the next stage of discussions regarding a summit meeting should be held, with the approval of NATO, at the diplomatic level in Washington. The British still wanted to fix a date and place for a summit meeting "without further probing," Dulles said, but they had accepted the U.S. position that preliminary negotiations must precede those decisions (Dulles to Eisenhower, Mar. 11, 12, 1958, AWF/D-H).

[5] Dulles had told Eisenhower that on the following day the delegates would prepare the communiqué. "I hope I have your sympathy at this trying, but apparently inescapable, ordeal." At the end of the conference he would cable the President that his "prayers with reference to the communiqué were answered, and after three nerve-wracking hours, a reasonably satisfactory agreement was reached" (Dulles to Eisenhower, Mar. 12, 13, 1958, *ibid.*; for the communiqué see State, *American Foreign Policy, Current Documents, 1958*, pp. 1116–19).

606   *EM, AWF, Name Series*

TO PERCY WALTER THOMPSON   *March 12, 1958*

Dear Percy: As I wrote you early in February, I asked the State Department to give me their reaction to the proposal by Professor

Ganong for "limited reciprocal citizenship" between the United States and Canada. I send along to you their memorandum on the subject.[1]

If you are talking to Professor Ganong, I would simply say—if anything is necessary—that you know the proposal has been given serious consideration.

As I am sure you are aware, I have had the children and grandchildren here at the White House during Mamie's absence in Arizona.[2] It was tremendous fun for me to have them around (and I managed to gain at least five pounds by virtue of the fact that I ate most of my meals with the children). I hope that Barbara enjoyed her respite from household chores as much as I enjoyed having her act as my "hostess" for the period.

With warm regard, *As ever*

P.S. I particularly request that you do not furnish any of the attached documents to the Professor.[3]

---

[1] Thompson had told Eisenhower that Canadian-born Carey E. Ganong, a friend, former neighbor, and professor at Purdue University, had proposed a plan whereby native-born American citizens who resided permanently in Canada would receive the rights of Canadian citizenship, except for the right to hold federal-level office. Canadian citizens residing in the United States would receive reciprocal privileges. "Such a move to cement the ties of friendship with Canada might have special world-wide significance at this time," Thompson wrote, "and if feasible it has the added merit of positive offensive action in the right direction" (Thompson to Eisenhower, Feb. 1, 1958; Eisenhower to Thompson, Feb. 6, 1958; and Eisenhower to Dulles, Feb. 6, 1958, all in AWF/N). The idea, although interesting, was "one of broad scope," Dulles had answered, and required further study before he could comment (Dulles to Eisenhower, Feb. 10, 1958, AWF/D-H).

Under Secretary Herter later wrote Eisenhower that after careful study, State Department officials had determined that the proposal presented legal difficulties and would not benefit the United States in any substantial way. He pointed out that resident Canadians already enjoyed all the privileges of citizenship except the right to hold office and vote. Although Professor Ganong's proposal was "an intriguing and appealing one at first glance," Herter said, the benefits seemed to be more apparent than real and would not justify a treaty with Canada (Herter to Eisenhower, Mar. 11, 1958, AWF/D-H).

[2] Mamie Eisenhower was vacationing at Maine Chance Farm in Phoenix, Arizona (see no. 579). Thompson was John Eisenhower's father-in-law.

[3] Thompson would tell Eisenhower that the documents had not arrived with his letter. "Considering their confidential nature," he said, "I feel obliged to report this to you." He assured the President that he would follow his suggestions regarding the information he might give to Professor Ganong (Thompson to Eisenhower, Mar. 24, 1958, AWF/N).

TO ARTHUR LARSON   *March 13, 1958*

Dear Arthur: Please look over what Mrs. Whitman will give you with this note, and let me know at once whether there is any virtue in this talk at all. If not, I must abandon it at once.[1]

If we go ahead with the idea, there will have to be still further reduction in its size, of course. I particularly request that you cut the pages 12 through the middle of 16 to not more than 1½ page. I know I wrote most of the material, but there is a great deal of repetition in it.[2]

With warm regard, *Sincerely*

[1] Eisenhower is referring to a speech on the cold war that he was scheduled to give before the American Society of Newspaper Editors on April 17, one day after the fifth anniversary of his 1953 speech before the same group (see Bernau to Dulles, Mar. 6, 1958, Dulles Papers, Telephone Conversations; for the President's 1953 speech see Galambos and van Ee, *The Middle Way*, no. 132). According to Ann Whitman, an earlier version of the draft had disappointed the President because Larson "had made no attempt to polish or interject new thoughts." When Whitman had explained to Eisenhower that Larson had "felt that the President had worked so much on it" that he did not want changes made. Eisenhower said that he had indeed asked Larson for substantive revisions. The President then ordered that he not be disturbed by anyone in order to work on the draft himself (Ann Whitman memorandum, Mar. 12, 1958, AWF/AWD).

On the following day the President would explain to his brother Milton that he wanted the speech to show the impact that enormous defense expenditures had on the economy. He also believed that the United States must accept the reality that the Soviet Union had a different form of government and then go on to search for ways toward a common understanding of the world's problems. He was "tired of working with mature men already set in their prejudices," he told Milton, and wanted to try "a different angle" by working with children. He outlined his idea for inviting 10,000 Russian students to spend a year in U.S. universities. Students would be "so busy learning our life, recreation, [and] studies," he said, that they would "have no time to subvert or convert and will get to know the heart of America" (Telephone conversation, Eisenhower and Milton Eisenhower, Mar. 14, 1958, AWF/D; see also Larson, *The President Nobody Knew*, pp. 70–71. For background on Eisenhower's ideas regarding Soviet students see no. 552.

[2] For developments see no. 617.

608   *EM, WHCF, Official File 149-B-2 Oil*

TO JAKE L. HAMON   *March 14, 1958*
Personal

Dear Jake:[1] At our recent meeting here in the office it is quite true that all of us agreed that voluntary quotas were not solving the oil problem. Several of us remarked that there seemed to be only one reasonable answer and that was compulsory quotas.[2]

The reason that I wrote to you to say that the point of "decisions" had not been reached was because of the very nature of the broad and comprehensive problem.[3] It is no simple matter to cover the United States with a regulation that will

(a) among other things stand the test of Constitutionality and accordance with law;

(b) bring about the just and fair conditions that the authors intend, and

(c) be immune to great loopholes.

The one thing I can assure you is that the people who are working on these things are wasting no time. They are really applying themselves.[4]

With warm regard, *Sincerely*

[1] For background on Dallas independent oil producer Hamon see Galambos and van Ee, *The Middle Way*, no. 1851.

[2] Hamon had written on March 5 to thank the President for meeting with the oil producers on March 3 (see no. 596). Hamon had praised Eisenhower's decision to invoke mandatory oil controls, saying that a "quick issuance of a mandatory order limiting oil imports will undoubtedly stimulate activity in the domestic oil industry." On March 6 Senate Majority Leader Lyndon Johnson had also written the President urging a mandatory reduction of oil imports by 20 percent, saying that the domestic oil industry was "reeling" under the impact of imports (Mar. 6, 1958). In his March 15 reply, Eisenhower would say that while mandatory controls might be necessary at some point, he believed that "universal acceptance and practice by the industry of voluntary quotas, adjusted to the present production situation with such flexibility as to meet future contingencies, would avoid many difficulties and would be the best approach to this vexing problem."

[3] In a March 7 letter to Hamon, Eisenhower had explained that no decision had yet been made on invoking mandatory controls pending the findings of the special committee on crude oil imports. Hamon had replied (Mar. 11, 1958) that he had never intended to try to commit the President to any decision. He added: "Obviously, stronger curtailment measures on imports are needed to keep us able to find oil in this country, and being prejudiced, I guess that I assumed that you were in agreement with us."

[4] Oil import policy would be discussed at the Cabinet meetings on both March 14 and 21 (AWF/Cabinet, Cabinet meeting minutes). At the meeting on March 14 Defense Mobilization Director Gordon Gray had reported that his agency could find no evidence that residual fuel oil imports would endanger national security. At the March 21 Cabinet meeting, Secretary of Commerce Weeks would report that the special committee on petroleum imports would soon recommend continuing the voluntary program, while making it more effective by applying the "Buy American Act" when oil purchase contracts were issued (for background on the Buy American Act see Galambos and van Ee, *The Middle Way*, no. 250). On March 27 Eisenhower would order cuts in crude oil imports by 14.8 percent and the establishment of procedures to compel compliance by importers (*New York Times*, Mar. 28, 1958; *Public Papers of the Presidents: Eisenhower, 1958*, p. 230; see also Chester, *United States Oil Policy and Diplomacy*, pp. 32–34). Eisenhower would later explain that he believed voluntary measures would be sufficient "to bring current supply into a more normal relation-

ship with present demand" while a drastic cut in imports would "set in motion a series of actions that might seriously impair, if not destroy, our relations with countries from whom we import petroleum" (see Eisenhower to Simpson, Apr. 15, 1958; all correspondence is in same file as document). For developments see no. 706.

609 *EM, AWF, International Series:*
Macmillan

To Harold Macmillan *March 14, 1958*
Confidential

Dear Harold: Our initial position at Geneva has been the same as your own—to support the three mile limit without qualification, until it becomes clear that it will not be accepted.[1]

While we are fully appreciative of the difficult decision that is to be made at Geneva, we are convinced that unless we are prepared to give vigorous support to a compromise proposal enlarging the coastal states' rights over nearby fisheries, we probably will not be able to halt the mounting momentum for Conference approval of a twelve-mile territorial sea. We are also convinced that fishery conservation measures alone will not solve the problem. Some concession in the nature of a special rights fishery zone for the coastal states is necessary and a nine-mile zone is the minimum likely to gain acceptance. This is the Canadian compromise proposal.

I am impressed by the statement in your message about the timing of the different steps that may become necessary during the proceedings of the Conference. My own feeling is, based upon the urgent advice of the United States delegation, that we have now reached the stage where inflexibility can damage us.[2]

It seems to me, therefore, that within the next few days we shall be faced with the choice between three miles of sovereignty plus nine additional miles of fisheries control, or Conference approval of a twelve-mile limit which we find wholly inadequate for strategic reasons.

You should also note that the Canadian compromise proposal involves control over a contiguous fisheries zone by the coastal state, and does not necessarily involve the exclusion of all other nations. In Latin and South American waters, our fishing interests, as a *modus vivendi*, have negotiated licenses which permit them to fish without molestation within coastal areas claimed by those states and even up to the shore. If the Canadian compromise proposal is adopted and your government so desires, the United States would be prepared to exert its good offices in an effort to assist the United Kingdom to obtain similar arrangements in areas of concern to your government.[3]

With warm regard, *As ever*

[1] For background on the U.S. and British positions at the Law of the Sea Conference, which had opened on February 24, see no. 589.

[2] Eisenhower had added this paragraph to the State Department draft of this letter after meeting with Under Secretary Herter earlier on this same day (see Ann Whitman memorandum, Mar. 14, 1958, AWF/AWD). In his March 12 letter Macmillan had told Eisenhower that he thought it would be "premature and even dangerous" to introduce a compromise at that stage of the conference, before they had determined the amount of support for the three-mile limit. He also believed that mentioning the twelve-mile limit for fisheries would enable conference participants to accept that figure for other purposes as well (AWF/I: Macmillan; see also State, *Foreign Relations, 1958–1960*, vol. II, *United Nations and General International Matters*, p. 657).

[3] The British subsequently would reject the Canadian compromise in favor of a proposed six-mile limit with rights of passage for warships and for flights by aircraft within the outer three miles. Another proposal, introduced by Mexico and supported by India and the Soviet Union, would provide for flexible limits ranging from three to twelve miles. In an attempt to help the conference reach agreement and to assure the stability of maritime law, the United States would present its own compromise proposal, providing for a six-mile territorial sea plus an additional six-mile fishing zone. The compromise included a clause that would protect the fishing rights of countries that had fished for the previous ten years in the outer six miles of the coastal state's territorial waters. The U.S. proposal was defeated by seven votes, and the conference adjourned on April 27, without agreement on this issue (*ibid.*, pp. 659–708; see also State, *American Foreign Policy, Current Documents, 1958*, pp. 259–88; Dulles to Eisenhower, Apr. 24, 1958; and Dean to Department of State, Apr. 21, 1958, AWF/D-H). For developments see no. 671.

610   *EM, AWF, DDE Diaries Series*

MEMORANDUM   *March 17, 1958*

Memorandum of Conversation with Roger Kyes: On Saturday, March 15, I had a talk with Roger Kyes.[1] He had two ideas that he suggested might have some virtue, one in the foreign field, the other in the domestic.

The Foreign Field. He gave only the barest outline of what he has in mind, but he has promised to send me a copy of a letter he has previously written on the subject.[2] As I understand the matter, he wants to set up a huge international corporation, in effect a holding company.

Trading would be accomplished under the auspices of the holding company, and one of the purposes of the company would be to promote the flow of profitable trade for participants.

Each country desiring to trade with others would purchase stock in the holding company, but free enterprise would be encouraged by making it possible, in countries such as ours, for a business firm to purchase such stock directly. His idea was that countries that derived income from the export of raw materials (such as oil) could pay for their stock out of earnings. His big purpose is to get each country to have a stake in the prosperity of each of the others; in other words, to have a powerful influence for peace.

The actual financial details are something we did not go into, and I am most interested in hearing what the explanation of them will be. Moreover, I will be waiting to hear what he says on tariffs.[3] But he is a smart man and I am sure that he believes that he has an idea that would be most beneficial to every country involved.[4]

Stimulation of the Domestic Economy. In this field he has been thinking about the effects of tax reduction.[5] He is very fearful that tax reduction would leave us with such a gap in revenue that we would quickly be going into deficit spending at an indefinite rate and for an indefinite period. The inflationary effect of this would wipe out, he is sure, any beneficial effects to be expected. He seems to have this conviction whether we are talking about reducing income tax or excise tax.

So his simple idea is that we should have a percentage *refund* on the 1957 personal income tax. This would be a "one time" affair and would immediately put a lot of money into the hands of the population and would spur buying all along the line. He thinks it would spur the weakest phase of our consumer buying—namely, consumer hard goods—for example, automobiles, refrigerators, house and farm appliances of all kinds.

He suggested the possibility of requiring that all refunded amounts over a particular level would have to be used as venture capital of some kind. In thinking it over, I do not see how this could be done because while an individual might make a purchase of this kind, he could resell it at his own convenience. (Possibly there should be a maximum limit on any single refund!)

With the 36 billion dollars collected in taxes on 1957 personal income, he thought that even a 25% refund would not be out of order. This 9 billion he believes would have a tremendous effect both materially and psychologically.

The Treasury Department is thinking of a similar idea, although probably on a smaller basis. Since I know he has been talking to Secretary Anderson, it is probable that it was by his initiative that this thought came under study. In any event, I shall keep it completely secret.

I talked about the philosophy under which the Administration is pushing ahead with its effort to stimulate the economy.

(*a*). We are basically conservative. We believe, for example, that frantic efforts now to put the Federal Government into a large-scale building program will have most unfortunate financial consequences in the years immediately ahead. We believe in a private enterprise rather than a "government" campaign to provide the main strength of recovery forces.

(*b*). We want to avoid a succession of budgetary deficits because of the inflationary effect.

(*c*). We want to do everything that has a stimulating effect on the economy, but so far as expenditure programs are concerned, we prefer to limit these expenditures to projects that are useful and needed. The idea is to do them *now* rather than later. We want to do everything that is feasible and practical to stimulate recovery, and at the same time keep our own financial house in order.

I told Roger that we expect to push forward with the things we have already undertaken administratively and with those we have already recommended to the Congress. (The easing of credit and reducing bank reserves slightly was, of course, done by the Federal Reserve Board, but with the approval and urgent support of the financial section of the government). This memo does not enumerate all the particular programs, but I attach hereto two statements, one written on February 12th and the other March 8th.[6]

*   *   *   *   *

There is one idea I have been discussing with the Treasury which I believe could become important. This concerns the railways, which by every discernible statistic are in real trouble. Only a few seem to be doing well. The majority are in bad shape and it is my belief that unless something is done, there will be bankruptcies looming for a number of railway systems within a matter of a few months.[7]

I believe it is important for the railways to achieve a truly competitive status with respect to other forms of transportation. To my mind success demands real cooperative studies as between the railways and other transportation systems if we are to get the highest form of efficiency from the several types. Take for example, railways and trucks. If the public could be informed as to what is really the most efficient form of freight transportation measured by such criteria as distance of haul, bulk, weight and conditions of delivery, it would certainly be to the benefit both of the shipper and of all transportation systems.

Here are some things to consider:[8]

(*a*). The elimination of the transportation tax, at least the three percent that is applied to the transportation on things.

(*b*). The placing before Congress a list of the restrictive laws that are preventing the railways from being truly competitive with respect to the other transportation systems. These laws were largely written when the railways had a monopoly on transportation and in many instances may be no longer applicable. I believe that one of their worst effects (this is possibly as much administrative as it is legalistic) is that railway complaints, protests and recommendations cannot even be heard and acted upon within a matter of one or two years. This is unconscionable. The railways now have the right to reorganize into a fewer number of systems, so long as the Attorney General does not find a reason for taking action against them under the Anti Trust Act. But the I.C.C. must find that the consolidation is in the public interest. I believe that if an application is not protested in a reasonable time, there should be a presumption of public interest in the consolidation. An appeal could be taken to a hearing. Reorganization could get rid of duplicatory service and mileage—and would be most helpful in a number of other ways.

(c). The whole question of feather-bedding under existing laws and union procedures should be thoroughly considered by the Congress. This would take considerable time, but it would be hopeful if the Congress would at least have the courage to undertake the examination.

(d). Assuming that (a) and (b) could be done, the railways could certainly gain so much efficiency, better their service, lower costs and increase revenues, that the way would be open for them to begin the renovation and reorganization of the railroad systems. The federal government could then well undertake the same kind of responsibility that it did with both the maritime and air industries, in guaranteeing loans for new equipment and general renovation.

(e). To my mind this is a project that must be undertaken promptly because of its effect on the whole transportation capacity of the country and its significance for the nation's defensive strength.

In the case of the railways the program would be not only important in itself, but incidentally would be one of the greatest possible spurs to economic recovery because of the wide-spread character and the volume of the work that would be immediately necessary.

Today I have a draft of a Report of the Transportation Study Group. I find that it suggests some of the same things to which I have adverted.[9]

Finally, I have asked Bob Anderson to confer with Dr. Saulnier to establish a Committee on Economic Development.[10]

[1] On Eisenhower's opinion of Kyes, former Assistant Secretary of Defense (1953–1954), see Galambos and van Ee, *The Middle Way*, no. 188. Kyes had returned to General Motors after leaving the Defense Department. The President had met with him for more than an hour on Saturday, March 15, 1958.

[2] On March 21 Kyes would forward to the President his ideas for an international holding company that he hoped would "instill new enthusiasm in the American people's concept of foreign affairs" (AWF/D-H). Kyes envisaged a stock company which would provide "a manageable common denominator so far as economic affairs are concerned" in dealing with problems as disparate as oil, minerals, Suez Canal tolls, "British pride or French instability." "Stock would be purchased by the United States and such other Western Allies who could afford to do so. Stock also would be allotted to countries who would pay for it over a period of years. For example, a country in the Middle East could pay with oil run. An African country with mining could pay with metal or equivalents of the metal." The holding company would then invest in self-liquidating projects around the world, providing its country shareholders with an equity that would lend stability to international politics.

[3] Kyes's letter did not provide detailed financial data or any information on tariffs.

[4] On March 26, 1958, Eisenhower would forward Kyes's letter to Secretary of State Dulles, saying that he found the idea "intriguing." "I believe he has discussed this whole proposal with Bob Anderson. Perhaps, if you see any virtue in the proposal, the three of us might sometime get together to discuss some of its ramifications." Dulles would respond on April 2, 1958 (AWF/D-H). He had consulted "some of our people concerned with the Middle East and with international economic problems" and promised to provide the President with an analysis of the proposal.

[5] For background on the economy see nos. 572 and 604.

[6] On February 8, 1958, Eisenhower had issued a statement on the economic situation, giving his reasons for believing that the economy would recover later that year (*Public Papers of the Presidents: Eisenhower, 1958*, pp. 151–52). On the March 8 statement see no. 598.

[7] Because of the growing financial losses of the nation's railroads in the post-World War II period, Eisenhower had begun to review federal transportation policy in 1954 (for background see no. 377; see also Galambos and van Ee, *The Middle Way*, nos. 790, 1097, and 1130). The President had appointed Sinclair Weeks to chair an Advisory Committee on Transport Policy and Organization. In 1955 a bill based on the recommendations of the Weeks committee was introduced in Congress, but no action was taken for three years. Beginning in January 1958, the Senate Interstate and Foreign Commerce Surface Transportation Subcommittee had held hearings on problems of the railroads in relation to both the national transportation system and the current recession (see *Congressional Quarterly Almanac*, vol. XIV, *1958*, pp. 244–49).

[8] In April Secretary of Commerce Weeks would send Eisenhower a copy of a letter that he proposed to send to the Surface Transportation Subcommittee of the Committee on Interstate and Foreign Commerce (see Weeks to Eisenhower, Apr. 21, 1958, and Eisenhower to Weeks, Apr. 22, 1958, AWF/A). In the proposed letter (Weeks to Smathers, n.d., AWF/A) Weeks would set forth the Administration program for change. Weeks called for a number of measures to help the railroads, including an enlarged ICC jurisdiction, revised federal rate-making policies, and temporary financial assistance in the form of short-term private loans for capital additions, improvements to plants and facilities, and the purchase of improved freight cars.

[9] Congress would pass the Transportation Act of 1958 on July 30, and Eisenhower would sign it into law on August 12. In its final form, the legislation authorized the ICC to make short-term loans to railroads for purchase of capital equipment or property maintenance; gave the ICC full authority to adjust intrastate rail rates that gave an "unreasonable" advantage to other carriers engaged in interstate commerce; gave

the ICC power to permit railroads to discontinue interstate and intrastate service under certain conditions; exempted truckers of certain agricultural products from ICC regulations; and closed the loophole which had enabled truckers to evade ICC regulation by assuming ownership of goods in transit. See Richard D. Stone, *The Interstate Commerce Commission and the Railroad Industry: A History of Regulatory Policy* (New York, 1991), pp. 44–50.

[10] Eisenhower had met with Anderson for a half-hour that day. There is no further record of this committee in AWF; Eisenhower was not referring to the Committee for Economic Development (CED) founded in 1942 as an independent, nonpartisan organization of business and education leaders committed to policy research on major economic and social issues.

611   *EM, AWF, International Series:*
                                                           Macmillan

To Harold Macmillan   *March 17, 1958*
Secret

Dear Harold: I was glad to get your letter which I received today, discussing the Summit and other matters.[1]

Foster, who is due back in Washington tomorrow evening, has been giving a lot of thought to the next moves on the Summit problem since talking with Selwyn and Pineau. I would therefore like to discuss the matter with him before giving you a full reply.[2]

With warm regard, *As ever*

[1] For background on the planning for a summit meeting see no. 588. After mentioning the unsettled conditions existing in the Middle and Far Eastern regions, Macmillan had told Eisenhower that he was concerned that the Russians would back out of summit preparations and place the blame for failure on Great Britain and the United States. "I think so far we are in quite a good posture but we always have to keep ahead of the Russians and not fall into any of their traps." He and Foreign Minister Selwyn Lloyd were working on a statement of the Western position that would, he said, "put the burden firmly back on the Russians and be understood to do so." This statement would make the point that there should be a meeting if there were a reasonable chance of agreement and that any meeting should include a "discussion of the main problems whether agreement is likely or not" (Macmillan to Eisenhower, Mar. 17, 1958, PREM 11/2327; see also Macmillan, *Riding the Storm*, pp. 477–78).

[2] Secretary Dulles was returning from the SEATO Council meeting, where he had held a number of discussions with Lloyd and French Foreign Minister Christian Pineau. For developments see no. 628.

To Aksel Nielsen

Dear Aks: At the urging of Mr. Bechtel, I went over to the BAC meeting one evening last week—I stayed for about a half hour before the dinner began.[1] I was looking around for you and then suddenly remembered that you had gone down to the Southwest. It was nice, at any rate, to talk with some of the other of my old friends.[2]

Just this morning I received the report on the University Hills Shopping Center. I went over it in detail and noted that more than a dozen of the establishments are paying more than the minimum. This seems to me to be very good and I assume that it is up to your expectations.[3]

Regarding the residential loan rate, you were for a rate, as I recall, that would have been sufficiently high to eliminate discounts. Of course the VA loans are fixed by law (even just last week the Senate declined to free them more than ¼ of 1%). I think that we here felt that to let the FHA loans go at 6 percent, with the VA loans frozen at least 1¼ percent lower, would have been something of a paradox. However, I hope that the situation soon improves.[4]

This morning I saw an article discussing the stock market and other investment activities. Quite naturally I am hopeful that a plentiful supply of money, available at cheaper rates, will be a real spur to the home building industry. It would be too bad if the stock market gets too much out of line and absorbs too much money.[5]

Thanks a lot for your news on Min. Mamie talked to her last evening and afterwards seemed rather depressed. But I think Min's two daughters try to make too much of a detailed diagnosis of her condition out of the sound of her voice over the telephone. Al Gruenther, who saw her only last Tuesday, thought that she was in very good form. If she could talk to you for an hour and a half, she certainly still has some interest in life.[6]

Thanks for sending me the fine report.[7]

With warm regard, *As ever*

---

[1] Stephen Davison Bechtel was president of the Bechtel Corporation, a large engineering firm whose work encompassed such activities as the construction of oil and natural gas pipelines, marine terminals, oil refineries, and industrial plants. He also served as Chairman of the Business Advisory Council (BAC) of the U.S. Department of Commerce. Bechtel may have issued his invitation to Eisenhower during a dinner at the White House on March 10. On March 13, accompanied by Sinclair Weeks and Bechtel, Eisenhower had joined a pre-dinner group of the BAC at the Mayflower Hotel in Washington, D.C.

[2] In addition to Bechtel, the Executive Committee of the BAC included James Byers Black, Roger M. Blough, Harold Boeschenstein, Ernest R. Breech, Paul Codman Cabot, Lucius D. Clay, Ralph J. Cordiner, Eugene Holman, Theodore V. Houser, De-

vereux Colt Josephs, Theodore Scarborough Petersen, Joseph Peter Spang, Jr., Frank Stanton, and Charles Allen Thomas.

[3] Nielsen had written on March 14, 1958 (AWF/N), and had enclosed an analysis of Eisenhower's University Hills investment. "They are small figures compared to what you are used to looking at," he said, "but they certainly affect you. Remember that 5% of this company belongs to you." For background on the University Hills property and Eisenhower's investments with Nielsen see no. 309.

[4] See no. 598.

[5] Eisenhower may have been referring to an analysis of the effect of the economy on the stock market in that day's *Wall Street Journal* (Mar. 17, 1958), which had reported that speculation about tax reductions, anti-slump measures, and maneuvering by short sellers had raised the Dow-Jones industrial average.

[6] Nielsen had written that he had visited with Mrs. Doud for an hour and a half on March 13. He hoped that Eisenhower "would tell Mamie that she is certainly doing very well, and that the visit with the girls has turned out to be a real blessing, as it gives her something new to talk about, and think about, and to be enthused about." On Nielsen's interest in the health of the First Lady's mother, Elivera Carlson Doud, see no. 321. On Mamie Eisenhower's sister, Mabel "Mike" Moore, see Susan Eisenhower, *Mrs. Ike: Memories and Reflections on the Life of Mamie Eisenhower* (New York, 1996), pp. 283–84.

[7] Nielsen would respond on March 25 (AWF/N). He would tell the President that "a good big portion of our troubles is all the conversation that is coming out of Congress," and that as far as he was concerned, in the first two months of 1958 business was "ahead of the same two months last year." Nielsen would say that "thinking" people were opposed to a tax cut for fear that it would "create a psychology that business is really much worse than it is and it would tend to scare more people into saving more money rather than keep the economy rolling."

613   *EM, AWF, Dulles-Herter Series*

DIARY   *March 18, 1958*

I spoke to the Secretary of State about a mistake in the public relations section of the State Department which was reported to have said yesterday "The State Department announces that the United States rejects the Soviet proposals on outer space.'[1] The Secretary of State was already aware of the implications of such a statement and has taken steps to correct any future occurrence of the kind.[2]

The Secretary himself was at some pains at a press conference when he arrived in Washington to point out that the original proposal was mine and that I was the one who had to make decisions as to acceptance or rejection of any Soviet counter proposals.[3]

[1] In a statement released on March 15 the Soviet Union had proposed a United Nations agency to administer a ban on military uses of space and to oversee the liquidation of foreign military bases in other countries. In response, State Department officials had said that the Soviet Union had attached "wholly unacceptable condi-

tions" to the proposal by asking for the removal of U.S. military bases in Europe, the Middle East, and North Africa (*New York Times*, Mar. 16, 17, 18, 1958).

[2] Dulles had told Eisenhower that he had discussed the incident with Under Secretary Herter, who had said that the statement was made without his knowledge. For his part Eisenhower acknowledged that there were "some good things" in the Soviet proposal, but it was "more detailed than we want to go" (Telephone conversation, Eisenhower and Dulles, Mar. 18, 1958, Dulles Papers, Telephone Conversations).

[3] Dulles, who had been at the SEATO conference in Manila, had told the press on March 17 the Russian ideas were "not in a very acceptable form" but that at least the Soviets were beginning to respond to Eisenhower's January 12 letter to Premier Bulganin (see no. 521) and other U.S. proposals on outer space made at the United Nations (*New York Times*, Mar. 18, 1958).

614   *EM, AWF, Administration Series*

To Neil Hosler McElroy   *March 18, 1958*

Dear Neil: I read with natural interest and mild astonishment the account by Professor Stevens of the Military-Scientific Dinner.[1] I would hope that no scientist who is working in the best interests of our country would ever feel for a moment that his work is not "appreciated" by those of us who are charged with the responsibility for such programs. If a simple gesture such as the recent dinner does anything to convince the many thousands such individuals who are dedicating their knowledge and skills to the scientific advancement of our country, I am more than gratified.[2]

And I am also a little surprised that the Harvard Alumni Bulletin saw fit to give the story so much space!

With warm regard, *Sincerely*

[1] Stanley Smith Stevens (Ph.D. Harvard 1933), professor of psychophysics and director of Harvard's Psychological Laboratory, was an authority on the physics of sensory perception. He had been a guest at a dinner for military and scientific officials that the Eisenhowers hosted on February 4. Stevens had written an account of the dinner for the Harvard alumni magazine (S. S. Stevens, "State Dinner," *Harvard Alumni Bulletin* 60, no. 9 [Feb. 22, 1958], pp. 391–92); Secretary of Defense McElroy, a Harvard alumnus, may have called the article to the President's attention.

[2] Stevens had described the "excitement" within the scientific community upon receiving engraved invitations to attend the state dinner—"a precedent-setting sign of the times." By the time the evening was over, "some of this country's scientists had enjoyed the heady experience of feeling appreciated in high places." For background see no. 434.

To Arthur Frank Burns   *March 20, 1958*
Personal

Dear Arthur: Some days ago I became convinced that the March figures were not going to be such as to cause me any great rejoicing.
Nevertheless, I continue to believe that the economy is now in a
"dragging-the-bottom" condition and could, very soon, show real
signs of upward movement.[1] I make no claim to gifts of prophesy,
but the above is my personal reaction to the various facts and de-
ductions that are, as you know, placed before me constantly.

A recent article by Bill Martin, which you undoubtedly saw, makes
the observation that one of the primary causes of the recession is
that it is a reaction from the prior period of inflation.[2] Personally I
think this generality can be made more specific by saying that the
1955 inflationary splurge by certain automobile companies had a
very great deal to do with subsequent economic movements. Of
course you were then one of those who did everything he could by
argument and discussion to get the companies to adopt a more moderate policy. George Humphrey and I were also in the same effort.
All of us failed.[3]

This morning there is an important housing bill that will be sent
to me. It has some bad features. I shall have to examine it with a
jaundiced eye, and I am quite sure that some of my advisers will be
as uneasy about it as I am. I hope its virtues outweigh its defects.[4]

I shall be looking forward to seeing a copy of your talk.[5] *As ever*

---

[1] For background see no. 604. On the recession and subsequent recovery see Saulnier,
Constructive Years, pp. 111–16. Burns's letter of March 17, 1958, is in AWF/A.
[2] Eisenhower was referring to William McChesney Martin, Chairman of the Federal
Reserve Board. We have been unable to find the article to which Eisenhower refers.
[3] On Eisenhower's concern over the interaction between the automobile industry
and the economy see Galambos and van Ee, *The Middle Way*, nos. 1272 and 1843.
[4] On the housing bill see no. 598. The President would sign the bill on April 1 (see
Congressional Quarterly Almanac, vol. XIV, *1958*, pp. 229–30). He would, however, say
that "the legislation ignores the responsibility and ability of private enterprise to function without imposing a direct burden on the Federal purse." Eisenhower would also
call upon Congress to enact legislation adjusting interest rates for guaranteed government loans "so that in this field our free enterprise system may have the fullest
opportunity to work" (*Public Papers of the Presidents: Eisenhower, 1958*, pp. 257–58).
[5] Burns had said that he was scheduled to give a talk on the recession on March 22
and would send the President a copy of the speech (for background see no. 577).
For developments see no. 620.

To Ezra Taft Benson   *March 20, 1958*
Personal and confidential

Dear Ezra: I am glad to have your note of March eighteenth, but frankly I feel that there is little need for you to enumerate again all the advantages both of us believe should result from our present farm program. I am not only familiar with these but have time and time again supported them publicly.[1]

In your efforts to improve Federal programs affecting agriculture I have always supported you enthusiastically; I shall continue to do so. But in what follows I shall attempt to give you some of my thinking about the legislative procedures through which we hope to secure an improvement in those and other necessary laws.[2] I think my text could well be the old German aphorism, "Never lose the good in seeking too long for the best," or as some say it, "The best is always the enemy of the good."[3]

I was impressed by the *apparent* attitude of some of the leaders at the meeting Tuesday. They, while announcing their continuing approval of the flexible price support system believe that *we*, the members of the Administration, are now guilty of *inflexibility*.[4] Conversations with Joe Martin and Bill Hill confirm this impression of their attitude.[5]

A number of Republican Congressmen have been advised by such individuals as Senator Schoeppel to run for the Congress on their own individual platforms, repudiating completely such items of the Administration programs as they do not like.[6]

One of the programs leading toward this kind of division is the Reciprocal Trade Bill. Others are the Mutual Security Program, and specific features of the Farm Program.[7]

I thoroughly believe that the majority of Americans approves of the direction of movement of the Administration's Farm Program. I believe the same thing about our Mutual Security and Foreign Trade Programs. But, as I noted in our conversation yesterday morning, there are often considerable differences, at any one time, between the political thinking of the country and the political actions taken by the Congress.

It is clear that if this kind of trend toward political individualism is going to continue in the current session of the Congress, there will be an increasing number of defections. The result will be that the most vitally important legislative measures for the long term good of the United States will be weakened or defeated, and the Republican strength in future elections will be badly damaged.

For five years we have been working hard to get Federal Programs affecting American agriculture on a sounder basis. I most sincerely believe that we have done this and for this great progress you have been primarily responsible. But we should observe that never in any one year have we gotten exactly what we wanted. Even when we first got some flexibility in farm prices, we had to take it on a step by step basis.

All I want to say here is that I believe it is *not* good *Congressional* politics to fail to listen seriously to the recommendations of our own Congressional leaders. Charlie Halleck, Les Arends, Joe Martin and Bill Hill from the House, as well as Bill Knowland, Everett Dirksen and others from the Senate, will find it difficult to keep their cohorts solidly together in critical moments unless we are ready to make what they consider are some necessary concessions from time to time.

So far as you and I are concerned, we certainly can have nothing to lose or to gain, except the satisfaction that we may derive from doing the very best job within our power for the country's good. But, sometimes in the workings of a democratic society, it is not sufficient merely to be completely right. We recall that Aristides lost the most important election of his life because the Athenian people were tired of hearing him called "The Just."[8]

As of this moment, I can see no way in which you can logically take action that our best Congressional friends would consider as an amelioration of their legislative difficulties. But I do believe that in future planning we should avoid advanced positions of inflexibility. We must have some room for maneuver, or we shall suffer for it.[9]

With warm regard, *As ever*

[1] Benson had written on March 18 (AWF/A) to reiterate his opposition to the so-called price freeze bill introduced in the Senate on March 7 (for background see no. 580). The bill was an attempt by Congress to help farmers and curb the recession by blocking the scheduled reductions in price supports for corn, rice, wheat and dairy products (see *Congressional Quarterly Almanac*, vol. XIV, *1958*, pp. 270–71).
[2] In his January 16 message to Congress on agriculture, Eisenhower had outlined a nine-point program designed to ease the burden of federal regulations on agriculture and to reduce the subsidies paid to farmers (see *Public Papers of the Presidents: Eisenhower, 1958*, pp. 100–107; for background see Galambos and van Ee, *The Middle Way*, nos. 1071 and 1841; on the Agricultural Act of 1958 see *Congressional Quarterly Almanac*, vol. XIV, *1958*, pp. 269–70).
[3] The French philosopher Voltaire had used the expression "The best is the enemy of the good" in a 1772 work entitled "La Begueule" (Elizabeth Knowles, ed., *The Oxford Dictionary of Phrase, Saying, and Quotation* [Oxford and New York, 1997], p. 156).
[4] Eisenhower had met with the legislative leaders on March 18 for his weekly scheduled session. Ann Whitman would note that the meeting lasted an "extraordinarily long" time and involved "considerable controversy about many subjects, principally the farm problem" (Ann Whitman memorandum, Mar. 18, 1958, AWF/AWD; see also Legislative Supplementary Notes, Mar. 18, 1958, AWF/D).

[5] William S. Hill, Republican Congressman from Colorado, served on the House Agriculture Committee. He and Congressman Martin had met with the President on March 19 to complain about Benson's supposed "inflexibility" (Ann Whitman memorandum, Mar. 19, 1958, AWF/AWD). Martin and Hill, speaking for the House Republican Policy Committee, urged the President and Secretary Benson to modify the order reducing the price supports on milk and butterfat. They suggested that the Secretary could phase in the reduction over a two-year period, rather than cutting the supports all at once. In this way, they felt, the Secretary could both recognize that conditions had changed since the order was issued in December 1957 and modify his position without sacrificing his principles. Eisenhower told Benson that "political considerations were involved" and that sometimes it was necessary to "sacrifice a battalion in order to win a battle." While he would not tell the Secretary what he should do, he urged him to "reexamine his position with his top policy people." Benson would later tell Sherman Adams that "after a thorough discussion of the milk order with his policy staff he felt that he could not in good conscience modify the order in any way" (Anderson memorandum, Mar. 19, 1958, AWF/D).

[6] Andrew F. Schoeppel, Republican Senator from Kansas since 1948, was chairman of the Senate Republican Campaign Committee. During the March 5 news conference, Eisenhower was asked about a statement Shoeppel was reported to have made the previous weekend, claiming "that it would be detrimental in some States for Republican candidates to campaign in support of your administration" (Public Papers of the Presidents: Eisenhower, 1958, p. 205).

[7] On the reciprocal trade bill and the mutual security act see nos. 524 and 753.

[8] Aristides (5th century BC) was an Athenian statesman and general and founder of the Delian League, the precursor to the Athenian Empire. On his reputation as "the Just" and his banishment from Athens, see John W. McFarland, Pleasant Graves, and Audrey Graves, eds., Lives from Plutarch (New York, 1972), pp. 21-32.

[9] On March 31 Eisenhower would veto Senate Joint Resolution 162, the price freeze bill. The President would say that, "With regard to government controls, what the farm economy needs is a thaw rather than a freeze." Eisenhower would propose an alternative five-point program, which included measures to help the dairy industry that did not involve freezing support levels. Dairy products acquired under the price support operation would be used outside the regular domestic market, in, for instance, donations to the school lunch program, charitable institutions, and the needy. When appropriate, surplus dairy products would be exported. See Public Papers of the Presidents: Eisenhower, 1958, pp. 250–56. On the Agricultural Act of 1958 see no. 809.

617 *Dulles Papers,*
White House Memoranda Series

To John Foster Dulles *March 21, 1958*

Dear Foster: Herewith a draft of the talk I am planning to make before the Editors on April seventeenth. There is still quite a bit of work to be done on it.[1]

My theme is that *we* must find ways of reducing the *need* for armaments. I mention various proposals that we have put forward during the past five years to ease tensions and promote peace—for example disarmament, atoms for peace, science for peace, control of outer space for peaceful purposes, exchanges of students, leaders of thought and so on, and a general diminishing of the barriers between free intercourse of ideas, persons and things. But I have wanted to make a rather startling new proposal.

I wanted to suggest that, if the Soviets were interested, I would recommend to Congress the inviting of several thousand students for one year.[2] Maybe this idea is not completely sound, but we need some vehicle to ride in order to suggest to the world, even if ever so briefly, that we are not stuck in the mud. We realize that the world is asking for something that is almost impossible when it insists that we should give to all peoples complete assurance that we are not only peaceful and friendly, but that we shall "hold the initiative" in striving for peace.[3]

Our public relations problem almost defies solution. The need always for concerting our views with those of our principal allies, the seductive quality of Soviet promises and pronouncements in spite of their unreliability, the propaganda disadvantage under which we operate because of the monolithic character of Soviet news broadcasts, and the readiness of many nations to take a virtual blackmail position as they make more and more urgent requests for aid—all serve to make us appear before the world as something less than persuasive in proclaiming our peaceful purposes and our effectiveness in pursuing them.

I didn't mean to write at this length. I only want to ask for your comments on the draft as it stands now. Any penciled notes in the margin would be completely satisfactory.

If you could let me have the draft back some time the early part of the week, I would be grateful.[4]

With warm regard, *As ever*

P.S. Your note of this morning, enclosing some comments by your staff, seems to condemn my idea as futile. But I'm not yet certain that, as presented in the accompanying draft, it may not have some value.[5]

---

[1] For background on Eisenhower's proposed speech to the American Society of Newspaper Editors see no. 607.

[2] On Eisenhower's plan to invite Soviet students to the United States see no. 552.

[3] After Dulles's return from the SEATO conference, he and Eisenhower had discussed the "militaristic image" of the United States as portrayed by newspapers in the Far East (Memorandum of Conversation, Mar. 19, 1958, Dulles Papers, White House Memoranda Series).

[4] Dulles would tell Eisenhower that the speech seemed to him "unnecessarily somber." He cited many American foreign policy successes, including the termination of both the Korean and the Indochinese wars, the Austrian State Treaty, the International Atomic Energy Agency, the development of a European community, and the "apparent abandonment by the Soviet leaders of methods of violence." Although arms limitation had eluded them, Dulles was still hopeful. "I am not particularly con-

fident of evolving any complicated, formal agreement with the Soviets," he said, "but I think that there could be perhaps parallel unilateral acts which would slow down the pace consistently with our safety." Dulles also suggested that Eisenhower point out that the United States did not need to develop every military potential, but only that necessary to deter attack. "I suspect that it might draw a positive response from the Russians," he said, "if only because they must be even more burdened than we by the cost of modern weapons" (Dulles to Eisenhower, Mar. 25, 1958, Dulles Papers, White House Memoranda Series).

[5] For Dulles's note see the following document; for developments see no. 623.

618   *EM, AWF, Dulles-Herter Series*

To John Foster Dulles   *March 21, 1958*

Dear Foster: With respect to your memorandum of March twentieth, attaching some staff notes discussing problems involved in US–USSR student exchange:[1]

I did not propose an exchange of students. My idea is to propose an invitation to a large group of these people to enter undergraduate schools here for one year.

The arguments for doing something of this kind are not to be found exclusively in the propaganda field. They are more compelling when we consider the benefits to be derived by us and the free world if Iron Curtain people could get a clearer understanding of American life and intentions.

Only this morning you were pointing out the great disadvantages that we incur by reason of the fact that people in the Far East do not understand America and what is going on here.[2] Even though a supposedly "free press" reaches those nations, that misunderstanding is not only very noticeable but its consequences are serious to us. The proposal I am considering would be aimed at clearing up such misunderstanding.

Now, with respect to some of the problems mentioned.

(*a*). I checked the security matter with Edgar Hoover, who said that the volume of the security problem would be slightly increased, but in reality it would be little more difficult.[3] Personally, he was in favor of the idea, saying, in effect, "It is high time that we were doing something positive; we cannot always be merely negative."

(*b*). If the information provided to me is reasonably accurate, there is a period for the next two or three years during which our undergraduate bodies will *not* be filled; I am told that numbers of undergraduate institutions are anxiously striving to fill up their student bodies.

(*c*). Of course the program would not be cheap. I had been calculating a total of $3,000 per student for one year, and I was thinking of something on the order of 5,000 students. This would cost us $15,000,000 per year.[4] *As ever*

[1] For background see the preceding document. Among the problems State Department officials had raised were: the expected Soviet resistance to an exchange of more than thirty students; possible visa problems associated with those students that were members of a Communist youth organization; the reluctance of American universities to assume security responsibilities for Soviet students; the extensive public funds necessary to cover the costs involved in an exchange; and the inability of the United States to offer similar exchange opportunities to other countries, particularly in Eastern Europe (Dulles to Eisenhower, Mar. 20, 1958; and "An Estimate of the Problems Involved in U.S.-U.S.S.R. Student Exchanges," n.d., both in AWF/D-H).
[2] At the Cabinet meeting that morning Dulles had reported on his Far East travels in connection with the SEATO conference. The news relating to the United States in that part of the world was "all bad," Dulles said. "In contrast to the careful control of all news out of Russia so as to show the Soviets off to good advantage, the United States is seriously hurt by the great play given to any statement of any US official that can be used to show the United States as being militaristic" (Cabinet meeting minutes, Mar. 21, 1958, AWF/D).
[3] For background on John Edgar Hoover, Director of the Federal Bureau of Investigation since 1924, see Galambos, *Chief of Staff*, no. 719.
[4] For developments see no. 640.

619   *EM, AWF, International Series:*
                                                              Bulganin

To Nikolai Aleksandrovich Bulganin   *March 22, 1958*

Dear Mr. Chairman:[1] I have received your letter of March 3. In my view, the substantive points which you make with regard to a possible Summit meeting do not appear to differ from those contained in the Aide Memoire which Mr. Gromyko gave Ambassador Thompson on February 28.[2] A full reply to the Aide Memoire has already been given to the Soviet Ambassador in Washington.[3] We are now awaiting, therefore, the Soviet Government's response in the hope that this response will facilitate progress toward resolution of the important problems to which I have drawn attention in my previous communications to you.[4]

In your letter you also make certain allegations with respect to American policy with which I cannot agree and on which I may wish to comment at a later date.[5] *Sincerely*

[1] State Department officials drafted this letter to the Soviet leader; it would not be sent, however, after receiving a subsequent Soviet aide-memoire (see n. 5; Dulles to

Eisenhower, Mar. 21, 1958, AWF/I: Bulganin; and Dulles to Eisenhower, Apr. 3, 1958, AWF/D-H).

[2] Bulganin had assured Eisenhower that the Soviet Union was willing to consider proposals recommended for discussion by other participating nations; those proposals, however, could not include the internal affairs of other states or the reunification of Germany (AWF/I: Bulganin). For the Soviet aide-memoire see no. 588.

[3] The U.S. reply, delivered to Ambassador Mikhail A. Menshikov on March 6, acknowledged the willingness of the Soviet Union to have preliminary meetings of the foreign ministers but maintained that the summit meeting envisioned by the Soviets would not reduce international tension. The United States wanted a meeting that would resolve such political issues as the limitation of armaments and would create an atmosphere conducive to further settlements (State, *American Foreign Policy, Current Documents, 1958*, pp. 763–66).

[4] See nos. 521 and 574.

[5] Bulganin had criticized those in the United States who had called for a preventive war against the Soviet Union. Although he acknowledged that this was not the official policy of the United States, Bulganin told Eisenhower that the Soviet Union could not ignore these statements, especially since the U.S. government did not condemn them. Bulganin also objected to assertions that the Soviets were to blame for the failure to achieve nuclear disarmament.

On March 24 Soviet Foreign Minister Andrei Gromyko would give Ambassador Thompson an aide-memoire, answering the U.S. note of March 6. The note, Dulles would later report, demanded "a very high political price" as a condition for a summit meeting. The Soviets had asked for the recognition of the East German government; the ending of the 1955 Geneva agreement to work toward the reunification of Germany; and the acceptance of an agenda based on premises the Western nations did not accept (Dulles to Eisenhower, Mar. 25, 1958, AWF/D-H; and State, *American Foreign Policy, Current Documents, 1958*, pp. 771–77). For developments see no. 628.

620

To ARTHUR FRANK BURNS   *March 24, 1958*
Personal

Dear Arthur: I have just finished reading a copy of your talk made in Chicago on March twenty-second.[1] I assume you have already sent Saulnier a copy and I am sending mine on to Anderson and to Hauge for their information.[2]

I particularly like the approach you take in examining the economy and in suggesting various methods by which business leaders, as well as the government, can be helpful.[3]

Incidentally, you said nothing about responsibilities of labor leaders.[4]

With respect to your discussion of a tax reduction, it seems to me that there is little difference between your attitude and what might be called the consensus here in the Administration.[5] There is one fact in this connection that has not been emphasized. It is this: costs of governmental programs already undertaken are certain to mount. This is not only because of the added unit costs due to the inflationary effect of anti-recession measures, but because these programs themselves have the tendency to mushroom. In the defense category we have had much experience in seeing how the aggregate of expenses goes up each year due to the reluctance to abandon old programs and the anxiety to add new ones.[6]

The best estimates I can now get for the probable costs of programs already scheduled or practically certain of adoption at the moment is something like *80 billion dollars in 1961*. This of course assumes no general or drastic change in the world outlook.

This means that alongside the advantages to be gained out of the tax reduction, including the expectancy of a widened tax base, we must also take into account the effects of great deficits—and the additional amounts that must be included in the costs of shelter, food and clothing.

Not easy, is it?[7] *As ever*

[1] For background see nos. 577 and 615. Burns had written on March 21, 1958 (AWF/ A), to forward a copy of his talk, entitled "The Current Business Recession," to be delivered at the Sixth Annual Management Conference of the University of Chicago. Eisenhower might, Burns said, find the talk "somewhat helpful at this difficult time."

[2] Eisenhower would send a copy of the talk to Treasury Secretary Anderson on that same day (AWF/A). He would comment that although Burns advocated a "prompt tax reduction," he was "very careful to give a balanced picture of our economy as it is now operating and tries to get the tax cut proposition placed in perspective." The President would also ask Chairman of the Council of Economic Advisors Raymond J. Saulnier whether he had received a copy of the Burns talk (Mar. 24, 1958, AWF/ A). In his March 26 reply (AWF/A), Saulnier would state that Burns's talk contained "much with which I agree, though I take a slightly different view on taxes and a completely different one on the question of amending the Employment Act to make price stability an explicit objective of governmental policy. The latter, in my judgment, could prove very troublesome and I hope we never amend our law to this effect."

[3] After reviewing what he believed to be the causes of the recession, Burns had suggested several government measures he believed would promote "speedy recovery and a sound prosperity." These included "a broadly based tax reduction," and "the improvement of the unemployment insurance system." Businessmen, however, should not wait to see what the government would do next, Burns added. Firms might need to intensify selling efforts, relax credit standards within prudent limits, introduce new products earlier than planned, accelerate research and development, and maintain or even increase dividends if profits were still ample and capital expenditures declining.

[4] For Eisenhower's views on the responsibilities of business leaders see Galambos and van Ee, *The Middle Way*, no. 1805.

[5] Burns had suggested that a tax reduction was a better method of dealing with a mild recession than was a large public works program. Burns argued that "a sizable and broadly based tax reduction, applicable to high as well as low incomes and to businesses as well as individuals," could have a powerful economic effect: "Such a

tax cut would increase promptly the spending power of both consumers and business firms. More important still, it would change the atmosphere or climate within which the spending decisions of consumers, businessmen, and investors are made."
[6] On rising defense expenditure see no. 448.
[7] For developments see no. 633.

621   *EM, AWF, Name Series*

To William Edward Robinson   *March 24, 1958*

Dear Bill: I have read the several articles contained in the advertisements of McCann-Erickson, Inc. They are good—I hope that the public will read them carefully and absorb their meaning promptly.[1]

The articles are directed to the people as a whole. This is as it should be because the purpose is to combat the apathy and complacency of a population that, the fortunate possessors of leisure and material rewards elsewhere unknown, is as much preoccupied with its own pleasures, entertainment and recreational opportunities as it is with the consequences to the whole free world of the potential Soviet threat.

For too long we have indulged in the habit of shrugging off disagreeable problems and possibilities in the hope that government will pick these up. We seem, at the same time, to assume that the abandonment of our own studies and duties will somehow give us still more time for self-indulgence.

For example, the articles point out that we must give more attention to the scientists and to our educational processes, so as to produce better citizens, including scientists. What government has done in this direction has been little enough, but the public is almost unaware of the need itself. For several years I have personally tried to get established what might be described as an Academy of the Arts and Sciences.[2] In addition, through the Atomic Energy Commission there has been established the Fermi Award,[3] while the Ford Foundation picked up my idea of awarding scientists for accomplishments in the peaceful use of the atom and established another award.[4] Each of these, I believe, is for $75,000. But while both Drs. Bohr and Lawrence in the past few months have received these awards, there has been almost no mention of them in the press.[5] It is difficult to believe that Americans would be more widely interested in a Swedish award than in an American one of much greater size and for which the scientific standards are certainly as strict.[6]

So, I repeat, I hope that the several advertisements will be helpful. In fact, it seems to me that they are certain to be.

I cannot tell you how delighted I was that we could go together to Augusta even though the trip was only a little over twenty-four hours in duration. Both of us have to do something drastic about our golf.[7] *As ever*

[1] International advertising agency McCann-Erickson had begun a series of five consecutive-day full-page advertisements in the March 24, 1958, *New York Times*. Seeking to spur the United States forward in its competition with the Soviet Union, the first article ("Who Has the Ultimate Weapon"), recognized the "immense scope of the Russian challenge" but also tried to reassure the American people that "no source of power yet discovered can match the energy that freedom can release in the minds and hearts of its people." Subsequent articles extolled the virtues of a free economy as an "economy of abundance," argued that the United States needed to provide scientists with the means, including "respect and status . . . [and] financial reward," to do their jobs, and called for a reevaluation of education in terms of its critical importance in the national scene.

On March 28 the *New York Times* published the fifth and final article: "How do We Look in the Space-Age Mirror?" It declared that the Soviet Sputnik had done a great service by clarifying the task facing America: "It has held up a yardstick to freedom and made us study each of its strengths against space-age demands. In every department—weapons, science, industrial production, education—America has the means of victory. Beyond that, it needs only the will." Freedom would provide the "ultimate weapon for survival and the ultimate promise of peace."

[2] For background see Eisenhower, *Waging Peace*, pp. 216–18; see also Clowse, *Brainpower for the Cold War*, pp. 5–16.

[3] The Fermi Award, named in honor of nuclear scientist Enrico Fermi who had died in 1954, was authorized by Congress that same year. This $50,000 prize, the government's oldest science and technology award, was given for a lifetime of achievement in the field of nuclear energy (see *New York Times*, Apr. 29, 1956).

[4] In 1955 the Ford Motor Company established the $75,000 Atoms for Peace Award as a memorial to Henry and Edsel Ford.

[5] Niels Henrik David Bohr, winner of the 1922 Nobel Prize for Physics, had been awarded the first Atoms for Peace Award on October 24, 1957 (see *Public Papers of the Presidents: Eisenhower, 1957*, pp. 766–68; *New York Times*, Mar. 14, 1957). Ernest Orlando Lawrence, winner of the 1939 Nobel Prize for Physics for his invention of the cyclotron, had been awarded the Fermi Award in 1957 (*New York Times*, Oct. 30, Dec. 3, 1957). Following Lawrence's death in August 1958, Eisenhower would establish an annual Ernest Orlando Lawrence Award for "especially meritorious achievements in the broad field of atomic endeavor" (*New York Times*, Aug. 31, 1958).

[6] The Nobel Prize, the value of which amounted to $38,700 in 1956, had been awarded since 1901. See Peter Wilhelm, *The Nobel Prize* (Stockholm; London, 1983), pp. 22–36; see also *New York Times*, April 2, 8, 1956.

[7] The President had played golf in Augusta on March 22 and March 23 with John Eisenhower, Clifford Roberts, and William Robinson. Robinson would respond on March 26 (AWF/N). He believed it would be possible to build some "real awareness" of the Fermi Award over the next year and told the President that he intended "to speak to some of my friends who might have some competence in this direction." Eisenhower would reply (Mar. 28, 1958, AWF/N) that if Robinson spoke to his friends about the Fermi Award, he hoped he would "also include mention of the Ford Foundation award for accomplishments in the *peaceful* use of the atom. Both are highly important."

To Edward Everett Hazlett, Jr.   *March 25, 1958*

Dear Swede: I understand from my private intelligence system that you are still undergoing tests out at Bethesda.[1] I know you realize how strongly I pray that medical science will finally find the answer to your difficulty and some way to alleviate it.

Over the weekend, as perhaps you know, I went to Augusta in search of the elusive sun and a decent game of golf.[2] The sun I found but there was absolutely no consolation in the brand of game I exhibited.

Perhaps these flowers will be a spot of color in your room; at the very least they will assure you that I am thinking of you.[3]

With warm regard, *As ever*

[1] Hazlett had been undergoing tests and treatments for high blood pressure and severe headaches since January 1957 (see nos. 41 and 457).
[2] While vacationing, the President played eighteen holes of golf on Saturday, March 22, and two separate rounds of nine holes on Sunday. For developments see no. 651.
[3] For developments on Hazlett's health see no. 645.

To John Foster Dulles   *March 26, 1958*
Personal and confidential

Dear Foster: I called you on the phone, but find you are still on the Hill. I wanted to talk to you about your conclusion that I was becoming a pessimist.[1]

In trying to produce a draft of a talk before the Editors, an effort which I am now disposed to postpone, I deliberately wanted to stress the difficulties *now* confronting the world. Of these, the greatest are:

(*a*). The costs of relative security with the attendant possibilities of, either:

(1). Seeing the American people get so tired of these huge expenditures as to cause them to refuse to support necessary appropriations and thus expose us to unacceptable risks.

(2). Imposing upon our people such political and economic controls as would imply a dangerous degree of regimentation.

(*b*). The task of reaching some reliable agreements with the Soviets that will make it possible, with confidence, to reduce armaments.

To my mind this transcends all other objectives we can have. Security through arms is only a means (and sometimes a poor one) to an end. Peace, in a very real sense, is an end in itself.

It is, of course, quite comforting to recite all of the international difficulties that have, over the five years, been either surmounted or ameliorated. I've personally recited these in a number of speeches.[2]

But these specific successes cannot blind us to the most potentially dangerous of all the situations now developing. This is the credence, even respect, that the world is beginning to give to the spurious Soviet protestations and pronouncements. As their propaganda promotes this world confusion, the tone of Soviet notes and statements grows more strident. The more the men in the Kremlin come to believe that their domestic propaganda is swallowed by their own people and by the populations of other countries, including some we have counted upon as allies, the greater the risk of American isolation. One great step we can take to counteract this trend is to make sure our own people are not deceived.

It is not pessimistic to face up to difficulties and to seek ways to overcome them. We must never confess that we have gotten to the bottom of the barrel in searching for ideas to stem and turn the tide of Soviet propaganda success.

I personally believe that one of the main objectives of our own efforts should be to encourage our entire people to see, with clear eyes, the changing character of our difficulties, and to convince them that we must be vigilant, energetic, imaginative and incapable of surrender through fatigue or lack of courage.

So, no matter what the preoccupations we daily have with the unfolding scene—both international and domestic—I feel that our principal responsibility is to try unceasingly to create both general and specific situations under which the consummation of reliable agreements conforming to our ideas of right and justice can be more probable.

I have not the temerity to argue that any idea I have advanced is necessarily good; I just say that we have one basic job to do. A part of this is educating and informing our own people—so that they will support every burden we must carry, and will dedicate themselves to helping seek out new ways to dispel the basic differences between us and the Soviets that, becoming more and more unyielding in character, could finally lead to consequences that could be most unpleasant.

My own feeling about this business is simple. Optimism is not the ability to smile because of a refusal to face disagreeable facts; it is the seeking unceasingly (and, if possible, intelligently) for the methods and means to overcome difficulties.[3]

With warm regard, *As ever*

[1] Eisenhower is referring to Dulles's reaction to the draft of a speech the President was to give before the American Society of Newspaper Editors on April 17. For Dulles's comments see no. 617.

[2] Dulles had suggested that Eisenhower emphasize such accomplishments of his Administration as the Korean Armistice, the Austrian State Treaty, and the International Atomic Energy Agency (Dulles to Eisenhower, Mar. 25, 1958, AWF/D-H; see also no. 617).

[3] After a meeting with Presidential Assistant Arthur Larson regarding the speech, Eisenhower had contemplated abandoning the idea because Dulles had taken "a dim view" of the proposed student exchange. The President thought the speech was "unworthy" without the exchange proposal (Ann Whitman memorandum, Mar. 26, 1958, AWF/AWD). Eisenhower would later tell Dulles that he had cancelled the speech. Unless he could provide a fresh approach, he said, he did not want to "belabor the subject." He really wanted to make the American people understand that they had "a blood, sweat, and tears problem" and unless they accepted it, the United States was "going to be in a hell of a fix" (Telephone conversation, Eisenhower and Dulles, Mar. 26, 1958, Dulles Papers, Telephone Conversations, and AWF/D).

As it turned out, Eisenhower would address the editors on the subject of defense reorganization, a topic that he would call "more national than international in scope." The speech would, however, include a list of his Administration's foreign policy successes (see *Public Papers of the Presidents: Eisenhower, 1958*, pp. 325–34; see also Dulles to Harlow, Apr. 9, 1958, Dulles Papers, Chronological Series; and Ann Whitman memorandums, Apr. 7, 9, 17, 1958, AWF/AWD).

624   *EM, AWF, Administration Series*

To Charles Douglas Jackson   *March 26, 1958*
Personal

Dear C. D.: This morning I read in my daily paper a reprint of *Life's* editorial on education. To say that I concur with its purpose and I am delighted with its tenor and tone is to express the understatement of the week.[1]

Since I suspect that you are the author, I want your permission to register one protest, involving nothing but two words in the editorial.[2]

The first is "existentialism."[3] Through the years I have done a bit of reading about some of the thinkers like Plato, Kant and Nietzsche, not to mention such proponents of more particularized ideas, such as Tom Paine, Thoreau and Machiavelli. But I confess ignorance of even the existence of the pseudo-philosophical Frenchman who developed the doctrine of existentialism.[4]

You use the word "lamaseries," probably to remind the average reader that it would be wise to check his impressions against the dictionary.[5] (I happened to know this one, but only because the working out of a cross-word puzzle suggested it to me.)

Now, I do not question the accuracy of the meaning you were expressing—I just doubt that Lincoln, a master of expressive prose, would have used these words.

Having, through the means of this protest conveyed an apology for my own unfamiliarity with long and little used words, I go back to my song of praise. Frankly, I hope that you are not content with the publication of one such editorial. Five years in my present post have more and more convinced me of not only the value but the indispensability of reiteration. Educators, parents and students alike must be continuously stirred up by the defects in our educational system. They must be induced to abandon the educational path that, rather blindly, they have been following as a result of John Dewey's teachings. I quite agree that so long as he was striving only to improve methods, his work was of the greatest possible value. But when he (or his followers) went free-wheeling into the realm of basic education they, in my opinion, did a great disservice to the American public.[6]

I should like to see a return to fundamentals in both high school and indeed in the higher grades of the elementary schools. We should stress English, history, mathematics, the simple rudiments of one or more of the sciences, and at least one language. We should demand real concentration on these subjects.

It is a reform that I believe could come about fairly promptly if a sufficient number of our respected periodicals, lecturers, speakers, business and other leaders would make such an effort a personal and primary objective.[7]

After this long note it seems ridiculous to say that my simple purpose was just to shout, "Me, too." Actually, that is all I have said.

With warm regard, *As ever*

[1] The March 31, 1958, *Life* magazine had published an editorial entitled "The Deeper Problem in Education: It is to Dig Out Educationists' Debris and Rediscover Learning's True Nature." The author of the article argued that the emphasis placed by the exponents of progressive education on pedagogical methodology had come at the expense of mastery of a body of knowledge. While praising the "worthwhile innovations in method" that modern educators had instituted, the article warned that "their exclusive devotion to techniques and group adjustment should never again be allowed to hide the fact that American education exists first of all to educate the individual in a body of learning, with a tradition and purpose behind it."
[2] In his April 8, 1958, reply (AWF/A) Jackson would say that while he was "flattered" by Eisenhower's belief that he wrote the editorial, in actuality "it was written by Frank Gibney, who works with Jack Jessup on the *LIFE* editorial page."
[3] The *Life* editorial had stated "in a kind of country club existentialism," those favoring progressive education had "genially contended that the traditional ends of education—and indeed of human life—like God, virtue and the idea of 'culture' were all debatable and hence not worth debating." Existentialism, a philosophy dating from about 1930, stressed the concreteness and problematic character of human existence in the world. See William Barrett, *What is Existentialism?* (New York, 1964),

and Robert Denoon Cumming, *Starting Point: An Introduction to the Dialectic of Existence* (Chicago and London, 1979),

[4] Eisenhower may have been referring to Gabriel-Honoré Marcel, usually regarded as the first French existential philosopher, or to Jean-Paul Sartre, an influential French novelist and exponent of existentialism (see James Collins, *The Existentialists: A Critical Study* [Chicago, 1952], pp. 128–67).

[5] A lamascry is a monastery for lamas. The editorial had complained that following Dewey's philosophy, "teachers' colleges assumed the dignities of lamaseries."

[6] John Dewey (A.B. University of Vermont 1879) had died in 1952. A philosopher and psychologist, he had played a major role in developing the philosophy of pragmatism; he had also been a leader in the progressive education movement. See George Dykhuizen, *The Life and Mind of John Dewey* (Carbondale and Edwardsville, Ill., 1973), and Richard J. Bernstein, *John Dewey* (New York, 1966).

[7] Jackson would note in his reply that letters from teachers' college circles were pouring in. "A really distressing aspect of it all is that so many of the letters say, 'As a teacher I don't dare approve of your editorial publicly, but I want you to know privately that I agree.'"

625   *EM, AWF,*
Administration Series

To Christian Archibald Herter   *March 26, 1958*

Dear Chris: In view of our intense preoccupation with Indonesia and Morocco and the Middle East (to say nothing of the furious correspondence we are having with Mr. Bulganin) birthday anniversaries have a habit of creeping up on us almost unaware. So I send you this note simply to be certain that on Friday morning you are assured of my warm felicitations and best wishes.[1]

    With personal regard, *As ever*

[1] On the deteriorating relations between the Netherlands and Indonesia see no. 501; on French difficulties in North Africa see no. 586; and on the proposed union between Eqypt and Syria see no. 560. Eisenhower's latest letter to Bulganin is no. 619. Herter would celebrate his sixty-third birthday on March 28.

626   *EM, AWF, Name Series*

To Clifford Roberts   *March 27, 1958*

Dear Cliff: When we were talking the other day, I pointed out that I could support enthusiastically any Republican candidate for office, provided that he and I could agree on two or three fundamentals of world import.[1] I have never felt that a good Republican has any compulsion to agree with me, or I with him, on every detail of our respective beliefs and convictions relating to politics. I went on to say that I could work earnestly with any Republican who held, with me, common convictions as to several subjects, basic in their character.

(1). The Republican Party is essentially conservative with respect to its approach to the American economy. We believe in fiscal responsibility and deplore deficit spending except when clearly necessary.

Specifically we believe that individuals should have the greatest amount of freedom in making their own economic decisions. As a corollary we believe that governmental control over the economy should be limited to that which can be logically demonstrated as necessary.

These convictions, applied to conditions of the moment, dictate that the Federal government should do its very best to point the way toward and to stimulate the economy toward greater activity. But it should not undertake unwise and unjustified activity that would, by its very nature, either be largely futile as an immediate spur to the economy or might have a serious aftermath leading toward inflation or other unpleasant consequences.[2]

(2). We believe we must assure the security of our own country, first of all, by maintaining with the utmost economy adequate and efficient defense forces. We help our own security by cooperating with other nations which stand with us in opposition to the Communist threat and which provide bases from which our own defensive forces can operate with the greatest efficiency. In carrying on this cooperative effort we provide some special military assistance to some of these nations.[3]

(3). We believe in building greater cooperation among the nations of the free world and in helping them raise their living standards. The purpose is to assure that they will become increasingly insensitive to Soviet pressures and will, in each case, become a self-reliant and sturdy people who will not succumb to Soviet blandishments.

To do this we must promote freer trade and we must in certain instances provide economic aid to nations, particularly in the form of loans for capital investment. So far as possible this last should be done by private agencies.[4]

The nation's needs in (2) and (3) above, are about as described in the appropriate programs already recommended to the Congress.[5]

All this is very roughly written, but to my mind little more is necessary[6] These are the most important aims and jobs of the United States today, internally and externally. If an individual is a loyal supporter of these simple ideas and views, then I am for him and I hope all my friends will be for him. If he is an opponent then I cannot support him. Again, however, I express a word of caution. What I am talking about is overall agreement on these objectives and upon the scale and level of the programs recommended, not necessarily on every detail thereof.

With warm regard, *As ever*

[1] The President had played golf with investment banker Roberts in Augusta, Georgia, on both March 22 and March 23. Eisenhower also sent a copy of this letter to Republican National Committee Chairman Meade Alcorn (Mar. 26, 1958, AWF/A).
[2] On the debate over the federal government's role in bringing an end to the recession see nos. 598 and 620.
[3] For Eisenhower's views on mutual security see nos. 60, 90, and 147.
[4] On the reciprocal trade agreement and the World Bank see nos. 75 and 524.
[5] For developments on the Mutual Security Act see no. 762 and *Congressional Quarterly Almanac*, vol. XIV, *1958*, pp. 183–88.
[6] Eisenhower had also added a longhand *p.s.*: "All this *could* have been said in many fewer words. Sometimes it takes a long time to carve a clumsy article down to a neat size." In his March 31 (AWF/N) reply, Roberts would say that he had re-read Eisenhower's letter several times. "I think I understand you completely but I agree that the three fundamentals might be expressed in a little more concise form." Roberts said that he would ask their friend Burt Peek, who was then at Augusta, to do a little "boiling down" work. In an April 17 letter (AWF/N), Roberts would note that he had continued to think about the President's letter. Although it was difficult to express the complex ideas succinctly, he promised to list the three points in the future "as being (1) fiscal responsibility, (2) adequate defense and (3) economic and military cooperation with the nations of the free world."

627

EM, WHCF,
Official File 114

To Martin Withington Clement   *March 27, 1958*

Dear Clem: I want to answer your note, if only to tell you how refreshing it is to find, in the daily grist of complaining letters that come to my desk, one such as yours. I agree completely with all you say as to the causes of our present difficulty and am, as you can well understand, more than a little disappointed when any group refuses to admit its responsibility. At the same time, there were other contributing factors to the present recession.[1]

As I said in a press conference recently, I feel we are experiencing the worst of the difficulty at the present time, and I am getting some encouraging reports from certain sections of the country.[2]

Thanks for your "cheers."

With warm regard, *As ever*

---

[1] Clement had written on March 20, 1958 (same file as document), in support of Eisenhower's economic policies. "Since you have been in office, you have balanced the budget, reduced taxes, given the dollar a sound value, brought integrity to all our transactions, and but for the wage spiral would have stopped inflation. You have maintained courage in saying that you will do everything that you can constructively do to bring about a resurgence of employment and production and saying that you will not get into such activities that would make hardships not temporary but chronic. That is the danger today." Clement had charged that the "spiraling of labor's wages" had caused the current recession and that the failure of labor leaders to demonstrate "statesmanship" by taking "a reduction in wages" was prolonging the downturn. See nos. 615 and 620. On labor pressure on wages see no. 583.

[2] Asked at his March 26 news conference whether he saw any sign that "the downward movement of the economy" was coming to an end, Eisenhower had responded that he thought there were "many factors that would imply that the bottom is certainly close, or possibly even now reached" (*Public Papers of the Presidents: Eisenhower, 1958*, p. 236).

---

628   *EM, AWF, International Series:*
                                                              Macmillan

To Harold Macmillan   *March 28, 1958*
Top secret

Dear Harold: I have not replied earlier to your letter of March 17 about a "Summit" meeting because the subject has been under such active, almost hourly, consideration between Foster and Harold Caccia that I knew you were aware that your point of view was being actively and sympathetically considered by us.[1]

Foster has just told me about the NATO meeting yesterday and I gather that aside from drafting questions you and we and our NATO partners are in agreement to take a step along the general lines which you wanted us to pursue.[2]

There is a problem about Italy. The Soviets have suggested the participation of Italy—with many others—and the Italians have taken hold of this very vigorously and are pressing us. I do not think we can deny them a role without injuring the prospects of our Italian friends in the forthcoming elections. On the other hand, it seems to me that the initial approach pattern ought to be the same as the last, namely, the three of us to the Soviet Union.[3]

I do feel, however, that this matter of composition is of the utmost importance and that we ought not in this respect to pay a costly political price for a ticket to the Summit—particularly since no one has yet suggested any really worthwhile result that might come out of that meeting.

I also have your letter of March 27.[4] We gave very serious thought to anticipating a possible Soviet move on suspension of testing by a statement of our own. I would, of course, have gotten in touch with you had we felt disposed to take this course. However, after weighing all of the factors, including your own problem, we concluded that it was on the whole best to do nothing at the moment. I do feel, however, that we are being pushed into a rather difficult position from the standpoint of world opinion and that we shall have to alter somewhat the four-power proposals in this respect. But of course we would not do so without full consultation with you.[5]

I hope that the amendment to the Atomic Energy Act can be put through in time to get our relationship in this respect on a new basis before the end of this Congress. I think, however, that Foster has told Harold Caccia that Congress is very sensitive to our now conducting negotiations on the assumption that the Act will be amended. I hope, however, in any event, that matters will move fast enough in Congress so that we could deal with this between us, when you are here in June.[6]

With warm regard, *As ever*

[1] For background on the proposed summit meeting and for Macmillan's letter see no. 611.

[2] Macmillan had suggested that the ambassadors begin discussions by formulating an agenda that had both subjects where some progress, however small, was likely, and subjects requiring serious discussion "if a Summit Meeting is to be worthy of the name." He also thought that Soviet officials might be willing "to bargain" about agenda items. By eliminating "Satellite States" as an agenda topic, he said, the Soviets might accept "European Security and Germany" (Macmillan to Eisenhower, Mar. 17, 1958, PREM 11/2554; see also Ann Whitman memorandum, Mar. 28, 1958, AWF/AWD; and no. 611).

[3] In their February 28 aide-memoire the Soviets had proposed that the foreign ministers of all the NATO and Warsaw Pact countries participate in the preliminary meetings (State, *American Foreign Policy, Current Documents, 1958*, p. 751). In an earlier discussion Eisenhower had told Secretary Dulles that he wanted foreign ministers from the same countries that had met after the Geneva Summit Conference in 1955 (the United States, Great Britain, France, and the Soviet Union) to decide the feasibility of a summit meeting. The President agreed that the Italians should participate in a summit meeting, but he believed that "you have to start from someplace and . . . just the four foreign ministers should start" (Telephone conversation, Eisenhower and Dulles, Mar. 25, 1958, Dulles Papers, Telephone Conversations and AWF/D).

[4] Macmillan had received reports that the Soviet Union was preparing to announce the unilateral suspension of nuclear testing or the manufacture of nuclear weapons, or both. The Russians would make this decision in order to avoid controls, he told Eisenhower, and "to tempt us to give up some of our positions in advance of Summit talks and, therefore, without any *quid pro quo.*" A means of verification should

accompany any decision to suspend testing, Macmillan said. "We should therefore keep this subject for negotiation at the Summit and not be drawn into proceeding by unilateral declarations" (Macmillan to Eisenhower, Mar. 27, 1958, AWF/I: Macmillan).

[5] Macmillan had opposed the suspension of testing as long as the Atomic Energy Act of 1954 limited the exchange of nuclear information between the United States and Great Britain. He told Eisenhower that he had an "extreme interest" in the progress of the amendments to the act, since the relaxation of restrictions would determine Great Britain's position on disarmament in talks with the Russians (see nos. 409 and 508 for background; see also Macmillan, *Riding the Storm*, 323–24, 476). On the four-power disarmament proposals signed by the United States, Great Britain, France, and Canada in August 1957 see no. 364.

[6] On Macmillan's visit to Washington see no. 581. For developments see no. 718.

629   *EM, AWF, Administration Series*

To Harold Edward Stassen   *March 28, 1958*
Personal

Dear Harold: I appreciate your taking the time to write me about the ridiculous question that confronted me at the press conference Wednesday, but it truly was not necessary. Of course I knew that you would not authorize such a badge, and I paid no further attention to the matter. I hope you won't, either.[1]

Many thanks for keeping me informed as to developments. As you can imagine, I am watching the situation with great interest.[2]

With warm regard, *As ever*

[1] Stassen was running for governor of Pennsylvania. At his March 26 news conference the President had been asked by a correspondent for the *Los Angeles Times* whether he had authorized badges circulating in Pennsylvania bearing Eisenhower's picture and the slogan, "I like Stassen for Governor." The President had responded: "I have always refused in advance of any primary or of any selection of Republican candidate for any office to intervene in any way, and I wouldn't want to be used either directly or indirectly in such a campaign" (*Public Papers of the Presidents: Eisenhower, 1958*, p. 242). Stassen had written to Eisenhower on March 27, 1958 (AWF/A) to assure him that there were "no such badges in circulation in Pennsylvania, and that I have at all times made it clear that I did not expect you to participate in the primary but would hope for your support after the primary is over."

[2] Stassen would lose his bid for election. For background on his candidacy see no. 594.

To Andrew Jackson Goodpaster, Jr.   *March 30, 1958*
Memorandum

With respect to the National Defense Reorganization Plan, I believe it is so long that we should have a short, strong summary at the beginning.[1]

I. The purpose of the plan is to remove legal restrictions upon the functioning of the entire Defense establishment and otherwise amend the law as needed, in order to facilitate unified direction and control.

II. Changes in the substantive law are not numerous, but they are important.

A. Remove restrictions applied to the authority and responsibility of the Secretary of Defense so that he is enabled:

1. To organize task forces and unified commands according to tactical needs and assign to each appropriate missions.

2. To organize the military staff under the Joint Chief of Staff at such strength and as needed by planning and operational requirements. Size of staff to be increased or as of such strength as determined by the Secretary of Defense.

III. Make a moderate reduction in the number of additional Assistant Secretaries in the several Services.

IV. Enable the Secretary of Defense, through a responsible Assistant, to organize, supervise and control Research and Development. The Secretary of Defense should be authorized to decide whether work is to be done directly or through one of the Services as agent.

V. Give to the Secretary of Defense great flexibility in managing financing through both direct appropriations or power of transfer. Particularly it is important that all Research money be appropriated directly to the Secretary of Defense.

VI. The Secretary of Defense, upon the recommendation of the Joint Chiefs of Staff, to recommend for appointment or removal all three and 4 star officers. Such appointments will be temporary and made according to positions held.

VII. Any other changes required in the law.

With these changes the Secretary of Defense will control unified commands through the Chiefs of Staff directly. There will be no executive agent.

VIII. The control of each unified commander over his own forces to be strengthened. (This may require law).

IX. The Secretary of Defense to be responsible for unified action in legislative contact activities and in public relations. (Again I am not certain whether or not law is involved).

Any other principal purposes of revision plans or Administrative action to be taken upon the enactment of necessary legislation should be included here as part of the summary.

It is important that the summary be as short as possible and conclude by merely saying: "The report herewith attached is historical reason for these changes and the details of the plan itself."[2]

---

[1] On the President's 1953 defense reorganization see Galambos and van Ee, *The Middle Way*, nos. 207, 353, and 693. Continuing problems with the defense structure and concerns that competition among the services was delaying missile development and deployment had led Eisenhower to seek a new reorganization (*ibid.*, 1663 and 1963). Although the 1956 reorganization plan had died in Congress, the successful launch in October 1957 of the Soviet earth satellite, Sputnik, had given impetus to the effort (see nos. 389, 390, 401, and 464). In his State of the Union Address on January 9, 1958, Eisenhower had called for changes in the Department of Defense and had cited the need for "real unity in the Defense establishment" and an end to interservice rivalries. His call for action would culminate in a special message to Congress on reorganization of the defense establishment (see *Public Papers of the Presidents: Eisenhower, 1958*, pp. 7–9, 274–90). See also *Congressional Quarterly Almanac*, vol. XIV, *1958*, pp. 133–39, and Watson, *Into the Missile Age 1956–1960*, pp. 246–62. Eisenhower dictated this memorandum during a weekend visit to his Gettysburg farm. The memorandum summarized proposals outlined earlier by General Goodpaster (Ann Whitman memorandum, Mar. 29, 1958, AWF/AWD).

[2] For developments see the following document.

9

"The problems inherent in this job"

To Henry Cabot Lodge, Jr.   *April 1, 1958*
Personal

Dear Cabot: Thanks for your note of yesterday. I agree with every word you say and I am, if I may use the expression, "going to town" on the issue of Defense Reorganization.[1]

Over the weekend I spent a great deal of time on the final draft of the document; I am determined to make it, in all respects, "mine."[2]

With warm regard, *As ever*

[1] Lodge had written on March 31 (AWF/A) to suggest that Eisenhower "vigorously (and both in private and in public) take the lead with Congress in favor of greater unity among the armed services." For background see the preceding document. Lodge said that Eisenhower's authority as Commander in Chief under the Constitution, as well as his personal experience, had given the President an "unparalleled right to speak." Presidential leadership in the campaign to reorganize the defense establishment would put the subject "on the front page where it belongs and would take the present politically-inspired anti-recession campaign off the front page" (for background see, for example, nos. 577 and 615). According to Lodge, congressional opposition to unification of the armed services was due to "Spokesmen for certain of the regular services [who] have worked with certain individual members to block and to obstruct." "But the point to remember," Lodge said, "is that these Members of Congress do not speak for any considerable body of opinion in the country and that opposition to unification is purely the work of a small congressional clique acting in response to certain professional military prompting. The weight of public opinion is all on the side of eliminating inter-service bickering and towards greater unity."

[2] Eisenhower was referring to his "Special Message to Congress on Reorganization of the Defense Establishment," which he would deliver on April 3 (see *Public Papers of the Presidents: Eisenhower, 1958*, pp. 274–90; see also *New York Times*, Apr. 4, 1958). The President would ask that all operating forces be organized into "truly unified commands" that were separated from the military departments; that the traditional military departments be downgraded into administrative agencies of a strengthened and centralized Defense Department; that the Joint Chiefs of Staff be empowered to provide greater central direction for operations and strategic planning; that a Director of Defense Research and Engineering be appointed to "eliminate unpromising or unnecessarily duplicative programs; and that Congress appropriate all defense funds to the Secretary of Defense rather than to the military departments (see *Congressional Quarterly Almanac*, vol. XIV, *1958*, pp. 133–39). For developments see no. 655.

To A. J. HARDENDORF   April 1, 1958
Personal

Dear Mr. Hardendorf: Thank you for your letter and for bringing to
my personal attention the major problems you encountered in your
recent trip covering the southwestern states.[1] Each of the points you
raise suggesting action on the part of the government would require
an extended reply. I cannot possibly argue the matters in detail in
a letter such as this.

However, your suggestion in paragraph two may indicate something that could and should be done. I am not sure. I shall send it
to the Interior Department.[2]

Frankly, I may say that if any thoughtful man cannot discover real
differences in the philosophies and doctrines of the two major political parties, then, in my opinion, he has not been paying very close
attention to the record. Possibly I may be able to send you documents that can point up some of these differences.[3]

I am delighted that you knew my father during the thirties; that
was a period when, unfortunately, I saw very little of him.[4]

With best wishes, *Sincerely*

[1] Hardendorf, a "lifelong" Republican and former Kansan, was a member of the
Wyoming State Legislature. His March 24 letter, which he also sent to Wyoming Senator Frank A. Barrett and Congressman Keith Thomson, is in the same file as the
document. Hardendorf said that after a four-month combined "business and pleasure" trip through ten states in the southwest, he had observed that livestock growers who supported Secretary of Agriculture Benson, were happy that livestock prices
were up, and "wanted no part of government interference." He also said that small
oil and gas producers needed "relief from excessive imports," and that all small businesses were "suffering from high taxes and government regulations."

[2] Hardendorf had commented that "Uranium mining companies in Wyoming need
more mills to process their ore and may face bankruptcy and ruination if they are
not built. These cannot be built without Government approval—private industry is
eager and willing to furnish the money for this." On the minerals stabilization plan
see no. 700.

[3] Hardendorf had written that everywhere he traveled, businessmen, ranchers, and
workmen seemed to feel that "for the past two years there had been no difference
in the two major political parties—it is all tax and spend." On April 7 Presidential
Secretary Ann Whitman would send Hardendorf, at Eisenhower's request, documents that "pointed up the basic differences between the philosophies of the two
major parties" (same file as document).

[4] Hardendorf had written that he had met Eisenhower's father during the 1930s in
the course of business dealings in Abilene. "All admired and respected his ability,"
he said, and his "frugal handling" of business transactions was "approved by all parties on both sides."

To Arthur Frank Burns   *April 2, 1958*
Personal

Dear Arthur: I have no quarrel whatsoever with your thesis that the
presentation of a government package program for stimulating economic recovery would be better than piece-meal accomplishment
or announcement.[1]

One difficulty that occurs to me instantly is that caused by the laborious and tortuous channels that must be pursued in Washington
in the process of translating any good idea into action that even remotely resembles the original thought. Even if, in unusual circumstances, the proposal and the result should be identical, yet there
always intervenes time consuming argument and pulling and haul-
ing that erodes the psychological effect sought in the original plan.

With respect to your item (1): When I contemplate the minimum
size of the Federal budget that we are now certain to have about
1961, I am alarmed by the amount of deficit spending we shall probably have to do.[2] As I try to peer just a bit down the road into the
future, I cannot fail but be impressed by the inflationary factors that
we shall likely have to combat. A sizeable tax reduction may become
one of these; I have not yet been convinced of proof of its necessity. And if it is not needed at the moment then I am quite sure its
future effect would be inflationary.

With respect to item (2): I agree to the objective you seek.[3] But
what law could bring about the result you seek? Certainly I do not
believe you are advocating Federal price controls.

I completely agree with item (3).[4] As you know, we are urging
some temporary benefit supplements, but I have a feeling that the
permanent improvement of the law should wait some definite signs
of economic improvement. Otherwise we shall have unwise legislation.[5]

I agree also with (4).[6]

With respect to (5), I think we have to do much more than merely
get rid of some of the restrictive regulations and laws.[7] The railways
need more self-help, as well as more understanding on the part of
the government and the public. Also, *less* feather bedding!

I do not have before me your "Prosperity Without Inflation," and
so must confess that I do not recall the outline of your proposal
about reconstruction of the Advisory Board on Economic Growth
and Stability.[8]

As you know, I finally felt compelled to sign the latest Housing
Bill, even though certain of its provisions seemed to me to be unwise, if not completely stupid. The freezing of interest rates on vet-

erans' mortgages with the requirement that the government purchase them at par, is demagoguery at its worst.[9]

I find that as time goes on, the Republicans in Congress show much more of a disposition to stand by the Administration firmly in legislative activity. But the pity is that we do not have a Republican majority in either house.

With warm regard, *As ever*

[1] Burns had written on March 31, 1958 (AWF/A), with suggestions for "fresh measures" to deal with the recession (for background see no. 615). Saying that "we've had enough of *individual* anti-recession actions," which had given the impression of Administrative "drift," Burns offered a "*concerted program* that will build a firm bridge of confidence between the present and the future." Burns suggested that Eisenhower should announce such a program himself and include in his announcement both a list of the anti-recession measures already undertaken and a statement that the steps being taken were "entirely adequate to stem the recession," were "designed to minimize risks of later inflation," and were going to be given a "reasonable trial" before further measures could be seriously considered.

[2] Burns had suggested as the first item in his program "a broadly based tax reduction for both individuals and business firms."

[3] Burns had called for an "amendment of the Employment Act, so that reasonable stability of the consumer price level would become an explicit objective, at law, of Federal economic policy."

[4] As his third item, Burns had suggested "permanent improvement of the unemployment insurance system, besides temporary benefit supplements."

[5] See no. 598.

[6] Burns's fourth proposition called for an amendment of the Highway Act of 1956, "so that two-way flexibility in construction outlays would become possible" (see *ibid.*).

[7] Burns had called for "relief to railroads from the constricting regulations now imposed upon them" (see no. 610).

[8] As his final item, Burns had suggested reorganization of the Advisory Board on Economic Growth and Stability "along the lines sketched in the last chapter of my *Prosperity Without Inflation*" (see nos. 216 and 512). "The Board might continue to function as it now does, except that its deliberations would be preparatory to periodic—say, monthly or semi-monthly—meetings at the highest level of our government." These meetings, to be chaired by Eisenhower and attended by the heads of the departments of State, Treasury, Commerce, Labor, Agriculture, HEW, as well as the Bureau of the Budget, Federal Reserve Board, the Council of Economic Advisors and the White House Office, would turn the Board into a "consultative body" with "a weight comparable to that of the National Security Council in its sphere" (see Burns, *Prosperity Without Inflation*, pp. 86–87).

[9] See no. 615.

634   *EM, WHCF, President's Personal File 1771*

To Lorraine P. Knox   *April 2, 1958*

Dear Lorraine: If I am not mistaken, you celebrate on Easter Sunday your birthday anniversary.[1] I hope the day will be a truly happy one for you, and that the years that lie ahead will each bring you increasing satisfaction — satisfaction that can come only from your dedication to your particular job.

A few weeks ago Sergeant Vaughn wrote me.[2] In his letter he intimated that you were shortly to be transferred. If this is true, I trust that you will find your new assignment interesting and enjoyable, and I hope that you will keep me posted as to your whereabouts.

Washington has experienced one of its most miserable winters, but at least there are signs that spring is really just around the corner. The sun has shown brightly for three days (which constitutes a record that you people in Denver will scarcely credit) and even the cherry blossoms are showing evidence that they are finally going into their act.

I am feeling as well physically as I have any right to expect, but the problems inherent in this job seem as complex and difficult as ever, if not more so.[3] But as I look back over the last five years I realize that there has scarcely been a day when some seemingly insoluble problem did not arrive on my desk; certainly there have been no such days since July of 1956. I try to be as philosophical about the constant stream of difficulties as humanly possible and do the best I can, even if often I am not satisfied with the "solution" we finally reach.[4]

This letter was simply meant to say "Happy Birthday" and already it has grown to outsize proportions. It brings you, in addition to my warm felicitations, my affectionate regard.[5] *Sincerely*

[1] Captain Knox would celebrate her birthday on April 6. The President frequently corresponded with the nurses who had cared for him while he recovered at Fitzsimons Army Hospital in 1955 (see, for example, Galambos and van Ee, *The Middle Way*, no. 1823, and no. 290 in these volumes).
[2] Joseph B. Vaughn was a medical corpsman at Fitzsimons Army Hospital. Vaughn's letter is not in EM.
[3] On March 1 Eisenhower had undergone a neurological examination at Walter Reed Army Medical Center (see no. 584).
[4] July 1956 marked the beginning of the Suez crisis; see Galambos and van Ee, *The Middle Way*, nos. 1932 and 1946 (see also no. 439 in these volumes).
[5] For developments see no. 1402.

635
EM, AWF, International Series:
Macmillan

To Harold Macmillan
April 3, 1958

Dear Harold: This letter is a personal one. If it presents to you any problem whatsoever it is unintentional, because in the suggestion I shall describe you will have complete freedom of decision without *any* slightest possibility of embarrassment to yourself.

About forty miles away, in the City of Baltimore, is one of our very fine universities, Johns Hopkins University. Its President is my youngest brother, Dr. Milton Eisenhower, a distinguished educator. He and his Trustees are very anxious to invite you to come over to the University on Tuesday, June tenth, to receive an Honorary Degree from them and to make a commencement talk. The hour of their ceremony is apparently set up at, I think, 10:30 in the morning. However, I am informed that it could be as easily moved to something on the order of 2:30 in the afternoon.

Because of my sentimental attachment to the institution and, of course, to my brother, I would volunteer to go along with you for the visit, if you should so desire, and if you should decide to accept the invitation. My idea would be for us to take a helicopter from the White House grounds directly to the University grounds (a trip of some twenty to thirty minutes), attend the ceremony, and return here at once.

My own "shot gun" opinion is that you will feel too rushed and your time will be too crowded to make room for this additional chore. But I do know that the University and my brother would be most highly honored if you should find it possible to accept.

I repeat that this letter must not under any circumstances occasion you the slightest hesitation in making any reply that you choose.[1] At any event it does not pose any question having to do with the Summit, nuclear tests, or outer space!

With warm regard, *As ever*

[1] On April 2, at a White House meeting, Milton Eisenhower had asked the President if he would invite British Prime Minister Macmillan to receive an honorary degree and to speak at the Johns Hopkins University commencement on June 10. The President had offered to write to Macmillan and added that if the Prime Minister agreed he, Eisenhower, would also come to Baltimore to receive an honorary degree (Ann Whitman memorandum, Apr. 2, AWF/AWD). On April 10 Macmillan would accept the invitation. He knew of the university's reputation, he would write, and would like to meet its president. His only regret, he added, was that taking the morning off to go to Hopkins would further reduce the time he spent with Eisenhower (AWF/I: Macmillan). On April 14 Eisenhower would thank Macmillan for responding "so quickly and favorably" (AWF/D; see also Telephone conversations, Eisenhower and Dulles, and Dulles and Caccia, Apr. 11, 1958, Dulles Papers, Telephone Conversations). For background on Macmillan's plans to visit Washington in June see no. 581. For developments see no. 652.

To Aksel Nielsen   *April 4, 1958*

Dear Aks: I am dictating this over the phone from Gettysburg.[1] Recently we sold a few good steers and I thought you would be interested in the prices. We thought them remarkable.

The price was $40 a hundred. We got $536 for one steer. The steer dressed out at 64.59 per cent.[2] We shipped the steers to the Baltimore Packing House, and they told us that if we had any more like these they would be greatly interested. *As ever*

[1] The Eisenhowers were celebrating the Easter holiday weekend (Apr. 3–6) at their farm.

[2] The price for the steers was "good news," Nielsen would write on April 14 (AWF/N). He characterized the "dressing out" or meat yield (i.e., the percentage of meat available after the steer had been dressed) as "excellent." He added that the recent "top fat steer price" around Denver was 32 cents per pound. Nevins also checked with a local packing company to learn that "they attempt to get a steer that will dress out at 62 to 63" percent. See also no. 644; and American Meat Institute, *Meat: Reference Book of the Industry* (Chicago, 1941), p. 37.

To John Stewart Bragdon   *April 7, 1958*

Dear Stewart: Below I quote a rough draft of a paragraph I have been trying to make as expressive, but at the same time as brief, as possible. I have studied your memorandum of March 21st, which gives me certain facts that I can fill in in this paragraph, but I wonder whether you would not try your hand at giving me a draft that would seem to you better and stronger.[1]

"Out of these 200 billions of our military money, we might have, in a peaceful world, financed either through public or private effort our entire highway program, built all the hospitals needed in the next decade, provided money for every worthwhile hydroelectric project programmed by our experts, allocated some 10 billions a year for more modern security forces and still reduced our national debt by some _____ million dollars."

As ever

[1] Eisenhower was preparing a speech to be delivered before the American Society of Newspaper Editors and the International Press Institute (April 17, 1958) in support of his plan for defense reorganization (see no. 607; see also *Public Papers of the Presidents: Eisenhower, 1958*, pp. 325–34; and *New York Times*, Apr. 18, 1958). Neither Brag-

don's March 21 memorandum, nor his reply to Eisenhower is in AWF, but the President would say:

> It is hard to grasp the enormity of our military expenditures. In only five years, they are almost 200 billion dollars. This colossal expenditure has cost us far more than dollars alone. In a less threatening world, how much it could have meant to us. In private or public spending, this 200 billion dollars could have bought:
> —of highways, the entire, nation-wide system;
> —of hydro-electric power, every worth-while project in America;
> —of hospitals, our needs for ten years to come;
> —of schools, our next decade's requirements, including catching up on present shortages.
> And even had we additionally allocated 10 billion dollars a year for security, some 50 billion dollars would still have been left over to reduce the national debt.

638   *EM, AWF, Administration Series*

To Robert Bernerd Anderson   *April 7, 1958*

Dear Bob: Attached is a strong recommendation for a man named Albert J. Gould, of Denver, for appointment to the Tax Court of the United States.[1]

The recommendation is signed by Jack Foster, a friend of mine in Denver, whom I respect and like very much.[2] I send you the letter for your consideration and decision.[3]

I should like to point out that as a matter of practice I normally appoint no one to a Federal judgeship after he is beyond 62 years old. I have made one or two exceptions. In this case the individual seems to be completely within the bracket, so this difficulty does not occur.[4]

After you have made a decision in this case, please return Mr. Foster's letter to me.[5]

With warm regard, *As ever*

[1] Albert J. Gould (LL.B. University of Denver 1921) was an attorney in Denver, Colorado.

[2] Foster, editor of the *Rocky Mountain News*, had written Eisenhower on March 31 about a vacancy in the U.S. Tax Court left by the death of Judge Stephen Ewing Rice (AWF/A, Anderson Corr.). Foster said that he had known Gould for "almost twenty years," and found him "unexcelled in his knowledge of tax matters, especially in his knowledge of income tax law and regulations, as I am sure our mutual friend, Judge Orie L. Phillips, would agree."

[3] Eisenhower would include a *P.S.* saying, "another strong supporter of Mr. Gould is Aksel Nielsen, whom I am sure you know well."

[4] Gould was born January 1, 1897.

[5] Gould would not receive the appointment.

To Nikita Sergeyevich Khrushchev   *April 8, 1958*

Dear Mr. Chairman:[1] I have your communication of April fourth repeating, in substance, the already widely publicized statement of the Soviet Government with reference to the suspension of nuclear testing.[2]

It seems peculiar that the Soviet Union, having just concluded a series of tests of unprecedented intensity, should now, in bold headlines, say that it will not test again, but add, in small type, that it may test again if the United States carries out its already long announced and now imminent series of tests.[3]

The timing, wording, and manner of the Soviet declaration cannot but raise questions as to its real significance.

The position of the United States on this matter of testing is well known. For several years we have been seeking a dependable ending to the accumulation of nuclear weapons stockpiles and a dependable beginning of the steady reduction of existing weapons stockpiles. This was my "Atoms for Peace" proposal, made in 1953 before the United Nations.[4] Surely, the heart of the nuclear problem is not the mere *testing* of weapons, but the weapons themselves. If weapons are dependably dealt with, then it is natural to suspend their testing. However, the Soviet Union continues to reject the concept of an internationally supervised program to end weapons production and to reduce weapons stocks. Under those circumstances of the Soviets' making, the United States seeks to develop the defensive rather than the offensive capabilities of nuclear power and to learn how to minimize the fissionable fallout.

It goes without saying that these experiments, so far as the United States is concerned, are so conducted that they cannot appreciably affect human health.

Perhaps, Mr. Chairman, you recall the Joint Declaration made by the Governments of the United Kingdom and the United States at Bermuda on March 24, 1957.[5] We then declared that we would conduct nuclear tests only in such a manner as would keep world radiation from rising to more than a small fraction of the levels that might be hazardous. We went on to say that we would continue publicly announcing our test series well in advance of their occurrence with information as to their location and general timing. We further said that we would be willing to register with the United Nations advance notice of our intention to conduct future nuclear tests and to permit limited international observation of such tests if the Soviet Union would do the same.

The Soviet Union has never responded to that invitation. Its latest series of tests was conducted behind a cloak of secrecy, so far as the Soviet Union could make it so. Nevertheless, as I recently stated, it is the intention of the United States to invite observation by the United Nations of certain of our forthcoming tests.[6]

Not only did the Soviet Union ignore our Bermuda proposal on testing, but it has persistently rejected the substance of my "Atoms for Peace" proposal. It refuses to agree to an internationally supervised cut-off of the use of new fissionable material for weapons purposes and the reduction of existing weapons stocks by transfers to peaceful purposes. During the five years since I first proposed "Atoms for Peace," the destructive power in our nuclear arsenals has steadily mounted, and a dependably controlled reduction of that power becomes ever more difficult.

Mr. Chairman, now that you have become head of the Soviet Government, will you not reconsider your Government's position and accept my proposal that fissionable materials henceforth be manufactured only for peaceful purposes?

If the Soviet Union is as peace-loving as it professes, surely it should want to bring about an internationally supervised diversion of fissionable material from weapons purposes to peace purposes.

If the Soviet Union is unwilling to accept "Atoms for Peace," there are other outstanding proposals by which the Soviet Union can advance the cause of peace. You will recall, Mr. Chairman, my "Open Skies" proposal made to you and Chairman Bulganin at Geneva in 1955.[7] You will also recall my proposals for the international use of outer space for peaceful purposes emphasized in my recent correspondence with Chairman Bulganin.[8] These proposals await Soviet acceptance.

The United States is also prepared, in advance of agreement upon any one or more of the outstanding "disarmament" propositions, to work with the Soviet Union, and others as appropriate, on the technical problems involved in international controls. We both recognize that international control would be necessary. Indeed, your present letter to me speaks of "the establishment of the necessary international control for the discontinuance of tests."

What is "necessary"? The question raises problems of considerable complexity, given the present possibility of conducting some types of tests under conditions of secrecy.

If there is ever to be an agreed limitation or suspension of testing, and the United States hopes and believes that this will in due course come about as part of a broad disarmament agreement, plans for international control should be in instant readiness. Why should we not at once put our technicians to work to study together and advise as to what specific control measures are necessary if there is to be a dependable and agreed disarmament program?

The United Nations General Assembly has called for technical disarmament studies, in relation both to nuclear and conventional armaments.[9] The United States says "yes." I urge, Mr. Chairman, that the Soviet Union should also say "yes." Then we can at once begin the preliminaries necessary to larger things.[10] *Sincerely*

[1] On March 27 the Supreme Soviet had elected Nikita Khrushchev chairman of the Council of Ministers to succeed Nikolai Bulganin. After consulting with Eisenhower, State Department officials had drafted this letter and had cabled a copy of the draft to British Prime Minister Macmillan on April 6. Dulles had told Eisenhower that Macmillan's comments were "reflected" in the final draft (Dulles to Eisenhower, Apr. 6, 1958, AWF/D-H; see also Telephone conversations, Eisenhower and Dulles, Apr. 4, 5, 7, 8, 1958, Dulles Papers, Telephone Conversations; NSC meeting minutes, Apr. 4, 1958, AWF/NSC; State, *Foreign Relations, 1958–1960*, vol. III, *National Security Policy; Arms Control and Disarmament* [1996], pp. 589–90; and Macmillan, *Riding the Storm*, p. 485).

[2] Soviet Ambassador Menshikov had delivered Khrushchev's letter to Secretary Dulles on April 4 (Howe to Goodpaster, Apr. 4, 1958; and Khrushchev to Eisenhower, Apr. 4, 1958, AWF/D-H). On March 31 the Soviet Union had announced the suspension of nuclear weapons testing and had called on the United States and Great Britain to do the same. Testing would resume, the statement said, if the two western nations refused to comply (*New York Times*, Apr. 1, 1958).

Having learned from intelligence sources that the Soviets would announce the cessation of testing after their current series of tests, Dulles had suggested on March 23 that the President designate the next series of tests as the last that would be conducted during his Administration (Telephone conversation, Eisenhower and Dulles, Mar. 23, 1958, Dulles Papers, Telephone Conversations). On the following day Eisenhower and Dulles had met with Defense Secretary McElroy, Deputy Defense Secretary Quarles, JCS Chairman Twining, and AEC Chairman Strauss to discuss an American response to the predicted Soviet announcement. Secretary Dulles again advocated taking the initiative. The United States had been losing the confidence of the free world, he said, and testing throughout the summer after the Soviet proposals for a test ban and a summit conference would place the country "under heavy attack worldwide." Dulles said that he felt "desperately the need for some important gesture . . . that would beat the Soviets to the punch."

After the Defense Department officials and Admiral Strauss expressed opposition, Eisenhower dropped Dulles's idea but asked the group to think about ways to eliminate "the terrible impasse" they had reached regarding disarmament (Goodpaster, Memorandum of Conversation, Mar. 28, 1958, AWF/D; see also Legislative Leadership Meeting, Apr. 1, 1958, AWF/D; Dulles to Eisenhower, and Dulles to Strauss, Apr. 1, 1958, Dulles Papers, Chronological Series; NSC meeting minutes, Apr. 4, 1958, AWF/NSC; and *Public Papers of the Presidents: Eisenhower, 1958*, pp. 261, 262, 265. For the statement prepared by State Department officials in advance of the Soviet announcement see Telephone conversations, Dulles and Hagerty, Mar. 30, 31, 1958; Dulles and Eisenhower, Apr. 1, 1958; and Draft #4, Mar. 30, 1958, Dulles Papers, Telephone Conversations).

[3] The Soviet Union had completed an intensive series of tests that had begun in August 1957. The detonations, sometimes two or more megaton bombs in a single day, had sharply increased global fallout levels. The Atomic Energy Commission had announced in the spring of 1957 that Operation HARDTACK, a series of tests to estab-

lish accurate data on local rather than worldwide fallout, would begin in May 1958 (State, *Foreign Relations, 1955–1957*, vol. XX, *Regulation of Armaments; Atomic Energy*, pp. 698–701; Hewlett and Holl, *Atoms for Peace and War*, pp. 362, 389, 456–57, 477–79; and *New York Times*, Feb. 28, Mar. 22, 1958).

[4] See Galambos and van Ee, *The Middle Way*, no. 598.

[5] For background on the Bermuda Conference see no. 78. The joint declaration is in State, *American Foreign Policy, Current Documents, 1957*, pp. 631–33.

[6] Eisenhower had announced at his March 26 news conference that "for the first time at any test" the United States would invite the United Nations to select a group of qualified scientific observers to witness the HARDTACK explosions (*Public Papers of the Presidents: Eisenhower, 1958*, pp. 232–33).

[7] See Galambos and van Ee, *The Middle Way*, no. 1523.

[8] See nos. 521 and 574.

[9] A United Nations General Assembly resolution passed on November 14, 1957, called for the Disarmament Commission to establish a group of technical experts to study inspection systems for disarmament (see U.S. Department of State, *Documents on Disarmament, 1945–1959*, 2 vols. [Washington, D.C., 1960], vol. II, *1957–1959*, pp. 914–15; see also no. 521).

[10] For developments see no. 665.

640   *EM, WHCF, Official File 225*

To Robert E. Matteson   *April 8, 1958*

Dear Mr. Matteson:[1] Thank you for your memorandum of April second. I have read, also, the accompanying record of the speech you made on February eighteenth. Of course I am glad to receive your suggestions and comments.[2]

With a great deal of your document I am in complete agreement. I strongly believe that there is great benefit to be gained through *association* of the peoples of the United States and the USSR.[3] The difficulty seems to be that their suspicion and mistrust of us are unfortunately such that all negotiations for interchange of scientists, scholars and so on move at a snail's pace. I should very much like to help develop a workable plan by which such contacts could be many times multiplied in number. One beneficial result of exchanging visitors by the thousands would be that of preventing any possibility that the USSR could select, as visitors to the United States, only those trained in subversion.

Obviously I cannot here comment in detail on your memorandum. I do appreciate very much your thoughts, based upon your experience working with Governor Stassen in the disarmament field.[4] *Sincerely*

[1] Robert E. Matteson, aide to Harold Stassen, had been director of the White House disarmament staff since 1955. He would become a member of the Board of National Intelligence Estimates of the Central Intelligence Agency in 1958.

[2] The United States should take maximum advantage of the fact that Nikita Khrushchev had assumed leadership of the Soviet Union, Matteson had written. Khrushchev's leadership, Matteson reasoned, was "different enough in degree" from the former rulers to facilitate a relaxation of tensions—a goal Khrushchev seemed to support. Matteson proposed joint U.S.-Soviet undertakings in the fields of thermonuclear research, economic support for underdeveloped areas, and exploration of outer space: multilateral development of the Antarctic for peaceful scientific purposes and multinational efforts to establish regional inspection zones and security pacts would also be possible, Matteson said. By associating with the Soviets, the United States could "win them gradually over to our way" (Matteson to Eisenhower, Apr. 2, 1958, same file as document).

Matteson had spoken about the disarmament dilemma before the University of Minnesota Conference on National Security in the Nuclear Age. Eisenhower had sent Secretary Dulles a copy of the speech and in a handwritten note at the top of the first page had called Dulles's attention to Matteson's remarks regarding the success of the London negotiations on disarmament (*ibid.*).

[3] For Eisenhower's proposal to invite ten thousand Russian students to visit the United States see no. 618.

[4] On Stassen's resignation as Eisenhower's special assistant for disarmament see no. 594.

641   *EM, WHCF, Official File 117-C-2*

TO ISIDOR SCHWANER RAVDIN   *April 8, 1958*

Dear Rav: Thanks for your letter.[1] I have asked some of my experts to take that good second look at the needs of hospitals (and schools) in the light not only of need, but of the recession we are presently experiencing.[2] Of course any look, including the second one, must comprehend a view of our defense needs, our foreign requirements and commitments, and at the same time encompass all the things in a thousand different directions that fall to the lot of the Federal government.[3]

Completely agreeing with you as to the need for the continuous modernization of hospital and medical facilities, I still feel that primary responsibility must always remain local. The Federal government can lead, assist and, occasionally, be a partner on a fairly massive scale, particularly in an emergency. However, the more that all such humanitarian activities depend for support upon the central government, the more we lose the effect of private initiative and local sense of responsibility.

These views, I have always understood, are identical with yours.[4]

Please convey my warm greetings to Betty and, of course, all the best to yourself. *As ever*

[1] Ravdin, Professor of Surgery at University of Pennsylvania School of Medicine, had assisted at Eisenhower's ileitis surgery in June 1956 (see Galambos and van Ee, *The*

Middle Way, no. 1912; see also Clarence G. Lasby, *Eisenhower's Heart Attack* [Lawrence, Kans., 1997], pp. 208–14). Ravdin had written the President on April 4, 1958, to praise Eisenhower's support for the extension of the program of federal grants for hospital construction under the Hospital Survey and Construction Act (Hill-Burton) (see *Public Papers of the Presidents: Eisenhower, 1958*, p. 309).

[2] Ravdin had said that the Hill-Burton bill would "'prime the pump' more than many people will imagine, and at the same time, be of tremendous value to the people of this country. . . . I do not know how funds can be better spent for the benefit of the people of this country."

[3] See no. 637 on the conflicting demands of defense and social welfare spending. On funding for public works to stimulate the economy see no. 598.

[4] Ravdin would respond on April 11. While he agreed with the President that, wherever possible, the primary responsibility for maintaining hospitals and schools should rest with the community, "the cost of maintaining these is becoming excessive and financing them I feel will necessarily become, in part, a responsibility of the Federal Government, if high standards are to be maintained." All correspondence is in the same file as the document.

642   *EM, WHCF, Official File 150-A*

To Ward Murphey Canaday   *April 8, 1958*
Personal

Dear Ward: Needless to say, I have discussed your note very seriously with a number of my most trusted associates. I find no specific disagreement with your basic idea that sales would be improved by a temporary moratorium on the excise tax on automobiles.[1] But I do find a very positive conviction that we should not, at this time, touch our tax structure. To do so will open flood gates in the Congress that will never be closed. Moreover, I do not know by what process we could insure a moratorium on wage increases during the period that the tax moratorium would be in effect.

I assure you that my associates and I are watching these matters every day. Of course it is my prayer and hope that there will soon be distinct signs of real recovery. If business can again start on the road to real increasing prosperity, the government's fiscal problems will be less severe.[2]

With warm regard, *Sincerely*

[1] Canaday, president of the Overland Corporation, had first broached the idea of removing automobile excise taxes in a meeting with Eisenhower on April 2 (see Ann Whitman memorandum, Apr. 2, 1958, AWF/AWD). In an April 4 letter (same file as document) he detailed "the important reasons which support my suggestion." He argued that the "immediate effect" of the tax cut would be "to change the trend of unemployment and bring *encouraging headlines* into the newspapers. This will break the trend of discouragement and fear among buyers of all classes of commodities

and turn up the curve of earnings which are essential to create income taxes." On the recession see nos. 598 and 615.

[2] Canaday would respond on April 10 (same file as document). Asking the President to forgive his "persistence," he suggested a temporary increase in depreciation allowances for machines purchased by manufacturers from May through December 1958. Canaday would also urge that the Administration exert more pressure to ensure "the reduction of interest rates to the consumer."

643   *EM, AWF, International Series:*
                                                  Philippine Islands

To Carlos Polestico Garcia   *April 8, 1958*

Dear Mr. President: On this 16th Anniversary of the Fall of Bataan, an event which we commemorate with sadness, but with pride, I extend best wishes to you and to the people of the Philippines on behalf of the people of the United States.[1]

The symbol of Bataan, the offering of the ultimate sacrifice by friends for one another, is an ideal so rarely witnessed that it will inspire freedom-loving men always. That together we have carried on our struggle for the preservation of liberty with justice does honor to the memory of our fallen sons and comrades.

Our mutual friendship has been nourished by the spirit of Bataan. May it continue to grow.[2] *Sincerely*

[1] 1958 marked the third consecutive year that Eisenhower had recognized Bataan Day (April 9) with a letter to the Philippine president. The State Department's original draft of this sentence had read, "... commemorate with pride and sadness. ..." After Eisenhower revised the message, State Department officials sent it to the American embassy in Manila (see Howe to Goodpaster, Apr. 8, 1958, AWF/I: Philippine Islands). For background on the surrender of American forces on April 8, 1942, see Chandler, *War Years*, nos. 23 and 229; on plans for President Garcia's June visit to the United States see no. 605.

[2] President Garcia would tell Eisenhower that his message, "coming from a renowned soldier who himself was in the thick of the battle against the forces that were out to stifle individual human freedom ... was both inspiring and encouraging" (Garcia to Eisenhower, Apr. 11, 1958, AWF/I: Philippines).

644   *EM, AWF, Gettysburg Series*

To Arthur Seymour Nevins   *April 8, 1958*

Dear Art: Whenever Bob Hartley thinks one of the steers is properly ready, I would be delighted to have another one butchered.[1]

There are two points I should like to discuss!

First, will you tell Mr. Grim that when it comes to the actual butchering and wrapping (after the period of curing has been completed), I should like the shanks to be cut off *without* stripping any of the meat from them. The bone, with the meat still on it, is to be used for making soup. The rear shank should be cut off above the hock, right up against what is normally called the "lower round." The front shank should be cut high enough up so that the brisket would remain with it.

Otherwise Mr. Grim's butchering was exactly as I should like it. All the large better steaks, taken out of the back, should be about 2 inches thick. (The small "club" steaks should be 1 inch only.) The round should be about the same, possibly 1¼ inches.

Second: After the steer has been killed, could you have the carcass brought back to the farm and put in the cool room in the garage. This is because I would like to cure it at a slightly higher temperature than Mr. Grim uses at the store. After the curing process is done, then you could send it back to Mr. Grim for butchering and packaging.

About twelve hours before you send the steer up to Mr. Grim to butcher, I think the cool room should be started in operation. If there is any doubt about its mechanism, Sergeant Dry could run up to start it. He is completely familiar with the operation. This reminds me that there ought to be in the cool room an ordinary thermometer, so that we could keep the temperature as near 35 degrees as possible.

I have put all this down so you can have a record of it. If there is any question you want to ask me, don't hesitate to call either Mrs. Whitman or me directly.[2]

It was good to see you and Ann—both of you looked in the finest of health. Give her my love and, of course, warm regard to yourself.[3]

As ever

P.S. Many thanks. I do hope I am not causing you too much trouble.

[1] For background on Eisenhower's interest in the butchering of his steers see no. 486. On April 10 Nevins would reply that according to Hartley, Eisenhower's herdsman, a steer would be ready by the second week in May.

[2] Nevins said he would give the President's instructions to Grim, the operator of the slaughterhouse at Lowes Country Store in Table Rock, Pennsylvania. He also said he would procure a thermometer that would accurately determine the cool room temperature, and he would have the cooling system operating by the time the carcass returned.

On April 29 Nevins would direct Hartley to select the steer. The steer would be trucked to Table Rock on May 6. The following day the carcass would be picked up and delivered to the President's barn for hanging in the cooling room (see Nevins to Hartley, Feaster, West, Apr. 29, 1958). All papers are in AWF/Gettysburg.

Leonard D. Dry, Jr., had served Eisenhower from 1942–1952; he would be Mrs. Eisenhower's driver until 1962 when he would return to and remain on the White House staff through the Johnson Administration (for background see *Eisenhower Papers*, vols. VI–XIII).

[3] The Eisenhowers had spent the Easter holiday at their farm (see no. 636).

645

To Elizabeth Hazlett

Dear Ibby: My Naval Aide tells me that Swede is to be operated on tomorrow because of some difficulty with his lung. The second-hand report I have from the doctors is that they are completely optimistic about the outcome. Nevertheless, I know that this will be a period of tension and strain for you, and this note is simply to assure you that the thoughts and prayers of Mamie and myself will be with you.

When Swede comes out of the anesthetic and again feels like talking, tell him that we will be pulling for his quick and full recovery.[1] *Affectionately*

[1] Eisenhower had visited Hazlett in Bethesda Medical Center on April 4. For background on Hazlett's health see no. 622. On April 14 Hazlett would undergo surgery for the removal of his left lung. The President would receive a report on this same day (AWF/N, Hazlett Corr.), and Hazlett would remain in the hospital until July 3 (Eisenhower to Hazlett, July 3, 1958, *ibid.*). For developments see no. 906.

646

Memorandum

Subject: Okinawa. For some time the Secretary of State and I have been much concerned about our failure to make with the Japanese an acceptable and mutually agreeable arrangement for the Okinawa Base.[1]

The problem is rather simply stated. We will obviously have the need for the Base for some years. At the same time the natives on Okinawa are growing in number and are very anxious to repossess the land that they once owned.

Regardless of legal or treaty arrangements, this conflict creates problems not only with our relationships with the people of Okinawa and Japan but could, if they become acute, be used for ammunition in the Communist propaganda attacks upon us. The situation could become unpleasant. While I do not expect the matter to assume the importance of the Cyprus difficulty with Britain, nor of the Algerian with France, still there could easily develop a situation that would create much embarrassment for us.[2]

We feel certain that in the cases of Cyprus and Algiers the local populations would have readily accept[ed] some five to six years ago privileges and rights that the respective mother countries would now gladly accord them. But the undercover struggles in these regions have for their purpose the expulsion of foreign troops from the area and so aroused emotions, misunderstandings and hatreds that nothing less than complete independence will seemingly satisfy the bulk of these populations.

The lesson is that we should be forehanded with offers that the Okinawans will clearly recognize as generous and understanding and which will have the effect at least for some years of forestalling trouble.

The Secretary of State informs me that he and the Defense Department are working actively on the problem. I personally hope that there will be an offer made of some division of territory so that there may be established an American enclave of minimum size to meet our needs.[3]

I would think that such a political agreement could be established together with reasonable financial remuneration. We might make of all these peoples firm allies rather than latent enemies.[4]

[1] The U.S.-Japan Security Treaty of 1952 had established U.S. policy toward Japan and the administration of the Ryukyu Islands (see Galambos and van Ee, *The Middle Way*, no. 457; see also Galambos, *Chief of Staff*, no. 1384 and p. 2293). Since December 1956 State and Defense Department officials had been discussing policy changes that would accommodate the mounting pressure for a return of the islands to Japanese authority without jeopardizing U.S. military bases in the area. After a thorough study of Administration policy toward the Ryukyus by the National Security Council, however, Eisenhower had issued an executive order (June 1957) continuing U.S. control over the administrative, legislative, and jurisdictional affairs of the islands.

U.S. Ambassador to Japan Douglas MacArthur II had discussed the security treaty with Dulles. He had made specific recommendations for changes in U.S. policies toward Okinawa where, he said, time was "running swiftly and remorselessly" against the United States. In a meeting with the President on April 1 Dulles had suggested the idea of an enclave that the United States would control, with Japan administering the rest of the island. Eisenhower thought that the idea was "well worth exploring" (*U.S. Department of State Bulletin* 37, no. 941 [July 8, 1957], 51–58; State, *Foreign Relations, 1955–1957*, vol. XXIII, pt. 1, *Japan*, pp. 52–62, 197–201, 244–46, 281–82, 346–49, 359, 436–37, 513–16, 524–27; State, *Foreign Relations, 1958–1960*, vol. XVIII, *Japan; Korea*, pp. 4–21; and NSC meeting minutes, Oct. 18, 1958, AWF/NSC).

[2] For background on the Cyprus situation see nos. 78 and 488; on Algeria see Galambos and van Ee, *The Middle Way*, nos. 1792 and 2108, and no. 451 in these volumes.

[3] Before writing this memorandum, Eisenhower had asked Dulles about the progress toward developing a new policy regarding Okinawa. If something could be done

quickly, the President said, relations with Japan and particularly with Prime Minister Kishi would be strengthened. Later this same day Dulles would tell Eisenhower that the U.S. High Commissioner of the Ryukyu Islands wanted permission to announce to the legislature that the United States was reviewing its policy regarding land acquisition. The President said: "Tell him to keep his damn mouth shut" (Telephone conversations, Eisenhower and Dulles, Apr. 9, 1958, AWF/D; see also Dulles Papers, Telephone Conversations).

[4] After consultation with State Department officials and Ambassador MacArthur, Dulles would tell Eisenhower that "the moment was not opportune" to return control of Okinawa to the Japanese. The military installations were so scattered that limiting U.S. jurisdiction to one or two enclaves would not be possible, he said. The Defense Department should begin a program to "rearrange their affairs" on the island so that in three to five years Japan could regain control of most of the administrative responsibilities. Eisenhower thought that was "a sound approach" and asked Dulles to explain the situation to Defense Secretary McElroy (State, *Foreign Relations, 1958–1960*, vol. XVIII, *Japan; Korea*, pp. 21–22; see also NSC meeting minutes, June 3, 1958, AWF/NSC). For developments see no. 724.

647   *EM, AWF, Name Series*

To ANDREW JACKSON GOODPASTER, JR.   *April 9, 1958*

Andy:[1] The most important part of this informal report is that dealing with Kerala. It *could* be sent to Allen Dulles. State *may* have a plan of action for its embassy personnel that need not condemn Kerala's material and social progress; but should seek the progress of other states in India.[2]

[1] Eisenhower had handwritten this note to Staff Secretary Goodpaster.
[2] We have been unable to locate the report that Eisenhower mentions. In the April 1957 Indian elections, the Communist party had secured control of the state of Kerala, India's most populous and least developed area. The Communist government had continued to allow U.S. activities, including those sponsored by the International Cooperation Administration and United States Information Service. Closely monitoring the political situation in the area, the Administration had sought to increase economic and technical assistance to neighboring Indian states while at the same time discouraging American investment in Kerala (State, *Foreign Relations, 1955–1957*, vol. VIII, *South Asia*, pp. 363–66, 379, 394–95; see also NSC meeting minutes, May 17, 1957, AWF/NSC).

Communists would continue to control the state government of Kerala until July 1959, when widespread agitation would lead the central government to overturn the regime and institute direct presidential control. In February 1960 the Communists would fail in their attempt to regain power when they were defeated in the Kerala elections (State, *Foreign Relations, 1958–1960*, vol. XV, *South and Southeast Asia*, pp. 494–96, 502, 509, 532–33). As of this writing, information regarding Allen Dulles and possible CIA involvement in Kerala remains unavailable.

To Sherman Adams   *April 9, 1958*

Memorandum for Governor Adams: Attached is a letter from Cabot
Lodge.[1]

I have great respect for Cabot's political sense. Therefore I think
that possibly you should make a date for Senator Cooper to come
in. If you do, I should like for you to be present also. If Cooper happens to be in Washington now we might see him tomorrow.[2]

Privately I am afraid this is just another "spending" proposition.

[1] Lodge had written on April 8, 1958 (Lodge Papers), to suggest that a talk with John
Sherman Cooper of Kentucky "would pay dividends." Cooper believed, Lodge said,
that when Congress returned from its recess there were things Eisenhower could do
"notably in the field of unemployment compensation, which will enable you to seize
the initiative."
[2] Eisenhower would meet with Senator Cooper on April 10. The majority of the meeting would be spent discussing the plan for defense reorganization (see no. 631).
There is no record of any talks about anti-recession planning (see Goodpaster, Memorandum for Record, Apr. 10, 1958, AWF/D).

649   *EM, AWF, Name Series*

To Louise Sondra Grieb Eisenhower   *April 9, 1958*
Personal

Dear Louise:[1] To answer first the latter part of your letter, I must tell
you that I have never heard of Mr. Kornitzer's intention to publish
another book.[2] In fact, when I was at Columbia I refused to provide
information to him for use in his first one. Even though, later, all
the other brothers were interviewed by him, I refused to do more
than to meet him briefly one day. I never gave him any anecdote or
story of any kind.

You can be quite certain that I shall not offer or give any assistance to Mr. Kornitzer in producing another book. I shall send this
letter to Edgar, Earl and Milton so that they will know of my intention. They can, of course, make their own decisions.[3]

I think it is only fair to say, however, that I know of no way that
an author can be prevented from writing a book provided, of course,
a publisher will take the risks of printing it. Although I have had
some pretty tough things said about me in books, there was nothing that I could—or indeed would—do to have stopped the publication of them.

It occurs to me that if your own volume is practically ready for publication, you should get it out as soon as possible. If you are ahead of Mr. Kornitzer in his effort then I think that his book would be practically stymied and no publisher would undertake its printing.[4]

Beyond this I think there is very little for me to say. Of course if any publisher should ask me (which none has ever before done) about the issuing of such a book I would state my negative preference.

I am glad that your own effort has served to occupy your time during the last two months. I know your adjustment is a difficult one, and assure you that Mamie and I think and speak of you often.

With affectionate regard, *As ever*

[1] Mrs. Arthur Eisenhower had been widowed in January. She had written on April 2 (AWF/N) to thank the President for attending her husband's funeral services in Kansas City. For background see no. 558.

[2] The President's sister-in-law planned to publish an Eisenhower family album on which she and her husband had worked before his death. She had continued the project, she said, for three reasons: it was a tribute to Arthur and his family; it had kept her focused after Arthur's death; and it would be a source of income. Her publisher had informed her, however, that Bela Kornitzer was working on another Eisenhower family volume. Louise told the President that Arthur would have wanted her to "respectfully request" the surviving Eisenhower brothers to deny Kornitzer any information or pictures about Arthur for the new publication. She added that she hoped the entire family would "refuse to cooperate" with Kornitzer because Kornitzer's publisher, Doubleday and Company, would not publish the book without the family's approval. For background on Eisenhower's views of Kornitzer and his book, *The Great American Heritage: The Story of the Five Eisenhower Brothers*, see Galambos and van Ee, *The Middle Way*, nos. 106, 288, 1469, 1994. See also Ann Whitman memorandum, April 9, 1958, AWF/AWD.

[3] On April 14 (AWF/N) Edgar Eisenhower would tell the President that he was "all through" helping those who wanted to write about him. Let them "use their own imagination about anything they want to print," he added.

[4] For developments see no. 742.

650   *EM, AWF, International Series: France*

To Félix Gaillard   *April 10, 1958*
Secret

Dear Mr. President:[1] The "Good Offices" mission established by your Government and that of Tunisia seems now to have thoroughly explored all aspects of the matter with which it was charged.[2] It would appear that the moment of decision cannot be much longer delayed. Since this decision may have fateful consequences for us all,

I take the liberty of addressing you personally. I do so in broad terms, perhaps beyond those heretofore presented by the "Good Offices" mission. I do so in the spirit of friendship which has always prevailed between our nations and which I was privileged again to appreciate in Paris last December when I had the opportunity for intimate exchange of views with you personally.[3]

I have followed closely the work of the "Good Offices" mission and it seems that the final word may now rest with France. In saying that, I do not mean to imply that you might not have legitimately hoped for acceptance by the Tunisian Government of further aspects of the French viewpoint. But it seems that this is not now possible and that France faces the question of whether or not it is consistent with France's own vital interests to accept the practical limits which seemed to be imposed upon the Tunisian Government by sentimental and even emotional ties, as well as geographical factors, which inescapably lead the people of Tunisia to sympathize with the aspirations of the Moslem nationalist elements in Algeria. May it not be that to take these practical factors into account is not only consistent with French interests, but is indeed a way to promote them? I hope that you may find an affirmative answer to this difficult problem.[4]

If the "Good Offices" mission fails to achieve at least a limited *modus vivendi* between France and Tunisia, larger aspects of the problem are almost sure to erupt violently. On the other hand, if the immediate crisis can be surmounted, there may be an opportunity to deal constructively with the larger aspects of the problem, perhaps within some such context as a broad European-North African association as you yourself have already, with statesmanlike vision, suggested.[5]

I recall that at our NATO Meeting in Paris last December, the Heads of Government expressed their common belief that there should be cooperation between the countries of Africa and other parts of the free world; and that historic, economic and other friendly ties between certain European countries and Africa would make such cooperation particularly desirable and effective.

I am convinced that such cooperation can still be achieved. But time is running out in the vital North African area. Under these circumstances, will it be possible for France to continue to enjoy the close relations with North Africa which the French nation understandably seeks unless that relationship is freely accepted in North Africa?

I cannot but view with great concern a future which will further protract, and perhaps enlarge and intensify, a military struggle in North Africa. That could, despite our wishes, seriously undermine the strength and cohesion of the Atlantic Community, of which our two nations form part and to the preservation and strengthening of which we and the other members of that Community have dedicated a vast effort in war and in peace.

Western civilization, to which France has greatly contributed, has over the centuries not only served the West but it has served humanity. It has spread freedom and respect for the rights of man. Indeed the United States owes much to the sympathy and help which France gave us in our early struggle for independence.

Now those concepts are challenged by a vast and powerful conspiracy represented by Communist imperialism. It would deprive all nations of genuine independence and it denies the dignity of man. In its efforts to spread its power throughout the world, International Communism seeks to disintegrate and weaken the Atlantic Community and to divide the free world. Is it not the task of the West to seize the initiative and to demonstrate that human aspirations can best be brought to fruition through close association with the West?

I realize that, as I said, I speak in broad terms and touch on matters which perhaps go beyond the scope of the "Good Offices" mission. However, I have devoted so many years of my life, both in war and in peace, to a safeguarding of the heritage of the West that this, I hope, is permissible. I would indeed feel derelict if I did not respectfully but earnestly express my estimate of the mounting danger to the West which looms in North Africa.

I know that the immediate decision on the matters presented by the "Good Offices" mission is one to be made by France. But the implications of that decision seem to me to be so far-reaching that I trust that these observations will not be considered to be inappropriate, prompted as they are by the historic friendship of our two nations and our oft-demonstrated cooperation for the achievement of high ideals.[6]

I am, dear Mr. President, *Sincerely*

[1] Eisenhower and Secretary Dulles had collaborated in drafting this letter, incorporating suggestions from British Prime Minister Macmillan (Telephone conversation, Eisenhower and Dulles, Apr. 4, 5, 1958, Dulles Papers, Telephone Conversations; Eisenhower and Dulles, Apr. 10, 1958, AWF/D; see also Telephone conversations, Dulles and Murphy, Apr. 2, 1958; Dulles and Rountree, Apr. 3, 1958; Dulles and Palmer, Apr. 5, 1958, Dulles Papers, Telephone Conversations).
[2] For background on the conflict between France and Tunisia and on the good offices mission see nos. 586 and 600.
[3] Eisenhower and Gaillard had met at the Heads of Government meeting of the NATO countries (see nos. 493 and 501).
[4] On March 15 Tunisian President Habib Bourguiba had approved the text of an agreement with France that had been presented to him by Robert Murphy and Harold Beeley, representing the United States and Great Britain on the good offices mission. Neutral observers were to replace French military personnel at four Tunisian airfields; French military personnel were to withdraw outside the perimeter of

the airfield at Bizerte; and the jurisdiction of existing French consulates in Tunisia was to be extended to those areas where consulates had recently closed. Bourguiba maintained that he could not accept French demands for a border commission unless all French troops were withdrawn from Tunisia (State, *Foreign Relations, 1958– 1960*, vol. XIII, *Arab-Israeli Dispute; United Arab Republic; North Africa*, pp. 838–41; see also Becker to Herter, Mar. 14, 1958, AWF/D-H; and Murphy, *Diplomat Among Warriors*, pp. 394–96).

Reporting to the National Security Council on March 20, Dulles warned that Gaillard would not be able to convince the French parliament to accept the agreement; any attempt to do so would lead to his overthrow. The situation, Dulles said, "was tragic" (NSC meeting minutes, Mar. 21, 1958, AWF/NSC).

In a subsequent conversation with Dulles, the President had expressed "a good deal of sympathy" toward Bourguiba's position, and Eisenhower said that France had caused him "almost more worry than any other problem in the world." A political settlement giving Algeria a chance for independence was the only solution to the North African problem, the President said, and he was willing to "accept considerable risks as far as France's role in NATO was concerned in an effort to get France to take such a position" (State, *Foreign Relations, 1958–1960*, vol. XIII, *Arab-Israeli Dispute; United Arab Republic; North Africa*, p. 841).

[5] Gaillard had discussed his views on the North African situation with Eisenhower in Paris (see State, *Foreign Relations, 1955–1957*, vol. XVIII, *Africa*, pp. 772–73).

[6] Murphy and U.S. Ambassador Amory Houghton would deliver this message to Gaillard. Murphy would tell Secretary Dulles that the letter "had not apparently caused any resentment," although it obviously had evoked "a sense of seriousness" (Memorandum of Conversation, Apr. 11, 1958, Dulles Papers, White House Memoranda Series; see also Telephone conversations, Dulles and Murphy, Apr. 11, 1958, Dulles and Eisenhower, Apr. 12, 1958; Dulles and Hagerty, Apr. 13, 1958; and Dulles and Eisenhower, Apr. 13, 1958, Dulles Papers, Telephone Conversations).

On April 15 communists and moderates would combine to defeat the French cabinet's decision to accept the proposals of the good offices mission, resulting in the fall of the government. French Minister of Foreign Affairs Christian Pineau would tell Murphy and Houghton that some members of the French government attributed the collapse of Gaillard's government to Eisenhower's letter (State, *Foreign Relations, 1958–1960*, vol. VII, pt. 2, *Western Europe*, pp. 5–7; see also Telephone memorandum, Apr. 12, 1958; Telephone conversations, Dulles and Jandrey, Apr. 13, 1958; and Dulles and Mansfield, Apr. 14, 1958, Dulles Papers, Telephone Conversations; and Wall, "The United States, Algeria, and the Fall of the Fourth French Republic," pp. 494, 504–5). For developments see no. 753.

651   *EM, WHCF, Official File 102-B-3*

To Ralph Emerson McGill   *April 11, 1958*
Personal

Dear Ralph: This morning the Attorney General, Bill Rogers, sent to me a copy of your editorial appearing in the *Constitution* of the 20th of March last. To my mind you have accurately portrayed the Administration's position on this issue. Charged as it is with emotionalism and prejudice, which are fed on ignorance, it is indeed difficult to express any view that seemingly points the way toward progress. I think you have.[1]

With warm regard, *Sincerely*

P.S. This morning I am planning to take off once more for Augusta to find one good golfing day during the spring. This is about my last opportunity, so I am praying that Thor and Neptune and all the rest of the Gods who may have some influence on the weather will be at peace over the weekend.[2]

---

[1] McGill's editorial described the Administration's policy on school integration. It was not based on a desire to "ram anything down the throats of people. There was not, and is not," he wrote, "anything the government can do save to insist on due process of law." The Administration had "no hostility toward the South or its people, no wish to force anything, but there is a full determination to enforce due process of law— North, South, East or West" (*Atlanta Constitution*, Mar. 20, 1958). Rogers had sent a copy of the editorial to Ann Whitman (Apr. 10, same file as document) with the explanation that he had recently spoken to McGill "for background purposes."

[2] On Eisenhower's April 11–13 visit to Augusta see no. 659.

---

652   *EM, AWF, Name Series*

To Milton Stover Eisenhower   *April 14, 1958*

Dear Milton: Yesterday, Sunday, I spoke to Foster Dulles asking whether he would not make the necessary contacts with the British so as to arrange that the visit of the Prime Minister to your University would be simultaneously announced by his office and by yours.[1]

For the moment I am not so certain that we should announce my planned visit, but this is a point that possibly I should speak about to Foster. If my acceptance should be announced at some later date it might possibly be a bit embarrassing, but it could be worse in the event I might have to check out after having announced it.

Of course if we should use a helicopter we could be back here at the White House in a matter of twenty minutes. While I believe that the Prime Minister's luncheon date is at one, I am quite sure that they could delay the function for a short time if necessary. I understand from Mrs. Whitman that you are planning for Macmillan and me to leave right after his talk. I do think that you should think some of the propriety and smoothness of our exit. By this I mean that it would be too bad for him to make such a nice gesture as coming to Johns Hopkins and making a short talk, and then conceivably spoiling it by too rapid an exit. On this matter I am merely speculating; I have no idea at what hour your exercises would normally terminate.[2]

When we last talked about this subject, I thought we had agreed that I personally should not take the honorary degree in the belief that I might be able, at some future date, to accept one from the University. I am not making any objection—and if you feel it would be the normal procedure under the circumstances it is quite satisfactory to me. At the same time I think we should talk over, between us, the ceremonial demands so that we make sure that everything goes smoothly. For example, I want to raise the point of my planned part, that of introducing Harold. My feeling would be that the audience might consider it presumptuous on my part. But we should talk it over.

I am answering Harold's letter today. Please let me know as quickly as you are back from California so that we may get ironed out any preliminary details, particularly those of timing of the announcement.[3] *As ever*

---

[1] On the plan to award an honorary degree from Johns Hopkins University to British Prime Minister Macmillan see no. 635. See also Milton Eisenhower's April 12 letter to Macmillan (AWF/N).

[2] Macmillan had said that he planned to attend a luncheon at the British embassy at one o'clock on the afternoon of the commencement exercises—June 10. In his April 12 letter Milton Eisenhower had assured the Prime Minister that he would arrange to have Eisenhower and Macmillan escorted to their helicopter immediately following Macmillan's address (*ibid.*).

[3] Following the conferring of the honorary degrees, the President would introduce Macmillan, who would deliver a short address urging expanded trade and more aid for the underprivileged. Immediately afterward, the President and Prime Minister left the stage, boarded the helicopter and returned to Washington, D.C. (see Program, 1958 Commencement, Johns Hopkins University; *News Letter*, vol. LXII, no. 29; *Baltimore Sun*, June 11, 1958; *New York Times*, May 29, June 8, 11, 1958; and Ann Whitman memorandum, June 10, 1958, AWF/AWD).

Macmillan's June 11 thank-you letters to the President and Milton Eisenhower, as well as Milton Eisenhower's thank-you letter to the Prime Minister of the same date are in PREM 11/2462. See also Macmillan to Green, June 11, 1958, *ibid.*

653   *EM, WHCF, Official File 3-VV*

To Ira Clarence Eaker   *April 17, 1958*
Personal

Dear Ira: Thank you very much for your encouraging note. Though I was already confident that our thinking along military organization lines was somewhat similar, it is good to know that you are in the same corner with Tooey and the rest of us.[1]

I suggest that one way you might help is by placing facts before your business friends. Some of these seem to have an unholy fear

that they might be in less favorable position to get procurement contracts if they have to submit to the overall supervision of the Defense plant. In this connection it seems that some non-military organizations such as the Navy League are asserting for themselves a
competence in the field of military organization. One is forced to
look with a jaundiced eye at such self-created experts.[2]

I understand you are now in Washington, at least temporarily. Why
not give my office a ring some day to see if we could have a few minutes chat?[3]

Thanks again for your note.

With warm regard, *As ever*

[1] Eaker, former Chief of the Air Force Air Staff, had been appointed vice-president
of the Eastern Office of the Douglas Aircraft Company in 1957 (for background see
Galambos, *NATO and the Campaign of 1952*, no. 130). He had written on April 14,
1958, in support of Eisenhower's plan for defense reorganization (see no. 631). Eaker
reported that conversations he had held during recent travels in Oklahoma and Texas
indicated that the President had "the confidence and support of a tremendous majority of our people in the courageous program you have launched." Eaker offered
his assistance to Eisenhower, saying, "it would be a pleasure to join your team again."
"Tooey" was former Air Force Chief of Staff Carl Andrew Spaatz (see Galambos and
van Ee, *The Middle Way*, no. 197).

[2] Founded in 1902, the Navy League of the United States saw its mission as one of
awakening the interest of American citizens in matters that would help improve and
develop the efficiency of American naval and maritime forces and equipment. On
April 12, 1958, the League had released a statement strongly opposing the Administration's proposed defense reorganization (see *New York Times*, Apr. 13, 1958). In a
set of resolutions adopted by its executive committee, the League had condemned
the proposal to reduce the three military services to the subordinate status of agencies within the Defense Department. It expressed support for retaining a requirement of existing law that the military departments be "separately administered." The
League also characterized Eisenhower's plans for strengthening the Joint Chiefs as
measures "establishing or leading to" a national general staff.

[3] Eisenhower would meet with Eaker for fifteen minutes on April 30. In a May 1 letter the President would thank Eaker for his eagerness to support the defense reorganization plan. The President said that he had "passed the word along" and was
certain that Eaker would "be called upon at some time or other to make public your
convictions." See Eisenhower to Eaker, May 1, 1958; and Eaker to Eisenhower, May
6, 1958. All correspondence is in the same file as the document.

654   *EM, AWF,*
                                                    Administration Series

To Christian Archibald Herter   *April 21, 1958*

Dear Chris: Before taking the time to worry myself about the draft
that C. D. Jackson prepared, won't you let me have your general

comments on it—especially that portion in which he proposes a new position for the United States to take in this matter of lessening the threat of nuclear war?[1]

With warm regard, *As ever*

[1] For background on Acting Secretary Herter's request that Jackson prepare a speech on disarmament see no. 603; see also no. 607. Jackson had sent a draft to Herter on April 16, the fifth anniversary of Eisenhower's speech in 1953 before the American Society of Newspaper Editors (see Galambos and van Ee, *The Middle Way*, no. 132). If the President made a speech on this topic within six weeks of the exact anniversary, Jackson had told Herter, "a lot of psychological mileage could be gained" (Jackson to Herter, Apr. 16, 1958, AWF/A, Jackson Corr.).

Emphasizing the efforts made by the Eisenhower Administration to solve the disarmament dilemma, Jackson had proposed that at the conclusion of the scheduled series of tests the United States announce the suspension of all testing that might contaminate the atmosphere. In addition, the United States could propose to suspend unilaterally the production of fissionable material for military purposes and to submit to inspections by neutral United Nations observers. If the Soviet Union failed to reciprocate within six months, Jackson wrote, the United States would then reconsider its position (*ibid.*; see also Jackson to Whitman, Apr. 16, 1958, *ibid.*).

Herter would tell Eisenhower that he had discussed the draft with Jackson. "My own feeling with respect to the dramatic suggestion at the end," he said, "is that, if we were operating alone, it might be a useful suggestion to advance. However, as of now, I think it ought to be placed in the context of our whole study of a joint position which might be advanced at the time, if ever, of a Summit conference" (Herter to Eisenhower, Apr. 21, 1958, AWF/A; see also Eisenhower to Jackson, Apr. 18, 1958, *ibid.*). For developments see no. 818.

655   *EM, WHCF, Official File 3-VV*

To Ralph Jarron Cordiner   *April 21, 1958*

Dear Ralph: I am grateful for your recent letter. Two points caught my eye at once. The first one was the aptness of your analogy between proper organization within a business company and within the Defense Department.[1]

The other point was in your offer to be of practical help in spreading an understanding of the need for effective organization in the Defense Department. I take you up on this by sending to you for criticism a draft of a letter that I expect to write to every business man of my acquaintance.[2]

I request that you examine this draft carefully and give me any suggestions that you believe would make it more concise, hard-hitting and persuasive. As quickly as you do this, I plan to start my letter-writing campaign![3]

With warm regard, *Sincerely*

¹ Cordiner had written on April 16, 1958, to express his support for the Administration's proposed reorganization of the Department of Defense (for background see no. 630). Citing his background as Vice-Chairman of the War Production Board during World War II and Chairman of the Defense Advisory Committee on Professional and Technical Compensation in 1956 and 1957 (see no. 73), Cordiner said he found the average citizen "very uninformed as to the impact of technology on the activities of the Department of Defense." He believed, moreover, that the average citizen did not understand how difficult it was for the President and the Secretary of Defense to provide leadership under current law. "The present situation within the Department," he wrote, "is not too dissimilar to a procedure in corporate operations that would permit each individual officer to report separately and independently to the Board of Directors, bypassing the chief executive officer entirely. This, of course, would be a completely unworkable arrangement and would not be tolerated very long, as measurement through profit and loss criteria with aggressive competitors organized on a basis of delegated authority would soon show the fallacy of such a procedure." He urged the President to "take this issue to the people in a series of presentations."

² Cordiner had said that while it was obvious that he was cheering "from a comfortable seat in the grandstand," he offered to join Eisenhower "on the playing field and run interference," if he could be of any help. On Eisenhower's letter to members of the business community see no. 878.

³ Cordiner would respond on April 24 with several suggested changes in the draft document. He would suggest that the President emphasize the necessity for changes in the organization of the Defense Department that would permit flexible responses to technological innovations in defense strategy. Eisenhower appears to have adopted this suggestion; see Eisenhower to Cordiner, May 2, 1958. All papers are in the same file as the document.

656   *EM, AWF, Dulles-Herter Series*

To John Foster Dulles   *April 21, 1958*
Secret

Dear Foster: I have your memorandum of April seventeenth, containing a proposal looking toward the settlement of the India-Pakistan differences.¹ I am all for the approach you indicate, to be undertaken in the utmost secrecy. In fact, if there should ever be realized sufficient progress in negotiations to warrant the hope that a personal gesture might help assure success, there is no inconvenience at which I would balk. For example, I'd be ready to welcome and entertain the Prime Ministers simultaneously—I would even go out there.² *As ever*

¹ With the exception of this introductory sentence, Eisenhower had handwritten this message at the top of Dulles's memorandum. For background on the conflicts between India and Pakistan see Galambos and van Ee, *The Middle Way*, no. 2139, and nos. 113 and 443 in these volumes.

² Dulles had told Eisenhower that two issues continued to plague relations between the two countries—the dispute over Kashmir and the division of the waters of the Indus River. Mutual distrust had led to the buildup of military arms by both countries, thus creating a third subject of dispute. Dulles had suggested a new approach that would closely relate the three problems and might lead to a compromise. He suggested that Eisenhower offer to assist the leaders of both countries in resolving their differences and included the draft of a letter along these lines to both Indian Prime Minister Nehru and Pakistani President Mirza. If the President approved, Dulles said he would ask the United Kingdom to participate in a good offices mission (Dulles to Eisenhower, Apr. 17, 1958, AWF/D-H). For developments see no. 696.

657 *EM, WHCF,*
Official File 101-L

To Sarah Newcomb McClendon *April 21, 1958*
Personal

Dear Mrs. McClendon: It was kind of you to write as you did concerning the press conference of last Wednesday. I appreciate your thoughtfulness. Actually no apology was needed because I am quite sure that you had a special interest in the matter of community public works.¹

I am grateful also for your comment on the usefulness of the presidential press conferences.²

With best wishes, *Sincerely*

¹ McClendon, a news correspondent with the *Austin American-Statesman*, had apologized for referring to golf in her question to Eisenhower during his April 16 news conference (Apr. 17, 1958, same file as document). McClendon had said that Eisenhower's "energetic" fight against the communities facilities bill had bewildered some congressmen. A representative from Texas, she commented, suggested that the President "leave off" his golf and go out and visit small cities and towns in need of the immediate help the bill would provide. She acknowledged that she and many of her editors had a keen interest in community public works, but, she said, the reference to golf had just "slipped in." The Democrat-sponsored Community Facilities Act of 1958 (S. 3497) proposed funding loans to municipalities for various public facilities. The bill had passed, amended, by the Senate in a 60–26 roll-call vote that same day (see *Public Papers of the Presidents: Eisenhower, 1958*, p. 315, and *Congressional Quarterly Almanac*, vol. XIV, *1958*, pp. 71, 151–53). For developments see no. 784.
² McClendon said the news conferences provide a "worthwhile service . . . for the nation and for democracy." She also thanked Eisenhower for "making it possible for little as well as big papers to question you in these unusual sessions, which are quite unique in our world." See Galambos and van Ee, *The Middle Way*, no. 1857, for similar correspondence between Eisenhower and McClendon.

To Arturo Frondizi   *April 22, 1958*

Dear Mr. President: It is with great pleasure that I convey to you through the Vice President of the United States, Richard Nixon, my sincere greetings and congratulations upon the occasion of your inauguration as President of Argentina. I am very sorry that I was unable to accept the kind invitation to attend your inauguration personally.[1]

Your inauguration, Excellency, marks without a doubt a key event in Argentine history, and a moment of hope and anticipation for the future. The re-establishment of constitutional government following free and exemplary elections has been watched with warm and sincere admiration by all the people of the Hemisphere. It is, therefore, with special pleasure that I send you these words of greeting on this occasion.

I am impressed with the similarities in ideals and principles which mark our two nations, and the importance and necessity of close relations between them for the strength and peace of the Hemisphere. I know that Argentina shares with the United States its cherished belief in the dignity of the individual and in the sanctity of personal civil liberties. Not only do the peoples of our two countries share similar ideals and principles, but their historic development contains many striking similarities, and both look to the future with the same determination to build for our children a more secure and fruitful life. I know also that Argentina shares our earnest desire to realize an effective international cooperation dedicated to the achievement of peace and justice.

It is with these thoughts that I should like to assure you of the hope and desire of the United States to expand and strengthen cooperation between our two countries in the years to come in order further to secure their steadfast friendship for the benefit of the peace and prestige of the Americas.

May I extend to you and your countrymen on this happy occasion the best wishes of the people of the United States for a successful and fruitful administration and my personal best wishes for your good health and well-being.[2] *Sincerely*

[1] For background on U.S.-Argentine relations see no. 116; NSC meeting minutes, Feb. 28, 1958, AWF/NSC; and State, *Foreign Relations, 1958–1960*, vol. V, *American Republics*, pp. 460–74. On February 23 Arturo Frondizi, leader of the leftist wing of the Civil Radical Union party and an exponent of economic nationalism and government control of industry, had assumed the presidency of Argentina in the first democratically elected government since the overthrow of Juan Domingo Perón in September 1955. Frondizi had invited Eisenhower to attend his inauguration in order to form a permanent "personal link" between Argentina and the United States.

Eisenhower, in a reply drafted by State Department officials, had declined the invitation and had told Frondizi that Nixon would head the U.S. delegation (Frondizi to Eisenhower, Mar. 26, 1958; and Eisenhower to Frondizi, Apr. 17, 1958, both in AWF/I: Argentina; see also Dulles to Eisenhower, Apr. 16, 1958, *ibid.*; and NSC meeting minutes, Feb. 28, 1958, AWF/NSC).

In preparation for Nixon's good will trip to eight Latin American nations, Eisenhower would also send personal greetings to the leaders of Bolivia, Colombia, Ecuador, Paraguay, Peru, Uruguay, and Venezuela (all letters are in AWF/I). For more on the Vice-President's trip (April 27–May 15) see no. 711; State, *Foreign Relations, 1958–1960*, vol. V, *American Republics*, pp. 222–48; and Richard Milhous Nixon, *RN: The Memoirs of Richard Nixon* (New York, 1978), pp. 228–38.

[2] Eisenhower would write President Frondizi in June regarding U.S.-Argentine relations, and Frondizi would visit the United States in January 1959 (Eisenhower to Frondizi, July 1, 1958, AWF/I: Argentina; see also Frondizi to Eisenhower, June 4, 1958, *ibid.*; and State, *Foreign Relations, 1958–1960*, vol. V, *American Republics*, pp. 527–35).

659   *EM, AWF, DDE Diaries Series*

To Clifford Roberts   *April 22, 1958*

Dear Cliff: On the plane the other day you showed to me a letter that detailed some of the planned improvements at Augusta.[1] You suggested that each member should purchase $500 worth of bonds that could be used, in part for greens fees and rent. You also said that you would be sending out some specific notices about the matter.

I have received no communication from you, but I do assure you that I am quite ready to purchase the $500 worth of bonds. You don't need to bother sending me any official letter because I think it would be easier for Mrs. Whitman to call Mrs. Harris and find out exactly how I write the check out and how the credit is set up at the Club.[2] I remember that some years back I put in some money for similar bonds, but I do not think I received a certificate. I believe that Mrs. Harris just keeps a running account for each of us.

In any event, I want you to know that I have not forgotten the obligation.

Ann tells me that you "recommend" a visit to Augusta for this coming weekend. I may take you up; my schedule these days is far from easy and so I must wait until the last minute to make the decision.[3]

All the best. *As ever*

[1] The President had played golf at Augusta National Golf Club April 11–13. Roberts, chairman of the executive committee at Augusta, had accompanied Eisenhower on the return flight to Washington, D.C.

[2] Helen N. Harris was the club's office manager.

As it turned out, Eisenhower would travel to Augusta for the weekend (Apr. 25–28). There is no further correspondence in AWF on this subject. Eisenhower may have settled the matter of the bonds while he was in Georgia.

660   *EM, AWF, Dulles-Herter Series*

To John Foster Dulles   *April 23, 1958*

Dear Foster: Herewith a note from Cabot that points up again one of the great crosses we have to bear in the international world because of loose talking.[1] I should like to have the letter back for my files.

In the meantime I am trying to think of something to say to the Defense establishment that may be really effective.[2] *As ever*

[1] U.N. Ambassador Lodge had written Eisenhower after an April 21 speech by Soviet U.N. Representative Arkady A. Sobolev, criticizing the United States for sending planes with atomic and hydrogen bombs through the Arctic zone toward the Soviet Union. He had cited statements by American generals that the flights had been recalled when radar signals were discovered to have been caused by electronic interference or falling meteorites. Although the flights had returned to their bases, Sobolev said, such actions indicated that very little provocation was needed "to place mankind on the edge of the abyss" (*New York Times*, Apr. 22, 1958). Lodge had written: "I realize that our Pentagon friends probably have good internal reasons for what they say, but I wish that they could have been here yesterday to see the harm which it does us in the world forum" (Lodge to Eisenhower, Apr. 22, 1958, AWF/D-H).

[2] On this same day Dulles would tell Eisenhower that leaks and uncleared statements were "a matter of great concern," and although the problem could never be completely corrected, "keeping the pressure on at least prevented the situation from getting worse." Eisenhower indicated that he would speak to Defense Secretary McElroy about this (Memorandum of Conversation, Apr. 23, 1958, Dulles Papers, White House Memoranda Series; for more on Defense Department leaks see Galambos and van Ee, *The Middle Way*, no. 508).

661   *EM, AWF, Administration Series*

To Arthur Larson   *April 23, 1958*

Dear Arthur: Obviously the speech for May sixth (which I am returning with a few pencilled notations) is meant to be a partisan speech. How can we therefore justify the first six and a half pages of the talk? The subjects of national security, including their corollaries mutual aid and reciprocal trade, are by our own contention bi-partisan rather than partisan in their character.[1]

This bothers me and I don't see any way around it, even though discounting the sincerity of some of the pledges made for the practice of bipartisanship.[2] *Sincerely*

[1] Eisenhower was referring to the address to the Republican National Committee's dinner to honor the Republican members of Congress, scheduled for May 6, 1958. The President would say that although the two major political parties differed on many domestic policies, three issues then before Congress were of such "grave importance" to the United States and to world peace that they "demand our attention as Americans, without regard to partisanship" (see *Public Papers of the Presidents: Eisenhower, 1958*, pp. 378–86; *New York Times*, May 7, 1958). Modernization of the defense establishment would help the United States meet the Soviet military challenge. Support for the mutual security program would help block the Soviet's "economic assaults on free world positions." Finally, to face Khrushchev's declaration of war "in the peaceful field of trade," the United States had to extend its reciprocal trade program for an additional five years. The speech was televised nationally. For background on these issues see nos. 524 and 630.

[2] The President would deliver his more partisan remarks at the end of his speech. He would promise his personal support to those Republican candidates in the upcoming November elections who backed his legislative program on these issues. Although he saluted "those members of the opposite party who have supported these programs with a zeal equal to that of many ardent Republican supporters," he declared that "the more nearly unanimous our Republican support for these programs, the stronger will be our country, the more effective the Republican Party in its leadership, and the greater our pride in our Party's service." For developments see nos. 678, 753, and 762.

662   *EM, AWF, International Series:*
Macmillan

To Harold Macmillan   *April 24, 1958*
Top secret

Dear Harold: I have your letter of April eighteenth, suggesting, as I understand it, military planning by the two of us plus Australia and New Zealand with reference to Southeast Asia.[1] I certainly see no objection to this provided it can be done, as you say, unobtrusively and in a way which will not run the risk of undermining SEATO and alienating the Asian members. However, it does seem to me that before there can be any very useful military talks, there is need for political discussion. I think this perhaps should occur in the first instance between our two countries. I wonder whether this could not be one of the matters we talk about when you are to be here in early June?[2]

The rebellion in Sumatra seems to have flattened out so that the problem there, while certainly as grave as ever, does not have the same time factor that seemed at one time to be the case.[3]

If you want Caccia to have some talks with Foster about this before you come over, I would see no objection. However, I must repeat my opinion that four-power military planning, in advance of political decisions by them, would incur more risk than advantage.[4]

Incidentally, Foster has the impression, derived from the SEATO meeting, that Prime Minister Nash of New Zealand is much less disposed than was his predecessor to vigorous action that could have military implications.[5]

With warm regard, *As ever*

[1] Although he had proposed a joint four-power defense strategy in the area, Macmillan had opposed anything that would weaken the South East Asia Treaty Organization. "At the same time," he wrote, "I think you will agree that we cannot honestly put all our cards on the table in the SEATO forum." He suggested informal discussions "held so unobtrusively as to attract no attention" (Macmillan to Eisenhower, Apr. 18, 1958, AWF/I: Macmillan). After receiving Macmillan's letter, Eisenhower had told Secretary Dulles that he thought he should reply "fairly promptly" (Eisenhower to Dulles, Apr. 23, 1958, Dulles Papers, White House Memoranda Series). The matter was delicate, Dulles said, because Macmillan's proposals were covered by the ANZUS Treaty. Australia and New Zealand wanted to maintain the three-power arrangement, which did not include Great Britain (Memorandum of Conversation, Apr. 23, 1958, *ibid.*).

[2] Macmillan would tell Eisenhower that he readily accepted his point and agreed that they should discuss the issue when the two men met in June (Macmillan to Eisenhower, May 15, 1958, AWF/I: Macmillan). On the prime minister's visit see no. 635.

[3] Communist strength in Indonesia had increased steadily since anti-colonialist leader Achmed Sukarno had declared the island archipelago independent from the Netherlands in 1945 (see Galambos, *Chief of Staff*, no. 600, n. 9). Recent nationalistic moves against Dutch interests in New Guinea (see no. 501) had provided additional opportunities for the communists to strengthen their position. Anti-communist groups, including a large group of orthodox Moslems, comprised the majority of the population, but rivalries had prevented united action. Dissatisfaction with the corruption and inefficiency of Sukarno's leftist-oriented government had resulted in an ultimatum demanding a new Indonesian cabinet free from communist influences. Rejection of the ultimatum by the government had led Moslem and Christian leaders in Sumatra, an area rich in oil and other natural resources, to establish a revolutionary anti-communist government headed by former Vice-President Mohammed Hatta. CIA Director Allen Dulles had told the National Security Council on February 27 that if the dissident movement failed, Indonesia would move into the Communist camp. At this point Eisenhower told the council that the United States "would have to go in" to prevent a Communist take-over (NSC meeting minutes, Feb. 28, 1958, AWF/NSC; see also State, *Foreign Relations, 1958–1960*, vol. XVII, *Indonesia* [1994], pp. 14–24, 31–37, 44–63, 68–89, 92–100; and NSC meeting minutes, Jan. 23, Feb. 7, 14, Mar. 7, 14, 21, 28, and Apr. 15, 1958, AWF/NSC).

As the situation worsened, Secretary Dulles and other State Department officials had discussed with Eisenhower the possibility of covert assistance to the rebels. The President authorized a confidential message to the rebel leaders, telling them that if they mounted a "stubborn resistance" to the expected attack by government forces, the United States would offer some form of recognition, which would in turn permit overt U.S. support (Memorandum of Conversation, Apr. 15, 1958, Dulles Papers, White House Memoranda Series; see also Telephone conversation, Dulles and Herter,

Apr. 8, 1958, Dulles Papers, Telephone Conversations; and State, *Foreign Relations, 1958–1960,* vol. XVII, *Indonesia,* pp. 109–10).

On April 17 President Sukarno had sent airborne troops into central Sumatra in the area near the oil fields of the American-owned Caltex Pacific Oil Company. The government forces had met only feeble resistance from the rebels. On the day this letter was written, Allen Dulles had reported to the National Security Council that the rebellion had "practically collapsed," although future actions by the Jakarta government were difficult to predict (NSC meeting minutes, Apr. 25, 1958, AWF/NSC; see also Telephone conversations, Dulles and Allen Dulles, Apr. 15, 17, 23, 1958, Dulles Papers, Telephone Conversations). On the CIA's involvement in the insurrection see Howard Palfrey Jones, *Indonesia: The Possible Dream* (New York, 1971), pp. 143–46; and Paul F. Gardner, *Shared Hopes, Separate Fears: Fifty Years of U.S.-Indonesian Relations* (Boulder, Colo., 1997), pp. 145–62; see also Audrey R. Kahin and George McT. Kahin, *Subversion as Foreign Policy: The Secret Eisenhower and Dulles Debacle in Indonesia* (New York, 1995). For developments see no. 753.

[4] Eisenhower had changed this sentence from the one in Dulles's original draft, which had read: "However, I think that four-power military planning at this stage carries more risks than advantages at least in advance of political decisions" (see State, *Foreign Relations, 1958–1960,* vol. XVI, *East Asia–Pacific Region; Cambodia; Laos* [1992], p. 40).

[5] Sidney Holland, prime minister of New Zealand from 1949–1957, had resigned in August 1957. Walter Nash, New Zealand's finance minister during World War II and leader of the Labour Party opposition in Parliament from 1950 to 1957, had become prime minister and minister of external affairs in December 1957 on a platform calling for the recognition of Communist China. Dulles had told Eisenhower that he thought Nash would "go slow in any such course of action. He is having quite a good education here, and I think he will end up in a mood of good cooperation" (Dulles to Eisenhower, Mar. 12, 1958, AWF/D-H; see also State, *Foreign Relations, 1958–1960,* vol. XVI, *East Asia–Pacific Region; Cambodia; Laos,* pp. 12–13; and Macmillan, *Riding the Storm,* pp. 398–99).

663   *EM, AWF,*
                                                       Administration Series

To Nelson Aldrich Rockefeller   *April 24, 1958*

Dear Nelson: Thank you for sending me an advance copy of the most recent panel report of the Special Studies Project of the Rockefeller Brothers Fund, Inc. Such study as I have been able to give to "The Challenge to America: Its Economic and Social Aspects" indicates the tremendous amount of conscientious effort and expert analysis of a subject which is, of course, one of the broadest and most difficult areas of concern to the government.[1]

With regard to the tax recommendation, I can sense from the wording of the report the problem of composing the different views of the members of the panel on the timing and amount of a tax cut which your group apparently thought was desirable. As you so well know, I am faced hourly with the same division of opinion among people in the Administration and my good friends in the business world.[2]

Incidentally, the editorial in the New York Times of Monday expresses far better than can I in a brief letter the belief, which I share, as to the long term value of the project.[3]

With warm regard, *As ever*

[1] The Rockefeller report, the second in a series studying important national questions, had been released on April 20, 1958 (see *New York Times*, Apr. 21, 1958). It recommended a six-point program to end the recession and clear the way for industrial expansion and social improvement that would create a more "abundant America." It also offered a ten-year blueprint for social improvement. Nelson Rockefeller, who headed both the fund and the project, had established the Special Studies Project of the Rockefeller Brothers Fund in 1956.

[2] The Report had also called for an immediate federal tax reduction, which would be the most effective short-time economic stimulant. Although the size of the proposed tax cut was not specified, the Rockefeller report made it clear that a reduction of several billions of dollars was intended. A cut of $5,000,000,000 had been in the preliminary draft but had been eliminated because of disagreements among the panel members. On Eisenhower's position regarding a tax cut see no. 604.

[3] The *New York Times* had called the Rockefeller report a "remarkable document which deserves the close attention and study of all thinking citizens and of government officials at all levels of local, state and Federal administration." The paper praised the report as the "finest statement in many years of the economic choices and opportunities before the American people." The *Times* favored many of the recommendations for short-term recession relief and called the long-term goals of expanded social and economic investment a "useful" blue-print "for a stronger, richer and progressive America. . . ."

664 *EM, AWF, Name Series*

To EMANUEL GOLDMAN *April 24, 1958*
Personal

Dear Mannie:[1] I am sending you the enclosed check because I feel that I simply must make, each year, some kind of gesture to express my gratitude to you and your brothers other than just to say "thank you" for the many courtesies you extend to me. I am not trying to discharge the obligation I feel—that would be an impossibility.

This spring, so far as I know, I am fully and amply supplied with all the clothes that I could possibly need. But I know that you and Bob Schulz often talk together and discuss, between yourselves, something that I am bound to like. Thereafter I am likely to find myself the recipient of one of your generous gifts. This explains my feeling that prompts this note.

With warm regard to you and to the members of your family, *Sincerely*

---

¹ Goldman was vice-president of William P. Goldman & Bros., the New York City firm that made most of Eisenhower's clothes (for background see Galambos and van Ee, *The Middle Way*, no. 261).

665   *EM, AWF, International Series:*
                                                                    Khrushchev

To Nikita Sergeyevich Khrushchev   *April 28, 1958*
Secret

*Dear Mr. Chairman:*¹ I have your communication of April twenty-second in reply to mine of April eighth. I regret that it is not an affirmative response to my proposal.²

You refer in your letter to the question raised recently by the Soviet Union in the United Nations Security Council which also touches upon the disarmament question.³ I am sure that you would agree that with the growing capabilities in the Soviet Union and the United States of massive surprise attack it is necessary to establish measures to allay fears. The United States has just asked the Security Council to reconvene in order to consider the establishment of an international inspection system for the Arctic zone. The United States has submitted a constructive proposal to this end.⁴ I urge you to join with us in supporting the resolution of the United States now before the Council. Your support of this proposal and subsequent cooperation would help to achieve a significant first step. It would help to reduce tensions, it would contribute to an increase of confidence among states, and help to reduce the mutual fears of surprise attack.

The United States is determined that we will ultimately reach an agreement on disarmament. In my letter of April eighth, I again proposed an internationally supervised cut-off of the use of new fissionable materials for weapons purposes and the reduction of existing weapons stocks by transfer to peaceful purposes; an agreed limitation or suspension of testing; "open skies", and the international use of outer space for peaceful purposes.

As an effective means of moving toward ultimate agreement on these matters and other disarmament matters, I proposed that we start our technical people to work immediately upon the practical problems involved. These studies were called for by the United Nations General Assembly. They would include the practical problems of supervision and control which, you and I agree, are in any event indispensable to dependable disarmament agreements.

The solution of these practical problems will take time. I am unhappy that valuable time is now being wasted.

You say that we must first reach a final political agreement before it is worthwhile even to initiate the technical studies. But such studies would, in fact, facilitate the reaching of the final agreement you state you desire.

For example, why could not designated technical people agree on what would be required so that you would know if we violated an agreement to suspend testing and we would know if you should commit a violation?

Would not both sides be in a better position to reach agreements if we had a common accepted understanding as to feasibility of detection or as to method of inspecting against surprise attack?

Studies of this kind are the necessary preliminaries to putting political decisions actually into effect. The completion of such technical studies in advance of a political agreement would obviate a considerable period of delay and uncertainty. In other words, with the practicalities already worked out, the political agreement could begin to operate very shortly after it was signed and ratified.

I reemphasize that these studies are without prejudice to our respective positions on the timing and interdependence of various aspects of disarmament.

Mr. Chairman, my offer to you still and always will remain open. I hope you will reconsider and accept it. In that way we both can make an important contribution to the cause of just and lasting peace.[5] *Sincerely*

[1] State Department officials drafted this letter to the Soviet leader. It was sent to Great Britain and to NATO headquarters before transmission to Moscow on April 29 (see Telephone conversation, Greene and Hagerty, Apr. 25, 1958, Dulles Papers, Telephone Conversations).

[2] Eisenhower's letter is no. 639. The President had proposed restricting the international use of outer space to peaceful purposes and the initiation of the technical studies necessary for international controls of atomic energy.

[3] On April 21 the Soviet Union had introduced a draft resolution in the Security Council calling upon the United States to end flights of military aircraft carrying atomic and hydrogen bombs toward the frontiers of other states "for the purpose of creating a threat to their security or staging military demonstrations." The council would reject a similar Soviet resolution on May 2 (State, *Documents on Disarmament, 1945–1959*, vol. II, *1957–1959*, p. 990).

[4] The U.S. resolution is in *ibid.*, p. 1005. On April 23 Dulles had shown Eisenhower a draft of the resolution, which the President approved (Memorandum of Conversation, Apr. 23, 1958, Dulles Papers, White House Memoranda Series).

[5] For developments see no. 712.

To John Foster Dulles   *April 30, 1958*
Personal

Dear Foster: I had a meeting with Joe Martin yesterday. In the course of the conversation he brought up the names of two people who would like to have positions in the State Department. They are Congressman Wigglesworth and Clare Luce. I think you already have been informed of these desires.[1]

I believe you told me that you would be glad to appoint Wigglesworth to an Ambassadorial post, provided there was any vacancy in the area where he would want to serve. This area I understand is the European region, and I think that all, or certainly most, of these posts are already filled with "political" appointees. In Congressman Wigglesworth's case, Mr. Martin says that he needs an answer within the next week or ten days because he has to make his decision as to whether or not he will run again in the spring primary for nomination as Congressman.[2]

Mr. Martin was far less specific in the Luce case. He merely pointed out that Mrs. Luce was recognized as a very capable individual and he thought it would be a fine thing if we could find a real job for her. He gave the impression that she was thinking of something on the order of a "free-wheeling" post—one that would give her opportunity to do some speaking.[3]

I send this information to you because of my own personal belief that both these individuals are more than average in ability. I shall be glad to talk to you about them at your convenience.

With warm regard, *As ever*

---

[1] Henry Luce had discussed with Eisenhower Mrs. Luce's desire for another ambassadorial appointment as early as October 25, 1957 (Ann Whitman memorandum, Oct. 25, 1957, AWF/AWD; for background see Galambos and van Ee, *The Middle Way*, no. 167). On April 10, 1958, Secretary of State Dulles had brought to the President's attention Congressman Richard Wigglesworth's (Rep., Mass.) desire for an ambassadorial appointment in Europe (Dulles, Memorandum of Conversation, Apr. 10, 1958, Dulles Papers, White House Memoranda Series). Eisenhower had told Dulles that he liked Wigglesworth but did not want to make a commitment. He directed that Wigglesworth should, however, be given a "certain priority" if and when a vacancy occurred. On Eisenhower's April 29 breakfast meeting with Massachusetts Congressman Martin, Republican leader of the House of Representatives, see Ann Whitman memorandum, April 29, 1958, AWF/AWD.

[2] Wigglesworth would receive an appointment as United States Ambassador to Canada (*New York Times*, Oct. 30, 1958).

[3] Luce, United States Ambassador to Italy from 1953 to 1957, would be named Ambassador to Brazil in February 1959 (see *New York Times*, Feb. 27, 1959). For developments see no. 1145.

To Jawaharlal Nehru   *April 30, 1958*
Secret

My dear Mr. Prime Minister:[1] I have just received news reports from New Delhi that you are thinking of laying down your official and heavy responsibilities, at least for the time being.[2]

You, if anyone, Mr. Prime Minister, deserve a long and restful vacation after all these years that you have guided your vast country toward economic, political, and social progress. However, I and countless others hope that you will not go too far away or for too long a time.

Are there not at least faint indications that the world may be at a turning point when some important problems can be solved, when perhaps the sharpness of conflict between the Soviet Union and the West may be sufficiently moderated to become tolerable? Certainly considerable progress has been made from the days when it seemed, to us at least, that the Soviet leaders were relying primarily on violence to attain their objectives. Their goals, and of this Mr. Khrushchev makes no secret, are still expansionist, [but] their methods seem to have somewhat moderated in the face of the world's opposition to violence as a technique for bringing about change. I also have in mind that we might be reaching a time when some of those problems which have persistently beset Indo-Pakistan relations might be susceptible to solution. I had indeed, been thinking of communicating with you in this matter.[3]

Under all these circumstances, it would indeed be a misfortune, perhaps for all of us, if at what may prove to be a critical, formative period, your own influence were not actively present over any really protracted period.[4] *Sincerely*

[1] On this same day Secretary Dulles had sent Eisenhower the draft of a letter he was planning to send to the Indian Prime Minister, since the two men had maintained "a somewhat intermittent but significant correspondence." Dulles added that he was confident that the President would share the sentiments he had expressed (Dulles to Eisenhower, Apr. 30, 1958, AWF/D-H). Eisenhower told Andrew Goodpaster that he wanted to send his own cable to Nehru and asked Dulles to incorporate some of the substance of his message in a shorter presidential message. Dulles agreed and said that in that case he might not send his own letter (Telephone conversation, Apr. 30, 1958, Dulles Papers, Telephone Conversations; see also State, *Foreign Relations, 1958–1960*, vol. XV, *South and Southeast Asia*, pp. 428–29).

[2] On the preceding day Nehru had told a meeting of the Congress party that he wanted to be relieved of the day-to-day burdens of his office. He had not said that he wanted to retire, and he agreed to leave that decision in the hands of the party (*New York Times*, Apr. 30, May 1, 1958).

[3] For background on the conflict between India and Pakistan see no. 656. Eisenhower would write to Nehru regarding this issue on May 14 (see no. 696).

tell Eisenhower. His health was good, he said, "but the mind gets stale and tired." He intended to travel through the mountains for a period of time and then visit with the people in various parts of the country. "Such contacts always refresh me" (Nehru to Eisenhower, May 4, 1958, AWF/I: Nehru). Nehru would remain Prime Minister of India until 1964.

668   *EM, AWF, DDE Diaries Series*

To Winston Spencer Churchill   *April 30, 1958*

Dear Winston: Last Thursday afternoon Mamie and I spent a delightful hour at the exhibition of your paintings at the Smithsonian.¹ Our one regret was that you and Clemmie could not have been with us.² The show was intriguing beyond even my expectations, and I wished for an opportunity to talk to you about your methods.

As I am sure you know, the exhibition is proving to be the artistic "hit" of the season in every city in which it is shown. I understand that on a normal Sunday some six or seven thousand people visit the Smithsonian; last Sunday, in wretched weather, forty thousand jammed the Museum to see your paintings.³

There are so many that I like that I beg leave to ponder, until the completion of the American tour, the choice of one. You see I am still hopeful that you will feel able to come over, and that together we can select the one that will be the pride of the Eisenhower family for generations to come. For the moment my choice is the scene of the Ourika River and the Atlas Mountains.⁴

With warm personal regard, and the hope that you are feeling better with each passing day, *As ever*

¹ In March 1957 Churchill had agreed to exhibit thirty of his paintings in several U.S. cities (see no. 86). On April 24 the Eisenhowers had attended a private viewing of his art (see *New York Times*, Apr. 25, 1958).

² The Churchills had planned to stay at the White House for the opening of the exhibition at the Smithsonian Institution (for background see nos. 445 and 568).

On April 8 the former British Prime Minister had written that he had suffered a "setback" in his health and would have to postpone his trip to Washington, D.C. He had been suffering from obstructive jaundice caused either by a stone or an infection of the bile passages (Lord Charles Moran, *Churchill: Taken From the Diaries of Lord Moran* [Boston, 1966], p. 782; see also Churchill to Eisenhower, Apr. 11, 1958). "Your health must take priority over everything else," the President had cabled that same day. Eisenhower would restate these sentiments in a letter on April 14.

³ The show had premiered on January 22 in Kansas City, Missouri (see no. 568). For a review of the Smithsonian exhibit see *Washington Post*, April 25, 1958.

⁴ Churchill had offered Eisenhower any painting in the exhibit (see no. 222). In his

letter of April 8 Churchill had expressed his hope to make a "rendez-vous later in the year." For developments see no. 909.

All correspondence is in AWF/I: Churchill.

669   *EM, AWF, Name Series*

To Earl Dewey Eisenhower   *April 30, 1958*

Dear Earl: I am delighted to learn that you have agreed to act as my personal representative at the dedication of the Eisenhower State Park in Denison, Texas, on May eighteenth.[1] Mr. R. L. McKinney, Jr., Director of the Dedication Program, will shortly be in touch with you regarding details.[2]

Within a day or so Mrs. Whitman will send you a memorandum containing what information she has on the restored birthplace which is, I understand, a corollary project, although different people seem to be in charge of the Park and the Birthplace. It might be useful for you to have available some of the background on the projects.

I shall, of course, be glad to send you a message to read at the ceremony.[3]

With all the best, *As ever*

P.S. I expect you to take Kathryn with you and, as Ann told you, I want to have the bill for your transportation.[4]

P.S.II I want to emphasize that the dedication of the Park has nothing to do with the dedication of the Birthplace, but I understand the Birthplace is open and I think you will want to see it.[5]

[1] Presidential Secretary Ann Whitman had asked Earl Eisenhower if he would attend the dedication ceremonies (Telephone conversation, Whitman and Eisenhower, Apr. 30, 1958, AWF/D). Eisenhower State Park, acquired by the Department of the Army in 1954, comprised 480 acres directly on Lake Texoma in Grayson County, northwest of Denison, Texas. On May 20 Earl would report that although the park was "nothing but rolling grassland and trees," it will be "a beautiful affair."

[2] We have been unable to identify McKinney.

[3] In his message, read by Earl Eisenhower, the President would say that while he lived in Denison only for his first year, he was "proud to be a native son of Texas" (*New York Times*, May 19, 1958; see also Signatures, May 12, 1958, AWF/D).

[4] On May 13 Eisenhower would enclose a check to cover expenses for Earl and his wife Kathryn (AWF/N). Earl would return a check for the unused portion of the money with his report on May 20.

[5] After visiting the birthplace Earl would tell the President that it was "a rather remarkable little place." The exterior had been well maintained, but the inside, he would report, had not seen as many improvements. The wallpaper, furniture, and coal stove were all from the 1890s and resembled those used by the Eisenhowers in Abilene. The front room contained a picture of General Lee and his staff, which Earl

was "sure Mother and Dad didn't have and would not have had." He had, however, made no objection.

Eisenhower would thank his brother on May 24 and would say that he gathered from Earl's account and from friends in Denison that Earl performed "nobly" at the dedication ceremonies (AWF/N; see also Signatures, May 26, 1958, AWF/D).

670   *EM, AWF,*
                                                                        Administration Series

To Alfred Maximillan Gruenther   *April 30, 1958*

Dear Al: I have friends who play a good game of bridge. I have at least one friend who talks a good game of bridge. But there is a certain individual who has proved beyond all doubt his superiority in teaching the game of bridge.

The other day, to commemorate that memorable feat, I, by virtue of the authority vested in me, did confer on Pete Jones a permanent appointment. In all fairness you should have a copy for your archives.[1]

With warm regard, *As ever*

P.S. You will note that the "Secretary" joins me in confirming the legality of the appointment.[2]

[1] Eisenhower had spent the evening of April 19 at Camp David with friends playing bridge and celebrating Jones's birthday (Ann Whitman memorandum, Apr. 18, 1958, AWF/AWD). In a thank-you letter to the head of the White House social office, Eisenhower would say the mock certificate was the "hit" of the birthday party (Eisenhower to Tolley, Apr. 23, 1958, WHCF/PPF 504). See also no. 122.

[2] Mrs. Whitman noted that Eisenhower requested "a special commission made up for Pete Jones" (Ann Whitman memorandum, Apr. 19, 1958, AWF/AWD). The certificate, a copy of which is in the Gruenther Papers, conferred upon Jones a "DCL" (Doctor of Card Law) degree and appointed him "PROFESSOR and INSTRUCTOR of Al Gruenther and Others in the Laws, Rules, Techniques and Skullduggery of Bridge . . . during the pleasure of the President of the United States for the time being."

10

Restructuring for National Security

To John Foster Dulles   *May 1, 1958*

Dear Foster: I have read the cablegram from Arthur Dean sent to me by your note of April twenty-fourth.[1] The most disappointing thing to me is the readiness of all the Latin American countries to desert our position. Maybe we have got to get a little bit more quid pro quo and do some of our agreements with supposed friends, particularly with an eye on future conferences where the principal sport might seem to be "cutting us down."

On another subject, why does Japan seem to oppose everything we want to do in Okinawa, but makes no effort to get Russia out of the Kuriles?[2] *As ever*

[1] Arthur H. Dean headed the U.S. delegation to the Geneva Law of the Sea Conference, which had concluded on April 27. For background see nos. 589 and 609. On April 21 Dean had cabled State Department officials regarding the problem of groups of nations, such as the Latin American countries, which voted as a bloc without regard to the merits of a particular issue. Such procedures raised serious questions for U.S. policy, Dean said. Even countries that had received extensive U.S. aid and had long friendships with the United States seemed determined "as newly emancipated nations to vote solidly with their brethren against their former masters and those associated with them." New nations had little realization of the actual meaning of such terms as "territorial sea" or of the duties involved in policing larger off-shore territories but favored expanded territorial limits because they seemed more compatible with their sovereignty as new nations. "Time and again the three-mile breadth was attacked and ridiculed," Dean said. "The ingenuity, ability, capital and markets of the older powers is [*sic*] resented and the use of large mother ships off coastal waters is frequently denounced as taking the bread out of the mouths of local coastal fishermen out of port on a small ship—on [a] one day basis" (State, *Foreign Relations, 1958–1960*, vol. II, *United Nations and General International Matters*, pp. 700–704; see also Ann Whitman memorandum, May 1, 1958, AWF/AWD). For developments see no. 1307.

[2] For background on the Okinawa controversy see no. 646. The Treaty of St. Petersburg between Russia and Japan in 1875 had given Russia control over Sakhalin Island and had given Japan the Kurile Islands. On the Soviet occupation of the islands after World War II see Galambos and van Ee, *The Middle Way*, no. 1336. Japan had made "strong efforts" to get the Russians to return some portion of the Kuriles, Dulles would tell Eisenhower. "It is true that the Japanese press and public ride us harder than they do the Russians" (Dulles to Eisenhower, May 1, 1958, AWF/D-H; see also Telephone conversation, Dulles and Robertson, May 1, 1958, Dulles Papers, Telephone Conversations). For developments see no. 724.

To Isidor Schwaner Ravdin   *May 1, 1958*

Dear Rav: As I understand it, you are now the Czar of Carvers. Regardless of title, I want to tell you how delighted I am that this great honor has come to you, one that all of your friends will applaud.[1]

I am sorry that as a Honorary Fellow of the College of Surgeons, I was not allowed to vote for you.[2] Could I have done so your unanimous vote would have been reinforced by one additional number.

My most sincere felicitations. Please convey my warm greetings to Betty and, of course, all the best to yourself. *As ever*

[1] Ravdin, who had assisted at Eisenhower's 1956 abdominal surgery, had been elected president of the American Surgical Association.
[2] On February 6 a delegation from the American College of Surgeons had conferred the honorary fellowship upon Eisenhower (see no. 160; see also President's daily appointments, Feb. 6, 1958).

673   *EM, AWF,*
                                                  Administration Series

To Arthur Ellsworth Summerfield   *May 2, 1958*

Dear Arthur: Thank you very much for your letter of the first. With the general thesis of your paper I am in agreement.[1]

With respect to the program of activity that you outline as one required if we are to change the American psychological attitude from pessimism to optimism, I should like to point out some of the items you suggest have already received considerable treatment.

Under item two, for example, I know of several meetings that have already taken place or are now scheduled. I am personally to make a talk to an Economic Mobilization Conference in New York on the night of May 18th, and during the preceding two days both the Secretary of Commerce and the Vice President will do the same.[2]

With respect to item three, the Federal Reserve Board has, in recent months, acted very decisively. Possibly a little needling of the commercial banks might be effective.[3]

I think item five would be particularly good.[4]

In any event, I will have some of the staff look over your memorandum.[5] Thank you for taking the trouble to send it to me.

With warm regard, *As ever*

[1] Summerfield's letter had addressed the recession by offering "a planned program of improvement" that would not increase the national deficit (May 1, 1958, AWF/A).

There was a danger, he believed, that "public psychology will cause actions which will cause the recession to feed upon itself and worsen." A "well-planned" program by the Administration in concert with commerce and industry, could "strengthen the psychological attitude of our citizens." On the recession see, for example, no. 698.

[2] Summerfield had suggested holding a conference "of industrialists and commercial magnates to arrange for concrete announcements or explanations by all of these companies of plant equipment, etc." On Eisenhower's speech and the Economic Mobilization Conference see nos. 675 and 691.

[3] Summerfield had suggested that "commercial bankers should be called upon to reduce interest rates to borrowers to encourage new projects. The bankers should also announce readiness to make loans on real estate, homes, etc." See nos. 598 and 675.

[4] Summerfield's fifth point dealt with GOP unity. "The party should present a solid front in the psychological campaign and should lose no opportunity to disprove any statement made by anyone which would indicate that the recession was deepening. I think it is particularly important," he said, "that Republicans show that the Democrat Congress is trying to sabotage the Administration's efforts to improve business, and that Republicans make this an issue in the forthcoming campaign." For developments see no. 850.

[5] Eisenhower would send a memorandum to Chairman of the Council of Economic Advisers Saulnier regarding Summerfield's letter on this same day (May 2, 1958, AWF/A). On May 5 Saulnier would reply that he was skeptical of "deliberate, planned efforts to bolster confidence." While he "instinctively" relied on the "tendency of Americans to respond quickly to favorable events that come along in the regular course of business," there might, as Summerfield had suggested, be ways "to speed up 'favorable events' and, especially, to bring them more clearly and forcibly to the attention of the public generally."

674   EM, WHCF, Official File 114

To Lewis Williams Douglas   May 2, 1958

Dear Lew: Thank you very much for your two letters of the nineteenth. I am only sorry to learn that you are, to some extent at least, still a captive of the doctors and I trust that before too long you will once again be feeling completely like yourself.[1]

First, as to your paper regarding the relationship between our own economic welfare and foreign exchange, in connection with our efforts to obtain adequate support for foreign aid and an adequate reciprocal trade bill. We are, as you know, following the third alternative you outline, the one you call prudent. I am, of course, grateful to you for the statement you prepared; I am certain it will have a helpful impact.[2] Incidentally, I asked Dr. Hauge to prepare for me a memorandum on this whole field; I am enclosing a copy of his comments.[3]

Now as to the current recession. There is no day, literally no hour, when the subject is not before me. We are of course giving attention to the problem of counteracting the slump by means that will be constructive over the long run, as well as in the immediate present. I assure you that purely financial considerations would not stand in the way of a reduction program if this is indicated, as I judge you believe it is, and there would be no disposition to favor large increases in public works' expenditures as an alternative.[4]

I know you realize, however, that a very considerable increase in Federal expenditures is inevitable under present commitments, without our undertaking any more, and this fact must be considered in any decision deliberately to reduce tax revenues.[5] What to do to benefit the present and not to harm our future economy presents one of the toughest problems I have had in a lifetime of difficult ones!

Take care of yourself, and know that I greatly appreciate your support and your thoughts.

With warm personal regard, *As ever*

[1] Former Under Secretary of the Treasury and former U.S. Ambassador to Britain Douglas had written twice on April 19, 1958. He apologized that poor health had kept him from testifying before Congress on behalf of a four-year extension of the Reciprocal Trade Agreements Act. (Hearings on the bill had begun in February and had continued for six weeks; see no. 524; see also *Congressional Quarterly Almanac*, vol. XIV, *1958*, pp. 165–79). Douglas enclosed a statement about trade and economic welfare, which he had also forwarded to many members of Congress.

[2] Douglas's paper, entitled "Will We Repeat the Errors of 1929 and 1930," examined the relationship between foreign aid, foreign trade, and the stability of exchange rates as they affected domestic economic activity. Douglas argued that restrictive tariffs after World War I had weakened world currencies and contributed to the severity of the Great Depression in the United States. This historical experience suggested three possible contemporary foreign aid strategies: the U.S. could abandon efforts to cut barriers to trade and reduce or eliminate appropriations for foreign aid; the U.S. could reduce tariffs substantially and quickly, allowing other countries to earn enough dollars to preserve stability of exchange rates; or the U.S. could "pursue a course of gradual reduction of interferences with the flow of trade and appropriate enough funds for foreign aid to insure us against the probably unpleasant internal consequences of a depreciation of major world currencies against the dollar." Douglas called the third strategy the "more prudent" one.

[3] See Hauge memorandum, April 25, 1958. Hauge had said that Douglas's proposed third course of action was "essentially the one this Administration is following. We seek a long-term extension of the Trade Agreements Act with broadened authority to negotiate further reciprocal reductions in tariffs. We seek a substantial mutual security appropriation with emphasis on the Development Loan Fund. We have asked for a $2 billion increase in the lending authority of the Export-Import Bank. We are retrenching nowhere on this international trade and finance front in the field of public policy." For developments see no. 753.

[4] Douglas's second letter concerned his "apprehension" that the recession was "deepening instead of receding," and that, if "positive intervention in the form of an appropriate tax reduction" was not taken soon, "even this may prove to be inadequate to stem the tide." For background see nos. 598 and 633. This portion of Eisenhower's reply had been suggested by Raymond J. Saulnier, Chairman of the Council of Economic Advisers, who had prepared a memorandum on Douglas's letter for the President (see Saulnier memorandum, Apr. 24, 1958).

[5] This sentence, too, Saulnier had suggested (*ibid.*). Secretary of the Treasury An-

derson had also prepared remarks to use in a reply to the Douglas letter (Anderson memorandum, Apr. 28, 1958; all correspondence is in same file as document).

675   *EM, AWF, Administration Series*

TO RAYMOND J. SAULNIER   *May 2, 1958*
Memorandum

Here is a suggested draft of a speech I am to give in New York on May eighteenth.[1] In general it seems to me to have quite an appeal. I would like, however, to have you examine it closely in the light of the following questions:

1. Are all the analogies accurate?
2. Are the inferences logical?
3. Is the entire thesis of the paper sound?
4. There is no mention of taxes at all. Should there be?[2]
5. Should I take the opportunity in the talk to needle commercial bankers with the suggestion that they should reduce interest rates?[3]

If feasible, you can put your comments and notes on the margin of the paper. Otherwise you may want to write me a memorandum and bring it to my office so that we might have a short talk about it.[4]

[1] Eisenhower was referring to his speech (May 20, 1958) to the Economic Mobilization Conference of the American Management Association (see *Public Papers of the Presidents: Eisenhower, 1958*, pp. 413–21; *New York Times*, May 21, 1958). The President would make a strong plea for voluntary action by industry and labor to reduce prices and avoid inflationary wage raises. He would term economic recovery a "joint effort in which business leaders, labor leaders, farm leaders, professional leaders, consumers, together with government, must all play a part" and would detail the steps the Administration had taken to counter the recession.

[2] The President would address the taxation issue. The Administration's goal was to assure maximum equity in the tax burden and adopt "a tax structure which least interferes with sound economic growth." The timing of such changes, however, was difficult. "In a time like the present, with its rising government expenditures, we are particularly sensitive to tax burdens, but there is likewise great concern with the future impact of increasing current deficits." Eisenhower would promise to make a decision on a tax cut shortly (for background see no. 663).

[3] The President would make no mention of interest rates.

[4] Eisenhower would discuss the speech with Saulnier for forty minutes on May 7 (see Ann Whitman memorandum, May 7, 1958, AWF/AWD).

To Pauline Riedeburg Mills   *May 2, 1958*

Dear Mrs. Mills: Rarely have I read a letter which has so profoundly moved me as yours. It is first of all a remarkable tribute to the character, accomplishments and high purposes of your late husband. Beyond that it reveals, on your part, both a clear understanding of some of America's most critical and complex problems and the need for intelligence, competence and dedication in their solution.[1]

Because of the fine and deep patriotism that you and your husband so obviously shared, and because of the feeling and skill with which you have expressed your and his selfless dedication to our country, I have shown your letter to several of my closest associates.[2] I could truly wish that every American might have the opportunity to read it.

With my lasting appreciation of the courageous spirit and sense of obligation to our country and to your husband's memory that inspired your letter, I assure you that you and your children will be remembered in my prayers and have an enduring place in my admiration and respect.[3]

With best wishes, *Sincerely*

[1] On April 20 Mrs. Mills had thanked the President for his letter of condolence (same file as document). Her late husband, Mark Muir Mills, had been killed in a helicopter accident at Eniwetok Proving Ground in the Pacific on April 7. Mills, a leading U.S. weapons designer and deputy director of the University of California's radiation laboratory at Livermore, was preparing for the upcoming atomic test series (*New York Times*, Apr. 8, 1958). Eisenhower had written that he had "a sincere admiration" for Mills and "for the outstanding work he had accomplished for our nation" (Apr. 7, 1958, WHCF/PPF 21).

Mrs. Mills wrote of her husband's "deep conviction that the United States must continue its weapons testing program." He had thought that most people equated "testing with war" and he felt that this "ostrich philosophy" endangered national security. She added that her husband "wanted peace with all his being," and asked the President to continue atomic testing so that her husband would not have given his life in vain. For background on the effort to suspend atomic testing see no. 628. For developments see no. 822.

[2] On April 25 the President had sent copies of Mrs. Mills's letter to the Joint Chiefs of Staff (WHCF/PPF 21).

[3] The Millses had two children, Ann and Mark John.

To Charles Ernest Chamberlain
May 3, 1958

Dear Mr. Chamberlain: Thank you for your recent letter. I appreciate your thought that I might stimulate consumer buying by endorsing a nation-wide "President's Sale" campaign.[1]

I share your belief that our economy would benefit from an increase in consumer buying. I also believe this buying should be selective, so that manufacturers and processors will be encouraged to offer products the American public wants. However, while I endorse this idea of buying, I am inclined against giving special endorsement to a particular sales venture such as the nation-wide "President's Sale" you have in mind. I think I can render a better service by preaching the general importance of consumer purchasing to our economy. This I will continue to do.

Other factors, of course, have a bearing on our economic well-being. Among these factors are some things the Government can do to help promote sustainable economic growth. My associates and I are watching the developing situation closely, so that we may take such actions as promise to be helpful over the long run as well as in the immediate present.[2]

With warm regard, *Sincerely*

[1] Chamberlain, a Republican Congressman from Michigan since 1957, had written on April 14, 1958 (same file as document). He had expressed concern over "increasing unemployment and current economic conditions" and had commended Eisenhower's view that "more aggressive salesmanship on the part of the nation's business community would do much to increase buying and restore confidence" in the economy. Chamberlain suggested that a nation-wide "President's Sale," "urging all merchants throughout the country to participate in stimulating business activities and offering their merchandise at lowest possible prices," might serve to bring about "an upturn in business and employment." For background on the economy see nos. 598 and 633.
[2] Eisenhower had asked Presidential Aide Wilton "Jerry" Persons to confer with Council of Economic Advisors Chairman Saulnier on this matter (Memorandum, Apr. 29, 1958, same file as document). He reminded Persons that an upcoming meeting in New York on May 20 would preach "optimism to businessmen and to the public with a view of increasing sales" (see no. 691; on the economy see nos. 675 and 753). Edward Aeneas McCabe, the President's Associate Special Counsel, may have drafted this letter.

To John Jay McCloy
May 5, 1958

Dear Jack: I am sure it is no news to you that I am engaged in an all-out effort to secure legislation under which the Defense Department may be organized to meet modern security requirements with maximum efficiency and minimum cost. In a number of instances I have detailed publicly my reasons for urging this action; I hope you believe these sound.[1]

Because of your business experience, it seems to me that you may be particularly impressed by an analogy suggested to me lately by a good friend who heads one of our great corporations.[2] He suggested that present operations within the Department of Defense are similar to a corporate operation that would permit each important subordinate to report separately and independently to the Board of Directors, bypassing the Chief Executive entirely. This, of course, would be completely unworkable; it could hardly be tolerated long, because tough competition with better organized units would soon produce a profit and loss statement that could spell disaster.

As of today, the Defense Department must operate under a system, or lack of system, similar to one that, as I say, would not be tolerated by a successful business corporation. All of us know that the competition faced by the Defense Department is the sternest in the world, that provided by the military might of the Soviet Union. The single objective of the Defense Department is the nation's security; in this it *must* be successful.

Of course, in a successful company the Board of Directors operates through its Chief Executive Officer. He is trusted to make, within the limits prescribed by the Board, decisions regarding details of general programs and operations as necessary.

I believe that, in a similar manner, the Secretary of Defense must, under broad policies prescribed by the Congress, make sure that the Defense establishment operates under single direction, is responsive to changing needs, and is in addition economically administered. Moreover, he must have the flexibility, within guide lines adopted by the Congress, to make detailed changes in programs, organization and doctrine as required by the rapidly changing technology of defense. In fact it is this technology, the advance of which is accelerated more and more each year, that is one of the most compelling reasons for according to the Secretary of Defense the necessary authority to keep the entire Defense establishment completely fit and ready for performance of whatever task may fall to it, night or day.[3]

If this little comparison with corporate practices appeals to you as helpful in appreciating the crying need for Defense modernization, I hope that you, and others, will find it useful in awakening the public to the grave seriousness of this matter. I am sending this letter, or one nearly identical, to a number of my good friends in the business world.[4]

With warm regard, *As ever*

[1] For background see nos. 630 and 631. In addition to his Special Message to Congress on Reorganization of the Defense Department on April 3, Eisenhower had also spoken on April 17 to the American Society of Newspaper Editors about the need for defense reorganization (see no. 637; see also *Public Papers of the Presidents: Eisenhower, 1958*, pp. 274–90, 325–34). Ann C. Whitman, the President's secretary, may have drafted this letter. See Donovan, *Confidential Secretary*, pp. 61–62.
[2] See no. 655. McCloy had been chairman of the board of the Chase Manhattan Bank since 1953.
[3] On April 16, 1958, Eisenhower had sent to Congress a defense reorganization bill that had been modified to accommodate criticisms of the Administration's plan to appropriate defense funds directly to the Secretary of Defense and grant him flexibility in allocating funds to the services. The House of Representatives had begun deliberations on the bill on April 22 (see *Congressional Quarterly Almanac*, vol. XIV, *1958*, pp. 135–36, and *New York Times*, Apr. 17, 1958). For developments see no. 687.
[4] Eisenhower would send copies of this letter to approximately 200 business leaders (see Eisenhower to Cordiner, May 2, 1958, same file as document).

679   *EM, WHCF, Official File 72*

To William Fife Knowland   *May 5, 1958*

Dear Bill: Your bill to establish a "National Freedom Board" and the comments of the various agencies have had my close attention.[1]

I agree, of course, that private citizens can make important contributions in the national security area. They have done so a number of times in this administration. However, dependable advice and planning in this area requires complete familiarity with operational problems, and only agency heads have this familiarity in the required degree. The National Security Council provides the President with a mechanism for regularly receiving the comprehensive advice and information from these agency heads. Similarly, the Operations Coordinating Board, which is now incorporated within the Council structure, assists the President in coordinating plans and actions and in developing new proposals for carrying out national security policies. As a matter of fact, this OCB operation, which I started only last year, strikes me as performing very nearly the exact function you apparently have had in mind.[2]

Our present integrated mechanisms are extremely useful and, I believe, are effective. I doubt that a significant continuing contribution would be made by non-governmental people who would have no continuing operational responsibilities.

One other point especially gives me concern. The President, responsible as he must be for the conduct of foreign relations, needs a considerable latitude in directing the administrative machinery which advises him on national security. Legislative specifics in this area seem to me to be very unwise for any President and for our country.

Knowing of your deep interest, I wanted you to have this brief outline of why in my judgment enactment of your proposed bill would be inadvisable.

With warm regard, *Sincerely*

[1] Knowland had written earlier to Eisenhower concerning a bill he had introduced authorizing a National Freedom Board (see no. 538 for background). The board, Knowland said, would review all the government's psychological warfare activities and then submit a program for effective coordinated action to the President and the National Security Council. Knowland strongly believed that only the creation of a separate organization could produce a unified government policy (Knowland to Eisenhower, Jan. 14, 1958). In a staff-drafted reply, Eisenhower had told Knowland that the interested agencies would reexamine the need for such a board and that he would carefully reconsider their reports (Eisenhower to Knowland, Jan. 17, 1958, *ibid.*). Both State and Defense department officials had reported that the proposed organization would unnecessarily duplicate the functions of existing governmental agencies, including the National Security Council and the Operations Coordinating Board. Presidential Assistant Bryce Harlow had asked Robert Cutler to draft this reply to Knowland. "We need a powerful one;" he said, "Knowland is likely to ricochet" (Macomber to Brundage, Feb. 5, 1958; Dechert to Brundage, Feb. 12, 1958; Stans to Harlow, Feb. 27, 1958; Persons to Knowland, Mar. 24, 1958; Harlow to Cutler, Apr. 4, 1958; Cutler to Harlow, Apr. 18, 1958; and Harr to Harlow, Apr. 28, 1958). All papers are in the same file as this document.
[2] Knowland's bill would not be enacted. On the responsibilities of the Operations Coordinating Board see Galambos and van Ee, *The Middle Way*, no. 1095.

680   *EM, AWF, Administration Series*

TO JOHN HAY WHITNEY   *May 5, 1958*
Personal

Dear Jock: I know that you are highly pleased with the Derby result. While I realize that you do not personally own Tim Tam, it must be a deep satisfaction to know that your great stake horse sired the recent winner. (I suppose it will not seriously damage his fees!).[1]

After your recent visit to me you took off for New York City where you expected to make a decision, one way or the other, about the newspaper deal that had occupied your attention for some time. I do not know what your decision was; certainly from this end I would not even attempt to inquire. But from the continued presence in the paper of a column written by one for whom I have no respect, no admiration and no liking—a feeling that I am sure you at least partially share—I conclude that your decision was negative.[2]

Weekend before last I went down to Augusta with Bill Robinson,

Barry Leithead, Cliff Roberts and one or two others.[3] I am having a very peculiar experience this spring with my golf. I always have more trouble than the average in trying to round into what I like to consider my "golf form." Even so, I am having trouble this year that I can't explain at all. I have played seven rounds and in each case I had one nine that was very good and the other was one to make me weep. Most often my good nine is the first, but at least once I reversed that order.

Washington becomes more political day by day. This is a statement that of course can be made every day of each year. But I think it is also true to say that nowadays the increase is annual as well as daily.[4]

If you and Betsey decide to go to the Prestwick area for a couple of weeks of golf, I do hope you will stay at Culzean. I have never been there in mid-summer, but many others have told me that the place is at its best at that period.[5]

Give my love to Betsey and, as always, the best to yourself. *As ever*

P.S. Assuming that you are here during the Prime Minister's visit in early June, please make a special effort to come in for a personal visit. If this is impossible during office hours, maybe we can arrange one of these six o'clock dates. I think it would be best to call Mrs. Whitman as soon as you get here. She will know details of my schedule.[6]

[1] Whitney owned Greentree Stables (see no. 130). Tim Tam, the winner of the Kentucky Derby (May 3), had been sired by Whitney's stallion Tom Fool (*New York Times*, May 4, 1958).

[2] Eisenhower was referring to Whitney's interest in acquiring the *New York Herald Tribune* (for developments see no. 748). In all likelihood the columnist that the President disliked was either Walter Lippmann or Joseph Wright Alsop, Jr. (see nos. 807 and 1713).

[3] Barry T. Leithead was president and director of Cluett, Peabody, Inc., a New York clothing manufacturer (for background see *Eisenhower Papers*, vols. X–XVII). On Eisenhower's trip to Augusta see no. 659.

[4] Earlier this day Eisenhower had been photographed with the cochairman of the National Citizens for Eisenhower-Nixon 1958 Committee (Ann Whitman memorandum, May 5, 1958, AWF/AWD; for background on the committee see no. 51). For the President's role in support of Republican efforts in the 1958 elections see, for example, nos. 708 and 842.

[5] On Eisenhower's apartment in Culzean Castle in Ayrshire, Scotland, see no. 55. The President had invited the Whitneys to stay at Culzean in May 1957 (see nos. 158 and 159). For developments see no. 1305.

[6] British Prime Minister Harold Macmillan would visit Washington, D.C., June 10–11 (see nos. 635 and 652). Whitney, who would be in Washington June 5–11, would visit with Eisenhower and attend a state dinner in Macmillan's honor (see also Telephone conversation, Dulles and Eisenhower, May 26, 1958, AWF/D).

To Samuel James Campbell   *May 5, 1958*

Dear Sam: It was a pleasant surprise to find you among those present at the Stratford ceremony yesterday. Additionally, of course, I felt it a great honor to meet Mrs. Campbell.[1]

You and I talked Aberdeen Angus a bit, but I didn't get a chance to ask you anything about the quality and purpose of the Stratford herd. Does it have good families and a satisfactory herd bull? Is it operated primarily to sell to other breeders or principally for the production of beef? If the latter is true, does the Foundation raise any grain to fatten out the steers or what is their condition upon disposal?[2]

These questions have no particular point other than the satisfaction of curiosity. I had only the briefest glimpse of the cattle; in fact as our car was coming along the road they left the area and headed for the woods, some of them at a trot. I guess they were tired of waiting for all the VIPs and could no longer stand the heat.

The circumstances of our leaving—right after the ceremony—were such that I did not have the opportunity to say goodbye to you both. So I send greetings to your charming bride and, of course, all the best to yourself. *Sincerely*

[1] Campbell, chairman of Kable News Company in Mount Morris, Illinois, raised Aberdeen Angus cattle at Argyle Terrace in Mount Carroll, Illinois. The Eisenhowers had motored to Stratford Hall in Stratford, Virginia, the birthplace of Confederate General Robert E. Lee. As guest of honor and principal speaker at the annual meeting of the Robert E. Lee Memorial Foundation, Eisenhower appealed for public support for his Administration's foreign aid and reciprocal trade programs (see *New York Times*, May 5, 1958). Campbell's wife was the former Ileen Bullis.
[2] Campbell would reply on May 13 that the Stratford herd was still in the developmental stage. The cows had been registered, he said, but the herd lacked the services of a satisfactory herd sire. For the most part, the operators sold the cattle to breeders. Although Campbell said he did not know the pedigrees, he offered to get them for the President. Eisenhower would thank Campbell on May 17. Both letters are in WHCF/PPF 1-JJ-1; see also Campbell to Eisenhower, January 25, 1957, and Eisenhower to Campbell, January 29, 1957, both in AWF/Gettysburg.

To Barry T. Leithead   *May 6, 1958*

Dear Barry: I have delayed giving you my personal opinion about the excellence of the steaks you sent to me from Chicago, primarily because I wanted at the same time to answer a question you posed,

"How do you cook good meat, especially this particular type of steak, to avoid ruining it?"[1]

In my opinion the first requirement is a meat thermometer and the second is the avoidance of "excessive" heat. The adjective "excessive" is a variable one. For some cuts and under particular conditions a very considerable heat is quite satisfactory, but by and large most people use too much.

As a general rule the thicker the steak, the greater the distance it should be from the broiler. In the present instance I had them bring the rack in the oven down to the point where the top surface of the steak was at least 7 inches below the broiler (I personally think it could have been 8 inches without hurting it). The broiler was turned on full, and the temperature of the oven itself should not show anything over 300 degrees.

The thermometer should be inserted into the steak from the heavy end, with the point of the thermometer reaching as near to the middle of the steak as you can gauge. The exact temperature of the interior of the steak at the time of its removal from the oven is a matter for the individual taste. One hundred and forty degrees is normally stated as rare. I personally take off steaks or roasts as the pointer is passing the 130 mark.

As usual, when you take a steak off salt and pepper it—but I do not think with steaks of this excellence you need to put any butter over them.

Under separate cover I am sending you a meat thermometer. While it is not exactly the same type as I have normally used, the instructions on the box and in the little booklet give you a perfectly good method of testing its accuracy.[2]

I trust this all works for you, because I assure you that Mamie and I had the best steaks the other evening that I can remember.

With warm regard, *As ever*

---

[1] On April 28 Eisenhower and Leithead had played golf at the Augusta National Golf Club (see no. 680).
[2] Leithead would thank Eisenhower for the "dope" about the steaks and the thermometer on May 12 (WHCF/OF 3-VV).

683   *EM, AWF, Dulles-Herter Series*

To John Foster Dulles   *May 7, 1958*
Secret

Dear Foster: I was tremendously interested in your conversation with Selwyn Lloyd on the subjects of Liba and Lebanon.[1] Press reports this morning indicate that Lebanon has made some extraordinary demands upon us, accompanied by warnings that can be scarcely regarded as anything else than threats. Of course the press reports may be unreliable. At the very least it would appear that Lebanon expectations are much greater than we had anticipated. I believe the figure of 170 million dollars over a 7 year period was mentioned.[2]

Thank you very much for your report. I hope you are keeping well.[3] *As ever*

---

[1] For background on U.S. relations with Libya see Galambos and van Ee, *The Middle Way*, no. 1784; on Lebanon see nos. 124 and 230 in these volumes. Secretary Dulles had cabled Eisenhower from Copenhagen, where he was attending the Ministerial Meeting of the North Atlantic Council (see State, *Foreign Relations, 1958–1960*, vol. VII, pt. 1, *Western European Integration and Security; Canada* [1993], pp. 320–49). In April 1957 British Foreign Secretary Lloyd had informed the pro-Western Libyan government that because of financial pressures Great Britain would curtail future economic aid and reduce its military forces in Libya. At that time U.S. and British officials had begun talks regarding the possibility of increased American aid to off-set the British reductions. Concerned about an unstable Libyan government and its vulnerability to Egyptian political pressures, Lloyd and Dulles had agreed that a joint approach could best serve Libyan needs. In his May 5 cable Dulles had told Eisenhower that the British were "doing a little bit more than expected in Libya" and that Lloyd wanted the United States to do the same (Dulles to Eisenhower, DULTE 7, AWF/D-H; State, *Foreign Relations, 1955–1957*, vol. XVIII, *Africa*, pp. 479–510; and State, *Foreign Relations, 1958–1960*, vol. XIII, *Arab-Israeli Dispute; United Arab Republic; North Africa*, pp. 720–24).

The six-year term of Lebanese President Camille Chamoun, a pro-Western Christian supported by the United States, was to end in September 1958. Only a constitutional amendment would permit Chamoun to succeed himself—a move that Moslems in Lebanon, as well as those in Egypt and Syria, strongly opposed. Although the Lebanese president had not decided to pursue reelection, he had asked the United States for support. At the same time Lebanon had requested additional economic and technical aid for highway construction, agricultural development, and irrigation and electrification projects (State, *Foreign Relations, 1958–1960*, vol. XI, *Lebanon and Jordan* [1992], pp. 10–33; see also Eisenhower, *Waging Peace*, pp. 265–66; Douglas Little, "His Finest Hour?: Eisenhower, Lebanon, and the 1958 Middle East Crisis," *Diplomatic History* 20, no. 1 [1996], pp. 31–38; and Irene L. Gendzier, *Notes from the Minefield: United States Intervention in Lebanon and the Middle East, 1945–1958* [New York, 1997], pp. 230–42).

On May 2 Eisenhower told Dulles that the United States should try to assist the Lebanese—"it was much cheaper to try to hold the situation than to try to retrieve it." He would do anything necessary, he said, "to insure prompt action" (Memorandum of Conversation, May 2, 1958, Dulles Papers, White House Memoranda Series). Three days later Dulles had told Eisenhower that the British were "particularly anxious" about Lebanon and hoped that the United States could do something (Dulles to Eisenhower, DULTE 7, May 5, 1958, AWF/D-H).

[2] Newspapers in Beirut had reported that the Lebanese government was expected to ask the United States for a total of $160 million over a six-year period and would renounce any U.S. aid offer that was conditional and insufficient (State, *Foreign Relations, 1958–1960*, vol. XI, *Lebanon and Jordan*, p. 34; see also Telephone conversation, Dulles and Allen Dulles, Apr. 28, 1958, Dulles Papers, Telephone Conversations; and *New York Times*, May 6, 7, 1958).

[3] On the following day CIA Director Allen Dulles would tell the National Security Council that the question of presidential succession in Lebanon was very serious. He also told the council that the aid Lebanon had requested was much more than it needed and was really "a kind of economic blackmail" (NSC meeting minutes, May 9, 1958, AWF/NSC). For developments see no. 753.

684   *EM, AWF, Dulles-Herter Series*

TO JOHN FOSTER DULLES   *May 7, 1958*
Secret

Dear Foster: I have just seen your report on the second day of the Conference.[1] The Iceland crisis brings again to mind that old expression "the tyranny of weakness." I am asking Herter to get a little group together to begin study of this latest problem involving the Island, and he will try to have as much preparatory work done as possible before you come back. I agree with you that we had possibly better try to keep some strength in the Island if its political weakness is as marked as the Foreign Minister seems to think.[2]

With warm regard, *As ever*

[1] Secretary Dulles was attending the ministerial meeting of the North Atlantic Council in Copenhagen. He had told Eisenhower that "quite a crisis" was developing because Iceland was expected to announce an extension of its territorial sea to twelve miles. The British, Dulles said, were particularly concerned. Foreign Secretary Selwyn Lloyd had told Dulles that "in the old days they would break relations and send a battleship." Now, Dulles added, "they dare not break relations and have no battleship." Iceland's foreign minister had told the conference participants that unless his country extended the limit, "the communists" would "take over" and would "buy all the fish." The episode prompted Dulles to wonder if the United States ought to continue planning to remove all American ground forces (Dulles to Eisenhower, May 6, 1958, AWF/D-II, for background on the territorial sea controversy see no. 589; see also Hannes Jónsson, *Friends in Conflict: The Anglo-Icelandic Cod Wars and the Law of the Sea* [London, 1982], pp. 69–83).

[2] Discussions regarding the situation had continued with "obvious tension," Dulles would tell Eisenhower, and he hoped that as a result Iceland would move more cautiously (Dulles to Eisenhower, May 9, 1958, AWF/D-H). On June 30, however, the Icelandic government would extend Iceland's fisheries limit from four to twelve miles, effective September 1. Several countries protested, but only Great Britain refused to honor the new limit. The British would send warships into the area to protect British trawlers (Jónsson, *Friends in Conflict*, pp. 83–108). For future discussions regarding U.S. troops in Iceland see State, *Foreign Relations, 1958–1960*, vol. VII, pt. 1, *Western European Integration and Security; Canada*, pp. 488–94. For more on territorial rights of the sea see no. 1307.

TO ARTHUR FRANK BURNS   *May 7, 1958*
Personal

Dear Arthur: Thank you very much for your letter. I am intrigued by some of your observations, but there is one question I have to ask. You mention the possibility of a tax reduction. The only amplification of this idea in your letter of March 31st is the statement that any tax reduction should be broadly based for both individuals and business firms.[1]

If you had to detail a tax reduction program that would strike you as being designed for the long pull rather than temporary stimulation, what would be your formula? I agree we should have reform—indeed, we have urged this for some years. But some reforms would be far from popular even though they would probably be most helpful to the economy over the long term.[2]

Certainly I agree as to the weakness of piecemeal action.
Your notes are always interesting. Thanks for writing them.[3]
With warm regard, *As ever*

---

[1] Burns had written on May 5 (AWF/A) to advise Eisenhower against further increases in government spending. While he was opposed to deficits, Burns said, they might find them to be a temporary necessity; if so, "let us get them from now on by the route of tax reduction." Should Eisenhower decide on a tax reduction, it would be best if he presented the proposals along with other ideas for promoting the nation's economic strength: "a package of proposals, announced at one time, is likely to have a much stronger psychological impact than the same proposals announced one by one." (On Burns's March 31 letter see no. 633.)

[2] Burns had suggested that proposals for economic reform be "*designed* and *presented* as a rounded program for promoting the nation's long-range economic growth, rather than merely as a miscellaneous set of anti-recession measures." The negative psychological effects of adopting anti-recession measures could be avoided "by putting the accent where it belongs—on building a stronger economy, not only for this year, but even more for the years ahead. Once people feel that they can look forward to a better future for themselves and their kids, they will not lose time in expanding their economic activities."

[3] For developments see no. 698.

TO HAROLD MACMILLAN   *May 8, 1958*
Cable. Top secret

Dear Harold: I have your note of May sixth. I recognize your problem and I am quite certain that we can meet your requirements.[1]

All the Departments concerned are instantly going into procedures and techniques that would be necessary so that we can make
certain that the effort is put on a practical basis.

We should have specific suggestions very soon.[2] *As ever*

[1] In his letter, portions of which Eisenhower had underlined, Macmillan had recounted the mounting "agitation" in Great Britain regarding flights over the country by American aircraft carrying nuclear weapons. He had reminded the President
that in allowing flights over U.S. territory for its Christmas Island nuclear test trials,
the United States had required Great Britain to disclose information regarding the
safety precautions taken, the flight paths of the aircraft, and the nature of the cargo.
"This is just the kind of information and assurance about your flights over this country which I now lack," Macmillan had written (Macmillan to Eisenhower, May 6, 1958,
AWF/I: Macmillan).

[2] Eisenhower had met with Acting Secretary of State Herter, Defense Secretary McElroy, and JCS Chairman Twining before the National Security Council meeting on
this day. After the meeting General Goodpaster had told Ann Whitman that British
officials already had all the information Macmillan had requested "but they do not
tell the Prime Minister!" (Ann Whitman memorandum, May 8, 1958, AWF/AWD).
For developments see nos. 739 and 710.

687   *EM, WHCF, Official File 3-VV*

To John Jay McCloy   *May 10, 1958*

Dear Jack: Thank you for your thoughtful letter of the seventh. Like
you I have been struck by the number of witnesses that testify that
they are "apprehensive." They are fearful, they say, that some particular part of one of the services may be combined with a similar organ-
ism in another—to the betterment of both—and that in this process
some traditional prerogative or perquisite will have been lost. The
people who talk this way seem to think that each of the services is of
itself held exclusively responsible for the defense of the United States.[1]

Of even more interest to me was your observation that "the inter-
service game extends right down through the corporations, depending upon which branch their contracts flow from and it even
goes into the academic institutions depending from where their research grants flow." It is from these vested interests that a great deal
of the objection to unification springs. I hope that you will emphasize this point in the several talks that you are scheduled to make.[2]

With warm regard and once again my thanks for your letter.[3] *As ever*

[1] McCloy's reply to Eisenhower's letter of May 5 is in the same file as the document;
see no. 678. Writing in support of the defense reorganization legislation, McCloy had

said that he would have gone even further "in the way of unifying the services." After reading much of the congressional testimony and talking to "a good many of the old hands in the Navy, Air Force and Army," he had concluded that none of the services wanted to lose any weapons or functions: "They all want unification provided the unification centers on their service."

[2] McCloy had said that he was scheduled to deliver the commencement address at the War College and intended to talk about interservice rivalries. "I do believe they have the beginning of wisdom there, whatever service they may come from." He added that he also planned to speak at the MIT commencement and was "thinking of perhaps saying something up there."

[3] McCloy would respond on May 14, 1958 (same file as document). He would include with his letter a copy of a letter on defense reorganization he had sent to the Chairman of the House Armed Services Committee, and he would note that he intended "shortly to write to the other members of the Committee as well very much along the same lines." For developments see no. 690.

688   *WHCF, President's Personal File 1-L*

To Robert Tyre Jones, Jr.   *May 10, 1958*

Dear Bob: Thank you very much for interesting yourself in the explosion of the head of my number five wood. It is correct that I was using the older clubs because they felt somewhat heavier than this year's set. Even though I had personally wanted to try the lighter style, I found that I was swinging better with the older ones. That was the reason for the accident.[1]

This afternoon I asked Mrs. Whitman to call Mr. Parker on the phone, stating that I agree completely with the thoughts you have on the matter. She also asked Mr. Parker, at my request, whether the shafts I am using are slightly on the soft side. My trouble is that I am not expert enough on the matter—I am not even aware of the gradation in stiffness of the shafts. I just believe I might do a little better with the next stiffer grade of shaft.[2]

Please don't bother personally about this matter any further. I simply repeated these ideas to Mr. Parker and he can use his own judgment.[3]

I had tentatively planned to get down to Augusta this weekend, but circumstances prevented.[4] I am still looking for a chance to ask you to be my partner in a challenge bridge match against a couple of good, high-bidding, reckless players like Schooey and Frank.[5]

Again my thanks, and, as always, warm personal regard. *As ever*

[1] During a recent round of golf, the head of Eisenhower's number four wood had broken off after the President had hit the ball solidly. Jones, who had heard about the mishap, had written on May 8, through mutual friend Cliff Roberts. In January

Jones had given the President a new lighter set of clubs that had been constructed using a method which would, Jones hoped, eliminate the problem (see no. 559).

[2] Edwin Lynch Parker was president and director, A. G. Spalding & Bros., Inc. Jones said he had asked Parker for a new set of woods of the new construction, but slightly heavier than the set the President received in January.

[3] In his June 11 thank-you letter to Jones the President would say that he "liked the feel" of the new woods "immensely." Eisenhower would also express his "heartfelt" appreciation to Parker and the people at Spalding (June 11). Parker's June 18 acknowledgment and all the correspondence are in the same file as the document.

[4] See Telephone conversation, Eisenhower and Whitman, May 9, 1958, AWF/AWD. The President would next visit Augusta November 20–December 2.

[5] Clarence John Schoo and Frank Alexander Willard were old friends of Eisenhower. Schoo was founder and president of General Fibre Box Company. Willard had been a general partner in the New York investment firm of Reynolds and Company since 1934. For background on both men see *Eisenhower Papers*, vols. X–XVII.

689   *EM, AWF, Administration Series*

To William Pierce Rogers   *May 12, 1958*
Personal

Dear Bill: I have a considerable curiosity concerning several phases of the arguments that now center around the functioning of the Supreme Court. In order to obtain specific information on some of the points bothering me, I wonder whether it would be possible for someone in your office to prepare me a succinct study—in layman's language—to guide my own thinking in certain of these matters.

There are several things that I think would be helpful to me:

(*a*). A very short summation of certain recent decisions of the Court that have attracted considerable editorial comment and, from some quarters, some resentment. For example, the case denying the States the right to prosecute Communists;[1] (2) the Mallory case;[2] (3) the purchasing of America back from the Indians;[3] (4) the decision denying the States the right to set up standards by which lawyers are admitted to the Bar;[4] and (5) other cases which do not come immediately to mind—but I am sure that you well know which the more important ones are.[5]

(*b*). The arguments centering around the so-called "legislation" by the Court. Who determines whether the Court is legislating or whether it is merely making a decision and issuing necessary orders therewith.[6] For example, I was somewhat confused by the David Lawrence column in the Herald Tribune this morning, May twelfth.[7]

(*c*). What are the main purposes of the two pieces of legislation that have been introduced in the Congress and, in one case, reported favorably out of a Senate Committee?[8]

(d). While I understand that you have reported adversely against these particular bills, is there any necessity for any kind of additional legislation respecting the functioning of our Courts, especially the Supreme Court?[9]

(e). I believe that the Constitution accords to the Congress the right to pass certain laws affecting the Courts. Does this right extend to the passing of laws affecting the functioning of the Courts and the kinds of cases they may properly decide?

*   *   *   *   *

I realize that the foregoing covers a lot of ground, but I repeat that what I need is a series of statements, rather than legal arguments. Seemingly I get more confused every time the Court delivers another opinion. *As ever*

[1] Rogers would respond on May 27, 1958 (AWF/A). In *Commonwealth of Pennsylvania* v. *Steve Nelson* (350 US 497), the Supreme Court had upheld the Pennsylvania high court decision overturning a conviction for violating the state's Sedition Act. The Court had held that the federal Smith Act (prohibiting the knowing advocacy of the overthrow of the government of the United States by force and violence) superseded the Pennsylvania Sedition Act under which the defendant had been convicted. Rogers would reply that the Court's ruling merely held that "Congress did not make clear that it intended the states to prosecute Communists. Congress may now amend the federal law to permit the states the right to prosecute Communists. There is now and has been for some time a bill before Congress to do that. The Department of Justice favors this bill and the administration is on record favoring it." See also *New York Times*, August 6, 8, 1958.

[2] The case of *Mallory* v. *United States* (354 US 449) had caused some confusion among district judges and police officers, Rogers would write. The Supreme Court had ruled a confession inadmissable because an accused person in the District of Columbia had not been "taken before a magistrate as the rule required 'without unnecessary delay.'" Rogers believed that similar pending cases would clarify the ambiguous language in the opinion. There were also several bills regarding the topic then before Congress, Rogers wrote: "The FBI has had no difficulty with the case and therefore we have taken no position on the legislation up to the present time." See also *New York Times*, August 5, 1958.

[3] Eisenhower was referring to the 1946 Indian Claims Commission Act and a subsequent federal court interpretation, which had given Indian tribal groups for the first time widespread authorization to sue for wrongs committed against them by the government. Tribal groups were authorized to present not only claims arising under the constitution, laws and treaties, but also claims based upon "fair and honorable dealings" not recognized by any existing laws (see Wilcomb E. Washburn, comp., *The American Indian and the United States: A Documentary History*, 4 vols. [New York, 1973], vol. III, pp. 2218–27; see also Wilcomb E. Washburn, *Red Man's Land/White Man's Law: A Study of the Past and Present Status of the American Indian* [New York, 1971], pp. 101–59). Rogers would explain that the law required the United States "to pay Indian tribes for land as to which their only claim of right is based on aboriginal pos-

session (Indian title)." The Justice Department estimated that there were approximately 1,300,000,000 acres of land involved, and that total U.S. liability could amount to a billion dollars. Rogers would explain that the Administration had made several unsuccessful efforts to exclude land claims based on aboriginal tribal title. He would write, however, "Congress has not done this and there is very little likelihood that it will."

[4] The Supreme Court had ruled on two cases regarding admission to the state bar: *Schware v. Board of Bar Examiners of New Mexico* (353 US 232), and *Konigsberg v. State Bar of California et al.* (353 US 252). Rogers would explain that "in both cases the applicants were denied admission to the Bar almost solely on the ground that many years back they had been members of the Communist party. This fact alone, the Supreme Court held, is not an adequate basis for concluding that the applicant is now disloyal and is now a person of bad character."

[5] Rogers would discuss two additional recent Supreme Court decisions. In the case of *Watkins v. United States* (354 US 178), the defendant had challenged the jurisdiction of the House Committee on Un-American Activities to ask certain questions which were "outside the proper scope of the committee's authority and not shown to be relevant to its work." The Supreme Court had held that a congressional contempt conviction could not be sustained under the due process clause of the Constitution "unless the Committee accorded the witness a fair opportunity to determine whether the questions which the Committee sought to have answered were pertinent to its work." See also *Sweezy v. New Hampshire* (354 US 234), in which the Court applied the same rule to an inquiry by the New Hampshire attorney general.

In *Oleta O'Connor Yates et al. v. United States* (354 US 298) and several other related cases, the Supreme Court had overturned a conviction of conspiracy to violate the Smith Act by the violent overthrow of the government. The Court had ruled that the prosecution had not distinguished between advocacy of forcible overthrow of the Government as an incitement to action and as an abstract principle. Expressed as an abstract principle, such advocacy was protected by the constitutional right to freedom of speech.

[6] Charges that the Supreme Court was "legislating," wrote Rogers, usually meant that the Justices were injecting too much personal philosophy into their decisions. While the complaint was sometimes a careless charge made primarily because a critic disagreed with a particular court decision, the criticism more often stemmed from a "grossly over-simplified notion of law." Rogers would explain that "The law in many areas is bound to lack certainty for words [that] do not have fixed and unvarying meanings as applied to the million varied factual situations which arise." Moreover, statutes frequently had "gaps, ambiguities, and inconsistencies, with which the courts must deal." The judge's role in interpreting the Constitution, the statutes, prior court decisions, and congressional intent was not an easy one. Rogers would conclude that, "If the Congress determines that the Supreme Court is legislating—that is making decisions that Congress did not intend when it passed the law—the Congress can correct this by a new law. In other words, Congress may determine if the Court is legislating and Congress is the final authority on all matters except those involving the Constitution."

[7] Lawrence's column, entitled "Troops-Withdrawal Order Revives Little Rock Issue," had appeared in the *New York Herald Tribune* on May 12, 1958. He had argued that many "prominent lawyers throughout the country" believed that "the position taken by the Federal government in ordering the troops sent in was in violation of the Constitution and the laws of Congress." Lawrence believed that no law authorized the President to use troops to enforce court decrees, and that the lawful method of enforcing judicial decrees was for the Administration to deputize private citizens as assistant U.S. marshals. By sending federal troops into Little Rock, the Administration had set a dangerous precedent.

[8] The President's inquiry had to do with congressional efforts since 1954 to restrict the power of the Supreme Court. The so-called Jenner bill (S. 2646) was the broadest of the more recent proposed bills. Originally introduced in July 1957 by Senator William E. Jenner (Rep., Ind.), the bill sought to bar the Supreme Court from accepting appeals in five categories: cases involving the powers of congressional committees and contempt of Congress proceedings; cases involving federal laws governing the hiring and firing of government employees on security grounds; cases involving state laws punishing subversive activities; cases involving school regulations regarding subversive activities by teachers; and cases involving state regulations for admission to the bar (see *Congressional Quarterly Almanac*, vol. XIV, *1958*, pp. 287–97).

Before being reported out of committee, the Jenner bill would be substantially amended; only the section of the original version barring the Supreme Court from reviewing state bar admissions would be retained. Rogers would write the President that he opposed the Jenner bill because it represented "a retaliatory approach of the same general character as the court-packing plan of 1937"; and because it left "the important questions covered by the proposal to be decided by eleven federal courts of appeal and 48 state supreme courts, without any authoritative nation-wide arbiter; and because this type of legislation threatens the independence of the judiciary." The Senate would table the Jenner bill in August and no further action would be taken.

Congress would also introduce a bill to limit the Court's right to strike down state laws under the doctrine of federal legislative preemption. Of all the proposals, the Federal Preemptive Doctrine (H.R. 3) would come the closest to enactment. For developments see no. 731.

[9] Rogers would address Eisenhower's fourth and fifth queries together. Noting that the Constitution had given the Congress the authority to limit the jurisdiction of the Supreme Court, Rogers would state that he was opposed to such plans: "Our legal system requires one final arbiter. Only once—after the Civil War—has Congress limited the jurisdiction of the Court, and this was soon recognized as a mistake and corrected." Nonetheless, Rogers also believed that the Court too often decided cases based on what it thought the law should be, and that the Court's opinions were too long and "often confusing even to an experienced lawyer." Most important of all was "stability in law." "It is a serious mistake," Rogers would write, "for the Court to change its decisions on the same set of facts, especially within short periods of time."

690   *EM, WHCF, Official File 3-VV*

To Dillon Anderson   *May 12, 1958*

Dear Dillon: Thank you for your letter of the eighth. Both it and its attachment were more than interesting. Of course, from past conversations I was sure that in principle you agreed with the proposals for defense modernization. In turn I want to express my agreement most enthusiastically with the paragraph in which you comment on the sources of the opposition to the reorganization plan.[1]

Of all these sources probably none is more vocal than the interested labor and management groups. In a note from Jack McCloy he made this same observation.[2]

Now, turning to the message you sent to Senator Johnson, I find myself again in your corner. If I had to express any critical comment whatsoever, it would be merely that you did not make even more emphatic the beliefs and convictions you express on the last page of your letter.[3]

I note that you expect to be in Washington during the final week of this month. If you have the opportunity to drop in to the White House, please make sure you come to see me.[4]

With warm regard, *Sincerely*

[1] Anderson had been one of the recipients of Eisenhower's letter to enlist support for defense reorganization (see no. 678). In his response (May 8, same file as document), he had described congressional opposition to the defense plan as stemming "from much more than divergent views as to organizational structure or symmetry. The opposition is more deep seated in my opinion; it is part and parcel of an old struggle, amongst our constitutionally coordinate branches, for more congressional power. In this instance the effort is to retain congressional prerogatives which, in my mind, go beyond the providing of policy guide lines and tend to encroach upon executive functions." Anderson had included with his letter a copy of a letter he had written to Lyndon Johnson (Anderson to Johnson, May 8, 1958, same file as document).

[2] See no. 687.

[3] Anderson had written Johnson of his opposition to tax cuts, deficit spending, and the "philosophy that prosperity flows from the Government down to the people." "I still cling," he said, "to the backwoods notion that our strength, economic and otherwise, must flow upward from the people to the Government." Anderson questioned whether "all of the precipitate public works spending, accelerated Rivers and Harbors programs, or any kind of made work that might be fostered by the Government" would lead to prosperity. He believed instead that "the thing that will restore healthy growth to the economy is for all of us on the producing end to work a little harder and observe some of the precepts of Benjamin Franklin about thrift and saving, etc." Anderson disagreed with Johnson's assessment that the problem faced by the Congress was one of "running headlong into Presidential vetoes and administrative slow-downs."

Eisenhower would quote parts of Dillon Anderson's letter to Johnson in a memorandum to Treasury Secretary Robert Anderson on May 12, 1958 (AWF/D).

[4] Eisenhower would meet with Anderson for a half-hour on May 29, 1958.

691   *EM, AWF, DDE Diaries Series*

TO CHARLES HARTING PERCY   *May 12, 1958*

Dear Chuck: Permit me the opportunity to add to your fan mail. Unfortunately, I did not get to see the televised program in which you participated yesterday afternoon, but my reports on your performance are more than glowing. You really struck a blow for world trade and its indispensability to the United States and to freedom.[1]

With warm regard, *As ever*

P.S. This morning Mrs. Whitman and I are working on the draft of the May 20th talk. I get so many ideas that I feel should be expressed that the final job becomes one more for the blue pencil than for the typewriter. I want to be sure that I am finished in not more than thirty minutes.[2]

---

[1] Percy, president of the Bell & Howell Company and vice-chairman of the Republican National Finance Committee, may have been a guest on "The Big Issue," which had featured a debate on the President's Reciprocal Trade Program during its May 11 show.

[2] Eisenhower would deliver the closing remarks at the two-day meeting sponsored by the American Management Association in New York on May 19 and May 20, 1958 (see no. 677; see *Public Papers of the Presidents: Eisenhower, 1958*, pp. 413–21). He would note that the latest reports indicated that the "economic decline of recent months is slowing down," and that the future was "bursting with vitality and promise." The President's speech would be seen as the "strongest plea he had yet made for voluntary action by industry and labor to reduce prices and avoid inflationary wage rises" *(New York Times, May 21, 1958)*. Vice-President Nixon and Secretary of Commerce Weeks would also address the conference.

692   *EM, AWF, International Series:*
                                                                                      Churchill

To Winston Spencer Churchill   *May 12, 1958*

[*Dear Winston:*] I have just learned of the plan to establish at the University of Cambridge a new College to be named in your honor. It seems to me that no other project could so well commemorate for posterity your contributions to your country, to the British Commonwealth, and to the Western world.[1]

The prospectus of Churchill College appeals greatly to me, particularly because, as I understand it, the College will concentrate primarily in the advancement of technological and scientific education.[2] We here in America are working toward the improvement of our own educational processes in these and other fields, and in the world I visualize where interchange of scientific information among friends is a matter of course, such a development as is envisioned in Churchill College is bound to have vast benefits for all mankind.

Quite naturally, I applaud the project; I know that it will find great popular support in the United States as well as in your country.[3]

With warm regard, [*As ever*]

---

[1] On May 7 Special Assistant Robert Cutler had written Eisenhower about a proposal to establish Churchill College at Cambridge University. A group of distinguished En-

glish and American businessmen had undertaken to raise $3.5 million for this purpose (AWF/I: Churchill). The President also had received background on the project from U.S. Ambassador to Great Britain Whitney. The British had responded favorably, Whitney had written, because of the need for increased technological education and because it was a way to memorialize Churchill. Eisenhower would tell Whitney that he had sent a note to the former British Prime Minister expressing "enthusiastic approval" (May 12, 1958, WHCF/PPF 833).

[2] For background on the President's call for advanced scientific and technological education see, for example, nos. 485 and 678.

[3] On May 23 Churchill would write Eisenhower that it was "very encouraging" to receive his "support" of the idea. He acknowledged the need for "technologists of the highest standing" in the United Kingdom and the United States (AWF/I: Churchill).

As it turned out, approximately $3 million would be raised by October 1958 (Cutler to Knollys, Oct. 6, 1958; Knollys to Cutler, Oct. 9, 1958; Cutler to Whitman, Oct. 15, 1958; and Eisenhower to Cutler, Oct. 17, 1958, all in WHCF/PPF 833). Churchill College, one of thirty-one constituent colleges of the University of Cambridge, would receive funds from British industry, major charitable trusts in Great Britain and the United States, and from the Transport and General Workers Union. The college would admit its first students in 1960 and would become a full college of the university in 1966 (Churchill College, "About the College" [World Wide Web, 1997]).

693   *EM, WHCF, President's Personal File 1783*

To Robert Lee Frost   *May 12, 1958*

Dear Mr. Frost: Your letter of April twenty-ninth I shall treasure, as eventually will my young grandson.[1] This acknowledgment of your beautifully expressed thoughts is woefully inadequate, but at least my thanks are deep and sincere. I pray that you will for many years to come continue to enrich America's cultural life.

The book of poetry you have promised to send me will have a place of honor in my personal library at Gettysburg.[2] For your thoughtfulness I am deeply grateful.

With the assurance that it was a privilege to entertain you at the White House, and with warm regard, *Sincerely*

[1] Frost, the Pulitzer Prize-winning poet, had thanked the President for offering a toast to him at a February 27 luncheon in the White House staff dining room. Frost had been the guest of the Assistant to the President Adams and Attorney General Rogers (*New York Times*, Feb. 28, 1958; see also Frost to Adams, Apr. 29, 1958, Minnich to Frost, May 2, 1958, Adams to Frost, May 8, 1958). "To be stood up for and toasted alone in such august company by the ruler of the greatest nation in the world," Frost wrote, left him nearly speechless "on the thrill of the moment." Following the lunch, Eisenhower had taken Frost aside to see some portraits hanging in the White House. Frost said he would "treasure the memory" and, he added, he still could envision the President's "vivid portrait" of David Eisenhower reflecting "the fine young All-there-and-ready-to-take-on-the-world. . . ."

On January 16 Eisenhower had praised Frost in a tribute read at the annual meeting of the Poetry Society of America where Frost received a distinguished service award (*New York Times*, Jan. 17, 1958).

[2] Books, paintings and music, Frost wrote, helped "temper the harshness of politics." He had urged Eisenhower to take the poems to the Gettysburg farm. We have been unable to find any further correspondence regarding the volume in EM (see also Adams to Frost, May 8, 1958). All correspondence is in the same file as the document.

694   *EM, AWF, DDE Diaries Series*

To Samuel Taliaferro Rayburn   *May 13, 1958*

Dear Mr. Speaker: In view of the importance of the Scandinavian countries to American interests and to the NATO Alliance, I was particularly gratified that you were able to attend the luncheon this noon, in spite of a critical day on the House calendar.[1]

Moreover, I considered it as a fortuitous circumstance that you and I both had opportunities to talk to the Prime Minister of Norway.[2] His country, because of its geography, has on the one hand a common boundary with the USSR, and on the other is a particularly important factor in all our calculations concerning the defense of the North East Atlantic. While it was difficult to talk to him intimately, because of the need for an interpreter, yet I know that he was very pleased to have even a brief chat with you.

I do hope that you were not too long delayed in getting back to the House, and I trust that everything is going along there this afternoon as you would wish. Thanks again for coming.[3]

With warm regard, *Sincerely*

[1] On this day Eisenhower had given a stag luncheon to honor the Prime Ministers of Norway, Denmark, and Finland (see the President's Appointment Calendar and Ann Whitman memorandum, May 13, 1958, AWF/D). The "critical day" involved the mutual security legislation; for background see no. 674. The bill was scheduled to face its first major test in the House of Representatives later this same day when members were to vote on an amendment that would eliminate all economic aid.

[2] Einar Gerhardsen, leader of the Norwegian Labour Party, had become prime minister in January 1955.

[3] The House would defeat the amendment that afternoon and would pass the bill on the following day (*Congressional Quarterly Almanac*, vol. XIII, *1958*, p. 185). For developments see no. 762.

To John Foster Dulles   *May 13, 1958*

Dear Foster: Would Doug Dillon have any ideas on the main thought in this letter? As you know, Felix Wormser is not a man who goes off half-cocked.[1]

While I can think of a dozen reasons why this idea should never reach the light of day, yet the ultimate result could be tremendous.

I have sent a mere acknowledgment to Felix, but some day I should like you, or Doug, or one of your other assistants to talk to me about the matter.[2]

With warm regard, *As ever*

[1] Before returning to his position as vice-president of St. Joseph's Lead Company in 1957, mining engineer Felix Edgar Wormser (E.M. Columbia 1916) had been Assistant Secretary for Mineral Resources in the Department of the Interior (see also Galambos, *NATO and the Campaign of 1952*, no. 327). He had written Eisenhower on May 9, after learning that the President planned to visit Canada in July. Canadians were "critical, and perhaps resentful" of U.S. trade policies, he said, and the visit could provide the opportunity to improve relations. He suggested that Eisenhower offer the Canadians "full and complete trade reciprocity" (Wormser to Eisenhower, May 9, 1958, WHCF/OF 149-B).

[2] Eisenhower had told Wormser that he had discussed the idea with some of his Canadian friends in 1951 and had been told that the time was not right. "In any event," he said, "I am going to do a lot of searching around here to see whether it is possible to start something along this line" (Eisenhower to Wormser, May 13, 1958, AWF/D; see also Galambos, *NATO and the Campaign of 1952*, no. 18)

On the following day Dulles would tell Eisenhower that U.S. Ambassador to Canada Livingston Merchant believed that any suggestion of free trade between the two countries "would produce a violent negative reaction" in Canada. The country was in a nationalistic mood, Dulles said, with trade preferences more toward the United Kingdom than the United States. Recent industrial growth in Canada would suffer under a free trade agreement with the United States; the country would become a producer of raw materials for the more efficient American industries (Dulles to Eisenhower, May 14, 1958, AWF/D-H). Eisenhower would write Wormser on May 19, reporting the opinion of State Department officials (WHCF/OF 149-B).

Eisenhower and Dulles would discuss economic problems with Canadian Prime Minister John Diefenbaker and other government officials during their visit to Canada in July (see State, *Foreign Relations, 1958–1960*, vol. VII, pt. 1, *Western European Integration and Security; Canada*, pp. 686–721). For developments see no. 720.

To Jawaharlal Nehru   May 14, 1958
Secret

Dear Prime Minister:[1] You are aware, I am sure, of the concern I have
had during the last few years over the economic problems which
face both India and Pakistan and which continue to resist easy solution.[2] I have long admired the resolute manner in which both
countries have tackled the complex of difficulties facing them and
the United States has given, I think, ample evidence of willingness
to provide financial and technical assistance in various forms. The
people of the United States have expressed their basic sympathy with
your people by supporting these actions. I am confident that this
understanding will continue unabated.

It is, however, a source of real concern to us that the effective economic development of both countries is being hindered by the continued existence of unresolved political and economic issues. The
consequences are that both countries are now devoting increasing
amounts to their defense budgets at the expense of development,
and that mutually profitable economic cooperation is much lessened.

I am convinced that the national interests of both Pakistan and
India make it highly desirable that mutually acceptable solutions of
the major outstanding issues be found. The peaceful, progressive
economic development which each nation desires and which the
foreign assistance program of the United States is designed to promote cannot succeed if these issues remain unresolved. In order to
utilize the available resources of our three countries most effectively
for the common good, I am writing you personally to offer the
friendly assistance of my Government to help in exploring the possibility of settling these major issues which are crucial to good relations between India and Pakistan and to the peaceful, cooperative
development of the area.

I have asked Ambassador Bunker to deliver this letter to you in
person and to arrange for negotiations if you desire. I have asked
Ambassador Langley to do likewise with the President of Pakistan.[3]

If you and Ambassador Bunker agree that it would be helpful, I
should be glad to designate a special representative to visit India for
further general talks with you. You and I could then determine
whether it might be useful for the United States to continue its good
offices in helping bring about more formal and detailed negotiations.
I cannot forget that this was a procedure which proved of considerable value in resolving the serious Trieste question.[4] An important part
of any such procedure must, I think, be its confidential character.

If negotiations are undertaken and successfully concluded, I pledge my Government to help in any way that it can in making the settlement effective and in assuring that it contributes to the economic development of India and Pakistan.

I cannot emphasize too strongly my deep personal concern with this problem and my great desire, and that of the American people, to help bring about its solution. We have a strong historic association with the people of the subcontinent. I hope very much, Mr. Prime Minister, that you will feel that I and my country can be of service in a further endeavor to promote their peace and well-being.[5] *Sincerely*

[1] State Department officials drafted this letter to Indian Prime Minister Nehru; an identical letter was sent to the President of Pakistan, Iskander Mirza. Both letters were originally dated May 2. In telegrams sent to the American embassies in New Delhi and Karachi, however, State Department officials had instructed the U.S. ambassadors to change the dates to May 14 (see Dulles to Eisenhower, May 2, 1958, AWF/I: Pakistan; Memorandum of Conversation, May 2, 1958, Dulles Papers, White House Memoranda Series; and State, *Foreign Relations, 1958–1960*, vol. XV, *South and Southeast Asia*, p. 106).

[2] For background see no. 656.

[3] Ellsworth Bunker had been U.S. Ambassador to India since March 1957; James M. Langley had assumed his position in July 1957.

[4] On the Trieste negotiations see Galambos and van Ee, *The Middle Way*, nos. 441 and 1060.

[5] Nehru would tell Eisenhower that the settlement they both wanted could not happen if "aggressive intransigence" against India continued. Although he appreciated Eisenhower's proposal, only direct contacts between India and Pakistan could resolve the problem, he said. "If third parties intervene, even though that intervention proceeds from goodwill, the position becomes entirely different. The aggressor country and the country against whom aggression had taken place, are put on the same level, both pleading before that third party."

Pakistani leaders would be more receptive, telling Ambassador Langley that the timing of the proposal was "most fortuitous." The long-standing dispute had done "immense harm" to both countries, Mirza would reply, and was "hampering the interests of the free nations in many ways." He hoped that Eisenhower's "great prestige" would help resolve the dispute (Nehru to Eisenhower, June 7, 1958, AWF/I: Nehru; Mirza to Eisenhower, May 26, 1958, AWF/I: Pakistan; see also State, *Foreign Relations, 1958–1960*, vol. XV, *South and Southeast Asia*, pp. 102–16). Although the United States would not play an active role in the Kashmir dispute during the remainder of Eisenhower's Administration, the President was able to visit both India and Pakistan in December 1959, and the United States continued to seek a reduction in tensions between the two countries. For developments see no. 1393.

697   *EM, AWF, Gettysburg Series*

To Arthur Seymour Nevins   *May 14, 1958*

Dear Art: Admiral Strauss has transferred to me a third interest in Brockmere 10, a son of Mr. Eileenmere, the International Grand

Champion in 1954. I am sending you his pedigree, together with an extract from Admiral Strauss' letter telling about something of the record of Mr. Eileenmere and his ancestors.[1]

I know nothing about the dam except that Admiral Strauss said she was a very fine cow.[2] Since Brockmere 10 will not be a year old until June 26, 1958, I think we would want to wait until somewhere along August before using him once or twice. However, we could, of course, breed them by artificial insemination merely by going down to the Admiral's farm to pick up semen.

Soon I will have a picture to send you, and at a convenient time within a couple of months perhaps Bob Hartley—and you, too, if you wanted to—could go down to the Lewis' farm and take a look at him.[3]

If everything goes favorably, then I would hope that you could save out two or three of my younger heifers that look pretty good to breed to him. Since I own a third interest, it could be done artificially. We could, of course, take one or two heifers of the Allen-Byars herd along for natural breeding in the event that he looked so good that we wanted to test him out on more than two or three heifers during this coming fall.[4]

I do not know when I shall be coming to the farm again, but I shall talk the matter over with you further.[5] I am sending a copy of this letter and the enclosures to Bob Hartley. *As ever*

[1] Strauss had written on May 13. For background on his offer to provide a herdsire for the Eisenhower Farms see Galambos and van Ee, *The Middle Way*, no. 1215; no. 96 in these volumes; and Nevins, *Five-Star Farmer*, p. 125.

[2] Hartley, Eisenhower's herdsman, would agree that the dam had a "fine pedigree" (Nevins to Eisenhower, May 18, 1958).

[3] Strauss had offered to take a photograph of the bull. Nevins would say he had admired the bull's sire at a sale at Brandy Rock Farm, Lewis Strauss's farm in Brandy Station, Virginia (*ibid.*). For developments see no. 736.

[4] On the George E. Allen-Billy G. Byars partnership see Galambos and van Ee, *The Middle Way*, no. 1463; see also no. 70 in these volumes.

[5] As it turned out, the President would visit his farm the afternoon of May 18. All correspondence is in AWF/Gettysburg.

698   *EM, AWF, Administration Series*

To Arthur Frank Burns   *May 15, 1958*
Personal

Dear Arthur: I agree with the five suggestions that you make on page one of your letter, for beneficial, long-pull effects on our economy.

Of these the only one on which I have a question is number four. You did not define "long term holdings."[1]

As of now the Internal Revenue Code defines long term as anything over six months. I personally would be content to make the minimum time one year, with the present tax rate. Thereafter I think we should reduce the percentage each year by a given amount so that at the end of five or more years of holding there would be no tax whatsoever on capital gains. I think the graduated reduction would tend to discourage the so-called "long term" investment that was really nothing but speculation, but at the same time would not impose a penalty on transfers of legitimate investment. I have not discussed this particular idea with others—you may see something wrong with it.[2]

As you well know, the suggestions of your second page occupy our attention here all the time.[3] The leaders of the Congress are quite fearful that any attempt to reduce any tax will open the doors to an overwhelming assault by amendments. Various pressure groups are waiting at those doors to initiate their attacks. It is difficult indeed to believe that logic and good hard common sense can, seemingly, not prevail over the wails and screams of political demagogues and selfish interests. As you so well know, however, any legislative effort of the kind we are now discussing has to be handled by legislative leaders—and I mean the good ones—with an eye on the political behavior of the members of Congress rather than on the basic growth and health of the economy.[4] *As ever*

[1] For background see no. 685. Burns's letter of May 12 (AWF/A) had contained five proposals for reform that would promote long-range economic growth: shorten the depreciation periods "in recognition of our dynamic technology and increasingly rapid obsolescence"; reduce the personal income tax rate from its maximum of 91 percent to 75 percent or below "so that young men of daring and ambition can have reasonable incentive for greater effort"; reduce the corporate income tax rate from 52 to 49 percent so that the Treasury Department would stop being "a senior partner in every corporate business"; reduce capital gains taxes on long-term holdings; and carry out the tax proposals recommended by the Cabinet Committee on Small Business (see Galambos and van Ee, *The Middle Way*, no. 1957).

[2] In his June 2, 1958, reply (AWF/A), Burns would say that Eisenhower's proposed reform of the capital gains tax would be "eminently desirable." Since Congress would be unlikely to accept such a broad revision, however, Burns would propose a more limited reform, such as lowering the maximum capital gains tax from twenty-five to twelve and a half percent on investments held over a year. "Any such proposal would of course need to be coupled with a strong plea that present practices with regard to the capital gains tax be tightened up so that loopholes for converting ordinary income into capital gains be closed."

[3] See n. 1 above.

[4] For developments see no. 733.

To Carl Vinson   *May 16, 1958*

Dear Mr. Chairman: I have just been shown your Committee's revision of the defense reorganization legislation which I sent to the Congress two months ago.[1] From a quick reading I have these impressions:

First, on the whole the bill clearly reflects constructive efforts to correct the main difficulties which have troubled our defense establishment in recent years. I congratulate you and your Committee colleagues for the progress made toward developing a sound defense structure.[2]

Second, by and large the bill seems to deal positively with every major problem I presented to the Congress.

Third, in certain respects—two quite important—I believe that changes would make the Committee's revision clearer in intent and more clear-cut in effect within the Defense Department, and therefore would result in greater departmental and operational efficiency. I am requesting a member of my staff to give you my views on such items. I hope this language will be suitably adjusted on the House Floor.[3]

With warm regard, *Sincerely*

[1] For background see nos. 630, 687, and 690.

[2] The House Armed Services Committee had begun hearings on April 22 on proposals to reorganize the Defense Department. The questions directed to the Secretary of Defense, the Chiefs of Staff of the Army, Navy, and Air Force, and the commandant of the Marine Corps, revealed apprehension that the reorganization would create a "Prussian general staff." After the hearings closed on May 12, the Committee drafted its own reorganization bill which, while incorporating most of the provisions requested by the White House, sought to reduce the concentration of power. See *Congressional Quarterly Almanac*, vol. XIV, *1958*, pp. 134–37; see also Watson, *Into the Missile Age*, pp. 264–74.

Ann Whitman noted that the President was "a little leery" of this letter, which presidential assistant Bryce Harlow had promised Vinson (Ann Whitman memorandum, May 16, 1958, AWF/AWD; see also no. 719).

[3] The Committee would reject Eisenhower's request to give the Secretary of Defense the authority to administer the departments under him, and require instead that the departments be "separately organized," with the line of command running from the Defense Secretary through the Secretaries of each military force. This organization was ostensibly designed to prevent the office of the Defense Secretary from becoming "a huge overcentralized and unmanageable administrative conglomeration." Moreover, safeguards would protect against a merging of the military departments and the establishment of a single Chief of Staff or Armed Forces General Staff. The Committee would also reject Eisenhower's second point and give to Congress the right to override any proposal by the Secretary of Defense to abolish or reorganize major combatant functions. It said that the Administration's request to give such power to the Secretary would "constitute a complete surrender of a Constitutional responsibility imposed upon the Congress." See also *New York Times*, May 17, 24, 1958. For developments see no. 716.

To SHERMAN ADAMS   *May 16, 1958*
Memorandum

I have signed the attached letter to the Secretary of Agriculture on
the mineral stabilization plan.[1] Although the letter seems to me satisfactory, I believe it would be stronger if we had pointed out the
following:

(*a*). That minerals are *not* in surplus production in the United
States as agriculture is. You will remember that a subsidy
plan seemed to be better than any other scheme for the
wool growers; we have a somewhat similar set of circumstances in the case of minerals.[2]

(*b*). While it is true that subsidies may have some effect in de-
pressing the world price and therefore hurting our South
American friends, the imposition of a tariff wall against
these minerals would inescapably damage them. I believe
that Mexico, Peru and Chile, for example, would react most
bitterly to such an effort.[3] Indeed, the mere suggestion that
we might allow the automatic tariff of 2¢ per pound [to]
become operative in the case of copper caused President
Ibanez to cancel his good will visit to the United States.[4]

(*c*). There are no completely satisfactory answers to such problems as these, but one measure of the seriousness of the
international problem is the amount of money we are
putting into defense and mutual aid and so on.[5] Any policy of ours that would completely divorce some of the mineral producing countries from the society of friendly nations we are trying so hard to build up could have eventual
consequences of the gravest nature.[6]

[1] Eisenhower had written to Agriculture Secretary Benson in response to Benson's
criticisms of the Domestic Minerals Stabilization Plan (May 17, 1958, AWF/D). The
plan had been designed to assist the mining industry, then facing competition from
foreign imports, by establishing a five-year price support program for lead, zinc, tung-
sten and acid-grade fluorspar. The plan also proposed incentive payments for scarce
strategic minerals and a one-year stock purchase plan for copper. (On problems in
the uranium mining industry see no. 632). Benson had expressed concern that support for mineral subsidies would compromise Administration efforts to deal with
chronic agricultural surpluses. Eisenhower's letter, while agreeing that Benson's fears
were "very real and very troublesome," had supported the stabilization plan as "the
best of the alternative courses of action available."
[2] On agricultural price supports see no. 616. For background see Galambos and van
Ee, *The Middle Way*, nos. 391, 445, 1595, and 1841.
[3] See no. 597.
[4] See no. 563; see also State, *Foreign Relations, 1958–1960*, vol. V, *American Republics*,
p. 800, and *New York Times*, April 17, 1958.

[5] The Minerals Stabilization Plan had been seen by some as an effort by the Administration to win senatorial support for its Reciprocal Trade Program. The plan had been designed to increase domestic mine production and help employment in the Western states. Its passage would give Eisenhower reason to reject the Tariff Commission's April recommendation for higher tariffs on lead and zinc. See *Congressional Quarterly Almanac*, vol. XIV, *1958*, pp. 321–24; see also Eckes, *The United States and the Global Struggle for Minerals*, pp. 222–24. On the Reciprocal Trade Program see nos. 674 and 753; for developments on the Mineral Stabilization Plan see no. 774.
[6] For developments see no. 859.

701 *EM, AWF, DDE Diaries Series*

To Jack E. Manning *May 17, 1958*

Dear Jack: As I told you, when you visited me in company with Dan Thornton and Randolph Scott, I have no objection to your naming of the United States Air Force Academy golf course as the "Eisenhower Golf Course."[1]

While this letter will serve as written evidence of my consent, I do make the suggestion that before making any announcement of this kind you should receive the consent and approval of either the Superintendent of the Air Force Academy or the Secretary of the Air Force, Mr. Douglas, or both.[2] After you have taken care of this formality, my own consent may be considered final.

Incidentally, because of the length of my name I should prefer to see the designation only "Eisenhower Golf Course" rather than using my full name.[3]

With greetings to both Dan Thornton and Randolph Scott, and with warm regard to yourself, *Sincerely*

[1] Manning was chairman of the Air Force Academy Golf Course Foundation. He, together with former Republican Governor of Colorado Daniel I. J. Thornton and movie actor Randolph Scott, had met with Eisenhower on April 24. Scott, widely acclaimed for his roles in Westerns, had appeared in various major motion pictures. He also produced films.
[2] Major General James Elbert Briggs was superintendent of the Air Force Academy. On June 4 Douglas would approve the proposal (Douglas to Manning; letter from R. A. Muenger, Apr. 30, 1993, both in EP; see also Ann Whitman memorandum, May 17, 1958, AWF/AWD).
[3] Although the Eisenhower Golf Course would open for play on Labor Day 1959, it would not be formally dedicated until July 1963 (for background see Galambos and van Ee, *The Middle Way*, no. 1498).

To William Pierce Rogers   *May 20, 1958*

Memorandum for the Attorney General: At the legislative meeting this week I was asked a question by Charlie Halleck, which I promised to relay to you. He pointed out that only two years ago the government was using its influence to get drug companies to produce Salk vaccine as promptly as possible. Now it seems that these same drug companies have been cited under the anti-trust law. Mr. Halleck voiced a question as to this action on the part of the government.[1]

Will you send me a memorandum regarding this—if possible, before the meeting on Tuesday of the leaders?[2]

[1] For background see Galambos and van Ee, *The Middle Way*, no. 1401. The legislative leaders had held their weekly meeting on May 19. On May 13, 1958, the *New York Times* had reported that a federal grand jury had charged five manufacturers of the polio vaccine with violating the Sherman Antitrust Act. Eli Lilly & Company, Allied Laboratories, Inc., American Home Products Corporation, Merck & Company, Inc., and Parke Davis & Company, had each been accused of setting prices at "uniform, artificial and non-competitive levels," and denying all other pharmaceutical concerns the "opportunity to compete in the sales of the vaccine to public authorities" (*New York Times*, May 13, 1958).

[2] Attorney General Rogers would respond on May 26 (AWF/A). He had discussed the case against the drug companies with House Majority Leader Charles Halleck subsequent to the Cabinet meeting. Research and development of the polio vaccine at the University of Pittsburgh had been funded by the National Foundation for Infantile Paralysis, which had "made the process, 'know-how' and even some of the raw materials available to the manufacturers." Moreover, the Foundation had "insured all manufacturers against loss resulting from their polio vaccine operations throughout 1954 and until announcement of the success of the vaccine in April 1955. Thus, the costs and risks involved by the manufacturers were substantially less than those which would normally be encountered in the production of a new product."

Between April 1955 and January 1958 the federal government had issued invitations for bids for the contract to provide for the immunization of school children. "In all cases, identical bids were received from the manufacturers. . . . despite the efforts of procurement officials to obtain competitive prices," Rogers would explain. Following the termination of the federal allocation program, the states and localities solicited bids for local programs. Rogers would report that again, "*thousands of sealed identical bids were received on the hundreds of solicitations issued. And, except in a rare case, these bids were all identical. . . . These deviating bids were later corrected or withdrawn under circumstances indicative of pressure by the manufacturers to maintain uniform prices*" (emphasis in original). Rogers would say that because the case was before the Grand Jury in New Jersey, the law did not permit him to comment further on profits realized by the manufacturers. He did, however, point out that the largest producer (Eli Lilly), "experienced large rises *in their general profits* before taxes concurrent with the commencement of commercial exploitation of the polio vaccine."

In December 1959 the five pharmaceutical concerns would be cleared of charges of price fixing and criminal conspiracy on the grounds that the federal government had failed to substantiate its accusations (*New York Times*, Dec. 1, 1959).

TO HARRY S. TRUMAN

May 20, 1958

Dear President Truman: I am in the midst of making arrangements for the official ceremonies this coming May thirtieth at Arlington National Cemetery to honor the Unknowns of World War II and the Korean Conflict. It occurred to me that because, though in different capacities, we both bore heavy responsibilities during critical periods of those conflicts, it would be only fitting and proper for us, together, to attend these solemn ceremonies. I should feel honored by your participation.

If this suggestion appeals to you—and I greatly hope that it will—I suggest that Mrs. Truman and you join Mrs. Eisenhower and me for a one-thirty luncheon at the White House before the four of us travel together to Arlington for the ceremonies.

If your plans permit your coming, we can consult later on how best to handle any necessary public announcement.[1]

With good wishes, *Sincerely*

---

[1] On May 23 Truman would decline the "highly appreciated" invitation due to plans to travel to Europe (AWF/N; *New York Times*, May 27, July 10, 1958; see also Goodpaster to Whitman, May 23, 1958, AWF/N).

During the ceremony, the President would place Medals of Honor on the coffins of unknown soldiers from World War II and the Korean War. The ceremony was climaxed by a funeral cortege and entombment at Arlington National Cemetery (*New York Times*, May 31, 1958).

TO BARRY T. LEITHEAD

May 20, 1958

Dear Barry: I was of course delighted to learn from you, as President of the National Father's Day Council, of the award to be given to my brother Milton as the "Father of the Year." May I ask you to give my greetings to those gathered in his honor at luncheon this Thursday in New York City?

It is difficult to picture one's youngest brother as the "Father of the Year" even though he has, for many years, been one of my most respected and trusted counsellors and associates. In addition to the esteem in which I hold him, I have long admired—with far more than the typical pride of a fond uncle—the character and ability of his children, my nephew Milton, Jr., and my niece Ruth. In my opinion his devotion to his own children, together with his contribution to all the splendid college students he has helped develop over the years, more than put Milton in the class of outstanding fathers.[1]

Congratulations to him and best wishes to all.[2] *Sincerely*

[1] On May 23 Milton Eisenhower would receive the award at a luncheon in the Waldorf-Astoria Hotel (*New York Times*, May 22, 1958).

[2] During the ceremony the committee would read a portion of this letter to the gathering (*ibid.*).

705   *EM, WHCF, Official File 134-F-3*

TO ALLAN SHIVERS   *May 21, 1958*
Personal

Dear Allan: From the press you have learned that the Attorney General has filed a brief in the Supreme Court in the case pending in that court to determine the exact meaning of the law passed three or four years ago affecting the Tidelands.[1]

In filing his brief, the Attorney General was careful to quote every public statement I have ever made affecting the matter. All of these add up to my personal conviction that whatever rights the United States has or claims in the sub-soil under the ocean out to the limit of three leagues from the coastline of Texas belong, in equity, to Texas. His brief also points out that I have never changed my opinion but that I have not expressed an opinion on what the Submerged Lands Act means because that is a legal question which should be decided by the Supreme Court.[2]

As we all know, before any controversy arose the coastal states had for years treated all the tidelands as their own and much money had been invested on that assumption. When the Supreme Court, in the first submerged land cases, held that the states had no rights beyond low tide many of us felt that legislation was appropriate to grant the states rights to the sub-soil. I recommended to Congress that it pass a law giving these rights to the states.[3]

Speaking for me, and expressing my long time conviction,[4] the then Attorney General, Herbert Brownell, urged Congress to draw a definite line on a map so there would be no question about it. In the case of Texas he recommended three leagues. Mr. Rogers, who was then the Deputy Attorney General, was in accord with that recommendation.

It was pointed out that if such a line was not drawn to make it perfectly clear what Congress intended that the court would have to decide the question. Congress, however, did not draw the line, but rather left the law unclear. Therefore, the legal decision as to what the Congress granted to the states has to be decided by the Supreme Court. That is why the case is in court now.[5]

The individual who is appointed and serves as the Attorney General in the President's Cabinet is also an officer of the Supreme Court. He has a duty to represent the federal government's interest in any suit which may be involved. In the case before the court now, he necessarily has to argue that Texas has no right beyond the three mile limit. Thus the decision as to the meaning of the Submerged Lands Act is left to the Supreme Court and, as the debate in the Congress clearly shows, that is what the Congress intended.[6]

You are already acquainted with the facts as I have outlined them in this letter, but for my own personal satisfaction and so that you may clearly understand that I have never changed my position in this matter, I wanted you to have this in writing.[7]

Please remember me warmly to Marialice[8] and your nice family and, of course, with lasting regard to yourself, *As ever*

[1] For background see nos. 438 and 473. Former Texas Governor Allan Shivers had served as chairman of the board of Western Pipe Line, Inc., since 1957. On May 16, 1958, the *New York Times* had reported that the Justice Department had filed a "massive" brief with the Supreme Court claiming all rights to undersea oil beyond the three-mile mark in the Gulf of Mexico, and rejecting the claims of Texas and four other Gulf Coast states to oil rights within a distance of three marine leagues, or ten and one-half miles, of the Gulf Coast. The 425-page brief made specific note, however, of Eisenhower's 1952 campaign opinion that the "Texas boundary was three leagues from the coast." See also Ann Whitman memorandum, May 17, 1958, AWF/AWD.

[2] Attorney General William Rogers had prepared a revision of a May 17 draft of Eisenhower's letter to Shivers (n.d., same file as document; the May 17 draft is also in *ibid.*). Rogers had added the clause clarifying the fact that the President had not expressed an opinion on the Submerged Lands Act. On the Act of 1953 see *Congressional Quarterly Almanac*, vol. IX, *1953*, pp. 388–96.

[3] Rogers had added this paragraph to the Eisenhower draft. The paragraph replaced one originally dictated by the President:

> As you know, at the time of the passage of the law, both Brownell and his principal associate, Mr. Rogers, agreed with my attitude in the matter. So far as I know, these *personal* opinions have never changed. It should be remarked, of course, that due to my ignorance of the fine points of the law, through those years I often used the expression "owned" the subsoil to three leagues from the Texas shoreline. Manifestly what I meant was that Texas, from my viewpoint, had the same subsoil rights as could be accorded under Federal law and international agreements. This I felt meant three leagues.

[4] Eisenhower had added this phrase to Rogers's draft paragraph.
[5] This paragraph was suggested by the Attorney General.
[6] Rogers added the last sentence in this paragraph.
[7] The Supreme Court would hear arguments in the case in October 1959 and announce its decision on May 31, 1960 (see *New York Times*, Oct. 13, 14, 19, 1959, June 1, 1960. The Court would decide that the Submerged Lands Act granted both Texas

and Florida a three marine-league belt of land under the Gulf of Mexico for domestic purposes. In both cases the decision was based on previously accepted boundary claims. The Court would rule that Louisiana, Mississippi and Alabama were not entitled to rights in submerged lands lying beyond three geographical miles from their coast (see United States *v.* Louisiana *et. al.* [363 US 1], and United States *v.* Florida *et. al.* [363 US 121]; see also Nash, *United States Oil Policy 1890–1964*, pp. 190–94). Shivers would write Eisenhower on May 31, 1960 (same file as document) thanking him for his "endorsement and leadership" of Texas's case and noting "the tremendous debt the people of this State owe to you for your courageous stand on this issue."

[8] Shivers's wife, the former Marialice Shary.

706

EM, WHCF,
Official File 149-B-2 Oil

To William Alvin Moncrief

May 21, 1958

Dear Monty: Your telegram of May twelfth requests me to invoke mandatory controls on crude oil imports as well as petroleum products.[1]

The fact is that the limitations placed on crude oil imports on a voluntary basis have been observed to a gratifying degree by a great majority of importers from the inception of the program. A further tightening up in the voluntary program was accomplished in March when I issued an Executive Order to require that petroleum product purchases by the United States Government be made under "Buy American" procedures.[2] In this order it was required that the source of crude oil from which the products were refined, when partly of foreign origin, be from importers who were in compliance with the voluntary program. This has had the effect of insuring agreement by importers who previously had not been in complete compliance. They are now voluntarily accepting the quotas assigned to them.

The enclosed report of the Cabinet Committee indicates that the matter of petroleum products has constantly been under surveillance by the Committee. The Director of the Office of Defense Mobilization, in reporting to the Committee, stated that in his opinion there is no threat to the national security from the present level of imports of petroleum products.[3]

While the imports of residual oil, which account for the largest part of all product imports, have increased in the last several years, the imports of other products have not increased. Domestic production of residual oil has actually declined. In order to meet our own energy requirements, which are increasing every year, it would be inadvisable at this time to limit the importation of residual fuel oil.

Under the voluntary program the percentage of crude oil imports to domestic production has been maintained at approximately the same level as 1954. There is, therefore, no logical determination that can be made to invoke mandatory controls.

I appreciate your good wishes and assure you that we are making every effort to seek an equitable solution to these vexing problems.[4]

Sincerely

[1] The telegram from Eisenhower's friend Moncrief, an independent oil producer, is in the same file as the document. Moncrief's request that the President "issue a mandatory order limiting oil imports and products" to the 1954 ratio of imports to domestic production may have been prompted by a domestic oil glut caused by the economic recession (see Vietor, *Energy Policy in America Since 1945*, p. 112). U.S. oil producers, said Moncrief, would prefer a presidential order over federal legislation because it was flexible and "could be changed forthwith if found necessary in the national interest." Moncrief's telegram had been sent to Secretary Weeks in the Department of Commerce for preparation of a draft reply (see Morgan to Weeks, May 15, 1958, and other correspondence in same file as document). Eisenhower heavily edited Weeks's draft, which had first been revised by White House aide Gerald Morgan. For background see Galambos and van Ee, *The Middle Way*, nos. 1392 and 1748. See also Chester, *United States Oil Policy and Diplomacy*, pp. 32–34.

[2] For background see nos. 596 and 608.

[3] The March 21, 1958, supplement to the January 1955 report of the Cabinet Committee on Energy Supplies and Resources Policy is in AWF/A, Weeks Corr.; the original report is in AWF/Cabinet. Gordon Gray was director of the Office of Defense Mobilization.

[4] Moncrief would reply on June 5, 1958 (same file as document). He was deeply appreciative of Eisenhower's "determined efforts to do something about excessive petroleum imports" and gratified with recent developments that plugged "a serious loophole in the voluntary program." Nonetheless, he believed that there were still "glaring defects" in the voluntary program. For developments see no. 1098.

707   *EM, AWF, Name Series*

To Aksel Nielsen   *May 21, 1958*

Dear Aks: Despite the rugged hours (which I admit were a bit difficult for a self-styled "Colorado cowboy") I gather you found the Costa Rican experience interesting and enjoyable. Particularly I am glad that the calibre of our Embassy people struck you as strong and sound.[1]

(Incidentally did you wear the entire Ambassadorial regalia, *including* pearl gray gloves?)

I hope I shall see you soon; meantime thanks for anything you can do on behalf of the Defense modernization plan.[2]

With warm regard, *As ever*

[1] Nielsen, who had recently served as the President's representative at the inauguration of the new Costa Rican president, had referred to the trip as a "strenuous five days" (May 17, AWF/N). He also described the "marvelous education" he had received a during a briefing by the staff at the U.S. embassy in San Jose. He had been impressed by the American diplomats he met and by the amount of respect the Central Americans had for them. "As your representative," he added, "I think I behaved myself." For background on Eisenhower's list of long-time friends who served as his personal representative to foreign functions see no. 246. Presidential Secretary Ann Whitman may have drafted this letter.

[2] On June 17 Eisenhower would meet with Nielsen at the White House (see also Nielsen to Whitman, May 17, 1958, AWF/N). Nielsen said he had "read with interest" the President's letter on defense reorganization and vowed to inform as many people as possible of Eisenhower's plan. The President's letter is no. 678.

708

TO CLIFFORD ROBERTS

EM, AWF, Name Series

May 21, 1958

Dear Cliff: I understand you will now send me the informal pledge signed by my friends at the table.[1] I will modify it (and I assure you in a way that will not make the obligations of my friends any lighter) and send it on to Lloyd. My own contribution directly to him is already on the way.[2]

I hope that our political conferences were really helpful. It seemed to me that the enthusiasm of the individuals present was of a high order.[3]

With warm regard, *As ever*

[1] The preceding evening Eisenhower had addressed more than two thousand business leaders attending the Economic Mobilization Conference of the American Management Association at the Hotel Astor in New York City. The President's speech, broadcast by radio and television, focused on slowing inflation and plans for a decision on tax cuts. Following the speech, Eisenhower dined with several prominent Republican businessmen who had pledged to support the National Citizens for Eisenhower-Nixon 1958 by signing the conference program. Roberts had telephoned Eisenhower earlier this same day (see *New York Times*, May 20, 1958; Program, American Management Association, Inc., May 21–22, 1958, AWF/D; and Telephone conversation, Roberts and Eisenhower, May 21, 1958, AWF/D). For background on Eisenhower's other efforts to strengthen the Republican party prior to the 1958 elections see nos. 51 and 680.

[2] Across the top of the program the President would write his own promise: "I hereby pledge $500–to the Citizens for Eisenhower for 1958 as my *initial* contribution." Twelve of his friends, including Roberts, would also sign the pledge. Eisenhower would send the document to Lloyd F. MacMahon, a New York attorney and chairman of the National Citizens for Eisenhower-Nixon 1958 Committee. In a separate letter to MacMahon Eisenhower would send his "modest financial contribution" (May 22, 1958, AWF/N, Roberts Corr.).

[3] In his May 26 reply (AWF/N) Roberts would call Eisenhower's signature on the

fund-raising document a "master stroke." Roberts predicted that it would cause a great "chain reaction."

709   *EM, AWF, Dulles-Herter Series*

TO JOHN FOSTER DULLES   *May 23, 1958*

Foster: Most of this letter is fine. I'm somewhat at a loss, however, to understand how inspection *in* the Arctic Zone alone, could give much protection. I feel the attack would come *through* rather than *from* the Arctic.???[1]

[1] For background on the U.S. proposal for an international inspection system for the Arctic area see no. 665. In a May 9 letter Soviet Chairman Nikita Khrushchev had told Eisenhower that the proposal provided no protection against surprise attack because the United States had not agreed to suspend flights of American bombers in the direction of the Soviet Union (Khrushchev to Eisenhower, May 9, 1958, AWF/ I: Khrushchev). A draft reply, prepared by the State Department, had assured Khrushchev "that if there were dependable and adequate safeguards against surprise attack in the Arctic area, no US alert flights whatsoever would enter this area." A note from Andrew Goodpaster informed the President that Dulles wanted his "general reaction" to the soundness of the approach. Eisenhower's handwritten reply, which appears below Goodpaster's note, is printed above (Goodpaster to Eisenhower, May 23, 1958, AWF/D-H; and Dulles to Eisenhower, May 23, 1958, *ibid.*). The letter to Khrushchev was not sent. For Eisenhower's response to other items in the Soviet leader's May 9 letter see no. 712.

710   *EM, AWF, International Series: Viet Nam*

TO NGO DINH DIEM   *May 23, 1958*
Personal and confidential

Dear Mr. President: I am taking the occasion of Ambassador Durbrow's return to Saigon to send this direct message to you.[1]

Your friendly visit to the United States about a year ago continues to stand out vividly in my mind. The opportunity which we had to discuss the Communist problem confronting the free world, the political and military progress of Viet-Nam since 1954, and the relations between our two countries was invaluable.[2]

Since that time, I have observed with much interest the visits that you have made to Thailand, Australia, Korea, India, and the Philippines. It is clear that by these visits you have increased the prestige and understanding of your Government abroad. The visits have also given you the opportunity to demonstrate to leaders of these countries that a new member of the family of free nations can overcome almost insurmountable obstacles to preserve its sovereignty and independence.

I have also been highly impressed by your Government's declaration of April 26, 1958, on the reunification of Viet-Nam.[3] It lays bare the propaganda nature of the proposals of the Communist regime in Hanoi. The positive suggestions put forth in your Government's declaration place the burden on the Communists to create conditions which will enable the peaceful reunification of your country.

May I extend to you my warmest personal greetings and my best wishes for your continued success in the development of Viet-Nam in the free world.[4] *Sincerely*

[1] For background on President Ngo Dinh Diem and the situation in Vietnam see Galambos and van Ee, *The Middle Way*, nos. 985 and 1140. Elbridge Durbrow, former U.S. minister in Singapore, had been U.S. Ambassador to Vietnam since March 1957. Secretary Dulles had recommended sending this letter, drafted by State Department officials, to reaffirm the "continued high esteem" that the United States had for President Diem. Diem, said Dulles, was the strongest anti-Communist leader in Southeast Asia (Dulles to Eisenhower, May 22, 1958, AWF/I: VietNam).

[2] On Diem's visit to Washington (May 8–12, 1957) and his discussions with Eisenhower see State, *Foreign Relations, 1955–1957*, vol. I, *Vietnam* (1985), pp. 762–63, 794–817; see also Diem to Eisenhower, May 28, 1957, AWF/I: Vietnam.

[3] The statement had labeled as propaganda a plan for reunification proposed by the Democratic Republic of Vietnam. Diem's statement had called for proof of a change in attitude by the communist leaders; evidence of such a change would consist of permission for refugees to leave the North, a reduction in military forces, a renunciation of terrorism, and restoration of democratic liberties (State, *Foreign Relations, 1958 1960*, vol. I, *Vietnam* [1986], p. 39).

[4] For developments see no. 1085.

711   *EM, AWF, DDE Diaries Series*

To Urbanus Edmund Baughman   *May 23, 1958*

Dear Chief Baughman:[1] When the Vice President reported to me on the unpleasant incidents in connection with his trip to South America, he stressed particularly the fine work of the Secret Service men who accompanied him.[2] Since then I have seen in the press, and had other first hand accounts, of the remarkable manner in which they conducted themselves. I tremendously admire the judgment, calmness and effectiveness all of them showed in the face of a most difficult and dangerous situation.

Won't you please convey to all of the members of the Secret Service who accompanied the Vice President a feeling of my pride and confidence? I would particularly like to thank, through you, the three members of the White House detail who were assigned to the mission.[3]

With warm regard, *Sincerely*

[1] Baughman, former supervising agent in both Washington and New York City, had been Chief of the United States Secret Service since 1948.

[2] For background on Vice-President Nixon's trip to eight South American countries see no. 658. Although most South American countries had suppressed Communist party activities, the CIA had told Nixon that he might face occasional demonstrations. Only minor heckling had marred his otherwise warm receptions in Uruguay, Argentina, Paraguay, and Bolivia, but a violent demonstration erupted when the Vice-President attempted to visit San Marcos University in Peru. During a stop in Colombia, Baughman had notified Nixon that the CIA had advised the Secret Service of an assassination plot against him in Venezuela. After Venezuelan officials had assured him of the tightest security, Nixon and his party continued to Caracas, where upon arrival at the airport he encountered angry mobs. As his motorcade approached the city, demonstrators, armed with rocks and iron pipes, attempted to overturn the Vice-President's car. Escaping with minor injuries (primarily from shards of glass), his party was able to reach the American embassy, where they remained until returning to the United States the following day (Richard M. Nixon, *Six Crises* [New York, 1962], pp. 183–234; and Nixon, *Memoirs*, vol. I, pp. 228–37; see also State, *Foreign Relations, 1958–1960*, vol. V, *American Republics*, pp. 222–38; Eisenhower, *Waging Peace*, pp. 519–20; Ann Whitman memorandums, May 13, 15, 1958, AWF/AWD; Telephone conversation, Dulles and Eisenhower, May 13, 1958, Dulles Papers, Telephone Conversations; *Public Papers of the Presidents: Eisenhower, 1958*, p. 395, *New York Times*, May 14, 1958; and Stephen G. Rabe, *Eisenhower and Latin America: The Foreign Policy of Anticommunism* [Chapel Hill, 1988], pp. 100–108).

After the incident in Peru, Eisenhower had sent a message to Nixon praising the Vice-President for his "courage, patience and calmness" during the demonstrations—actions which, Eisenhower said, would bring Nixon "new respect and admiration" in the United States (State, *Foreign Relations, 1958–1960*, vol. V, *American Republics*, pp. 225–26). In a telephone call to the embassy after the Caracas demonstrations, Eisenhower had told Nixon that he was sorry about what had happened, but that he had "carried it through splendidly" and would be "the bigger for it" (Telephone conversation, May 14, 1958, AWF/D). After his return, Nixon had reported on the incidents to both the National Security Council and the Cabinet (see NSC meeting minutes, May 23, 1958, AWF/NSC; and Cabinet meeting minutes, May 16, 1958, AWF/Cabinet; see also Memorandum of Conversation, May 18, 1958, Dulles Papers, White House Memoranda Series).

[3] Jack Sherwood was the agent in charge of Secret Service protection for Nixon; he was aided by Agent Wade Rodham (see Nixon, *Six Crises*, pp. 188, 197, 201–4, 210, 216–20). For developments in U.S.-South American relations see no. 730.

To Nikita Sergeyevich Khrushchev   *May 24, 1958*
Secret

Dear Mr. Chairman:[1] I have your letter of May 9, 1958. I note with
satisfaction that you accept, at least partially, my proposal that technical persons be designated to ascertain what would be required to
supervise and control disarmament agreements, all without prejudice to our respective positions on the timing and interdependence
of various aspects of disarmament.[2]

Your letter of May ninth states that "the Soviet Government agrees
to having both sides designate experts who would immediately begin
a study of methods for detecting possible violations of an agreement
on the cessation of nuclear tests with a view to having this work completed at the earliest possible date, to be determined in advance."

Experts from our side will be prepared to meet with experts from
your side at Geneva, if the Swiss Government agrees, within three
weeks of our learning whether these arrangements are acceptable
to you. On our side, experts would be chosen on the basis of special competence. I have in mind, for example, experts which might
be contributed not only from the United States, but from the United
Kingdom which, like the Soviet Union and the United States, has
conducted nuclear tests, and from France, which has advanced plans
for testing, and possibly from other countries having experts who
are advanced in knowledge of how to detect nuclear tests. We assume that the experts on the side of the Soviet Union would be similarly chosen on the basis of special competence, so as to assure that
we get scientific, not political, conclusions.[3]

I also suggest that the experts should be asked to make an initial
progress report within thirty days after convening and to aim at a final report within sixty days or as soon thereafter as possible.[4]

In view of the Charter responsibilities of the General Assembly
and the Security Council of the United Nations in the field of disarmament, we would propose to keep the United Nations and its
appropriate organs informed of the progress of these talks through
the intermediary of the Secretary General.

I will write you further shortly regarding your statements on the
problem of surprise attack and the Arctic Zone of inspection which
we have proposed.[5] *Sincerely*

---

[1] State Department officials drafted this letter after consultations with Defense Secretary McElroy, AEC Chairman Strauss, and Special Assistant for Science and Technology Killian. A copy was also sent to the British Foreign Office for approval (State,
Foreign Relations, 1958–1960, vol. III, *National Security Policy; Arms Control and Disar-*

mament, p. 610; see also Telephone conversations, Dulles and McElroy, Strauss, and Killian, May 14, 1958, Dulles Papers, Telephone Conversations).

[2] After reviewing Khrushchev's letter (AWF/I: Khrushchev), Eisenhower had asked Dulles if he believed the Soviet acceptance depended on a prior agreement to suspend testing. Dulles had interpreted the letter to mean that the Soviets had agreed to have experts study controls without prior commitments (Memorandum of Conversation, May 12, 1958, Dulles Papers, White House Memoranda Series).

[3] Eisenhower had discussed the composition of the team of experts with Dulles on May 18. Officials from both the United States and Great Britain believed that the Western delegation should include France, Dulles said, even though the Soviets might then insist on including representatives from the Eastern European satellites or Communist China. Dulles had shown Eisenhower two drafts of this paragraph: one reflecting the participation of several nations in the Western delegation and only the Soviet Union on the Communist side, and a draft suggesting two sides, with each selecting experts on a technical, non-political basis, from countries of their own choosing. Eisenhower approved the latter and also suggested substituting the concept of "contributed by" other countries for "chosen by" the United States.

Killian had urged the selection of three distinguished scientists to head the American team in order to force the Soviets to do the same (Memorandum of Conversation, May 18, 1958, Dulles Papers, White House Memoranda Series; see also Telephone conversations, Dulles and Killian, May 14, 1958; Dulles and Strauss, May 17, 1958; and Dulles and Eisenhower, May 17, 1958, Dulles Papers, Telephone Conversations). The Swiss had quickly agreed to host meetings of the technical experts in Geneva (State, *Foreign Relations, 1958–1960,* vol. III, *National Security Policy; Arms Control and Disarmament,* pp. 607–12).

[4] Killian suggested setting this deadline for the final report (*ibid.,* p. 607).

[5] On the surprise-attack problem and the Arctic inspection zone see no. 709. For developments see no. 737.

713   EM, AWF, DDE Diaries Series

To Ann Cook Whitman   May 28, 1958

O.K. I'd tell the W. S. J. that it must be composed of a bunch of babies![1]

[1] The President had written his comment on a note from his secretary Ann Whitman regarding a message from Treasury Secretary Robert Anderson. The *Wall Street Journal* had asked Anderson if Eisenhower's comments on interest rates during that morning's news conference had "passed judgment" insofar as future Treasury Department operations were concerned (see *Public Papers of the Presidents: Eisenhower, 1958,* pp. 429–39). Fearing "speculation in the bond market," Anderson had told the *Journal* that the President's comment that he hoped long-term interest rates would decline was directed toward "the problem in a general sense in relationship to the whole economy, and without reference to the refunding of more than nine billion in government securities which the Treasury Department must announce later this week." Anderson had added that no decision had yet been made as to what the refunding offer might or might not include.

To John Hay Whitney   *May 28, 1958*
Cable

Dear Jock: This is in the nature of a personal request. General Arthur Nevins' daughter, Mary Ann, has been studying at Cambridge this past year. She is being married June eleventh or twelfth. Neither her father nor mother can attend the ceremony, and Mary Ann has asked for an introduction to you or some one at the Embassy so that arrangements can be made for an American stand-in to take her father's place at the wedding. Since her father is a retired officer, it might be fitting to ask your military attache to undertake the chore.[1] Mary Ann will get in touch with you or your secretary, but her address in case you want it is 1(one) Union Road, Cambridge.

I look forward to seeing you early in June when you are in Washington.[2] *As ever*

[1] Mary Ann Nevins, a Pfeiffer Bye-Fellow of Girton College at Cambridge, would be married on June 16. Major General William Henry Hennig (USMA 1928), a military attaché at the United States embassy in Great Britain, would escort the bride and represent her father at the ceremony (*New York Times*, June 17, 1958; see also Whitman to Nevins, June 7, 1958, AWF/Gettysburg).

[2] See no. 680.

To Philip Young   *May 29, 1958*

Dear Phil: Thank you for your letter of the twenty-first.[1] The central point of your comment is, of course, disturbing and very difficult to understand. I shall discuss some of its aspects with our friends in the State Department. And perhaps—if I see you when you are in the States for Faith's wedding—we can talk a little bit about the problem.[2]

With warm regard, *As ever*

[1] Philip Young, U.S. Ambassador to the Netherlands, had written Eisenhower about the lack of morale and spirit which he had observed at a Paris meeting of the U.S. ambassadors in Western Europe. After Secretary Dulles had spoken to the group about the controversial areas in the world, few of the ambassadors had taken advantage of the opportunity to ask questions, Young reported. Most had exhibited a "marked lack of interest and intellectual curiosity." Equally disturbing was the fact that only three other ambassadors had elected to accompany Dulles to the airport when he returned to the United States. Young had praised the selection process that

had produced enthusiastic young men in the foreign service. "But then," he said, "something happens and enthusiasm wanes, a touch of cynicism begins to show, individual initiative is dulled, and talents tend to become rusty" (AWF/N).

[2] Young's daughter was to be married on June 21 in Van Hornesville, New York. We have found no record that Eisenhower spoke with State Department representatives regarding the European ambassadors. Young would meet with Eisenhower on June 26.

716 *EM, WHCF, Official File 3-VV*

TO REUBEN BUCK ROBERTSON, JR. *May 29, 1958*

Dear Reuben: Neil McElroy and others have shown me your May twentieth letter which powerfully—and cogently—supports the proposed reorganization of the Defense Department.[1] Congratulations on a fine piece of work!

I am told that Karl Bendetsen, among others, is also busy in this effort and has recently sent out correspondence dealing with the amendments discussed in the attached statement issued yesterday to the press.[2] The need now is to do the job right; if we accept the Committee's decision to hold to the concept of disunity and separatism, America is certain to have the same troubles inside the Pentagon in future years that have plagued us for more than a decade. I hope we can encourage our friends to be vigorously helpful on these amendments during the next ten days. This period is not only critical in the House but also has much to do with the decisions to be reached later on in the Senate.[3]

So that you will have a clear-cut picture of the items at issue, I enclose a marked copy of the bill. On the surface these amendments may seem relatively insubstantial; in them, however, is the kernel of the unification struggle. They give us a choice of having a truly unified defense program or contenting ourselves with the doctrine and the practice of separatism, with all that the latter means in dilution of military power, costly duplication and interservice strife.

I greatly appreciate all that you are doing to help advance this cause.[4]

With warm personal regard, *Sincerely*

[1] In letters addressed to "Fellow Champion," president of Champion Paper and Fiber Company and former deputy defense secretary (1955–1957) Robertson had expressed his support for the President's defense reorganization proposal (same file as document; for background see nos. 630, 678, and 687). Robertson had explained: "Past concepts of warfare have been completely outdated, and our defense mechanism must be overhauled in recognition of this cold fact. The President's proposal for reorganization has been worked out in concurrence with our most able military and civilian defense advisers, and they have worked with the President all along the

line in the development of his recommendations to the Congress." It was his hope, he said, that his audience of 1,200 executives and supervisors at Champion would feel strongly enough about the issue to pressure their representatives in Congress. Eisenhower had written on Robertson's letter, "I'll write a note." See Watson, *Into the Missile Age*, pp. 264–74; see also Ries, *The Management of Defense*, pp. 167–92. Presidential Assistant Bryce Harlow may have drafted parts of this letter.

[2] Karl Robin Bendetsen (A.B. Stanford 1929, LL.B. Stanford 1932) was a vice-president with Champion and former Under Secretary of the Army. Eisenhower's May 28, 1958, statement detailing his objections to the congressional bill can be found in *Public Papers of the Presidents: Eisenhower, 1958*, pp. 439–43.

[3] The Armed Services Committee had reported the bill to the House of Representatives on May 22. Despite the President's misgivings (see no. 699), the Committee had retained provisions requiring that the military departments be organized separately, with the line of command running from the Secretary of Defense through the service secretaries. The House Committee had also insisted on language giving Congress the right to override any attempt by the Secretary of Defense to abolish or reorganize major combatant functions. Eisenhower had also objected to a section of the bill that allowed a department secretary or a member of the Joint Chiefs of Staff to present to Congress, on his own initiative, recommendations regarding the Department of Defense. Eisenhower had called this "legalized insubordination." See *Congressional Quarterly Almanac*, vol. XIV, 1958, pp. 194–99.

[4] For developments see no. 802.

717   *EM, WHCF, Official File 111-C-1*

To Charles G. Mortimer   *May 29, 1958*

Dear Mr. Mortimer: It was gratifying and reassuring to read your letter and to find that, amidst all the pressing claims of your heavy business responsibilities, you are thinking so deeply about one of the most critical problems confronting our country.[1]

I could not agree with you more as to the vital necessity of according education higher priority in our scheme of things and of focusing on the teacher as the key to improvement.[2] Mark Hopkins' reference to a school as a log with a teacher at one end and student at the other still gets pretty close to the heart of the matter.[3]

Your suggestion about making the earned income of teachers exempt is provocative and I shall ask Secretary Anderson's comment on it. I fear he will tell me that granting such an exemption will require extending similar treatment to other groups.[4] I was pleased with the new Treasury regulation making expenses of teachers for additional training, including summer school, generally tax deductible. That is a constructive step.[5] Believe me, I would like to find others that we could live with that would not entail unacceptable consequences in other directions. In any event, I am going to see what the Secretary has to say on your suggestion.

Again my thanks for your interest with respect to this key problem.

With warm regard, *Sincerely*

[1] Mortimer, president and chief executive officer (since 1954) of General Foods Corporation in White Plains, New York, had written on May 22. Mortimer said he had become increasingly concerned over the country's "crisis in education" since the successful launch of Russia's two earth satellites in 1957 (for background see nos. 389 and 434). Sputnik had "dramatized the weakness" of the American educational system, Mortimer wrote, and had posed the question of how the United States could compete successfully with Russia in this area.

[2] Mortimer felt that teachers were held in "low esteem" by the public, which had an "appalling . . . apathy toward so fundamental an institution of democracy" as education. He suggested adequate compensation for teachers and college professors and an increase in the status of the profession, "as the Russians have done."

[3] Mark Hopkins (B.A. Williams College 1824; M.D. Berkshire Medical College 1829), American educator and theologian, was president of Williams College (1836 to 1872), where he also taught moral philosophy and rhetoric. Eisenhower's reference was to a statement by U.S. President James A. Garfield, who reportedly had commended his former teacher by saying: "The ideal college is Mark Hopkins on one end of a log and a student on the other" (Peskin, *Garfield*, pp. 34, 619–20).

[4] Mortimer suggested that if salaries could not be increased, then spendable income could be raised by "*making the earned income of teachers tax exempt,* at least for a period of years." This action would "make teachers a specially recognized class in our society, as they are in Russia where, with calculated effect, they are given the best homes and apartments and other material evidences of their 'pedestal status.'"

Secretary of the Treasury Anderson would tell Mortimer (June 13) that his proposal had been discussed thoroughly. As the President had predicted, Anderson would tell Mortimer that such a tax exemption would lead to demands for similar relief by other groups. Such tax cuts could also lead to resistance to salary increases on the presumption that teachers received economic advantages which made pay raises unnecessary. Mortimer would thank Eisenhower (June 5) and Anderson (June 27) for their replies. All correspondence is in the same file as the document.

[5] The President had requested passage of the measure in his budget message to the Congress on January 13, 1958 (*Public Papers of the Presidents: Dwight D. Eisenhower, 1958*, pp. 17–74, esp. p. 48; see also nos. 416 and 767). On September 2 Eisenhower would sign into law the requested legislation, the Technical Amendments Act of 1958, P.L. 866 (*Congressional Quarterly Almanac*, vol. XIV, *1958*, p. 298).

718   *EM, AWF, International Series:*
                                                                                      Macmillan

To Harold Macmillan   *May 30, 1958*
Secret

Dear Harold: I have received your letter of today's date. I believe we will be in a position to go over the situation with Plowden when he arrives next Wednesday and that very shortly thereafter we can decide on the dispatch of the balance of your team of experts to complete the negotiations.[1]

It is difficult to foretell whether these discussions by the experts can in fact progress quickly enough so that you and I will be able to come to some agreement in principle when we meet, but we will make every effort to do so.[2] You realize however that there may be very real limitations arising from our legislative processes since the Congress has not yet acted on the Committee report, which itself is not yet available. In addition, the technical nature of the discussions may take a short time.

I am fully conscious of the time factor and we are moving with all possible speed. In view of the Congressional situation I feel it is important that no publicity should be given to the fact that even preliminary discussions are under way.[3]

With warm regard, *As ever*

[1] The State Department drafted this letter to the British prime minister (see Memorandum of Conversation, Herter and Eisenhower, May 30, 1958, Dulles Papers, Chronological Series). For background see no. 628. On May 28 the Agreements for Cooperation Subcommittee of the Joint Committee on Atomic Energy had approved amendments to the Atomic Energy Act of 1954, allowing an increased exchange of atomic information and materials with U.S. allies. Macmillan had suggested that U.S. and British officials meet as quickly as possible to formulate an agreement between the two countries. "As you know, we have fully accepted the view that it would have been dangerous to have held discussions between us . . . until the present stage," Macmillan said. "I trust, however, that the way is now open for our experts and yours to begin substantive discussions urgently" (Macmillan to Eisenhower, May 29, 1958, PREM 11/2554). Eisenhower had told Acting Secretary Herter that he agreed with Macmillan and urged him to take immediate steps (Telephone conversation, Eisenhower and Herter, May 30, 1958, AWF/D). After consulting AEC Chairman Strauss, Herter told Eisenhower that he thought they could step up the "time table" and be ready for preliminary discussions with Edwin Noel Plowden, chairman of the British Atomic Energy Authority (Memorandums of Conversation, Herter and Eisenhower, and Herter and Strauss, May 30, 1958, Dulles Papers, Chronological Series).

[2] Eisenhower had added the words "by the experts" to the first sentence of this paragraph (*ibid.*). Macmillan would be in Washington from June 9–11 (see no. 635).

[3] The committee would report the bill to the floor of the House of Representatives on June 5 (for congressional action regarding the amendments see *Congressional Quarterly Almanac*, vol. XIV, *1958*, pp. 253–55). For developments see no. 725.

To Arthur Krock   *May 30, 1958*
Personal and confidential

Dear Arthur: Your column this morning had as its subject a matter that has occupied a great deal of my waking time for several months. You point out that I am flatly determined to accomplish military reform in the interests of our country's future. I hope you are in accord with that purpose.[1]

My special reason for writing a note to you is merely to explain a point. You believe that I experienced a change in my thinking between the date of May sixteenth and the statement I made on May twenty-eighth.[2]

In the first instance I employed a manner of expression—as in the military service I employed it in positions of command—that was intended to be mild in tone, polite in tenor, but unmistakable so far as my dissatisfaction with important details was concerned. Actually, on the evening I wrote the letter to the Chairman, I had in front of me for study and was referring to in terms of disapproval exactly the same three points that led to my later statement. But, by that time, I decided that in the existing circumstances I should use a terminology and tone that might be more effective in political circles than did those I was accustomed to using. Incidentally, as these political problems come up from time to time, I am not again going to make the mistake of assuming that a polite indication of disagreement—which in my former life was taken seriously indeed—can be interpreted as a weakness in will.

When this thing is all over, you may be interested in learning either from me, or from one of my close associates in this work, like Mr. Harlow, the exact circumstances which brought out the requested letter of May sixteenth. The approval of the Committee's work was sincere, subject to certain exceptions that I deemed important. But I failed to see that the general statement of approval could be used to hurt the program while the exceptions were disregarded.[3]

I would not bother you with this long note this morning except that since it happens to be Memorial Day, the offices of the government seem largely deserted and I have a few minutes belonging to myself.[4]

Did I say that I enjoyed your column? I should have.

With warm personal regard, *As ever*

---

[1] Krock's column, "In the Nation," had addressed Eisenhower's criticisms of the defense reorganization bill, which had been reported by the House Armed Services Com-

mittee on May 22, 1958 (*New York Times*, May 30, 1958; see no. 716). Krock had written that the President's May 28 statement indicated that "he now fully subscribes to the adverse analysis of the committee changes in his reorganization plan. . . ." Also implicit in the statement, Krock said, was the President's realization that "if he is to get from Congress certain actions he considers vital to the national interest, his preferred tactic of moderation must be replaced by all-out attack. This foreshadows a fight to the finish on the Pentagon legislation with very influential members of Congress."

[2] Krock had pointed out the differences between Eisenhower's "quick impressions" of the defense reorganization bill as expressed in his May 16 letter congratulating the House committee and his "mature conclusions" as expressed in his May 28 public statement. See no. 699.

[3] On May 30, 1958, Krock would thank Eisenhower for his letter (same file as document), and would profess himself eager to learn the background of the May 16 letter to Vinson. "It is not from want of trying, however, that I have not had a talk with you on a number of subjects since late 1956. . . . But my efforts have been unsuccessful, though anything you might say for my ears only would be held in the same confidence as your letters have been" (see Galambos and van Ee, *The Middle Way*, no. 442).

[4] Krock would add that he was not only "in accord" with Eisenhower on the Pentagon bill but also that he had "been a steadfast believer in you and in all your purposes and principles since we met long ago. Within my narrow limitations I have sought ever to advance them."

720   *EM, AWF,*
                                                 Administration Series

To CHRISTIAN ARCHIBALD HERTER   *May 30, 1958*

Dear Chris: I would be grateful if you would have some staff officer develop either a draft or an outline for my talk in Ottawa—particularly one that will bring out in the open the major problems that are common to both our countries.[1]

I feel that it would be useless to make one of the regular "hands across the border" talks. It would be better to identify problems of imports and quotas and foreign markets and so on and so on, and to suggest (*a*) that we certainly hope to be reasonable and tolerant of their views in discussions and (*b*) the belief that answers can be found that will not be unacceptable to either country.

The talk should not be long—20 to 25 minutes is ample. A half hour should be the extreme limit. If you can find someone that could do this, I should like for him to get at it fairly promptly. I like to have a lot of time to ponder over these things, and to correct and edit.[2]

Thanks. *As ever*

[1] For background on Eisenhower's upcoming visit to the Canadian capital see no. 695.

Herter would thank Eisenhower for his guidance and would tell the President that the speech he contemplated was exactly the kind that should be made. Presidential Assistant Gabriel Hauge would also assist in preparing the talk (Herter to Eisenhower, May 31, 1958, AWF/A; and Ann Whitman memorandum, June 26, 1958, AWF/AWD). In his address to the Canadian Parliament on July 9 Eisenhower would discuss the U.S. wheat disposal policies (see no. 24), the imbalance in mutual trade, private U.S. investments in Canada, and Canadian fears regarding future U.S. trade policies (*Public Papers of the Presidents: Eisenhower, 1958*, pp. 529–37). For more on the Canadian visit see State, *Foreign Relations, 1958–1960*, vol. VII, pt. 1, *Western European Integration and Security; Canada*, pp. 686–721.

721   *EM, AWF, Administration Series*

To Neil Hosler McElroy   [May 30, 1958]

My dear Mr. Secretary: The military pay bill, H. R. 11470, which I recently approved, represents an important step forward in our efforts to attract and retain highly qualified personnel in the armed forces.[1] It is now incumbent upon those of us in the Executive Branch who are charged with responsibilities for the operation of our military establishment to see that the maximum benefits are realized from the substantial increases in compensation which have thus been authorized and from the substantially greater expenditures which will be necessary to finance these increases. To this end, supporting administrative actions should be pressed vigorously within the Department of Defense, especially with respect to such matters as improved personnel management, promotion policies and practices, retention criteria, and the like. These are matters which I believe to be sufficiently important to warrant your personal attention.

In enacting the military pay bill, the Congress provided for an alternative proficiency pay system for enlisted personnel in addition to the one already authorized. It also authorized added compensation for officers serving in positions involving "unusual responsibility." The authority for proficiency and responsibility pay is clearly permissive in nature.[2]

In order to achieve the bill's purposes, it is essential that great care be exercised in designating the categories of enlisted personnel which should be granted entitlement to proficiency pay. Similarly, great care must be exercised in deciding upon implementation of the authority for officer responsibility pay. In this connection, it will be necessary not only to evaluate the effect of the new rates of compensation but also to study the implications of a responsibility pay system with its consequent problems of administration. We must not forget that officers are trained for, and expected to assume, increasingly heavy responsibilities in varying assignments and that present promotion systems afford those of demonstrated ability recurring opportunities for periodic advancement to higher rank.

I would appreciate it if you would submit, for my review and approval, through the Bureau of the Budget, any proficiency or responsibility pay programs which the Department may subsequently wish to put into effect.[3] *Sincerely*

[1] The military pay raise bill (H.R. 11470), incorporating the major recommendations of the 1957 Cordiner Committee report (see nos. 73 and 226), had been prompted by a large turnover in military personnel and was designed to retain skilled military men of all ranks (*New York Times*, Mar. 26, May 13, 1958). Passed by the House on March 25, the Senate on April 29, and signed into law on May 20, 1958, the legislation increased the basic pay for almost all military personnel with more than two years' service, set up two new higher pay grades for officers and enlisted personnel, and established a program of "responsibility pay" and "proficiency pay" to reward officers and enlisted men holding positions involving "unusual responsibility" or special expertise (see *Congressional Quarterly Almanac*, vol. XIV, *1958*, pp. 235–36). The bill also increased pensions for all personnel retired prior to the effective date of the legislation, and authorized additional increases in retirement pay for Vice-Admirals, Lieutenant Generals, four-star Generals, and Admirals (see no. 564).

[2] See Watson, *Into the Missile Age*, pp. 152–53.

[3] For developments see no. 969.

Forcing the President's Hand

JUNE 1958 TO OCTOBER 1958

11

"Take time by the forelock"

To Charles André Joseph Marie de Gaulle   *June 2, 1958*

Dear Mr. President: I wish to extend to you my personal greetings and good wishes on this occasion of your assuming leadership of the French nation.[1]

You may be confident that I retain vividly in mind the important and friendly association which we had during the critical days of the Second World War.[2]

You know of my deep and lasting affection for France. You may be sure that you have my sympathetic understanding in the great tasks which you are about to undertake.[3]

Please accept, Mr. President, my best wishes for the success of your mission.[4] *Sincerely*

[1] On May 14 French colonists in Algeria had staged an insurrection and demanded that Charles de Gaulle be brought to power; the French Army was later reported to have supported the insurrection in both Algeria and Corsica. De Gaulle offered to form a new government if the National Assembly agreed to adjourn for four months and to give him full power to rule by decree for six months as well as a mandate to write a new constitution (State, *Foreign Relations, 1958–1960*, vol. VII, pt. 2, *Western Europe*, pp. 8–24; see also NSC meeting minutes, May 23, 29, 1958, AWF/NSC; and no. 451.

     Shortly before de Gaulle came to power Secretary Dulles had given Eisenhower a draft of this letter. Eisenhower thought the draft was appropriate and said he "would hold it on a contingency basis" (Memorandum of Conversation, May 26, 1958, Dulles Papers, White House Memoranda Series; see also Herter to Eisenhower, May 31, 1958, Dulles/Herter Papers, Chronological Correspondence Series).

[2] On Eisenhower's relations with de Gaulle see Chandler, *War Years*, vols. I–IV; see also Frank Castiglioga, *France and the United States: The Cold Alliance Since World War II* (New York, 1992), pp. 121, 124–25, 127.

[3] After reading an editorial in *Life* citing the problems posed by de Gaulle's return to power, Eisenhower had taken a more optimistic position. He told Ann Whitman that he had had many "satisfying and revealing" conversations with the French leader, and that some of the constructive steps de Gaulle had taken in North Africa as early as 1943 led Eisenhower to believe that he could "stabilize relations between France and Algeria, to say nothing of Tunisia and Morocco" (Whitman to Jackson, June 5, 1958, AWF/A; see also McCrum to Whitman, June 6, 1958; and "De Gaulle: The Risks, the Rewards," *Life*, June 2, 1958).

[4] For developments see no. 765.

To John Foster Dulles[1]   *June 4, 1958*

United States policy comprehends those programs that are designed to protect and promote the interests of the United States in the international field. It is based upon certain facts and convictions:

(*a*). That the peoples of the world, as distinguished from their governments, universally desire the elimination of war and the establishment of a just peace;

(*b*). That the designs of aggressive Communist imperialism pose a continuous threat to every nation of the free world, including our own;

(*c*). The security of this nation can be maintained only by the spiritual, economic and military strength of the free world, with this nation the most powerful of the partners committed to this purpose;

(*d*). That the effectiveness of our collective security measures depends upon the economic advancement of the less developed parts of the free world, which strengthens their purpose and ability to sustain their independence;

(*e*). That in all international associations and combinations within the free world, in which the United States is a member, it considers all nations, including itself, as equals. The sovereignty of no nation will ever be limited or diminished by any act of the United States.

Since American policy is designed to protect and promote the interests of the United States, we list them as follows:[2]

[1] Eisenhower had dictated these suggestions after Secretary Dulles had asked him to comment on a statement he was scheduled to make before the Senate Foreign Relations Committee on June 6 (Dulles to Eisenhower, June 3, 1958, AWF/D-H; see also Memorandum of Conversation, June 4, 1958, Dulles Papers, White House Memoranda Series).

[2] The full text of Dulles's statement is in John Foster Dulles, "The Challenge of Change: The Basic Philosophy, the Rationale, Which Underlies U.S. Foreign Policy," *U.S. Department of State Bulletin* 38, no. 991 (June 23, 1958), 1035–42. The Secretary of State would list the interests that American foreign policy was designed to serve.

In a telephone conversation after his presentation Dulles would tell Eisenhower that the session had gone very well and that the points the President had made were very effective (Telephone conversation, June 6, 1958, AWF/D).

To John Foster Dulles   *June 4, 1958*

Memorandum for the Secretary of State: I return herewith without my approval the draft of the letter you recommended that I sign to the Prime Minister of Japan regarding the currency conversion proposed for the Ryukyu Islands.[1]

This proposal seems to be one of doubtful wisdom, particularly because of its possible effect within Japan. I am sure that the use of American currency in the Islands would be interpreted in Japan as an unexpressed but nevertheless latent ambition of this country to annex those Islands. The mutual friendship and trust that have been built up between our country and Japan are extremely valuable and I do not see why we should chance damaging them in the effort to achieve a greater administrative efficiency.

If the Prime Minister of Japan himself recommends the use of American currency because of a favorable effect upon the Ryukyu economy, and would agree that the consideration would in his mind outweigh any fear of possible future attempts on our part to annex the Islands, then I would be ready to give my approval to the project.

In the meantime I suggest that Ambassador MacArthur be instructed to lay before Premier Kishi all the anticipated advantages and potential disadvantages of the proposal and to make a complete report to you.

After the matter has been so studied and reported on, I will be ready to consider the paper again.[2]

[1] For background on U.S. policy regarding the Ryukyu Islands see no. 646. Discussions regarding the introduction of dollar currency in the islands to replace the circulating B yen (occupation currency) had taken place during Japanese Prime Minister Nobusuke Kishi's visit to the United States in June 1957. At that time, however, State Department officials opposed the measure. They had, instead, proposed a plan whereby the B yen would be backed 100 percent by U.S. currency and therefore freely convertible into dollars (State, *Foreign Relations, 1955–1957*, vol. XXIII, pt. 1, *Japan*, pp. 265, 436–37, 516).

In the memorandum to Eisenhower that accompanied the draft letter to Kishi, Dulles had told the President that the prime minister had received a large vote of confidence in the recent Japanese elections and that State and Defense department officials now wanted to proceed with the conversion. Eisenhower had written "I'm doubtful" at the bottom of Dulles's memorandum (Dulles to Eisenhower, June 3, 1958, WHO/OSS: Subject [State Dept.] State Dept.; see also MacArthur to Dulles, May 23, 1958, State, *Foreign Relations, 1958–1960*, vol. XVIII, *Japan; Korea*, Microfiche Supplement no. 453). In a meeting held on this day Dulles had told Eisenhower that he had misgivings about the conversion and had "only with reluctance" agreed to the plan because of the strong views of the Defense Department. Eisenhower said that he would explain his views in writing and would send a copy to Defense Secretary McElroy (Memorandum of Conversation, June 4, 1958, Dulles Papers, White

House Memoranda Series; see also Telephone conversations, Dulles and Robertson, June 4, 1958; and Dulles and Brucker, June 5, 1958, Dulles Papers, Telephone Conversations).

[2] U.S. Ambassador to Japan Douglas MacArthur II would discuss conversion with Kishi on June 18 and would tell the prime minister that President Eisenhower wanted "his frank reaction." Although the proposal would create some difficulties, Kishi replied, "he could live with conversion as long as [the] timing was right." He asked that the United States postpone any action until after the Diet had adjourned on July 4 and until the United States had reached a favorable decision on Okinawan land compensation policy. MacArthur would tell Dulles that Eisenhower's handling of the problem had "touched Kishi deeply" and had led him to withdraw his original objection to currency conversion (Dulles to MacArthur, June 16, 1958, State, *Foreign Relations, 1958–1960*, vol. XVIII, *Japan; Korea*, Microfiche Supplement no. 460; and MacArthur to Dulles, June 19, 1958, *ibid.*, no. 461). For developments see no. 813.

725 *EM, AWF, DDE Diaries Series*

TO LEWIS LICHTENSTEIN STRAUSS *June 4, 1958*
Secret

Memorandum for the Chairman, Atomic Energy Commission: Prime Minister Macmillan has written me to express the hope that U. S. and U. K. experts could, on a strictly confidential basis, get ahead with discussion of atomic cooperation so as to be able to report to the Prime Minister and myself during his visit to Washington. Such a report might give us a basis for agreeing in principle on the general content of a bilateral agreement.[1]

I understand that U. K. atomic weapons experts are arriving in Washington at the end of this week and that our own staff work is well under way.[2]

Accordingly, I hope that your experts will be able to work with the British in preparing a joint report along the lines suggested by Prime Minister Macmillan. Such a report would be an appropriate sequel to the report which we had from you, Under Secretary Quarles, Sir Edwin Plowden and Sir Richard Powell during the Prime Minister's visit in October, 1957.[3]

I have asked the Secretary of State to advise the British Ambassador of this proposed procedure.[4]

[1] Eisenhower sent an identical version of this memorandum, which was drafted by State Department officials, to Secretary of Defense Neil McElroy (AWF/D; see also Memorandum of Conversation, June 4, 1958, Dulles Papers, White House Memoranda Series). For background on Macmillan's letter, atomic cooperation, and the proposal for a bilateral agreement see no. 718.

[2] In an earlier conversation, Strauss had told Acting Secretary Herter that his staff was working on a preliminary draft of a bilateral agreement. Minor differences with

the Defense Department had delayed the discussions, Strauss said, but he was certain that they would be ready to meet with the British experts (Memorandum of Conversation, Herter and Strauss, May 30, 1958, Dulles-Herter Papers, Chronological Correspondence Series).

[3] On the 1957 visit see nos. 409 and 433; see also State, *Foreign Relations, 1955–1957*, vol. XXVII, *Western Europe and Canada*, pp. 802–39. Plowden had been chairman of the British Atomic Energy Authority since 1954; Powell had been Permanent Secretary of the Ministry of Defence since 1956. The report had included recommendations regarding the transfer and exchange of nuclear materials for military purposes, the allocation of specific weapons design and development projects between the two countries, and the reduction of waste in the duplication of material and talent (Report to the President and the Prime Minister, Oct. 25, 1957, PREM 11/2329).

[4] Harold Caccia was the British ambassador. For developments see no. 740.

On the following day Strauss would send Eisenhower his formal resignation as chairman of the Atomic Energy Commission. Although he was "gratified" that Eisenhower had wanted to reappoint him, Strauss, alluding to disagreements with the Congressional Joint Committee on Atomic Energy, told the President that "circumstances beyond the control of either of us make a change in the chairmanship of the Commission advisable" (Strauss to Eisenhower, and Eisenhower to Strauss, June 5, 1958, AWF/A, AEC; see also Strauss to Eisenhower, June 9, 1958, *ibid.*; Telephone conversation, Dulles and Goodpaster, June 5, 1958, Dulles Papers, Telephone Conversations; Hewlett and Holl, *Atoms for Peace and War*, pp. 426–29, 497; and Divine, *Blowing on the Wind*, pp. 217–18). Eisenhower would nominate Strauss to be Secretary of Commerce in the fall of 1958. After a protracted and bitter debate, however, the Senate would reject the appointment in June 1959 (see nos. 1134 and 1215).

726   *EM, WHCF, Official File 142-A*

To Jack Roosevelt Robinson   *June 4, 1958*

Dear Mr. Robinson: Thank you very much for taking the time to write me some of the thoughts you had after the meeting of the Negro leaders here in Washington.[1] While I understand the points you make about the use of patience and forbearance, I have never urged them as substitutes for constructive action or progress.[2]

If you will review my talk made at the meeting, you will see that at no point did I advocate a cessation of effort on the part of individuals, organizations, or government, to bring to fruition for all Americans, the enjoyment of all the privileges of citizenship spelled out in our Constitution.

I am firmly on record as believing that every citizen—of every race and creed—deserves to enjoy equal civil rights and liberties, for there can be no such citizen in a democracy as a half-free citizen.

I should say here that we have much reason to be proud of the progress our people are making in mutual understanding—the chief buttress of human and civil rights. Steadily we are moving closer to the goal of fair and equal treatment of citizens without regard to race or color.[3]

This progress, I am confident, will continue. And it is gifted persons such as yourself, born out of the crucible of the struggle for personal dignity and achievement, who will help lead the way towards the goals we seek.[4] *Sincerely*

[1] Jackie Robinson, the first African-American baseball player in the U.S. major leagues, had played for the Brooklyn Dodgers from 1947 through 1956. He would be elected to the Baseball Hall of Fame in 1962. Robinson had written on May 13 (same file as document) in response to Eisenhower's remarks to the Summit Meeting of Negro Leaders in Washington on May 12, 1958 (see *Public Papers of the Presidents: Eisenhower, 1958*, pp. 391–92). White House aide E. Frederic Morrow may have helped prepare Eisenhower's letter (see E. Frederic Morrow, *Black Man in the White House* [New York, 1963], pp. 218–19).

[2] Eisenhower had said that every American "must have respect for the law. He must know that he is equal before the law. He must have respect for the courts. He must have respect for others. He must make perfectly certain that he can, in every single kind of circumstance, respect himself. In such problems as this, there are no revolutionary cures. They are evolutionary." Eisenhower had cited the integration of the armed forces and the federal government as evidence that progress had been made, but he also urged "patience and forbearance" because the solution to these "human problems" would require "better and more profound education" rather than new laws. Robinson had written that when he heard Eisenhower call for "patience," he had "felt like standing up and saying, 'Oh no! Not again.'" "I respectfully remind you sir," he wrote, "that we have been the most patient of all people. When you said we must have self-respect, I wondered how we could have self-respect and remain patient considering the treatment accorded us through the years."

[3] Robinson had said that by his constant calls for "forbearance," Eisenhower "unwittingly crush[ed] the spirit of freedom in Negroes" and had given "hope to those pro-segregation leaders like Governor Faubus who would take from us even those freedoms we now enjoy." The President's personal experience with Governor Faubus should have been "proof enough that forbearance and not eventual integration is the goal the pro-segregation leaders seek."

[4] Robinson had called on the President to make "an unequivocal statement backed up by action such as you demonstrated you could take last fall" [*i.e.*, sending troops to Little Rock] to "let it be known that America is determined to provide—in the near future—for Negroes—the freedoms we are entitled to under the constitution."

Robinson would reply on June 10 (same file as document). He was "very pleased" with Eisenhower's letter, but was still concerned about "the part 17 million loyal Negro Americans can play in bringing about equality for all Americans." He asked that the President consider meeting with Negro leaders: "Unfortunately, too many Negro leaders and Negro masses, misinterpret your statement about patience. They consider that you favor patience alone rather than patience backed up when necessary with law enforcement." A meeting with "responsible Negro leadership" would "help clarify and advance the cause of equal rights and . . . thus eliminate some of the unfavorable propaganda used by our enemies abroad." For developments see no. 784.

To Maurice Hubert Stans   *June 4, 1958*

Memorandum for the Director of the Bureau of the Budget: Regarding HR
1466. In the cited bill the Board of Commissioners of the District
of Columbia recommended disapproval. The Bureau of the Budget
recommended approval.[1]

This is the last day for action. I have no time nor opportunity to
argue its soundness in principle.[2] My instant reaction is that the
Board of Commissioners was absolutely correct and that you were
wrong.

Because of the doubt in my mind and because I would rather
make a mistake on the part of mercy rather than on the side of
harshness, I have signed the bill. Another reason is that only a small
amount was involved.

At some future opportunity I want to talk to you about the matter.[3]

[1] H.R. 1466 directed the Secretary of the Treasury to pay, out of District of Columbia funds, the sum of $159.87 to a physician from Brooklyn, New York. The sum rep-
resented reimbursement to the doctor for repairing his automobile, which was damaged while being towed from an illegal parking space at the direction of the District's
Metropolitan Police Department in September 1954. En route to the impounding
lot, a bolt connecting the automobile to the tow truck pulled loose, causing the car
to strike the rear of the tow truck, damaging the front bumper and grille. The District's Board of Commissioners agreed that the reimbursement sought was consistent
with the damage sustained but held that the District of Columbia was not liable. Congress, however, concluded that relief should be granted because the automobile was
under the control of the District of Columbia at the time of the accident (*U.S. Statutes
at Large*, vol. 72, pt. 2 [1958], p. A33, and *Congressional Record*, 85th Cong., 2d sess.,
1958, pt. 16:834).
[2] The bill (Private Law 409), introduced and referred to the House Committee on
the Judiciary on January 3, 1957, had been presented to the President on May 23.
The Constitution allows the President ten days (excepting Sundays) to approve a bill
or return it to the House with his objections.
[3] The President would meet with Stans on June 16.

728   *EM, AWF, Administration Series*

To William Pierce Rogers   *June 4, 1958*
Personal

Dear Bill: The attached telegram does not mean much to me except
that old friends of my boyhood are very anxious to acquire a Federal facility that seems to be planned for the region.[1] Will you have
the matter studied and give me your conclusions?

I can see no reason why my old home town could not have some such recognition, assuming other considerations to be equal. On the other hand, I would certainly not urge anything that would compel additional costs on the Treasury.[2]

With warm regard, *As ever*

[1] On June 2 Henry B. Jameson, editor and general manager of the *Abilene Reflector-Chronicle* since 1955, had written Eisenhower about the Abilene Chamber of Commerce's bid for a federal youth center that the Bureau of Prisons proposed to build in the midwest. Jameson said that Eisenhower's "loyal friends" had guarded against seeking favors, but in this case Abilene wanted a federal facility that would benefit its economy and bolster community growth.

[2] On June 11 Attorney General Rogers would reply that although Congress had appropriated funds for planning both a youth guidance center and a new maximum security prison, no decision had been made on the sites because Congress had not authorized construction. The Bureau of the Budget had not approved the projects for Fiscal Year 1959, but seemed "kindly disposed" to approving them for Fiscal Year 1960. Rogers had spoken to the Director of Federal Prisons, who advised that the representatives of Abilene should communicate their views to him as soon as possible. Thomas E. Stephens, Secretary to the President, would pass this information to Jameson on June 20 (see also Whitman to Stephens, June 15, 1958). All correspondence is in WHCF/GF 133-A.

The federal government would not place any correctional facility in Abilene. In February 1959 the Administration would select 1200 acres at Crab Orchard Lake, a national wildlife refuge in the Marion-Herrin-Carbondale area of southern Illinois, for the site of a new federal prison. The U.S. Penitentiary in Marion, Illinois, would open in April 1964 (see *Congressional Quarterly Almanac*, vol. XV, *1959*, pp. 331–33; *New York Times*, Feb. 7, May 11, 27, June 24, July 2, 14, 1959, Apr. 9, 1960, Jan. 20, 1961, July 15, Oct. 4, Dec. 19, 1962, and Nov. 17, 1963).

729   *EM, AWF, Dulles-Herter Series*

To JOHN FOSTER DULLES   *June 5, 1958*

Dear Foster: Late this afternoon I hurriedly dictated a draft of a possible answer to President Kubitschek, which is enclosed. I believe we should send him a reply at the earliest moment.[1]

I am delighted that he has seized the initiative in this matter and I think it provides a favorable portent for the future. That is the reason I should like personally to get off a reply as soon as possible.

At the same time I realize that you will be responsible for carrying on the negotiations and bringing about anything constructive.

I have no pride of authorship whatsoever about the attached draft. Its sole purpose is to get something down on paper.[2] *As ever*

[1] Brazilian President Kubitschek's letter was prompted by what he called the "aggressions and vexations" Vice-President Nixon had experienced on his recent trip to

South America. Although most South Americans had deplored the conduct of a factious minority, he wrote, "those disagreeable events . . . have nevertheless imparted an inescapable impression that we misunderstand each other on this Continent." Anti-American propagandists were now claiming that there was "incompatibility and even enmity between the free countries of the American community" (Kubitschek to Eisenhower, May 28, 1958, AWF/I: Brazil; see also Ann Whitman memorandum, June 5, 1958, AWF/AWD; State, *Foreign Relations, 1958–1960*, vol. V, *American Republics*, pp. 676–79; and Rabe, *Eisenhower and Latin America*, p. 110. On Nixon's trip see no. 711).

[2] Secretary Dulles would suggest that Assistant Secretary of State for Inter-American Affairs Roy R. Rubottom, Jr., personally deliver Eisenhower's letter. This would not only strengthen the reply, Dulles said, but would allow Rubottom to explore Kubitschek's ideas. Eisenhower agreed but told Dulles that discussions should include a wide range of subjects and not just focus on the Communist threat (Telephone conversation, Eisenhower and Dulles, June 6, 1958, AWF/D and Dulles Papers, Telephone Conversations). For Eisenhower's response to Kubitschek see the following document.

730   *EM, AWF, International Series:*
Brazil

To Juscelino Kubitschek de Oliveira   *June 5, 1958*

Dear Mr. President: This morning your Ambassador delivered to me the letter you wrote under date of May 28th.[1] I found it intensely interesting.

To my mind you have described accurately both the existing situation and the desirability of corrective action. I am delighted, therefore, that you have taken the initiative in this matter.

While Your Excellency did not suggest any specific program to improve Pan American understanding, it seems to me that our two governments should consult together as soon as possible with a view to approaching other members of the Pan American community, and starting promptly on measures that would produce throughout the continent a reaffirmation of devotion to Pan Americanism, and better planning in promoting the common interests and welfare of our several countries. There is a wide range of subjects to be discussed and explored, including for example, the problem of implementing more fully the Declaration of Solidarity of the Tenth Inter-American Conference held in Caracas in 1954.[2]

Because I deem this matter so important I am instructing Mr. Roy Richard Rubottom, Jr., Assistant Secretary of State for Inter-American Affairs, to deliver my letter to you personally in Rio de Janeiro, to explore with you further your thinking on these matters. Your thoughts and ideas thus obtained at first hand can be the subject of further consultation through normal diplomatic channels, preparatory to a later visit to Brazil by the Secretary of State. With your concurrence, Mr. Rubottom will make final arrangement with your government for the timing of Secretary Dulles' visit.[3]

With assurance of my highest consideration, and with best wishes for the continued well-being of Your Excellency and of the Brazilian people, I remain *Sincerely*

[1] For President Kubitschek's letter, delivered by Brazilian Ambassador Erani do Amaral Peixoto, see the preceding document.

[2] The State Department added the last sentence of this paragraph to Eisenhower's original draft (see Draft of Letter to the President of Brazil, June 5, 1958, AWF/D). For background on the Caracas Conference see Galambos and van Ee, *The Middle Way*, no. 568.

[3] After Dulles had discussed this letter and its delivery with Eisenhower, State Department officials substituted this paragraph for one in the President's original draft. Eisenhower's original read: "For our part we will be quite ready through normal diplomatic channels to cooperate with you in such consultations in order that we may jointly approach others interested and quickly bring about a counter force against the aggressive thrusts of Communists, who are always inimical to each of our governments and to our peoples" (see Howe to Goodpaster, June 6, 1958, AWF/I: Brazil).

After receiving Eisenhower's letter on June 10, Kubitschek would tell Rubottom that his initiative was not designed to consider U.S.-Brazilian relations but to strengthen Pan-Americanism. He proposed a meeting of the heads of the American states and gave Rubottom an aide-memoire detailing his ideas for consultations. Dulles would tell Eisenhower that Kubitschek's memorandum would be answered through diplomatic channels and that the U.S. ambassador would encourage bilateral consultations pending Dulles's trip to Brazil in August (Dulles to Eisenhower, June 20, 1958, AWF/I: Brazil; and State, *Foreign Relations, 1958–1960*, vol. V, *American Republics*, pp. 679–83, 685–88). For developments see no. 967.

731   *EM, AWF, Administration Series*

To William Pierce Rogers   *June 5, 1958*

Dear Bill: Many thanks for your letter concerning two recent decisions by the Supreme Court on cases involving labor unions. I much appreciate your thoughtfulness, and I hope, if it does not involve too much of a burden on you, that you will continue to send me brief summaries of actions in which you know I have a special interest.[1]

With warm regard, *As ever*

P.S. I found this morning at the Legislative meeting that there is very sharp difference of opinion on the so-called "Pre-emptive" bill. In these troublesome days it is very hard to keep our leadership all on the same track. I think you better come talk to me about this matter.[2]

[1] Attorney General Rogers had summarized the two cases in his letter of June 4 (AWF/A). In *United Automobile Workers* v. *Russell,* a worker had sued the union because he was prohibited from entering the workplace by mass picketing and threats of violence. The court held for the plaintiff. In *International Association of Machinists* v. *Gonzales,* a worker's union membership was reinstituted following what was held to be unlawful expulsion. In both cases the Court had based its ruling on the finding that since Congress had not completely preempted the field of labor legislation, state governments were allowed to act to protect workers' rights against union infringement. Rogers noted that the two decisions were "very significant and may have considerable effect on union activity. They also are a partial answer to some of the critics of the Court who contend that the Court is legislating by interpreting federal laws in the manner which incorrectly supersedes state laws. Now the attack on the Court is coming from the unions."

[2] Eisenhower would meet with Rogers the following day to discuss H.R. 3, the federal preemption doctrine bill (June 6, 1958, AWF/AWD). Inspired by congressional dissatisfaction with Supreme Court decisions since 1954, and in particular with the recent decision setting aside the conviction of a Pennsylvania Communist, the bill sought to limit the Court's right to strike down state laws under the doctrine of federal legislative preemption (for background see no. 689). That doctrine was based on the provision of the U.S. Constitution that established federal law as the "supreme law of the land." Federal law thus superseded state law when Congress stated an intention to take over a given field of legislation, when there was a direct conflict between a federal and a state law, and when congressional intention to preempt a field of legislation could be inferred, even though it had not been specified by Congress (preemption by implication). H.R. 3 barred the "preemption by implication" doctrine and stated that no act of Congress should be construed as indicating congressional intent to bar state legislation on the same subject unless Congress so specified or unless there was a direct and irreconcilable conflict between the state and federal law. It also specified that no act of Congress already passed should be construed as indicating congressional intent to bar states from passing laws punishing subversive activities against the federal or state governments (see *Congressional Quarterly Almanac,* vol. XIV, *1958,* pp. 289–92; see also *New York Times,* July 16, 17, 18, 1958). The House would pass the measure on July 17, but on August 21 the Senate would recommit it to the Judiciary Committee, effectively killing the bill.

732   *EM, AWF, Name Series*

TO MILTON STOVER EISENHOWER   *June 5, 1958*

Dear Milton: In our spare time let's set up a speech-writing business. Somewhat to my surprise our joint effort on the Annapolis talk seems to have met with a pretty good reception. At any rate I thought you would be interested in the attached editorial from the New York Daily News; much of the credit for not being a "bore" belongs, of course, to you.[1] *As ever*

¹ Eisenhower had given the commencement address at the U.S. Naval Academy on June 4, 1958 (*Public Papers of the Presidents: Eisenhower, 1958*, pp. 450–56). He had told the graduates that their most important function was one of "helping prevent war and of furthering a just peace" and offered them a list of ways to make themselves "crusaders for peace." The President's call to "keep up to date on the principles and techniques of effective management" seemed to support the Administration's defense reorganization plan (see no. 716). The President had warned that outmoded military management and organization was "as dangerous to our nation as obsolescence in weaponry" (*New York Times*, June 5, 1958). The *New York Daily News* had praised Eisenhower's speech, saying that while most commencement addresses were "pretty boring productions," the President had "performed the near-miracle of delivering a commencement address which was not boring and was loaded with excellent advice and counsel for young people—any young people anywhere."

The President's brother would respond the following day (AWF/N). He would thank Eisenhower for "sharing the success of the Naval Academy talk with me." He had noticed "that every press story carried your thought that war is now 'preposterously and mutually annihilative.' Sometimes a verbal mouthful is quotable."

733   *EM, AWF, Administration Series*

To Arthur Frank Burns   *June 6, 1958*
Personal

Dear Arthur: Thank you for your letter. I comment briefly on its final paragraph. I assure you that I put a very heavy weight on tax *reform*. The only question I raise is regarding your phrase "I believe politically realizable." I cannot tell you how many Senators and Representatives I have talked to on this subject. I yet have to encounter anyone who believes that we could initiate a well-conceived program and get it passed. The general consensus is that any bill that would get through both Houses would be so loaded down with indefensible and illogical proposals that a veto would be practically compulsory.¹

If we can possibly get the renewals on the corporate and excise taxes accomplished promptly and without crippling amendments, we could then have more breathing space if we should come to conclude that an effort toward some reform should be undertaken.²

Just one thought on your first paragraph in which you suggested that a more limited reform in the capital gains tax would seem more desirable than the one I previously outlined in a former letter to you. My feeling on this is that any reform would be an advance. I was merely trying to think of something that might be more palatable for the politically minded.³

With warm regard, *As ever*

[1] Burns had concluded his letter (June 2, 1958, AWF/A) by saying that he understood fully and shared Eisenhower's concern for fiscal soundness. "If there is any difference between us, it may merely be this: that I put a heavy weight, perhaps a heavier weight than you do, on the power of well-conceived (and I believe politically realizable) tax reforms to energize the economy and thereby to raise the tax base."
[2] On June 5 the House of Representatives had passed a bill extending for one year corporate tax rates, while repealing certain transportation excise taxes including those on coal and oil. Amendments proposing cuts in excise taxes, personal income taxes, and taxes on small business had been defeated. Corporate income tax rates were kept constant at 52 percent. The President would sign the bill (H.R. 12695) into law on June 30 (*Congressional Quarterly Almanac*, vol. XIV, *1958*, pp. 145–46). In August Congress would also pass H.R. 7125, the first comprehensive administrative and technical revision of the general excise tax provisions since 1932 (*ibid.*, pp. 263–67).
[3] See no. 698.

734   *EM, WHCF, Official File 124*

To John Michael Budinger   *June 6, 1958*
Personal

Dear Jack: I quite agree with your feeling that unless there is intelligent action taken with respect to the management-labor problem in this country, we are going to suffer from very serious consequences. By all odds the preferable method of solving the problem would be voluntary action of labor leaders and of business executives and groups. Adequate and just laws would be difficult to write, even more difficult to enact.[1]

As to whether or not an anti-trust law could be so devised as to keep the power of labor leaders within proper bounds and yet not clash with the inherent rights of individuals is something that I would not even attempt to answer without long study and after a great deal of conferring with the legal fraternity.

No one could more fully share your dislike of socialism than I.[2] While I feel that we have not yet come to the threshold of such a result, your letter has suggested to me the desirability of making some very serious studies both in the Labor and Justice Departments in order to see what, if anything, *government* should do. With this once decided, we should then agree how things should be done.[3]

Thanks for your letter.

With all the best, *As ever*

[1] In his June 2 letter (same file as document), Bankers Trust executive Budinger had praised Eisenhower's speech to the American Management Association dinner on May 20, 1958 (see nos. 675 and 691). Budinger called upon the President to intro-

duce legislation that would subject the labor unions to the same antitrust laws as the business institutions. "Unless and until present conditions are corrected and stabilized, whereby labor and business are subject to the same laws and rules governing our free enterprise system, the present parade of mergers and amalgamations—many of them necessitated by survival—will result in a limited number of large companies controlling substantially all the output and locking horns with one or two powerful labor unions," he wrote. "Inevitably this must result in the government controlling prices and wages, and of course squeezing the life blood out of capital." See also no. 627.

[2] Budinger had argued that failure to control the labor unions could lead to socialism, "and under a weak or unscrupulous national leadership we would be ripe for some form of Communism after our moral fabric had been perforated by a loss of spirit because of the failure of the flesh and blood."

[3] For developments see no. 905.

735   *EM, AWF, Dulles-Herter Series*

To Memorandum for Files   *June 9, 1958*

This morning I noted in the papers a report that an American helicopter was down in East Germany. Some difficult[y] was being incurred in our attempts to get the people back because of Soviet insistence that we deal with East Germany, and our insistence that we wanted to deal with the Soviets because we do not recognize East Germany.[1]

Having forgotten the incident until about 12 noon, I called the Secretary of State on the telephone to remind him that under somewhat similar circumstances we had dealt directly with Red China, which we do not recognize.[2] When I had the Secretary on the phone, he remarked that my call was a remarkable coincidence because he was just reaching for the phone to call his staff to remind them of the same circumstance and to express his opinion that we should not be too stiff-necked in our attitude. To do so might easily create a situation that could bring about a prolonged stalemate such as we have had in China.[3]

[1] Eight Army officers and a sergeant were detained after navigational difficulties had forced their helicopter to land in Zwickau, near the Czechoslovakian border on June 7. Negotiations to return the men were being conducted through the U.S. mission in Potsdam in order to deal directly with the Soviet military command for East Germany (*New York Times*, June 9, 1958).

[2] Eisenhower had told Dulles that he hoped we would not put ourselves in a position to have to back down "and lose face about it" (Telephone conversation, June 9, 1958, Dulles Papers, Telephone Conversations). For background on the 1953 downing of a U.S. plane over North Korea and the detention in Communist China of eleven airmen see Galambos and van Ee, *The Middle Way*, no. 1200.

[3] On the following day Dulles would tell Eisenhower that the Czech government had indicated that the East Germans were prepared to communicate with U.S. officials regarding the matter. Eisenhower repeated his desire to avoid "any stiff-necked attitude" and told Dulles that a delay would make a "cause celebre" out of the matter when there was no reason for it (Telephone conversation, June 10, 1958, AWF/D). Dulles would later tell newsmen that even though the standard procedure was to deal with the Soviets, the United States would not "stand on ceremony" where American lives were concerned. "When you have people kidnapped, you deal with the kidnapper," he said, although he denied that such negotiations would constitute recognition of East Germany (*U.S. Department of State Bulletin* 38, no. 992 [June 30, 1958], 1087).

Both the Soviet Army command and East German government officials would continue to maintain their position, forcing the International Red Cross to broker an agreement that would allow their release of the Americans on July 19 (Dulles to Eisenhower, June 26, 1958, AWF/D-H; and *New York Times*, July 20, 1958).

736   *EM, AWF, Gettysburg Series*

To Arthur Seymour Nevins   *June 9, 1958*

Dear Arthur: Attached is the original and a photostat of the registration certificate of Brockmere 10.[1] I notice that there is no mention of a third interest—just the names of the Eisenhower Farms and Brandy Rock Farms appear, a partnership in which I take a great deal of satisfaction.[2]

Admiral Strauss has told me that he has already put up seven thousand bales of hay, with his first crop in the barn. While they have had a considerable amount of rain, he has had a great deal of success in curing hay quickly by the use of a machine which is attached to the mower. This machine picks up the hay and crushes the stems thoroughly. This makes it possible for rapid curing in a single day. They cut one morning and bale the next.

I asked him whether the machine was an expensive piece of equipment and he said "less than $1,000."

This may be something to be examined; you could, of course, drop a note to Admiral Strauss and ask him the name of the machine if you are really interested.[3]

I have been thinking that I might take an afternoon to see Admiral Strauss' farm. If I do so, any time in the near future, that might be a fine time for Bob Hartley—and you if you should like to come—to meet me at his farm and see the new bull. If any such opportunity occurs, I shall of course get in contact with you at once.[4]
As ever

---

[1] For background on the herdsire, a gift to Eisenhower from Admiral Strauss out of his Brandy Rock Farms herd, see no. 697.

[2] On the third interest, the Allen-Byars partnership, see no. 70.

[3] Nevins would reply (June 11, AWF/Gettysburg) that he had leased the machine and had been "using it with good results. . . ." Eisenhower would visit his farm June 13–15.

[4] As it turned out, Nevins and Hartley, Eisenhower's herdsmen, would not accompany the President to the Strauss farm in Brandy Station, Virginia, on June 28 (see also Eisenhower to Mrs. Lewis Strauss, June 30, 1958, AWF/D, and Nevins to Eisenhower, Allen, Byars and Jones, July 23, 1958, AWF/Gettysburg).

Strauss would send a snapshot of Brockmere 10 in June 1959. By that time he had been bred to several cows and heifers on the Eisenhower Farms (Strauss to Eisenhower, June 18, 1959; and Nevins to Whitman, June 29, 1959, AWF/Gettysburg; see also the related material in *ibid.*).

In July 1959 Strauss would transfer to the President's name a one-third interest in another bull (see Whitman to Nevins, July 15, 1959, and Nevins to Whitman, July 16, 1959, *ibid.*).

737   *EM, AWF, International Series:*
                                                        Khrushchev

To Nikita Sergeyevich Khrushchev   *June 10, 1958*

Dear Mr. Chairman:[1] I have your letter of May thirtieth and am glad to note you have accepted my proposal that technical experts meet to study the possibility of detecting violations of a possible agreement on suspension of nuclear tests.[2] These talks would be undertaken without commitment as to the final decision on the relationship of nuclear test suspension to other more important disarmament measures I have proposed.

I propose that these discussions begin on or about July first in Geneva. While we appreciate your offer to hold these talks in Moscow, we believe that Geneva would be preferable from our standpoint, and note that it would be acceptable to you. The Swiss Government has agreed to this location.[3]

With respect to participation I suggest that initially at least we adhere to the concept expressed in your letter of May 9, 1958, where you say, "the Soviet Government agrees to having both sides designate experts."[4] As indicated in my letter of May 24, 1958, our side at this discussion will include experts from the United States, United Kingdom, France and possibly from other countries which have specialists with a thorough knowledge in the field of detecting nuclear tests, and we note that you have no objection to this. With regard to the inclusion on your side of experts from Czechoslovakia and Poland, we have no objection to this. With respect to experts of nationalities not identified with either side, we have no objection in principle to their joining later in the discussions if it is agreed during the course of the talks that this is necessary or useful from the point of view of the purposes of the technical talks.

It may be possible for the experts to produce a final report within three or four weeks as you suggest. However, I believe that there should be enough flexibility in our arrangements to allow a little longer time if it is needed to resolve the complex technical issues involved.

I propose that further arrangements for the meeting be handled through normal diplomatic channels.[5] *Sincerely*

[1] Eisenhower approved the State Department draft of this letter, "subject to coordination with the British, French, and NATO" (see Dulles, Memorandum of Conversation, June 2, 1958, Dulles Papers, White House Memoranda Series; see also Herter to Eisenhower, May 31, 1958, Dulles-Herter Papers, Chronological Series).
[2] For background see no. 712.
[3] Khrushchev had told Eisenhower that the Soviets preferred that the conference be held in Moscow and assured him that they would provide all the facilities necessary for the experts to conduct their work (AWF/I: Khrushchev).
[4] For Khrushchev's May 9 letter see no. 712.
[5] For developments see no. 822.

738   *Hagerty Papers*

To James Campbell Hagerty   *June 10, 1958*
Memorandum

I have your inquiry regarding the story reported to LIFE by General William H. Wilbur. My suggestion is that you tell Mr. Wilson that the story should *not* be published.[1]

The general tenor of the story is correct, but there are two important differences from actual facts. First, the Medal of Honor was not "offered" to me. In one or two instances the Medal of Honor has been awarded to individuals for accomplishments that did not involve "action against the enemy and gallantry over and beyond the call of duty."

In this pattern a message was brought to me by a responsible officer that perhaps a suitable notice of the first successful Allied venture would be the presentation to the commander of the Medal of Honor. (The officer who brought me the message was General Walter Bedell Smith.) The suggestion was never officially couched as an "offer" at the time. Since my reaction was completely negative, nothing further was ever done.[2]

Another inaccuracy in the story is the statement that the incident took place at the close of the war. Actually it took place late in 1942.[3]

I can well understand that when General Wilbur visited me the incident might have come up, since just at about that time he himself was awarded the Medal of Honor and we were unquestionably reminiscing about the incidents of November and December, 1942.

In view of the fact that there has never been any kind of official record of this incident, and there is no documentation of any kind concerning it, I consider that it would be very unwise to mention it. Consequently I suggest

(a) that by note to General Wilbur you tell him that informal and personal conversations with friends should never be published by anybody; and that while the tenor of his letter is accurate, because the whole matter was handled on an informal and unofficial basis there are no grounds for treating the original suggestion as an "offer." You might also say that I have never mentioned this incident to more than a few personal friends and that I deplore any suggestion that it appear in a publication of any kind.

(b) I suggest that you tell Mr. Wilson that the story is not wholly accurate and I would be very embarrassed if it should ever appear in publication in any form, and that I make a personal request that he refrain from so doing.[4]

---

[1] Donald Malcolm Wilson (B.A. Yale 1948), Chief Washington Correspondent for LIFE magazine, had written to Hagerty about a story he had received from William Hale Wilbur, warden of Cook County Jail in Chicago since 1950 (for background see *Eisenhower Papers*, vols. I–IX, XII–XIII). Wilbur had written that at the end of World War II Eisenhower had been offered the Congressional Medal of Honor, but had refused it because he had "never performed any act or acts of heroism which the award of the Medal of Honor requires." Wilson had asked Hagerty to "confirm or deny the facts" in Wilbur's story. Wilson also wanted to know, if the facts were true, who had offered Eisenhower the medal and when (see Wilbur to Wilson, June 2, 1958, and Wilson to Hagerty, June 3, 1958).

[2] The first Allied combined offensive—the invasion of North Africa—began on November 8, 1942. Smith and his staff had arrived in Gibraltar on November 7. Wilbur had also taken part in the landings (see Eisenhower, *Crusade in Europe*, and Chandler, *War Years*, no. 509 and *passim*, vols. I–V).

During World War II Eisenhower had opposed conferring the Medal of Honor to General Douglas MacArthur because, in his opinion, MacArthur had not demonstrated the sort of valor in close combat that normally was associated with the award (James, *The Years of MacArthur*, vol. II, *1941–1945* [1975], pp. 129–33, 844–45, n. 32; see also Chandler, *War Years*, no. 274).

[3] Wilbur said he had discussed the award with General Eisenhower at his SHAPE headquarters in 1952.

[4] In an undated memorandum Hagerty would write: "This has been done. Life will not use it." All correspondence is in Hagerty Papers.

To HAROLD MACMILLAN *June 11, 1958*
Top secret

Dear Harold: Your letter of May sixth suggested that the procedure for the conduct of United States air operations over the United Kingdom which involve hazardous cargo be standardized with U.S. requirements for similar U.K. operations over U.S. territory.[1]

I have been informed that the technical safety conferences between representatives of our countries have been quite successful in establishing a mutual understanding of our respective safety rules and procedures while conducting air operations involving hazardous cargoes.[2]

The standardization of procedures seems to fall beyond the intended scope of the safety conferences. There was some discussion of the individual countries procedures in this forum. We might, with additional instructions to our conferees, utilize the channels and contacts that have been established for conferences on the standardization of the flight procedures and your requirements for information. In the previous conferences, the United States representatives were the Cmdr, 3rd Air Force; Cmdr, 7th Air Division and representatives from the U.S. Embassy, London.[3]

If you agree, I will make the necessary arrangements for the above United States representatives to re-establish contact with your designated representatives to determine what additional operational information you feel the United Kingdom requires to make consistent the United States-United Kingdom procedures involving the transport of hazardous cargo.[4]

With warm regard, *As ever*

[1] For Macmillan's May 6 letter and background on the transportation of hazardous cargo over the United Kingdom see no. 686.

[2] There are no documents regarding these conferences in AWF.

[3] The commander of the Third Air Force was Major General Ernest Moore; the commander of the Seventh Air Division was Major General William H. Blanchard.

[4] Concurring with Eisenhower's suggestion, Macmillan would say that British representation would be the same as it was at the previous conferences, except for eliminating representatives from the Home Office and other departments that were more concerned with safety issues (Macmillan to Eisenhower, July 4, 1958, AWF/I: Macmillan).

To Harold Macmillan   *June 12, 1958*
Secret

Dear Harold: Quite naturally I am highly pleased that you found your visit interesting and informative.[1] Frankly it was the kind of international meeting, especially between ourselves, that I prize so highly. It is the kind that, for these past five years, I've hoped might become routine. But my frequently-presented arguments about the value of agenda-less visits have always been met by objections from others, from both sides of the water, who seem so plainly to see the risks and difficulties. I share the hope with you that we may find a way of repeating this experience.

With respect to your note of June tenth to which you attached a memorandum of specific observations or suggestions, I have already written to you about the plan for concerting the programs of our two governments in the matter of carrying nuclear weapons.[2]

As far as the other specific points you mention—Exchange Officers, Security Clearance for British Controlled Firms, and Scientific and Defense Cooperation—I shall have these matters examined with a view to sending along to you the available information.[3]

Trusting you have a pleasant journey home—and with warm regard, *As ever*

[1] After delivering the commencement address at De Pauw University in Greencastle, Indiana, Macmillan had arrived in Washington on June 9 for informal talks with Eisenhower and Secretary Dulles. Among the subjects discussed were the situation in the Middle East, relations with Egyptian President Nasser and French President de Gaulle, the British plans for Cyprus, the defense of Southeast Asia, and the proposed amendments to the Atomic Energy Act (see State, *Foreign Relations, 1958–1960*, vol. VII, pt. 1, *Western European Integration and Security; Canada*, pp. 810–18; see also Macmillan to Eisenhower, June 11, 1958, AWF/I: Macmillan). On June 11 Macmillan had left for a two-day visit to Ottawa. Eisenhower had asked the State Department to deliver this letter to the prime minister in the Canadian capital (see Whitman to Howe, June 11, 1958, *ibid.*).

[2] See the preceding document.

[3] The value of an arrangement to exchange officers had diminished, Macmillan told Eisenhower, because the knowledge of nuclear equipment possessed by U.S. officers had to be kept from British officers. Some posts had to be redesignated as liaison rather than exchange. The British hoped that U.S. officials would review the restrictions as soon as legislation amending the Atomic Energy Act was passed.

Macmillan had also said that firms owned by the British were handicapped in bidding for contracts in the United States because of Defense Department regulations denying them security clearances. He asked that the new and more lenient regulations "be brought into force without delay."

After the Eisenhower-Macmillan meetings of October 1957, two study groups had been established to make recommendations in the fields of nuclear cooperation and military defense. Progress had been hampered by the difficulty of assembling suit-able experts, Macmillan told Eisenhower, and no group had been able to put for ward specific proposals. He hoped that things would move forward, "now that the machinery has been set up and has begun to turn" (Macmillan to Eisenhower, June 10, 1958, PREM 11/2316; see also *U.S. Department of State Bulletin* 37, no. 959 [November 11, 1957], 739–41; on the Atomic Energy Act amendments see no. 718).

Following consultations among the Joint Chiefs of Staff, the military departments, and other Defense Department agencies, Eisenhower would tell Macmillan in a letter drafted by the State Department that satisfactory progress was taking place in each of these areas. Although the changes in the Atomic Energy Act would facilitate the exchange of information, he said, improvement in the exchange of officers might come slowly because of problems in control and access to the information exchanged. Eisenhower added that the Defense Department had made progress with respect to security clearances for British firms, and that he had requested that every effort be made to speed the activities of the subcommittees working on atomic cooperation (Eisenhower to Macmillan, Sept. 24, 1958, AWF/I:Macmillan and PREM 11/2316).

741   *EM, WHCF, Official File 23-D-2*

To FRANKLIN G. FLOETE   *June 12, 1958*

Dear Mr. Floete: It is good to learn of the advancing work of the National Historical Publications Commission. This Commission has made splendid progress toward enlarging the basic stock of source materials of American history.[1]

Written history is as important to civilization as human memory to an individual. The free world must have histories written by men and women in search of the truth—not by those seeking to rewrite the records of the past to their own advantage. This underlines the essential need of a broad and incorruptible supply of our Nation's documentary resources.

Incidentally, I have asked the Director of the United States Information Agency to consider placing in our overseas libraries the documentary publications resulting from the Commission's work.[2] There is no better way to gain a true understanding of America's traditions and objectives than through a direct study of the writings of our national leaders and the records of our free institutions.

Please give my congratulations and best wishes to the members of the Commission and to the historical editors assembled in conference here next week. At that time, I want you to give special thanks to the sponsors and donors who are helping in this program.[3] *Sincerely*

[1] Floete (A.B. University of Wisconsin 1908; LL.B. Harvard 1912) had been appointed to head the General Services Administration following the resignation of Edmund

Mansure in 1956 (see no. 752). Floete had written White House Chief of Staff Adams on March 3 (same file as document) on behalf of the Chairman of the National Historical Publications Commission, who had requested a meeting with the President. Floete had reminded Governor Adams that in 1954 the Commission had given Eisenhower "a recommended national program for the publication of historical documents. The President warmly approved the program as one that would 'be of lasting benefit to all Americans.'" The Commission had supported publication projects covering the papers of Benjamin Franklin, John and John Quincy Adams, James Madison, and Alexander Hamilton, as well as a project for the publication of documents related to the ratification of the Constitution and the Bill of Rights. A draft of this letter was prepared by Wayne C. Grover, the Archivist of the United States. On Eisenhower's interest in the publication of presidential papers see Memorandum of Conference with the President, May 15, 1958, AWF/D.

[2] Arthur Larson was director of the United States Information Agency.

[3] Eisenhower's letter was read at a luncheon during the National Historical Publication Commission conference in New York on June 17, 1958 (*New York Times*, June 18, 1958).

742   *EM, AWF, Name Series*

To Louise Sondra Grieb Eisenhower   *June 12, 1958*

Dear Louise: You raise a question that has never before entered my head.[1] In thinking of the suggestion there are so many factors involved that I simply could not attempt to put them down in a letter. I am convinced, however, that the idea is not practical and I shall ask Colonel Schulz to telephone you and present the picture as I see it.[2]

Edgar, as the oldest living Eisenhower of our particular family, is now the family's head. I do not know what his own reaction to the matter will be, but I do think you should consult with him.[3]

So far as the presentation of any documents or mementos is concerned, I would think that should be a matter between you and the officers of the Museum.[4] From all I have heard about the scrapbook you have prepared, I am certain they would like to have it.[5]

With affectionate regard, *As ever*

[1] Arthur Eisenhower's widow had written on June 7 regarding the creation of a final resting place for her late husband at the Eisenhower Foundation (see Edgar Eisenhower to Milton Eisenhower, June 19, 1958). Arthur had died in January (see nos. 558 and 649). Mrs. Eisenhower's letter is not in EM.

[2] On June 16 Eisenhower's military aide Robert Schulz would telephone Louise Eisenhower. Refusing to discuss the matter with him, she asked, instead, for an appointment with the President (Note for Files, June 16, 1958). In a June 20 letter Schulz would remind her that only the President's parents were buried at the Abilene Cemetery; other family members were buried elsewhere. He also said he would send a

copy of Mrs. Eisenhower's letter and the President's reply to Edgar so that Edgar could correspond with her directly.

[3] In a letter to Milton Eisenhower, Edgar would say that although he disagreed with Louise's proposal, he would not give her an unsolicited opinion (June 19, 1958).

[4] Mrs. Eisenhower would tell the President on June 19 that she was "quite disturbed" because he seemed to miss the point of the proposal. She explained that she would not write to Edgar because the President's was the only opinion she desired. She added that she would not "pursue the matter further" even though it had been her understanding that the Foundation had been established "as a memorial for the achievements of the whole family." All correspondence is in AWF/N, Mrs. Arthur Eisenhower Corr.

The controversy would prompt the President to discuss his own plans. He "supposed" he would be buried in either Washington, West Point, or Denver. Eisenhower did not mention interment in Abilene as a possibility ([Ann Whitman] memorandum, June 24, 1958, AWF/D).

[5] The collection of Louise Eisenhower Papers consists of thirteen large scrapbooks covering the years 1941–1952. The items were donated to the Dwight D. Eisenhower Library in 1988 (Correspondence, H. L. Pankratz, Jan. 30, 1998, EP).

743   EM, WHCF,
                                       President's Personal File 472

To Freeman F. Gosden   June 12, 1958

Dear Freeman: To the other two musketeers I have ventured to present a bit of sound and exceedingly well-meant advice. In your case, of course, it would be presumptuous of me to make even so much as a suggestion. Rather, expressing my confidence in your reliability, wisdom and your keen awareness of the need for impeccable deportment when donning gray toppers and cutaways, I merely observe that it is to you I will look to make certain of the safety, sanity and security of your fellow hobos.[1]

Needless to say, from you I should like a complete report on the peregrinations of the wandering trio. Such details as favorite restaurants, dishes and race tips should be included. I should like to know also whether the fashions this year are blondes or brunets, tall or short, and have they ever learned to speak English? Incidentally, I hope that your report will be submitted through Jane—I am sure that she will make certain that you have omitted no lurid details.[2]

With warm regard, *As ever*

P.S. Actually, I have made arrangements with Jock Whitney to have your adventures in Britain recorded through the secret police and the United States Marines.[3]

[1] Gosden wrote and produced the "Amos 'n Andy" program. For background on his friendship with the President see *Eisenhower Papers*, vols. I–XVII. On June 14 Gosden,

Barry Leithead, and Clifford Roberts would travel to London on business (see Roberts to Eisenhower, May 30, 1958; Eisenhower to Roberts, June 4, 1958; Roberts to Eisenhower, June 13, 1958, all in AWF/N; see also Eisenhower to Leithead, June 12, 1958; and Leithead to Eisenhower, July 7, 1958, both in WHCF/PPF 305). On this same day Eisenhower advised Roberts to "stay out of dark alleys, the Black Market, and French taxicabs" (AWF/N).

[2] Gosden's wife was the former Jane Stoneham. On Gosden's report see no. 781.

[3] For developments see no. 757.

744   *EM, AWF, International Series: Turkey*

To ADNAN MENDERES   *June 13, 1958*
Cable. Secret

Dear Mr. Prime Minister: I am, of course, aware that our governments have been in communication concerning recent Cyprus developments, including the current violence on the Island.[1] In view of my great concern over the possible consequences of a failure to bring about a peaceful solution to this problem, and one which will not disrupt the very foundations of western defense to which both of our countries have made such a great contribution, I would like to share with you personally my own apprehensions.

The United States is not directly a party to the dispute, although we have endeavored to be of assistance to our friends in bringing about an amicable settlement. I believe that such a settlement is both possible and desirable, and I am confident you share with me views upon the overriding importance of letting nothing happen which will make it more difficult and which would bring about grave losses in terms of the type of cooperation among our allies which is vital to the whole free world. In the present situation emotions are running high and I fear that unless immediate and effective steps are taken to bring about a calmer situation one event, in Cyprus or elsewhere, might lead to another with ultimate effects unwanted and unwelcomed by all of us.

This matter is currently being considered by the North Atlantic Council. It is my fervent hope that the deliberations in the Council can lead to constructive measures which not only will contribute to a solution to the Cyprus problem itself but will immediately bring about a lessening of tensions and an improvement in the general atmosphere.[2]

I understand that proposals are now being formulated within the Council to accomplish this end.[3] While I do not yet know what their content will be, I do know the motivations which lie behind them, and I earnestly hope that when they are received you will on your part give them most serious consideration in the context of the great importance of finding some way out of the present impasse. I am confident that you will do so, Mr. Prime Minister, and that you will use your great influence to the end that a harmonious atmosphere will quickly be restored.

I know you agree that we should do everything to avoid placing in jeopardy the objective of peace and security for which our two governments and peoples have made such great sacrifices.[4]

With high regard, *Sincerely*

[1] For background on the Cyprus situation see nos. 78 and 488. Sir Hugh Foot had assumed the governorship of Cyprus on December 3, 1957, and within a month had told officials in the British Foreign and Colonial Offices that a long-term settlement of the Cyprus problem was not possible at that time. He recommended: a seven-year period of limited self-government for Cyprus under the sponsorship and protection of the British, self-determination on equal terms for both Greek and Turkish Cypriots at the end of this period; and the retention of British bases on the island. The British agreed to accept at any time any solution that had the support of the Greek and Turkish governments and the two communities on Cyprus. They also agreed to end the state of emergency on Cyprus and to release persons detained by British authorities. The Greek government gave qualified approval to the Foot Plan but rejected self-determination because it would result in partition of the island. The Turks rejected the plan, called for partition, and proposed that representatives from the Greek and Turkish governments meet to formulate a final disposition of the island.

Searching for an interim solution that would satisfy all parties, British Prime Minister Macmillan then proposed another seven-year period, when community assemblies and a ministerial council would deal with local problems on the island. During this time Great Britain would maintain sovereignty; however, the governments of Greece and Turkey would be represented on the ministerial council and would provide advice to the governors. Greek and Turkish Cypriots would become citizens of their respective countries as well as retaining British citizenship. In this way the British hoped to end the state of emergency in effect since November 1955 and eventually provide for shared responsibility (tridominium) on the island.

On June 7 mob violence had erupted on Cyprus after a bomb exploded outside the Turkish press office in Nicosia. Five days later Under Secretary Herter told Eisenhower that the Greek government was close to severing diplomatic relations with Turkey and withdrawing from NATO. The British proposals, Herter said, had "made both sides mad." He suggested that Eisenhower send messages to both countries urging restraint. Eisenhower had approved the draft of this letter and a similar one to Greek Prime Minister Konstatine Karamanlis but asked Herter to add something at the end of the messages to the effect that "the great sacrifices your people and ours have made for peace must not be lost" (State, *Foreign Relations, 1958–1960*, vol. X, pt. 1, *Eastern Europe Region; Soviet Union; Cyprus*, pp. 564–69, 591–92, 610–24, 641–42; see also Telephone conversation, Eisenhower and Herter, June 13, 1958, AWF/D; Ann Whitman memorandum, June 13, 1958, AWF/AWD; and Macmillan, *Riding the Storm*, pp. 665–70). For the message to Karamanlis see the following document.

[2] After hearing from representatives of the Greek and Turkish governments, the North Atlantic Council had recommended that a more active role be taken by NATO in the search for a solution. The council believed that further deterioration of Greek-Turkish relations could lead to armed conflict between the two countries, the collapse of NATO unity and its defense effort in Southern Europe, and a British with-

drawal from Cyprus (State, *Foreign Relations, 1958–1960,* vol. X, pt. 1, *Eastern Europe Region; Soviet Union; Cyprus,* pp. 624, 628–29).

[3] Council members would be hindered by the fact that Greece wanted bilateral talks only with the United Kingdom, and the Turks wanted a tripartite conference. Neither country would accept the British proposals as a basis for discussion (*ibid.,* pp. 672–75; see also NSC meeting minutes, June 20, 1958, AWF/NSC; and Goodpaster, Notes for Record, June 13, 20, 1958, AWF/D).

[4] In his reply (June 15) Menderes repeated his position that partition of the island offered the best chance for a peaceful solution. He would do his best to "calm down" the Turkish people, but, he said, it was "an extremely difficult course for governments to act against the justified feelings and emotions of public opinion" (State, *Foreign Relations, 1958–1960,* vol. X, pt. 1, *Eastern Europe Region; Soviet Union; Cyprus,* pp. 653–54).

Eisenhower would later ask Herter if the Turks could be removed from Cyprus and placed "in a better position elsewhere." When he learned that 20 percent of the island's inhabitants were Turks, Eisenhower said that ended the idea of resettlement, and "all we can do is pray" (Telephone conversation, Eisenhower and Herter, June 14, 1958, Dulles Papers, Telephone Conversations).

For developments see no. 872.

745   *EM, AWF, International Series:*
                                                                    Greece

TO KONSTANTINE KARAMANLIS   *June 13, 1958*
Cable. Secret

Dear Mr. Prime Minister: Ambassador Riddleberger has, of course, reported to me his conversations with you and Foreign Minister Averoff with respect to recent developments in the Cyprus question.[1] I am therefore fully aware of the deep concern that you have regarding the situation. I would like for you to know that I am also gravely concerned, particularly that the ramifications of this problem have been such as to impair relations among our valued friends and allies. The recent losses in life and property among the Cypriots of Greek origin have saddened all of us.

The United States wishes to cooperate fully in bringing about a tranquil atmosphere and in achieving progress toward a settlement of the Cyprus dispute itself. A consideration of vital importance in this whole affair is, of course, that the situation should not develop so that it would result in any permanent weakening of our alliances and collective security system which are so vital to the survival of free nations.

I have learned from Ambassador Riddleberger your observations concerning the possible effects of certain contingencies upon your Government's policies.[2] I fervently share the hope that such contingencies will not occur. I know that in the present situation the free world can count upon the statesmanship of yourself and other Greek leaders to see to it that developments do not result in any actions which might place in jeopardy the achievement of our common objectives upon which our common policies have been based, and for which our two governments and peoples have made such great sacrifices.

You may be sure that the United States is using its influence in seeking to avoid any occurrences in Cyprus or elsewhere which might exacerbate the situation.

I am happy that your Government has seen fit to bring the Cyprus question before the North Atlantic Council.[3] I understand that the Council is now deliberating the matter, and that there are in preparation suggestions as to what might be done constructively in the present circumstances. While I do not yet know the content of the proposals, I do know the motivations which lie behind them. I earnestly hope that you will give them most careful consideration and that no opportunity will be lost in achieving progress through this forum.[4]

With high regard, *Sincerely*

[1] State Department officials had drafted this message and a similar one to Turkish Prime Minister Adnan Menderes. For background on the Cyprus situation, the British proposals for an interim government on Cyprus, deliberations in the North Atlantic Council, and the letter to Menderes see the preceding document. Seeking to gain support for Macmillan's plan, James W. Riddleberger, U.S. Ambassador to Greece since March 1958, had met with Foreign Minister Evangelos Averoff-Tossizza on the preceding day. He had told Averoff that the British plan included a Greek majority on the administrative council and did not exclude eventual self determination—two provisions that should appeal to the Greek government. The most serious defect of the plan, Averoff maintained, was the legal power it gave Turkey over the government of Cyprus. It provided Turkish citizenship for Turkish Cypriots and gave the Turkish government a role in the creation of the government of Cyprus; no Greek government could accept those provisions. Averoff also told Riddleberger that his government believed that the United States was pro-Turkish. Although Greece would always have sentiments of gratitude and friendship for the United States, he said, on the Cyprus issue "it has been ill-treated in [a] manner which is politically unpleasant and morally unjustified" (State, *Foreign Relations, 1958–1960*, vol. X, pt. 1, *Eastern Europe Region; Soviet Union; Cyprus*, pp. 631–33).

[2] In an aide-mémoire handed to Riddleberger on this day, the Greek government had declared that if Turkish attacks on Greek Cypriots continued and the reported intentions of the Turkish government to expel Greeks from Istanbul were carried out, it would sever ties with Turkey and consider withdrawing from NATO (*ibid.*, pp. 637–68). Eisenhower had asked Under Secretary Herter to add the sentiments expressed in the last sentence of this paragraph (see the preceding document).

[3] For the NAC discussions see the preceding document.

[4] Intelligence sources would inform Eisenhower ten days later that young Greek and Turkish officers, including those in NATO units, were becoming more and more agitated; older officers were exercising restraint. Embassy officials in London would suggest that the U.S. government refrain from diplomatic discussions with the governments of Greece, Turkey, and the United Kingdom until the British proposals

and the results of NATO discussions could be fully assessed (Goodpaster, Notes for Record, June 23, 1958). For developments see no. 872.

746   EM, AWF, International Series: Turkey

To CELAL BAYAR   *June 13, 1958*

Dear Mr. President:[1] I have read with great interest and care your letter delivered to me on June 3 concerning the economic problems of your country.[2]

The desire evinced by you, Mr. President, and your Government to provide your country with a strong and healthy economy that will better the life of the Turkish people and enable them to bear their share of the collective defense effort, has always received a most sympathetic response by the Government and people of the United States. The aid which we have extended and continue to extend to Turkey, our friend and ally, has been given in the spirit of the partnership which characterizes our very close relations.[3]

I have naturally been following with close interest recent developments having a bearing upon these matters. I have been concerned over the fact that, not withstanding the progressive increase in the amount of aid rendered to Turkey, the economic difficulties have become still more pressing. I believe there is a general recognition now that the answers to these problems do not lie solely in the amount of aid which might be extended by Turkey's friends, but rather, to a very important degree, in measures of economic stabilization which, I am pleased to learn, are being considered by your Government. The importance of effective measures of this kind is underlined by the fact that it has become more and more clear that your economic problems have acquired such a scope that outside help alone will not be able to cure these problems, however sympathetic we and your other friends may be.

I am, therefore, glad to know that you have enlisted the assistance of the International Monetary Fund and the Organization for European Economic Cooperation, and that the missions representing these organizations are visiting Turkey. The views of these respected international institutions will be of great value, not only directly to your Government, but also to your friends, in considering how, together, we can effectively assist. I sincerely hope that your Government will be able to put before these missions an integrated program to stabilize the Turkish economy so that external resources can be successfully used in support of this objective.

I can assure you that, in the spirit of cooperation which always prevails in our relations, we will be prepared, in collaboration with our other friends and with the international organizations, to do what we can to help Turkey in implementing a specific and effective program to restore the stability and good health of the Turkish economy. Within this context I need not emphasize that my Government will always be happy to discuss this matter with its friend and ally.[4] *Sincerely*

[1] State Department officials, with the approval of the Treasury Department, drafted this letter. Secretary Dulles had told Eisenhower that the economic situation in Turkey had seriously deteriorated and required "prompt and effective action by the Turks themselves, which they have thus far been reluctant to take." The government had applied to the International Monetary Fund and the Organization for European Economic Cooperation for direct assistance, Dulles said, and the two organizations had agreed to send missions to Turkey (Dulles to Eisenhower, June 12, 1958, AWF/I: Turkey).

[2] In his letter, dated May 29, Bayar had cited Turkey's low standard of living and sluggish economy which, he said, had made the country's military burdens increasingly more difficult to sustain (State, *Foreign Relations, 1958–1960*, vol. X, pt. 2, *Eastern Europe; Finland; Greece; Turkey* [1993], pp. 747–50).

[3] For background on U.S. economic aid to Turkey see no. 237.

[4] After reading Eisenhower's letter, President Bayar would assure the U.S. Ambassador that the Turkish government would take the necessary steps to stabilize the country's economy. In meetings held in Paris from July 28–31 representatives from the United States, the United Kingdom, France, and West Germany would discuss the Turkish economic situation and would approve a program of economic aid. The OEEC would provide $100 million in loans; the IMF would grant drawing rights of up to $25 million; and the United States would supply $234 million in loans, grants, supplies, and debt waivers (State, *Foreign Relations, 1958–1960*, vol. X, pt. 2, *Eastern Europe; Finland; Greece; Turkey*, pp. 753–56; and *U.S. Department of State Bulletin* 38, no. 1000 [August 25, 1958], 322–24). For developments see no. 814.

747   *EM, WHCF, Official File 111-C*

TO JAMES BRYANT CONANT   *June 13, 1958*

Dear Jim:[1] Yesterday the Commissioner of Education, Dr. Derthick, brought to my office three individuals from Huron, Ohio (population five thousand) to tell me about a program of community action undertaken there to strengthen the public schools.[2] I was so interested that I send you this brief summary (even though I realize you may already be aware of the Huron effort).

The people who came in with Dr. Derthick were R. L. McCormick, Superintendent of Schools; Robert Bowers, President of the School Board; and Henry M. Miles, who is a chemist by profession and who, I understand, conceived the original idea of bringing in experts from industry to give supplementary talks and demonstrations to the science classes.[3] The PTA, the School Board, and other citizens' groups got interested in the project; a special community science committee was formed; funds were raised to buy new laboratory equipment; special lectures were given to the students by industry scientists and engineers; the curriculum has been expanded; the hours of attendance were increased, etc.[4] And the crowning achievement was when the salary of the science teacher was raised to equal that of the football coach! The program has apparently been highly successful both in actual accomplishment and in the arousing of public and student interest.

This seemed such an excellent example of what a community *can* do itself, on its own initiative, that I thought you would be as enthusiastic as I.[5]

With warm regard, *As ever*

[1] Conant, former Harvard University president and U.S. Ambassador to Germany, was conducting a study of the condition of American secondary schools for the Carnegie Corporation (for background on Conant's appointments and his work with Eisenhower on peacetime planning for wartime manpower see Galambos and van Ee, *The Middle Way*, nos. 51, 60, 1698). On May 23 Conant had sent the President a copy of his report (see "Can Our High Schools Do the Job?" *Carnegie Corporation of New York Quarterly*, vol. VI, no. 2 [Apr. 1958]). See James B. Conant, *My Several Lives: Memoirs of a Social Inventor* (New York, 1970), pp. 613–21; see also the correspondence in the same file as the document.

[2] Lawrence Gridley Derthick (LL.D. University of Chattanooga 1954) had been superintendent of city schools in Chattanooga since 1942. In 1956 Eisenhower appointed him U.S. Commissioner of Education. Recently he had traveled to the Soviet Union as a member of the U.S. Office of Education team to study schools there. He had returned from the trip, a part of the cultural exchange program, on June 10.

[3] McCormick had attended Ball State Teachers College and Columbia University. He was also a member of the Ohio Education Association and had been superintendent of schools in Huron for nineteen years. Robert E. Bowers, a graduate of the University of Toledo, was a salesmen for the Dutchess Underwear Company and was serving his third term as president of the Huron School Board. Miles, a graduate of Kalamazoo College and a former director of supervisory training at the Ford Motor Company plant in Sandusky, Ohio, was a placement manager for Dreher Employment Service in Cleveland. McCormick would thank the President on June 17 and Eisenhower would reply (June 23) that he had written Conant about the Huron program.

[4] There was widespread national concern over Soviet scientific achievements in the wake of Sputnik (Nov. 13, 1957). The President had stressed the need to train scientists and engineers in order to remain competitive with the Soviet Union. (For background on Sputnik see no. 389; on Eisenhower's radio and television address on "Our Future Security," see *Public Papers of the Presidents: Eisenhower, 1957*, pp. 807–17, and nos. 447 and 448). One of the responses to Eisenhower's call for educational improvements was the Huron program, which had been recognized as one of "the Nation's leading examples of school-community cooperation to improve instruction." See also Ann Whitman memorandum, June 12, 1958, AWF/AWD.

[5] In his thank-you letter to the President (June 21) Conant would say he had not

known about the project in Huron. The results, he wrote, proved that with "effective community action" American schools could be "greatly improved without any radical change in our pattern of education."

All correspondence and related papers are in the same file as the document.

748 *EM, AWF, DDE Diaries Series*

To John Hay Whitney *June 13, 1958*
Personal and confidential

Dear Jock: Last evening, Thursday, Helen Reid telephoned Mrs. Whitman to say that it was imperative that she, Helen, see me this morning. My morning was a high pressure one and I really had no time for a conversation, but she was so insistent that I agreed to the meeting.[1] She has just left my office.

She seems to have two main worries:

a. She believes that an erroneous impression has been created, apparently by young Brown Reid, that he was *not* ready to step out of the Herald Tribune operation the instant that Mr. Hills could take charge. This, she thinks, is not the case. In Helen's view Brown did nothing except express a *willingness* to stay on the job as long as Mr. Hills might want him—but this was to be understood as a voluntary act and Brown has never had any other thought except that of leaving the instant he would be relieved.[2]

b. She felt that I had never made clear to you my own conviction that the Herald Tribune has a great and valuable function to perform for the future of America.[3] On this point I told her that you and I had often talked; that you knew of my feeling that I looked upon your proposed venture of taking over the Herald Tribune as a civic service of the highest order—one that I thought would bring a challenge and opportunity to you and would be of tremendous advantage to the cause of good government in the future.

I told Helen of my talk with you on Wednesday afternoon and I was very frank in telling her that your great concern sprang from the feeling on the part of Mr. Hills that he was not to have as free a hand as he had anticipated.[4] I said that from my various conversations with you I felt that you believed the acquiring of Mr. Hills' services and making certain that neither Brown nor any other official in the organization would interfere in its operations were two indispensable conditions of the deal if it was to be successful. I told her that you would probably not go ahead unless the man that you put in to run the paper would not only have your complete confidence but would have authority independent of any other person except yourself or your designated representative.

To all of this she agreed and professed herself as being nonplused by the road block that suddenly seemed to bar progress in the consummation of the deal. I told Helen, once more, that I did attach the most tremendous importance to the project and that I, of course, would be most happy to see it go through, provided that the conditions which you believed necessary would be completely fulfilled.

Finally, I told her that while you and I had talked on the telephone yesterday afternoon about 2:15, I did *not* know of the final outcome of your conversations in New York and I would not until you had had time to communicate with me. But she obviously attaches such tremendous importance to your taking over the Herald Tribune and is so confident of the complete readiness of the Reid family (especially Brown) to comply with the conditions you have laid down that she wanted me to reassure you on these points as well as of my own abiding interest.[5]

Give my love to Betsey and, as always, the best to yourself, *As ever*

---

[1] Helen Rogers Reid was former chairman of the board of the *New York Herald Tribune*. For background on Whitney's plans to acquire the *Herald Tribune* see no. 680.

[2] Thirty-three-year-old Ogden ("Brown") Rogers Reid had been chief executive officer and editor of the paper since April 1955, when his mother stepped down as chairman of the board. He would remain in his post throughout 1958. For background on Mrs. Reid see *Eisenhower Papers*, vols. I–XVII; on Ogden Reid see *ibid.*, vols. XII–XVII.

On June 7 the Reids had met with Whitney and his choice for executive editor, Lee Hills (LL.B. Oklahoma City University School of Law 1934), to discuss the acquisition and management of the paper. Hills had been executive editor of the *Miami Herald* and the *Detroit Press* since 1951. He also had won a Pulitzer prize for reporting in 1956. Negotiations with Whitney would, however, break down (see no. 757).

[3] Eisenhower had taken a great interest in the *Herald Tribune*, which was oriented toward the progressive wing of the Republican party. For background on his efforts to help Reid when the paper ran into financial difficulty see, for example, Galambos and van Ee, *The Middle Way*, no. 1350.

[4] Eisenhower had met with Whitney at the White House on June 11.

[5] For developments see no. 757.

749

EM, WHCF, Confidential File: State Department

To EDWARD IAN CLAUD JACOB   *June 16, 1958*
Personal and confidential

Dear Ian: Your note of May 30th of course strikes a very responsive chord, especially because of my friendship with you and with Field

Marshal Montgomery. My first reaction was to comply at once with your request.[1] But before agreeing to do so, I want to present some questions that bother me. Among the older and very senior men of the British uniformed services who have stood high in my respect, admiration and affection are such people as Peter Portal, Andrew Cunningham, Arthur Tedder, Pug Ismay, Harold Alexander and, of course, Montgomery.[2] There are others.

So far as I know, the BBC has never staged any special ceremony to mark the retirement of any of these people; if it has, I have not been invited to participate. So the specific questions I have are:

(*a*). If I should now participate in any public ceremony noting the retirement from active service of Montgomery, would the others consider me as having been indifferent when their own retirements took place?

(*b*). Does it not place before me a very delicate problem in differentiating among my British military friends so far as any public expression of my admiration of their abilities?

(*c*). Would participation on my part create for me a precedent both with respect of my American friends and associates as well as those British figures for whom at some future date some special ceremony will be planned?

It is questions such as these that bother me. I should like your own opinion about them.[3]

Because of the confidential and delicate nature of any problem involving personalities, I hope that this matter may be kept on an "EYES ONLY" basis between you and me.[4]

With warm regard,

[1] Brigadier Jacob, who had served as Military Assistant Secretary to the War Cabinet throughout World War II, was Director-General of the British Broadcasting Company (BBC). For background see *Eisenhower Papers*, vols. I–V. Jacob had asked the President to record a short message for the special program marking the retirement of Field Marshal Bernard Law Montgomery of Alamein, then serving as NATO's Deputy Allied Supreme Commander, Europe. Referring to Eisenhower's "close association" and "personal friendship" with Montgomery, Jacob said the program would be "incomplete" without the President's "personal 'appreciation.'"

[2] Marshal of the Royal Air Force Charles Frederick Algernon Portal, Viscount of Hungerford, had been Chief of Air Staff during World War II. British Admiral of the Fleet Viscount Andrew Browne Cunningham of Hyndhope had served as First Sea Lord and Chief of Naval Staff, 1943–1946. Following the war he had been Lord High Commissioner to the General Assembly of the Church of Scotland. Sir Arthur William Tedder, Marshal of the Royal Air Force, had been Deputy Supreme Commander under Eisenhower during World War II and the United Kingdom representative on the NATO Standing Group until 1951. He was currently chairman of Triumph-International Ltd. General Lord Hastings Lionel Ismay had served as Deputy Secretary to the War Cabinet during World War II and as Secretary-General of NATO from 1952 until 1957. Field Marshal Sir Harold Rupert Leofric George Alexander of Tunis had served as Supreme Allied Commander Mediterranean The-

atre, 1944–1945. He had been Governor General of Canada, 1946–1952, and Minister of Defense, 1952–1954. For background on all these men see *Eisenhower Papers*, vols. I–XVII.

[3] Press Secretary Hagerty would offer "no objection" to the idea on June 9. The State Department would report on June 13 that Eisenhower's participation in the program would be an "appropriate gesture" to Montgomery and would be received "most warmly" in the United Kingdom (Hagerty to Whitman, and Howe to Whitman). We have been unable to locate any reply from Jacob.

[4] On September 17 more than 300 Allied officers would attend the dinner in Paris marking the end of Montgomery's fifty years of service in the British Army. In his tribute, the President would acknowledge Montgomery's "distinguished wartime record" and his "great contribution" to the establishment of NATO (*Public Papers of the Presidents: Eisenhower, 1958*, p. 704, and *New York Times*, Sept. 18, 1958).

For developments on Eisenhower's view of Montgomery see no. 948. All correspondence is in the same file as the document.

750   *EM, AWF, DDE Diaries Series*

To Bernard Mannes Baruch   *June 17, 1958*

Dear Bernie: Thank you very much for your note of June twelfth. Sam Lubell is, of course, a keen observer.[1] He has already talked to Secretary Anderson, who was impressed by Lubell's findings. I also repeated your note to George Humphrey.[2]

Beyond this, I am asking my economic people to give it a good long look. Action in this field would be a matter of public relations and persuasion rather than governmental edict.[3]

Some of my British visitors here a few days ago, told me that our old friend is noticeably losing his vigor. Nevertheless, they said that for a two or three hour period of every day he is still much like his old self. Every once in a while I see a picture of him, but have not had a letter from him in about two months.[4]

With warm regard, *As ever*

[1] Baruch had written that Samuel Lubell, Polish-born journalist and author of *The Future of American Politics* (New York, 1952), had interviewed laborers throughout the United States. Lubell had told Baruch that the workers in the steel, auto, and other industries indicated a willingness to forego wage increases "if prices could be stabilized." Baruch added that Lubell believed the public would overwhelmingly support "any action" taken to "hold the line on prices and wages" (AWF/A).

[2] The President had telephoned Secretary of the Treasury Anderson, who said the public should be represented at the bargaining table with industry and labor. Eisenhower had also telephoned former Treasury Secretary Humphrey, who since retiring in July 1957 had continued to advise the President about economic matters (Telephone conversations, June 17, AWF/D). For developments on the recession see no. 753.

[3] Baruch thought that the President's economic advisers would have little trouble

finding a "basis of agreement on the part of the leaders of industry and labor, particularly in steel and autos." He also thought prevention of "another wage spiral" would improve the economy and rally public support.

[4] British Prime Minister Macmillan had visited Washington, D.C., June 9–11 (for background see no. 635). Eisenhower was referring to former British Prime Minister Winston Churchill, who last had written to the President on May 23 (see no. 692).

751   *EM, AWF, DDE Diaries Series*

To Richard King Mellon   *June 17, 1958*

Dear Mr. Mellon: As you know, your invitation to visit Fort Ligonier has a great attraction for me. I am keeping it on my tentative schedule.[1] However, with the usual uncertainty as to when Congress will adjourn and the present state of the world today, I cannot as yet make any detailed plans for the future months.[2] I venture that it will be at least mid-August before I can possibly give you any reasonably accurate prediction as to whether I can accept. If this is satisfactory, I shall ask my Appointment Secretary, Thomas E. Stephens, to get in touch with you at that time.

Meantime, I much appreciate your assurance that should I be able to be with you, you would personally look after the details of the visit.

With warm regard, *Sincerely*

P.S. It suddenly occurs to me that the 26th of September in 1918 was the beginning of the Argonne Battle in World War I. It is scarcely possible to realize that that important event will be forty years behind us as Fort Ligonier celebrates its bicentennial.[3]

[1] On June 9 Mellon had reminded the President of his tentative agreement, made in 1957, to attend the bicentennial celebration of Fort Ligonier in Ligonier, Pennsylvania, on September 26. Mellon was the chief financier and promoter on the restoration of the fort as a national monument. Fort Ligonier, the first British fort west of the Allegheny Mountains, had operated as a depot and a military post. See also Mellon to Eisenhower, May 28, 1957, Eisenhower to Mellon, June 5, 1957, and Mellon to Eisenhower, June 20, 1957. All correspondence is in WHCF/PPF 1-F-113.

[2] The second session of the Eighty-fifth Congress would adjourn on August 24.

[3] At the time of the Argonne offensive, one of the final campaigns of World War I, Eisenhower was commander of the Tank Corps at Camp Colt in Gettysburg, Pennsylvania (see Eisenhower, *At Ease*, pp. 137–51).

For developments see no. 866.

To Edmund F. Mansure   June 19, 1958

Dear Mr. Mansure: I have your letter of June second in which you indicate a wish to come back into Government as Administrator of the General Services Administration, or possibly in some other capacity.[1] Mr. Floete, the present Administrator, is doing an outstanding job, and the likelihood of his replacement is virtually nil, unless, of course, he indicates a desire to be relieved and submits his resignation.[2] Even then I would be reluctant to let him go. If—as seems most likely—a vacancy should occur in that office, you may wish at that time to express an interest in it.[3]

With personal regard, *Sincerely*

[1] On Mansure's resignation in February 1956, following charges of political favoritism by the GSA, see Galambos and van Ee, *The Middle Way*, no. 1748. Mansure had written on June 2, saying, "Now that you are calling back some of those who were in Gov't at the beginning of your Administration I would sure like to have a chance to finish the work I started." White House counsel Gerald Morgan may have helped draft Eisenhower's reply.

[2] Franklin G. Floete had been an Assistant Secretary of Defense from 1953 to 1956, when he was appointed to head the General Services Administration.

[3] Mansure would respond on June 30, 1958. He "did not even mean to infer the replacing of Frank Floete," and was "sorry if my letter was misunderstood." "Just wanted you to know if there is a place where my administrative experience can be of use I would like to help" (all papers are in same file as document).

753   *EM, AWF, Administration Series*

To Paul Gray Hoffman   June 23, 1958
Personal and confidential

Dear Paul: It has been far too long since we have had an informal visit—indeed, it seems equally long since I last heard from you directly either by letter or otherwise.[1] Until recently we seemed to have more frequent opportunities to discuss questions and problems that, if not always of earth-shaking proportions, were at least most interesting and sometimes burdensome to me. As of this moment the things that seem constantly on my mind are:

>   Lebanon
>   Cyprus
>   France
>   Indonesia
>   Defense Reorganization

Mutual Trade Renewal
Mutual Aid Appropriations
Economic Recovery
Governor Adams
Racial Relations

These I have listed in random order; there is no connection between their sequence and the importance of each, or the burden they place upon me.

The Lebanon situation has been reported by the newspapers with what seems to be fair accuracy.[2] Chamoun is most friendly but indecisive. Chehab seems to be playing some political game of his own rather than to take energetic action in suppressing the rebels. There are, of course, wheels within wheels, conflicting reports, cross currents of personal ambition and religious prejudice, and, above all, a great internal campaign of subversion and deceit, possibly communistic in origin. Unless the United Nations can be effective in the matter, it would appear that almost any course that the United States could pursue would impose a very heavy cost upon us. The two alternatives could become intervention and non-intervention.

Intervention has been frequently mentioned in the press. Under certain circumstances to avoid intervention might be fatal. On the other hand, to intervene would increase, in the Arab world, antagonism toward the West and might even bring Nasser closer to his Pan-Arab ambition. We give to Chamoun every kind of aid he desires—but the problem of sustaining him by force—if he so requests—will be difficult to solve.[3]

Cyprus presents a problem that is equally knotty—possibly worse.[4] Five years ago I had a friendly argument with Winston Churchill here in the White House. I urged that a forward-looking, generous British policy would have to be adopted and followed in the Cyprus question unless he was ready to face a real difficulty.[5] I expressed a belief that a solution, satisfactory to all the parties concerned, could be reached provided that we were ready to recognize the inevitability of eventual self-determination on the part of dissatisfied peoples everywhere. I ventured to say further—actually I finally wrote to Winston a long letter on the whole subject of enlightened treatment for colonial peoples—that if we should take time by the forelock and insist upon, rather than reluctantly acquiesce in, the eventual independence of colonies, the mother country would have better relations and more profitable trade with such areas.[6]

Since you know Mr. Churchill intimately, you can well imagine the character of his reply. In this one field he seemed to me to be singularly blind, if not overly stubborn. He went so far as to say in almost these exact words, "I am not so sure but that history will yet render a judgment that the elimination of British domination over India was an unalloyed disaster to Western civilization."

In Cyprus we now find the British desperately seeking for any solution that will satisfy the conflicting claims and arguments of the Greeks and the Turks. Unfortunately the Turks have finally reached the point where they believe that partition presents the only solution they can accept. This is the one solution that the Greeks will not even consider. The final result cannot presently be foreseen. But certain effects are already noticeable. The NATO Alliance has been weakened on a critical flank, and the mutual antagonisms between Greece and Turkey can reopen problems and difficulties that we have hoped were things of the past.

Politicians seemingly love to sow the wind and reap the whirlwind.

France presents a twelve year history of almost unbroken moral, political and military deterioration. After her re-emergence as a free and independent nation in 1945, most of us hoped that the selfishness, petty ambitions and national self-indulgence of the French people had been purged by the years of suffering under the Nazi regime. That hope has long since flickered out.

A principal cause for this deterioration has been the same blindness on the part of French leaders toward colonialism that, in my view, afflicted Winston Churchill and some of his associates.

France came out of World War II seemingly believing, although it had been defeated, overrun and occupied, that it would still remain the unchallenged head of a great empire, including Indochina, Madagascar, French Equatorial Africa and, of course, Morocco, Algeria and Tunisia. In addition there were some important islands in the South Pacific.

The post-war insurrections that began in Vietnam should have awakened the French to the true situation and to the fate that was almost certain to overtake them unless they should act with respect to colonial peoples in a more enlightened fashion.

Instead of that, they undertook the formidable, even impossible, task of subduing an insurrection by force. French politicians insisted on regarding the Vietnamese war as one of rebellion against legitimate French authority and as directed against a legal and moral French right to control these people, thousands of miles away from the seat of government, according to French objectives and interests.

The French had plenty of warning and some of them well understood the situation. But the only French leader that then had the courage to speak openly about the matter was General de Lattre. At my suggestion he came to the United States to make a television address in which he insisted that the Indonesian war must be considered as part of the free world's struggle against Communism and was not to be regarded as an effort of the French to re-establish the integrity of its so-called French empire.[7] To furnish proof of this better intent, he argued that the French should immediately and publicly offer complete independence to the Vietnamese, on their own terms. He hoped the French government would pledge its help to Vietnam in attaining and maintaining that independence. Failure of politicians to back up and support this pronouncement by de Lattre (who was then commander of the French forces in Vietnam) became a disaster for France. This failure made it impossible for the United States to intervene as a partner with France in establishing Vietnamese independence.

Further warnings were given to the French to the effect that this incident in far-off Indochina would have its repercussions in other parts of the French empire; again the warnings fell on deaf ears.

After a long, dismal history of political failures, indecision, all comingled with French ambitions for a restored and strengthened world position, and a fatuous belief that the nation could sustain that position by force, finally brought about the fantastic situation that almost demanded the presence of a "strong man"—in the person of de Gaulle.[8]

Fortunately, so far, de Gaulle has seemed to tread the path of statesmanship and conciliation. If he is smart enough to go along with the legitimate aspirations of the Algerians and do it in such a way as to win Algerian confidence and trust (this also includes Tunisia and Morocco) he may be able to develop with that great area such cultural, trade and mutual assistance relations as will give France a stronger rather than weaker position in the world. Here the difficulty will be to persuade French politicians and, indeed, the entire French nation. The old catch words of "honor, glory and prestige" could yet defeat de Gaulle's efforts to establish ties based upon true friendship and cooperation rather than on the brittle bonds of military force.[9]

Economically the French internal situation is good. If French capital would stay home to invest in the machinery of expansion and if French tax laws were somewhat more skillfully formulated and rigidly enforced, de Gaulle should have a good economic base from which to work. At the very least I think that the Western world should do everything possible to support him, assuming that he continues along the lines that he seems to have chosen.

There is very little to be said about Indonesia that you do not already know, except to observe that it remains a worry to the Administration. With Sukarno's ambitions and his leftist leanings, with his readiness to take Communist support, and his seeming preference for the radicals rather than the more conservative sectors of Moslem people, the situation could well become serious in that area of the world. At the moment we can do little more than remain alert.[10]

Defense reorganization remains one of my continuous preoccupations.[11] Until the problem is resolved with sufficient clarity and resolution to make sure that the spirit of separateness has been eliminated, I shall have to continue to work intensively for the necessary legislation. This matter is one of the country's security and solvency. It is absurd to assume that the Congress can give separate missions and responsibilities to the Air, Navy and Ground when there is only one country to defend and only one strategic plan can be used for doing this. Until the present situation is completely corrected, this nation will be compelled to pay far more for its security than it should and will not have the confidence in the effectiveness of the military establishment that it deserves.[12]

To the subjects of Reciprocal Trade and Mutual Aid you have probably given as much study as any other man alive.[13] I am hopeful that the Congress will act favorably and promptly on the necessary legislation. It appears that the authorizing legislation for Mutual Aid will give us almost what we regard as the minimum we need.[14] But we always have additional trouble with the Appropriations Committee. A man named Passman in the Appropriations Committee of the House has been a real road block in obtaining needed funds for this purpose. Because of his ignorance and stubbornness, he is a menace to our nation's best interests.[15]

In the House a satisfactory bill was passed respecting Reciprocal Trade. If the Senate does as well, our hope of bettering international relations—as well as the economic situation for our friends and ourselves—will be vastly strengthened. To fail to pass satisfactorily legislation in this regard would be an unforgivable disaster.[16] Why both Senators Knowland and Bridges found it necessary to advocate, gratuitously, a shortening of the five year period to three, is beyond my comprehension.[17] We shall have a very difficult negotiation with Western Europe as the development of the common market progresses. Their own decisions in this critical area will probably be drawing near crystallization in four or five years. At the very least our own period for confident negotiations should be that long—if the result is to be beneficial for both sides.[18]

In the domestic field Senator Knowland seems to be, normally, in my corner. But I have great difficulty in understanding his prejudices and comments in the field of foreign relations. I have discussed this matter with him in the past, but I am afraid with not too much effect.[19]

Quite naturally the subject of economic recovery comes to my desk in one form or another every day. Right now the majority of the indices seems favorable, but it is still too early to have any great confidence in predictions of immediate upturn. If, of course, the automobile business would pick up markedly, our outlook would be defined as most promising. Throughout this troubled period, the Administration has favored efforts that, in our judgment, would be effective in the short term but which would not have an undesirable aftermath. For example, in the field of public construction, we have tried to confine our operations to things that we know to be necessary, but with additional emphasis on the effort to speed things up, both in authorization and in financing. In credit we have, in conjunction with the independent operations of the Federal Reserve Board, tried to make more money available and at easier terms. We have hoped to keep at a minimum those expenditures that are not immediately productive in stimulating recovery, so as to avoid the creation of huge deficits that will further cheapen our money.[20]

The next two or three months should give us a clearer picture of the future than is now possible.

I come next to the subject of Sherman Adams. Nothing that has occurred has had a more depressive effect on my normal buoyancy and optimism than has the virulent, sustained, demagogic attacks made upon him. Without denying that he was something less than alert in foreseeing the difficulties that could be brought about by his acceptance of Goldfine favors, I can still understand the long history of friendship between the two families that explained such mistakes as were made.[21]

The fact remains that he is not only honest, effective and dedicated, but in most cases, *his attackers know this to be true*. At the very least we could have expected that Republicans would not have added fuel to the flame. I grow to despise political expediency more every day. The whole affair has added a heavy burden upon me—especially when I realize how much it has damaged his own peace of mind.

I was going to take up the question of racial relations, but just at this moment I have the news that you are coming to see me Wednesday morning.[22] This eliminates any desirability for making this long letter even longer—even if I had anything to add of a constructive character. *As ever*

[1] For Hoffman's most recent correspondence with Eisenhower see no. 534; he had last visited the President in February. According to Ann Whitman, this letter was "a good analysis of the President's thinking and state of mind" at the moment (Ann Whitman memorandum, June 23, 1958, AWF/AWD).

[2] For background on the political upheaval in Lebanon see no. 683.

[3] Unrest in Lebanon over the possibility that President Camille Chamoun would amend the constitution and seek an unprecedented second term in office had turned violent when the popular publisher of an opposition newspaper was assassinated on May 8. Opposition leaders had demanded the immediate resignation of Chamoun

and called for a general strike, which resulted in antigovernment rioting and the burning of the USIA library in Tripoli. According to General Fuad Chehab, Commander in Chief of the Lebanese armed forces and a possible successor to Chamoun, the country was saturated with arms smuggled into Lebanon from Egypt, Syria, and the Soviet Union and was threatened with imminent civil war. Eisenhower had discussed the possibility of U.S. intervention with State and Defense Department officials on May 13. A properly worded request for aid from the Lebanese government, saying that such aid was essential for the preservation of that country's independence, would almost force the United States to respond, Eisenhower stated. He agreed that the Marines should start moving eastward.

In response to Secretary Dulles's question regarding a Soviet reaction, Eisenhower said that he doubted that the Soviets would react if the intervention were limited to Lebanon. If U.S. forces were to attack Syria, however, "that would be something else again." Later that same day Eisenhower asked Dulles to inform Chamoun that the United States would honor a request for troops under three conditions: that he understand that U.S. intervention was not for the purpose of securing him an additional term in office; that he obtain support from at least one other Arab nation; and that he accept United Nations help in resolving the crisis. In spite of a subsequent governmental statement that rejected the possibility of a constitutional amendment, thus eliminating the possibility of Chamoun's reelection, Allen Dulles had told the National Security Council on May 29 that the situation remained "delicate." Rebels were controlling parts of the countryside as well as the Moslem quarters of Beirut, Dulles said, and General Chehab was doing little to control the situation.

On May 22 Lebanese officials had asked for an emergency session of the United Nations Security Council based on the infiltration of arms from the United Arab Republic. As a result, a resolution passed on June 10 provided for an observation team of representatives from Ecuador, India, and Norway—later supplemented by ninety-four military officers from eleven member nations—to prevent further infiltration of arms and men. In an emergency meeting at the White House on June 15, called to discuss the deteriorating situation and the possibility of intervention, Eisenhower questioned the justification for sending U.S. forces into Lebanon "to save a country from its own leaders," especially before the U.N. observation team had had an opportunity to stabilize the situation. The lack of evidence of aggression from dissident elements from either Egypt or Syria would make the case for intervention doubly difficult, and he professed "little, if any, enthusiasm" for intervening at that time.

Eisenhower agreed with Dulles, however, that to refuse a request for help would mean "the end of every pro-Western government in the area" and that if the request were made, the United States would have to fulfill its commitments (State, *Foreign Relations, 1958–1960*, vol. XI, *Lebanon and Jordan*, pp. 28–45, 57–67, 81–83, 93–98, 100, 107–8, 120–22, 130–37, 166–69; State, *American Foreign Policy: Current Documents, 1958*, pp. 940–44; Goodpaster, Memorandum of Conversation, May 15, 1958, AWF/D; Legislative Supplementary Notes, May 19, 1958, *ibid.*; NSC meeting minutes, May 23, 29, June 3, 19, 1958, AWF/NSC; Telephone conversations, Dulles and Eisenhower, June 6, 12, 14, 19, 1958; Dulles and Rountree, May 14, 17, 19, June 21, 1958; Dulles and Lodge, May 16, 21, 26, June 18, 20, 1958; and Dulles and Allen Dulles, June 19, 20, 1958, Dulles Papers, Telephone Conversations and AWF/D; and Eisenhower, *Waging Peace*, pp. 264–69; see also Gendzier, *Notes from the Minefield*, pp. 242–70; Little, "His Finest Hour?" pp. 39–42; and Caroline Pruden, *Conditional Partners: Eisenhower, the United Nations, and the Search for a Permanent Peace* [Baton Rouge, 1998], pp. 268–75). For developments see no. 770.

[4] For background on the Cyprus situation see no. 770.

[5] On Eisenhower's discussions with Churchill in June 1954 see Galambos and van Ee, *The Middle Way*, no. 963; for their correspondence regarding Cyprus see *ibid.*, no. 1031.

[6] Eisenhower's letter to Churchill on colonialism is in *ibid.*, no. 991

[7] Eisenhower meant to say, "Indochinese war." General Jean de Lattre de Tassigny, then French high commissioner in Indochina and commander in chief of French forces in the Far East, had met with State and Defense Department officials for twelve days in September 1951 (see Galambos, *NATO and the Campaign of 1952*, nos. 360, 361, and 362).

[8] De Gaulle had become head of the French government on June 1 (see no. 722; see also NSC meeting minutes, June 3, 20, 1958, AWF/NSC).

[9] For background on French relations with the countries in North Africa see no. 451. For developments see no. 860.

[10] For background on the Indonesian situation see no. 662. The power of both the rebel forces opposed to the growing Communist influence in Indonesia and the Indonesian army, the most anti-Communist branch of the armed forces, had gradually weakened during the spring. U.S. officials continued to fear that the desire of President Sukarno for greater authority would enable the Communists to impose a type of dictatorship that would effectively move Indonesia into the Communist camp through the electoral process. Recent shifts in the cabinet of the central government, designed to weaken Communist representation, had been insignificant, and dissident forces had threatened to attack U.S. oil installations on Sumatra unless the United States offered military assistance.

In July President Sukarno would assure U.S. officials that he would strengthen his government's position against the Communists and provide a long-range plan for economic development. This commitment would prompt the United States to provide $7 million in limited military aid to the Indonesian armed forces, to support Export-Import Bank loans to the Indonesian government, and to aid in various airport and shipping projects (State, *Foreign Relations, 1958–1960*, vol. XVII, *Indonesia*, pp. 125, 155–62, 167–68, 191–93, 196–99, 201–2, 213–35, 240–61; see also NSC meeting minutes, May 2, 9, June 27, 1958, AWF/NSC; *U.S. Department of State Bulletin* 39, no. 1002 [September 8, 1958], 384; Gardner, *Shared Hopes, Separate Fears*, pp. 154–60; and Jones, *Indonesia: The Possible Dream*, pp. 151–54). For developments see no. 1043.

[11] See nos. 630 and 699.

[12] See nos. 716 and 719. For developments see no. 802.

[13] See, for example, nos. 60, 90, and 524.

[14] On the President's special message to Congress regarding the Mutual Security program see *Public Papers of the Presidents: Eisenhower, 1958*, pp. 160–68. The House of Representatives had passed the Mutual Security Act of 1958 on May 14, 1958, and the Senate on June 6. The measure authorized appropriations of over $3 billion, in addition to the $644 million previously authorized for 1958. The Administration was aware, however, that the authorization measure lacked fiscal obligation and that the real fight over foreign aid would come during the appropriations process, which would begin in the House on June 27 (see *Congressional Quarterly Almanac*, vol. XIV, *1958*, pp. 183–88; Kaufman, *Trade and Aid*, pp. 133–38).

[15] Otto Ernest Passman (Dem., La.) had been a member of Congress since 1947, and Chairman of the House Appropriations Foreign Operations Subcommittee since 1955. Passman had voted for the reduction of foreign aid since his election to Congress. In May 1947 he voted to limit assistance abroad to $200,000,000; he also voted against establishing the Voice of America in 1947. Since assuming the chair of the House Foreign Operations Subcommittee, Passman had consistently opposed foreign aid. See *Congressional Quarterly Almanac*, vol. XIV, *1958*, pp. 188–90. For developments see no. 802.

[16] For background see no. 674. On June 11 the House had passed a Reciprocal Trade bill that included a five-year extension of the Trade Agreements Act and measures for tariff cutting authority. The House had defeated an amendment that would have

extended the Trade Agreements Act for only two years. In a June 10 letter to the Chairman of the House Ways and Means Committee (see *Public Papers of the Presidents: Eisenhower, 1958*, pp. 461–63), Eisenhower had warned that the proposed amendment would have "irreparably" damaged the Reciprocal Trade Program. The Senate had begun hearings on the bill on June 20 (see *Congressional Quarterly Almanac*, vol. XIV, *1958*, pp. 165–71; Hoffman, *Trade and Aid*, pp. 115–26).

[17] On June 12, 1958, Senate Minority Leader Knowland had said he would support efforts in the Senate to cut the five-year extension of the Reciprocal Trade bill to three years (see *New York Times*, June 13, 1958). New Hampshire Republican Senator Bridges had said: "Nobody knows what will happen in the 1960 elections and I see no reason for taking any chances and extending this authority for five years" (*New York Times*, June 17, 1958). For developments see no. 802.

[18] For background on the Organization for European Economic Cooperation (OEEC), created in 1948, see Galambos, *NATO and the Campaign of 1952*, no. 16; see also Galambos and van Ee, *The Middle Way*, no. 244. On March 25, 1957, France, Germany, Italy, Belgium, Luxembourg, and the Netherlands had signed the Treaty of Rome, which authorized the establishment of the European Economic Community (EEC). The EEC, or Common Market, came into being on January 18, 1958 (Martin J. Dedman, *The Origins and Development of the European Union 1945–95* [London and New York, 1996], pp. 33–69, 93–129; see also no. 1415 in these volumes for background on the formation of the European common market.

[19] See, for example, no. 311.

[20] On the Administration's efforts to counter the recession through public construction and other measures see no. 598; on public construction see also no. 604; on actions by the Federal Reserve Board see no. 610; and on automobile sales and the recession see no. 642.

[21] On June 5, 1958, the Legislative Oversight Subcommittee of the House Interstate and Foreign Commerce Committee had begun hearings on whether Sherman Adams, the Assistant to the President, had pressured the Federal Trade Commission and the Securities and Exchange Commission on behalf of Bernard Goldfine, a Boston textile industrialist who had paid nearly $2000 for Adams's Boston hotel bills. On June 12 Adams had acknowledged that Goldfine had paid his hotel bills but said that Goldfine had never received favored treatment from federal agencies in return (see *New York Times*, June 11, 12, 1958). In his June 18, 1958, news conference, Eisenhower had addressed the growing storm surrounding Adams. The President would emphasize the difference between a "gift" and a "bribe," saying, "One is evil, the other is a tangible expression of friendship." "Anyone who knows Sherman Adams has never had any doubt of his personal integrity and honesty. No one has believed that he could be bought; but there is a feeling or belief that he was not sufficiently alert in making certain that the gifts, of which he was the recipient, could be so misinterpreted as to be considered as attempts to influence his political actions" (*Public Papers of the Presidents: Eisenhower, 1958*, p. 479). See Eisenhower, *Waging Peace*, pp. 311–18; Adams, *Firsthand Report*, pp. 435–51; see also *Congressional Quarterly Almanac*, vol. XIV, *1958*, pp. 690–99, and Frier, *Conflict of Interest in the Eisenhower Administration*, pp. 11–25. For developments see no. 842.

[22] Eisenhower would have breakfast with Hoffman on Wednesday, June 23. Hoffman would encourage the President to make a speech to the United Nations urging neutral nations, and particularly India, "aggressively to wage the peace" (Ann Whitman memorandum, June 25, 1958, AWF/AWD).

To John Foster Dulles *June 23, 1958*

Dear Foster: In accordance with our telephone conversation, I am returning to you for some editing the draft reply to Khrushchev's letter of June eleventh. With the changes made so as to clarify the meaning in the portion of the text at the end of page two and the beginning of three, I think the draft is satisfactory.[1]

I will keep in my files a copy of Macmillan's reply to Khrushchev's note of June eleventh, as well as our draft reply to Khrushchev's note of June second. This latter document seems to me satisfactory as it stands. I assume you have retained copies of these two documents.[2] *As ever*

[1] For background on the controversy regarding the agenda for the proposed summit meeting see no. 628. On this day Secretary Dulles had told Eisenhower that the prime ministers of Great Britain and France had received similar letters from Khrushchev regarding the meeting. Although the State Department and the embassies of the other two countries had drafted a uniform response, the British and French governments had subsequently decided to send individual replies. The U.S. draft followed the "general lines of the tripartite draft," Dulles said, but differed in some respects (Dulles to Eisenhower, June 23, 1958, AWF/D-H; see also Telephone conversation, Dulles and Eisenhower, June 23, 1958, AWF/D and Dulles Papers, Telephone Conversations).

Dulles would send Eisenhower a redraft, clarifying the portions that concerned the President. He also "revised the language in the penultimate paragraph, omitting specific reference to the items of German reunification and the situation in Eastern Europe" (Dulles to Eisenhower, and Draft Reply, June 24, 1958, AWF/D-II). For Khrushchev's letter and Eisenhower's response see no. 761.

[2] For Macmillan's reply to Khrushchev's letter, which, according to Dulles, differed only slightly from the tripartite draft, see Macmillan, *Riding the Storm*, p. 499. For Eisenhower's reply to Khrushchev's note of June 2 see no. 768; see also Draft Reply to Khrushchev's Letter of June 2, n.d., Dulles Papers, White House Memoranda Series.

755 *EM, AWF, International Series:*
Ceylon

To Solomon West Ridgeway Dias Bandaranaike
June 23, 1958

Dear Prime Minister:[1] Your Ambassador very kindly transmitted your message of May twenty-third to me, which placed before this Government the urgent and critical financial problems which have arisen in your country.[2]

We welcomed the visit of your Finance Minister as your special representative and I am pleased that he had the opportunity of meeting Secretary Dulles and the heads of the various agencies of our Government concerned with economic assistance programs.[3] I am informed that as a result of these meetings Ceylon's financial problems with respect to development are receiving careful consideration. We are approaching these problems with the same friendly interest that we displayed during the difficulties your country experienced because of the floods some months ago.[4] *Sincerely*

[1] State Department officials drafted this letter to Bandaranaike, who had become prime minister of Ceylon in May 1956, after having served as minister of health and local government.

[2] In the letter that Ambassador R. S. S. Gunewardene had presented to Secretary Dulles, Bandaranaike had asked Eisenhower to give his "earnest consideration" to the request for economic aid that the Ceylonese finance minister would present to U.S. officials (Bandaranaike to Eisenhower, May 23, 1958, AWF/I: Ceylon). Dulles had advised Eisenhower to delay a reply until the Ceylonese delegation had concluded its visit (Dulles to Eisenhower, June 20, 1958, AWF/I: Ceylon; see also Howe to Goodpaster, May 26, 1958, *ibid.*).

[3] Ceylonese Finance Minister Stanley de Zoysa had told officials from the Department of State, the International Cooperation Administration, and the Export-Import Bank that the country was seeking funds from the United States and Canada to offset a budget deficit of $50 million. The aid would increase the general welfare of the people, he said, and would help to prevent the country from turning toward communism (State, *Foreign Relations, 1958–1960*, vol. XV, *South and Southeast Asia*, pp. 376–89).

[4] After heavy monsoon rains had flooded eighteen thousand acres of rice-paddy land and left hundreds of thousands homeless in December 1957, Eisenhower ordered the U.S. Navy to deliver supplies of medicine and food to the stricken area. Later, the United States had sent 10,000 tons of wheat flour, an additional 30,000 metric tons of foodstuffs, and loans totaling $2.5 million for relief and rehabilitation (*ibid.*, pp. 371–72, 375; *Congressional Quarterly Weekly Report* 21, May 23, 1958, p. 651; and *New York Times*, Dec. 30, 1957).

On July 1 the State Department would announce that the Development Loan Fund had authorized a loan to Ceylon of $750 thousand for its railroad system; an agreement under the Agricultural Trade Development and Assistance Act would provide additional aid in 1959 (*U.S. Department of State Bulletin* 39, no. 996, [July 28, 1958], 156; *ibid.* 40, no. 1033 [April 13, 1959], 537). Bandaranaike would express his appreciation to Eisenhower for the "spirit of helpful friendship" that U.S. officials had shown to the Ceylonese delegation (Bandaranaike to Eisenhower, July 12, 1958, AWF/I: Ceylon).

To Howard Stix Cullman   *June 26, 1958*
Confidential

Dear Howard: George Allen came in to see me a day or two ago to give me the results of his visit to the Fair and talk with you last week. He has now furnished me a written report of his principal impressions and observations, which will be made public tomorrow or the next day.[1]

It was gratifying to me, as I know it will be to you, to have his confirmation of the many excellent features of the exhibit. In addition, he has suggested a number of areas in which improvements would seem possible.[2] I would appreciate it if you would give them your consideration, and let me have a brief report as to which of these— and any others that suggest themselves to you—you think could advantageously be introduced into the exhibit.

In addition to George Allen's summarized report, I have received many verbal and written comments from returning Americans who have visited the Fair. My general impression of these comments is that, on the average, they reflect the points made by Mr. Allen, although I believe that more people have criticized than praised to me the exhibit on "Unfinished Business."[3] (Incidentally, I am sending you by mail copies of two brief articles on the Fair which I have just read, that are appearing in the Atlantic Monthly.)[4]

Another feature that seems to be creating an unfavorable impression at times is what is regarded as an over-abundance of futuristic or abstract art.

You know me too well to believe that I would set myself as a critic of any artistic exhibition. I send you this communication for study and not as a directive.[5]

A copy of his report is attached. *With warm regard*

[1] For background on U.S. participation in the Brussels Universal and International Exhibition, which had opened in April see no. 405. George Venable Allen, former U.S. Ambassador to Greece, had become director of the United States Information Agency in November 1957. He had told Eisenhower (June 24) that Cullman "was very unhappy and depressed" because of negative comments about the fair from several congressmen. Because press reports had stated that the President was "irritated," Cullman had asked that Eisenhower send him a letter "backing him up for what he had done."

The *avant garde* concept of the art exhibit, which had been determined by the curator of the Modern Art Museum in Cambridge, Massachusetts, was the "prime difficulty," Allen had reported. Many visitors had also objected to an exhibit titled "The Unfinished Work," which portrayed three problems the country faced and the plans to correct them: racial tensions as evidenced by the Little Rock incidents; tenement housing for the poor; and the waste of natural resources through farmland erosion. Cullman had agreed to close that particular exhibit within the following two weeks,

Allen said, despite the protests and the threatened resignation of the curator. The country should put its best foot forward in such an exhibit, Eisenhower stated, and although there was a place for modern art, he doubted if the fair was "the place to try to teach sophistication to the public of Europe or to American tourists" (Goodpaster, Memorandum of Conference, June 25, 1958, AWF/D; see also Ann Whitman memorandum, June 24, 1958, *ibid.*; Robert H. Haddow, *Pavilions of Plenty: Exhibiting American Culture Abroad in the 1950s* [Washington, D.C., 1997], pp. 70–200; and *New York Times*, Apr. 24, May 11, 1958; on the negative comments of Senator Styles Bridges and other congressmen see Legislative Leadership meeting, Supplementary Notes, June 17, 1958, AWF/D; and *New York Times*, June 18, 23, 1958). Allen's report to the President was attached to this cable.

[2] Among the exhibits Allen had praised was the building itself, which, he said, was brilliant from both an architectural and engineering viewpoint. He also cited the Circarama exhibit, a 360-degree film presentation of American life; the technical exhibits, which included a color television demonstration, an "electric brain" machine, an atomic energy show, and the voting machines, which he called "a great hit." He suggested that the exhibit on "unfinished work" be broadened to include issues such as public health and that the art exhibit should include more traditional works (see the official guide book to the fair, in AWF/Cabinet).

[3] Eisenhower had asked Raymond J. Saulnier, who was to be in Paris on business, to visit the fair and give him his impressions. He subsequently told Eisenhower that the American exhibit was the most popular one at the fair and that the President "had nothing to worry about" (Conversation with Saulnier, Mar. 5, 1997).

[4] One of the articles described the fair as having projected the "spirit and diversity" of the American people. "You must measure the impact as much by what it does to the foreigners as by what it does to yourself, and I suspect that such sour notes as emanated from some of the American correspondents were written in advance, before the crowds responded" (Edward Weeks, "The Peripatetic Reviewer," *Atlantic Monthly* 202, July 1958, pp. 81–82; see also Madeleine May, "Overheard at the Fair," *ibid.*, Aug. 1958, pp. 69–70).

[5] For developments see no. 853.

757   *EM, AWF, Administration Series*

To John Hay Whitney   *June 27, 1958*

Dear Jock: I was astonished as well as amused by the quotation you sent me from Helen Reid's letter, written before my recent meeting with her. My first impulse was to send it on to Helen, but I decided there was nothing to be gained and that I certainly didn't want to inject my self again into the situation.[1]

The three musketeers apparently performed to my full expectations while they were with you. I am certain their final report will be completely biased, totally inaccurate and highly colorful. At the very least their trip sounds a lot more enjoyable than facing, day after day, problems that are insoluble.[2]

Give my love to Betsey and, as always, the best to yourself. *As ever*

[1] Ambassador Whitney had been negotiating with the Reids to acquire the *New York Herald Tribune.* Shortly before a final meeting to discuss announcement of the takeover, Helen Reid had sent a letter to Whitney which, according to the Ambassador, had effectively ended the negotiations. Mrs. Reid had discussed the situation with the President on June 13. Eisenhower then wrote to Whitney to explain Mrs. Reid's position and to encourage Whitney to continue working on the acquisition (see no. 748). On June 23 Whitney sent excerpts of Reid's letter to Eisenhower (AWF/A). She had threatened to bring in other investors who might care more for the *Herald* and "the Reid identity and investment." Moreover, while her son might represent her in the future, "'in the final analysis'" she reserved the right to make the decisions herself. See also E. J. Kahn, Jr., *Jock: The Life and Times of John Hay Whitney* (Garden City, N.Y., 1981), pp. 260–62, and Richard Kluger, *The Paper: The Life and Death of the* New York Herald Tribune (New York, 1986), pp. 545–84. For developments see no. 759.

[2] While vacationing in London, the President's good friends, Freeman Gosden, Barry Leithead, and Cliff Roberts had visited Whitney at the American embassy (see no. 743).

758   *EM, AWF, Dulles-Herter Series*

To Lewis Lichtenstein Strauss   *June 28, 1958*

Dear Lewis: I have your letter of June twenty-fifth. It is fully in order for you to speak to your laboratory directors and key staff along the lines you suggest.[1]

With warm regard, *Sincerely*

[1] Strauss had told Eisenhower that newspaper reports of a possible suspension of weapon development had resulted in some losses of personnel in U.S. weapons laboratories. He wanted Eisenhower to sign a letter he had drafted that could be used to emphasize the importance of maintaining the laboratories "in vigor," because testing might resume later (Strauss to Eisenhower, June 25, 1958, AWF/A: AEC).

After seeing Strauss's letter and the enclosed draft, Secretary Dulles had suggested that Eisenhower give the AEC director the authorization to reassure his personnel. He did not believe, however, that Eisenhower should sign the letter Strauss had requested. "I doubt that it is wise at this juncture," Dulles wrote, "to attempt to reexpress in a letter from you which would become public our attitude on the suspension of testing problem." Dulles drafted this short reply after discussing the issue with Strauss (Dulles to Eisenhower, June 28, 1958, AWF/D; see also Telephone conversation, Strauss and Dulles, June 27, 1958, Dulles Papers, Telephone Conversations).

To John Hay Whitney   *June 30, 1958*
Personal and confidential

Dear Jock: As I wrote to you on June twenty-seventh, I was astonished
by the paragraphs in your letter of the twenty-third, quoting Helen
Reid. That astonishment was all the greater because of the conversation I had had with Helen on the day succeeding your departure
for London, in which she expressed herself as being completely bewildered by your termination of the negotiations affecting the Herald Tribune. At that time one reaction I had to your information
was that any further effort on your part to save the Herald Tribune
was probably useless. But the matter has continued on my mind—
I cannot wholly forget it.[1]

Of course this affair is none of my business. But since I think it
necessary to preserve sound and moderate government and that a
successful Herald Tribune, operated under your political philosophy, could help to do this, I have concluded to write to you once
more on the subject.

Having a belief in the potential value of your operation of the paper, I feel that possibly you should continue to explore every avenue
that could lead to that end. Some of the thoughts I now entertain
may have been previously considered and discarded by you. Nevertheless I present several observations or suggestions that may have
some validity.

I am confident that, when you've finished your tour of duty in
Britain you will want to do something that will truly appeal to you
as a public service. There are a number of ways in which you can
do this; one would be to take the responsibility of making the Herald Tribune a forceful voice in supporting the policies in which you
believe.

One of my "second thoughts" has been this: I believe that Helen
Reid did not fully understand that her message to you, delivered
during your conference with Brown and Lee Hills just before your
departure for London, would constitute a conclusive decision. She
was, mother-like, expressing a hope or prayer affecting something
that, with respect to her son, in her heart she knew to be impossible of fulfillment. She was voicing the ambitions of a troubled
mother for her child—maybe also, her pride in him. She seemingly
felt a personal anguish because those ambitions and that pride were
obviously not fully shared by you.

This conclusion seems to me to be at least partially warranted by
the statements she made to me the succeeding day. Those statements
were unequivocal in their meaning that Brown was to have no more

direction or controlling influence in your operation of the paper than you desired. She clearly implied that there was no need even to have him on the premises if you decided otherwise. Yet this happened the very next day after she sent to you the seemingly decisive written message.

If I am reasonably accurate in this conclusion, it would appear that the conditions upon which a contract satisfactory to you could be drawn have not appreciably changed.

I have had long talks with Bill Robinson, whose views coincide with mine—and yours—as to the need for rehabilitation of the paper as a guiding influence on present and future policies important to our government and people. My respect for his opinions and for his dedication to the country is high indeed. I repeat some of the things he said because I believe you also like him and respect his judgment.[2]

Out of his long newspaper experience, he talked about advertising, and its function in producing the principal part of the revenue of a newspaper. He spoke of integrity, of editorial and reporting ability, and of salesmanship in making a newspaper successful. Incidentally he mentioned the extraordinary success experienced by the Herald Tribune during the years 1946–50 when it was operated in accordance with these considerations.

He said that Lee Hills was a man that he, Bill, did not know too well, but he was certain that your selection of Mr. Hills was perfect. This opinion Bill based on information gained from a wide acquaintance in the newspaper world.

Then he made this observation: Every newspaper, no matter how well financed initially, should, to be successful, have a virtual partnership between two men—one of whom is the editorial, make-up and news boss, the other the director of management, advertisement, promotion, circulation and so on. Only, Bill declared, when this combination is a real partnership based upon mutual friendship, respect and ability can a paper become outstanding. No one man—unless he be a genius—can fill satisfactorily both positions.

In Mr. Hills you have, Bill believes, one of the men you need. He wonders whether you have found the other. (Of course, Mr. Hills could be one of those rare men who could function well in both positions).[3] I have never heard you mention the idea Bill suggested to me; possibly you feel you've already solved this part of the anticipated problem, if the project ever reaches fruition.

In the event that you do need to search further to complete your management team, I know that you could count on Bill for help if you should ever solicit it. His devotion to the paper and friendship for you would guarantee his cheerful assistance in any way that might seem fitting to you.

His first love is the newspaper profession—I truly believe that under challenging circumstances and in a friendly climate he would go back to it without a moment's hesitancy. In this I may be wrong—but my conviction illustrates, at the least, how much his interest is absorbed by the problem of influencing public opinion; how deeply he believes such an effort, when unselfish, to be a great public service, whether as owner, editor or publisher.

All this is personal. I hope it does not sound like an exhortation. I do not mean to offer advice gratuitously. But my interest in the whole project is such that I cannot fail to present to you any thought that may seem to me pertinent.

In any event, this letter requires no reply—if it provides any new peep hole through which you may peer from another angle at this complex problem, I shall be more than repaid for writing it. In any event, already I've said too much considering the little I *know*.[4]

Love to Betsey—all the best to you. *As ever*

[1] Eisenhower's letters regarding Whitney's plans to acquire the *New York Herald Tribune* from the Reid family are nos. 748 and 757.
[2] During his tenure at the *Herald Tribune* (1936–1954), William E. Robinson had served as business manager and executive vice-president (see Galambos, *Columbia University*, no. 28; see also Kluger, *The Paper*, p. 564).
[3] For developments on Hills see no. 816; on the selection of a management team see no. 1026.
[4] Whitney would acquire the paper in August (see no. 825; see also 799).

760   *EM, AWF, Name Series*

To Jacob Loucks Devers   *June 30, 1958*

Dear Jake: I am sorry that there has been a delay in getting to you the promised list of names that might be considered as candidates for the Sylvanus Thayer Award next year.[1] My brother, with whom I wanted to consult, was on a leisurely motor trip to Wisconsin and it took some time to contact him.[2]

The suggests we both like are:

1. Dr. James Conant (I personally think he would be a splendid choice).[3]
2. Dr. James Killian[4]
3. Dr. Franklin Murphy (Chancellor of the University of Kansas)[5]
4. Dr. Arthur Adams (President of the American Council on Education)[6]
5. Dr. Arthur Flemming (although by the time the award is

made, he will not be actively in education; as you know I have sent his name to the Senate as Secretary of Health, Welfare and Education).[7]

I hope these will be helpful.[8]

With warm regard, *Sincerely*

---

[1] Eisenhower had met with Devers (USMA 1909), a personal friend and technical assistant to the president of Fairchild Engine and Airplane Corporation since 1951, at the White House on June 12. Devers chaired the committee to select an American who best exemplified the principles of the West Point motto: "Duty, Honor, Country." The Thayer Award was given annually by the Association of Graduates of the United States Military Academy.

[2] Milton Eisenhower had arrived at his hotel in Land O' Lakes, Wisconsin, on June 25. Writing on June 23, Presidential Secretary Ann Whitman had asked him to send the names of some educators who were "pre-eminent in this field." Milton had replied on June 25, listing the five men the President would nominate (both in AWF/N).

[8] Conant was former president of Harvard University and a former U.S. Ambassador to Germany. He currently was doing research on methods of stimulating talented students (see no. 747).

[4] Killian, president of MIT, was Special Assistant to the President for Science and Technology (see no. 396).

[5] On Murphy see no. 307.

[6] Arthur Stanton Adams (USNA 1918; Sc.D. Colorado School of Mines 1927) was former president of the Association of Land Grant Colleges and State Universities and former president of the University of New Hampshire. He had served as president of the American Council on Education since 1951.

[7] Arthur Sherwood Flemming had assumed the presidency of Ohio Wesleyan University while also serving on the Hoover Commission on Organization of the Executive Branch of the Government. Eisenhower had named him Director of the Office of Defense Mobilization in March 1953. He would become Secretary of HEW later this year (see no. 930; for background see *Eisenhower Papers*, vols. XII–XVII).

[8] As it turned out, John Foster Dulles, then dying of cancer, would receive the award (*New York Times*, May 21, 1959).

12

America Invades
the Mideast

To Nikita Sergeyevich Khrushchev   *July 2, 1958*

Dear Mr. Chairman: I was frankly surprised by your letter of June eleventh. You complain about delay in preparations for a Summit meeting precisely at the moment when the Western powers have submitted a proposal for a serious and effective procedure for conducting these preparations. This refutes the allegation contained in your letter that the three Western powers are creating obstacles and impeding progress toward a Summit meeting.[1]

The position of the Western powers concerning holding of a meeting of Heads of Governments has been clear from the outset. They consider such a meeting desirable if it would provide an opportunity for conducting serious discussions of major problems and would be an effective means of reaching agreement on significant subjects. From the known positions of the Soviet Government, there is no evidence so far that such is the case. That is why the Western powers insist on adequate preparatory work and why they have put forward their proposal to facilitate satisfactory completion of this work.

The Soviet Government instead has disrupted the discussions in Moscow by taking upon itself to publish with bare hours of warning and no attempt at consultation the documents exchanged between it and the Western powers, including diplomatic documents originating from the Western powers. This action is scarcely consonant with the spirit of serious preparation in which the Western powers entered into these diplomatic exchanges. It cannot but cast doubt on the intentions of the Soviet Government concerning the proper preparations for a Summit meeting.[2]

Following receipt of the Soviet agenda proposals on May fifth the three Ambassadors in interviews on May twenty-eighth, thirty-first, and June second presented in return the Western agenda proposals. They also outlined to Mr. Gromyko a suggested procedure for overcoming the difficulty caused by the fact that the two sets of proposals were widely divergent. The Western Ambassadors are quite ready to offer comments on the Soviet agenda proposals and to clarify certain points in their own proposals on which the Soviet Government seems to have misconceptions. But the Western Governments cannot agree that the discussions between their Ambassadors and Mr. Gromyko should be based exclusively on the Soviet list any more than they would expect the Soviet Government to agree to base the discussions solely on the Western list. Since the topics in both lists fall under certain general headings, the Western proposal was that preparatory discussion of the individual topics put forward by the two sides should take place within the framework of these general headings. Had this been accepted by the Soviet Government, the Soviet Foreign Minister and the Ambassadors could have proceeded to examine the positions of the various governments on the topics in both lists and establish what subjects should be submitted for examination by the Heads of Government. Neither side would, during the preparatory stage, have been able to veto the inclusion of any topic for discussion and an opportunity would have been afforded to find some common ground, for later consideration by Heads of Government.

Mr. Gromyko promised an official reply to the above proposal. Instead, however, the Soviet Government has now addressed communications to the Heads of Government of the three Western powers, in the form of your letters of June eleventh, which repeat the arguments in favor of the Soviet set of proposals of May fifth and criticize some of the Western proposals which it happens not to like. The procedural proposal put forward by the Ambassadors has been ignored altogether.

You allege in your letters that the Western powers by including, as possible subjects of discussion at a meeting of Heads of Government, some of the great political issues that create grave tension are trying to prevent the holding of a Summit meeting.[3] There is no warrant for this allegation. A meeting of Heads of Government would not respond to the hopes and aspirations of mankind if they met under an injunction that seals their lips so that they could not even mention the great political issues that gravely trouble their relations and endanger world peace.

In spite of the arbitrary action of the Soviet Government and its apparent unwillingness to negotiate seriously on concrete points at issue, the Western powers do not propose to abandon hope or to relax their efforts to seek solutions of the major outstanding problems. If the Soviet Government is equally serious in pursuing this goal, it will accept the procedural proposal put forward by the Western powers or advance some equally effective and workable alternative.[4] *Sincerely*

[1] For background see no. 754. On May 28 the governments of the United States, Great Britain, and France had given Soviet Foreign Minister Andrei Gromyko a draft agenda of questions to be considered at a summit conference. Among the items included were the control of fissionable material production and the reduction of existing stockpiles of such materials, the suspension of nuclear tests, the use of outer space for peaceful purposes, the reunification of Germany, and European security arrangements (State, *American Foreign Policy, Current Documents, 1958*, pp. 802–9). In his letter Khrushchev had objected to the inclusion of German reunification. "We have already repeatedly stated that we regard it inadmissable to raise such a ques-

tion at an international conference," he wrote. "The Soviet Union does not intend to interfere in the international affairs of other sovereign states and is of the opinion that no one can claim the right to such interference" (Khrushchev to Eisenhower, June 11, 1958, AWF/I: Khrushchev).

[2] These documents are in State, *American Foreign Policy, Current Documents, 1958*, pp. 787–88, 780–800, 802–9.

[3] The Soviet leader appeared to doubt that the Western powers really wanted a summit meeting. They had chosen agenda items that were not "ripe" for settlement, Khrushchev said, so that they could later claim to have predicted the failure of the conference (Khrushchev to Eisenhower, June 11, 1958, AWF/I: Khrushchev).

[4] For developments see no. 783.

762   *EM, WHCF, Official File 114*

To Lewis Williams Douglas   *July 2, 1958*

Dear Low: Your letter of May twelfth regarding the desirability of a tax reduction of the right sort posed too many questions of a technical nature for me, and I sent it along to Bob Anderson for advice on how best to answer you.[1] To his embarrassment — and to mine — the letter was misplaced in his office, and only now have they provided me with a memorandum discussing the pros and cons of your recommendation. I found it so interesting that I am sending you a copy of the entire memorandum.[2]

At the moment one of my major matters of concern is the cut in mutual security funds. You perhaps will see the statement with which I opened the press conference today. I might add that I simply cannot understand, try as I will, the thinking that approves huge expenditures for the maintenance of a military establishment, yet cuts eagerly and substantially our minimum requirements for the waging of the peace.[3]

With warm regard, *Sincerely*[4]

[1] In his letter dated May 7 (same file as document), Douglas had discussed Senate reactions to his statement supporting foreign aid and the Reciprocal Trade Bill (see no. 674). He had also outlined his thoughts on tax reduction, suggesting that the Administration needed to preempt the Democratic party by making its own tax reduction proposal. Any Democratic program would place the Administration "on the defensive and be a source of real embarrassment to you," he said. On the other hand, if the Administration proposed its own tax reduction program, the "demagogues" would "be compelled to disregard your recommendations or, by the logic of your proposals, be pressed to support them." An appropriate tax reduction, he suggested, could increase revenues by stimulating investment and by "the creation of employment by private initiative." "Accordingly, the appropriate sort of tax reduction recommended at this time might be not solely an anti-cyclical measure but a part of a longterm program, as well."

² Treasury Secretary Anderson's memorandum of June 30, 1958, is in the same file as the document. He had stated that Douglas's argument was "probably correct." "Judicious tax reduction through tax reform could actually increase revenue within a short period." Since it would "give relief primarily to middle and upper bracket individuals and to business," however, it would be unpopular.

³ For background see no. 753. On June 27 the House Appropriations Committee had reported a bill recommending a total foreign aid appropriation of $3,078,092,500, which represented a cut of $872 million from the President's original request for funds, and $597.5 million less than the amount authorized for fiscal 1959 foreign aid spending (see *Congressional Quarterly Almanac*, vol. XIV, *1958*, pp. 188–90). On July 2, prior to the full House vote appropriating the funds as recommended by the Committee, Eisenhower had issued a statement, calling the cuts "reckless." "It is my deep conviction," he said, "that reductions of a size contemplated by the Committee will have grave consequences in portions of the free world and to our nation's security—and will encourage Communist imperialists" (*Public Papers of the Presidents: Eisenhower, 1958*, pp. 519–20). For developments see no. 782.

⁴ Douglas would respond on August 4, 1958 (same file as document). While thanking the President for his letter, he noted that economic recovery had made his suggestions regarding taxes "past history." "I agree completely with your views on mutual security funds," he noted.

763   *EM, WHCF, Official File 151-A*

To Paul Dudley White   *July 2, 1958*

Dear Dr. White: Immediately after I received your letter of June seventeenth, I got in touch with the State Department to determine their reaction to your request for a special assignment to go to Communist China.[1] I am sorry that I must give you a reply that will, I know, be disappointing to you. In general, I consider that it must continue to be a United States policy not to authorize travel of American citizens to the China mainland even in cases like your own, where, if normal conditions obtained, worthwhile contact would result.

The Department has prepared for me a memorandum of further considerations relating to travel of Americans to Communist China which I believe will be of interest to you. A copy of that memorandum is enclosed.[2]

With warm regard,[3] *Sincerely*

[1] White had written following his return from a trip to New Zealand and Australia where he had helped establish a National Cardiac Research Foundation. While there he had been intrigued by reports of physicians who had recently visited mainland China. He recalled that in September 1956, he had received official invitations to lecture at medical schools in Mukden, Shanghai, and Peking. Although he had put off accepting the offers, he believed that the "invitations could be revived at any time if it were considered worthwhile." White asked for a "special assignment to go medically to China with some of the Australian, British, or Mexican physicians. Perhaps

a very few of us might be able to go if it were in any way possible. I feel that we could do a useful job in a medical contact" (June 17, 1958). The invitations to White may have represented efforts by the Chinese government to open an informal channel of communication with the American government in the light of increasing tensions with the Soviet Union (see Chang, *Friends and Enemies*, pp. 161–62).

[2] Secretary of State Dulles had prepared a memorandum regarding the proposed visit to the People's Republic (July 1, 1958). He noted that there had been only four exceptions to the general U.S. policy against authorizing travel to the Chinese mainland. "In each of these instances there were clear considerations of overriding importance to the national interest which do not appear to exist in Dr. White's particular case." Dulles had also enclosed a draft reply to White for the President's use.

[3] White would respond on July 12, thanking the President for the "trouble" he took on White's behalf. "I appreciate the situation and will be patient," he said. All correspondence is in the same file as the document.

764   *EM, AWF, Name Series*

To AKSEL NIELSEN   *July 2, 1958*

Dear Aks: Mamie and I both deeply appreciated the message we received yesterday from you and Helen. We did have a particularly happy anniversary.[1]

The high point of the day was a short trip down the Potomac on the Barbara Anne, with John and Barbara and all the grandchildren. We escaped for a few hours the oppressive humidity and heat that is hanging over Washington, and I—in addition—managed to dismiss for a little while some of the current knotty problems.

I am sorry that you are having all that trouble with the Broomfield dam, but I quite agree that you must be sure that the water system is of the best, whatever the cost.[2]

Incidentally, while I am delighted to have those new flies, I am not certain that I approve either the "official" or the nickname. But I think any patriotic trout ought gladly to rise to those colors, don't you?[3]

With warm regard, *As ever*

[1] The Nielsens' telegram, misdated June 31, is in AWF/N. The Eisenhowers were married on July 1, 1916 (for background see Eisenhower, *At Ease*, pp. 122–23, and Susan Eisenhower, *Mrs. Ike*, p. 41).

[2] For background on the real estate investment program Nielsen had developed for the President in 1955 see Galambos and van Ee, *The Middle Way*, no. 1252; see also Eisenhower to Nielsen, June 21, 1958, AWF/D. On June 25 Nielsen had written about the water system in Broomfield, a real estate development project in Boulder, Colorado (AWF/N). After construction the dam had started to settle, forcing the builders to empty the reservoir and make extensive repairs. In October Eisenhower

would travel to Colorado, and on October 18 he would visit Broomfield with Nielsen (see Nielsen to Eisenhower, Oct. 7, 1958, AWF/N).

[3] Nielsen had sent the President some red, white, and blue flies that he said were "named Ike but some people seem to call them by the name of Vicuna." The "Vicuna" reference was to the recent attacks made upon the Assistant to the President Sherman Adams; see no. 753.

765

EM, AWF,
Dulles-Herter Series

To Charles André Joseph Marie de Gaulle   *July 3, 1958*

Dear Mr. President: I am glad that you are giving Secretary Dulles the opportunity of having a talk with you and with Couve de Murville.[1] I hope there will be close understanding and cooperation between our countries and the basis for this is such an informal and frank expression of views as I know will take place. I recall with deep satisfaction our own relations in the past. I trust that our relationship will be the same again and that we may thus work together in facing the great problems of this era.

I look forward very much to meeting you again. It would give me particular pleasure to welcome you to Washington and I know that the American people join me in the hope that the man who symbolizes the liberation of France and who guides its present destinies will pay this country a visit in the not too distant future. You are deeply preoccupied, I realize, with pressing problems at home. But when such a trip may seem feasible and desirable to you, I would be happy if you would so inform me, so that we could arrange a mutually convenient date.[2]

With warm regard and the assurance of the highest esteem from your friend and former comrade-in-arms, *Sincerely*

[1] For background on Charles de Gaulle's election to the French presidency see no. 722. Secretary Dulles had left Washington on this same day for talks with de Gaulle and other French officials. He had told Eisenhower that a letter from him to the French president "would be very helpful," and had proposed this message. He also told Eisenhower that Canadian Prime Minister John Diefenbaker had written de Gaulle, asking him to visit Canada (Dulles to Eisenhower, July 2, 1958, AWF/D-H; see also Goodpaster memorandum, July 3, 1958, AWF/D; and NSC meeting minutes, July 5, 1958, AWF/NSC. For British Prime Minister Macmillan's meetings with de Gaulle in Paris on June 29 and 30 see Macmillan, *Riding the Storm,* pp. 446–50). Maurice Couve de Murville, French diplomat and economist, had been commissioner of finance in the Free French government under de Gaulle. After serving as ambassador to Egypt, the United States, and most recently the Federal Republic of Germany, he had become foreign minister in June.

[2] In meetings on July 5 Dulles and de Gaulle would discuss Communist threats and NATO cooperation, economic subversion by the Soviet Union, the future of Germany, a possible summit conference, and problems in the Middle East and Algeria. Dulles would tell Eisenhower that the two men "had covered the waterfront, and although some differences of viewpoint had emerged, there was no sharpness at any point" (Dulles to Eisenhower, July 5, 1958, AWF/I: de Gaulle; see also State, *Foreign Relations, 1958–1960*, vol. VII, pt. 2, *Western Europe*, pp. 53–71).

After Dulles returned on July 6 and briefed the President on his meetings, Eisenhower would write de Gaulle in appreciation of the opportunity "for each of us to express to the other in all frankness and honesty our respective points of view" (Eisenhower to de Gaulle, July 7, 1958, AWF/D-H). De Gaulle would make a state visit to the United States in April 1960; Eisenhower would visit Paris that September. For further developments in U.S.-France relations see no. 901.

766   *EM, AWF, DDE*
                                                         Diaries Series

To Robert Montgomery   *July 3, 1958*

Dear Bob: This is to confirm our oral understanding regarding the literary and dramatic rights to a story on my life. I hereby confirm that as long as you are interested in obtaining these rights I will not give or assign them to anyone else.[1] In the event there are any inquiries from others regarding such rights, I will get in touch with you immediately.

In the meantime, this letter will be my authority to you to inspect any papers or records which you may believe necessary to familiarize yourself with for a dramatic literary effort based on my life when, as and if we undertake such a project. The papers and records which I have in mind are those to which I have access.

Respecting the paragraphs just preceding, it is agreed between us that no formal instrument of a contractual nature will be proposed by either of us as long as I occupy my present office, nor will any preparatory action be taken in anticipation of a future formal agreement except that above described herein.

In the event we decide to undertake such an effort, I assure you I will make every effort to secure the necessary releases from the immediate members of my family.[2]

With warm regard, *Sincerely*

[1] Former actor Montgomery, the President's television consultant, also produced and directed films. There is no other reference to the oral understanding in AWF.
[2] For developments see no. 1758.

To Stuyvesant Wainwright ii

Dear Mr. Wainwright: It was a pleasure to meet with you and your associates and to receive later your letter concerning the action of the House Committee on Education and Labor on H.R. 13247.[1]

I am pleased, of course, with your report that the Committee has approved many provisions which generally follow the recommendations I made last January.[2] I believe enactment of the emergency four-year program, recommended by the Administration, would have far-reaching benefits to education and to national security in the years ahead. There is a compelling national need for Federal action now to help meet emergency needs in American education.

This bill fulfills most of the objectives I outlined in my message to Congress last January. As I told you and your colleagues, I am in general sympathy with the provision for a loan fund which has been added.[3] I do suggest, however, that the addition of this provision should lessen the need for scholarships. I hope, as the bill progresses, that adjustments will be made to reduce the number of scholarships. The Committee bill, while adding the loan fund, also increases the scholarships from the 10,000 recommended by the Administration to a figure somewhere between 18,000 and 23,000 a year. I also hope that the payment of scholarship stipends will not only be restricted to those students who show outstanding ability, but will also be paid only to the extent that such students need financial help in order to get a college education.

The passage of a sound educational bill is a top-priority objective for this session of Congress and I heartily support your efforts to achieve this objective. If the United States is to maintain the position of leadership and if we are further to enhance the quality of our society, we must see to it that today's young people are prepared to contribute the maximum to our future progress and strength and that we achieve the highest possible excellence in our education.[4]

With warm regards to you and your associates, I am *Yours sincerely*

[1] On New York Republican Congressman Wainwright see Galambos and van Ee, *The Middle Way*, no. 1782. On July 2, 1958, Wainwright and a group of Republican congressmen had met with Eisenhower to discuss the status of the National Defense Education Act (see Wainwright to Eisenhower, July 2, 1958, AWF/D). On that day the Education and Labor Committee had approved the bill, which authorized federal money for college scholarships, student loans, and foreign language teaching. Administrative Assistant to the President Edward A. McCabe drafted this letter for Eisenhower.

[2] In a special message to Congress on education on January 27, 1958, Eisenhower had recommended "certain emergency Federal actions" to meet the challenge posed

by the Soviet Union's advances in science and technology as demonstrated by their successful launch of Sputnik the previous fall (see *Public Papers of the Presidents, Eisenhower, 1958*, pp. 127–32; for background see nos. 389 and 422). The Administration had recommended a five-fold increase in appropriations for the scientific education activities of the National Science Foundation, to be divided among teacher education, improvement of science courses, encouragement of science as a career, graduate fellowships, and new programs for secondary school science teachers. Eisenhower had also recommended additional funding for upgrading secondary school science education, increasing the supply of college teachers, improving foreign language training, and for strengthening the Office of Education (see *Congressional Quarterly Almanac*, vol. XIV, *1958*, pp. 213–16; see also Clowse, *Brainpower for the Cold War*, pp. 54–104).
[3] Eisenhower was referring to the provision of the bill authorizing a $220 million federal student loan fund. As approved by Committee, H.R. 13247 had also authorized funds for 23,000 new college scholarships per year; grants of $240 million in matching funds to states for equipment to help teach science, language and mathematics; grants of $18 million to train foreign language teachers; $20 million for federal fellowships for graduate students and graduate schools; $8 million for research in visual aids; and $84 million to test and guide high school students and to train guidance counselors.
[4] For developments see no. 784.

768   *EM, AWF, International Series:*
                                                    Khrushchev

To Nikita Sergeyevich Khrushchev   *July 14, 1958*

Dear Mr. Chairman: I have read with interest your letter of June 2, 1958, proposing a considerable increase in U.S.-Soviet trade.[1] As I made clear at the Geneva Conference of Heads of Government in 1955 and more recently in my letter of January 12, 1958 to Premier Bulganin, the United States favors the expansion of peaceful trade with the Soviet Union.[2] Expanded trade between our countries could, under certain conditions, be of mutual benefit and serve to improve our relations in general. This would especially be true if it were accompanied by broad contacts between our peoples and a fuller exchange of information and ideas aimed at promoting mutual understanding as a basis for lasting peace.

Americans believe that the economic welfare of each contributes to the economic welfare of all. Therefore they cannot but welcome the emphasis you place in your letter on striving to expand the supply of consumers goods and housing available to the Soviet people. Our people have done a great deal in recent years to promote higher standards of living through expanded trade with many countries. They would like to trade with the Soviet Union as well, for the same purpose.

As you know, United States export and import trade is carried on by individual firms and not under governmental auspices. There is no need, therefore, to formalize relations between United States firms and Soviet trade organizations. Soviet trade organizations are free right now, without any need for special action by the United States Government, to develop a larger volume of trade with firms in this country. They may not be taking advantage of all available possibilities. In recent years, United States firms have bought far more from Soviet trade organizations than the latter have purchased from the United States. Furthermore, many of the more important Soviet trade items mentioned in your letter are accorded duty-free entry into the United States. Thus, the situation favors the expansion of Soviet purchases in this country. While the extension of long-term credits for Soviet purchases in the United States would raise complex legal and political questions, the normal commercial credit terms presently available to Soviet trade organizations permit the further expansion of trade between our two countries.

I am asking the Department of State to examine the specific proposals contained in your letter and to communicate further with your government.[3] *Sincerely*

[1] For background see no. 754. State Department officials drafted this reply to Khrushchev's letter, which Secretary Dulles described as "relatively amiable" (Dulles to Eisenhower, June 23, 1958, AWF/D-H; see also Draft Reply, n.d., Dulles Papers, White House Memoranda Series). Khrushchev had told Eisenhower that "great and so far unused opportunities" existed to improve trade relations between the United States and the Soviet Union. In the previous ten years, he said, trade between the two countries had decreased to negligible levels. He had suggested that the Soviet Union purchase industrial equipment for its plants and factories from the United States to enhance the production of consumer goods. The Soviet Union could provide, in exchange, certain ores and alloys, paper and chemical products, furs and other goods (Khrushchev to Eisenhower, June 2, 1958, AWF/I: Khrushchev).

[2] Dulles advised the President to delay sending this reply because the Soviets had recently executed Hungarian leader Imre Nagy, whose actions had prompted them to intervene in the 1956 Hungarian revolt; see Galambos and van Ee, *The Middle Way*, no. 2067. For background on the 1955 Geneva Conference see *ibid.*, no. 1723; Eisenhower's letter to Bulganin is no. 521.

[3] For developments see no. 1150.

769   *EM, AWF, Administration Series*

To Gabriel Hauge   *July 14, 1958*

Dear Gabe: Over the past six years there have been many occasions when I have addressed a note to you, but never have I begun one so reluctantly as I do this. Even though we have discussed several times the prospect of your departure from the White House Office later this year, still I think there remained with me a subconscious hope that your plans might somehow change, enabling you to continue as my Special Assistant and so provide the highly valuable advice and support that I—and many others in government—have been accustomed to receiving from you.[1]

I recognize the importance of the personal considerations that have led to your decision, one that I realize has been reached with no less difficulty than I have in accepting it.[2] Fortunately, several months remain before you will necessarily leave, and a mutually convenient date for your departure can be set later on, as you suggested.

You have made a very real contribution to the Administration's work of fostering the economic health of the nation. You know well the complexity of the countless activities and relationships that constitute a highly developed economy such as ours, as well as the critical sensitivity of such an economy to changing trends in any part of it. To the Administration's handling of the many and varied problems that had to be met in this area, you brought wisdom, technical knowledge, and especially an understanding of the human considerations that must never be neglected in fulfilling the basic purposes of our democracy.

For all of your devoted work I am deeply grateful. I have particularly appreciated the clarity and conciseness in which you have so frequently in public appearances expounded the principles that govern the Administration in the development of economic policy. Two of your most notable expositions of this character were before the Commonwealth Club of San Francisco and the Economic Club of Detroit.[3] And I must make special mention of the passage in your letter of resignation which, in the guise of expressing respect for my own efforts toward creating a stronger American dedication to the timeless principles of competitive enterprise, actually present in succinct terms your own economic philosophy. Of course I agree in your economic convictions; I cannot help wishing that I could express them so well.[4]

Along with my thanks for your constant strong support and valued friendship through these years, I send best wishes to you and your fine family for every success and happiness in the future.[5] Mamie joins me in these sentiments, I know.

With warm personal regards, *As ever*

[1] In his letter of resignation (July 7, 1958, AWF/A), Hauge had mentioned that he had previously discussed with the President his desire to become finance chairman of the Manufacturers Hanover Trust Company (see Ann Whitman memorandum, June 6, 1958, AWF/AWD). His resignation was to be effective "sometime early in the autumn." See *also New York Times,* July 16, 1958.

[2] "I have had happier tasks than to write this letter and to take the decision which requires it," Hauge had written. Terming his work for the President as "the most satisfying of my life," Hauge commended Eisenhower's economic policy: "You have been concerned not only with remedying what is wrong in our economy but with invigorating what is right. You have restated the traditional American belief in incentive and reward for individual effort and excellence. . . . You have reminded us that only sensible economics, not razzle-dazzle substitutes, can truly serve the ends of equity and social justice."

[3] These speeches are not in AWF.

[4] A draft of this letter, with Eisenhower's extensive handwritten emendations is in AWF/A. Hauge had also commended Eisenhower for having "stressed integrity of the currency as essential both to healthy economic growth and to sturdy national character," and for having "reasserted America's vital interest in strengthening rather than weakening economic ties with other nations." Because of the President's influence, "the climate of controversy regarding economic matters has undergone a heartening change for the better."

[5] For developments see no. 858.

770   *EM, AWF, International Series:*
                                                                    Canada

To John George Diefenbaker   *July 14, 1958*
Cable. Secret

Dear John: In order to amplify what I could give you only guardedly in our telephone conversation, these are our plans. Two United States Marines landing battalions will land in Lebanon at 3:00 P.M. Lebanon time (9:00 A.M. EDT) Tuesday, July 15.[1] Soon thereafter our representative at the United Nations will report this action to a special session of the Security Council which Lebanon or we will have urgently asked be convened. Our representative will report that we have received an urgent appeal from President Chamoun for assistance in maintaining the independence and integrity of Lebanon and that, having concluded that the United Nations observers now in the Lebanon cannot suffice to preserve Lebanon's independence under the circumstances now prevailing, we have affirmatively responded to Chamoun's request. We contemplate that these United States forces are in the Lebanon not as combat troops but to assist in stabilizing the situation there. We hope that the United Nations will be able to organize a force quickly to take over this function and as soon as such a force arrives in the Lebanon United States forces will withdraw.[2]

I will issue from the White House at about the same time, a statement outlining what we are doing and later in the day will make a fuller statement to the people of the United States.[3]

I have been in touch with Harold Macmillian about our plans.[4]

As you can well imagine, I greatly appreciate your assurance of support. Please treat these plans on an "eyes only" basis until the events take place.[5]

With warm regards, *Sincerely*

[1] After calling Canadian Prime Minister Diefenbaker, who had offered his full support, Eisenhower had asked Secretary Dulles about sending this secret cable giving details of the troop movement. Every "once in a while his opinion of a man" went up, Eisenhower had told Dulles, and Diefenbaker had been "very fine about it" (Telephone conversation, Eisenhower and Dulles, July 14, 1958, Dulles Papers, Telephone Conversations).

For background on the situation in Lebanon see no. 753. In June Lebanese President Camille Chamoun's cabinet had authorized him to request military intervention from the United States and other Western countries. Chamoun had decided, however, that the need for military intervention was not imminent. He had also assured U.S. officials that he had no intention of succeeding himself in office.

On June 26, Secretary General Hammarskjöld had met with both Chamoun and Egyptian President Nasser and afterward described the political situation as "an absolute stalemate." The army could not be trusted to support the government, and the rebels lacked a common goal beyond opposition to Chamoun. Furthermore, U.N. observers had no definite evidence of United Arab Republic involvement. Hammarskjöld had reported that Chamoun was making no attempt either to reach a settlement with the opposition or to exercise a firm hand with the government.

The situation seemed to change, however, when earlier this same day young left-wing army officers staged a sudden and successful coup against the pro-western government of Iraq, prompting Chamoun to ask for rapid U.S. military intervention. Dulles told Eisenhower that if the United States went into Lebanon, the Soviet Union might threaten Turkey and Iraq, unfriendly Arab nations could cut off oil supplies, and Egypt might block the Suez canal. Inaction, however, would lead to worse consequences. Eisenhower, who would later write that his mind was "practically made up" before the meeting, agreed and stated that the United States must act or get out of the Middle East entirely—"to lose this area by inaction," he said, "would be far worse than the loss of China" (Eisenhower, *Waging Peace*, pp. 264–78; and Goodpaster memorandum, July 14, 1958, AWF/D; see also State, *Foreign Relations, 1958–1960*, vol. XI, *Lebanon and Jordan*, pp. 143–243, and Microfiche Supplement; State, *Foreign Relations, 1958–1960*, vol. XII, *Near East Region; Iraq; Iran; Arabian Peninsula*, pp. 307–11; Telephone conversations, Dulles and Eisenhower, July 14, 15, 1958, AWF/D and Dulles Papers, Telephone Conversations; Goodpaster memorandums, July 15, 16, 1958, AWF/D; NSC meeting minutes, June 20, 27, 1958, AWF/NSC; *Public Papers of the Presidents: Eisenhower, 1958*, p. 141; Andrew Wellington Cordier, Wilder Foote, and Max Harrelson, eds., *Public Papers of the Secretaries-General of the United Nations*, 8 vols. [New York and London, 1969–77], vol. IV, *Dag Hammarskjöld, 1958–1960*, edited by Andrew Wellington Cordier and Wilder Foote [1974], pp. 120–51; Little, "His Finest Hour?" pp. 43–47; Gendzier, *Notes from the Minefield*, pp. 263–317; and Pruden, *Conditional Partners*, pp. 275–80).

[2] Soon after dispatching this letter, State Department officials would ask U.N. Ambassador Lodge to request an urgent meeting of the Security Council. Later the following day Lodge would introduce a draft resolution asking the United Nations to take over the defense of Lebanon (State, *Foreign Relations, 1958–1960*, vol. XI, *Lebanon and Jordan*, pp. 238–39; Lodge's statement and the resolution are in State, *American Foreign Policy; Current Documents, 1958*, pp. 960–64, 967–68).

[3] For Eisenhower's statements see *Public Papers of the Presidents: Eisenhower, 1958*, pp. 549–57.

[4] Eisenhower had spoken to the British prime minister by telephone earlier this same day. Macmillan had supported the U.S. decision but thought the crisis would "set off a lot of things throughout the whole area." Eisenhower told Macmillan that his decision was limited to Lebanon and that they should not be considering "the initiation of a big operation." They agreed that a British force of 3,700 should be held in reserve. Macmillan would subsequently suggest that Eisenhower inform Prime Minister Diefenbaker, after which he would send his own letter to the commonwealth countries (Telephone conversation, Macmillan and Eisenhower, July 14, 1958, AWF/D; see also Macmillan to Eisenhower, July 14, 1958, PREM/11 2380 and AWF/I: Macmillan; Dulles to Eisenhower, July 15, 1958, AWF/D-H; and Macmillan, *Riding the Storm*, pp. 510–24).

[5] Eisenhower had directed Dulles to add this final sentence to the State Department's draft (Telephone conversation, Eisenhower and Dulles, July 14, 1958, Dulles Papers, Telephone Conversations). After his public statements regarding the Lebanon landings, Eisenhower would cable Diefenbaker again, expressing the hope that "in general principles, at least" the Canadian leader would approve of his actions (Eisenhower to Diefenbaker, June 15, 1958, AWF/I: Canada; see also Whitman to Bernau, July 15, 1958, Dulles Papers, White House Memoranda Series; and Macmillan to Eisenhower, July 16, 1958, AWF/I: Macmillan). For developments see no. 776.

771   *EM, AWF, DDE Diaries Series*

DIARY   *July 15, 1958*
Memorandum.[1] *Secret*

The true issue in the Middle East is whether or not the Western world can maintain its rightful opportunity to purchase vitally needed oil supplies peaceably and without hindrance or payment of blackmail.[2]

Since the need is so obvious, involving as it does the economy and welfare of all Western Europe, if not the entire Western world, the problem revolves not about the fact that we must obtain the supplies, but whether we can do so peaceably and freely.

Were the Western world organized under a single dictatorship, the issue would not be the peaceable purchase of supplies; it would be merely the degree of certainty and sufficiency of the oil flow to the West. However, the Western world comprising, as it does, a series of independent nations, most of them organized under democratic process, cannot entertain the thought of the use of force in satisfying these needs, except in bitter extremity. Only by the exhaustion of every peaceful means to sustain the opportunity to purchase from those who want to sell these we justify to ourselves the taking of any action beyond the diplomatic and economic.

Another factor that enters the problem is the right of all peoples, recognized by the United States, to self-determination. This means that governments should be maintained by the consent of the governed and if any outside improper influence is brought to bear on the destruction of such a government, then the United States cannot fail to show concern.

Outside improper influence can take many forms, the most obvious of which is direct military aggression. But today aggression is more subtle and more difficult to detect and combat. Its forms include propaganda barrages, bribery, corruption, subversion, and export into the affected countries of arms, munitions, supplies and, sometimes, so-called "volunteer" combatants. This type of aggression is carried on under the name of "civil war," a term that connotes domestic difficulty not directly affected by outside influences. By falsely invoking, and using as a cover for actual aggression, the right of revolution, inherent in the people of any nation desiring to change their form of government by force when such is necessary, the aggressor confuses the issue. They bitterly denounce any support rendered to the lawful

---

[1] According to a notation by Ann Whitman, this uncompleted memorandum, dictated by Eisenhower, was "not used."
[2] For background on the landing of U.S. forces in Lebanon see the preceding document.

---

772 *EM, AWF, Name Series: Favors*

To John Merryman Franklin *July 15, 1958*
Personal

Dear John:[1] This note is to acknowledge receipt of your telegram of today about the bill authorizing two new superliners.[2] By the time this reaches you, you will know that I have signed the bill into law, but I do so with considerable misgiving. The statement that I make public on the occasion of the signing will give you my principal objections. I enclose a copy.[3]

Needless to say, I trust that the venture will prove to be in the best interests of the United States; I have no other criterion by which to form a judgment in these matters.

I do appreciate the trouble you took to give me a summation of your views, and though, as my statement points out, I disagree with some of them, I have no disagreement whatsoever with the basic purpose of keeping on hand a respectable American merchant marine.

With warm regard, *Sincerely*

[1] Franklin (B.A. Harvard 1918) had been president of the steamship company United States Lines since 1946. During World War II he had served as a transportation officer in the Office of the Quartermaster General and as Assistant Chief of Transportation in the War Department.

[2] Franklin had written (July 15, AWF/N: Favors) urging the President to approve H.R. 11451 (P.L. 521), "An Act to authorize the construction and sale by the Federal Maritime Board of a superliner passenger vessel equivalent to the steamship United States, and a superliner passenger vessel for operation in the Pacific Ocean, and for other purposes." In accord with the legislation, the sister ship to the *United States* was to be sold to U.S. Lines for $47 million. U.S. Lines would pay down one-fourth of its share and the government would pay the rest, to be paid off by the company over twenty years at roughly 3.5% interest. The ship would cost approximately $128 million, and after the deduction of defense features and the U.S. Lines share, the remainder would be subsidized federally.

Without the bill's passage, Franklin said, the ship would never be built, resulting in "great loss" to national defense, the American Merchant Marine, U.S. servicemen and American shipyards and suppliers.

[3] Although the President did not criticize the subsidy, he had misgivings about financing with government aid. He noted that government, instead of private, mortgage financing was a reversal of Administration policy and would call for an additional $90 to $100 million in appropriations. He urged postponing initial appropriations until fiscal 1960. Eisenhower also added that he would recommend private financing when the matter appeared before appropriations committees if the Secretary of Commerce found that government-guaranteed private financing on reasonable terms was available. See *Congressional Quarterly Almanac*, vol. XIV, *1958*, pp. 249–51; *Public Papers of the Presidents: Eisenhower, 1958*, p. 548, and *New York Times*, July 16, 1958. The copy of Eisenhower's statement is in AWF/N: Favors.

773   *EM, AWF, International Series:*
                                                               Sweden

To Tage Fritiof Erlander   *July 16, 1958*
Cable. Secret

My dear Mr. Prime Minister:[1] I take the liberty of sending this personal communication to you because I am deeply disturbed at the report that you disapprove of our action in responding to the desperate appeal of the Government of Lebanon.[2] That the appeal had justification is shown by the fact that within the space of a few hours the lawful government of Iraq was wiped out and the country sought to be forcibly taken over by those who have no claim to this position other than that they were able forcibly to liquidate the lawful incumbents. Our own independent intelligence demonstrates beyond the shadow of a doubt that the civil war in Lebanon has been fomented from without. This has been done not in terms of isolated acts but by persistent, substantial and continuous course of conduct over the past two months during which men, materiel and money have been supplied to overthrow the freely elected lawful government of that democratic country.[3] Similar plotting has been disclosed in relation to Jordan and the fate of that country is still in doubt.[4]

It would of course have been far better if the United Nations had been able to deal adequately with this situation. It was our considered judgment that it could not and we accordingly went to the aid of this friendly country as requested by its President with the approval of every member of its Cabinet. At the same time we went to the United Nations to report our action and to seek from it aid to Lebanon which would be adequate to meet the threat, the full proportions of which have only now been revealed by the action in Iraq and the threat against Jordan. Then, and as quickly as practical, our own forces would be withdrawn.

I think you must be aware of the dedication of the United States and of myself personally to the cause of peace. We showed that by our action in the Suez crisis when we acted vigorously to save Egypt when it was under attack. We believe that Lebanon also is entitled to be saved and that our failure to act with the utmost promptness would have led to a series of disasters which would be apt to culminate in general war as was the case when the free world did not react to the aggressions that occurred during the 1930s.

The fact that this aggression is indirect, being carried out by the fomenting of civil strife, does not make it any the less aggression as has been determined by the "Essentials of Peace" Resolution of the United Nations General Assembly of 1949 and the "Peace through Deeds" Resolution of 1950.[5]

We share the high regard which all the world holds for Sweden and we value greatly your cooperation and good opinion. I believe however that our own course of conduct is such as to justify us in asking you to put faith in our peaceful purposes and our regard for international law and order. I hope that your Representative on the Security Council can be guided accordingly.[6]

With warm regard, *Sincerely*

[1] Eisenhower approved this State Department draft after making one change; he also asked that the letter not be published (Telephone conversation, Eisenhower and Dulles, July 16, 1958). Erlander had held several ministerial positions with Social Democratic governments from 1938 until he became prime minister of Sweden in 1946. He was the major architect of Sweden's welfare state.

[2] For background on U.S. intervention in Lebanon see no. 770. Dulles had told Eisenhower that initial reports had indicated "a rather widespread, adverse reaction" in Sweden to the U.S. decision. He suggested that the President not only write to Erlander but also discuss U.S. objectives in the Middle East with the new Swedish Am-

bassador, Gunnar Jarring, when he presented his credentials the following day (Dulles to Eisenhower, July 16, 1958, AWF/I: Sweden; see also Telephone conversations, Eisenhower and Dulles, Dulles and Lodge, July 16, 1958, Dulles Papers, Telephone Conversations).

³ Eisenhower had added the words "freely elected" to this sentence.

⁴ For background on the Jordanian situation see no. 124. In June a number of army officers had been arrested in connection with a plot to assassinate Jordan's King Hussein, and the political situation had become unstable. After the United States had landed troops in Lebanon, Hussein asked both the United States and Great Britain to insure the independence and integrity of Jordan. In a meeting on this same day CIA Director Allen Dulles had informed Eisenhower of a plot by Egyptian agents in Jordan to assassinate Hussein and overthrow his government (State, *Foreign Relations, 1958–1960*, vol. XI, *Lebanon and Jordan*, pp. 282–316; State, *Foreign Relations, 1958– 1960*, vol. XII, *Near East Region; Iraq; Iran; Arabian Peninsula*, pp. 312–14; and Goodpaster memorandum, July 16, 1958, AWF/D; see also Telephone conversations, Dulles and Macmillan, July 16, 1958, Dulles Papers, Telephone Conversations; and Macmillan to Eisenhower, July 14, 1958, AWF/I: Macmillan).

⁵ The "Essentials of Peace" Resolution called upon all nations "to refrain from any threats or acts, direct or indirect, aimed at impairing the freedom, independence or integrity of any State, or at fomenting civil strife and subverting the will of the people in any State" *(Yearbook of the United Nations, 1948–1949* [New York, 1950], p. 344). The "Peace Through Deeds" Resolution stated that prompt united action would be taken against any aggression, committed openly or by fomenting civil strife, directed toward a state in order to change its legally established government *(Yearbook of the United Nations, 1950* [New York, 1951], pp. 203–4).

⁶ On this same day Ambassador Jarring, who continued to represent Sweden at the United Nations, would tell the Security Council that U.S. intervention into Lebanon was not justified under the United Nations Charter since no armed attack had occurred. He questioned the ability of the U.N. observation team to carry out its mission under the circumstances and threatened to introduce a resolution suspending observer activity. After reading Eisenhower's letter, Erlander would tell the American Ambassador that although the United States certainly had committed no acts of aggression, Sweden still considered the matter an internal Lebanese question. He doubted that infiltration of arms or subversive agents from other countries had contributed to the crisis (White to Dulles, July 17, 1958, AWF/I: Sweden; *New York Times*, July 17, 18, 1958).

In Washington Eisenhower would tell Jarring that the United States supported the United Nations whole-heartedly and would leave Lebanon the minute U.N. forces took over. The President professed himself "peaceful and conciliatory and ready to talk if there was an honest desire to do so" (Memorandum of Conversation, July 17, 1958, AWF/I: Sweden).

The State Department would also draft presidential letters to Indian Prime Minister Nehru, Japanese Prime Minister Kishi, and the leaders of several other Asian and African nations regarding the U.S. decision (Telephone conversation, Eisenhower and Dulles, July 16, 1958, Dulles Papers, Telephone Conversations; Eisenhower to Nehru, July 16, 1958, AWF/I: India; and Eisenhower to Kishi, July 16, 1958, AWF/I: Japan; see also MacArthur to Dulles, July 18, 1958, *ibid.*; Eisenhower to Chiang Kai-shek, July 19, 1958, AWF/I: Formosa; Eisenhower to Diem, July 19, 1958, AWF/I: Indochina; Eisenhower to Zahir, July 21, 1958, AWF/I: Mid East; Eisenhower to Ruiz Cortines, July 22, 1958, AWF/I: Cortines; Eisenhower to Idris, July 22, 1958, AWF/I: Libya; Eisenhower to Tubman, July 22, 1958, AWF/I: Liberia; Eisenhower to Mohamed V, July 22, 1958, AWF/I: Morocco; Eisenhower to Bourguiba, July 22, 1958, AWF/I: Tunisia; and Eisenhower to Selassie, July, 22, 1958, AWF/I: Ethiopia).

For developments see no. 785.

To Adolfo Ruiz Cortines   *July 17, 1958*

Dear Mr. President: Since writing you briefly on March seventh, I have
given much additional thought to the concern you expressed in
your courteous letter of February seventeenth. In that communication you indicated that higher tariffs would cause serious harm
to the economy of Mexico through the creation of new import barriers.[1]

Developments looking toward a solution of this vexing problem
have been the subject of frequent consultations between representatives of our two Governments and I believe that the steps which
have been taken provide ample evidence that the views of those
countries most concerned have been fully and sympathetically considered.[2]

Because of the long-standing friendship between our two countries, so frequently renewed and strengthened not only on such occasions as you and I have enjoyed at the inauguration of the Falcon
Dam, at White Sulphur Springs, and at Panama, but also through
the many daily associations between our two peoples, I have felt that
I wanted to write you again at this time to tell you personally how
the matter stands at the present time.[3]

On April twenty-fourth the United States Tariff Commission reported its finding that domestic lead and zinc producers are experiencing serious injury as a result of imports of these products. One
group of Commissioners recommended maximum increases in
United States tariffs with quantitative limitations; the other Commissioners recommended a return to the statutory rates of duty provided in the Tariff Act of 1930, without quantitative limitations.[4]

Partly because of my desire to avoid taking any measure which
would be detrimental to the economies of Mexico and other friendly
countries, I have suspended action on the recommendations of the
Tariff Commission and have expressed to the Congress my hope that
it will expedite its consideration of the Minerals Stabilization Plan
which has been submitted by the Secretary of the Interior to the
Congress. I am hopeful that the Plan will be approved by the Congress in a form which will meet the immediate needs of the mining
industry in my country and also lay the basis for continuing trade
in lead and zinc between our two countries.[5]

While it is, I am sorry to say, still too early for me to give you any
definite news about the eventual outcome of these particular developments, I want you to know that the frank expression of your
views is always greatly valued. My own efforts to resolve the prob-

lem, now and in the past, have been motivated by a desire to give substance to a deep conviction: that the circumstances which fortunately link our two nations so closely together require us in all our undertakings to maintain a sincere concern for the avoidance of any ill effects which our independent actions may sometimes tend to bring upon our separate interests. In expressing appreciation for your past generous public recognition of my Government's understanding of and friendship for its Western Hemisphere neighbors, I venture to hope that my present efforts with regard to lead and zinc will also demonstrate the high esteem in which I continue to hold our personal and official relationship.[6]

Accept, Mr. President, my cordial good wishes for your continued personal well-being, and for the welfare of the Mexican people. *Sincerely*

[1] See no. 597. Secretary Dulles had told Eisenhower that another letter to the Mexican president was "timely and appropriate" after the U.S. Tariff Commission had determined that imports of lead and zinc had seriously affected domestic producers. State Department officials drafted this letter, which was transmitted to the Mexican president by U.S. Ambassador Robert C. Hill (Dulles to Eisenhower, July 15, 1958, AWF/I: Cortines).

[2] See n. 5.

[3] On the dedication of the Falcon Dam see Galambos and van Ee, *The Middle Way*, no. 214; on the meetings at White Sulphur Springs, West Virginia, see *ibid.*, no. 1810; and on the Panamanian meetings, *ibid.*, no. 1925.

[4] See State, *American Foreign Policy; Current Documents, 1958*, pp. 1491–93, 1496.

[5] On April 28 the Administration had outlined a plan that would allow mineral producers to sell their products on the open market, while receiving subsidies to compensate for the difference between the market price and a fixed support price of 14.75 cents for lead and 12.75 cents for zinc (see no. 700). Although the Senate passed the bill, which increased stabilization payments beyond those recommended by the Administration, the House would defeat it by a narrow margin on August 21 (*Congressional Quarterly Almanac*, vol. XIV, *1958*, pp. 321–24; and State, *Foreign Relations, 1958–1960*, vol. IV, *Foreign Economic Policy* [1992], pp. 168–73, 175–76; see also State, *American Foreign Policy; Current Documents, 1958*, pp. 1524–26.

[6] After delivering this message, Ambassador Hill would tell Secretary Dulles that Ruiz Cortines "was profoundly touched by the President's warmth and understanding" and praised the action taken by the United States (Hill to Dulles, July 22, 1958, AWF/ D-H; and Dulles to Eisenhower, Aug. 2, 1958, *ibid.*).

After defeat of the stabilization plan and the failure of subsequent multilateral negotiations to determine a temporary solution to the problem of oversupply, Eisenhower would finally institute import quotas on lead and zinc in September (see no. 859; see also Eckes, *The United States and the Global Struggle for Minerals*, pp. 224–25).

To Harry S. Truman   *July 17, 1958*

Dear President Truman: I deeply appreciate your forthright support of the action, so reminiscent of one you took in somewhat similar circumstances, in order to protect the freedom of an independent nation and to help keep the peace.[1] Your statement should assist the world more fully to understand that in the purpose of opposing direct and indirect aggression against free democratic countries, America does not divide on partisan lines.

With best wishes, *Sincerely*

[1] Eisenhower was responding to press reports that Truman had supported his decision to send U.S. troops to Lebanon (see *Eisenhower, Waging Peace*, p. 276). He may also have been referring to a newspaper article written by the former president, in which he had characterized Eisenhower's actions as "heartening." In a subsequent article Truman, who had just returned from the Mediterranean area, would say that Eisenhower's momentous decision to send U.S. troops to Lebanon (see no. 770) "proclaimed a policy which every citizen of the United States should support." Although both he and Eisenhower would have preferred to place the decision before the United Nations, Truman said, the United States could not have done so because the Soviet Union would have delayed action "until help of any kind would have been rendered futile." He agreed that the United States should withdraw its troops as soon as a U.N. force could replace them (*New York Times*, July 20, 1958; see also *ibid.*, Aug. 17, 1958; and Bernau to Dulles, July 17, 1958, Dulles Papers, Telephone Conversations).

In June 1950 Truman had ordered American forces to aid the Republic of South Korea after it was invaded by North Korea.

776   *EM, AWF, International Series:*
                                                        Macmillan

To Harold Macmillan   *July 18, 1958*
Draft cable. Secret

Dear Harold:[1] Your cable of July 18 has just now reached me. Foster and Selwyn have had useful talks and I believe that our thinking on the common problem is identical. Our operations seem to be satisfactorily co-ordinated.[2]

One factor that has helped create for us the serious Mid East problem has been the Western failure to counteract or effectively neutralize the Nasser propaganda in that region.[3] For ourselves we have long seen the danger growing out of this failure and felt we knew what material means we needed to wage an effective campaign. But the Congress has never seen eye to eye with us on this point. So we have lacked facilities, to say nothing of the needed technicians and local cooperation and cover.[4]

We know that Nasser has won the enthusiastic and even idolatrous support of the largely illiterate populations in the region. One reason has been his use of the slogan of nationalism, which is one force stronger than communism.[5] We have failed to attract the spirit of nationalism to the support of Western ideals, while he has inspired it to support the concept of a Pan-Arab State. As a result, the government of other Mid East countries, in most cases based on feudalist traditions rather than on any popular sentiment, have been living in a precarious situation.[6]

While this subject could be enlarged upon both in its history and in its clamor for future attention, it is enough to say for the moment that I think we must concert our propaganda efforts not only in the countries already disaffected, but even more so in those regions which are still loyal to the West—or at least neutral. Libya, Sudan and Ethiopia need help.[7]

Naturally, no matter what we do in the field of information, education and propaganda, in nearly all cases we must also help friendly governments economically, militarily and politically.

We must try to bolster up both the loyalties and the military strength of Lebanon and Jordan.

Probably even more important is the area of the Persian Gulf. It seems to me that in this region we should exert ourselves on a very broad front—by this I mean political, propaganda, economic and military—to make sure of its retention in the Western orbit.

In a very definite sense Turkey and Iran have become key regions in the defense of the Mid East. We should bestir ourselves to see that they are sturdy allies, first in quality and second in quantity— insofar as that quantity can be provided and maintained.

Pakistan is important but the fears of India compel some caution in the extent of help to be given.

There is much to do and our resolution must measure up to the difficulty of the task. Moreover, the true source of our strength is the thoroughness of the understanding of our own people of these intricate problems. Democracies exert a tremendous power for accomplishment when there exists an overwhelming and favorable public opinion. An informed public opinion requires mass understanding. The evidence that our understanding is not all that it should be is found in the reluctance of Congress to appropriate money for information programs and mutual security costs, and economic improvement of less developed nations.

There is no question in my mind of the need for success in creating an informed public opinion here, and possibly in your country.

If we can do this well it will spread throughout the whole Western world. If a vast majority of both our peoples stand four-square and sturdily behind the great effort to preserve the Mid East we need not fear either the dictators in the Kremlin or a puppet in Cairo.[8]

In the meantime, together, we have to keep plugging along with such wisdom as the Lord gives us to bring about a more prosperous and peaceful world.[9]

With warm regard, *As ever*

[1] Eisenhower had dictated and edited this message draft, which after substantial editing was sent to London for Prime Minister Macmillan. According to a notation by Ann Whitman, the draft was kept as a "matter of record" since it was "so much more to the point the President was making than the final one that the State Department submitted and that was sent." At the bottom of a copy of Eisenhower's cover letter, which told Secretary Dulles to send the message if he were to "agree with it," Whitman had written, "State re-wrote[.] Bah!" (Eisenhower to Dulles, July 18, 1958, AWF/D-H). Two earlier drafts of this message with Eisenhower's handwritten emendations are in AWF/D; the final, State-drafted version, which Eisenhower approved, is in AWF/I: Macmillan. For background on the landing of U.S. troops in Lebanon see no. 770.

[2] The State Department's version of the cable would include a reference to British troop landings in Jordan at the end of this paragraph: "I recognize that your decision as regards Jordan was a very close and difficult one. We have of course fully supported your decision." Macmillan had cabled the President regarding his decision to send two battalions of paratroops into Jordan after King Hussein had requested British aid to protect his country's independence. He had wanted to defer the decision until after Foreign Secretary Lloyd and Secretary Dulles had concluded their Washington meetings. "Clearly this is a situation in which we ought ideally to have had a proper joint long-term plan before embarking on any operations." Macmillan also said that he "very much" disliked "from the military point of view, the sort of operation to which we are now committed in Jordan where our own troops will have no port, no heavy arms and no real mobility" (Macmillan to Eisenhower, July 18, 1958, PREM/11 2380; see also Macmillan to Eisenhower, July 16, 1958, AWF/I: Macmillan; Macmillan, *Riding the Storm*, pp. 513–20; Eisenhower, *Waging Peace*, pp. 278–80; Uriel Dann, *King Hussein and the Challenge of Arab Radicalism: Jordan, 1955–1967* [New York, 1989], pp. 88–90; and State, *Foreign Relations, 1958–1960*, vol. XI, *Lebanon and Jordan*, pp. 308–22). On the Dulles-Lloyd talks see Memorandum of Conversation, July 17, 1958, AWF/I: Macmillan; and Hood to Macmillan, July 17, 1958, PREM/11 2380.

Eisenhower had told Dulles that Macmillan's message "seemed to imply a loss of spirit" and that the letter he had drafted was an attempt "to buck him up a little . . . in the guise of making a review of the problem" (Telephone conversation, Eisenhower and Dulles, July 18, 1958, AWF/D).

[3] For background on Egyptian President Nasser's impact on Middle Eastern affairs see no. 450.

[4] This sentence was omitted from the final version of the cable.

[5] Eisenhower's statement that nationalism was a stronger force than communism was not used; the outgoing message referred to regions "where more emphasis can be put upon nationalism which, in fact, Soviet Communism tries to destroy."

[6] The State Department removed this sentence from the cable.

[7] The specific references to Libya, Sudan, and Ethiopia were omitted from the final version of Eisenhower's message.

[8] The State Department condensed the two preceding paragraphs into one:

> Of course, the foundation for all that we do is understanding here at home. I am struggling hard these days to overcome the reluctance of Congress to appropriate money for information programs and mutual security costs and the economic development of the less developed nations.

[9] The reference to "plugging along" was dropped from the outgoing cable. The State Department also inserted the following language:

> The problems are immense and we are not free of danger. We can, I think, however, recognize that the danger is not here *because* of what we have done. What we have done has made apparent and overt a danger *that was always* there.

For developments see no. 785.

777   *EM, AWF, Name Series*

TO HENRY ROBINSON LUCE   *July 18, 1958*
Personal

Dear Harry: I gather from the tone of your letter to me of the 17th that you, Mr. Larson and I are all agreed that there should be a great world-wide push to enthrone law over force as a means of settling the world's differences.[1]

When I go beyond this, I am most uncertain of the meaning you intend to convey. I refer specifically to the second paragraph of your letter where you say ". . . preparing a program for leadership in this cause at the highest governmental level."[2]

Would you mind dictating to Mr. Larson a short statement that amplifies your ideas sufficiently so that I may know exactly what you are proposing? Of course this nation, like many others, subscribes to the United Nations Charter. But in spite of the brave words of that Charter, it is manifest that the world is not yet ready to adopt and observe the principles of international law. Consequently I had assumed that the effort we are now talking about was to be largely a private one, carried on through the Bar Associations of several countries and with Duke University spearheading a drive within the United States. In other words, I had not visualized a specific governmental function. So I should like you to tell Mr. Larson what you think he could do in preparing such a program, whether you think his function should be a continuing one or should rather be temporary in character, and how any governmental activity of this kind would be coordinated with private action.

By no means am I quarreling with your idea; I am simply asking you to explain it a little bit more to Mr. Larson who, I think, could probably make sure that I labor under no misapprehension and could unquestionably save a bit of my time by undertaking this chore in lieu of my trying to comprehend all its details and possibilities by myself.[3]

With warm regard, *As ever*

[1] Responding to an effort by the American Bar Association to promote the theme of "peace through law," Eisenhower had proclaimed May 1, 1958, as Law Day. "In a very real sense," the President said (in a statement prepared by Presidential Assistant Arthur Larson), "the world no longer has a choice between force and law. If civilization is to survive, it must choose law." Luce had echoed these sentiments in his letter, saying that "the most hopeful alternative to global catastrophe is the extension of the Rule of Law" (AWF/N). Larson previously had talked with Luce regarding an invitation he had received to establish a Rule of Law Research Center at Duke University to provide ideas and materials in support of the peace-through-law effort (Larson, *Eisenhower: The President Nobody Knew*, pp. 101–4; *Public Papers of the Presidents: Eisenhower, 1958*, pp. 362–63; see also Henry R. Luce, "Our Great Hope: Peace Is the Work of Justice," *American Bar Association Journal* 43 [1957], pp. 407–11).
[2] In his letter Luce had supported the idea of a research center but had suggested that Eisenhower should keep Larson in the Administration and should assign him the task of preparing such a program within the government. Eisenhower and Larson had discussed Luce's letter earlier this day (Luce to Eisenhower, July 17, 1958, AWF/N; and Ann Whitman memorandum, July 18, 1958, AWF/AWD).
[3] Luce would tell Eisenhower that a "fruitful interplay" between the principles involved and their day-to-day application through U.S. foreign policy would best prepare the world for the rule of law over force (Luce to Eisenhower, July 22, 1958, AWF/N). For developments see no. 803.

778   *EM, AWF, International Series:*
                                                                          Mid East

To Harold Macmillan   *July 19, 1958*
Cable. Secret

Dear Harold: I have your message of July 10, regarding our discussion, when you were in Washington, of the level of British forces in Germany.[1]

I am in agreement with your suggestion that our two representatives on the NATO Council should be authorized to discuss the problem of the financial gap and to see whether a solution to the problem can be found. Accordingly, Foster is sending appropriate instructions to Ambassador Burgess, asking him to concert with Sir Frank Roberts.[2]

Naturally I would wish any such discussions to be without prejudice to the basic question we discussed when you were here. If it should develop that no way can be found within NATO to bridge the financial gap, I would still very much hope that you and your colleagues would find it possible to reconsider your decision to reduce the level of British forces in Germany.[3]

With warm regard, *As ever*

[1] For background on British force levels see no. 57. At the time of the Washington discussions (June 9–11), Macmillan had agreed to maintain the current level of British troops in Germany in 1959 if NATO would bridge the financial gap between the current 55,000 and the proposal to economize by cutting the British force to 45,000. Eisenhower had asked Macmillan to reconsider the decision even if no financial aid was available. Macmillan said that he would make no decision before talking with General Norstad (State, *Foreign Relations, 1958–1960*, vol. VII, pt. 2, *Western Europe*, pp. 817–18; and State, *Foreign Relations, 1958–1960*, vol. VII, pt. 1, *Western European Integration and Security; Canada*, pp. 327–28; see also Macmillan, *Riding the Storm*, pp. 246–48, 501). In his letter to the President Macmillan had acknowledged the political importance of the British force and his reluctance to cause dissension within the alliance. He told Eisenhower that he would defer the decision until October 1 to allow time for further negotiations. Nevertheless, he said, the ultimate goal was 45,000 regular British troops—"a very powerful force" (Macmillan to Eisenhower, July 10, 1958, PREM/11 2325 and AWF/I: Macmillan).
[2] W. Randolph Burgess was the chief of the U.S. mission to NATO; Frank Kenyon Roberts, career diplomat and former British Ambassador to Yugoslavia, was the British permanent representative.
[3] After subsequent negotiations the United States would agree to provide $25 million to the United Kingdom for their mutual weapons development program, thus permitting the British to announce in mid-October that they would maintain their current force levels through 1959 (State, *Foreign Relations, 1958–1960*, vol. VII, pt. 1, *Western European Integration and Security; Canada*, p. 348; see also Foreign Office to Roberts, July 10, 1958, PREM/11 2325).

779   *EM, AWF, International Series:*
                                                                    Iran

To Mohammed Reza Pahlavi   *July 19, 1958*
Cable. Secret

I know that Your Majesty, like ourselves, is concerned about the recent developments in Iraq and the effect that those developments may have on certain aspects of the collective security planning we have undertaken through the mechanism of the Baghdad Pact.[1] Although we believe it would be premature at this time to make final decisions as to how the coup d'etat in Iraq may modify our collective security planning, we wish Your Majesty to be assured that the United States Government is fully aware of and actively following the possible implications. Moreover, I recall that Your Majesty in our recent talks indicated your belief that there should at this time be additional strengthening of the Iranian armed forces beyond that already contemplated.[2]

With the foregoing in mind, we believe it is important to begin now to reconsider our collective security planning. It is also our belief that your armed forces as now supported should be brought up to agreed operational strength and to a high level of operational efficiency. I have, therefore, already directed that the delivery of a wide range of equipment for your present forces be further accelerated and I am prepared to provide your armed forces with additional training assistance on a selected but intensified basis. As you with our assistance are able to provide adequately trained manpower, my government is prepared to consider with you the desirability of activating additional units as well as the possibility of our assisting in the equipping of such units.

We fully recognize that the strengthening of Iran's military power and its efforts to achieve economic development will result in strains on the Iranian economy. You may depend on the sympathetic and prompt consideration by the United States within our available means of Iran's needs for economic assistance as they may develop.

I have every confidence that through our combined efforts with our other friends, the recent events will not be permitted to undermine joint security arrangements. It is our purpose to help assure the political independence and integrity of your country as an integral part of those security arrangements.[3]

[1] On the July 14 overthrow of the pro-Western government of Iraq see no. 770; on the formation of the Baghdad Pact see Galambos and van Ee, *The Middle Way*, no. 1681, and no. 78 in these volumes. Soon after the Iraqi coup, the Shah had told U.S. embassy officials that arms were "life and death to Iran now." Iraq possessed the defense plans of the Baghdad Pact, he said, and those plans would soon be made available to Egypt and the Soviet Union (State, *Foreign Relations, 1958–1960*, vol. XII, *Near East Region; Iraq; Iran; Arabian Peninsula*, p. 575). The United States had long promoted a regional military alliance that included the countries of Iran, Iraq, Turkey, and Pakistan—the northern tier of Baghdad Pact countries—and had provided aid to strengthen their defensive capabilities through the Military Assistance Program (MAP) (*ibid.*, pp. 42–45, 55–60, 77, 531–37, 546–47). On July 16 Eisenhower had received a cable from the Shah and the presidents of Turkey and Pakistan, supporting his "bold and appropriate decision" to protect the independence of Lebanon. After reading the message to the Republican legislative leaders, Eisenhower had discussed the need to increase economic and military support for the three Baghdad Pact countries (Telephone conversation, Eisenhower and Dulles, July 16, 1958, Dulles Papers, Telephone Conversations; Goodpaster, Memorandum of Conversation, July 19, 1958, AWF/D; and Eisenhower to Bayar, Palhavi, and Mirza, July 16, 1958, AWF/I: Mid East).
[2] The Shah had been in Washington from June 30 to July 2 (State, *Foreign Relations, 1958–1960*, vol. XII, *Near East Region; Iraq; Iran; Arabian Peninsula*, pp. 546–75).
[3] The American Ambassador to Iran would present this letter to the Shah and, on instructions from Secretary Dulles, would offer to discuss the internal security program in Iran with him. In his response (July 22) the Shah would write Eisenhower

that the change of regime in Baghdad made Iran as vulnerable to invasion from the west as it was from the north and northeast. He welcomed U.S. willingness to help increase the strength of the Iranian armed forces (AWF/I: Iran).

At a meeting of the members of the Baghdad Pact on July 28, Dulles would promise increased military assistance to Turkey, Iran, and Pakistan and would commit the United States to partnership in the alliance. On the following day Eisenhower would ask the congressional leaders to restore more than $500 million, previously cut from the mutual security program, to bolster the governments of Turkey and Iran (see no. 791; see also Consulate General to Department of State, July 17, 1958, AWF/I: Pakistan; Minnich to Stans, July 29, 1958, AWF/D; State, *Foreign Relations, 1958–1960*, vol. XII, *Near East Region; Iraq; Iran; Arabian Peninsula*, p. 78; and *New York Times*, July 30, 1958).

780   *EM, AWF, Administration Series*

To Neil Hosler McElroy   July 19, 1958
Confidential

Memorandum for the Secretary of Defense: I hereby approve the advanced space project set forth in your letter to me of July 11, 1958 concerning a large inflatable satellite.[1] I do so with the understanding that when the new civilian space agency comes into operation, this project will be subject to review to determine whether it will remain under the cognizance of the Department of Defense or pass to the cognizance of the new agency.[2]

My approval is subject also to the provision that the complete funding for this project will be provided by ARPA, without addition of Service funds. I desire that the identity of this project as an ARPA project be maintained throughout.[3]

[1] Eisenhower was referring to a memorandum written by McElroy's deputy, Donald A. Quarles (AWF/A). Quarles had asked the President for advance approval of this project for the Advanced Research Projects Agency (ARPA). Presidential action was necessary, Quarles wrote, in order to meet production schedules that would allow the launch of a 100-foot inflatable satellite in the late spring of 1959. The highly visible sphere, which would become the world's first communications satellite, was designed to reflect radio, television, and microwave transmissions sent from the surface of the earth (see Donald C. Elder, *Out From Behind the Eight-Ball: A History of Project Echo*, AAS History Series, ed., R. Cargill Hall, 17 vols. to date [San Diego, Calif., 1977–95], vol. 16 [1995]).

On February 6 Congress had passed H.R. 9739 (P.L. 325), an appropriations bill for special (one year) defense spending that had authorized the Secretary of Defense or his designee to engage in advanced projects essential to the Defense Department's responsibilities in the field of basic and applied research and development pertaining to space projects designated by the President (see *Congressional Quarterly Almanac*, vol. XIV, *1958*, p. 238; Eisenhower, *Waging Peace*, p. 257; and Watson, *Into the Missile Age*, pp. 189, 191, 362, 385, 392).

[2] Eisenhower had requested Congress to establish a National Aeronautics and Space Agency (NASA) in April. On July 29 he would sign the National Aeronautics and Space Act of 1958 (P.L. 568), which would create and fund a civilian agency to direct scientific activities relating to all non-military aspects of outer space. NASA would begin operating officially on October 1 (*Congressional Quarterly Almanac*, vol. XIV, 1958, pp. 160–64; Eisenhower, *Mandate for Change*, p. 257; *Public Papers of the Presidents: Eisenhower, 1958*, p. 573; Levine, *The Missile and Space Race*, pp. 70–71, 102–4; and *New York Times*, Oct. 2, 1958).

[3] As it turned out, on October 1 the President would sign Executive Order 10783, which authorized him to transfer to NASA specific ARPA projects relating to space activities. Among the transferred projects were lunar probes, scientific satellites (including inflatable satellites), and superthrust boosters (see *Federal Register*, vol. 23, no. 194, p. 7643; T. Keith Glennan, *The Birth of NASA: The Diary of T. Keith Glennan*, J. D. Hunley, ed. [Washington, D.C., 1993], p. 9; Glennan to Eisenhower, "Accomplishments of the National Aeronautics and Space Administration 1958–1960," Dec. 28, 1960, AWF/A; and Watson, *Into the Missile Age*, pp. 362, 385; see also *New York Times*, Sept. 11, 12, 1958). For developments on the space program see no. 1414.

781   *EM, WHCF, President's Personal File 472*

To Freeman F. Gosden   *July 19, 1958*

Dear Freeman: For over ten days I have waited patiently for the inspiration that I knew would come properly to acknowledge the saga of Tulips and his travelling companions.[1] While I refuse to admit the lack of talent to do justice to an appropriate reply, I do have the refuge of the assorted problems that have descended on me this last week.[2] So I can only say that I have read and re-read your masterpiece—and admit in all honesty that when I saw Cliff last weekend I did not dare call him "Tulips." Of course he exhibited with pride his photographs of all of you—placards included—done up for the Ascot.[3]

I suspect you are at Bohemian Grove. With a little encouragement, I could feel very sorry for myself on that score alone.[4]

I do have one grievance against you. Will you kindly tell me why it was impossible to travel from New York to Los Angeles by way of Washington? I had hoped very much that you would stop over.

At any rate, many thanks for your letter. If I were you—and if I had your talent—I'd write a scenario on the travels of the Musketeers!

With warm regards, *As ever*

[1] On July 8 Gosden had reported, as requested by Eisenhower, on his business trip to Europe with Cliff Roberts and Barry Leithead (see no. 743). Roberts had received the nickname "Tulips," Gosden explained, because "he fell in love" with the antique tulip vases in the American embassy in London. As a result of this affection, Gosden wrote, the travelers had visited "at least seventy-five antique shops and in each in-

stance our old bachelor friend, Cliff, would enter the shop and quietly say: 'Do you have any tulip vases?'" The remainder of Gosden's report described various comic mishaps that had taken place during the trip. See also Whitman to Champion, December 3, 1958, and Champion to Whitman, December 8, 1958. All correspondence is in the same file as the document.

[2] On the recent criticism of Assistant to the President Sherman Adams see no. 753. On the recent crisis in the Middle East see nos. 753, 770, 773, and 776. On July 7 White House aide Gabriel Hauge had submitted his resignation (see no. 769).

[3] On Sunday, July 13, Eisenhower and Roberts had played bridge at the White House (Ann Whitman memorandum, July 13, 1958, AWF/AWD).

[4] Eisenhower had attended the Bohemian Grove encampment, near San Francisco, California, in July 1950. Bohemian Grove was the site of the annual meeting of the Bohemian Club, which was originally organized in 1872 by journalists and writers for professionals who work in or appreciate literature, art, music and drama (for further background see Galambos, *Columbia University*, no. 388).

782   *EM, WHCF, Official File 99-V*

To SAMUEL TALIAFERRO RAYBURN   *July 21, 1958*

Dear Mr. Speaker: The moment I hung up the phone after our conversation I realized, to my embarrassment, that I must have kept you waiting while I came to the phone. I was out of my office for the moment, and had asked only that I be informed when you returned to your office so that I might call. I hope you were not long holding the wire yourself—but in any event, I am sorry.[1]

Needless to say, I am more than grateful for your help in securing the maximum funds for the mutual security effort—an effort that is more vitally important now than ever.[2]

With warm regard, *Sincerely*

[1] Eisenhower had unsuccessfully attempted to arrange a meeting with Rayburn (see Ann Whitman memorandum, July 21, 1958, AWF/AWD).

[2] For background see no. 762. On July 2 the House of Representatives had approved the appropriation of $3,078,092,500 for the fiscal 1959 Mutual Security Program, $872 million less than the President's original request. The Senate Appropriations Committee had begun hearings on funding for the bill on July 8, with Administration officials testifying that it was imperative to restore the $325 million cut by the House in order for the United States to compete with Soviet efforts in the underdeveloped countries and to maintain the free world defense system. On August 23 the Senate would pass funding for the bill, restoring some of the House cuts. On August 28 the President would sign the bill, which appropriated $3,298,092,500 (see *Congressional Quarterly Almanac*, vol. XIV, *1958*, pp. 188–90). Eisenhower would term the cuts in mutual security appropriations as his "greatest disappointment" with the 85th Congress, saying that he could "only hope" that the funds would be sufficient (*Public Papers of the Presidents: Eisenhower, 1958*, pp. 640–41).

To Nikita Sergeyevich Khrushchev   *July 22, 1958*

Dear Mr. Chairman: I have received your communication of July nineteen.[1]

May I assure you that the establishment and maintenance of a just peace is the dominant influence in American policy. I cannot agree that the United States has acted in Lebanon in a manner calculated to disturb the peace. Rather it is motivated by the purpose of helping stop acts of violence, fomented from without, designed to destroy the genuine independence and integrity of that small nation. Such a process, if unchecked, would have grave implications for all small nations everywhere.

The manner in which you have chosen to express yourself is hardly calculated to promote the atmosphere of calm reasonableness which, you correctly say, should replace the presently overheated atmosphere.

I am not aware of any factual basis for your extravagantly expressed fear of the danger of general war.[2]

What has happened in regard to Lebanon is this:

On Monday, July fourteen, the lawful Government of Iraq was violently overthrown. On the same day a comparable plot against the Kingdom of Jordan was discovered and barely thwarted. The Government of Lebanon, which had already for some months been subjected to indirect aggression from without, appealed to the United States for instant assistance. In the light of the developments in neighboring Iraq and Jordan, it felt that nothing less than immediate help would make it possible to preserve the independence and integrity of Lebanon. The United States responded to this appeal. We knew that the plea was based upon solid facts that showed that Lebanon was gravely menaced.

Surely, it is not "aggression" thus to help a small nation maintain its independence.

You speak of "armed conflict in the Near or Middle East".[3] There has been the bloody coup in Iraq, the plot to assassinate those who compose the Government of Jordan, and the civil strife in Lebanon fomented from without. Otherwise, I know of no "armed conflict". Unless those of aggressive disposition are far gone in folly, they would not start war because Lebanon with a population of about one and a half million, is helped to maintain its integrity and independence. The real danger of war would come if one small nation after another were to be engulfed by expansionist and aggressive forces supported by the Soviet Union.

We do not want to see a repetition of the progressive destruction of the independence of small nations which occurred during the 1930's and which led to the Second World War. To be acquiescent in aggression, be it direct or indirect, is not the road to peace.

This does not mean that the United States is dedicated to a perpetuation of the status quo in the Arab world. The United States recognizes and sympathizes with the yearning of the Arab peoples for a greater nationalistic unity. For example, the United States promptly recognized the United Arab Republic, bringing together Egypt and Syria, as soon as it was apparent that the change was accepted by the people concerned and after the new government had undertaken to meet the normally applied international standards.[4] But it is one thing to change the international status quo by orderly and peaceful processes, and another thing to change it by indirect aggression. Such processes cannot be reconciled with a peaceful world or with the ideals of the United Nations which recognizes the equal rights of nations large and small and the dignity and worth of the human person.

The action of the United States in relation to Lebanon was fully in accord with the accepted principles of international law and with the Charter of the United Nations. The Government of Lebanon was one which had been chosen by freely held, peaceful, nationwide elections only a little over a year ago. The appeal to the United States was made by the President of Lebanon with the full approval of the Cabinet. When last week the Soviet Union introduced in the United Nations Security Council a Resolution condemning our action in Lebanon, that Resolution received only one vote—that of the Soviet Union itself. I also note that efforts were made within the Security Council to provide Lebanon with increased protection from the United Nations so as to preserve its integrity and independence, thus permitting United States forces promptly to be withdrawn. There were two such proposals, each defeated by the one vetoing vote of the Soviet Union.[5]

How does the Soviet Union reconcile its allegation that United States forces in Lebanon endanger world peace with the veto of these two proposals?

Am I to conclude, Mr. Chairman, that the Soviet Union seeks by imputing to others war motives and itself boasting of its nuclear and ballistic missile power, to divert attention from the steady erosion of the independence of small nations? Are we as civilized peoples to accept the increasing use of violence, murder and terrorism as instruments of international policy? If so, this constitutes the real danger to peace. The United States will steadfastly oppose that danger and seek to strengthen the established processes of international law and order.

The Soviet Union, by its constant abuse of its veto power in the Security Council—its veto of today was the 85th—would tear down, and not strengthen, the orderly processes which the nations have established for the maintenance of international peace and security.[6]

Your present proposal seems further calculated to derogate from the authority and prestige of the United Nations. What you propose amounts in effect to five nations, without sanction of the United Nations and without conformity with its Charter, reaching what you call "recommendations" regarding the Near and Middle East which would then be submitted to the United Nations Security Council. But in reality such so-called "recommendations" would be decisions and the process would in effect make the United Nations into a "rubber stamp" for a few great powers.

Furthermore, Mr. Chairman, when procedures are sought to be improvised to meet what is alleged to be a situation of great urgency, this can scarcely be expected to save time. It raises a whole series of new problems which must be considered by the various nations that might consult together, and by others which might feel that they were improperly omitted and which are deeply concerned with the Near and Middle East.

If, indeed, the Soviet Union seriously believes that there is an imminent threat to world peace, it is bound by the United Nations Charter to take the matter to the Security Council. By Article 24 of the United Nations Charter, the Soviet Union, with other members of the United Nations, has conferred on the Security Council "primary responsibility for the maintenance of international peace and security" and all the members have agreed that, in these matters, it "acts on their behalf". It is also agreed that that Council has the responsibility to "determine the existence of any threat to the peace" and to "decide what measures shall be taken . . . to maintain or restore international peace and security". Surely this solemn undertaking ought to be respected.

The Security Council is already dealing with certain phases of the problem alluded to by your note. If you or we believe that other aspects of this problem or other problems should be urgently dealt with in the interest of peace, then it lies open to any of us to enlarge the scope of the Security Council consideration. Furthermore, under the Charter, members of government, including Heads of Government and Foreign Ministers, may represent a member nation at the Security Council. If such a meeting were generally desired, the United States would join in following that orderly procedure.

I do not, of course, exclude the discussion, outside the United Nations, of world or regional problems, not posing alleged imminent threats to the peace. I cannot but deplore the persistent refusal of your Government for so many months to agree to the adequate preparation of a "summit" meeting at which we could exchange considered views on the great problems which confront the world. The Ambassadors of France, the United Kingdom and the United States were negotiating at Moscow with your Foreign Minister to develop a list of topics which might lend themselves to considered and useful discussion at a summit meeting. These negotiations were broken off by your Government on June sixteenth.[7]

In conclusion, I venture to express in most earnest terms my hope that the Soviet Government will unite with us for real peace. The longing of mankind for peace is too precious to be used for ulterior purposes. I hope that ways can be found to act for peace in accordance with the standards prescribed by the Charter of the United Nations. All the world, I believe, knows that peace with justice is the dedication of the American nation. We have in the past sacrificed greatly for that devotion. We have loyally complied with the pledge we made, by the United Nations Declaration of January 1, 1942, to renounce any aggrandizement for ourselves. Just as we shall resist any efforts to use love of peace to mask aggression, so we shall equally never fail to take any step, at any sacrifice, which will genuinely promote the cause of peace and justice in the world.[8]
Sincerely

[1] Khrushchev had told Eisenhower that the U.S. decision to send troops into Lebanon (no. 770) and the British moves in Jordan (no. 776) had moved the world to "the brink of catastrophe." "Alarm is gripping the minds of people in all continents," he said, and "a war conflagration, wherever it begins, may spread to all the world." He called for an immediate conference of the heads of government of the Soviet Union, the United States, Great Britain, France, and India with the participation of the U.N. Secretary General. The conference would propose concrete recommendations to end the crisis in the Middle East and would submit them to the Security Council (Khrushchev to Eisenhower, July 19, 1958, AWF/I: Khrushchev). Khrushchev had sent similar letters to Prime Minister Macmillan, President de Gaulle, and Prime Minister Nehru. Eisenhower discussed the Soviet proposal and the draft of this reply with State and Defense Department officials and later with Secretary Dulles. After Dulles had told the President that the British and French had thought the original U.S. response "a bit too negative," Eisenhower agreed to accept the proposal of a special Security Council meeting, with participation by the heads of government and foreign ministers (Goodpaster, Memorandum of Conversation, July 21, 1958, AWF/D; and Dulles, Memorandum of Conversation, July 21, 1958, Dulles Papers, White House Memoranda Series; see also Telephone conversations, Eisenhower and Dulles, July 19, 22, 1958; Dulles and Nixon, July 21, 1958; Dulles and Hagerty, July 23, 1958, Dulles Papers, Telephone Conversations, and AWF/D; on the British, French, and Indian responses see *Public Papers of the Secretaries-General of the United Nations*, vol. IV, *Dag Hammarskjöld, 1958–1960*, p. 148; and Macmillan, *Riding the Storm*, pp. 523, 525–28).

[2] Eisenhower added the last portion of this sentence in a handwritten emendation to the eighth draft of this letter (Dulles Papers, White House Memoranda Series; see

also Greene, Memorandum of Meeting, July 22, 1958, *ibid.*). Before Eisenhower's changes the sentence had read: "I am not aware of any danger of war unless indeed war be the purpose of the Soviet Union." Khrushchev had warned Eisenhower that the Soviets possessed "atomic and hydrogen bombs, an Air Force and a Navy, and in addition Ballistic Missiles of all types in which are included intercontinental."
[3] Khrushchev's letter contained several references to the "aggression" and "armed conflict" which had "arisen in the area of the Near and Middle East."
[4] On the formation of the United Arab Republic see no. 560.
[5] On the Soviet resolution see State, *American Foreign Policy; Current Documents, 1958,* pp. 964–65. Following the vetoes, Lodge proposed another resolution calling for an emergency session of the General Assembly to consider Lebanon's complaint of aggression by the United Arab Republic (see *ibid.,* pp. 967–68, 980–81; see also State, *Foreign Relations, 1958–1960,* vol. XI, *Lebanon and Jordan,* pp. 252, 331–32).
[6] On this day the Soviet Union had vetoed a Japanese resolution that authorized Secretary General Hammarskjöld to take "additional measures" to protect the independence of Lebanon. Although the resolution failed to pass, Hammarskjöld stated that he would expand the activities of the U.N. Observation Group in Lebanon (*ibid.,* p. 968, see also *Public Papers of the Secretaries-General of the United Nations,* vol. IV, *Dag Hammarskjöld, 1958–1960,* pp. 140–48; State, *American Foreign Policy; Current Documents, 1958,* pp. 991–92; and Telephone conversations, Dulles and Hagerty, July 21, 1958; Dulles and Eisenhower, July 21, 1958; and Knowland and Eisenhower, July 21, 1958, Dulles Papers, Telephone Conversations, and AWF/D).
[7] For background on the summit negotiations see no. 761; see also State, *American Foreign Policy; Current Documents, 1958,* pp. 809–16.
[8] For developments see no. 789.

784

EM, AWF,
Administration Series

To George Magoffin Humphrey   *July 22, 1958*
Personal and confidential

Dear George: An incident that occurred at the legislative meeting this morning suddenly suggested to me that I could think of nothing else that would be so helpful at this moment as a good long talk with you.

There was under discussion in the meeting the current Housing Bill in the Senate. That bill seeks to authorize 2 billion 4 hundred million dollars for sundry purposes, even including, as part of a so-called Housing Bill, the building of "facilities" in universities. I assume that this could mean lecture halls, student unions, class rooms and the like.[1] This sum, of course, is in addition to one billion 8 hundred million appropriated a good many weeks back when the Congress passed, as an "anti-recession measure" a Mortgage Reinsurance Bill that compels the government to insure mortgages at a fixed rate.[2] This means that private financing will be, to that extent, excluded from home building.

Other items on the agenda this morning included the additions made by the House Appropriations Committee to the Administration's Defense Budget—something like one billion 250 million.[3] There were also under discussion certain cuts the House made in the Defense Budget and the reclamas from the Defense Department for the restoration of the major portion of these items.[4] Although I questioned the witnesses closely, it was impossible to find out exactly what would be the *net* addition to the Defense estimates.

Other money items we had to examine involved the Communities Facilities Bill[5], the Depressed Areas Bill[6] and the Educational Bill.[7]

The first of these bills is particularly bad. In the House version the Federal loans to communities can go up to 2 billion at a $2\frac{5}{8}\%$ interest rate. All in all, in these bills we were talking something on the order of 5 to 6 billion dollars *over and above budgetary estimates.*

There are many other bills still in the mill which have for their purpose the expenditure of additional amounts.

Only yesterday I had another conference of an entirely different kind. It was attended by Bob Anderson, Bill Martin, Steve Saulnier and Gabe Hauge.[8] Our subject was the condition of the money market and the prospects for satisfactory refinancing of some 70 billions of our debt over the next year, to which of course must be added the amount of next year's deficit. The prospects of successful financing, particularly if we hope to lengthen out any of our debt, are far from bright. They are not helped any by the number of measures that Congress tries to enact which contemplate the expenditure of Federal money at fixed interest rates, always lower than are practical.[9]

As you may know, I have already approved bills which I personally considered as imposing unwarranted drains on the Federal Treasury. The first of these was the Postal Bill. Arthur Summerfield would have had a heart attack and would now be in a sanitarium had I not approved this one. This was because of his long fight to reform the rate structure and his belief that unless the rate bill was approved now we would never get another. He argued that with this feature of the bill once out of the way, we could not *again* be blackjacked into approving a pay increase that was unwarranted by the rise in living costs, whereas the Postal Rate reform would stand permanently. While I was not too happy about this situation, the advice of all my associates on the bill was unanimous.[10]

At the same time we finally enacted the so-called Cordiner Plan for the military services, which in some instances made material increases in the amounts recommended by the Administration.[11]

With these two approved, it was manifestly impossible to veto the Civil Service pay raise.[12] On the other hand, I did veto the Public

Works Bill and the Omnibus Farm Bill. [13] Incidentally, neither of these vetoes has ever been brought up for overriding in the Congress and I am beginning to believe now that there will not be made any such attempt.

I have not really called your attention to bills that, by standards which we now seem to be observing, could be classed as inconsequential. For example, a Maritime Bill for two superliners at 224 million. Here again, however, a necessary and recommended item was inflated by the Congress almost beyond the point of recognition.[14]

(Exactly at this point Jerry Morgan brought me in a Supplemental request for 462 million dollars!)[15]

As I consider the credit of our country, the need for constant, orderly, and successful refinancing of our debt, and the prospect of a greater '59 deficit than we had contemplated, I would truly like to be somewhat more persuasive in my efforts to make the Congress understand the danger of unwarranted expenditures. Of course I understand that some individuals are simply careless and obsessed by the idea that by voting for every expenditure, particularly those that affect their states and districts, they hope to be re-elected. But there are others who, as a matter of political belief, are anxious to centralize additional functions in Washington, and to push us more and more to socialistic forms. To further this aim they are quite ready to burden our people with a debt that becomes more and more menacing in its proportions.

There is still another Congressional group that, in the opinion of many, is engaged in pushing preposterous money bills in the certainty that these will be vetoed by me. According to this theory, these individuals believe that the country will be no worse financially but they, by their "liberal" voting record, will fare much better at the polls this fall.

Finally, there is a group that believes (or pretends to believe) that we are still moving so rapidly downward in a recession that only lowered taxes and vast increases in spending will do us any good.

As you can see, I think that nothing is more necessary in our domestic affairs than to examine, each day, our economy as well as our governmental receipts and expenditures, and to act prudently. Others seem to overlook this problem; they get preoccupied with different items.

This morning I was visited by the Chairman of the Commission on Civil Rights, who voiced his conviction, after several months of intensive study, that the racial problem was the most critical of all those now facing the United States.[16] Others argue that there is no problem that is quite so important as that of bringing about a better level of leadership in labor and business circles so as to defeat the vicious inflationary spiral brought about by higher wages and higher prices. This is the only matter that concerns them. Other individuals think that only in a vastly increased scale of scientific training can our country be saved from destruction caused by its own ignorance.

Whether or not all these are correct, I cannot help but feel that all of us must help to stop the Congressional practice of passing huge money bills that, interlarded with "must" provisions, make vetoes either impractical or so misunderstood by the people that they are over-ridden.

(At this point Hagerty came in to tell me that there is a rumor to the effect that Khrushchev is going to come to a United Nations meeting).[17]

If there is anything left of coherence in this letter up to this point it is strictly coincidental and unintentional. I'm sure of one thing: with this list of things to command my attention, you can easily understand that calm, continuous, searching analysis of all factors in the complicated Mid East question is indeed difficult.

The story of our effort to preserve the peace and to avoid unacceptable deterioration of the United States position in the Mid East has been fairly well told in the press; I shall not bore you here with its details. The fact is that we will take any honorable and practicable solution to the Lebanese problem, so that we can remove our troops. But we must insist that the formula is both practicable and honorable.

So far Iraq has not taken some of the mob-like actions that normally we could expect. They have not destroyed any of the pipe lines or attempted to interfere with production of oil in the region. There is some slight indication that they may want to remain on good business relationships with the West, even though I suppose they will want to negotiate somewhat better contracts, probably in the pattern of the Standard of Indiana contract.[18]

The basic reason for our Mid East troubles is Nasser's capture of Arab loyalty and enthusiasm throughout the region. Foster and I have long struggled with the Congress to get the kind of propaganda campaign established in that area that could counteract anti-Western sentiment as it now pours out of the Cairo—and Soviet—radios.[19] We have never been able to get the money to do a good job, though today we are probably spending more by the month to solve this crisis than it would have cost us by the year to have been more effective in preventing it.

There is no use going over with you all of the ins and outs of our negotiations with the Russians. Admittedly they are masters in propaganda, in deceit, in distortion and in influencing ignorant populations. At the same time they seem to appeal also to a certain percentage of the intelligentsia. But one thing is certain. The men in the Kremlin are serving only their own selfish purposes. They are not trying to do anything decent for any other portion of humanity.

Of course I could have made this letter even more confusing by outlining some of our current difficulties with the Congress in reciprocal trade, mutual security, defense reorganization, as well as the difficulty of preventing a splendid public servant from being crucified by demagogues and columnists.[20] In all these, however, except for the last, I seem to be doing well at the moment. But I think Congress will not have the wisdom—and political courage—to give us what we so desperately need in M.S.A.[21] They would rather neglect a vital—but unpopular—program to spend billions elsewhere futilely.

Actually, of course, the sun is shining, we have had a better spring and summer so far as crops and vegetation are concerned than we have had in many years, the United States is still populated by relatively happy people, and by and large our grandchildren do not seem too much worried—yet—about some of the things today that cause me a mite of irritation.

Give my love to Pam and remember me to all the others in your nice family and, of course, all the best to yourself. *As ever*

P.S. You may be one of the lucky humans that finds himself out at the Bohemian Grove at this minute. If this is so, this recitation of Washington activities will be largely out of date for the reason that in one way or another some of the problems will have been settled by the time you read this. All of which may prove something—possibly that there is no real reason for bothering one's friends with his troubles.[22]

---

[1] On July 11, 1958, the Senate had passed S. 4035, an omnibus housing bill authorizing $2.5 billion in government spending on various housing programs. The bill extended the FHA program for insuring home improvement loans; raised FHA mortgage ceilings; established a new program to provide mortgage insurance for housing for the elderly; and increased urban renewal funding ($300 million a year for fiscal 1959–1964). It also authorized funds for low rent housing; extended the Capehart military housing program; expanded the number of lenders authorized to make VA loans; increased the maximum revolving fund for college housing loans, and established a $250 million revolving fund for guaranteeing loans to educational institutions for classroom and laboratory construction (see *Congressional Quarterly Almanac*, vol. XIV, *1958*, pp. 225–29; on Capehart housing see Galambos and van Ee, *The Middle Way*, no. 1775; see also Legislative Leadership meeting supplementary notes, July 22, 1958, and Minnich to Stans, July 22, 1958, AWF/LM).

[2] On the Emergency Housing Bill, passed by Congress on March 19 in an effort to counter the recession, see nos. 598 and 633.

[3] On July 24, the Senate Appropriations Committee would report H.R. 12738, recommending defense appropriations of $40,032,811,000. This amount was $1,245,841,000 more than the President had requested, and $1,623,250,000 more than the House version of the bill. Some of the increases included support for a 900,000-man Army, and additional funds for modernization of Army equipment.

[4] A reclama is a request to authority to reconsider its decision or its proposed action. On July 30 the Senate would authorize $40,042,992,000 for the 1959 Defense Department Appropriation Bill.

[5] The Community Facilities Bill, an anti-recession measure, sought to expand and liberalize a program of loans to municipalities to build various public facilities. Congress failed to pass the measure after delays and a recovering economy had seemed to render the bill unnecessary (see *Congressional Quarterly Almanac*, vol. XIV, *1958*, pp. 151–53).

[6] Eisenhower was referring to S. 3683, the Area Redevelopment Bill, which sought to authorize $280 million in federal aid for "distressed areas" suffering from chronic unemployment. The President would pocket veto the measure on September 6, saying that despite his three-year effort to promote the adoption of a program to aid communities, the current bill did not recognize that "the major responsibility for planning and financing the economic redevelopment of communities of chronic unemployment must remain with local citizens" (see *Public Papers of the Presidents: Eisenhower, 1958*, pp. 690–91; *Congressional Quarterly Almanac*, vol. XIV, *1958*, pp. 147–51; for background see Galambos and van Ee, *The Middle Way*, no. 1579).

[7] Eisenhower had discussed the National Defense Education Act with the legislative leaders and had stated his desire that this emergency program should be limited in duration. Agreement was reached that there should be a reduction in the number of scholarships in view of the additional provision that had been made for loans to students (see no. 767).

[8] Eisenhower had met with Treasury Secretary Anderson, Federal Reserve Board President Martin, Chairman of the Council of Economic Advisors Saulnier, and White House Special Assistant Hauge for one hour on July 21.

[9] On July 21, 1958, the Treasury Department and the Bureau of the Budget had reported that the U.S. government had incurred a 2.8 billion dollar debt for fiscal year 1958. The recession had reduced receipts below the original estimates. On July 28 Eisenhower would ask that the statutory debt limit be raised by $10 billion to $285 billion and a temporary increase over that amount of $3 billion be made available through June 30, 1960 (see *Public Papers of the Presidents: Eisenhower, 1958*, pp. 571–72; *New York Times*, July 22, 24, 25, 1958). This marked the Administration's second 1958 request for an increase in the debt ceiling. On August 23 Congress would pass H.R. 13580 raising the debt limit by $8 billion and authorizing an additional $3 billion temporary increase through 1960 (see *Congressional Quarterly Almanac*, vol. XIV, *1958*, pp. 267–68).

[10] In May Eisenhower had signed into law the Postal Bill (H.R. 5836) which raised rates by about $550 million and increased employees' salaries by $265 million annually. Postmaster General Summerfield had requested the rate increase in order to modernize the postal service and fund thousands of new post offices (see *Congressional Quarterly Almanac*, vol. XIV, *1958*, pp. 208–10; for background see no. 328).

[11] See nos. 564 and 721.

[12] On June 20, 1958, the President had signed S. 734, approving salary increases averaging 10 percent for all government employees (see *Congressional Quarterly Almanac*, vol. XIV, *1958*, p. 212).

[13] Eisenhower was probably referring to the omnibus Flood Control Bill, comprised of the Rivers and Harbors, Flood Control and Water Supply Acts of 1958, which he had vetoed on April 15, 1958. The bill, he said, had violated Administration policy that called for shared federal, state, and local expenditures when "substantial local benefits" would result. The President, saying that "significant steps" had already been taken to accelerate federal construction, had not been moved by arguments that the legislation was necessary to stimulate the economy (see *Public Papers of the Presidents: Eisenhower, 1958*, pp. 307–10; *Congressional Quarterly Almanac*, vol. XIV, *1958*, pp. 304–8). On Eisenhower's veto of the farm "price-freeze" bill see no. 616. The House Om-

nibus Bill, an assemblage of individual commodity, milk, and surplus disposal programs, would not be considered by the full House (see *Congressional Quarterly Almanac*, vol. XIV, *1958*, pp. 269–75).

[14] On July 2, 1958, Congress had authorized the Federal Maritime Board to contract
for the construction and sale of two very large passenger vessels at a cost of $221
million. Although the President had signed the legislation on July 15, he had criticized the bill's provision for "90 to 100 million dollars more than would be required
if these two vessels were constructed under existing law and practice." He had also
expressed disapproval of the bill's provision for government rather than private mortgage financing (see no. 772; *Public Papers of the Presidents: Eisenhower, 1958*, p. 548;
Congressional Quarterly Almanac, vol. XIV, *1958*, pp. 249–51; and *New York Times*, July
2, 16, 1958).

[15] Gerald D. Morgan was Deputy Assistant to the President.

[16] John A. Hannah, former president of Michigan State University and current Chairman of the U.S. Commission on Civil Rights, had met with Eisenhower and Sher
man Adams.

[17] On Soviet Premier Khrushchev's proposal for a meeting of the heads of government of the Soviet Union, the United States, Great Britain, France, and India, see
no. 783; on the deployment of U.S. and British troops in Lebanon and Jordan see
nos. 770 and 776.

[19] A violent coup had ousted the pro-Western government of Iraq and had led to U.S.
intervention in Lebanon (see no. 770). According to State Department intelligence
officials, the new regime desired friendly relations with the West, intended to maintain its international agreements, and would not nationalize oil production.

   On June 1 the government of Iran had ratified an agreement with Standard Oil
of Indiana for the exploration of offshore oil in the Persian Gulf. Iran would receive
75 percent of the net profits; the oil company would receive 25 percent. Standard
Oil also paid Iran a $25 million cash bonus for signing the agreement (State, *For-
eign Relations, 1958–1960*, vol. XII, *Near East Region; Iraq; Iran; Arabian Peninsula*,
pp. 330–31).

[19] See, for example, Galambos and van Ee, *The Middle Way*, nos. 1811 and 1920; and
nos. 450 and 776 in these volumes. See also Ashton, *Eisenhower, Macmillan and the
Problem of Nasser*, pp. 140–89.

[20] For background see no. 753.

[21] On funding for the mutual security program see nos. 762 and 782.

[22] Eisenhower had added an additional longhand postscript: "And keep watching for
some 'vetoes'!!"

---

785   *EM, AWF, International Series:*
                                                                    Macmillan

To Harold Macmillan   *July 23, 1958*
Cable. Secret

Dear Harold: I received yesterday your message about Jordan.[1] Taking up first the matter of supply, we are quite ready in principle to
help out further in this respect. I understand that we are flying POL[2]
from Lebanon to Jordan, overflying Israel close to the Syrian border. The Israelis acquiesce in this but do not like it. We have told

them that we think this need will be over by this week and that an adequate substitute can be found in Aqaba where, I believe, intensive work is being done to improve the facilities and communication route with Amman.[3]

We would be willing to use our Globemasters to assist you in flying from Cyprus supplies to your forces in Jordan. As you say, a smaller number of these larger planes could do the job you are doing. However, we would have to seek and find some accommodation with Israel. Foster has already talked with their Embassy here about the matter, and we hope to get a reply by tomorrow.[4] I am convinced that whatever be the immediate outcome, we cannot look upon these overflights of Israel as a permanent solution. We must concentrate upon getting what is needed into Aqaba, preferably by commercial vessels because of Arab sensitiveness about non-Arab naval vessels in the Gulf. Then we must quietly create better ways to get the cargoes to the Amman area.

The introduction of our ground forces raises much more difficult problems. Our public opinion and Congress would, I know, be extremely averse to seeing us take this further step.[5] We believe, as you indicate, that your forces there already stabilize the position and we hope that it will continue thus, until through the UN or otherwise you are able, logically, to lay down this burden.[6] *As ever*

[1] For background on the British decision to send troops into Jordan see no. 776. Macmillan had told Eisenhower that the Jordanian prime minister was convinced that increased ground forces were essential to protect his country against subversion. "It is clear," Macmillan said, "that unless reinforcements are sent there is a real danger that a *coup* may take place under our very noses." He asked for American ground troops to increase military and political support and also for American Globemaster cargo planes to aid in flying essential supplies to the British troops (Macmillan to Eisenhower, July 22, 1958, AWF/I: Macmillan; see also Goodpaster to Twining, July 30, 1958, WHO/OSS: Subject (DOD); Macmillan, *Riding the Storm*, pp. 523–25; and State, *Foreign Relations, 1958–1960*, vol. XI, *Lebanon and Jordan*, pp. 363–64, 366–67). Earlier on this same day Eisenhower had told Secretary Dulles that he thought perhaps Macmillan had "lost his nerve." The United States could supply six Globemasters, he said, but both men agreed that the United States could not "take the whole thing over" (Telephone conversation, July 23, 1958, Dulles Papers, Telephone Conversations).

[2] Petroleum, oil, and lubricants.

[3] Dulles had discussed the problem of overflights with the Israeli Ambassador Abba Eban (State, *Foreign Relations, 1958–1960*, vol. XIII, *Arab-Israeli Dispute; United Arab Republic; North Africa*, pp. 67–72; and NSC meeting minutes, July 25, 1958, AWF/NSC; see also Eban, *An Autobiography*, pp. 262–63; and Alteras, *Eisenhower and Israel*, pp. 309–10).

Eisenhower and Dulles had reviewed Macmillan's requests with State and Defense Department officials, CIA Director Allen Dulles, and JCS Chairman Nathan Twining. The supply problem could be solved, they reasoned, by reconstructing both road and railway routes from Amman to the port of Aqaba (State, *Foreign Relations, 1958–1960*, vol. XI, *Lebanon and Jordan*, pp. 374–76; and Goodpaster, Memorandum of Conversation, July 24, 1958, AWF/D).

[4] On August 2 Israeli Prime Minister Ben Gurion would ask the United States and Great Britain to stop flights over Israel immediately. He could no longer subject Israelis to the dangers involved, he said, and he had already exceeded the authority granted him by his cabinet. He would later agree to the overflights, however, provided that the United States initiate consultations designed to end the flights as soon as possible (State, *Foreign Relations, 1958–1960*, vol. XIII, *Arab-Israeli Dispute; United Arab Republic; North Africa*, pp. 79–87; *ibid.*, vol. XI, *Lebanon and Jordan*, pp. 426–27; see also Memorandum of Conversation, Aug. 3, 1958, Dulles Papers, White House Memoranda Series).

[5] At this point Eisenhower deleted a sentence in the original draft: "Our own intelligence does not suggest that it is needed now, and I hope we can postpone this decision" (see Dulles Papers, White House Memoranda Series).

[6] Before Eisenhower's revisions, the original draft of this last sentence had read: "We believe, as you say, that your forces there already stabilize the position and we hope that it will contain them. We shall, however, keep this under the closest review and keep in touch with you on this matter" (*ibid.*).

In his reply on the following day Macmillan would thank Eisenhower for the cargo planes and would tell the President that he had asked his planners to coordinate the operation with U.S. officials (AWF/I: Macmillan). For developments see no. 789.

786   *EM, AWF, International Series:*
                                              Adenauer

To Konrad Adenauer   *July 23, 1958*

My good Friend: I am glad that Foster is going to be able to get to Bonn for a talk with you on Saturday before he goes to London.[1] There are many matters to talk about—the Middle East, the new France under De Gaulle, and some of the hardy perennials like disarmament.

I want you to know that we keep you constantly in mind and while sometimes events force quick decisions, we try to act in the spirit of our intimate and close understanding.

I am asking Foster to take this little note to you as a visible expression—if indeed one is needed—of my highest regard and best wishes.[2] *Sincerely*

[1] Secretary Dulles would meet with German Chancellor Adenauer for several hours on July 26 on route to a meeting of the Baghdad Pact in London.

[2] For Dulles's report on his visit see no. 791.

TO LYNDON BAINES JOHNSON   *July 24, 1958*

Dear Lyndon: Although I mentioned this to you yesterday at luncheon, I did want to say thanks ever so much for your leadership and effective results in respect to the foreign trade legislation. You know, as I do, the importance of this measure to our country and to the cause of world peace. Congratulations on the results achieved.[1]

Now I hope that you will be praying with me that the remaining defects will be eliminated in conference.

With warm regard, *Sincerely*

---

[1] On July 17, 1958, White House aide Bryce Harlow had suggested that there might be "salubrious fallout" from the phone calls made by the President to Senators Johnson, Styles Bridges, and California Republican Congressman Gordon Leo McDonough, thanking them for their efforts on behalf of the extension of the reciprocal trade, defense reorganization, and space bills (see Harlow to Whitman, July 17, 1958, AWF/D; for background see no. 753; see also no. 782). The Senate had taken up debate on the reciprocal trade legislation on July 15, with Majority Leader Johnson leading the fight to approve the House version of the bill without, as Johnson phrased it, "crippling amendments." Johnson had been particularly outspoken in the successful opposition to two amendments introduced by South Carolina Senator Strom J. Thurmond, amendments that would have cut the trade extension to two years, and diluted presidential authority by requiring congressional approval of a presidential rejection of a Tariff Commission recommendation (see *Congressional Quarterly Almanac*, vol. XIV, *1958*, pp. 171–73; *New York Times*, June 13, July 8, 1958). Eisenhower would write McDonough on July 21, and Bridges on July 28, 1958. For developments see no. 802.

---

788   *EM, AWF, Gettysburg Series*

TO ARTHUR SEYMOUR NEVINS   *July 24, 1958*

Dear Art: The only question I have on the papers you sent to me regarding the cattle census involves Black Brutus. While it is true that by an exchange of letters of more than a year ago, I agreed with the Allen-Byars partnership that Black Brutus would be owned jointly by them and by me, yet Black Brutus is registered under the single ownership of Allen-Byars. This means nothing except that, as I understand it, we cannot use artificial insemination on my cattle with Black Brutus.[1]

I have filed this note with you just to keep the record straight as I understand it.

Thanks very much for your trouble. So far as I am concerned, all progeny of any of my Sunbeams should be either sent to the butcher or fattened for home butchering.[2]

With warm regard, *As ever*

[1] On July 23 Nevins had sent the President an inventory of the Eisenhower Farms herd and of the George E. Allen-Billy G. Byars Partnership herd as of July 1, 1958. The list included information about the predominant line of breeding and the families of the brood cows (all in AWF/Gettysburg). For background on the arrangement between the Eisenhower Farms and the partnership see no. 70.

Nevins would confirm Eisenhower's understanding of the arrangement in a letter of July 25 (AWF/Gettysburg). Despite the joint ownership by Eisenhower Farms and the Allen-Byars partnership, Nevins would write, Black Brutus had been registered in the name of Allen-Byars. Moreover, Nevins said, the herdsman understood that under the current registration the Eisenhower cows had to be bred naturally to this bull.

[2] Bulls from the Sunbeam family were largely responsible for the dwarfism that was beginning to appear in many Angus herds. They were thus relatively unsuitable for breeding (for background see no. 10).

789   *EM, AWF, International Series:*
                                                        Khrushchev

To Nikita Sergeyevich Khrushchev   *July 25, 1958*

Dear Mr. Chairman: I have studied your letter of July twenty-third. I find in it apparent misunderstandings of the views expressed in my letter of July twenty-second, which I would request you to read again more carefully.[1]

I then said that if, despite the facts established in the recent meetings of the Security Council, your Government still desires to allege that the situation in Lebanon constitutes an imminent danger to peace in the Middle East, the proper forum for appropriate discussion is the United Nations Security Council. I am glad that you now recognize the responsibility of the United Nations and have withdrawn your original proposal which would have gravely undermined the prestige and authority of the United Nations.[2]

My letter pointed out that the Charter of the United Nations authorizes members of government, and that of course includes Heads of Government and Foreign Ministers, to represent a member nation at the Security Council and that if such a meeting were generally desired, the United States would join in following that orderly procedure. It is, of course, not yet certain that such a meeting is in fact "generally desired," although that may prove to be the case.

You now make specific suggestions dealing with the composition of the Security Council and the conditions under which nations other than members of the Council may participate in discussions of the Council.[3] My letter to you of July twenty-second urged that one of the advantages of proceedings in the Security Council is that there are established rules on these matters and it is accordingly not necessary to rely on improvising. I pointed out that when rules of this kind are sought to be improvised, there is raised a whole series of new problems, notably as to the participation and non-participation of various states. The United States will adhere, in these respects, to the Charter, which lays down the conditions under which nations which are not members of the Council may participate in the discussions of the Council.[4]

As to the agenda, we agree that it should be limited to a discussion of the problems of the Middle East, including the causes of those problems. I would, however, be lacking in candor if I did not make clear that to put peace and security on a more stable basis in the Middle East requires far more than merely a consideration of Lebanon and Jordan. These situations are but isolated manifestations of far broader problems. In my opinion the instability of peace and security is in large measure due to the jeopardy in which small nations are placed. It would be the purpose of the United States to deal with the specific incidents you raise within that broad context. To do otherwise would be to be blind to the teaching of history.

You will recall, Mr. Chairman, that World War II was brought about by a series of acts of direct and indirect aggression against small nations. In March 1939 the then head of the Soviet Communist Party[5] pointed out that the failure of non-aggressive nations, among which he named Britain and France, to check direct or indirect aggression against small countries meant "giving free rein to war and, consequently, transforming the war into a world war." The forecast unhappily proved true.

You will also recall the 1950 "Peace through Deeds" Resolution of the General Assembly which condemns the "fomenting of civil strife in the interest of a foreign power" as among "the gravest of all crimes."[6]

It is my earnest hope that through the United Nations Security Council steps can be taken in regard to the Middle East which, by making peace more secure there, will help promote it elsewhere.

In conclusion, I suggest that the Permanent Representatives of the members of the United Nations Security Council in New York should exchange views, under arrangement made by the Secretary General, to ascertain that a meeting of the kind and under conditions I suggest is generally acceptable. If so they should also agree upon a date which would be generally satisfactory. The date of July twenty-eighth would be too early for us.

I am today authorizing our own Permanent Representative to act in this sense.[7] *Sincerely*

[1] For background and for Eisenhower's July 22 letter see no. 783. Several drafts of this letter with Eisenhower's handwritten emendations are in the Dulles Papers, White House Memoranda Series. Khrushchev had rejected decisively the assertion he claimed Eisenhower had made that the Soviet Union supported aggressive and expansionist forces in the world. After the U.S. intervention in Lebanon and the British in Jordan, he said, no one doubted who the aggressive countries were. Khrushchev supported a special session of the Security Council, at which the goal would be achieving agreement rather than the submission of resolutions that called for voting (Khrushchev to Eisenhower, July 23, 1958, AWF/I: Khrushchev; see also Telephone conversations, Eisenhower and Dulles, July 24, 1958, AWF/D and Dulles Papers, Telephone Conversations; and Telephone conversation, Dulles and Hagerty, July 25, 1958, *ibid.*).
[2] The Soviet leader had originally proposed a meeting of the heads of the governments of the Soviet Union, the United States, Great Britain, France, and India, outside the auspices of the United Nations (see no. 783).
[3] Khrushchev had recommended that India be included in the special session as the largest Asian nation promoting world peace. "Its participation," Khrushchev said, "would be really useful in contrast to the participation of one of the so-called permanent members [i.e.Nationalist China] who factually represent no one." The interested Arab states must also be included, he added.
[4] According to the United Nations Charter (Chapter V, Articles 23–32) any member of the United Nations which is not a member of the Security Council but is party to a dispute under consideration by the council can be invited to participate, without a vote, in any discussions related to that dispute (*Yearbook of the United Nations, 1946–17* [New York, 1947], pp. 323–26).
[5] Joseph Vissarionovich Stalin.
[6] On the Peace Through Deeds Resolution see no. 773.
[7] For developments see no. 800.

790   *EM, WHCF, Confidential File:*
                                                    State Department

To WILLIS P. DURUZ   *July 25, 1958*
Personal

Dear Bill: This note refers further to your letter of June 28th about the operations of ICA in Bolivia.[1] I understand that the program there has been of concern to responsible officials of the Administration, and that there is ground for your specific criticisms.[2] However, there is another side to the coin which, without going into details, is largely political in character.[3]

I simply want you to know that another look will be taken at the whole situation.

Again, my thanks for bringing this matter to my personal attention, and my warm regard, *Sincerely*

¹ Duruz, who had served in the Army under Eisenhower at Fort Lewis, Washington (see Chandler, *War Years*, no. 289), had been a horticulturist with the International Cooperation Administration for more than seven years. In his June 28, 1958, letter he had outlined what he believed to be serious problems with the American program of technical aid to Bolivia, where the mistakes were "frightening" and the waste "criminal." "The mission," he wrote, "could in my opinion, carry on more efficiently with one half the U.S. staff, and with almost half the money." There were enormous expenditures on agricultural machinery that was "rusting away and useless" because it was not suited to "primitive agriculture." New schools stood empty because they were flooded part of the year, having been built in poorly drained areas. Evaluation committees had been misled to the extent that it had become a "standing joke among people who really know the situation in the field."

Duruz urged Eisenhower to "place someone who is experienced in the field activities of this organization to check on the procurement and placement of U.S. personnel, to review critically the program planning, and the staffing patterns, and to severely examine the budgets for equipment and supplies going to the various countries."

The ICA was also under attack by Congress. On June 25, 1958, the House Government Operations Committee had charged the agency with "inadequate, indifferent and incompetent" handling of foreign aid projects. Six major deficiencies were named, ranging from inadequate advance planning to excessive reliance on political considerations to excuse deviations from sound procedures (see *New York Times*, June 26, 1958).

² Eisenhower had first responded to Duruz on July 2. He told Duruz that he was forwarding his letter to the Director of the ICA since there was little that he "personally can do about reported defects of this kind." On July 23, 1958, James Hopkins Smith, Jr., ICA Director, had responded in a letter to Sherman Adams. Smith had noted that the Bolivia program had been "a source of considerable concern" and was under review (see Smith to Dillon, June 30, 1958; and Dillon to Smith, July 15, 1958). He was deferring a final answer to the President until the review was complete. All correspondence is in the same file as the document.

³ For a discussion of American political concerns about Bolivia see State, *Foreign Relations, 1958–1960*, vol. V, *American Republics*, pp. 653–55; Kenneth Lehman, "Revolutions and Attributions: Making Sense of Eisenhower Administration Policies in Bolivia and Guatemala," *Diplomatic History* 21, no. 2 (1997), 185–213; and Rabe, *Eisenhower and Latin America*, pp. 77–82. According to Smith, the U.S. aid program was designed to keep the current noncommunist government in power, "and any incidental economic benefits should be considered as an added dividend."

791   *EM, AWF, Dulles-Herter Series*

TO JOHN FOSTER DULLES   *July 27, 1958*
Cable. Secret

*Dear Foster:*¹ Your report was most interesting. I was somewhat astonished by the Chancellor's estimate of French intention in the nuclear field.² While I respect the Chancellor's perspicacity, I cannot feel that at this moment the French would indulge in such a dangerous game as he suspects is possible. It seems to me their potential gains would in no way balance the undoubted risks.

We have of course long agreed that we should seek more effectively to concert with the British our independent conclusions and planning.[3] Whether or not Khrushchev is plotting more difficulties for us, and I do not doubt that he is doing so, or whether or not he personally runs out of the United Nations meetings, we must be alert in detecting his designs and circumventing them. More than this we should build up our capacity to neutralize, frustrate and eventually defeat the Kremlin.

Regarding a possible substitute for the Baghdad Pact, my present thoughts are about as follows: I believe we should listen and discuss but not now make decisions.[4] Our Mid East friends are currently tense and fearful, thus tending to make them more emotional than thoughtful. Their urgent and immediate needs we should seek to supply to the best of our ability but long-range planning should ordinarily be agreed on the basis of calm study and reflection.

We of course must be loyal and friendly but we need not be in a hurry to exchange marriage vows.

This is not especially helpful. But it is to be remembered that I just received your message a few minutes ago and of course I have had no opportunity for recent personal contacts with the responsible officials with whom you will be talking on Monday.[5]

My principal purpose now is to let you know that I shall be thinking of you and your work in the confidence that in your wisdom and knowledge we have an asset of incalculable value.

I shall be looking forward to seeing you on Tuesday.[6]

My warm greetings to all my friends and my best to you.

[1] This letter was transmitted early on July 28 to London, where Secretary Dulles was attending a meeting of the Baghdad Pact nations.

[2] Dulles had met for five hours with West German Chancellor Konrad Adenauer and Foreign Minister Heinreich von Brentano before arriving in London. The Chancellor, Dulles said, was "highly suspicious of French intentions" because of reports that the Soviet Union had offered France enriched uranium for their nuclear weapons program. De Gaulle had also canceled an earlier agreement on a French-Italian-German cooperative nuclear research program. Dulles had told Adenauer that he thought it "most unlikely the Soviets would help the French make nuclear weapons and thus expose themselves to demands from China" (Dulles to Eisenhower, DULTE 2, July 27, 1958, AWF/D-H).

The American Ambassador to France, David K. E. Bruce, had reported earlier that Germany was becoming increasingly anxious about de Gaulle. German officials questioned de Gaulle's ability to restore political stability in France, and they were concerned that he would take a more independent and aggressive role in NATO (State, *Foreign Relations, 1958–1960*, vol. VII, pt. 2, *Western Europe*, p. 76). In an earlier discussion regarding a possible meeting between Adenauer and de Gaulle, Eisenhower had told Dulles that the German leader was "a big enough man . . . to go to Paris to see De Gaulle and would in fact gain in stature by doing so" (Memorandum for the Record, July 25, 1958, Dulles Papers, White House Memoranda Series).

[3] Dulles and U.S. Ambassador John Hay Whitney had discussed with Prime Minister

Macmillan and Foreign Minister Selwyn Lloyd the dangers involved if Khrushchev backed away from the proposed heads of government meeting on the Middle East (see no. 789). They had agreed that more effective machinery for joint planning was necessary, Dulles said, and had decided to establish a working party in Washington "to crystallize some ideas." Both Macmillan and Dulles felt that the Soviet Union might "step up efforts to hit us at our weak points with the thought of 'teaching us a lesson' on the theory that Khrushchev offered us a chance to talk, we did not accept on his terms, and now we must face the consequences."

[4] Dulles, Macmillan, and their advisors had discussed the possibility of changing the name of the organization and of creating a new mechanism for the security commitments of the northern tier nations.

[5] Before the formal sessions of the Baghdad Pact conference began on the following day, Dulles would meet with Turkish Prime Minister Adnan Menderes and Foreign Minister Fatin Rustu Zorlu (State, *Foreign Relations, 1958–1960*, vol. XII, *Near East Region; Iraq; Iran; Arabian Peninsula*, pp. 111–12).

[6] After the morning session, Dulles would advise Eisenhower by telephone that the United States had to make some kind of declaration of intentions and purposes concerning Pakistan, Iran, and Turkey. The countries wanted the United States to join the pact, Dulles said, and he had explained that we could neither sign a treaty nor join the pact at that time. He read Eisenhower a proposed statement that, he assured the President, did not go beyond the terms of the 1957 Middle East Resolution (see no. 63).

After approving the statement, Eisenhower dictated the following to Ann Whitman: "Foster Dulles feels that it is absolutely necessary that we give some special reassurance to our support for Iran, Turkey and Pakistan. He apparently thought this might put him in disagreement with my statement in the telegram I sent him last evening, where I advised going slow in trying to establish some substitute for the Baghdad Pact. Since, however, he intends to make only a statement of our purpose of living up to the Mid East Resolution passed in March of 1957, I see no harm in making such a statement" (Telephone conversation, Dulles and Eisenhower, July 28, 1958, AWF/D, and Dulles Papers, Telephone Conversations; for the declaration and the communiqué issued at the end of the conference see *U.S. Department of State Bulletin* 39, no. 999 [August 18, 1958], 272–73).

On July 29 Dulles and Eisenhower would discuss the Baghdad Pact meetings and Dulles's talks with Adenauer and Macmillan. Dulles told Eisenhower of Adenauer's belief that if Egypt were given economic aid, Nasser "would then give up his grandiose political ambitions." Dulles and Macmillan had discussed the Soviet interest in a Mideast summit conference and also the "importance of trying to get the French back in line" (Dulles, Memorandum of Conversation, July 29, 1958, Dulles Papers, White House Memoranda Series).

792   *EM, AWF, Name Series*

To VERNON BIGELOW STOUFFER   *July 28, 1958*
Personal

Dear Mr. Stouffer: The other evening the cooking unit on my electronic oven apparently burned out.[1] The unit for browning continued to function, but the other unit not only ceased to cook but the timing dial also stopped moving. At the time I had a large rib roast in the oven. While I understand that the oven does not work at its best when the meat has not been boned, yet from the instructions it seemed to me that this merely delayed cooking and would not have any bad effect upon the oven itself.

In any event, we find upon inquiry that there is no individual or firm in the Gettysburg-York area of Pennsylvania authorized to repair the oven. I wonder if you could tell me who would be the closest individual to contact.

If it would be best to send the unit back to the factory for repair, could you have the factory give me directions as to exactly what should be removed, since it would be awkward indeed to send the whole piece of equipment back. If you can help me out in this matter, whether in identifying the person I should contact or in getting factory help in repairing it, please make certain that everybody understands that I am to be billed at regular rates like any other customer.[2]

Many thanks for the trouble I am causing you, and, of course, with warm regard to yourself, *Sincerely*

[1] Stouffer, chairman of the board of Stouffer Corporation, had installed the electric oven at Eisenhower's Gettysburg farm in 1957 (see no. 33). Eisenhower had visited his farm July 25–27.

[2] On August 4 Eisenhower would report to Stouffer that, as arranged, the oven had been repaired. Eisenhower also said that Chief West, a Naval Petty Officer stationed at Camp David who occasionally assisted in the operations at the farm, had received instructions "as to what should be done in case the oven is not used over a period of time. . . ." The President would also renew his offer to pay for the repairs (AWF/N; see also Telephone conversations, Eisenhower and West, July 27, 1958, and Eisenhower and Hartley, Aug. 1, 1958, in AWF/D).

---

793   *EM, AWF, Name Series*

To JULIAN BRADEN BAIRD   *July 29, 1958*
Personal

Dear Baird: I am not certain how the Treasury measures the degree of attrition when exchanging new obligations for old.[1] But according to my morning paper, the attribution on the non-bank holdings was about 50%.[2]

So I enclose a dollar in payment of my wager. (But it is a rather beaten up bill and possibly worth not over 95 cents!).

With warm regard, *Sincerely*

[1] On July 17 Under Secretary of the Treasury Baird had met with the President, Secretary of the Treasury Anderson, and Chairman of the Federal Reserve Board Martin to discuss the new rate for the certificates of indebtedness to be reissued on August 1. The Treasury Department had proposed a rate of 1 ⅝ percent. Eisenhower had written on the memorandum from Anderson: "gloomy prospects for success, fear as much as 30% attrition (I bet Baird 1.00 it would be less)" (see Anderson memorandum, July 17, 1958, AWF/A, Anderson Corr.; Ann Whitman memorandum, July 17, 1958, AWF/AWD; see also *Wall Street Journal*, July 28, 1958).

[2] On this same day Baird would write the President (AWF/N) to discuss the attrition rate, or the percentage of notes refinanced. "The attrition was $2,770 million. As a percentage of the $9,322 million of maturing debt publicly held on the day the refunding was announced, it figures out to 29.7 percent," he said. "From overhearing Secretary Anderson's telephone conversation with you last Friday, I realize you were under the impression that the 30 percent applied against the $16,264 million total outstanding, including the Federal Reserve holding. On this basis, the attrition amounts to 17 percent. So whichever way you figure it, you won the bet, and I am happy to send you the enclosed one dollar bill." Apparently, Eisenhower's letter crossed with Baird's in the mail, and on July 29 Eisenhower would again write Baird: "I find our dollars crossed in delivery. Since I have a new one I will call it square if I don't have to return this one from you!" (AWF/N). Baird would write in a follow-up letter that same day that he was "quite happy to call it a draw" (AWF/N).

794   *EM, AWF, International Series:*
                                                                            Macmillan

To Harold Macmillan   *July 30, 1958*
Cable. Confidential

Dear Harold: You will recall that on June 26th you sent me word concerning certain language that you desired eliminated from the draft text of the proposed agreement for military atomic cooperation and, although this was wording which had been used in the report prepared in this connection by Sir Edwin Plowden and Sir Frederick Brundrett for your side and by Lewis Strauss and Donald Quarles for ours, we dropped the clause which was objectionable to you.[1]

You may be interested to have the reasoning of our people in this connection. They believe it is possible that your Atomic Energy Authority has knowledge in the generation of atomic power by means of gas-cooled reactors which is not transmitted to us. Our planned expenditures might be different if we had all pertinent information on this type of reactor on which your people have specialized. In view of the fact that we are exchanging information on nearly every other aspect of atomic energy, it does not seem reasonable that we devote money and talent which might be saved or, at any rate, more wisely spent if the exchange of information is as broad as feasible. I am assured that we transmit to you freely all of our information on the generation of electricity by atomic power. I understand that there may be some patent or royalty difficulties in this area but, with good will on both sides, I am hopeful that they can be resolved.

The second point deals with the military usefulness of plutonium generated in atomic power reactors. It is widely believed that unless the uranium fuel elements in which plutonium is made are exposed only briefly and are frequently replaced with fresh fuel, that the plutonium is not of weapons grade. When the new military agreement becomes effective, our people will be in a position to tell yours that you can save considerable sums relative to your present costs of atomic power by leaving the fuel in the reactors for longer periods and nevertheless produce plutonium suitable for weapons. Thus, there will be a direct financial benefit to your civilian power program which will stem from the new military agreement. This is why in the draft of the agreement the principle of "interdependence" in the military and civilian areas was mentioned.[2]

With warm regard, *As ever*

[1] Frederick Brundrett, former chief of Royal Navy Scientific Research, was scientific advisor to the Ministry of Defence and chairman of the Defence Research Policy Committee. Plowden was chairman of the British Atomic Energy Authority.

For background on the amendments to the Atomic Energy Act and the negotiations for a bilateral treaty between the United States and Great Britain see nos. 718 and 725. Macmillan had told Eisenhower that although the British and American negotiators had settled on the terms of the agreement, controversy had arisen over some of the words American experts wanted to add to the preamble. "These words," Macmillan said, "would link the arrangements for exchange of defence information for our common security with the exchange of information in the civil field to which different considerations apply." Even though the wording was limited to the preamble and did not appear in the clauses of the agreement, Macmillan had asked that Eisenhower personally look into the matter so that the plans for the exchange of information would not become "bogged down on this point" (PREM/11 2554).

AEC Chairman Lewis Strauss, after learning of Macmillan's request, had told Secretary Dulles that the Defense Department also believed that civilian considerations should not be included with military agreements. In a later conversation Dulles had told Strauss that Macmillan was "adamant." Since the Defense Department agreed with him, Dulles said, perhaps the AEC should reconsider. The offending sentence was subsequently removed (Telephone conversations, Dulles and Strauss, June 26, 27, 30, 1958; and Dulles and Hood, June 27, 1958, Dulles Papers, Telephone Conversations; see also Macmillan to Eisenhower, July 1, 1958, PREM/11 2554).

On July 2 Eisenhower had signed the legislation amending the Atomic Energy Act and had authorized Dulles to sign the bilateral agreement. "We have acted at once," Eisenhower had told Macmillan, "to get this agreement before the Congress" (Eisenhower to Macmillan, July 3, 1958, AWF/I: Macmillan; see also Macmillan to Eisenhower, July 4, 1958, PREM/11 2554; and *U.S. Department of State Bulletin* 39, no. 1000 [August 25, 1958], 310–11).

[2] For developments on the information exchange see no. 822.

To Sherman Adams   July 30, 1958

Memorandum for Governor Adams: This draft was written for the same purpose, I assume, that George Allen had in mind when he sent me a similar one a couple of days ago.[1] Any speech in the foreign field has to be staffed thoroughly within the State Department both for fact and for its effect in areas or on individuals other than the one to which the talk is specifically directed.

There is very little use for me to do any real work on such a draft until after it has gone through this process in the State Department.

This particular one has some very good ideas, well stated. So I think it would be in order, just as in the former case, to ask the Secretary of State to have it looked over.

Incidentally, there is no need for identifying the author of the draft. It can merely be listed as one in which I am interested.

[1] The draft that Eisenhower mentions is not in EM. The speech draft USIA Director George V. Allen sent may have resulted from a meeting he had with the President on July 23. At that time Allen had expressed the hope that Eisenhower would address the people of the world at some appropriate time over the Voice of America (Goodpaster, Memorandum of Conversation, July 23, 1958, AWF/D).

796   EM, WHCF, Official File 116-SS
To Douglas McCrae Black   July 30, 1958

Dear Doug: Thank you so much for your recent longhand letter.[1] I think you realize that I live in a fairly sterile world, too remote for my own tastes from the thinking of the average American and too influenced by endless diplomatic cables and discussions to get a feel of the pulse of the people. Consequently, it does me no end of good to receive a communication such as yours.

I need not add that I deeply appreciate, too, your personal confidence and support.

With warm regard, *Sincerely*

[1] Black had praised Eisenhower for his recent letter to Soviet leader Nikita Khrushchev (see no. 783). Although he had not minimized the dangers that had frightened many Americans, Black wrote, Eisenhower had reassured them by the firmness of his response. "I hope you feel deeply the reaction of the people to your leadership" (Black to Eisenhower, July 23, 1958, same file as document).

Black had also complimented Eisenhower on the proposed reorganization of the Defense Department and the passage of the Reciprocal Trade Agreements Act (see

797   *EM, WHCF, Official File 116-R*

To Edward Lee Roy Elson   *July 31, 1958*
Personal

Dear Dr. Elson: Since my first note to you on the subject, I have been pondering carefully the interesting letter you left with Jim Hagerty.[1] Because of the earnest thought you have devoted to Mid East problems and your personal acquaintance with the region, I am stealing the time to write you again, at greater length than normally I could do. Even so I can do no more than to set out, in random fashion, a few of the factors in these problems.

First of all, as I said in my previous letter, I find myself in general agreement with your conclusions. I concur in the advice, "Keep Israel out of this crisis completely. If possible do not even mention the word." The difficulty here is that in any conversation with an Arab, *he* is the one that brings up the subject of Israel. Underlying all Arab thought is resentment toward the existence of Israel and an underlying determination, some day, to get rid of it. So while I agree that in this crisis we should try to prevent Israel from being a principal subject in our discussions and planning, yet it is necessary to remember that it is antipathy against that State, practically universal among all Arabs, that provides fertile ground for Nasser's hate propaganda.

I assure you that I never fail in any communication with Arab leaders, oral or written, to stress the importance of the spiritual factor in our relationships. I have argued that belief in God should create between them and us the common purpose of opposing atheistic communism. However, in a conversation of this kind with King Saud, he remarked that while it was well to remember that the Communists are no friends of ours, yet Arabs are forced to realize that Communism is a long ways off, Israel is a bitter enemy in our own back yard.[2] But the religious approach offers, I agree, a direct path to Arab interest.

Next, this Administration has never been antagonistic to Arab nationalism. Our own history as well as our sense of justice impel us to support peoples to achieve their own legitimate nationalistic aspirations. I think that possibly we have failed to make this clearly apparent to our Arab friends. The Cairo and Moscow radios have too long been falsely drumming in their ears the charge of Western imperialism and the clear purpose of Western nations, including the United States, to dominate all Arabs.

This brings to mind the need for a better and more consistent operation of our information services throughout the Arab region and indeed, through all the Muslim countries. George V. Allen, now in charge of our information services, is the most capable and knowledgeable man we have yet had in that post. He is struggling hard to find the facilities and the techniques whereby we, through friendly Arab spokesmen, can reach over good communications, the entire populations with the message of truth and fact about the West.

You refer to "a position of strength." I agree that we can be successful only when we operate from such a position. But we know that strength comprehends far more than military power.

For instance: There is an old military saying that "Nothing positive can be accomplished except from a strong base." So our position of strength must comprise not only the necessary military force in critical spots with proper support and reserves behind it, but the United States must itself be a "strong base" out of which positive action can be projected as necessary.

I want to pursue this thought a moment. The real strength of America must be described in values that are intangible. It is a truism to say that the strength of democracy is public opinion. When there is a truly unified public opinion there is a tremendous power generated by our free people. Further, when that public opinion is based upon knowledge and real understanding of the issues involved, then this tremendous power can produce and sustain constructive action, almost without limit.

But the prerequisite for such strength, I repeat, is knowledge and understanding. An important element is such an understanding that purely military defenses, no matter how powerful, can never insure any nation's security. Aggression that is political, psychological and economic can outflank military forces because of our failure to provide the necessary counter measures in those fields. The problem then is to create in the United States a true understanding of our proper relationship to the less developed countries, including the Mid East, as well as the measures necessary to keep those relationships healthy. I do not need to recite to you the efforts that have been made in this direction. That effort has been focused, in late months, primarily upon the Mutual Security Program. To inform the country on the essentials of this program there was organized under Eric Johnston a bipartisan army of crusaders.[3] There has been a very great deal of gratifying evidence that this message has reached a vast portion of our population; but there is still a serious question that the resulting understanding has been forcefully communicated, in turn, to the members of the Congress. Indeed, it is clear that there has not yet been created the determined, unified, aroused public opinion that would demand from the Congress the kind of support and action for these programs which must be carried out effectively, imaginatively and honestly if we are to preserve the peace and lead the world to a better life.

By and large you are well aware of the basic purposes, hopes and efforts of the American government in the foreign field. Those efforts in the Mid East are based upon convictions that largely parallel your own. Yet I feel that all of us must do more, here at home, if we are to be successful abroad. I have made speeches on this subject, three or four of them on nation-wide television.[4] But I believe teachers, business leaders, labor leaders and, indeed, including and especially the clergy, ought to be active in this work.

If all of us are to be active and effective, it must be on the basis that we have studied the problem realistically. Our purposes must be lofty and we must demand from ourselves a full measure of dedication to the principles that have inspired this nation in the great moments of its history. We may, and probably should, be emotional and sentimental in the proper sense, but we must come right down to earth if our conclusions are to be realistic and our efforts productive.

Even among some of our very able friends we apparently have not had this kind of thinking and conclusion. Just recently I had a letter from your close associate, Dr. Lowry, a man whom I respect and like.[5] But I cite some of his words, in communications he has sent to me, to support my belief that while his purposes are correct, some of his analyses and conclusions are wide of the mark.

I send along to you an article he wrote in which I have marked one paragraph.[6]

The charge he makes in that paragraph against three Presidents is, to my mind, completely unsupportable. He notes that in certain periods our military strength has been so great as to be awesome. Yet he deplores the fact that, possessing this strength, America has not so used it when needed, even though "No enemy would have dared stand against it."

The meaning that I get from this paragraph is that he believes that preventive war should either have been waged or at least threatened upon a number of occasions in the past two decades.

He ignores the fact that no Congress could ever have been induced to declare such a war. But his failure to ponder what such a venture would have brought about is mystifying. War is war, no matter by what adjective it is described. His idea is that all of these Presidents quailed before heavy responsibility. No matter what else might be said of President Roosevelt or of President Truman, I think that no one properly could charge them with being cowardly either in the physical or in the moral sense. Truman in standing firmly against Soviet intentions in Iran in 1946, his pronouncements on Turkey and Greece in 1947, and his reaction to the Korea invasion, even if that invasion came about as a result of our own neglect, were all examples of courageous action.[7] It seems to me that for a man who has never had the responsibility of conducting America's relationships with the remainder of the world to take it upon himself to make this sweeping criticism rather destroys my confidence in his judgment. This I say with some sadness because in his personal letter to me he expresses some thoughts that are more than appealing. They are in some instances very penetrating.

Incidentally he expressed some approbation concerning a column that I also enclose for you.[8] You will note that this column makes the charge that the sending of troops into Lebanon signified a complete turn-about in America policy. Actually it did nothing of the kind. The Lebanon incident was the natural outcome of doctrines, beliefs, convictions and policies that have been upheld by this Government, in every kind of situation through a number of years.

I think I need not recite them for you. You know of the Formosa, Viet Nam, Guatemala and Iran incidents.[9] In the solution of them real risks were run.

So what I am saying is that we cannot reach proper conclusions in these matters by thinking only with the top of our minds. We must get down to the fundamentals of human behavior, values and aspirations. We must be true to our religious heritage in recognizing clearly the basic principles by which we must attempt to guide our nation's destiny. But we must not fail to recognize that it is humans who must make temporal decisions. If those decisions are to conform to fundamental convictions, are to be logical and timely, there must be earnest and deep study and contemplation not only by officials, but by the people who produce the power through which such important projects are implemented.

The phrase "Will to Greatness" is an expression of a noble ideal; it will be achieved only if all of us, leaders and followers, each in his own sphere, uses his heart, his brain and his body to make it so.

With warm regard. *Sincerely*

P.S. I repeat that I very much liked your succinct, logical presentation of your ideas.[10]

---

[1] Eisenhower's first note to Dr. Elson, pastor of the National Presbyterian Church, is not in EM. Elson had praised Eisenhower's decision to send American troops into Lebanon (see no. 770) and compared that decisiveness to his handling of the Suez crisis in 1956—"one of your greatest moments." The military action would have "a salutary effect," he said, if the United States left the area "in a position of strength." Elson described the Arabs as a people who respected communication in spiritual terms. "We must find a way," he said, "to identify ourselves with the Arabs' natural

aspirations for freedom under God, for self fulfillment and the achievement of *an honorable national destiny consonant with their cultural and religious heritage.*" He made a number of suggestions that he believed would enhance relations with any Arab country: avoid mention of Israel, deal openly with Nasser, assure the Arabs of American friendship, help improve the lives of all Arabs, and eventually work toward a solution of the Palestinian problem (Elson to Eisenhower, July 24, 1958, same file as document; see no. 213 for more on Elson's interest in the Middle East).

[2] The Arabian monarch had visited Eisenhower in January 1957 (see no. 13).

[3] On Eric Johnston's group see nos. 524 and 582.

[4] Eisenhower's most recent speech was on May 6 (see *Public Papers of the Presidents: Eisenhower, 1958*, pp. 378–86; see also *ibid.*, pp. 160–68).

[5] Charles Wesley Lowry (D.Phil. Oxford n.d.), an Anglican clergyman, had contributed a number of articles to religious publications. He was chairman and executive director of the Foundation for Religious Action in the Social and Civil Order. Lowry had supported Eisenhower's decision regarding Lebanon and advocated a "dramatic and appealing" approach to the Arab nations, showing U.S. sympathy for their problems and their legitimate national aspirations (Lowry to Eisenhower, July 20, 1958, WHCF/OF 116-SS; see also Eisenhower to Lowry, July 24, 1958, *ibid.*). According to Ann Whitman, on July 28 Eisenhower had dictated a long letter to Lowry defending U.S. action in the Middle East but was "not sure whether to send it or not" (Ann Whitman memorandum, July 28, 1958, AWF/AWD).

[6] The article, "Wanted in the U.S.A.: A Will to Greatness!" is not in EM.

[7] For background on the Iranian situation, U.S. policy toward Greece and Turkey, and the Korean invasion see Galambos, *Chief of Staff*, nos. 809 and 1377; and Galambos, *Columbia University*, no. 865.

[8] The column, written by William S. White, is not in EM.

[9] On the crisis involving the islands off the shore of mainland China see Galambos and van Ee, *The Middle Way*, no. 1265; on Vietnam, vol. 15; on Guatemala, no. 965; and on Iran, no. 281.

[10] Elson would write again, primarily describing Egyptian President Nasser's background and its effect on his policies. He would also repeat his plea for the encouragement of Arab nationalism. While agreeing with Eisenhower's assessment of former President Truman's decisions, Elson would say that Truman's "action in the creation of Israel was the most colossal diplomatic debacle of our day" (Aug. 4, 1958, same file as document; see also Eisenhower to Elson, Aug. 12, 1958, *ibid.*).

On September 27 Elson would send the President a letter and a brochure that he and five other religious leaders had sent to Cabinet members, senators, congressmen, and military and academic leaders regarding the Arab-Israeli dispute and the threat it posed to peace in the Middle East and the rest of the world. (These letters and the brochure entitled "Peace By Persuasion in the Middle East" are in the same file as this document; see also Eisenhower to Elson, Oct. 3, 1958, *ibid.*).

798   *EM, AWF, DDE Diaries Series*

To NEIL HOSLER MCELROY   *July 31, 1958*
Top secret

Memorandum for the Secretary of Defense: There is disturbing evidence of a deterioration in the processes of discipline and responsibility within the Armed Forces. Setting aside earlier instances, I refer to recent occurrences which have special seriousness because of their operational character or connection. They include, in particular, unauthorized decisions which have apparently resulted in certain balloons falling within the territory of the Communist bloc,[1] a reported violation of the Soviet border in the Caspian Sea area by one of our reconnaissance aircraft following a route that contravened my standing orders,[2] and statements resulting in the disclosure of the location of certain of our atomic weapons storage and assembly sites within the United States.[3]

The harm done by this type of thing to the conduct of our international affairs, and to our national security, is obvious.

I believe it is essential that action be taken at once, with provision for the appropriate degree of security, to fix responsibility in those instances through formal investigation and report, and to institute a general tightening of discipline and command and executive responsibility within the defense establishment.

[1] On July 29, 1958, General Goodpaster had been advised that a reconnaissance balloon, part of the 461-L project that Secretary of State Dulles had approved earlier in July, had gone down in Poland the previous day. The project had envisioned that approximately eight balloons were to be released over the Pacific to fly over the United States, while at the same time two or three additional balloons equipped with cameras would be aimed specifically to pass over the Soviet Union. Any balloons detected over the Soviet Union would be explained as strays from the announced American launch. The balloon's descent in Poland was due to an error by an Air Force officer who had underestimated the time necessary for it to reach the Atlantic Ocean.

Goodpaster noted that the President had "deplored" the way in which this project had been handled and had told him to advise the Defense Department that the project was "to be discontinued at once and every cent that has been made available as part of any project involving crossing the Iron Curtain is to be impounded, and no further expenditures are to be made" (State, *Foreign Relations, 1958–1960*, vol. X, pt. 1, *Eastern Europe Region; Soviet Union; Cyprus*, pp. 168–69, 179–80; see also *New York Times*, Sept. 4, 7, Oct. 12, 1958). The National Security Council meeting on July 31, 1958, would discuss this issue and decide that presidential approval be required before the launching of any mechanism capable of reconnaissance over the Soviet Union (see State, *Foreign Relations, 1958–1960*, vol. III, *National Security Policy; Arms Control and Disarmament*, p. 211).

[2] On July 30, 1958, the Soviet Union had accused the United States of deliberately violating Soviet air space when a U.S. plane from Iran crossed the Soviet border over the Caspian Sea. The plane, a reconnaissance version of a four-engine medium jet bomber, had been forced back by Soviet fighters. The State Department had announced that it would investigate the Soviet complaint (*New York Times*, July 31, 1958).

[3] On July 30 the *Albuquerque Tribune* had reported the locations of seven atomic weapons storage sites in the United States, which it said were listed in the United States Postal Guide (see *New York Times*, July 31, 1958). The Atomic Energy Commission had declined comment.

Ann Cook Whitman, President Eisenhower's personal secretary.

Claude A. Barnett (*left*), Director of the Associated Negro Press, and E. Frederic Morrow (*right*), White House Aide for Special Projects, present President Eisenhower with a large copper tray from Tripoli, March 26, 1958.

President and Mrs. Eisenhower attend a private showing of Winston S.
Churchill's paintings at the Smithsonian Institution's Museum
of Natural History, April 24, 1958.

British Prime Minister Harold Macmillan with President Eisenhower
and Dr. Milton S. Eisenhower before commencement exercises at the
Johns Hopkins University, June 10, 1958.

President Eisenhower bids farewell to British Prime Minister
Harold Macmillan after two days of meetings in June 1958.

President Eisenhower greets Bernard Baruch, accompanied by Secretary of the Treasury Robert B. Anderson, April 2, 1958.

President Eisenhower congratulates Gordon Gray, newly appointed Special Assistant for National Security Affairs. Attorney General William P. Rogers, Secretary of the Treasury Robert B. Anderson, and Gray's wife Nancy observe the ceremony on July 23, 1958.

President Eisenhower greets Rajkumari Amrit Kaur, chairman of the Red Cross
Society of India, and General Alfred Gruenther, president of the American
Red Cross, November 13, 1958.

President Eisenhower and members of his staff meet with prominent Negro
leaders in his White House Office on June 23, 1958. *L to R:* Lester Granger,
Dr. Martin Luther King, Jr., White House aide E. Frederic Morrow,
the President, A. Philip Randolph, Attorney General William P. Rogers,
Special Presidential Assistant Rocco C. Siciliano, and Roy Wilkins.

South Korean President Syngman Rhee and Secretary of Defense
Neil H. McElroy, October 8, 1958.

President and Mrs. Eisenhower, Speaker of the House of Representatives Samuel T. Rayburn, his sister Medibel Bartley, and members of the armed services pose following a state dinner in honor of Rayburn, January 27, 1959.

To John Hay Whitney   *July 31, 1958*

Dear Jock: The ticker just brought me the news that you have bought Parade Magazine. I am delighted. It begins to look as if some of your plans are really coming to fruition.[1]

You can well imagine what I have been going through these weeks.[2] I wish that I had you here so we could have an occasional talk, about things both serious and trivial.

For example, I had an hour or so with George Humphrey just the other day. He reports that tropical red ants have invaded Georgia and that they are killing off the young quail.[3] Having served some years in the tropics, I know how vicious some of these ant varieties can be.[4] I do hope that they have some success in defeating them in Georgia. George tells me that at the moment the scientists are disagreeing violently as to methods that will be effective.

At least he brought me something to think about besides Khrushchev, Lebanon and deficits![5]

Give my love to Betsey and, as always, the best to yourself. *As ever*

[1] Whitney had purchased *Parade Magazine,* a syndicated Sunday newspaper supplement with a total circulation of 8.5 million, in an effort to support the financially suffering *New York Herald Tribune* (see *New York Times,* Aug. 1, 1958, Sept. 26, 1958; Kahn, *Jock,* pp. 262–63; and Kluger, *The Paper,* pp. 551, 553, 557). On July 10 (AWF/ A) Whitney had thanked the President for his "generous, friendly and as always unselfish interest" in Whitney's acquisition of the *New York Herald Tribune* (for background see no. 759). For developments see no. 825.

[2] On the recent attacks made upon Assistant to the President Sherman Adams see no. 753. On the decision to dispatch U.S. Marine landing battalions to Lebanon see nos. 753, 770, 773, and 776.

[3] The evening of July 29 the President and the former Treasury Secretary had motored from the White House to the Cosmos Club to attend a reception. For background on Eisenhower's turkey and quail hunts at Humphrey's Milestone Plantation and Whitney's Greenwood Plantation see nos. 7 and 525.

[4] Eisenhower describes his service in the Panama Canal Zone (1922–1924) and in the Philippine Islands (1935–1939) in his memoir, *At Ease,* pp. 182–95, 218–32.

[5] The President would write to Khrushchev the following day (see the following document). For developments in Lebanon see no. 916. On the economic recession, which had resulted in a federal budget deficit, see no. 784.

To Nikita Sergeyevich Khrushchev   *August 1, 1958*

Dear Mr. Chairman: For several centuries personal correspondence
between Heads of Government and Heads of State has been an extremely valuable channel of communication when the normal diplomatic channels seemed unable to carry the full burden. However, it
has always been recognized—not just as a matter of diplomatic form
but as a requirement of efficacy—that the essential ingredient in
such correspondence, whether confidential or public, was a tone of
serious purpose and an absence of invective.

It is in this tradition that I reply to your letter of July twenty-
eighth.[1]

I consider it quite inaccurate for you, both implicitly and explicitly, to convey the impression that the Government of the United
States has embarked on a policy of delay based on niggling procedural argument. The fact is that the differences between us are not
procedural but basic.

Very simply, the two basic points which the United States has
stated many times in the past, and which I repeat now, are (*a*) do
all of us, the Charter Members of the United Nations, agree that
the United Nations Security Council has the principal responsibility for the maintenance of international peace and security; and (*b*)
shall small nations as well as a few so-called "great powers" have a
part in the making of decisions which inevitably involve them?

As to my first point—What of the United Nations? It was created
out of the travail of World War II to establish a world of order and
of justice. It embodied and still embodies the hopes of mankind. At
this juncture, when you claim peace is endangered, you would push
it aside—we would invoke its processes.

This leads to my second point—What of the smaller powers of
this world? Shall they be ignored or shall the small nations be represented in the making of decisions which inevitably involve them?
History has certainly given us ample proof that a nation's capacity
to contribute to the advancement of mankind is not to be measured
by the number of divisions it can put in the field. You must be aware,
as I am, of the many very specific proposals made these last years
by the so-called smaller powers which have been of great value to
all of us.

The stated assumption in your letter that the decisions of five
great powers will be happily accepted by all other interested powers
seems to indicate an attitude on your part which could have dan-

gerous consequences in the future for the smaller powers of this world.

Your position, which means that the desires, the dignity, in fact the security, of the smaller nations should be disregarded, is one which the United States has consistently opposed and continues to oppose today. Essentially you are proposing that we should join you in a policy reminiscent of the system of political domination you imposed in Eastern Europe. The United States cannot accept that point of view.

The problem of the Middle East is not one of a threat of aggression by the United States but rather the threat, by others, of further indirect aggression against independent states. This problem is clearly the responsibility of the United Nations Security Council.

I am, therefore, instructing the United States Permanent Representative to the Security Council to seek a special meeting on or about August twelfth of the Security Council under Article 28(2), which would permit direct discussions among Heads of Governments and Foreign Ministers. I would hope that you would similarly instruct your Permanent Representative.[2] Such a meeting will make it possible for the Council to discharge its responsibilities in the manner contemplated by the Charter.

As for the place of the meeting, the United States agrees that the meeting might be held elsewhere than New York City but we could not agree to the meeting being held in Moscow. The memory of the well-organized mass demonstration and the serious damage to the United States Embassy in Moscow is too fresh in the minds of the American people.[3]

If such a meeting is arranged, I expect to attend and participate and I hope that you would do likewise.[4] *Sincerely*

[1] Khrushchev had responded to Eisenhower's most recent letter (see no. 789) which, the Soviet leader said, represented "a step backwards from the achieved agreement" regarding a meeting of the heads of government. He maintained that the United States was delaying the conference by insisting that it be held during a regular session of the Security Council (AWF/I: Khrushchev). In an earlier discussion regarding this response, Eisenhower and Secretary Dulles agreed that they should not abandon their emphasis on the United Nations and the role that smaller nations should play (Memorandum of Conversation, July 29, 1958, Dulles Papers, White House Memoranda Series; see also Telephone conversations, Eisenhower and Dulles, July 29, 1958; Dulles and Hagerty, July 30, 31, 1958; and Ann Whitman memorandum, July 30, 1958, AWF/AWD; see also Eisenhower, *Waging Peace*, pp. 283–85).

[2] Arkady A. Sobolev was the Soviet Union's permanent representative at the United Nations.

[3] On July 18 thousands of Muscovites had attacked the American embassy with stones, bricks, metal pellets, and ink bottles in protest over U.S. actions in Lebanon. Escalating the actions of an angry but peaceful crowd that had gathered the previous day, the protesters had broken two-thirds of the windows on the first floor of the embassy and had damaged furniture, rugs, and draperies. No one was injured in the

demonstrations. U.S. Ambassador Llewellyn Thompson had lodged a strong protest with the Soviet government and had demanded compensation for damages to the embassy (*New York Times*, July, 18, 19, 20, 1958).
[4] Writing his final letter to Eisenhower regarding the issue, Khrushchev would continue to criticize U.S. and British actions in the Middle East but would withdraw his proposal for a summit conference. Instead he called for an emergency session of the U.N. General Assembly to discuss the withdrawal of troops from Lebanon and Jordan. The Security Council had become "subordinated" to U.S. foreign policy, he said, and was not the proper forum for such discussions. He also proposed a separate meeting of "the great powers" to "facilitate the creation of trust and mutual understanding between states and aid in a more rapid thawing of the ice of 'the cold war'" (Khrushchev to Eisenhower, Aug. 5, 1958, AWF/I: Khrushchev; see also Dulles to Herter, Aug. 6, 1958, AWF/D-H; and State, *Foreign Relations, 1958–1960*, vol. XI, *Lebanon and Jordan*, pp. 429–31).

Eisenhower responded with a public statement calling Khrushchev's proposal "completely acceptable." The General Assembly session would open on August 8, and five days later Eisenhower would address the United Nations for the first time in nearly five years (see no. 818; see also State, *American Foreign Policy, Current Documents, 1958*, p. 1022; and State, *Foreign Relations, 1958–1960*, vol. XI, *Lebanon and Jordan*, pp. 455–61, 467–69).

On August 21 ten Arab nations would propose a compromise resolution, supported by the United States, calling on Secretary General Hammarskjöld to make "practical arrangements" that would uphold the principles of the U.N. charter with regard to Lebanon and Jordan and facilitate the withdrawal of U.S. and British troops from the area (State, *American Foreign Policy, Current Documents, 1958*, pp. 1047–48; see also State, *Foreign Relations, 1958–1960*, vol. XI, *Lebanon and Jordan*, pp. 510–12; and Telephone conversations, Dulles and Herter, and Dulles and Eisenhower, Aug. 21, 1958, Dulles Papers, Telephone Conversations). The crisis in Lebanon would ease with the parliamentary election on July 31 of General Chehab as president, and on August 11 General Twining would tell Eisenhower that the Joint Chiefs of Staff were making plans for a quiet and dignified withdrawal of U.S. troops. Air Force units would begin their departure on August 29, with the removal of military equipment and service units planned for mid-September. The last marines would leave Lebanon on October 25 (State, *Foreign Relations, 1958–1960*, vol. XI, *Lebanon and Jordan*, pp. 549–53, 563–75, 599–600, 615; and NSC meeting minutes, Aug. 1, 1958, AWF/NSC; see also Little, "His Finest Hour?" pp. 50–54; Gendzier, *Notes from the Minefield*, pp. 357–63; and Eisenhower, *Waging Peace*, pp. 286–88).

For developments see no. 916.

801   *EM, AWF,*
                                                    Administration Series

To SHERMAN ADAMS   *August 1, 1958*
Memorandum

Senator Bridges called me this morning to recommend a man named George Smith for membership on the Civil Service Commission.[1] He said Mr. Smith had been a professor of government at

Yale, has had a considerable experience in government and in political activity. Senator Bridges believes he would be one of the finest types we could appoint.

I told Senator Bridges we would be very glad to consider the man seriously if we found that it was impossible to find a woman that we believed to be completely qualified; I said we had been anxious to appoint another woman to a high post and that we felt a woman in this position would be desirable because of the large number of women in civil service.[2] Senator Bridges understood this very well and merely asked that if we did decide to take a man, that we give Mr. Smith serious consideration.[3]

I promised to do this.

[1] Political scientist George Howard Edward Smith (M.A. University of Michigan 1928), was an author, educator, and consultant to the U.S. Senate Republican Policy Committee—a committee on which Bridges served. See Telephone conversation, Eisenhower and Bridges, August 1, 1958, AWF/D.

[2] According to a 1958 publication by the Women's Division of the Republican National Committee, Eisenhower had appointed 123 women to key posts in the federal government, including positions in international affairs and on important committees and commissions ("Top Women Appointments in the Eisenhower Administration [1953–1958]," AWF/A: Administration Officials).

[3] Eisenhower would appoint Barbara Bates Gunderson, a Republican National Committeewoman from Rapid City, South Dakota, to fill the post. She had written to the President on several occasions to express her sentiments on women's roles in the political and national scene. Her term would expire in March 1961 (Galambos and van Ee, *The Middle Way*, nos. 377, 1001, 1452, and *New York Times*, July 16, 26, Aug. 1, 1958). See also Ann Whitman memorandum, August 8, 1958, AWF/AWD. For more on Eisenhower's efforts to place women in political offices see nos. 336 and 1530.

802   *EM, WHCF,*
                                                    Official File 3-VV

To Clarence Dillon   *August 1, 1958*

Dear Clarence: By now you of course know that the Defense Reorganization plan has been passed—happily, very much in the form I proposed it to the Congress. The law assures a stronger, more effective and more economical defense for our country. I am grateful to you for your help.[1]

Doug has been a tower of strength in his work with the Congress on reciprocal trade and mutual aid.[2] I am gratified by the results achieved on the trade bill; I am frustrated by our inability to create the determined, unified, aroused public opinion that would demand from the Congress the kind of support we need in this area.[3]

But, as I say, Doug's work is becoming increasingly effective in this difficult field.

With warm regard,[4] *As ever*

---

[1] New York banker Dillon was one of the businessmen to whom Eisenhower had written on behalf of his efforts to reorganize the Department of Defense (see no. 678; see also Eisenhower to Dillon, May 5, 1958). Dillon had responded by discussing the defense reorganization legislation with "a number of people." He had written on June 11 to report that despite initial unfamiliarity with the provisions of the bill, all the people he had spoken with "felt that the department must be streamlined to the maximum efficiency, and that Congress should grant all necessary authority to achieve this." On defense reorganization see also nos. 630, 699, and 716.

On July 24 Congress had passed the Defense Department Reorganization Act of 1958, granting Eisenhower most of what he had requested. The Administration was not successful, however, in its efforts to abolish legal restraints on executive power to abolish, merge or transfer functions. Neither were they able to convince Congress to remove language allowing the Service Secretaries and Joint Chiefs to bring complaints and recommendations to Congress on their own initiative (see *New York Times*, July 24, 1958, and *Congressional Quarterly Almanac*, vol. XIV, *1958*, pp. 133–39). Nevertheless, Eisenhower had commended Congress on the legislation, saying that, "Except in relatively minor respects, the bill adequately meets every recommendation I submitted to the Congress on the subject" (*Public Papers of the Presidents: Eisenhower, 1958*, p. 564).

[2] C. Douglas Dillon, Dillon's son, had been appointed Deputy Under Secretary of State for Economic Affairs on July 1, 1958.

[3] For background see nos. 674, 753, 762, and 787. For developments see no. 805.

[4] Dillon would respond on August 14. "The country is relieved," he would write, "that the Defense Reorganization Bill is passed and it now expects of the Congress the remaining legislation that you have asked, which may well prove to be equally vital to our defense." All correspondence is in the same file as the document.

---

803   *EM, AWF, Name Series*

To Henry Robinson Luce   *August 1, 1958*

Dear Harry: On the strength of your letter of July twenty-second I have talked again with Arthur Larson about concrete moves to forward the rule-of-law-for-peace idea.[1] He has shown me an outline sketch of actions which could be the concern of a Presidential Commission on Rule of Law for Peace. I understand he is sending you a copy for your comments.

The substance of this program seems to me to have real merit. Before moving on such an action as a Presidential Commission, however, I would like to see more work done on the precise job contemplated for such a group, its nature and composition, its relation to the various branches of our government as well as to people or governments abroad, and possible alternative methods of governmental encouragement of the program.

It seems to me that a way of giving effect to your suggestion might be this: Mr. Larson, while going forward with the initiation of the Rule of Law for Peace Center at Duke University, could also be appointed as a consultant to the President for the purpose of drawing up recommendations for appropriate action.[2]

As we have learned from the People-to-People program, there are important advantages in keeping efforts of this kind as nongovernmental as possible. My suggestion is intended to facilitate the maximum government "push," while preserving the basically private character of the activity.[3]

With warm regard, *As ever*

[1] For background see no. 777. Luce had told Eisenhower that a number of opportunities existed to help in the cold war by establishing the principle of the rule of law. He claimed that Latin Americans professed a "passionate interest in international jurisprudence" and noted promising developments in Europe, where the forthcoming Common Market (see no. 753) would establish procedures to resolve disputes. Luce added that he had urged Secretary Dulles to recommend formation of "a Presidential Commission to develop a strategic plan in the field of international law." He thought that such a commission could give answers to the questions that Eisenhower was asking. "Stress in these areas where forward motion is already apparent could be linked with demands for progress on other fronts," Luce had written (Luce to Eisenhower, July 22, 1958, AWF/N). Eisenhower had talked with Larson on this same day and also on July 25 (Ann Whitman memorandums, July 25, Aug. 1, 1958, AWF/AWD).

[2] On Larson's invitation to establish the center see no. 777; see also Larson, *Eisenhower: The President Nobody Knew*, pp. 103–9. Although Eisenhower would accept his resignation on August 11, Larson would remain as an unpaid special consultant to plan a government program in coordination with the Duke center (*New York Times*, Aug. 12, 1958).

[3] In his reply (August 4) Luce would commend the decision to appoint a special consultant as "highly symbolic as well as practical." He had received Larson's outline, which, he said, made "a rich and impressive agenda," and he was prepared to offer any assistance he could (AWF/N). For developments see no. 900.

804   *EM, WHCF, Official File 3-VV*

To Barry T. Leithead   *August 2, 1958*

Dear Barry: Within the last few days I have spent some of my "spare" time trying to thank my friends for their help on the matter of Defense reorganization. As you know, the law as finally passed assures a stronger, more effective and more economical defense for our country.[1] However, in re-reading your note of May twelfth, I am afraid we did not adequately answer your specific questions.[2] Sometime when I see you perhaps we can discuss in general terms just how business people like yourself can help in trying to convince the Congress of the necessity of legislation that is vital to the best interests of our country.

A case in point is my effort to secure the funds that I consider an absolute minimum for the mutual security program. As of now the chances of the conferees giving me what I need are anything but bright.[3] I realize that the Congress acts only if there is an aroused public opinion—and despite everything I have done (and the works of a band of crusaders under the direction of Eric Johnston) public opinion has *not* been aroused.[4] The issue will be resolved this week and at this point all I can do is pray.

Thanks for your note about Mr. Adler.[5] Both Gabe Hauge and I were amused by the entire exchange. Incidentally, Gabe tells me you are a member of the Board of the Manufacturers Trust Company. Losing Gabe creates a void that will be impossible to fill here at the White House; the bank is extremely fortunate to enlist his services.[6]

With warm regard, *As ever*

[1] See no. 802.

[2] In May Leithead had written that Eisenhower's efforts to secure legislation for defense reorganization had received an excellent response (see no. 678). The business community was still asking: "How can we be most effective and helpful?" Most businessmen, Leithead believed, knew "very little how to get things accomplished in Washington." Congressional representatives often listened "with a political ear" instead of being concerned about "what is good for their country." Leithead's letter is in the same file as the document. See also no. 682.

[3] See nos. 782 and 805.

[4] See nos. 524, 582, and 797.

[5] Herbert L. Adler of Adler's Department Store in Martinsville, Indiana, had written the President on July 10, 1958. Adler had responded to Eisenhower's "buy now" anti-recession appeal by cutting prices (see nos. 598 and 677). Although successful, the plan had hit a "snag" regarding the products of Eisenhower's "golfing partner," Leithead. Adler had offered a promotion on Arrow shirts and ties but had received a "severe warning from your golfing partner's firm that such a policy could only bring financial ruin to both of us and that in the future it would be better if all Arrow products were sold at the pre-ticketed price." Adler had raised prices on Arrow's products but told the President that it gave him "a lack of confidence in your administration when your own golfing partner's firm won't let me do what you told me to do." Eisenhower had forwarded the complaint to Leithead (see Eisenhower to Adler, July 25, 1958, and Eisenhower to Leithead, July 25, 1958). Leithead had responded on July 29, saying that his company "will work it out some way so that Mr. Adler is happy and is not down on the Administration." All correspondence regarding the Adler-Leithead matter is in WHCF/OF 122.

[6] See no. 769.

To Lyndon Baines Johnson   *August 4, 1958*

Dear Lyndon: As you know from our many conversations on the subject, the cuts in the mutual security appropriations have troubled me a great deal. The carefully planned program I submitted last February was cut by almost $275 million in the authorizing legislation recently enacted by the Congress. The appropriation bill recently voted by the House of Representatives was further reduced by nearly $600 million from this already reduced amount.[1]

I am advised of your view that the Senate is likely to restore only $440 million of the House cut. Of this $440 million, I understand that $90 million would be for defense support, $15 million for special assistance, $55 million for contingencies, and $280 million for the Development Loan Fund.[2] I have two reactions: first, that it falls short of the authorization by $157.5 million and is that much too low; second, that, at our calculated rate of expenditures, it would at least bridge the adjournment period without forcing program changes that would unduly increase our risks. Thereafter, unless world conditions should improve, I would expect to request additional funds to meet the cost of our required programs. On this basis a $440 million restoration would enable us to carry on our calculated programs until Congress returns.

It is, of course, the duty of Congress ultimately to determine how much this program requires. But before that decision is reached my duty is equally clear—to emphasize the utter gravity of the House cuts. The restoration of these funds is of the utmost importance to ourselves and to friendly nations throughout the world. I hope you will use this letter, to the degree you deem advisable, throughout the Senate, for in this matter the stakes for America are no less than crucial.[3] *Sincerely*

[1] See nos. 762 and 782.

[2] On August 5 the Senate Appropriations Committee would report a bill to provide $3,518,092,500 for mutual security funds, $440 million more than had been approved by the House of Representatives. The Senate increases followed the President's recommendations.

[3] The Senate would pass the committee bill on August 23. On the following day a Senate-House compromise version would be approved, appropriating $400 million instead of $580 million for the Development Loan Fund, and $750 million rather than $790 million for defense support. The total amount was over $420 million less than Eisenhower's original request (see *Congressional Quarterly Almanac,* vol. XIV, *1958,* p. 190; *New York Times,* Aug. 24, 1958; and Kaufman, *Trade and Aid,* pp. 139–41).

TO JAMES PAUL MITCHELL   *August 4, 1958*
Personal

Dear Jim: Following up on certain suggestions made at the Cabinet
meeting on August 1, 1958, I am writing to ask your comments on
the following proposition.[1]

I propose to establish, on a completely confidential basis, an ad
hoc Cabinet Committee under your chairmanship. Its purpose
would be to consider what steps the Federal government might
take to restrain the pressure of wage increases on production costs
and prices. At the same time it should consider what actions might
be suggested to discourage business from making unnecessary increases in prices.[2]

I believe that aside from yourself, the membership of the committee should include the Secretary of Defense, the Attorney General, the Secretary of Commerce, Dr. Saulnier, and such others as
you may desire to designate.[3]

I realize, of course, that most of the work would have to be done
by representatives designated by each member, but I would hope
that the principals themselves could keep in close touch with the
work, especially its findings and recommendations.

While I should like to have a preliminary report by October first,
I am aware that this is the kind of study that might have to continue
on into the next session of the Congress.[4]

May I have your comments at your earliest convenience? If you
agree with the proposal, I shall then promptly send to those concerned an appropriate letter of instructions.[5] *As ever*

[1] Cabinet members had discussed the growth of the national economy and the effects of inflation. Labor Secretary Mitchell had expressed doubt that voluntary action would serve to restrain inflation and had suggested that the government should
make an intensive study to determine whether it could do anything in this regard
(see Cabinet Committee minutes, Aug. 1, 1958, AWF/D).
[2] Eisenhower had written at the top of another copy of this letter: "No action. Handled verbally" (AWF/D).
[3] Mitchell would tell the President in a note of August 4 (AWF/D) that he was "ready
to proceed with the assignment." He suggested adding Postmaster General Summerfield to the committee.
[4] Mitchell would issue an interim report on October 1 (AWF/A). The committee had
organized a staff and was looking into the relative importance of the various factors
involved in inflation since 1939, he said. It had first concentrated on problems of
price policy and was planning to concentrate on wages and wage policy in its next
report. It also planned to study government programs directly affecting prices. The
committee recommended that the Administration should make "relative price sta-

bility a stated objective of national economic policy" by amending the Employment Act of 1946 (see Mitchell to Eisenhower, Jan. 5, 1959, AWF/A).

[5] The President would also request Treasury Secretary Anderson to establish a similar committee to prepare a program of tax reform and reduction. Eisenhower suggested that the agenda include "the types of tax changes that would do most to promote the growth and stability of the economy," the best sequence for these changes, and the most politically opportune times to revise the tax laws (Eisenhower to Anderson, Aug. 4, 1958, AWF/D). In his August 20 response (AWF/A), Anderson would outline his suggestions for an *ad hoc* committee to study tax reform and reduction and would propose that the committee complete its report in the latter part of November or early December, "in time to formulate a program for presentation to the next Congress." Eisenhower would note that he completely agreed with Anderson's proposed procedures and awaited developments with interest. See also Sloan, *Eisenhower and the Management of Prosperity*, pp. 119–25; H. Scott Gordon, "The Eisenhower Administration: The Doctrine of Shared Responsibility," in *Exhortation and Controls: The Search for a Wage-Price Policy 1945–1971*, ed. Craufurd D. Goodwin [Washington, D.C., 1975], pp. 122–25).

807   *EM, AWF, Administration Series*

To Charles Erwin Wilson   *August 4, 1958*
Personal. Eyes only

Dear Charlie:[1] I hope—in fact, I pray—that you did not today read the writings of a certain columnist who considers himself both profound and informed.[2] And, if you have not done so, please refrain unless you are courting a case of colic. At any rate, if you have seen the thing, I know that your good sense won't allow you to become upset over his senseless diatribe and that you will, instead, congratulate yourself on your admission to his bad-grace club.

Your friends and associates in the Administration will dismiss the column with due regard to its source; nonetheless I know they all join with me in resentment that a person of such low character is enabled by his access to the columns of a reputable newspaper to deprecate the abilities and dedication of one that we admire, respect and like.[3]

With affectionate regard to Jessie, and all the best to yourself, *As ever*

[1] Former Defense Secretary Wilson was director of the Bank of Detroit (see no. 369).
[2] Eisenhower was referring to author and journalist Joseph Wright Alsop, Jr., whose column, "Matter of Fact," appeared in the *New York Herald Tribune*. (For more on Eisenhower's opinion of him see no. 680.) Alsop had written a sardonic "letter of thanks" to Wilson, who recently had criticized Major General James Maurice Gavin (USA, ret.), an outspoken opponent of Eisenhower's military policies. Gavin, who in

March had retired as chief of Army Research and Development, had taken a post as vice-president and director of the industrial research and development firm of Arthur D. Little, Inc.; he had recently blamed "inertia" in the Defense Department for the Soviet lead in rocketry and space exploration. He faulted Wilson for disregarding the importance of Sputnik and accused him of dealing with the Chiefs of Staff as though they were "recalcitrant union bosses" (James M. Gavin, *War and Peace in the Space Age* [New York, 1958], pp. 18, 155, 169; *New York Times,* Jan. 5, 9, Feb. 19, Mar. 11, 31, Apr. 4, Aug. 10, 11, 1958). Alsop said that Wilson had minimized Soviet accomplishments and that as a result the Soviets were "now well on their way to gaining almost unchallengeable superiority in nuclear striking power. For this," he told Wilson, "we have you to thank." Alsop also charged Wilson with having unjustly belittled Gavin's military accomplishments (see Chandler and Galambos, *Occupation, 1945,* no. 2053; Galambos, *Columbia University,* no. 125; and Galambos, *NATO and the Campaign of 1952,* no. 287).

[3] In his thank-you letter to Eisenhower Wilson would characterize Alsop as a "bitter New Dealer" bent on belittling the Administration (Aug. 7, 1958, AWF/A). On this same date the President would send a copy of the Alsop column to U.S. Ambassador to Great Britain Whitney. In a cover letter Eisenhower would say that the article inspired "resentment toward the practice of newspapers of turning their columns over to liars, demagogues and worse, with the publisher's implied endorsement of all that is written" (AWF/D). Later this month Whitney would announce his acquisition of the *New York Herald Tribune* and its European edition (see no. 825). For developments see the following document.

808

EM, AWF, Name Series

To William Edward Robinson August 4, 1958
Personal and confidential

Dear Bill: You and I have often talked about the value we place upon the character and standing of a newspaper. One of the measures that we use in judging character in any periodical is our respect and admiration for the men and women who are responsible for its publication.

This kind of evaluation must certainly include the columnists, those people for whose competence and integrity any newspaper, in effect, vouches when it uses the material they submit.[1]

I have no objection to columnists as such; in fact there are a very few—I mention Krock, Drummond and Lawrence as outstanding examples—who in my opinion frequently contribute good ideas and seemingly always attempt to be factual in their writing.[2]

Others, who do not conform to what I consider acceptable standards in their writing, not only do a disservice to readers, but so far as I am concerned, tend to diminish or destroy the standing of a paper itself. It is easy enough to say "Well, just skip over this particular column when you read the paper." The fact is that the mere presence of the columnist on the paper's staff tends, so far as I am concerned, to bring the entire publication down to the level of written garbage.

For myself, from now on I am going to ask Mrs. Whitman to clip out for me daily the articles she finds from Drummond and Lawrence; otherwise I will keep on my desk as my reference newspaper the one that contains the Krock column.

There is no real reason to write you in this fashion. But you and I have so often discussed between ourselves the practices and standards of American journalism that I thought I might tell you how I have solved my personal problem with respect to it.[3]

With warm regard, *As ever*

[1] Robinson was former business manager, vice-president and director of the *New York Herald Tribune.* A column appearing in the *Herald Tribune* on this same date had prompted the President to write Robinson (see the preceding document, and Telephone conversation, Eisenhower and Whitman, Aug. 4, 1958, AWF/D, and Ann Whitman memorandum, Aug. 4, 1958, AWF/AWD).

[2] Journalist Arthur Krock's column, "In the Nation," appeared in the *New York Times* (see no. 44). Roscoe Drummond (B.S.J. Syracuse University 1924), chief of the Washington bureau of the *New York Herald Tribune*, was also a syndicated columnist. David Lawrence, another syndicated columnist, was founder, president and editor of *U.S. News & World Report* (see no. 120).

[3] Robinson would reply that the "irresponsibility" and "arrogant pretensions of authority" of some journalists "appalled" him. When he managed journalistic enterprises, he wrote, he cautioned columnists to be responsible for the paper's integrity. He also said that he agreed with Eisenhower's "formula" for reading the newspaper (Aug. 6, 1958, AWF/N).

809   *EM, WHCF,*
                                                                   Official File 106

To Joseph William Martin, Jr.   *August 5, 1958*

Dear Joe: Most of the time this morning I was simply nonplussed by the farm bill discussion.[1] The longer it lasted, the more I realized that the discussion dealt with parliamentary tactics which you, Charlie, Les, Leo and Bill Hill, as well as George Aiken, have forgotten more about than Ezra and I will ever learn.[2] Obviously our rightful concern—the farm program itself—was not in question; rather it was a question of how best to handle the bill. Once that became clear I felt impelled to comment as I did.[3]

One thing, however, I want you clearly to understand. Neither Ezra Benson nor I intended for an instant to subscribe to any move that could possibly embarrass you in this situation. That would be unthinkable. I wanted you to know this beyond any doubt and also to know how much I have appreciated the loyalty and vigor with which you have consistently advanced the cause of our Administration.[4]

With warm regard, *Sincerely*

[1] Eisenhower had met with the Republican legislative leaders for two hours that morning. Among the subjects discussed was pending farm legislation, and Agriculture Secretary Benson heatedly argued that Republicans should hold firm against any law that was contrary to the Administration's policy. The meeting had concluded, however, with an agreement that Republican congressional leaders were most capable of deciding on the best tactics to be followed in the House of Representatives (Legislative Leadership meeting notes, Aug. 5, 1958, AWF/LM; Benson, *Cross Fire*, p. 402). For background see nos. 616 and 784. White House aide Bryce Harlow drafted this letter for the President.

[2] Eisenhower was referring to Congressman Charles Halleck, House minority whip Leslie C. Arends, Illinois Congressman Leo E. Allen, Colorado Congressman William S. Hill, and Vermont Senator George D. Aiken.

[3] Following the failure to pass either the price freeze or omnibus farm bill, the Senate had again considered legislation to provide relief for farmers hurt by international competition and by perceived weaknesses in the acreage allotment system (see no. 358; and Galambos and van Ee, *The Middle Way*, nos. 1595, 1748, 1841). On July 25 the Senate had passed S. 4071, which established new price support and production control provisions for cotton, rice, corn and feed grains. The proposed legislation retained the parity principle but gave the Administration the authority it had sought to lower price supports and loosen federal planting controls (see *New York Times*, July 26, 1958). The bill had, however, run into trouble in the House, where the Agriculture Committee had removed the new price support formula from the cotton and rice sections of the bill, retaining it for corn only if approved by a farmers' referendum. The Committee had also raised the support price for all three commodities above the Senate figures. The Administration opposed these adjustments. House Republican leaders had proposed tactics that would defeat the bill in its current form, while allowing it to be brought up again in a revised version. See *Congressional Quarterly Almanac*, vol. XIV, *1958*, pp. 269–75. We have been unable to locate any record of Eisenhower's specific comments at the Legislative Leaders meeting.

[4] The House of Representatives would defeat the Agriculture Bill on August 6, 1958, and House Speaker Rayburn would say that it was "futile to consider any more farm legislation at this session" (*New York Times*, Aug. 7, 1958). Pressure from commodity groups would, however, force the Democrats to seek a new compromise with the Administration. On August 14 the House would pass a revised version of the bill that removed the dollars-and-cents price support floors on corn, cotton and rice, while leaving parity percentage price supports in place. The Senate would agree to the measure on August 18, and the President would sign the legislation on August 28, 1958 (see *New York Times*, Aug. 9, 15, 1958).

To Wilbur Daigh Mills   *[August 6, 1958]*
Personal

Dear Mr. Mills: A few moments ago I tried to telephone you only to find that, as is probably normal with you at this stage of a Congressional session, you are busy in Committee work. My purpose was to express to you my gratification over reports that have come to me, from friends on the Hill, relating to your effective work over a wide range of legislative activities.[1]

The reciprocal trade bill reflects not only your success in steering its initial passage through the House, but in effecting conference agreements that, if not in complete conformity to all that you and I might like, is nevertheless a satisfactory measure.[2] It is reported to me also that you have been largely responsible for the smooth passage of the debt limit measure through the House.[3]

Finally, I learn that you have expressed yourself most emphatically on the necessity of minimizing unnecessary Federal expenditures.[4] Nothing could please me more than your stand on this subject. Along with other multitudes of our citizens, I share your concern for mounting Federal costs, especially where these are devoted to activities that are either unnecessary or not necessary at this time. Because we recognize that there are unescapable costs imposed upon us by the world situation and by domestic responsibilities that cannot be avoided, your efforts in this direction are of real significance to the long-term interests of our country.

With personal regard, *Sincerely*

---

[1] Mills, Chairman of the House Ways and Means Committee, had served as Democratic congressman from Arkansas since 1939. Eisenhower had twice attempted to reach Mills by phone before completing the call at 6:35 P.M. A handwritten note on this document states: "Dictated but liaison people would not let Pres send." For Eisenhower's other messages of thanks to Congress see no. 787.

[2] For background see no. 753. On July 22, 1958, the Senate had approved a revised Reciprocal Trade Bill, having eliminated an amendment that would have restricted the President's authority to veto actions of the Federal Tariff Commission (*New York Times*, July 23, 1958). On August 6 House and Senate conferees had agreed on a bill that extended the Trade Agreements Act for four years. Final action would come several days later (see *Congressional Quarterly Almanac*, vol. XIV, *1958*, pp. 165–75; *New York Times*, Aug. 7, 1958). The President would say that while he believed "that a five-year extension would have best served the interests of the United States," the Congress was to be "particularly commended for enacting the longest extension in the history of the trade agreements program" (*Public Papers of the Presidents: Eisenhower, 1958*, p. 632).

[3] See no. 784.

[4] Mills was a member of the Joint Committee on the Reduction of Nonessential Federal Expenditures.

To François Duvalier   *August 8, 1958*

Dear Mr. President:[1] I had the pleasure of meeting and talking with your Minister of Foreign Affairs, Dr. Louis Mars, on Thursday afternoon, August seventh, and I have read with great interest your letter of August second which he handed to me at that time.[2] As my representative in Port-au-Prince, Ambassador Gerald A. Drew, stated to your Government on August first the United States deplores the involvement of its citizens in the revolutionary attempt against your Government on July 29, 1958, and appropriate agencies of this Government are conducting an inquiry to determine what violations of United States laws may have occurred.[3]

I have asked the Department of State and other agencies of this Government to give urgent and careful study to the request made in your letter. I have noted particularly your allusion to the dangers of an International Communist conspiracy against Haiti and other countries in the area. I appreciate your concern in this respect, and I believe it would be most helpful if you could convey more information on this matter to my Ambassador to assist in determining how best we can cooperate to preserve the integrity of our institutions against this threat.

With my best wishes for your personal happiness and for a prompt and full restoration of domestic peace and tranquility to the people of Haiti,[4] *Sincerely*

[1] In October 1957 Duvalier, a physician who had formerly directed the U.S. sanitary missions in Haiti, had become president of his country in an election that the opposition considered fraudulent.
[2] Louis Mars, psychologist and rector of Haiti University, had become foreign minister on June 17. Eisenhower had asked Under Secretary Herter to prepare an immediate reply to Duvalier and to have Mars transmit it to the Haitian president (see Howe to Goodpaster, Aug. 7, 1958, AWF/I: Haiti).
[3] On July 29 seven former army officers had led a group of over one hundred insurgents, including four Americans, in an unsuccessful attempt to overthrow the Duvalier government. The president himself had led the counter-attack, during which several of the rebels were killed. The State Department had instructed Drew to apologize to the Haitian government for the involvement of American citizens in the affair.

In his letter Duvalier had called the attempted coup an "act of international brigandage" and requested U.S. military assistance to help resist Communist "henchmen" (AWF/I: Haiti; see also *U.S. Department of State Bulletin* 39, no. 999 [August 18, 1958], 282; and *New York Times*, July 29, 30, 31, Aug. 1, 2, 1958).
[4] Although the United States had authorized $3.5 million in economic aid and technical assistance to Haiti in 1958, the unsettled political situation had brought the technical assistance programs to a standstill. Relations with the United States would improve, however, after a thorough investigation of the attempted coup, and in October a group of U.S. Marine Corps specialists would embark on a mission to help

reorganize Haiti's military forces (*U.S. Department of State Bulletin* 39, no. 1014 [December 1, 1958], 892; and *New York Times*, Oct. 6, Nov. 1, 1958, see also *State, Foreign Relations, 1958–1960*, vol. V, *American Republics*, pp. 152–53, 299–300).

812   *EM, AWF, Dulles-Herter Series*

To John Foster Dulles   *August 11, 1958*

Memorandum for the Secretary of State: I have a very fine friend named George Whitney. I am sure you are also acquainted with him.

After a long career in Morgan's Bank, I think that he finds himself with an unwanted amount of idle time, and I have detected occasionally in his correspondence a hope that we might find some place in government where he could serve usefully.

Because of my respect for his breadth of interest and his objective attitude, it is possible that you might want to communicate with him should any vacancy occur in which you think he could be unusually effective.[1]

P.S. I imagine he is something on the order of 67 or 68 years of age, but so far as I know he is in good health.[2]

---

[1] Whitney (A.B. Harvard 1907) was director of the advisory council of Morgan Guaranty Trust Company and a director of General Motors Corporation. He and the President had corresponded regarding the American economic and political scene since 1951 (see Galambos, *NATO and the Campaign of 1952*, no. 50).
[2] Dulles would say that Whitney was a personal friend whom he regarded highly. Although Whitney had, in fact, been born in 1885 Dulles said that he did not believe "incapacity automatically came at 73" (Memorandum of Conversation, Aug. 12, 1958). For developments see no. 1623.

813   *EM, AWF, International Series: Japan*

To Nobusuke Kishi   *August 12, 1958*
Confidential

Dear Prime Minister: Ambassador MacArthur has reported to me your views on the Ryukyuan currency question, which I had requested him to obtain following receipt of your letter to me of May twenty-third.[1] I appreciate very much your understanding the reasons which led us to a decision to replace the military occupation currency with United States currency. I also appreciate your helpful suggestions regarding the timing of the announcement and your understanding of our problems in the Ryukyus.[2]

As you know, the land compensation problem was thoroughly discussed with the Ryukyuan delegation during its recent visit to Washington.[3] As the result of these discussions I believe that we have arrived at the basis for a new land compensation program which will prove satisfactory to the Ryukyuans. The details of the new program will be worked out in discussions in Naha between United States officials and Ryukyuan leaders.[4] I believe that it would be appropriate to proceed with the conversion of currency as soon as the new program becomes public knowledge in the Ryukyus. Ambassador MacArthur will discuss with you the timing and form of the currency conversion announcement in advance of its publication.[5]

I remember with pleasure the cordial and frank talks we had last summer concerning problems affecting our two countries.[6] I am deeply gratified, as I know you are, that we have been able to handle this matter in the same spirit of mutual understanding. *Sincerely*

[1] State Department officials drafted this letter to the Japanese prime minister and, after the President approved, cabled the text to Tokyo on the following day (see Eisenhower to Dulles, Aug. 12, 1958, AWF/D-H). For background see no. 724.

[2] Although Prime Minister Kishi did not endorse the currency conversion, Dulles had told Eisenhower, he understood the reasoning behind the U.S. proposal. The change would cause some difficulties, Kishi had said, but the Japanese "could live with it." He asked that the announcement be delayed until after the adjournment of the Diet so as not to intensify the controversy over Okinawa (Dulles to Eisenhower, Aug. 11, 1958, AWF/I: Japan).

[3] Kishi had also asked that the United States postpone an announcement regarding currency conversion until negotiators had reached a favorable conclusion regarding land compensation. The Japanese had long disagreed with the U.S. policy for land requisitioned for military use, particularly on Okinawa. The United States had displaced one-third of the Ryukyuan population from their farmlands, forcing the islanders to pay rents on the open market far higher than the compensation they had received. The Ryukyuan delegation, which met with U.S. officials on July 1, had asked that the United States abolish the existing lump-sum payment program entirely and substitute indefinite leases with annual rentals renewable in three- to five-year periods. Dulles had told Eisenhower that the Departments of State, Defense, and the Army had reached an agreement on the compensation problem after meeting with Ryukyuans; annual rentals at a fair market price would replace the one-lump payment (State, *Foreign Relations, 1955–1957*, vol. XXIII, pt. 2, *Korea*, pp. 232–33, 391, 442–43, 476–79; Record of Meeting, June 30, 1958, State, *Foreign Relations, 1958–1960*, vols. XVII/XVIII, *Indonesia; Japan; Korea*, Microfiche Supplement no. 462; Robertson to Herter, July 2, 1958, *ibid.*, no. 463; MacArthur to Robertson, July 16, 1958, *ibid.*, no. 465; and New *York Times*, July 31, Dec. 22, 1958).

[4] Naha, a seaport city, was the seat of the Ryukyuan government.

[5] MacArthur would deliver Eisenhower's letter to Kishi on the following day. Kishi would ask MacArthur to tell the President of his "deep appreciation" for the consideration that Eisenhower had given his views. He also agreed with MacArthur that although the exact details of the land policy remained to be finalized, the announcement regarding currency conversion should not be postponed. He asked that

the announcement be made in Okinawa by the U.S. high commissioner as a routine administrative matter, rather than in Washington (MacArthur to Dulles, Aug. 14, 1958, AWF/I: Japan).
[6] On Kishi's June 1957 visit see State, *Foreign Relations, 1955–1957*, vol. XXIII, pt. 1, *Japan*, pp. 346–49, 357–415.

814   *EM, AWF, International Series: Turkey*

To Celal Bayar   *August 12, 1958*

Dear Mr. President: I appreciate and wish to reciprocate the kind thoughts you expressed in your letter delivered to me on August fifth on the conclusion of the negotiations in Paris concerning economic assistance to Turkey.[1]

As I said in my letter of June thirteenth, I have followed with close interest developments bearing on the economic situation in your country.[2] At my request, the Secretary of State, the Secretary of the Treasury and members of their staffs have devoted special attention to helping your Government in its endeavors to strengthen the economy of Turkey. I note that the International Monetary Fund and the members of the Organization for European Economic Cooperation have also contributed substantially to the financial assistance required by Turkey in connection with its stabilization program. However, these negotiations could not have succeeded if it had not been for the determination of your Government to adopt and carry out the measures necessary to stabilize the Turkish economy.[3] We wish you every success in this endeavor.

I regard the happy outcome of these negotiations as another example of the mutual cooperation between our two countries and of the effectiveness of the International Monetary Fund and the Organization for European Economic Cooperation.[4] *Sincerely*

[1] State Department officials drafted this message to the Turkish president. For background on Turkey's economic problems, President Bayar's request for U.S. economic aid, and the Paris conference, see no. 746. In his letter, which is not in AWF, Bayar had thanked Eisenhower for U.S. assistance in the recently concluded negotiations (Dulles to Eisenhower, Aug. 11, 1958, AWF/I: Turkey).
[2] Eisenhower's previous letter to Bayar is no. 746.
[3] For the announcement of these contributions, which would total $359 million, see *U.S. Department of State Bulletin* 39, no. 1000 (August 25, 1958), 322–24; for more on U.S. economic assistance to Turkey, see State, *Foreign Relations, 1958–1960*, vol. X, pt. 2, *Eastern Europe; Finland; Greece; Turkey*, pp. 756–62. The Turkish economic program included measures to balance the budget, end deficits incurred by state economic enterprises, and restrict credit expansion.
[4] For developments see no. 1438.

TO FRANK HAROLD NOTT   *August 12, 1958*

Dear Monsignor Nott: Thank you very much for your letter, which was forwarded to me by Assistant Secretary of State Walter S. Robertson.[1] I share your conviction that all of us should become constantly more aware of our dependence upon the Almighty for guidance in the vast affairs of humanity. I believe, with you, that the more we consciously seek that guidance the more men will be successful in solving the problems that are currently besetting them.

For this calendar year two different days have been set aside as National Days of Prayer. Under a Resolution of Congress the first of these was May 30th, which is annually proclaimed by the President as a Day of Prayer for Permanent Peace.[2]

In addition to the Memorial Day mandate, the Congress has provided "That the President shall set aside and proclaim a suitable day each year, other than a Sunday, as a National Day of Prayer."[3] Conforming to that Resolution I have designated the first day of October, 1958, and have called "upon my fellow Americans and all who may be visitors in our country, each according to his own faith, to join in prayer for our Nation and for all mankind." Incidentally, it is my hope that the first Wednesday of each October will become recognized as "The National Day of Prayer."[4]

Last year's response to the proclamation was disappointing. I found that the churches seemed generally to be unaware of its existence. Indeed, I had to make special, ad hoc, arrangements to attend a service that day because the pastor had not learned of the proclamation and its purposes.[5]

At the moment it seems to me that to proclaim another special Day of Prayer would not be very effectual. This by no means indicates any deprecation of your idea. Rather I feel that too frequent issue of such proclamations tends to diminish the attention paid by the public to each.

However, if a group of national religious leaders in the several branches of faith should take an initiative in this regard, I should most certainly be among those who would make every effort to be present at one of the services to be held.[6] By making advance public announcement of such intention my hope would be to support your efforts in this realm.

Needless to say I deeply appreciate your concern over the world difficulties of today, and am grateful for your thoughtfulness in expressing to me your idea.[7]

With best wishes, *Sincerely*

[1] Nott, rector of Holy Cross Parish in Lynchburg, Virginia, had written on August 7. Robertson, who had known Nott for several years, forwarded the letter through White House Press Secretary James Hagerty (Robertson to Hagerty, Aug. 8, 1958; see also Whitman to Robertson, Aug. 18, 1958).

[2] Nott had proposed that the President "issue a call to prayer" to end international tension and hostilities. In 1950 Congress, by joint resolution, had dedicated Memorial Day as a "day for Nation-wide prayer for permanent peace" (see Galambos and van Ee, *The Middle Way*, no. 183).

[3] In 1952 Congress, by joint resolution, enacted the second National Day of Prayer (*ibid.*).

[4] Eisenhower had issued Proclamation 3252 on August 6 (*Federal Register*, vol. 23, no. 153, p. 5947). In his news conference the morning of Wednesday, October 1, the President would ask the journalists present to remind their readers about the official announcement (see *Public Papers of the Presidents: Eisenhower, 1958*, p. 712). Later this same day the Eisenhowers would attend special services at the National Presbyterian Church.

[5] The President had designated Wednesday, October 2, 1957, as a National Day of Prayer and had attended services at the National Presbyterian Church.

[6] Nott had suggested that Eisenhower attend Protestant, Jewish, and Catholic services as a "demonstration" of his "personal dedication" to world peace.

[7] Nott would apologize on August 19, saying that he had heard of Eisenhower's proclamation only after sending his letter. He also said he was working to arouse interest in "this beautiful custom." All correspondence is in WHCF/OF 144-F.

816   *EM, AWF, Administration Series*

To John Hay Whitney   *August 12, 1958*

Dear Jock: I enjoyed every word of your letter of the sixth (until I got to the postscript about Lee Hills). Now I am wondering what your next step may be.[1]

Primarily this letter is for the purpose of expressing felicitations and good wishes on your birthday anniversary.[2] I wish you were here so we could celebrate it properly.

Incidentally, if I had any remote idea of what shape a vacation this year might take, I'd be tempted to urge you to forsake future quail for present golf.[3] But at the moment I simply can see no further than the possibility of going to the United Nations General Assembly, with a dim hope that the Congress may decide to adjourn a couple of weeks hence.[4]

Give my love to Betsey, and a special Happy Birthday to yourself. *As ever*

P.S. I have seen Bill several times; I don't think he is quite as worried as he was which, of course, in turn relieves his friends greatly.[5]

[1] Whitney's letter is in AWF/A. The postscript read: "Same as above. Lee Hills has [declared] himself out. Damn!" The President and Whitney had been correspond-

ing regarding Whitney's plans to acquire the *New York Herald Tribune*. Hills was Whitney's choice for executive editor (for background see no. 748). For developments see no. 825.

[2] Whitney was born on August 17, 1904.

[3] Recently tropical red ants had been killing young quail near the Whitney's Greenwood Plantation in Thomasville, Georgia (see no. 799). Whitney said that his estate manager had told him that the quail on his farm were unaffected, but if the ants were going to ruin his winter hunting, then Whitney would take his vacation when Eisenhower did and look for the President in Newport, Rhode Island, "or some even more salubrious golf-and-water-hole!" The Eisenhowers would vacation in Newport August 29–September 23 (*New York Times*, Aug. 30, Sept. 24, 1958).

[4] Eisenhower would address the Third Special Emergency Session of the United Nations General Assembly on August 13 (see no. 818). The second session of the Eighty-fifth Congress would adjourn on August 24.

[5] Whitney said he was distressed by news of Robinson's health, as relayed to Mrs. Whitney by Mrs. Eisenhower. Robinson had attended a dinner at the White House on July 31, and Eisenhower had written him on August 4 (see no. 808). Whitney and Robinson would visit the President at his vacation home in Newport on September 4 (see no. 842).

817

EM, AWF, DDE
Diaries Series

To Leslie Cornelius Arends

August 13, 1958

Dear Les: While I had the chance to tell you on the telephone this noon how gratified I am at the action of the House in preventing the overriding of a veto which would have caused an unconscionable amount of administrative confusion in the procurement services of the Defense Department[1]—and how proud I am of the leadership that you and Charlie[2] have displayed in bringing about this fine result—I still feel I would like to make a written record of my satisfaction. When the chips are down I can always count on you to perform, and I cannot tell you what a fine feeling of satisfaction I gain from that knowledge.

With warm regard, *As ever*

[1] On this day, the House of Representatives had sustained Eisenhower's August 4 veto of a bill that would have required the Navy to use the same pay scale for per diem employees at the Portsmouth, N.H., Navy Yard as was used at the Boston yard, where workers were paid more for the same type of work. On the previous day the Senate had voted to override the President's veto, the first time that either chamber had taken this action while Eisenhower was President (see *Congressional Quarterly Almanac*, vol. XIV, *1958*, p. 239; *New York Times*, Aug. 13, 14, 1958). Eisenhower had warned that the legislation would have had "broad and far-reaching implications on the entire Federal wage structure. . . ." While wage inequities should be reviewed, he argued that wages should not "be adjusted by legislation. To do so could ultimately

lead to the deterioration of the present wage board system" (*Public Papers of the Presidents: Eisenhower, 1958*, pp. 580–81).

[2] Indiana Congressman Charles Halleck.

EM, AWF,
Administration Series

To Charles Douglas Jackson *August 13, 1958*

Dear C. D.: All morning long I expected to see you, at least for a moment, in my suite. Apparently with the document all finished and put to bed, you decided yourself to hit the sack and stay there.[1]

In any event, I am sure you know how deeply I appreciate the fine result that you did so much to produce. On every side I have had compliments concerning the content of the talk—I am sorry you could not take over also its delivery.[2]

I feel I must voice two possibilities that you may take almost as warnings. The first is that Foster may feel a need for your continued collaboration in the presentations that he will probably be compelled to make during the next week or so. The second one is that when another international chore of this character falls to my lot, I shall be again sending out an SOS.[3]

Drop in and see me when you can—and, as always, my thanks.
As ever

[1] For background see no. 800. In discussing Soviet Premier Khrushchev's suggestion to place the Lebanon situation before the U.N. General Assembly, Eisenhower had told Secretary Dulles that he would be willing to "make a lead-off address couched in lofty terms that would be above the immediate occasions of controversy" (Memorandum of Conversation, Aug. 7, 1958, Dulles Papers, White House Memoranda Series). Eisenhower had then asked Jackson to prepare a draft that had no more than one paragraph about action in the Middle East. He wanted a speech that would deal with "constructive and useful proposals," he said. Jackson replied, "Bravo" and said that he would begin the draft immediately (Telephone conversation, Eisenhower and Jackson, Aug. 7, 1958, AWF/D; for more on the speech preparation see Dulles, Memorandum of Conversation, Aug. 12, 1958, Dulles Papers, White House Memoranda Series; and Telephone conversations, Dulles and Lodge, Aug. 8, 11; Dulles and Eisenhower, Aug. 9, 12; and Dulles and Whitman, Aug. 12, 1958, Dulles Papers, Telephone Conversations).

[2] After reviewing the circumstances that had precipitated the emergency session of the General Assembly, Eisenhower had pledged to withdraw U.S. forces from Lebanon when that country's independence and integrity were assured. He also called for a U.N. study of heavy armaments entering the area, a study that would be useful in future arms control arrangements. The main thrust of the talk, however, was his proposal to establish a regional economic development program to improve the living standards in the Arab states. Eisenhower indicated that the United States

would support a development organization established and governed by the Arab countries (*Public Papers of the Presidents: Eisenhower, 1958*, pp. 606–16; see also State, *Foreign Relations, 1958–1960*, vol. XI, *Lebanon and Jordan*, pp. 467–69).

According to Ann Whitman, the U.N. speech was the best Eisenhower had ever made. "He was forceful, dynamic, voice clear, words perfect, phrases underscored at [the] proper places," and the content was well received. Dulles had also told Eisenhower that the speech "was a great success" (Ann Whitman memorandums, Aug. 12, 13, 1958, AWF/AWD).

[3] On this same day Dulles would tell Jackson that he would be making a speech to the Veterans of Foreign Wars on "ballistic blackmail" and indicated that he would enjoy working with Jackson again (Telephone conversations, Dulles and Jackson, and Jackson and Dulles, Aug. 13, 1958, Dulles Papers, Telephone Conversations; see also John Foster Dulles, "Foundations of Peace," *U.S. Department of State Bulletin* 39, no. 1022 [September 8, 1958], 373–77). For developments see no. 848.

819   *EM, AWF, Administration Series: AEC*

To John Alex McCone   *August 16, 1958*

Dear John:[1] Mamie tells me that one of the things Rosemary misses in her transplanted life here in Washington is the swimming pool. I do hope that both of you will use the White House pool whenever you wish.[2]

Because of the lack of dressing rooms, normally ladies are requested to use the pool between 9:00 and 11:00 A.M. But I know that would not be satisfactory for the two of you, and I suggest that you simply telephone Sergeant Spanko (extension 154) whenever you wish to come over.[3] If he is not available, a call to the Usher will be all that is necessary.[4]

I shall feel much better if you will use the pool any time you feel like it.

With warm regard, *As ever*

[1] On June 6 the President had nominated McCone to succeed Lewis Strauss on the Atomic Energy Commission. On July 7 the Senate had unanimously confirmed the appointment, and McCone was officially designated as chairman of the AEC on July 14 (see *Congressional Quarterly Almanac*, vol. XVI, *1958*, p. 617; and *New York Times*, June 7, 1958). For developments see no. 826.

[2] McCone's wife, Rosemary, had exercised in their pool in San Marino, California. McCone would reply that Eisenhower's invitation was "welcome" (Aug. 18, 1958, AWF/A: AEC). He added that since his arrival in Washington, he had been "'submerged in the deep end'" and had "little time to miss the luxury of a swim."

[3] Master Sergeant Willie J. Spanko had served in the White House dispensary since March 1954.

[4] J. Bernard West had served as White House chief usher since the Franklin D. Roosevelt Administration.

To John Merrill Olin   *August 18, 1958*
Personal

Dear John: I have done a little investigating about the salmon matter and the information that I give you in this letter I would prefer that you keep on a confidential basis.[1] Apparently it is important to maneuver strategically so that any suggestion that fishing for Atlantic Salmon be restricted should come from the Canadians rather than us. To that end I believe informal contacts have been arranged with some prominent people in Canada (and I understand you yourself may be involved in some of them). I have every confidence that Mr. Leffler is proceeding properly and with due caution in this matter.[2]

With warm regard, *As ever*

[1] Olin Mathieson Chemical Company executive and sportsman John Olin had written Eisenhower in June regarding his work with Assistant Secretary of the Interior Ross Leffler on ways to protect Atlantic salmon in U.S. and Canadian streams. He believed that a treaty with Canada, similar to an earlier one regulating hunting of migratory birds, might be the only means to prevent the fish from "depletion approaching extinction" (Olin to Eisenhower, June 5, 1958, same file as document; see also Eisenhower to Olin, June 9, 1958, *ibid.*). In a subsequent letter Olin had told Eisenhower that although the numbers of salmon caught in Canadian streams in June exceeded those for the same month in 1957, the number was still below that of a normal year (Olin to Eisenhower, July 14, Aug. 7, 1958, *ibid.*).

[2] Leffler had told Interior Secretary Fred Seaton that the investigation would be "long, slow, and frustrating." He had to "explore with caution" all possibilities since he had learned through informal discussions that the Canadians would resent any U.S. suggestion of a restriction on commercial salmon fishing. He also told Seaton that the United States netted practically no Atlantic salmon; most were caught on the Canadian side. He was trying to interest a Canadian motion picture executive in the problem, with the hope that he could influence some of the government officials, Leffler reported. He would continue to meet with State Department and Canadian officials and keep in close contact with Olin, who seemed "reasonably satisfied with the progress that is being made" (Leffler to Seaton, Aug. 13, 1958, same file as document; see also Whitman to Seaton, Aug. 12, 1958, *ibid.*; for more on regulations regarding Atlantic salmon see Anthony Netboy, *The Atlantic Salmon: A Vanishing Species?* [Boston, 1968], pp. 345–70; Anthony Netboy, *The Salmon, Their Fight for Survival* [Boston, 1974], pp. 169–211; W. J. Christie, *A Study of Freshwater Fishery Regulation Based on North American Experience*, Food and Agriculture Organization of the United Nations, Fisheries Technical Paper No. 180 [Rome, 1978]; and Department of Fisheries and Fisheries Research Board of Canada, *The Commercial Fisheries of Canada* [Ottawa, 1957]).

TO EZRA TAFT BENSON   *August 18, 1958*

Dear Ezra: Thank you very much for your suggestions as to possible
individuals to replace Gabe Hauge.[1] For the moment I have decided
not to try to fill the position—but rather to apportion his duties
among a number of other people of experience on the staff.
    With warm regard, *As ever*

[1] On August 14 Secretary of Agriculture Benson had submitted the names of two
candidates for the position of Special Assistant to the President for Economic Affairs
(AWF/A). One, bank executive Jesse Washington Tapp, was an "Eisenhower Democrat" who had served on a number of government commissions; the other, Republican William Irving Myers, was dean of the New York College of Agriculture. For
background on Hauge's resignation see no. 769. At the bottom of Benson's letter
Eisenhower had written: "Please send to Dr. Hauge for comment—informally." For
developments see no. 862.

822   *Prime Minister's Office Records,*
                                                        PREM 11/2566

TO HAROLD MACMILLAN   *August 19, 1958*
Cable. Confidential

Dear Harold: I have just heard of Foster's talk with Selwyn concerning making a unilateral statement about cessation of testing provided the protocol at Geneva is signed in a completely satisfactory
form. In view of some doubts expressed by Selwyn to Foster, I want
to assure you that it is our purpose to be as completely generous
with your Government in the matter of passing information as the
law will permit. I am sure you will understand the need for something being done promptly in the event that the Geneva Protocol is
signed as expected.[1]
    With warm regard.

[1] On July 1 technical experts from the United States, Great Britain, Canada, and
France had begun meetings in Geneva with representatives from the Soviet Union,
Poland, Czechoslovakia, and Romania to discuss ways to detect violations of a possible agreement on the suspension of nuclear tests (see no. 737; State, *Foreign Relations, 1958–1960*, vol. III, *National Security Policy; Arms Control and Disarmament*,
pp. 607–13, 618–48; NSC meeting minutes, June 27, 1958, AWF/NSC; Hewlett and
Holl, *Atoms for Peace and War*, pp. 537–42; and Divine, *Blowing on the Wind*, pp. 215–
17, 225–26). On August 12 Secretary Dulles had told Eisenhower that the Geneva
negotiators were close to an agreement and that the Administration urgently needed
a policy decision on nuclear testing. The State Department was "working actively"

with the AEC and the Defense Department on the subject, Dulles said, and he believed that "some split would develop that the President would have to resolve." Eisenhower told Dulles that he was considering a total suspension of tests with the exception of those underground, even though the Defense Department and the AEC would probably disagree (Dulles, Memorandum of Conversation, Aug. 12, 1958, Dulles Papers, White House Memoranda Series).

During a private dinner in New York where both men were preparing for the special session of the United Nations General Assembly, Dulles had told Foreign Secretary Lloyd that the United States was considering a test suspension, possibly excluding underground tests, to begin on a date that would protect the next series of British tests. Macmillan later told Lloyd that he "did not see the urgency for an immediate statement." The nature of the tests to be excluded from the ban concerned him, he said, and he would have to be "fully satisfied" that the Americans would provide atomic information (Macmillan, *Riding the Storm*, pp. 559–60; on the General Assembly session see no. 818; on amendments to the Atomic Energy Act, which made possible the exchange of atomic information, see no. 794). For developments see no. 824.

823   *EM, AWF,*
                                                                        Name Series

To Louis Francis Albert Mountbatten   *August 19, 1958*

Dear Dickie: I was delighted to have your note telling me of your forthcoming visit to Canada and to this country. Needless to say, Mamie and I will be looking forward to seeing you both when you reach Washington.[1]

There is, of course, always the possibility that circumstances might compel my absence from the city during mid-October. Among other things we will be having an off-year election and this fact will somewhat complicate my schedule.[2] Nevertheless I assure you that unless something unforeseen and uncontrollable gets in the way, we shall be here to welcome you.

If matters follow a normal schedule what I would propose is this: that you and Edwina come to dinner on the sixteenth and, if it should suit your convenience, spend that night at the White House. The reason I say this is because whenever possible, we go to the farm for the weekend, leaving here, as a matter of routine, around noon on Friday. We would hope that the two of you would find this suggested schedule convenient to yours. It would be our thought, also, to get some of your old friends in for dinner on that evening, Thursday.[3]

With affectionate regard to you and Edwina from the both of us.
As ever

[1] Admiral of the Fleet Earl Mountbatten of Burma had served as First Sea Lord since 1955; for background on his long relationship with Eisenhower see *Eisenhower Papers*, vols. I–XVII. Mountbatten had written on August 8 (WHCF/PPF 1427) that he and his wife, the former Edwina Cynthia Annette Ashley, were planning to visit Canada and the United States in October and hoped to be in Washington, D.C., October 16–20.

[2] On the upcoming midterm election see no. 935.

[3] On September 8 Mountbatten would thank the President for the dinner invitation. He also would explain that he would come alone. His wife had undergone surgery, and although she was progressing well, her doctors had advised against her making the trip (Mountbatten to Eisenhower, Sept. 8, 1958, WHCF/PPF 1427, and Sept. 25, 1958, AWF/N). The President would decide later to host a black-tie, stag dinner in Mountbatten's honor (McCaffree to Stephens, Sept. 28, 1958, and Whitman to Mc-Caffree and Stephens, Oct. 2, 1958, both in WHCF/PPF 1427, and Eisenhower to Mountbatten Sept. 29, 1958, AWF/I: Australia).

On October 19 (AWF/N) Mountbatten would thank the President for a "wonderful, memorable experience." He enjoyed talking over old times, he said, and he deeply appreciated the dinner party at which Eisenhower had "succeeded in collecting so many of our old war-time friends and colleagues." See also the guest list and related correspondence in WHCF/PPF 1427, and *New York Times*, October 17, 1958.

As it turned out, the Mountbattens would visit Canada and the United States again in 1959, and the Eisenhowers would host a small dinner party for them on October 8 (see Mountbatten to Eisenhower, Oct. 9, 1959, AWF/N and *New York Times*, Aug. 21, 1959).

824   *EM, AWF, International Series:*
                                                        Macmillan

To Harold Macmillan   *August 20, 1958*
Cable. Secret

Dear Harold: This cable replies to your first message, the one referring to certain technical matters.[1] Foster is just now leaving for New York and during the trip will give to Selwyn his conclusions on the political side of the matter for immediate cabling to you. His cable will quote our statement as it has been revised, including such important points as timing.[2]

My personal comment about the political side is merely that the week's experience at the General Assembly clearly shows that much of the world opinion is shifting, if not toward the Soviets, at least away from the West because of our alleged intransigence about all aspects of nuclear testing and so on.[3] I feel that the publication of the report of the technical experts at Geneva may mark an opportunity for us to regain some of this world opinion. If we are to do so, I think we cannot wait for some weeks or days during which time

Russian propaganda would make it appear that we are being forced into a position that finally might become untenable.

Now with respect to the two questions of reduction of weight and invulnerability, under the law I am permitted to convey to you any information needed so long as that information will not endanger our security. The law requires that I make a certification to this effect. Since our joint purpose is to make certain that the weapons we both manufacture are for use by the free world in our common defense, there will be no difficulty in my making the necessary certificate for this type of exchange.[4] I understand that British and American technicians are having their first meeting on next Wednesday morning, at which time there will be some agreement as to the kinds of information in which both sides wish to delve. Out of that meeting will come to me further suggestions as to the certificates that I need to make.[5]

Incidentally, we do not see how we could establish and stand by a limit of 25 kilos for bomb testing. The findings of tests are not sufficiently exact to make this a feasible condition.[6]

I think this gives you the technical assurance you need.

I want further to say with respect to the whole matter that we are not trying to push you either politically or technically into an isolated or indefensible position. No matter what the exact language of the statement, which I think we will make no later than Saturday morning, we would hope that you could associate yourselves with it if you so desire. But in any event, we will do our best to make certain that our own action does not embarrass you.[7]

When you have both the messages to which I refer, I hope that you will reply as soon as you can because we do believe we are up against one of those moments that we regard as psychologically correct.[8]

With warm regard, *As ever*

---

[1] Responding to Eisenhower's assurance that the United States would provide atomic information as far as U.S. law would permit (see no. 822), Macmillan had told the President that notwithstanding their upcoming series of tests (which would provide some additional information), the British still needed to know more about the vulnerability of atomic weapons to enemy countermeasures and about the development of small yet powerful bombs. Macmillan promised to agree to the suspension of tests "with a clear conscience" if the United States could provide this information (Macmillan to Eisenhower, Aug. 20, 1958, PREM 11/2566; see also Macmillan, *Riding the Storm*, pp. 561–63).

[2] For background on the U.S. statement regarding test cessation see no. 822. In his second letter, also sent on August 20, Macmillan had told Eisenhower that although he agreed on the need for a response to the technical report, he questioned the need for haste. The report would "demonstrate the theoretical possibility of controlling a suspension of tests," he said, but there were "practical difficulties" with "putting this theoretical system into operation." If the two countries suspended all

tests, the Soviets "might refuse to agree to any genuine international control, calculating that the West would never be able to resume the tests which they had voluntarily suspended." Macmillan also expressed concerns over the failure to consult the French. "I do feel strongly that the whole economic future of Europe, and perhaps its political future too, may be jeopardized if we allow the French to feel isolated or roughly treated over this question" (Macmillan to Eisenhower, Aug. 20, 1958, AWF/ I: Macmillan and PREM 11/2566).

Secretary Dulles had been attending the special session of the United Nations General Assembly dealing with U.S. actions in Lebanon. He had returned to Washington to discuss Macmillan's two letters with Eisenhower (see no. 818; and Ann Whitman memorandum, Aug. 20, 1958, AWF/AWD). Dulles would tell Macmillan that unless the West responded to the report of the technical experts by formulating a "significant program," they would be "subjected to a serious propaganda barrage." He did not agree that a test suspension would preclude a future resumption if the Soviets refused to negotiate further, nor did he detect French reluctance to accept the U.S. proposal (Dulles to Macmillan, Aug. 21, 1958, AWF/D-H; see also Telephone conversation, Eisenhower and Dulles, Aug. 21, 1958, Dulles Papers, Telephone Conversations).

The technical committee's report, released on August 21, called for a system of between 160 and 170 land-based and ten ship-based control posts and described methods of detecting nuclear explosions at altitudes of thirty to fifty kilometers above the earth (State, *American Foreign Policy; Current Documents, 1958*, pp. 1331–32, 1336– 41; for the report of the chairman of the U.S. delegation see NSC meeting minutes, Aug. 28, AWF/NSC; see also Killian, *Sputnik, Scientists, and Eisenhower*, pp. 158–62).

In the President's statement, which was revised to accommodate the upcoming British tests, the United States proposed negotiations among the nuclear powers to suspend future tests and to establish an international control system based on the report of the technical experts. Unless testing were resumed by the Soviet Union, the United States would suspend the testing of atomic and hydrogen weapons for one year from the beginning of the negotiations (State, *American Foreign Policy; Current Documents, 1958*, pp. 1332–33; see also Divine, *Blowing on the Wind*, pp. 225–29; and Hewlett and Holl, *Atoms for Peace and War*, pp. 542–47. For disagreements among State and Defense Department officials, prominent scientists, and members of the Atomic Energy Commission regarding the U.S. statement see State, *Foreign Relations, 1958–1960*, vol. III, *National Security Policy; Arms Control and Disarmament*, pp. 631– 46; Goodpaster memorandums, Aug. 18, 19, 20, 1958, AWF/D and WHO/OSS: Subject [Alpha], Nuclear Testing; Ann Whitman memorandums, Aug. 18, 19, 1958, AWF/AWD; and Telephone conversations, Dulles and Herter, Aug. 19, 20, 21, 1958, Dulles Papers, Telephone Conversations).

[3] Eisenhower may have been referring, in part, to negative reaction at the special session to U.S. troop deployments to Lebanon.

[4] At a meeting on this same day Eisenhower had asked Deputy Defense Secretary Donald Quarles if the United States was planning to provide the British with the information they had requested. When Quarles told the President that the initial exchange did not include that information, Eisenhower heatedly replied that the United States could not conduct its relations on such a basis. He would later tell the acting chairman of the AEC that any exchange of information with the British "should be full and generous; any attempt to do otherwise with true allies," he said, "is bound to alienate them" (Goodpaster, Memorandums of Conversation, Aug. 23, 25, 1958, AWF/D).

[5] On the talks between British and American scientists see Macmillan, *Riding the Storm*, pp. 565–67.

[6] In his second message Macmillan had told Eisenhower that he would prefer to have any moratorium limited to those tests that could be detected by existing systems—

that is, above twenty-five kilotons. "A proposal on those lines would be consistent
with our past insistence on linking suspension to control," he said, "and would also
go a long way to meeting public criticism of tests on grounds of injury to health,
since it would eliminate all tests which release fission products into the stratosphere."
[7] The statement would be released on Friday, August 22.

[8] Macmillan would agree to release of the statement. Although his first reaction had
been "one of great concern," Macmillan said he was gratified by the President's assurances regarding the exchange of information. "I have never for one moment
doubted the sincerity of your desire to help us. . . . But this business has had a long
and chequered history, and I know you will understand my anxiety that there should
be no possible room for misunderstanding between us at this last stage." He told
Eisenhower and Dulles that he welcomed the revisions to the proposed statement
that accommodated the upcoming series of British nuclear tests and the qualification that test suspension would depend on Soviet acceptance of an international control system (Macmillan to Eisenhower, Aug. 21, 1958, PREM 11/2566; and Macmil
lan to Dulles, Aug. 21, 1958, WHO/OSS: Subject [Alpha], Nuclear Testing; see also
Eisenhower, *Waging Peace*, pp. 476–77; and Macmillan, *Riding the Storm*, pp. 563–65).
For developments see no. 943.

825   *EM, AWF, Administration Series*

To John Hay Whitney   *August 21, 1958*

Dear Jock: Your letter of the eighteenth contains much good news,
though I find disturbing your comment that Betsey's health has not
been consistently up to par.[1]

I am, of course, delighted that you are going to take the TRIBUNE
plunge. Incidentally—to answer your question—although I know
Mr. Amberg and like him, I did not personally select him as my representative to Paraguay.[2] My personally-directed choices have been
from our circle of intimate friends although I do approve all names
for such assignments.[3]

Mamie and I are still undecided as to where we shall try to get a
bit of rest after Congress adjourns. I think it would be good for both
of us to get away from this atmosphere for a while. You can easily
find me, and I shall, of course, look forward to seeing you, wherever I am, when you are here. We have much to talk over.[4]

With warm regard, *As ever*

[1] Whitney said his wife, whose health "fluctuates far too violently and too often,"
would leave Great Britain on August 18 for a checkup and a long-awaited rest in the
United States. Whitney planned to join her over the Labor Day holiday (AWF/A).
[2] For background on Eisenhower's interest in Whitney's plans to acquire the *New
York Herald Tribune* see no. 748. Official announcement of Whitney's acquisition of
the paper and its European edition would be released on August 28 (see *New York
Times*, Aug. 29, 1958). Whitney said he would remain in the United States after La-

bor Day to interview several editors to fill the *Herald Tribune* post. Richard Hiller Amberg (A.B. Harvard 1933; U.S. Naval War College 1943), publisher of the *St. Louis Globe-Democrat,* was a candidate under consideration (for background see no. 816). For developments see no. 1026.

[3] On August 15 Amberg had been among the U.S. representatives who attended ceremonies in Paraguay inaugurating Alfredo Stroessner for a second term (*New York Times,* Aug. 16, 1958; see also no. 1365). For background on Eisenhower's use of longtime friends as his personal representatives at foreign ceremonies see no. 246.

[4] The second session of the Eighty-fifth Congress would adjourn on August 24. The Eisenhowers would vacation in Newport, Rhode Island, August 29–September 23. Whitney would visit the President at his vacation home on September 4 (see no. 842).

826   *EM, AWF, Name Series*

To Charles S. Jones   *August 22, 1958*
Personal and confidential

Dear Charlie: Thinking of the California political situation this morning, I was impelled to pick up the phone and ask you to come in to see me. Momentarily at least I have stifled that impulse in favor of sending to you, in this letter, my convictions, the basic one of which is:

Knowland *must* win.[1]

The problem is how to bring this about. But first I want to dwell for a minute on why this is so important.

To begin: California is rapidly increasing in population; in fact before many years it will unquestionably be the number one state in size. Even by 1960 it will almost surely be allotted some six or seven additional representatives and the political complexion of the delegation will be more than ever before important. If the state machinery is in Democrat hands, re-apportionment will practically eliminate Republican representation in Congress.[2]

Because of the kind of migration into the state that has caused its mounting rate of growth, the natural conclusion is that the state would tend toward the liberal or leftish side. This is because the proportion of retired people becomes ever greater. Depending so heavily on pensions for their livelihood, they have a very human desire to see the pensions liberalized and increased. When old people are not covered by OASI, their interest in increased amounts for old age assistance is acute, with the Federal government carrying more and more of the burden.[3]

Republicans support proper programs in this field but, realizing that there can be no soundness in pension and insurance plans that are not based upon a stable dollar, they are equally concerned with fiscal responsibility and stability.

Fiscal irresponsibility is practiced by those people who, regardless of the size of deficits and the increasing inability to manage the nation's debt economically and effectively, insist upon higher and higher Federal expenditures. It is one of the characteristics of the ADA-CIO school of thinking.[4] If the entire California delegation becomes of this school—as so much of the Oregon and a great deal of the Washington delegations have become—we are going to have mounting deficits and difficulties in the Federal government accompanied constantly by a depreciating dollar—or, stating it another way, higher living costs.

If the California state political machinery is allowed to pass into the hands of the Democrats, all of the eventualities I have just mentioned will certainly come to pass. The Republican representation in the California delegation will become almost non-existent.

If, on the other hand, we can keep the state machinery in more conservative—that is, Republican—hands, then both the state and national outlook will be considerably brightened. So I repeat: Knowland *must* win.

There is no alternative!

I am not one to minimize the difficulties, particularly when we look squarely at all of the obstacles to be overcome. You are fully aware of these. Bill Robinson, George Allen and Al Gruenther have all told me something of your chagrin and resentment because of what you feel to be the ill-considered and arbitrary action of Senator Knowland in splitting the Republican Party when he determined to run for the governorship instead of continuing in the Senate.[5] Both you and I know that he has been called stubborn, a bit of a lone wolf, and likely to follow his own conclusions and decisions, disregarding the opinions and convictions of able people who would like to be his friends. In other words, he is considered by some to be a bit of a bull in a china shop.

But I feel the following is also true: Bill Knowland is impeccably honest, courageous, studious and serious, and he is physically strong and tireless. Regardless of any blunders that he may or may not have made, these attributes are not to be lightly dismissed.

Frankly, I admit that he and I have more than once disagreed, particularly in the foreign field, where I am bold enough to believe I have a greater competence than he. Sometimes I have considered him to be almost dense in his failure to comprehend factors that I have tried to present to him as of the utmost importance to the United States.[6]

But looking at the debit and credit sides of his political ledger, there can be no question in my mind that he would make an excellent Governor. In fact, I think he would be of greater service to the nation, and to the Republican Party and its principles, in the Governor's chair in California than he is in the United States Senate.

This rough evaluation of the man, which I dare say you largely share, gives, in a sketchy way, my reasons for saying that, despite any personal resentments as to his past actions and no matter how deep those resentments may be, we still have a good man as our Republican candidate for the governorship. I conclude, moreover, that with the stakes as high as they are, we must by no manner of means write off the November contest as a hopeless one. We must, rather, because of the additional difficulties that have been created by Knowland's decisions of last winter, work all the harder and more intensively, to make sure that he will win.

I do not know anything about the state of his political organization; I do not know the identity of his current finance chairman. John McCone was, I believe, in that post, but he had to give it up because of his appointment to the Atomic Energy Commission.[7]

But regardless of the efficiency of his organization or the identity of his money raisers, I want, on a personal basis, to appeal to *you* to get into this fight with everything you have. I can do so with confidence because you have, over these past turbulent and momentous years, supported me and the policies for which both you and I have stood without counting the cost and sacrifice.

I deeply believe that moderate government is the only thing that can stop the United States from sliding more and more into fiscal irresponsibility and consequent financial difficulties that would be bound to bring about profound changes in the procedures of our government, possibly even in its form. None of us can sit on our hands even though there are things in the background of the case that we dislike and resent. Even if Senator Knowland should prove to be so stubborn or even so proud that he does not come directly to people such as yourself and Ted Peterson and Harry Collier and Blackie McLaren and Norman Chandler and Freeman Gosden and George Murphy, and all of the hundreds of others I could name, I pray that you will independently take leadership in giving his candidacy every atom of political and financial support that you can.[8] It makes no difference to me whether you and my other friends do this from inside or outside the Party. Just so we win!

I believe these things so earnestly that I am planning to come to the Coast this fall to make a speech in the state (possibly in Los Angeles) even if that should be the only time I leave Washington during the political campaign. I have promised myself to do this in spite of the inconvenience and the hope I have had for a good long rest without constant political demands upon me.[9] I mention this intent only to show you that I am hopeful of doing my part, even as I ask you and others to rush into the breach.

This is a personal and confidential communication, written hurriedly and without any thought of covering the subject exhaustively. I well know that you are acquainted thoroughly with the political situation and the consequences of Republican failure in California this fall. My effort here has been merely to convey to you my own conviction that success is vital and that regardless of personalities and personal feelings, we must work and win.

I have no objection to your communicating these views, on a personal basis, to our common friends. In fact I should like for each to know how deeply my convictions are on the points I have adverted to in this letter.[10]

With warm regard, *As ever*

[1] Richfield Oil Company President Jones, a Californian, had been a strong supporter of Eisenhower's political efforts during the 1956 election; see Galambos and van Ee, *The Middle Way*, no. 2107. On Senate Minority Leader William F. Knowland's efforts to become governor of California see Gayle B. Montgomery and James W. Johnson, *One Step from the White House: The Rise and Fall of Senator William F. Knowland* (Berkeley and Los Angeles, 1998), pp. 228–54; and Totton J. Anderson, "The 1958 Election in California," *The Western Political Quarterly*, vol. XII, no. 1, pt. 2 (March, 1959), 276, 281–85.

[2] Eisenhower's fears were well-founded. Following the 1960 federal census, California created eight new congressional districts. The Democrats would capture seven of these in the 1962 elections (Winston W. Crouch, John C. Bollens, and Stanley Scott, *California Government and Politics*, 6th ed. [Englewood Cliffs, N.J., 1977], p. 50).

[3] The Old Age and Survivors Insurance program was administered by the Social Security Administration, a division of the Department of Health, Education, and Welfare; see Galambos and van Ee, *The Middle Way*, nos. 26 and 502, and no. 345 in these volumes. On August 29 Eisenhower would sign into law a measure increasing OASI benefits. At the same time he would criticize congressional tendencies toward assigning to the federal government an ever-increasing share of the costs for public assistance programs (*Public Papers of the Presidents: Eisenhower, 1958*, pp. 661–62).

[4] On the Americans for Democratic Action (ADA), a liberal political organization, see Galambos and van Ee, *The Middle Way*, no. 1163. The Congress of Industrial Organizations (CIO), a federation of labor unions, had merged with the supposedly more moderate American Federation of Labor (AF of L) in 1955; see *ibid.*, nos. 541, 1192, and 1313.

[5] Knowland had convulsed the faction-ridden California Republican party by announcing that he would leave the Senate and run for governor—a post then held by another Republican, Goodwin J. Knight (see *ibid.*, nos. 1076 and 1221). After meeting with Eisenhower and Vice-President Nixon in November 1957, Knight had abandoned his plan to thwart Knowland's campaign by running for reelection. Knight declared his intention to try instead for Knowland's Senate seat. This "Big Switch," as it came to be known, was not popular in California (Telephone conversation, Eisenhower and Nixon, Nov. 1, 1957, and Adams, Memorandum for Record, Nov. 5, 1957, AWF/D; Montgomery and Johnson, *One Step from the White House*, pp. 228–43; Anderson, "The 1958 Election in California," pp. 281–83).

[6] On Eisenhower's troubled relationship with Knowland see, for example, nos. 266 and 753.

[7] McCone, a Republican, had become Chairman of the AEC in July (see no. 819); he had also contributed to Eisenhower's 1956 campaign (see Eisenhower to McCone, Nov. 9, 1956, AWF/A).

[8] For background on Standard Oil Company President Theodore Scarborough Petersen see Galambos, *Columbia University*, no. 868. On former Standard Oil Company executive Henry DeWard Collier see Galambos, *NATO and the Campaign of 1952*, nos. 624 and 652. California businessman Norman Loyall McLaren was a former president of the Bohemian Club. Norman Chandler was publisher of the *Los Angeles Times*. Both Eisenhower's close friend Gosden and George Lloyd Murphy were in show business, Gosden as a creator of the radio program "Amos and Andy," and Murphy (see Galambos and van Ee, *The Middle Way*, no. 689) as an actor and movie executive.

[9] In October Eisenhower would make a campaign trip to California; see nos. 892 and 914.

[10] Eisenhower would also write his friend Cliff Roberts on this subject; see no. 829. For developments in California see no. 836.

827   *EM, WHCF, Confidential File:*
Atomic Weapons

To EDWARD H. TELLER   *August 22, 1958*
Confidential

Dear Dr. Teller: I am today announcing that the United States will suspend nuclear weapons tests for a period of twelve months and, under certain conditions of progress toward real disarmament, continue that suspension on a year-to-year basis.[1]

It will, of course, require an extended period to negotiate and install a genuine and assured disarmament arrangement. Even though we will not be doing any weapons testing, it will be necessary that we maintain our weapons development progress during the period and with no less urgency than in the past. It is necessary, in the interest of our country's defense, that the staff of your laboratory, and that of the other weapons development laboratories, continue their research and development in this field with their current vigor and devotion.[2]

I am instructing the Atomic Energy Commission to develop plans to see that these essentials are met and that the vitality of our laboratories is maintained.[3] *Sincerely*

[1] On Eisenhower's test suspension statement see no. 824.

[2] Fears expressed by AEC Chairman John A. McCone that a test moratorium would cause key personnel to leave atomic laboratories prompted Eisenhower to send this letter. Eisenhower also sent this letter to Norris Edwin Bradbury, director of the Los Alamos Laboratory, and to Dr. James Wilson McRae, president of the Sandia Corporation (same file as document; see also Goodpaster, Memorandum of Conference, Aug. 18, 1958, AWF/D; and Hewlett and Holl, *Atoms for Peace and War*, pp. 542–46).

³ Teller would assure Eisenhower that his colleagues would "work vigorously" under the limitations imposed by the moratorium to continue the development of nuclear explosives both as tools for defense and for peaceful purposes (Teller to Eisenhower, Aug. 28, 1958; see also Bradbury to Eisenhower, Sept. 18, 1958; and Goodpaster to Stans, Sept. 10, 1958; all in the same file as this document).

828   *EM, WHCF, Official File 8-F*

To Eric Harlow Heckett   *August 22, 1958*

Dear Mr. Heckett: Your letter of the fourteenth gives me some suggestions that cause some pondering. Of course it has often occurred to me—and been suggested to me—that there should be a "Foreign Service Academy." However, no one has before given me even a partial list of the subjects that, along with such things as world history and literature, should make up a suitable curriculum. Incidentally, I was intrigued by the variety of subjects that you thought it worth while to mention.[1]

Without delay I am going to send your letter to officials in the State Department and ask them whether they would not again study this whole subject in sufficient detail to develop a rough outline of a plan that would comprehend such things as numbers of students, cost of development, maintenance and operation, curriculum and so on. Even if the Congress should not be too impressed, there might be great value in making such a study and putting it on the record.[2]

Many thanks for writing me so fully.

With warm regard, *As ever*

[1] Heckett had suggested "a complete reorganization of thinking" concerning the U.S. system of educating foreign service officers. A "separate and distinct institution" was needed to prepare a person for diplomatic service. He visualized a school where students would take courses in languages, public speaking, history, physical education, world religions, and public relations, as well as chess, poker, bridge, fencing, jujitsu, and pistol shooting. "They have to learn how to slap a man on his back without hurting his shoulders, to tell a joke at the right time without hurting anybody's feelings, and to take drinks without bad consequences." Heckett also emphasized the importance of studying the personalities and writings of the great statesmen, diplomats, philosophers, and historians of the past (same file as document).
[2] On this same day Eisenhower would suggest to Secretary Dulles that he study Heckett's idea "in sufficient detail as to give a rough outline of a plan that would comprehend such things as numbers of students, costs of development, maintenance of operations, curriculum and so on." Admitting that the idea was not new and Congress had not accepted previous proposals, the President said that "it would be a good idea to have the whole thing on record" (Eisenhower to Dulles, July 22, 1958, AWF/D).
In his September 29 response Dulles would include a memorandum that outlined

cost estimates, personnel, and programs for a foreign service academy. The establishment of such an undergraduate institution, according to State Department officials, would be expensive and might result in a less diverse foreign service. It would also provide undesirable competition with American colleges and universities that were, with the Foreign Service Institute, currently training foreign service officers. Dulles reminded Eisenhower that the State Department had in the past "consistently expressed serious reservations" regarding such proposals and had indicated this to the Senate Foreign Relations Committee the previous May. Even though the disadvantages outweighed the advantages, he agreed to study the proposal further and to discuss it with the Bureau of the Budget and other executive agencies which might employ the graduates of such an academy (same file as document).

After receiving a copy of the memorandum from Eisenhower, Heckett would tell the President that his interest in the academy had been stimulated rather than discouraged. He asked for permission to correspond with the State Department to argue his case (Eisenhower to Heckett, Oct. 2, 24, 1958; and Heckett to Eisenhower, n.d., *ibid.*; see also Dulles, Memorandum of Conversation, Oct. 24, 1958, Dulles Papers, White House Memoranda Series).

Deputy Under Secretary for Administration Loy W. Henderson would explain to Heckett that although the State Department was not "entirely satisfied" with the existing training situation, the system had provided "a national flavor and a variety of talents" to foreign service personnel. "Training these young people in a single institution in accordance with a prescribed curriculum," he wrote, "would not . . . meet the needs of the Service" (Henderson to Heckett, Dec. 3, 1958, same file as document).

829   *EM, AWF, Name Series*

To CLIFFORD ROBERTS   *August 23, 1958*
Personal

Dear Cliff: I sent a confidential letter yesterday to Charlie Jones and I talked to Pete on the subject of Knowland's candidacy in California.[1] In spite of the many difficulties that will be encountered in electing Knowland—some of which are alleged to arise out of his own decisions and actions in California—the fact is that it is vitally important that he should win.

You are possibly already well aware of the many issues involved— if not, I will have a long talk with you whenever we can get together. It is enough here to say that the same forces and influences that tried so hard to defeat Senator Taft in 1950 are now the bitter opponents of Knowland.[2] In the Far West he is the symbol of moderate government—it is the radicals who want him out. Should he lose, the state political machinery will be used to take advantage of a need for the upcoming re-apportionment in that state, with the result that the Republican representation will come close to the vanishing point. So the effect will be far more than local; the influence will be felt throughout the country.

Bill will need more funds than he can probably obtain locally. I understand that a number of men out there are waking up to the potentialities of the situation and are beginning to bestir themselves both politically and financially. But since I think he will need outside help, I hope that you get Lloyd McMahon and his financial chairman steamed up in the effort. Mrs. Knudsen should also be most effective.[3] Further I hope that you will do some missionary work among your friends.

I have every confidence that Charlie will really get onto the ball if for no other reason than he has been my warm personal friend and, more than that, has extended himself throughout these recent years to support the policies in which all of us believe. You have done the same. So I am bold enough to put these thoughts before you in the hope—and even the belief—that you will agree with me that we must get going. I am sure that Pete feels the same way.[4]

This afternoon, Saturday, is lovely. It would be a fine time to play golf. But I am sweating out the final few hours (or what I hope are the final few hours) of the present Congressional session. It will be interesting to know how much foolish action can be crowded into the ten hours from now until midnight.[5]

With warm regard, *As ever*

[1] Eisenhower's letter to Jones is no. 826.

[2] Organized labor had fought against Robert A. Taft's 1950 bid for reelection to the Senate with large campaign contributions and energetic political workers. Taft, co-sponsor of the Taft-Hartley Labor Relations Act of 1947, had nevertheless defeated his Democratic opponent by a wide margin (see David W. Reinhard, *The Republican Right Since 1945* [Lexington, Ky., 1983], pp. 66–67, and William S. White, *The Taft Story* [New York, 1954], pp. 94–95, 99–102; see also Galambos and van Ee, *The Middle Way*, nos. 26, 397, and 431). Eight years later Knowland had aroused intense labor opposition to his candidacy by advocating an end to compulsory unionism (the so-called "right-to-work initiative") in California (Montgomery and Johnson, *One Step from the White House*, pp. 238–41, 244, 247; Anderson, "The 1958 Election in California," pp. 289–92). For developments see no. 836.

[3] Lloyd F. MacMahon, chairman of the National Citizens for Eisenhower-Nixon 1958 Committee, had met with Eisenhower on May 20. Valley Knudsen, the former Valley Filtzer, was the wife of California creamery executive Thorkild R. Knudsen (see Galambos and van Ee, *The Middle Way*, no. 851) and co-chairman of the committee.

[4] W. Alton "Pete" Jones had contributed to Eisenhower's 1956 reelection campaign and had pledged to support the 1958 Citizens for Eisenhower-Nixon effort; see Eisenhower to Jones, November 20, 1956, AWF/N, Eisenhower to [Mac]Mahon, May 22, 1958, WHCF/OF 138-C-4, and no. 708.

[5] The Eighty-fifth Congress would adjourn on the morning of August 24, following last-minute passage of the mutual security appropriation bill (see no. 782; see also *New York Times*, Aug. 24, 1958).

On this same day Eisenhower would send Knowland a strong letter of endorsement, which would be released to the press two days later (AWF/D; see also *Public Papers of the Presidents: Eisenhower, 1958*, p. 638). On August 25 Eisenhower would learn that Charles Jones would work for the Knowland campaign. This news, according to

Presidential Secretary Ann Whitman, "pleased the President greatly" (Ann Whitman memorandum, Aug. 25, 1958, AWF/AWD). For Roberts's reply see no. 842.

830   *EM, AWF,*
                                                      Administration Series

To NELSON ALDRICH ROCKEFELLER   *August 25, 1958*

Dear Nelson: To the surprise of no one word has just been received of your nomination as the Republican candidate for Governor of New York.[1] To say that I am pleased is the understatement of the year. I know that you will make a vigorous, honest and courageous fight, and I have every confidence that you will be successful. And, I need not add, to have you in the Governor's Chair in the State of New York will be quite the finest backstop I could hope to have for the next two years. All of your friends on the White House staff join in warm congratulations.

How you have managed to keep up your interest in your various other projects during what must have been a hectic period for you, I do not precisely know.[2] I am delighted to have the "Opinions of Parliamentarians in India and Japan" and when I get free of a little of the bill signing pressure, I shall have the time to study it carefully.[3] Many thanks, as always.

With all the best,[4] *As ever*

[1] Rockefeller had announced his candidacy on June 30 and had been nominated by the Republican state convention on August 25. The President would congratulate Rockefeller in a telephone conversation on August 26 (*New York Times,* July 1, Aug. 26, 1958, Telephone Conversation, Rockefeller and Eisenhower, Aug. 26, 1958, AWF/D; see also nos. 841 and 843).

[2] Among other duties, Rockefeller had served as a member and chairman of Eisenhower's Advisory Committee on Government Organization (see no. 965).

[3] Rockefeller had sent the President a study conducted among parliamentarians in India and Japan during March and April 1958 by the Institute for International Social Research in Princeton, New Jersey (Rockefeller to Eisenhower, and Rockefeller to Whitman, Aug. 21, 1958). The effort, which was part of a continuing project, focused on the issue of neutrality in the cold war. The twenty-six-page report and related correspondence are in AWF/A.

The second session of the Eighty-fifth Congress had adjourned on August 24. On the many bills the President would consider before departing for Newport, Rhode Island, on August 29 see, for example, no. 831, and *Public Papers of the Presidents: Eisenhower, 1958,* pp. 652–67.

[4] The President would add a longhand postscript: "Truly—I am delighted. D." Rockefeller would reply (Aug. 29, 1958, AWF/A) that he looked forward to the opportunity of running with such a "strong ticket"; one united in support of the President. For developments see no. 922.

To Robert Bernerd Anderson   *August 26, 1958*

Dear Mr. Secretary: I have read with great interest your letter concerning the adequacy of the present resources of the International Monetary Fund and the International Bank for Reconstruction and Development.[1]

I thoroughly agree with you that the well-being of the free world is vitally affected by the progress of the nations in the less developed areas as well as the economic situation in the more industrialized countries. A sound and sustainable rate of economic growth in the free world is a central objective of our policy.

It is universally true, in my opinion, that governmental strength and social stability call for an economic environment which is both dynamic and financially sound. Among the principal elements in maintaining such an economic basis for the free world are (1) a continuing growth in productive investment, international as well as domestic; (2) financial policies that will command the confidence of the public, and assure the strength of currencies; and (3) mutually beneficial international trade and a constant effort to avoid hampering restrictions on the freedom of exchange transactions.

During the past year, as you know, major advances have been made in our own programs for dealing with these problems. These include an increase in the lending authority of the Export-Import Bank; establishment of the Development Loan Fund on a firmer basis through incorporation and enlargement of its resources; extension and broadening of the Reciprocal Trade Agreements Act; and continuation of the programs carried forward under the Agricultural Trade Development and Assistance Act.[2]

Our own programs, however, can do only a part of the job. Accordingly, as we carry them forward, we should also seek a major expansion in the international programs designed to promote economic growth with the indispensable aid of strong and healthy currencies.

As you have pointed out, the International Bank for Reconstruction and Development and the International Monetary Fund are international instruments of proved effectiveness already engaged in this work. While both institutions still have uncommitted resources, I am convinced that the time has now come for us to consider, together with the other members of these two agencies, how we can better equip them for the tasks of the decade ahead.

Accordingly, I request, assuming concurrence by the interested members of the Congress with whom you will consult, that you take the necessary steps in conjunction with the National Advisory Council on International Monetary and Financial Problems, to support a course of action along the following lines:

First: In your capacity as United States Governor of the International Monetary Fund, I should like to have you propose, at the Annual Meeting of the Fund at New Delhi in October, that prompt consideration be given to the advisability of a general increase in the quotas assigned to the member governments.

The past ten years testify to the important role played by the International Monetary Fund in assisting countries which, from time to time, have encountered temporary difficulties in their balance of payments. We are now entering a period when the implementation of effective and sound economic policies may be increasingly dependent in many countries upon the facilities and technical advice which the Fund can make available as they meet temporary external financial difficulties. This is particularly true of the less developed countries with the great variability in foreign exchange receipts to which they are subject from time to time. It also applies to industrialized countries which are dependent on foreign trade. Through its growing experience and increasingly close relations with its members, the Fund can also help see to it that countries are encouraged to pursue policies that create stable financial and monetary conditions while contributing to expanding world trade and income. The International Monetary Fund is uniquely qualified to harmonize these objectives but its present resources do not appear adequate to the task.

Second: In your capacity as United States Governor of the International Bank for Reconstruction and Development, I should like to have you propose, at the Annual Meeting of the Bank, that prompt consideration be given to the advisability of an increase in the authorized capital of the Bank and to the offering of such additional capital for subscription by the Bank's member governments. Such additional capital subscriptions, if authorized, would not necessarily require additional payments to be made to the Bank; they would, however, ensure the adequacy of the Bank's lending resources for an extended period by strengthening the guarantees which stand behind the Bank's obligations.

The demands upon the Bank for development loans have been increasing rapidly, and it is in a position to make a growing contribution to the economic progress of the free world in the period which lies ahead. Moreover, it can do this by channeling the savings of private investors throughout the world into sound loans, repayable in dollars or other major currencies. But to meet the rising need for such sound development loans, it must be able to raise the funds in the capital markets of the free world. An increase in the Bank's subscribed capital, by increasing the extent of the responsibility of member governments for assuring that the Bank will always be in a position to meet its obligations, would enable the Bank to place a larger volume of its securities in a broader market, while still maintaining the prime quality of its securities and hence the favorable terms on which it can borrow and re-lend funds.

Third: With respect to the proposal for an International Development Association, I believe that such an affiliate of the International Bank, if adequately supported by a number of countries able to contribute, could provide a useful supplement to the existing lending activities of the Bank and thereby accelerate the pace of economic development in the less developed member countries of the Bank. In connection with the study of this matter that you are undertaking in the National Advisory Council pursuant to the Senate Resolution, I note that you contemplate informal discussions with other member governments of the Bank with a view to ascertaining their attitude toward an expansion of the Bank's responsibilities along these lines. If the results indicate that the creation of the International Development Association would be feasible, I request that, as a third step, you initiate promptly negotiations looking toward the establishment of such an affiliate of the Bank.

The three-point program I have suggested for consideration would require intensified international cooperation directed to a broad attack upon some of the major economic problems of our time. A concerted and successful international effort along these lines would, I feel certain, create a great new source of hope for all those who share our conviction that with material betterment and free institutions flourishing side by side we can look forward with confidence to a peaceful world.[3] *Sincerely*

---

[1] Anderson had prepared for Eisenhower's approval drafts of his letter to the President, as well as this reply, before the formal exchange of messages took place. Eisenhower approved both, and the two letters were released to the public on this day (see Eisenhower to Anderson, Aug. 12, 1958, AWF/A; and *New York Times*, Aug. 27, 1958). The United States had taken "major steps" in expanding its own programs to enhance the well-being of the industrialized nations as well as those in less developed areas of the free world, Anderson had written. He believed, however, that the International Monetary Fund and the International Bank for Reconstruction and Development (the World Bank group) needed strengthening. "Both of these organizations have staffs of internationally recruited experts who, with over a decade of experience behind them, have demonstrated their ability to act effectively and impartially," he wrote. "Both have established operating standards and policies which command the respect of their member governments." Anderson had recommended that the IMF and the IBRD consider at their upcoming annual meetings ways to increase their impact.

Anderson also referred to a recently passed Senate resolution calling for a feasibility study by the National Advisory Council on International Monetary and Financial Problems of an "International Development Association"—a new institution that would be affiliated with the World Bank. Such an association would finance projects in less developed areas on the basis of "soft" loans—those repayable in local currency or in hard currency at low interest rates with long repayment periods (Anderson to Eisenhower, Aug. 18, 1958, same file as document; for background on the IMF and the IBRD see Galambos and van Ee, *The Middle Way*, no. 1883; and nos. 746 and 75 in these volumes; on the proposal for an International Development Association and the Senate resolution see *Congressional Quarterly Almanac*, vol. XIV, *1958*, pp. 60, 256; and State, *American Foreign Policy; Current Documents, 1958*, p. 189). See also Edward S. Mason and Robert E. Asher, *The World Bank Since Bretton Woods: The Origins, Policies, Operations, and Impact of the International Bank for Reconstruction and Development* (Washington, D.C., 1973); and Galambos and Milobsky, "Organizing and Reorganizing the World Bank, 1946–1972," pp. 156–90.

[2] On the strengthening of the Export-Import Bank, the Development Loan Fund, and the Reciprocal Trade Agreements Act see no. 674; see also no. 755; and State, *Foreign Relations, 1958–1960*, vol. IV, *Foreign Economic Policy*, pp. 25–26, 174–75, 290–93. On the Agricultural Trade Development and Assistance Act see *ibid.*, pp. 176, 178; and *Congressional Quarterly Almanac*, vol. XIV, *1958*, pp. 277–80; see also no. 24.

[3] At its September 4 meeting the National Advisory Council would recommend a 100 percent increase in IBRD resources and no less than a 50 percent increase in World Bank resources. Anderson, who was the U.S. governor of both institutions, would propose the increases at the New Delhi meeting, and on December 29 the executive directors of the two organizations would recommend the increases to the member governments (State, *Foreign Relations, 1958–1960*, vol. IV, *Foreign Economic Policy*, pp. 86–88, 90, 93–95, 304–6).

In August 1959 Anderson would submit to the Senate Foreign Relations Committee the report of the National Advisory Council, stating that favorable reaction among World Bank members warranted the drafting of a resolution for the establishment of an International Development Association. Eisenhower would promote the association in his address to the annual meeting of the governors of the IMF and IBRD that September. In February 1960 the President would submit the articles of agreement to Congress and would urge legislation authorizing U.S. participation. He would sign the bill with an appropriation of $320 million in June. Three months later the IDA would begin operations with fifteen countries as members (Anderson to Black, July 31, 1959, AWF/A, Anderson Corr.; Anderson to Eisenhower, Aug. 14, 1959, Dec. 3, 1959, AWF/A; *Congressional Quarterly Almanac*, vol. XVI, *1960*, pp. 221, 630; State, *Foreign Relations, 1958–1960*, vol. IV, *Foreign Economic Policy*, pp. 371–72, 394–95, 398–99; *Public Papers of the Presidents: Eisenhower, 1959*, pp. 702–4; *Public Papers of the Presidents: Eisenhower, 1960–61*, pp. 180, 199–201, 381–82).

832   *EM, WHCF, Official File 8-N*

To Arthur Kittredge Watson   *August 26, 1958*

Dear Dick: As I wrote you on August twelfth, I asked the Secretary of State for his personal reaction to your suggestion that a series of what you called "friendship teams" made up of businessmen and educators visit the Soviet Union and the satellites "to promote friendship and understanding."[1] While the terminology is not quite the same, I think you will agree that many of your objectives are being fulfilled in the present program of exchanges with the Soviet orbit; I am enclosing a copy of the report for the first six months of the

U.S.-U.S.S.R. Exchange Agreement program. Progress, of course, is slow, but I am agreeably pleased with the number of exchanges that have been accomplished.[2]

As far as an appeal to the heads of state is concerned, the State Department feels that such a procedure could be embarrassing to Gomulka, and is, at the moment, not feasible with Hungary or Czechoslovakia.[3]

I understand that other programs are under consideration that embody elements of your ideas. I am in total agreement with the objectives of these programs, and shall report them whenever I have the opportunity.[4]

With warm regard, *Sincerely*

[1] IBM President Watson (B.A. Yale 1942) had told Eisenhower that his idea had been inspired by conversations with a number of banking and statistical experts in both Eastern and Western European countries. The Iron Curtain could not be raised "in the foreseeable future," Watson said, "unless we take the initiative away from the communists and start a real campaign to promote friendship and understanding followed by increased trade in non-essential materials" (Watson to Eisenhower, Aug. 8, 1958). In his August 12 response Eisenhower had told Watson that he agreed completely with the premise that friendship and understanding were "the basis of mutually beneficial trade, as well as the basis for the peace we so much want to assure." To Dulles he wrote that Watson's program had "a slightly different slant" that he found "appealing" (Eisenhower to Watson, and Eisenhower to Dulles, Aug. 12, 1958; Dulles to Eisenhower, Aug. 23, 1958).
[2] On U.S.-Soviet exchange programs see nos. 617 and 640.
[3] Recent moves by Wladyslaw Gomulka, First Secretary of the Central Committee of the Polish United Workers' Party, had strengthened government ties with the Soviet Union, even though most Poles apparently opposed the Communist system. The recent execution of former Hungarian Premier Imre Nagy in June and Czechoslovak surveillance of U.S. embassy staff and intimidation of embassy contacts had affected U.S. relations with the Communist governments of both countries (State, *Foreign Relations, 1958–1960*, vol. X, pt. 1, *Eastern Europe Region; Soviet Union; Cyprus*, pp. 48–51, 72–76; pt. 2, *Eastern Europe; Finland; Greece; Turkey*, pp. 123–33).
[4] Dulles had told Eisenhower that the State Department was developing a number of other exchange projects, including one proposed by U.N. Ambassador Lodge (Dulles to Eisenhower, Aug. 23, 1958).

Reassured by this response, Watson would write Eisenhower that he was pleased at the progress the President had reported (Sept. 2, 1958). All papers are in the same file as the document.

833   *EM, AWF, Administration Series*

To Robert Cutler   *August 27, 1958*

Dear Bobby: If I have timed this letter correctly, it ought to arrive in Belgrade to help celebrate the arrival of your forty-seventh grand-niece or grandnephew. At any rate, it will serve to bring my greetings to your niece and to your sister, if she is there with you.[1]

I have enjoyed greatly your cards and letter, although I am aghast at the statistics of your riding trip through Britain (in bad weather at that). But long ago I think we came to a truce as to bicycling versus golf.[2]

I suspect you can realize the relief that surrounded the White House on the closing of the Congressional session.[3] Although I don't think properly I should quote a Democratic Senator, but it did amuse me that Senator Lausche said publicly that in his opinion all acts of Congress during the last ten days should be declared unconstitutional.[4]

As to foreign affairs, I am sure you are up-to-date at least on the main currents, and more than that I cannot, of course, say in a letter.[5]

Mamie and I are trying to get away to Newport, but the specter of a month haunted by school difficulties is always with me. You probably know that the Supreme Court has called a special session tomorrow afternoon to consider the stay granted by the Eighth Court of Appeals.[6]

But problems are always with us. Personally, I am feeling well and looking forward to some respite from the White House routine.[7] *As ever*

---

[1] Cutler had resigned as Eisenhower's special assistant in June (see *New York Times*, June 25, 1958). Cutler and the family of his deceased brother were traveling throughout Yugoslavia. He would reply on September 9 (AWF/A) that he and his sister-in-law had just returned from a six-day tour of the Dalmatian Coast and Upper Slovenia. Cutler also thanked the President for the card he signed for his niece Mary's baby girl—"(No 47)."

[2] Cutler's letter included a description of ancient Yugoslav cities. His other cards and letters are not in AWF.

[3] The second session of the Eighty-fifth Congress had adjourned on August 23.

[4] Ohio Senator Frank John Lausche had made the statement the day Congress adjourned (*Washington Post*, Aug. 24, 1958).

[5] For Eisenhower's analysis of the situation in the Middle East see no. 797.

[6] For background on the desegregation crisis in Little Rock, Arkansas, in the fall of 1957 see nos. 320 and 330. In June, following widespread violent resistance, a federal district judge decided to delay the integration program in Little Rock until 1961. On August 18 the U.S. Eighth Circuit Court of Appeals overturned the order, but stayed its decision until the Little Rock school board could seek review in the Supreme Court (Burk, *The Eisenhower Administration and Black Civil Rights*, pp. 191–94, and *New York Times*, Aug. 26, 27, 29, 1958; see also no. 835). The Eisenhowers would vacation in Newport, Rhode Island, August 29–September 23. For developments on the Supreme Court decision see no. 840.

[7] For developments see no. 875.

To Lewis Bergman Maytag   *August 28, 1958*

Dear Bud: I am distressed to learn that Ed has been having angina pains.[1] I sincerely trust that he is consulting the finest specialist available and that he is doing exactly as the doctor orders.

One of my Cabinet officers, a man almost as old as I am, has had the same difficulty for a good many years. He is very careful in following the rules prescribed by his doctor; in addition he always carries with him nitroglycerine pills, one of which he takes whenever he feels any slightest distress. In this way he seems to get along in good fashion.

In any event, I join in your prayer that Ed will get no worse—I cannot imagine the game of golf without him somewhere in the offing and me always with the hope that I will get a chance to play him again. Incidentally this goes for you, too.[2]

With warm regard, *As ever*

---

[1] Maytag was president and director of the Maytag Company, manufacturers of washing machines; for background see *Eisenhower Papers*, vols. X–XVII. In his August 25 reply to Eisenhower's August 19 birthday greetings, Maytag had included a report on Ed Dudley's health. Maytag was a member of the Broadmoor Golf Club in Colorado Springs, Colorado, where Dudley was the summer golf professional. In 1957 Dudley had left his position as winter golf pro at the Augusta National Golf Club to accept the same post at the Dorado Club in Dorado, Puerto Rico (see no. 271).
[2] Maytag said he hoped that Dudley's condition would not become serious enough to force him to give up his work. He then went on to describe Dudley's golf swing as "the prettiest thing" he had ever seen.

As it turned out, Dudley's doctors would advise him to stay in Colorado Springs year round to take advantage of "'off season'" periods of inactivity (see Eisenhower to Maytag, Aug. 18, 1959, Maytag to Eisenhower, Aug. 24, 1959, and Eisenhower to Maytag, Sept. 8, 1959). All correspondence is in the same file as the document.

To Lucille Dawson Eisenhower   *August 30, 1958*

Dear Lucy: Of course I am glad to have your views on one of the gravest problems of our times.[1] I can't in a letter, discuss them as fully as I would like—perhaps one of these days we shall have the opportunity for a family chat on the subject.

But I must remind you that there are three equal *and separate* branches of our governmental system—a system, incidentally, that has served the people of America well for one hundred and seventy-five years. As President, I am sworn to uphold the Constitution and the Constitution, due to the wisdom of our forebears, is subject to the interpretation of one of those three separate branches of our government, the Supreme Court.[2]

At the same time, I have preached in every possible statement the need for moderation, for tolerance, for understanding, and for education. A deep-seated emotional attitude is of course something that cannot be corrected, certainly overnight, by law. Don't forget that I, too, have spent much time in the South and in border states, enough certainly to understand and be sympathetic to the views of the people there.[3]

Ed seems to have enjoyed his trip to Banff and—I hope I am not speaking out of school—suggests I arrange a similar jaunt to Bermuda this winter.[4] It's a wonderful idea, but—.

As I say, I should like to talk to you about all this sometime; meantime, my affectionate regard. *As always*

[1] Mrs. Edgar Eisenhower had written on August 26 regarding the special session of the Supreme Court that was dealing with school desegregation in Little Rock, Arkansas. On August 18 the U.S. Eighth Circuit Court of Appeals overturned a June ruling to delay the integration program in Little Rock until 1961, but stayed its decision until the Little Rock school board could seek review in the Supreme Court (see no. 833). For background on the 1957 desegregation crisis see nos. 320 and 330. Integration was a states' rights issue, Mrs. Edgar Eisenhower said, and federal enforcement would produce violence. She also stated her belief that African Americans were inherently inferior to whites and said she feared for the well-being of white girls who attended racially integrated schools. For developments on the Supreme Court's decision see no. 840.

[2] Mrs. Eisenhower had asked the President to "call off" Chief Justice Earl Warren and his "NAACP do-gooders!"

[3] Lucille Eisenhower, whose sister lived in Birmingham, Alabama, said that Southerners were no different from others, but only people who lived in the South could understand them. "And I don't mean the Maryland and Virginia Southerners. I'm talking about Alabama, Georgia, Tenn., Fla., La., and Texas." During his military career Eisenhower had been stationed in Texas, Maryland, and Georgia.

[4] Edgar Eisenhower had represented the President at the dedication of Mount Eisenhower in Banff National Park in Alberta, Canada (see Telephone conversation, Eisenhower and Diefenbaker, Aug. 4, 1958, AWF/I: Canada; *Public Papers of the Presidents: Eisenhower, 1958*, p. 637, and *New York Times*, Aug. 25, 1958). Edgar had thanked the President (Aug. 25) for appointing him and added that if a similar occasion arose in Bermuda, he would like to go. The President would reply to Edgar on this same date (Aug. 30). All correspondence is in AWF/N.

To Hugh Meade Alcorn, Jr.   *August 30, 1958*
Personal

Dear Meade: It has been reported to me that the Hearst papers are planning to support Brown rather than Knowland in California.[1] Isn't there something that you can do about this? If you are not personally in close touch with the Hearst people, you might get hold of Jim Hagerty or Bill Robinson or someone of that kind to try to get them on the right track.[2] *As ever*

[1] For background on Senator William F. Knowland's attempt to become governor of California see nos. 826 and 829. His Democratic opponent, Edmund Gerald ("Pat") Brown (LL.B. San Francisco Law School 1927), had served as attorney general of California (1951–1958) and as district attorney for the city and county of San Francisco (1943–1947). He had also been chairman of the Golden Gate Bridge and Highway District since 1942. The Hearst Corporation newspapers had supported Eisenhower in the 1956 election; see Eisenhower to Hearst, October 11, 1956, WHCF/OF 138 New York.
[2] Republican National Committee Chairman Alcorn would reply (Sept. 4, AWF/A) that he thought he had "taken some steps which will prove effective" and that he would make a personal report to Eisenhower later. Three of the four Hearst newspapers in California, however, would support Brown (Montgomery and Johnson, *One Step from the White House,* pp. 241, 252; Anderson, "The 1958 Election in California," p. 288; *New York Times,* Sept. 27, 1958). For developments see no. 842.

837   *EM, AWF, Name Series*

To Elwood Richard Quesada   *August 31, 1958*

Dear Pete: It is good news that you have been able to achieve an "agreement in principle" looking toward a single National Aviation Weather System.[1] Such a program has long been needed, and there is no doubt that it can be operated more efficiently, more economically, and with better results than have formerly been possible under the divergent systems that had grown up.

Won't you please, at some convenient time, convey to Mr. Reichelderfer my special thanks for his cooperation in the matter?[2]

And my personal congratulations to you on making such an achievement possible![3]

With warm regard, *As ever*

[1] Retired Air Force Lieutenant General Quesada, Chairman of the Airways Modernization Board, had been Special Assistant to the President for Aviation since the

passage of the Airways Modernization Act of 1957. For background on the legislation, which established a temporary Airways Modernization Board to coordinate proposals with the Federal Communications Commission and Civil Aeronautics Board in order to develop traffic controls for military and civilian planes, see no. 288. Quesada had written on August 28 (AWF/N) that the National Aviation Weather System would meet military, civil, commercial, and agricultural aviation needs. The Airways Modernization Board (and eventually the Federal Aviation Agency) would promote a unified research program and would consolidate the existing programs of the Civil Aeronautics Administration, the Weather Bureau, and the armed services.

Eisenhower had signed the bill (P.L. 726) to create the Federal Aviation Agency on August 23. The new agency combined the existing aviation functions of the Civil Aeronautics Administration, the Airways Modernization Board, and the Commerce Department (see *Congressional Quarterly Almanac,* vol. XIV, *1958,* pp. 233–34, and Stuart I. Rochester, *Takeoff at Mid-Century: Federal Civil Aviation Policy in the Eisenhower Years 1953–1961* [Washington, D.C., 1976]; see also *New York Times,* Nov. 30, 1958).
[2] Quesada had complimented Francis Wilton Reichelderfer (A.B. Northwestern University 1917), head of the U.S. Weather Bureau, for his cooperation. Reichelderfer had been with the U.S. Weather Bureau since 1938. During World War I he had served as a Naval meteorological officer, and he had directed the Naval Meteorological Organization from 1922 until 1928.
[3] On September 30 Eisenhower would appoint Quesada Administrator of the Federal Aviation Agency, effective November 1 (see *Public Papers of the Presidents: Eisenhower, 1958,* pp. 710–11, and *New York Times,* Sept. 14, Oct. 1, 4, 1958). For developments see no. 1635.

13

Quemoy and Matsu

To Chiang Kai-Shek   September 1, 1958
Cable. Confidential

Dear Mr. President: I have just read with great interest Ambassador
Drumright's reports of his most recent conversations with you.[1] You
may be assured that it is my Government's firm unwavering policy
to support the security and international prestige of the Government of the Republic of China. The military measures we have been
taking and will continue to take in cooperation with your forces are
all directed with that end in view.[2]

This message bears my warm personal regards to a leader of outstanding valor and highest principle. *Sincerely yours*

[1] For background on the earlier crisis involving the islands immediately off the coast
of the Chinese mainland see Galambos and van Ee, *The Middle Way*, vols. XV and
XVI. On August 7 CIA Director Allen Dulles had told the National Security Council
that the situation in the Taiwan Straits was "heating up." Chinese Communist air
forces had moved into previously unoccupied bases on the mainland opposite the
island of Quemoy, raising the possibility of an air blockade of the offshore islands.
At that time Eisenhower had said there would be "no excuse for U.S. intervention"
unless the activity was thought to be preliminary to an attack on Formosa. Since the
threat to the islands in 1954, however, Nationalist Chinese President Chiang Kai-shek
had gradually increased his forces on Quemoy and Matsu, increasing their strategic
importance. As a result, Secretary Dulles now doubted whether there could be an
"amputation" of the islands "without fatal consequences to Formosa itself" (NSC
meeting minutes, Aug. 8, 1958, AWF/NSC; and Dulles, Memorandum of Conversation, Aug. 12, 1958, Dulles Papers, White House Memoranda Series; see also State,
Foreign Relations, 1958–1960, vol. XIX, *China* [1996], pp. 44–68).

The Chinese Communists had started shelling the islands on August 23 and 24,
prompting the United States to deploy an aircraft carrier and five destroyers to the
Far East. A subsequent letter from Chiang to Eisenhower had described intense artillery bombardments, the strafing of ground troops, and the sinking of two vessels.
He asked that the United States assist him in defending the islands, provide convoy
vessels to make the straits safe for shipping, and authorize Nationalist bombing of
Communist artillery positions on the mainland (State, *Foreign Relations, 1958–1960*,
vol. XIX, *China*, pp. 83–86; see also Thomas J. Christensen, *Useful Adversaries: Grand
Strategy, Domestic Mobilization, and Sino-American Conflict, 1947–1958* [Princeton, 1996],
pp. 194–96).

In an earlier cable, drafted by State Department officials, Eisenhower had told the
Chinese leader that he could not offer an immediate reply because of the "magnitude and gravity of the issues involved" (Eisenhower to Chiang, Aug. 27, 1958, AWF/
I: Formosa [China]; see also State, *Foreign Relations, 1958–1960*, vol. XIX, *China*, pp.
89–96). On August 29, at a meeting with the chairman of the Joint Chiefs of Staff,
Eisenhower had approved U.S. convoy protection for Nationalist supply ships up to
the three-mile limit of coastal waters. He also approved the U.S. assumption of responsibility for the air defense of Taiwan, thus releasing Nationalist forces for defense of the islands (*ibid.*, pp. 86–102; see also Goodpaster memorandums, Aug. 14,
29, 1958, AWF/D; NSC meeting minutes, Aug. 15, 22, 1958, AWF/NSC; Dulles, Memorandum of Conversation, Aug. 23, 1958; Herter, Memorandum of Conversation,

Aug. 22, 1958; both in Dulles Papers, White House Memoranda Series; Telephone conversation, Eisenhower and Dulles, Aug. 22, 1958, Dulles Papers, Telephone Conversations; and Eisenhower, *Waging Peace*, pp. 292–304).

Everett F. Drumright, former Consul General in Hong Kong, had been Ambassador to the Republic of China since March 1958. He had informed the State Department that Chiang's reaction to the U.S. response to his requests was "the most violent I have ever seen him exhibit." He had called the U.S. attitude "'inhuman' and 'unfair' to his soldiers on [the] islands and destructive of public morale." Drumright had suggested that Eisenhower send a message of reassurance and support. After a meeting on the following day, Drumright reported that Chiang was "more at ease and relaxed . . . and argued his position rationally." He worried about his inactivity in the face of Communist assaults and its effect on the morale of his forces, Drumright said, but he understood U.S. reluctance to provide any basis for a Communist charge of aggression. In a telephone conversation on this same day Eisenhower had "expressed some annoyance" to Dulles over pressure from Chiang to involve the United States in this latest series of events (State, *Foreign Relations, 1958–1960*, vol. XIX, *China*, pp. 107–8, 109–13).

[2] Chiang would thank Eisenhower for his "positive measures of assistance." "Whatever may be their motives and objectives in launching the recent large-scale attacks," he wrote, "the Chinese Communists can be checked only by our joint demonstration of firmness in both pronouncements and actions" (Chiang to Eisenhower, Sept. 4, 1958, *ibid.*, Microfiche Supplement no. 82). For developments see no. 844.

839   *EM, AWF, Gettysburg Series*

TO ARTHUR SEYMOUR NEVINS   *September 1, 1958*

Dear Art: Quite naturally I am proud and delighted that the Erica heifer won first place in her class at the Ohio State Fair show. Congratulations to you and Bob Hartley![1]

I am dropping a note to Mr. Heckett and to Bill Ewing, as you suggest.[2]

So far I have managed to achieve a greater degree of isolation from problems and paper work than I could have thought possible. I have a great hunch, however, that this is only the Labor Day lull and cannot possibly last.[3]

With affectionate regard to Ann and all the best to yourself, *As ever*

[1] Nevins had written on August 30 that he had attended the Angus cattle show at the Ohio State Fair (AWF/Gettysburg).

[2] Nevins said he had visited with the Hecketts and that their entries won most of the competitions. Nevins also had suggested that the President send a congratulatory note to the Ewings regarding the showing of a calf dropped by their cow. On the Hecketts and the Ewings, who raised Angus cattle, see nos. 148 and 10, respectively.

[3] The Eisenhowers would vacation in Newport, Rhode Island, August 30–September 23.

To Ralph Emerson McGill   *September 3, 1958*
Personal

Dear Ralph: Your letter of the twenty-first did not reach the White House until just before we left for Newport, and this is the first opportunity I have had to acknowledge it.[1] Previously, however, Charlie Yates sent me the column entitled "The President as Professor."[2] Far from being off the mark, it demonstrated once again your understanding of my convictions.

The entire situation distresses me profoundly, as I know it does you and all other leaders of American thought.[3] There doesn't seem to be any solution in sight—for the simple reason that not even the principles of political and economic equality will be accepted in some of our states. Any start, any degree of progress toward practicing this kind of equality, even though many years might be required to reach fruition, would, in my opinion, reverse this situation. Lacking such a start, I rather agree with you that there will be a decline in the influence that the deep South has traditionally exercised.[4]

All of us, collectively, seem to lack the wisdom we should have to deal adequately with the entire problem.[5]

With warm regard, *Sincerely*

[1] Atlanta newspaper editor McGill had written in response to the comments on segregation that Eisenhower had made at his August 20 news conference (same file as the document). On August 18, 1958, the Eighth Circuit Court of Appeals had refused to postpone the desegregation of Little Rock's Central High School, and its decision had been appealed to the Supreme Court. Refusing to comment on the case itself, Eisenhower had emphasized "the solemn duty that all Americans have to comply with the final orders of the court." It was, he said, the responsibility of each state to ensure compliance with court orders and to ensure the suppression of unlawful forces: "The very basis of our individual rights and freedoms rests upon the certainty that the President and the Executive Branch of Government will support and insure the carrying out of the decisions of the Federal Courts" (see *Public Papers of the Presidents: Eisenhower, 1958*, pp. 621, 631–32). For background see no. 833; on the President's Newport vacation see no. 825.

[2] McGill had enclosed his front-page editorial from the August 22 *Atlanta Constitution*, in which he reviewed Eisenhower's position on the courts and civil rights decisions. Eisenhower felt, McGill wrote, "that some of those who have been most defiant of the court have obscured the issue and made many people believe that the President may, by his own decision, take some other course. Some, apparently, have been caused to believe the President himself is trying to force something upon them." Eisenhower's statement was intended to "remind the people of their government and its functions." Charles R. Yates of Atlanta, an executive with Joshua L. Baily & Company, was a golfing companion of the President (see Galambos, *NATO and the Campaign of 1952*, no. 852).

[3] On Eisenhower's stance on civil rights see, for example, no. 726.

[4] McGill had written that he had received reports that Southern opposition in the Senate to the Civil Rights Bill had led to a decline of Southern influence in the current session of Congress, and was likely to lead to further decreases in the future. McGill said that he was saddened to "think that the deep South blinds itself, not merely to what is happening in the rest of the South but to the great historical forces which are at work."

[5] For developments see no. 879.

841   *EM, WHCF, Official File 101-Y*

To Douglas McCrae Black   *September 3, 1958*

Dear Doug: Many thanks for your good note of the twenty-ninth. Actually Daisy did nothing more than delay my departure for Newport and the last three days here have been, weather-wise, ideal. I have managed, in addition, to get more time to myself than ever before, although of course I have to keep in close touch by telephone with Washington.[1]

I am quite naturally gratified that you feel there is in the atmosphere a greater spirit of confidence than the American people had a few months, or a year, ago.[2] One of my friends recently complained to me about a feeling of "hopelessness" that he said permeated, especially, the Republican party. My answer in part was that I can never permit myself to feel hopeless about anything, even problems that seemingly defy solution.[3] By contrast, your report sets about restoring my equilibrium.

I think Nelson will make a splendid, vigorous campaign, and I hope very much he will emerge the winner. Do help him in every way possible.[4]

With affectionate regard to Maudie and, as always, the best to yourself, *As ever*

[1] Black had feared that Hurricane Daisy, the first hurricane tracked from the Caribbean to New England by radar, would spoil the President's vacation (same file as document; on Daisy see Ann Whitman memorandum, Aug. 29, 1958, AWF/AWD, and *New York Times*, Sept. 13, 1958). Newport could be lovely in the late summer, Black said, but Eisenhower brought his "own climate, unfortunately, regardless of the weather." Black was referring to the desegregation crisis in Little Rock, Arkansas (see no. 833). The Eisenhowers had left Washington, D.C., on August 29.

[2] Black had praised the President's recent "noted accomplishments," which had stimulated the confidence of Americans. Referring to Eisenhower's U.N. speech as "one of the great papers of our time," Black said he thought world opinion was becoming more favorably disposed to the United States (on the address see no. 800). He also complimented the Administration's handling of the economic situation (see nos. 784 and 831) and called Eisenhower's agricultural program "a great success for the

country and the farmer" (see no. 831). He went on to note the President's accomplishments in the Mideast (see no. 800); defense reorganization, and foreign aid (see no. 802); international trade (see no. 831); and atomic testing (see no. 827).

³ This was Cliff Roberts. Eisenhower's reply to him is the following document.

⁴ For background on Nelson Rockefeller's nomination as the Republican candidate for Governor of New York see no. 830. Eisenhower's congratulatory letter to him is no. 922.

842   *EM, AWF, Name Series*

To Clifford Roberts   *September 4, 1958*
Personal

Dear Cliff: Thank you very much for your longhand letter.¹ I agree of course that it is better to use financial resources where there is a chance to win rather than to pour money down a political drain that cannot be filled up.²

Another thought is that California seems to be a fairly wealthy state and it should be possible to raise the needed money, if the spirit is there. I am encouraged by Charlie Jones' fighting attitude.

The thing that disturbs me most about your report is that a spirit of "hopelessness" seems to you to be a Republican attitude discernible throughout the country. This defeats me. The six-year record of the Administration has been remarkable in view of the political complexion of the Congress. One man (Adams) admittedly made a mistake, but no one has ever accused him of crookedness. Yet this circumstance, almost alone, seems to account for the alleged "hopelessness."³

When Ed Pauley was in the Cabinet under Truman he was accused of using confidential governmental information to make a lot of money out of speculating in wheat. For other offenses, officials of lesser rank were later indicted and convicted.⁴ In view of these circumstances, why is it that the Democrats are not plagued by a spirit of hopelessness?

No one could feel worse than I about the entire Adams affair. Indeed, in view of the fact that I know better than anyone else the extraordinary dedication the man has exhibited through six years, the constant pressure under which he has worked, the round-the-clock days that he has devoted to the service of the government and the country, all now seemingly forgotten by the public with a consequent readiness to make him a greater villain than almost anyone in current history, you can understand that I get not only puzzled but sometimes resentful as well.

But that is the way it goes, and I am forced to agree that the situation is not greatly different from your portrayal of it.

In any event, I am one that cannot afford to be hopeless. I am forced to give constant attention—even now when I am supposed to be on a vacation—to problems that defy solution and keep the most prominent members of the Administration in a state of watchfulness, if not tension.

If circumstances do not compel the shortening of my planned vacation, perhaps you can come over for an afternoon and evening and we can have a talk. Bill is coming over with Jock today. I hope that you and Pete can come over early next week. I don't mean to say that I want a long, exhausting discussion of Republican prospects. I do think, however, that it would be helpful to chat informally with two people who have been not only among my closest friends but also my staunchest political supporters.[5]

With warm regard and again thanks for your frank analysis of the situation as it appears to you, *As ever*

---

[1] Roberts's letter of August 29 is in AWF/N; for background see no. 829. He had written Eisenhower that he had become "painfully" aware of the political situation in California, where Senator William F. Knowland faced strong Democratic opposition in his campaign for the governorship. He added that even though the President's letter (no. 826) would make it easier for Charles Jones to secure donations, Republicans across the nation were having trouble raising funds for the campaign.

[2] Roberts had written: "We can agree, I'm sure, that we should not rob a state of money which has a chance to win in order to help a hopeless state," and he questioned "the wisdom of tearing our shirts for Knowland." He contrasted the bleak situation in California with that in New York, where there was "a reasonable chance" to elect a Republican governor and senator. Roberts argued that the "only money which should be diverted" from one state to another should "come from the big contributors who are willing to send checks to a number of states but these big contributors are so far not coming through."

[3] Roberts believed that the controversy involving Assistant to the President Sherman Adams (see no. 753) was hurting the Republicans' chances in the 1958 elections by limiting their ability to raise money. The furor over the Adams-Goldfine relationship had not subsided since Eisenhower had publicly supported Adams on June 18. A congressional subcommittee had revealed that Goldfine had listed his gifts to Adams as business expenses on his income tax returns, and the House of Representatives had cited Goldfine for contempt of Congress. From both public and private sources Eisenhower had also learned that Goldfine possessed a reputation as an unethical businessman in New England. In his letter to the President, Roberts had attributed many of the Republican party's current troubles to the scandal and had called for Adams's departure: "The Democrats are going to make Adams their number one campaign issue but it will be far less effective with him out of the White House." See Ann Whitman memorandum, September 4, 1958, AWF/AWD; Eisenhower, *Waging Peace*, pp. 315–16; and Adams, *Firsthand Report*, p. 446. For developments see no. 862.

[4] For background on independent oil producer, real estate developer, and Democratic party leader Edwin Wendell Pauley (B.S. University of California 1922) see Galambos, *Chief of Staff*, nos. 793, 1787. Early in 1948 Pauley, then Special Assistant to the Secretary of War, had been accused of profiting from unethical transactions

in commodity markets after World War II. Although he had admitted making over $000,000 in commodity speculations, he had denied that he had used insider information in the process (Robert J. Donovan, *Conflict and Crisis: The Presidency of Harry S. Truman, 1945–1948* [New York, 1977], pp. 349–50). The Truman Administration had also been marred by other corruption scandals, involving such agencies as the Reconstruction Finance Corporation and the Internal Revenue Service. See Galambos, *NATO and the Campaign of 1952*, nos. 75 and 109; Eisenhower, *Mandate for Change*, p. 65; and Alonzo L. Hamby, *Man of the People: A Life of Harry S. Truman* (New York, 1995), pp. 584–89.

[5] On this same day Eisenhower would call Republican National Committee Chairman Meade Alcorn and relay to him the substance of Roberts's August 29 letter. Both men would agree that Alcorn and Vice-President Nixon, rather than the President, should confront Adams and persuade him to resign (Ann Whitman memorandum, September 4, 1958, AWF/AWD). Eisenhower would meet with Roberts on September 8. He would also meet with his friends William E. Robinson, W. Alton ("Pete") Jones, and Ambassador John Hay ("Jock") Whitney on several occasions during his New England vacation. For developments see nos. 870, 881, and 905.

843   *EM, WHCF, Official File 138 New York*

To Leonard Wood Hall   *September 4, 1958*

Dear Len: At last I am able to carry out a purpose that I have held ever since Nelson was nominated for the Governorship of New York.[1] That purpose was to send you a note to express my admiration for the gallant struggle you made. More than this I want to assure you again of my gratitude for the work you have done both for the Republican Party and the current Administration, as well as of the personal esteem and affection in which I hold you.

To my mind it took real courage for you to withdraw your candidacy, which seemed to have behind it a healthy strength, to avoid a bitter convention fight and, by this avoidance, assure party harmony.[2]

I know that you will be an enthusiastic and working leader in the campaign. It would be completely out of character for you to be anything else. More than this, I know from experience that you are effective and that Nelson and the party are both most fortunate that your talents in this direction will be exercised to the fullest.[3]

At the moment, as you may have heard, I am on a so-called vacation; its termination date is in the lap of the Gods. However, either when I return to Washington or, if I should by chance be in New York, I should very much like to have a chat with you. I would have suggested you come to Newport, but the trip is a very difficult one and its inconvenience too high a price to pay for a mere office conversation. Nevertheless, I do hope that we can get together for a short talk.[4]

With warm regard and, of course, my affectionate greetings to Gladys,[5] *As ever*

[1] For background on Nelson Rockefeller's nomination as the Republican candidate for Governor of New York see no. 830. On June 2 Hall, former Republican National Committee chairman, had announced his candidacy in the New York gubernatorial race (*New York Times*, Jan. 13, June 3, 1958). For background on Hall see Galambos and van Ee, *The Middle Way*.

[2] On August 17 Hall had withdrawn from the race, assuring a first-ballot nomination for Rockefeller at the Republican State Convention (*ibid.*, Aug. 18, 1958).

[3] On Eisenhower's continued interest in Rockefeller's campaign see no. 841. For developments see no. 922.

[4] The Eisenhowers would return to Washington on September 23 (see no. 816). Hall would reply that he enjoyed the pre-convention battle. Rockefeller, he said, would make "inroads with the so-called 'liberal voters'" and ethnic groups (Sept. 9, 1958, same file as document). Hall would attend an off-the-record meeting with the President on January 5, 1959.

[5] Hall's wife was the former Gladys Dowsey.

844   *EM, AWF, International Series:*
                                                                        Macmillan

To Harold Macmillan   *September 6, 1958*
Cable. Secret

Dear Harold: I am in Washington today and have read the message which you sent to Foster in reply to the analysis of the Formosa situation which he dispatched at my request.[1] I am delighted that in the basic elements of this situation, as in so many others, we stand together.

One major factor which is not readily understood by those not in direct touch with the situation is Chiang's temperament and purposes. Any proposal that seems to him to imply retreat from his position as head of the only legitimate Chinese Government, any thought of abandoning a single foot of his defense perimeter, is automatically rejected. Indeed, such rejection is so emphatic as to imply that if coercive efforts should be made to override his objection, that would end his capacity to retain Formosa in friendly hands.

Foster will shortly be communicating with you again in greater detail, but I wanted first of all to let you know my appreciation for your helpful exchange of information with us and also to recall this one point which stubbornly stands in the way of what many would consider the reasonable solution.[2]

Since your message and since I have been in Washington, Chou En-lai has made his statement about resuming negotiations in the interest of peace. I hope this means that the immediate crisis will become less acute, at least temporarily. We have just issued a statement on our willingness to resume the Ambassadorial talks.[3]

With warm regard, *As ever*

[1] Eisenhower's handwritten draft of this message is in Dulles Papers, White House Memoranda Series. Macmillan had written the President regarding the escalation of hostilities in the Taiwan Straits. Although the two countries had different views regarding the legal and practical considerations concerning the offshore islands, Macmillan said, his "overriding concern" was that they "should not be divided or appear to be divided." He asked for a "private message" from either Eisenhower or Secretary Dulles giving him some indication of the way their minds were working (Macmillan to Eisenhower, Sept. 3, 1958, AWF/I: Macmillan; see also Macmillan, *Riding the Storm*, p. 545. For background on the situation in the Taiwan Straits see no. 838; see also State, *Foreign Relations, 1958–1960*, vol. XIX, *China*, pp. 114–36).

After meeting with Eisenhower in Newport, Rhode Island, where the President was vacationing, Dulles had written Macmillan that the United States had in the past tried to "bring about disengagement" of Chiang's Republic of China from the offshore islands. These efforts, however, had never gone "to the point of attempted coercion" due to "the hard fact that the ability to keep Formosa in friendly hands has not been separable from the National Government holding on to those islands." If Quemoy were lost through either assault or surrender, a weakened Taiwan government might eventually advocate union with Communist China. The Nationalists had significant capacity to resist a takeover of the islands, Dulles added, but if they could not, the United States "would probably act." The use of atomic weapons—"an unpleasant prospect"—was contemplated because the U.S. military establishment increasingly believed that their use "would become normal in the event of hostilities" (Dulles to Macmillan, Sept. 4, 1958, AWF/I: Macmillan; and Macmillan, *Riding the Storm*, pp. 546–48). Before asking him to send the letter to Macmillan, Eisenhower had told Dulles that the possible use of nuclear weapons was "the heart of the matter," and he noted that the Communists might retaliate with atomic weapons "against Taiwan itself and beyond rather than directed simply at Quemoy" (Dulles, Memorandum of Conversation, Sept. 4, 1958, Dulles Papers, White House Memoranda Series; for Dulles's statement see State, *Foreign Relations, 1958–1960*, vol. XIX, *China*, pp. 134–36).

In his response to Dulles, Macmillan had outlined what he believed would be the stand taken by the various Commonwealth countries. He said that public opinion in Britain would "not be easy to steer." He appreciated the U.S. position but noted that Dulles did "not hide from yourself or from me that we may be on the edge of operations which could be a prelude to a third world war." Macmillan believed that demilitarizing the islands would be a "good public position," whether the Communists agreed to it or not, "and would serve, if properly handled, to strengthen us where we are weakest—in the public opinion of all those countries upon which we normally rely" (Macmillan to Dulles, Sept. 5, 1958, AWF/I: Macmillan; and Macmillan, *Riding the Storm*, pp. 548–49).

[2] We have not found an additional letter from Dulles to Macmillan; see, however, Lloyd to Dulles, Sept. 11, 1958, FO 13711/133528.

[3] Between August 1955 and December 1957 the U.S. Ambassador to Czechoslovakia and the Communist Chinese Ambassador to Poland had held informal negotiations in Geneva, primarily to discuss the repatriation of prisoners but also to consider tensions in the Taiwan Straits. Negotiations had broken down, however, when the U.S. Ambassador moved to a post in another country, and the Communists refused to accept a replacement of lesser rank. In February 1958 Secretary Dulles had approved

the recommendation that the talks resume in Warsaw with the U.S. Ambassador to Poland as the American representative. Subsequent delays had resulted in a Chinese Communist accusation that the United States had sabotaged the negotiations (see State, *Foreign Relations, 1955–1957*, vol. III, *China*, pp. 657–59; State, *Foreign Relations, 1958–1960*, vol. XIX, *China*, pp. 1, 6–7, 16, 29, 34–35; *ibid.*, Microfiche Supplement no. 7; and State, *American Foreign Policy, Current Documents, 1958*, pp. 1129–30). For Premier Chou En-lai's statement see Royal Institute of International Affairs, *Documents on International Affairs 1958*, edited by Gillian King (London, 1962), pp. 179–82; see also Goodpaster, Memorandum of Conference, Sept. 8, 1958, AWF/D. A draft of the U.S. statement, with Eisenhower's handwritten revisions, is in Dulles Papers, White House Memoranda Series; the final statement is in *U.S. Department of State Bulletin* 39, no. 1004 (September 22, 1958), 446–47.

Dulles would instruct the U.S. Ambassador in Taiwan to tell Chiang that Chou En-lai's statement appeared to indicate a desire "to disengage at least momentarily" from the threatened attempt to seize the islands by force. It was a move that, if true, would be "heartening evidence" that Chiang's heroic resistance and the determination of the United States to "stand squarely by [the] side of free China has had [a] salutary effect" (State, *Foreign Relations, 1958–1960*, vol. XIX, *China*, Microfiche Supplement no. 90).

For developments see no. 883.

845   *EM, AWF, DDE Diaries Series*

To FREDERICK ANDREW SEATON   *September 6, 1958*

Memorandum for the Secretary of the Interior: I have just signed S-4085, only because it was supported in the Congress by Administration recommendations (made without my knowledge). It appropriates 17 million dollars plus for some kind of Jefferson National Expansion Memorial in St. Louis.[1]

It is difficult for me to see the virtue of appropriating Federal funds for this purpose, particularly when the ratio of Federal contribution is to be three to one of private donations.

For two or three years I supported very earnestly the efforts of a private group to memorialize the history of this nation on a suitable site just beyond the Potomac River. That project would have required no Federal expenditures whatsoever. The only Federal participation would have been first the authorization of the project and, secondly, the donation of a piece of ground already owned but unused by the Federal government. In spite of my personal support, I know of no particular part of the government that made any sustained effort to get it enacted into law.[2]

I request that hereafter no bill for memorializing anything in the United States be placed before the Congress with a view to obtaining appropriations for such a project until it has been first cleared with me.[3]

¹ S. 4085 was a bill to amend the 1954 act that provided for the construction of the Jefferson National Expansion Memorial at the site of old St. Louis, Missouri, in accordance with the architectural designs approved in 1948. It had been reported favorably in the Senate on August 13.

In its final form P.L. 936 authorized appropriations not to exceed $17.25 million to construct the memorial; it permitted construction of a 576-foot stainless steel arch, which the United States Territorial Expansion Memorial Commission had included in the plan in 1948; and it repealed the existing provision which made the authorization of federal appropriations contingent upon the occurrence or the forecast of a balanced budget. The funds would be appropriated in a ratio of $3 of federal funds for each $1 contributed by the city of St. Louis or other non-federal source for this purpose. The Gateway Arch for the Jefferson National Expansion Memorial would be completed in 1965 (*United States Code*, 85th Congress–Second Session 1958, vol. 1, p. 2162, *ibid.*, vol. 3, pp. 5345–47; *Congressional Quarterly Almanac*, vol. XIV, *1958*, pp. 481, 546; *Congressional Quarterly Weekly Reports* 16, 1958, p. 1214; *St. Louis Post-Dispatch*, Oct. 21, 25, 28, Nov. 4, 7, 1965, and *New York Times*, Oct. 24, 27, 29, Nov. 7, 1965, July 25, Aug. 27, 1967).

² Eisenhower probably was referring to his efforts to establish an Armed Services Memorial Museum (for background see no. 14).

³ On September 20 Seaton would say he had "simply inherited the project" to commemorate the Louisiana Purchase. It had been authorized in 1935, reaffirmed by the present Administration in 1954, and successful efforts had been made to secure private and municipal support (Telephone conversation, Seaton and Whitman, AWF/A).

846

To Clarence Francis

Dear Mr. Francis: I very much appreciated having your letter regarding the completion of the Citizens Committee's program of public information in connection with the recommendations of the second Hoover Commission.¹ I have had frequent evidence during the past five years of the enthusiasm with which the Citizens Committee carried on its important mission, and I have been delighted and encouraged by the effective support the Committee has given to the Administration in implementing recommendations of the Commission.²

In connection with the statistic you mentioned, it would, I believe, be interesting to the members of the Committee to take note also of these:³

Of the total of 497 distinct proposals, the Administration has accepted, in whole or in part, a total of 383 or slightly over 77%.

Of the proposals accepted, our present estimate is that more than 83% have been or are being implemented by the Executive Branch, and a number of others await Congressional action.

In the area of budget and accounting, 69% of the 26 distinct proposals have been wholly or substantially accepted by the Administration and the remaining 31% have been partially accepted or accepted as to objective. All but 2 of the 26 proposals have been fully implemented or are in the process of implementation.

In the limited field of food and clothing, 54% of the 26 distinct proposals have been wholly or substantially accepted by the Administration and 39% have been partially accepted or accepted as to objective. Twenty-three proposals have been implemented or are in process of implementation.

While no one can appraise precisely the monetary savings that will result, I know that the effect of implementing the recommendations of both Hoover Commissions throughout the Federal Government has been highly salutary—particularly from the point of view of uncovering unnoticed and dusty corners within the Government and bringing to public attention the need for corrections.

Government reorganization and administrative streamlining is necessarily a continuing task. The fact that the Citizens Committee has fulfilled its mission does not mean that no further effort is needed in this field. Quite the contrary. The Administration will continue to put into effect recommendations not yet undertaken and will, in the operations of the Government, apply day by day many of the principles featured in the Commission's work.[4] In addition, other reorganization plans, suggested as a result of the Hoover Commission studies, will be proposed from time to time.

The time will again come when there will be need for a new comprehensive review such as inspired Mr. Hoover's monumental missions. Meanwhile representative Government requires the day-by-day interest of thoughtful and able citizens who are alert to the organization and management problems of good Government and are willing to devote attention to them.

Through its fine work, the Citizens Committee has contributed significantly to the understanding of an interested and well informed public—a very real and lasting source of strength as we look ahead to the future.

As the Committee prepares to disband, I hope you will convey to all your associates my appreciation of the time and energy they have so generously contributed to these public affairs. Surely their work has counted in the results obtained. *Sincerely*

[1] For background see no. 157. The Citizens' Committee for the Hoover Commission had been organized as a private, voluntary group formed to support prompt enact-

ment of the commission's proposals for economy and efficiency in government (see Arnold, *Making the Managerial Presidency*, pp. 194–96). Among the recommendations of the second Hoover Commission were those involving the reorganization of the Department of Defense and the modernization of the federal budget system. Francis, chairman of the board of Federal Foods Corporation and chairman of the Citizens Committee (see Galambos and van Ee, *The Middle Way*, no. 621), had noted that both of these plans had been approved by Congress that year despite strong opposition (see nos. 802 and 810).

[2] See Galambos and van Ee, *The Middle Way*, nos. 743 and 1850.

[3] Francis had reported that the second commission had a success rate of sixty-four per cent, falling short of the seventy-two percent success rate of the first commission. He noted, however, that "a greater share of the second commission's recommendations were of fundamental and major importance."

[4] Francis had written that the elimination of the Citizens Committee did "not mean for a moment that there will be no further action on the Hoover reports." In addition to commitments from the President to seek implementation of the Hoover recommendations, "we have been assured by Congressional leaders of both parties that Congress will work for further action on my commission proposals." See *New York Times*, October 25, November 2, 1958; see also Gary Dean Best, *Herbert Hoover: The Postpresidential Years 1933–1964*, 2 vols., vol. II, *1946–1964* (Stanford, 1983), pp. 408–10. All correspondence is in the same file as the document and in WHCF/OF 103-A-1.

847 *EM, WHCF, President's Personal File 1817*

To Carline E. Koger

September 8, 1958

Dear Captain Koger: I was delighted to hear from you (as a matter of fact, I asked Mrs. Whitman some weeks ago to track you down). While I am sure that Fort Bragg and the surrounding area have many good points, I can never quite feel there is any place as delightful as Denver.[1] The friends from there whom I see from time to time tell me that the city is growing by leaps and bounds but that it still gives the impression of being uncluttered and spacious (and that the mountains, of course, are just as beautiful as ever).

News that Colonel Powell had been assigned to Womack came as a surprise to me; won't you give him and Mrs. Powell my very best wishes and warm regard?[2]

As usual, my "vacation" period seems replete with crises. But despite the fact that I must be able to be in touch with Washington almost instantly, the daily routine of office work is being kept at a minimum. I have played golf almost daily (with not too much success) and all in all both Mrs. Eisenhower and I are enjoying the change of pace and the comparative privacy that we have here.[3] Three of the grandchildren are here for a few days, and they have taken delightfully to all the new and intriguing things the Navy has to offer.[4]

I hope you will continue to keep in touch with me; I am ever mindful of my personal gratitude to you.

With warm regard, *Sincerely*

[1] Koger had been one of the nurses at Fitzsimons Army Hospital in Denver, Colorado, who attended the President following his heart attack in 1955 (for background see Galambos and van Ee, *The Middle Way*, no. 1626). She had written on September 2 (same file as document) that she had been transferred in April to Womack Army Hospital at Fort Bragg, North Carolina. She apologized for the delay in communicating. On Eisenhower's continuing correspondence with his Fitzsimons nurses see, for example, nos. 634 and 854.

[2] Doctor George Merle Powell had attended the President following his heart attack (see Galambos and van Ee, *The Middle Way*, no. 1629).

[3] The Eisenhowers were vacationing in Newport, Rhode Island. On Eisenhower's concerns regarding the desegregation crisis in Little Rock see no. 833.

[4] Ten-year-old David, nine-year-old Barbara Anne, and six-year-old Susan would spend September 6–11 in Newport. Eisenhower's youngest grandchild, Mary Jean, was born in December 1955.

848   *EM, AWF, Administration Series*

TO CHARLES DOUGLAS JACKSON   *September 9, 1958*

Dear C. D.: This afternoon I had an opportunity to read your three memoranda, the originals of which you sent to Foster. I like them.[1]

I am apparently going to have to make a foreign affairs speech somewhere in the East during the campaign—perhaps in New York, Boston or Philadelphia—and it seems to me that such a talk could well deal with *positive* efforts along the lines you have set forward. Question: Do you have any urge to send me a rough draft for a thirty minute talk?[2]

With warm regard, *As ever*

[1] Jackson had sent Secretary Dulles memorandums on Eisenhower's recent speech to the United Nations on a Middle East development plan (see no. 818), the reactivation of the Palestine Conciliation Commission, and the Eastern European satellite countries. Referring to the development plan, Jackson had urged an initiative that would "get the proposal off dead center." He recommended that either Dulles or U.N. Ambassador Lodge impress upon Secretary General Hammarskjöld the need to move forward—that "it would be counterproductive to the UN, to peace, to political and economic stability in the Near East area, if this proposal were allowed to drag interminably and eventually die." He also suggested that both Eisenhower and Dulles keep the subject alive through the release of news items, indicating that "this was not a one-shot effort by the President to divert attention from other aspects of the Near East problem."

The United Nations had established the Palestine Conciliation Commission in December 1948 to facilitate the implementation of U.N. resolutions regarding Palestine and to help the parties involved reach agreement on critical issues. In June 1958 the commission had submitted its sixteenth progress report, stating that the Middle Eastern governments had not taken advantage of its services. The commission, therefore, had concentrated on the solution of specific problems that could benefit the greatest number of refugees regardless of the reluctance of the parties to reach overall agreement (State, *American Foreign Policy; Current Documents, 1958*, pp. 896–901; see also United Nations, *Yearbook of the United Nations, 1948–49*, pp. 174–76). Jackson's Arab friends had told him that the time was ripe to reactivate the commission—that "Nasser will play." The commission, which included the United States, France, and Turkey, should be enlarged, Jackson wrote, to include representatives from a Scandinavian country, an Asian country, and a Latin American country. All the members should be in a position to devote their undivided time to current problems.

The third memorandum concerned the Eastern European satellite countries, particularly Hungary and Poland, which Jackson likened to the Achilles heel of international communism. "Time after time," he said, "we have failed to tweak that tendon, even when it was lying bare and exposed." Jackson suggested that the United States should vote to deny the inclusion of the newly-formed government in Hungary in the United Nations. Even if the United States lost the vote, "at least we would have brought the subject up like men; we would have stood up and been counted; and our moral position would be considerably enhanced—not to mention the repercussions behind the Iron Curtain." Poland, on the other hand, needed a series of economic, medical, health, educational, agricultural, and industrial missions that, in consultation with the Polish people, could determine how best to provide aid. "If we could crowd the Polish switchboard with American sounds that the Polish man in the street can hear," Jackson said, "it will be all the harder for Khrushchev to get on the line" (Jackson to Dulles, Aug. 29, 1958, AWF/A, Jackson Corr.).

[2] Although Jackson would send Eisenhower the draft of a speech on foreign affairs (see no. 900), the President would not speak on this issue during the campaign. Dulles had told Eisenhower that he was reluctant to interject foreign policy into a political speech, particularly when many Democrats supported the Administration's policies (Telephone conversation, Eisenhower and Dulles, Sept. 29, 1958, Dulles Papers, Telephone Conversations). For developments on the seating of the Hungarian delegates in the United Nations see no. 923.

849   *EM, WHCF, President's Personal File 371*

To David H. Marx   *September 9, 1958*

Dear David: As always you are more than kind—and I now find myself equipped for any sort of gift emergency that might arise. The grandchildren have taken over all the hoops[1] (George was adamant in refusing to perform for us),[2] and Ann tells me that she has a quantity of bubble-blowing monkeys on hand.[3] In addition, I understand there are stored away some special transistor radios that will be given to those people here who are particularly helpful to Mamie and to me. I truly can't thank you enough for your thoughtfulness.

We are having as good a vacation as possible in view of the critical situations that demand my daily attention.[4] The weather today has been almost perfect, an adjective I cannot possibly apply to the brand of golf I am displaying these days.

With much gratitude and warm personal regard, *As ever*

---

[1] Marx, toy manufacturer of Louis Marx & Company, was an old friend of Eisenhower (for background see Galambos and van Ee, *The Middle Way*, no. 1983). The Marx Company recently had manufactured the Hoop-Zing—a version of the latest fad in American toys—a large plastic hoop, called the Hula Hoop by another manufacturer. Persons using the toy tried to keep it spinning while swaying the torso in a hula-like motion (see *Washington Post*, Aug. 20, 1958, and *New York Times*, Sept. 8, 1958).

[2] Marx's wife, Charlene, had suggested that George Allen demonstrate the hoop (Charlene Marx to Eisenhower, Sept. 9, 1958, same file as document).

[3] Presidential Secretary Ann Whitman accompanied the President to his vacation home in Newport, Rhode Island, where he would remain until September 23.

[4] On Eisenhower's concerns about the desegregation crisis in Little Rock, Arkansas, see no. 833.

---

850   *EM, WHCF, Official File 138-A-9*

To James Cunard Black   *September 11, 1958*

Dear Jim: I am glad to hear that you are going to Colorado to raise funds for the present political campaign.[1] I want to send, through you, my best wishes to all my friends in Colorado and the hope they will enthusiastically support our Party candidates, both with money and with personal effort.

Just one of the issues of the campaign is, it seems to me, the question of moderate government against immoderate government, and sound fiscal policies versus fiscal irresponsibility. The Administration has, for the last six years, directed all its efforts toward solidly based programs; I am certain that my friends in Colorado—indeed, throughout the nation—will want to help the Party's efforts to continue that policy.[2]

Good luck and warm regard, *Sincerely*

---

[1] Eisenhower's frequent golfing partner Black was the Washington-based manager of the Republic Steel Corporation. In Colorado, as in California (see nos. 826 and 829), the Sherman Adams scandal and the right-to-work issue were major factors in the 1958 election; see Curtis Martin, "The 1958 Election in Colorado," *Western Political Quarterly*, vol. XII, no. 1, pt. 2 (March, 1959), 301–8.

[2] Black would thank Eisenhower (Sept. 13, same file as document) for his "splendid and gracious letter," which he thought "should be most helpful." In November, however, the Democrats would capture three of four congressional seats, as well as the offices of both governor and lieutenant governor. According to one analyst, a shortage of Republican campaign funds contributed to the result (Martin, "The 1958 Election in Colorado," pp. 301, 304; see also *New York Times*, Oct. 19, Nov. 6, 1958).

To Nikita Sergeyevich Khrushchev   *September 12, 1958*
Confidential

Dear Mr. Chairman: I have your letter of September seventh. I agree
with you that a dangerous situation exists in the Taiwan area. I do
not agree with you as to the source of danger in this situation.[1]
   The present state of tension in the Taiwan area was created directly by Chinese Communist action, not by that of the Republic of
China or by the United States. The fact is that following a long period of relative calm in that area, the Chinese Communists, without
provocation, suddenly initiated a heavy artillery bombardment of
Quemoy and began harassing the regular supply of the civilian and
military population of the Quemoys. This intense military activity
was begun on August twenty-third—some three weeks after your visit
to Peiping.[2] The official Peiping radio has repeatedly been announcing that the purpose of these military operations is to take
Taiwan (Formosa) as well as Quemoy and Matsu, by armed force.
In virtually every Peiping broadcast, Taiwan (Formosa) and the offshore islands are linked as the objective of what is called the "Chinese Peoples Liberation Army."
   The issue, then, is whether the Chinese Communists will seek to
achieve their ambitions through the application of force, as they did
in Korea, or whether they will accept the vital requisite of world
peace and order in a nuclear age and renounce the use of force as
the means for satisfying their territorial claims. The territory concerned has never been under the control of Communist China. On
the contrary, the Republic of China—despite the characterizations
you apply to it for ideological reasons—is recognized by the majority of the sovereign nations of the world and its government has
been and is exercising jurisdiction over the territory concerned.
United States military forces operate in the Taiwan area in fulfillment of treaty commitments to the Republic of China to assist it in
the defense of Taiwan (Formosa) and the Penghu (Pescadores) Islands. They are there to help resist aggression—not to commit aggression. No upside down presentation such as contained in your
letter can change this fact.
   The United States Government has welcomed the willingness of
the Chinese Communists to resume the Ambassadorial talks, which
were begun three years ago in Geneva, for the purpose of finding a
means of easing tensions in the Taiwan area.[3] In the past, the United
States representative at these talks has tried by every reasonable
means to persuade the Chinese Communist representative to reach

agreement on mutual renunciation of force in the Taiwan area but the latter insistently refused to reach such agreement.[4] The United States hopes that an understanding can be achieved through the renewed talks which will assure that there will be no resort to the use of force in the endeavor to bring about a solution of the issues there.

I regret to say I do not see in your letter any effort to find that common language which could indeed facilitate the removal of the danger existing in the current situation in the Taiwan area. On the contrary, the description of this situation contained in your letter seems designed to serve the ambitions of international Communism rather than to present the facts. I also note that you have addressed no letter to the Chinese Communist leaders urging moderation upon them. If your letter to me is not merely a vehicle for one-sided denunciation of United States action but is indeed intended to reflect a desire to find a common language for peace, I suggest you urge these leaders to discontinue their military operations and to turn to a policy of peaceful settlement of the Taiwan dispute.

If indeed, for the sake of settling the issues that tend to disturb the peace in the Formosa area, the Chinese Communist leaders can be persuaded to place their trust in negotiation and a readiness to practice conciliation, then I assure you the United States will, on its part, strive in that spirit earnestly to the same end.[5] *Sincerely*

[1] For background on the Communist Chinese shelling of the offshore islands see no. 838. Khrushchev had blamed aggressive U.S. policies for "the direct threat of the beginning of a military conflagration." The United States had seized the island of Taiwan by force, he wrote, and had cloaked the occupation of this "age-old Chinese territory" with references to the support of "the traitor of the Chinese people, Chiang Kai-shek." "If you look squarely at the truth," Khrushchev added, "you must acknowledge that the USA is trying to assume the functions of some sort of gendarme in this area" (AWF/I: Khrushchev).

[2] Khrushchev had visited the Chinese capital from July 31 to August 3 (*New York Times*, Aug. 4, 1958; see also Nikita S. Khrushchev, *Khrushchev Remembers: The Last Testament*, trans. and ed. by Strobe Talbott [Boston, 1974], pp. 258–63).

[3] On the resumption of these talks see no. 844.

[4] U. Alexis Johnson, former American Ambassador to Czechoslovakia, had represented the United States; Wang Ping-nan, Ambassador to Poland, had represented the People's Republic of China.

[5] Eisenhower had added this paragraph to the State Department draft of this letter (see Dulles, Memorandum of Conversation, and Bernau to Dulles, Sept. 11, 1958, Dulles Papers, White House Memoranda Series). The State Department cabled the text of this letter to the U.S. embassy in Warsaw on September 11. For developments see no. 883.

To Abbott McConnell Washburn   *September 12, 1958*

Dear Abbott:[1] Thank you very much for giving me your frank appraisal of our situation in the Far East and your recommendations as to the course of action we should pursue.[2] In many respects I am sympathetic to your point of view, and I want firmly to assure you that I weighed carefully your convictions before I did the final work on the broadcast of Thursday night.[3]

Of course you realize that there are many elements in the whole affair on which I could not touch in the talk I made: nonetheless what I there said represents my best judgment as to the stand our country must take.

Needless to say, I am gratified by the expression of your trust, particularly in a decision with which you disagree. I am, as always, grateful for your dedication to the people of our country and to the principles for which the Administration stands.

With warm personal regard, *Sincerely*

---

[1] For background on Washburn, Deputy Director of the United States Information Agency, see Galambos and van Ee, *The Middle Way*, no. 8; see also no. 546 in these volumes.

[2] For background on the situation in the Taiwan Straits see no. 838. Washburn opposed any policy that would link the defense of Formosa to that of the offshore islands—a position that he felt could lead to the use of nuclear weapons in an all-out war. World opinion would be "preponderantly opposed to U.S. intervention in Quemoy-Matsu with conventional arms," he had told Eisenhower, "and it would experience revulsion at any use by the U.S. of nuclear weapons in this area." Recommending an evacuation of the islands, which were a natural part of the mainland, Washburn admitted that a withdrawal would entail a short-term loss of prestige to the United States and would be a blow to Nationalist morale. He claimed, however, that "both these effects could be offset by a reaffirmation of our determination to defend Formosa and the Pescadores." If the first line of defense were Formosa, an island that was necessary to the security of the free world, the United States would have the support of its allies and could "present a strong argument in the U.N. or in any other forum" (Washburn to Eisenhower, Sept. 9, 1958, AWF/A: Quemoy-Matsu—Washburn).

[3] In discussing the speech with Dulles, Eisenhower had said that "he wanted to deal effectively with a major dilemma confronting the United States: On the one hand we must show both firmness and courage in our opposition to the use of aggressive force, combined with readiness to negotiate in a spirit of conciliation; on the other hand in the Taiwan Straits situation, we are committed, indeed over committed, to backing up Chiang Kai-shek in a policy of defending Quemoy and Matsu." Eisenhower added that "he was quite prepared to see the abandonment of Quemoy," but could not say so publicly at that time (Dulles, Memorandum of Conversation, Sept. 11, 1958, Dulles Papers, White House Memoranda Series; see also Telephone conversation, Eisenhower and Dulles, Sept. 11, 1958, *ibid.*). In his speech Eisenhower had reviewed the situation and cited the congressional resolution of support passed

during similar attacks on the islands three years earlier. "If the present bombardment and harassment of Quemoy should be converted into a major assault, with which the local defenders could not cope," he warned, then the United States might have to intervene militarily. He expressed the hope that even if bilateral talks with the Chinese were unsuccessful, the United Nations would "exert a peaceful influence on the situation" (*Public Papers of the Presidents: Eisenhower, 1958,* pp. 694–700; on the bilateral talks see no. 844; and on the congressional resolution, Galambos and van Ee, *The Middle Way,* no. 1265. For reaction to the speech in Taiwan see Dulles to Eisenhower, Sept. 12, 1958, AWF/D-H). For developments see no. 883.

853   *EM, WHCF, Official File 139-B-3*

To Howard Stix Cullman   *September 13, 1958*
Personal

Dear Howard: Thank you for sending me a copy of Leo Cherne's latest letter on the United States Exhibit. I agree with him that there has been in our press a definite swing from critical to favorable comment; I know you are as gratified as I am.[1]

The problems you faced were tremendous and the road blocks in your path would have defeated a lesser individual. I shall always be grateful to you for accepting an assignment we both knew at the outset would be difficult, and for carrying it through, at times under fire, so successfully.

I am sorry about your finger and your golf.[2] At that you have a fine excuse which you can use for any future miserable scores—if you ever have any. My present poor game I have to blame on such intangibles as "thinking-about-the-Formosa-Straits" at the top of my back swing.[3] And, try as I will, I can't conquer such bad habits.

With warm regard, *As ever*

[1] For background on the Brussels Universal and International Exhibition see no. 756; see also Haddow, *Pavilions of Plenty,* pp. 70–200. Economist Leo Cherne, executive director of the Research Institute of America (see Galambos and van Ee, *The Middle Way,* no. 783), had told Cullman that he was heartened to see that "the thoughtless and uninformed criticisms" of the U.S. exhibit had been "replaced by deserved and balanced praise." He complimented Cullman on his ability to mount the exhibition despite "the obstacles that were placed in your path and the unbelievable stupidity of some of the economies and decisions which were imposed upon you" (Cherne to Cullman, n.d., same file as document). Cullman told Eisenhower that he had recently shown the pavilion to Allen Dulles, Eleanor Roosevelt, and Paul Hoffman, and that Roosevelt intended to praise the exhibition in her syndicated newspaper columns (Cullman to Eisenhower, Sept. 10, 1958, *ibid.*).
[2] "My golf is temporarily on sabbatical leave," Cullman had written, "because some stupid youngster slammed the door of my car and left the top half of my left digit on the driving seat" (*ibid.*).

[3] On the crisis in the Formosa Straits see the preceding document.

Cullman would send Eisenhower additional reports and a description of the closing ceremonies, held on October 19. The Belgian government would keep the theater building, the esplanade, the pool, and the trees, Cullman said, and his preliminary figures indicated a balance of approximately $100,000 of revenue over expenditures. "This should be a wonderful memorial for America" (Cullman to Eisenhower, Oct. 14, 16, 17, 20, 1958, same file as document; see also Eisenhower to Cullman, Oct. 26, 1958, *ibid.*).

854   *EM, WHCF, President's Personal File 1454*

To EDYTHE P. TURNER   *September 15, 1958*

Dear Colonel Turner: Your letter of the fifth gives me precisely the reassuring news of you that I wanted to hear. I am delighted that your tour of duty in Hawaii is proving in every respect interesting and enjoyable.[1] Despite the wonderful climate there, I agree with you that Denver is still the best from that point of view.

As you know, we are spending our second summer "vacation" in Newport. This year Mrs. Eisenhower and I have managed to achieve a little more isolation than formerly, and—despite the fact that I have already been called back to Washington twice—I have managed to keep paper work to a minimum. Of course there are always trouble spots that give me great concern, but I have become reconciled to the fact that in this job there is always a crisis of some kind or other.[2] I am trying to get in as much golf (of a rather poor variety) as possible and in general charge my batteries for the months ahead.

Please give Mrs. Eisenhower's and my warm regard to General Schwartz and Captain Miller, and to you, as always, my lasting gratitude and best wishes.[3] *Sincerely*

[1] Turner had taken the position as chief nurse at Tripler U.S. Army Hospital in Honolulu in 1957 (see no. 111). She had written to the President in response to a letter from Presidential Secretary Ann Whitman, who had informed her that Eisenhower had requested news of her (see Whitman to Turner, Aug. 23, 1958; see also Turner to Whitman, Sept. 5, 1958, both in same file as document).
[2] The Eisenhowers' vacation in Newport, Rhode Island, began on August 24. They would remain there until September 23 (on the crises that developed during the Eisenhowers' 1957 vacation see, for example, no. 330). The President had been in Washington on September 6 to host a White House reception for educators from the Association of American Universities and the Association of Universities of the British Commonwealth. He also had returned on September 11 to deliver a televised report on the Formosa crisis (see no. 844). On Eisenhower's concerns regarding the ongoing desegregation crisis in Little Rock, Arkansas, see no. 833.
[3] Apparently General Schwartz was the commanding officer at Tripler. Lorene Miller

had attended the First Lady following her surgery in 1957 (see no. 291). Turner reported that Miller had been assigned to the Tripler's cardiology ward.

855

EM, AWF,
Administration Series

To Alfred Maximilian Gruenther   *September 16, 1958*

Dear Al: I am following your tennis-playing and speaking trail through Europe with interest and awe, not that I ever underestimate your capacity in either department. But I do greatly admire the stamina you demonstrate.[1]

You know that I could never rely on George to report, with any accuracy, on Newport activities. He has constantly complained about his bad luck—at bridge, at golf, and in fishing and shooting. His darkest moment came the other day when Brilliant Speed lost another race.[2]

Pete Jones' place, which is about twenty minutes from here by helicopter, is a veritable paradise. He has two well-stocked lakes, ducks and pheasants in abundance, and a well-equipped skeet range. We spent one fine day there and hope to manage another one before we leave.[3]

As you so well realize, the problems of the Formosa Straits and the closing of some of the high schools are constantly with me.[4] Additionally, there are lesser worries, some of them political. The results in Maine were anything but encouraging, and a linking of Senator Knowland with a character named Joseph Kamp isn't helping his campaign get off the ground.[5] But all this we can discuss when you return.[6]

Meantime continue to have a good trip, and give my greetings to any of our friends whom you chance to meet. *As ever*

[1] After an inspection tour of Red Cross activities at U.S. military bases in Europe and Morocco (*New York Times*, Sept. 2, 1958), Red Cross President Gruenther had written Eisenhower (Sept. 14, AWF/A). He had, he said, already delivered twenty speeches and anticipated giving four more. Gruenther also had referred to his tennis as "really hot." Before receiving this letter from the President, Gruenther again would report on his trip and tennis matches (Sept. 18, WHCF/PPF 373). On September 19 he would fly to Geneva for the meeting of the Executive Committee of the League of Red Cross Societies.

[2] George E. Allen had joined the President in Newport, Rhode Island. On the Eisenhowers' vacation (Aug. 29–Sept. 23) see no. 816; see also *New York Times*, August 31, September 2, 3, 4, 6, 8, 1958. On September 14 Gruenther jokingly had asked the President to "order that Good-for-Nothing Allen" to report on the golf and bridge at Newport. Again on September 18 Gruenther would refer to the portly Allen as

that "242 lb. monster who makes your life so miscrable." Brilliant Speed was apparently one of Allen's race horses (see no. 159). On September 23 Eisenhower would
cable Gruenther, then in Geneva, that, "not trusting George," he had sent a letter
on the Newport activities to Europe (AWF/A).

[3] Eisenhower had gone to Jones's farm at West Greenwich, Rhode Island, on September 13 and would pay another visit on September 19 (*New York Times,* Sept. 14,
20, 1958).

[4] Gruenther suggested that the crises involving Quemoy and Little Rock had so engrossed the President that he "justifiably" had no time to worry about Gruenther's
tennis game. On the situation in the Formosa Straits see no. 852. On the Supreme
Court decision regarding integration of public schools and governor Faubus's threat
to close the high schools in Little Rock see no. 879.

[5] On September 8 Maine had elected a Democratic governor, senator, and two of
three representatives (see Eisenhower, *Waging Peace,* p. 316; *Congressional Quarterly
Weekly Reports* 16, 1958, and *New York Times,* Sept. 9, 1958).

In an effort to help elect California Senator William Knowland, an opponent of
compulsory union membership (see no. 829), Joseph P. Kamp, a veteran pamphle-
teer of extreme right-wing causes, had written a tract attacking the president of the
United Auto Workers. Thousands of the pamphlets had been distributed in California at the request of Knowland's wife, Helen. On September 17 Knowland would
state that neither he nor his organization were using the Kamp booklet (Eisenhower,
Waging Peace, p. 376, and *New York Times,* Sept. 14, 15, 16, 18, 1958). The "right-to-
work" referendum would appear on the California ballot on November 4. For developments see no. 870.

[6] Eisenhower would meet with Gruenther on November 13 (see also *New York Times,*
Oct. 28, 1958).

856   *EM, AWF, DDE Diaries Series*

To Benjamin Franklin Fairless   *September 16, 1958*

Dear Ben: I am of course complimented that you and Hazel have
asked for "several" of my so-called "paintings" for exhibition in the
first Pennsylvania Artists Exhibit, sponsored by the Arts League of
Ligonier Valley.[1]

First I might tell you that over the years I have received numerous requests for the loan of some of my daubings in such amateur
shows. The only exceptions that have been made to my habitual refusal to comply have been where one or two of my pictures already
given to friends, have been exhibited by those friends. Another partial exception has been at times when I have given, to this kind of
exhibit, reproductions or color photographs of some of the paintings.[2]

But because of my friendship for you and because I am now a citizen of Pennsylvania, I am anxious to comply with your request so
far as I possibly can. So I am sending to you the following: (1) a
color photograph of three heads I once painted of Secretary Dulles,

Secretary Humphrey and Secretary Wilson; (2) a painting of the 16th Hole at Augusta—this is the property of Bob Jones and I have his permission for you to show the picture (I would appreciate it if it was identified as Bob's property); a painting of David contemplating a golf shot—this is the property of the Augusta National Golf Club and should be so marked.[3]

You may keep the reproduction if you so desire, but I should like the painting of David returned to me when the exhibit closes. Bob would like the one of the 16th Hole sent to Cliff Roberts' apartment in New York, 535 Park Avenue. If there is any desire on Bob's part to have the painting at Cliff's by the 14th of October, as he mentioned in passing to me, he will get in touch with you; I told him I assumed it could be arranged.

Incidentally, there is one other reproduction I can send to you if you should want it—of a snow scene in the Rockies. Just ask Mr. Parsons to get in touch with Mrs. Whitman if you want that, too.[4] But I am afraid that the show is going to be far too heavily weighted with "Eisenhowers" as matters stand now!

I assume that these paintings will be entered in a special class; they are sent to you for exhibition only—no competition.[5]

With warm regard. *As ever*

[1] Fairless, coordinator of the President's Citizens Advisors on the Mutual Security Program and former president of U.S. Steel, had written on September 3 (AWF/D). His wife was the former Hazel Hatfield Sproul. The exhibition, a feature of Fort Ligonier's bicentennial celebration, would run from September 21 to October 12. For background on the fort and Eisenhower's plans to speak at the ceremonies see no. 751). For developments see no. 866.

[2] For background on similar requests see, for example, no. 532 in these volumes and Galambos and van Ee, *The Middle Way*, no. 1567.

[3] For background on the President's portrait of his grandson David see no. 532.

[4] Lewis Morgan Parsons was vice-president of U.S. Steel's Washington and Philadelphia offices.

[5] Fairless said that the Arts League would award a gold medal to the artist winning first place and a silver medal to the "best entry from Western Pennsylvania."

857   *EM, AWF, Administration Series*

To WILLIAM PIERCE ROGERS   *September 17, 1958*
Personal and confidential

Dear Bill: The three men named on the list you provided me as possible appointees to the Supreme Court who, I believe, would be the most satisfactory Judges are, arranged alphabetically:[1]

Herbert Brownell[2]
Warren Burger[3]
Elbert Tuttle[4]

Anything further I have to say assumes that your own findings, including study of the opinions they have handed down in lower Courts, definitely reflect a middle-of-the-road political and governmental philosophy.

With respect to Brownell, in my opinion he has every qualification for a Court member. I believe he is a strong character and a man of high principle. The single thing that could be argued against him would be by Southern extremists who would point out that he was Attorney General when the Supreme Court's integration orders conforming to the decision of 1954 were promulgated.[5]

Burger's record seems to be without blemish and I believe his reputation as a citizen is exemplary.

The reason that I have put Tuttle's name with the other two is that he is of Southern origin. (I once before considered him for a Court position and for some reason that I cannot now recall, we dropped his name.) It is possible that it would be a good idea to have two Southerners on the court and I think Black is the only one now who would be classed in that category.[6]

So far as ability is concerned, I would put Kenneth Royall on the list in spite of the fact that he is sixty-four years of age.[7] One of the reasons I would do so is that he, too, is of Southern origin. But he is a Democrat and I do not want further to overbalance the Court as between the two major Parties. This we would do if we replaced a present Republican by a Democrat. Except for this objection, he would be almost ideally fitted for my conception of the kind of man we now need.

Of course you possibly by now may have some other names to add to your original list, but if we think of anyone who is not now in the judiciary or who has not previously been in government, there is a long investigatory procedure that must be followed.

You mentioned on the telephone this morning that you wanted to see me again about this matter and I think we should arrange for a meeting at an early date. Whether or not I come back to Washington on Monday, I must be there Tuesday noon to give a luncheon. We might have an appointment at some time just before luncheon Tuesday, if Monday afternoon is cancelled out.[8]

With warm regard, *As ever*

---

[1] Faced with the imminent retirement of Associate Justice Harold Hitz Burton due to ill health, the Attorney General had written the President to discuss candidates to fill the upcoming vacancy (see *New York Times*, Oct. 7, 1958). On Eisenhower's Supreme Court appointments see Galambos and van Ee, *The Middle Way*, nos. 444, 1334, and 1386.

[2] For background on Brownell's qualifications for a seat on the Supreme Court see no. 22.

[3] Eisenhower had appointed Warren Earl Burger (LL.B. St. Paul College of Law 1931) to the U.S. Court of Appeals for the District of Columbia in 1955. Burger had also served as Assistant Attorney General from 1953 until 1956. In 1969 President Richard Nixon would name Burger to succeed Earl Warren as Chief Justice of the Supreme Court.

[4] Elbert Parr Tuttle (LL.B. Cornell 1923), a supporter of racial integration of public schools, had served on the U.S. Court of Appeals for the Fifth Circuit since 1954. During World War II he had commanded an artillery battalion in the Pacific and later had served as General Counsel of the Treasury Department. Tuttle would be awarded the Presidential Medal of Freedom in 1981.

[5] See Galambos and van Ee, *The Middle Way*, no. 1353.

[6] Although born in California, Tuttle had practiced law in Atlanta since his admission to the Georgia bar in 1923 and had played a pivotal role in extending civil rights in the South in the 1950s and 1960s (see *New York Times*, June 25, 1996). Hugo Lafayette Black (LL.B. University of Alabama 1906), born in Clay County, Alabama, had been appointed an associate justice of the Supreme Court in 1937. Black, who had once been a member of the secret Ku Klux Klan, was known for his strong belief in the Bill of Rights as a guarantee of civil liberties.

[7] Kenneth Claiborne Royall (LL.B. Harvard 1917) had served as the last Secretary of War in 1947, and the first Secretary of the Army from 1947 to 1949 (see Galambos, *Chief of Staff*). He was a partner in the New York law firm of Royall, Koegel, Harris & Caskey. Royall would greet the President at Quonset Point Naval Air Station upon his return from Rhode Island.

[8] Eisenhower would meet with Rogers on the afternoon of September 23, following a luncheon for Latin American foreign ministers. (On the President's vacation see no. 841.) On October 7 the President would name Potter Stewart (LL.B. Yale 1941), a judge of the United States Court of Appeals since 1954, to the Supreme Court vacancy (see *New York Times*, Oct. 8, 1958).

858   *EM, AWF, DDE Diaries Series*

To Gabriel Hauge   *September 19, 1958*

Dear Gabe: I hear that tonight Clarence Randall and Fred Seaton are giving a dinner in your honor. By no means shall I consider it a "farewell" dinner; it is inconceivable that, despite your removal from the Washington scene, you will not still be—and be so considered by all of us—a member of the original Administration family.[1]

What precisely we shall do without your gentle prodding, without your stern—at times—conscience, and without the lift of your daily epigrams I do not quite know. We shall miss your contribution to the difficult problems of the day, and I assure you I do not mean merely clothes pins and brier pipes.[2]

One of the rewards of my job is the friendship and inspiration I receive from younger, dedicated people such as you. Your presence on the White House Staff has been a real gratification; your friendship I shall always cherish.[3]

With warm regard, *As ever*

[1] For background on Hauge's resignation see no. 769. He would continue to advise the President (see, for example, no. 976).

[2] On Hauge's epigrams see, for example, his memorandums to the President, May 21, July 8, 10, 1958, in AWF/A. Eisenhower would reflect on his relationship with Hauge in his memoir, *Waging Peace*, p. 320. On Hauge's role in the Administration's concept of "modern Republicanism" see Ewald, *Eisenhower the President*, p. 290. On the Reciprocal Trade Agreements Act and brier pipe imports, see Galambos and van Ee, *The Middle Way*, no. 26.

[3] On September 30 the President would meet twice with Hauge (Ann Whitman memorandum, Sept. 30, 1958, AWF/AWD).

859   *Diefenbaker Papers*

To John George Diefenbaker   *September 21, 1958*

Dear John: You will recall that among the problems we discussed during my visit to Ottawa last July was the depressed state of the United States lead and zinc industry.[1] It was pointed out that under the circumstances something would have to be done to improve conditions in the industry.

Contrary to my hopes and expectations, the minerals stabilization plan, which I proposed as an alternative to acceptance of the recommendations of the United States Tariff Commission to curtail imports sharply, although approved by the Senate, was defeated by a narrow margin in the House of Representatives.

The Department of State subsequently discussed with the major exporting countries, including Canada, the possibility of multilateral agreement to a temporary reduction of exports.[2] It was our feeling that this would allow time for study of the causes of the imbalance between world production of, and demand for, lead and zinc and for exploring the best way of coping with this problem. These discussions, and the subsequent talks which took place in London under the auspices of the United Nations, revealed that while a majority of the interested nations were willing to undertake a study of the longer term problem, a temporary international arrangement to deal with the present emergency would not be feasible. This was due in part to the difficulties Canada would face in implementing such an arrangement.[3]

I believe you will agree with me that all of the lead and zinc producing nations face a serious and immediate problem of oversupply. I cannot disagree with the unanimous finding of the Tariff Commission that the United States industry is in genuine distress. It has already reduced its production by very substantial amounts and in spite of the accumulation of large stocks and decreased demand, imports have continued at a very high level. I have, therefore, felt obliged to take immediate action. In searching for the type of action which would be consistent with the spirit of the multilateral discussions which are in progress, and which would operate to share equitably the burden of dealing with the present emergency, I have decided to institute import quotas. I am hopeful that one of the effects of this action will be to prevent a further decline in the prices which your exporters, as well as others, obtain in the United States market.[4]

Meanwhile, I have instructed the Department of State to continue its efforts in cooperation with representatives of your Government and other Governments to seek an early and equitable multilateral action looking toward elimination of the current imbalance between production and consumption.

I am hopeful that our efforts in this direction will soon bear fruit.[5]

Sincerely

[1] On Eisenhower's informal visit to Ottawa (July 8–11) see no. 720; and State, *Foreign Relations, 1958–1960*, vol. VII, pt. 1, *Western European Integration and Security; Canada*, pp. 686–721. For background on the problems of the lead and zinc industry, the recommendations of the U.S. Tariff Commission, and the minerals stabilization plan see no. 774. State Department officials had drafted this letter to Canadian Prime Minister Diefenbaker at Eisenhower's request. On the preceding day he had signed a similar message to Mexican President Ruiz Cortines (Dulles to Eisenhower, Sept. 21, 1958, AWF/I: Canada; Herter to Eisenhower, Sept. 19, AWF/I: Cortines; Eisenhower to Ruiz Cortines, Sept. 20, 1958, *ibid.*; State, *Foreign Relations, 1958–1960*, vol. V, *American Republics*, pp. 845–46; and Eckes, *The United States and the Global Struggle for Minerals*, pp. 224–25). Secretary Dulles cabled the text of the President's message to Ottawa for delivery to Diefenbaker on this same day (AWF/I: Canada).

[2] State Department officials had also met with representatives from Australia, Mexico, and Peru (see State, Foreign *Relations, 1958–1960*, vol. IV, *Foreign Economic Policy*, pp. 179–80).

[3] On September 8 forty nations had begun talks in London under the auspices of the Interim Coordinating Committee for International Commodity Arrangements of the United Nations. There they attempted to determine whether the production and prices of lead and zinc could be stabilized through international agreements (*ibid.*, pp. 179, 183; *New York Times*, Sept. 9, 10, 1958).

[4] On the following day Eisenhower would announce the imposition of quotas that would cut lead and zinc imports by one third—the first time that quotas had been used as a protective device under the escape clause of the Trade Agreements Extension Act (State, *Foreign Relations, 1958–1960*, vol. IV, *Foreign Economic Policy*, pp. 182–84; *U.S. Department of State Bulletin* 39, no. 1007 [October 13, 1958], 579–84; and State, *Current Documents, 1958*, pp. 1496–97; see also Galambos and van Ee, *The Middle Way*, no. 914; and Telephone conversations, Dulles and Eisenhower, Sept. 11, 1958, and Dulles and Dillon, Sept. 19, 1958, Dulles Papers, Telephone Conversations).

[5] The lead and zinc producing nations would denounce the U.S. action. Diefenbaker

expressed "deep concern" regarding the decision and the fact that Eisenhower had "felt compelled to take action" when the producing nations were attempting to reach a solution. He asked the President to review the decision as soon as possible and to "restore the traditional access which Canada and other friendly countries have had to your market for these commodities" (Diefenbaker to Eisenhower, Oct. 28, 1958, AWF/I: Canada). For Peru's reaction, which ranged from strong to violent, see Prado to Eisenhower, Sept. 24, 1958; Eisenhower to Prado, Sept. 21, 1958; Achilles to Dulles, Sept. 25, 1958, AWF/I: Peru; and State, *Foreign Relations, 1958–1960*, vol. IV, *Foreign Economic Policy*, p. 184). For Australian reaction see no. 868.

In a November 20 letter Eisenhower would tell Diefenbaker again that his decision was made "only after all other courses proved ineffectual." He reiterated his belief in the expansion of international trade and expressed the hope that restrictions could soon be relaxed (same file as document; see also Dulles to Eisenhower, Nov. 18, 1958; and Department of State to Canadian embassy, Nov. 7, 1958, *ibid.*). For developments see no. 959.

860   *EM, AWF, International Series: Tunisia*

To Habib Bourguiba   *September 22, 1958*
Confidential

Dear Mr. President: I have studied carefully your letter to me of August twenty-fifth, and wish to thank you for having taken the time to set forth your views on the dangers facing the Free World as a result of Soviet imperialist attempts at expansion in the Near East and North Africa.[1] I agree completely that the situation is most serious and that one of the most important tasks facing us all is to make clear the moral values and principles on which our free institutions are based.

Since 1945, the American people have given unstintingly to assist the other nations of the world to develop their economic life and preserve their territorial integrity and internal security in the face of external threats. This has been possible only through diversion of our efforts from many worthwhile programs which we would have liked to carry out here in the United States. Large as this aid has been, when one considers all the urgent requirements which have had to be met, it may well seem that our efforts have been, as you say, widely dispersed. However, although the idea of concentrating our assistance on a few countries and making them "show windows of the West" has great appeal, had we done this we would have had to refuse assistance to other countries whose needs were equally great. This would have been a denial of the fundamental principles on which our assistance to other nations is based. I hope that you will agree that it is as much in Tunisia's interest as in that of the United States that other Free World countries continue to develop economic and political strength.

Your suggestion that the leaders of the Free World should meet regularly to discuss and define their moral and political position with particular attention to the problems of nationalism and underdevelopment is most interesting. Such periodic consultations as you envisage might be most desirable but I fear they would tend to undermine important existing means of international cooperation. Unless a few nations are to arrogate to themselves the right to decide what should be done about the problems facing the whole Free World, the best forum for consultations and cooperation will probably continue to be the United Nations and its specialized agencies. In this connection, may I say that I am gratified that your Government has taken such an active part in the work of the United Nations and has been so ably represented there by your Ambassador to the United States, Mongi Slim.

The specific test which you feel that the Free World must face in the coming months is the question of Algeria.[2] Certainly, I need not reassure you that the United States has done and will continue to do everything it can to make a constructive contribution to a solution of this problem. Here again, however, our ability to make such a contribution is limited. Were the United States to take a partisan position our chances of influencing developments would be reduced still further. Similarly, an extreme approach in the United Nations General Assembly could be unproductive and most dangerous. I believe that General de Gaulle, for whom I have great respect, is trying to deal constructively with the problem. It would be unfair to discount the handicaps which he must overcome, but above all he requires time to work out a solution if he is to be successful. In your speech of July thirty-first, you advocated a moderate approach to this problem. Without question, the greatest contribution any of us can make is to urge all parties to exercise moderation and to keep ever in mind the over-riding importance of arriving at a just and fair settlement, even at the cost of some concessions.

In closing, I wish to repeat my appreciation of your frankness in expressing your thoughts on these basic questions, and to express my admiration for the moderate, constructive and helpful role which you and your country are playing in these troubled times.[3]
Sincerely

[1] Bourguiba had written Eisenhower in response to two earlier letters from the President regarding U.S. troop landings in Lebanon and Bourguiba's recent speech supporting U.S. foreign policy (see Eisenhower to Bourguiba, July 22 and Aug. 2, 1958, AWF/I: Tunisia; for more on Bourguiba's speech see Dulles to Eisenhower, Aug. 2, 1958, *ibid.*; and *New York Times*, July 26, 1958). Bourguiba had said that he wished to see Western values endure in the Near East but that vestiges of British and French colonialism had enabled the Soviet Union to expand its influence. The United States

had too often appeared "as the integral friend of old colonial powers" and was too slow to respond to the Soviet challenge. It had "dispersed its considerable efforts instead of concentrating them on two or three countries which could have been 'test countries' and show windows of the West." He suggested that Western leaders meet periodically to plan a more unified approach to their policies in the area (Bourguiba to Eisenhower, Aug. 25, 1958, AWF/I: Tunisia; see also State, *Foreign Relations, 1958–1960*, vol. XIII, *Arab-Israeli Dispute; United Arab Republic; North Africa*, pp. 857–58). The State Department officials who drafted this letter had told Acting Secretary Herter that Eisenhower's reply was designed to be "as friendly and responsive as possible" without conceding the validity of all of Bourguiba's arguments (see *ibid.*, p. 857; and Herter to Eisenhower, Sept. 18, 1958, AWF/I: Tunisia).

[2] For background on the Algerian situation see no. 451.

[3] Bourguiba would tell the American ambassador that he was "pleased and proud" to receive this letter. Eisenhower had studied his own letter, he said, and had answered all its main points (State, *Foreign Relations, 1958–1960*, vol. XIII, *Arab-Israeli Dispute; United Arab Republic; North Africa*, p. 858).

861   *EM, WHCF,*
                                      President's Personal File 233

TO IDELLA BARBARA RUTH BLACKADDER MARX
                                          September 22, 1958

Dear Idella:[1] Recently I have given some thought to the over-all problem of our educational processes and yet, when confronted with your specific question of the third language that Spencer Bedell and Emmett Dwight should study, I am not entirely sure that my instinctive answer is the proper one. But my feeling is that a thorough grounding in Latin and Greek is essential for anyone these days, especially for an individual who might have a scientific or mathematical bent. If, however, a choice must be made between the study of Latin and Greek and practical mastery of Russian, I personally would prefer the latter.[2]

I shall be interested in your final decision, but a great deal should depend, I believe, on what the boys themselves wish to do.

At any rate, there is the advice of a godfather, for what it may be worth.[3]

With warm regard to you and Lou and all the members of your family, *Sincerely*

[1] Mrs. Marx was the wife of toy manufacturer Louis Marx (for background on Eisenhower's friendship with Marx see *Eisenhower Papers*, vols. VI–XVII).

[2] On the President's views regarding education see nos. 16, 784, and 889. Mrs. Marx had written on September 13 (same file as document). Her sons, Spencer Bedell,

born August 28, 1949, and Emmett Dwight, born November 15, 1950, attended a French school and were tutored in English one hour per day. Now the boys were required to study a third language before entering prep school. The choices, Mrs. Marx wrote, were: Latin and Greek (taken simultaneously), Russian, Chinese, Spanish, German, or Italian. She said she had received varying advice from others but considered the President "best able to give . . . the most sound guidance."
[3] Eisenhower was godfather to both boys (see revised list of President Eisenhower's Godchildren, Apr. 30, 1953, WHCF/PPF 5). On Spencer Bedell's christening see Galambos, *Columbia University*, no. 625.

862   *EM, WHCF, Official File 1*

To Ezra Taft Benson   *September 24, 1958*

Dear Ezra: I was startled to hear that you found it necessary to enter the hospital, but have been reassured by reports of last evening that your illness is of less serious nature than it might have been.[1] Needless to say, I pray earnestly for your early and complete recovery.

Over the past several days I have been studying the Paarlberg matter, including your telephone message to me as to his value in your organization.[2] I have come to the conclusion that I must ask you to make a sacrifice and permit him to serve on my staff. I do this reluctantly because I know how preoccupied you are with your vital responsibilities and the need you have for an experienced and able staff. But only within a matter of weeks I have had to face up to the loss of Rabb, Martin and Larson, and shortly will lose Adams, Pyle and of course Hauge.[3] I simply cannot take in people who are inexperienced in government and expect them to perform in the way that my depleted staff must now do. I give you this explanation so that you will know that I have not lightly asked you to suffer this loss in your own organization.

Because of my urgent need, I have asked Mr. Paarlberg to make the transfer as soon as he possibly can. So I hope you will notify him of your acquiescence.

Incidentally, I should think that Mr. Paarlberg would still be of real assistance to you when agricultural matters come up for discussion here at the White House.

May I request you to convey to President McKay my warmest greetings and expressions of my highest esteem.[4] I repeat that my prayers will ask for your quick recovery.

[1] Secretary of Agriculture Benson had been admitted to Latter-Day Saints Hospital, in Salt Lake City, Utah, on September 23 for a mild infection. He had been dis-

charged earlier this same day (Whitman to Benson, Sept. 24, 1958, and *New York Times*, Sept. 24, 1958).

[2] Don Paarlberg (Ph.D. Cornell 1947) had been a professor of agricultural economics at Purdue University until 1953, when he became Assistant Secretary of Agriculture. Benson had said that Paarlberg was doing outstanding work in the Department of Agriculture. But if Eisenhower wanted Paarlberg as an economic adviser, Benson would "grin and bear it" (Ann Whitman memorandum, Sept. 20, 1958, AWF/D). Benson also suggested other candidates for the position the President wanted to fill (see no. 821, and Benson to Eisenhower, Sept. 26, 1958, AWF/A). On September 26 Eisenhower would appoint Paarlberg as Special Assistant to the President on Economic Affairs. For developments see no. 1321.

[3] Cabinet Secretary Maxwell Rabb had resigned on April 24 (*New York Times*, Apr. 25, Aug. 23, 1958). On August 26 Administrative Assistant I. Jack Martin had resigned to be sworn in as an Associate Judge of the U.S. Court of Customs and Patent Appeals (*New York Times*, Aug. 27, 1958). Eisenhower had accepted Special Assistant Arthur Larson's resignation on August 11 (see no. 803). For background on Sherman Adams's resignation as the Assistant to the President see no. 753. Administrative Assistant Howard Pyle had submitted his resignation in July (*New York Times*, July 12, 1958). On White House aide Gabriel Hauge's resignation see no. 769.

[4] David O. McKay was president of the Church of Jesus Christ of Latter-Day Saints and president of the board of trustees of Brigham Young University. McKay had written numerous Priesthood Manuals for the Church and a volume on *Ancient Apostles* (Salt Lake City, 1918).

863   *EM, AWF, Name Series*

To Malcolm Charles Moos   *September 25, 1958*

Memorandum for Malcolm Moos: Attached is a new draft of the Ligonier speech. As you can see I have eliminated one or two thoughts from your suggested talk, and have tried by certain deletions to emphasize only the idea of Fort Ligonier as a symbol of pioneer courage and, also, a symbol of the global struggle for peace and freedom today.

If you have any additional comments, please send them back to Mrs. Whitman early this afternoon.[1]

[1] Moos, a political scientist at The Johns Hopkins University, had been sworn in as an administrative assistant on September 24 (see Ann Whitman memorandum, Sept. 24, 1958, AWF/AWD). For background on the bicentennial celebration of Fort Ligonier, a historic British-built fort near Pittsburgh, Pennsylvania, see no. 751. During this day, Eisenhower would revise Moos's draft five times. Despite the President's significant editing and handwritten emendations, the final draft would roughly follow Moos's original outline. Eisenhower, however, would excise a reference to his own pioneer heritage (on the speech see no. 866). Copies of drafts two through five, showing Eisenhower's handwritten changes, are in AWF/Speeches. Moos would continue to draft speeches and statements for the President (see no. 1100; see also Ann Whitman memorandum, Sept. 30, 1958, AWF/AWD).

To Benjamin Franklin Fairless   *September 26, 1958*

Dear Ben: While it was a real pleasure to see you for one brief moment at the Ligonier ceremony, I was disappointed that there was no opportunity for us to have a little talk.[1]

There seems to be a curious—even inexplicable—apathy in the rank and file of Republicans. The Chairman of the National Committee is working to an extent that I already am hoping that he avoids a nervous breakdown. Yet he is handicapped not only by the existence of this widespread lack of enthusiasm, reported from every corner of the country, and even more so by lack of means through which we could get people on their toes and working.[2]

The situation is by no means hopeless. If we can get all the politicians, business and professional leaders who believe in moderate government and—above all—in a sound fiscal system to recognize the importance of the moment, I am sure this inaction would quickly disappear.[3]

I spoke to Dick Mellon and to Ed Martin. Dick promptly promised to help out in some specific instances and from what Ed said I believe the situation in Pennsylvania itself seems to be looking up.[4]

I hope you will do whatever you can to stir up everybody who thinks he can influence another voter in these brief weeks left to us.[5]

With my warm greetings to Hazel and all the best to yourself. *As ever*

[1] Earlier this day Eisenhower had attended the bicentennial celebration of Fort Ligonier, the historic British fort in Fort Ligonier, Pennsylvania (see nos. 751 and 856).
[2] On Chairman Hugh Meade Alcorn's efforts to boost Republican morale see, for example, nos. 836 and 885. For developments see no. 919.
[3] For background on the President's increasing concern regarding GOP morale see nos. 840 and 842. Eisenhower would deliver campaign speeches in California, Iowa, Illinois, West Virginia, Pennsylvania, and Maryland (see no. 908).
[4] Mellon had agreed to raise campaign funds for the Republican senatorial candidate (see no. 866). Former Republican Governor of Pennsylvania Edward Martin had served the state as a U.S. Senator since 1947. He had announced his retirement in July (*New York Times*, July 29, Oct. 9, 1958). For background on Martin see *Eisenhower Papers*, vols. XII–XVII, and no. 836 in these volumes. On November 4 Democrats in Pennsylvania would capture the governor's chair, but Martin's Senate seat would be filled by a Republican (*New York Times*, Nov. 5, 1958).
[5] For developments see no. 836.

EM, AWF, Name Series

To Harry S. Truman   *September 27, 1958*

Dear President Truman: I learn from General Cabell, the Acting Director of the CIA, that he has recently briefed you about the situation in the Far East.[1] I want you to feel that you can always get such briefings whenever you desire and we may from time to time take the liberty of suggesting them, if there seems to be a situation of grave national importance, as to which you would presumably wish to be impartially and authoritatively informed.

Let me express appreciation for the statement which you made on the Quemoy and Matsu situation, as reported on September fourteenth.[2]

With best wishes, *Sincerely*

[1] Charles Pearre Cabell (B.S. USMA 1925), former Director of Intelligence for the United States Air Force and Director of the Joint Staff of the Joint Chiefs of Staff, had become Deputy Director of the Central Intelligence Agency in 1953. CIA Director Allen Dulles was out of the country (see Telephone conversation, Eisenhower and Dulles, Sept. 12, 1958, Dulles Papers, Telephone Conversations). On the recent Communist shellings of the islands off the coast of the Chinese mainland see no. 838.

[2] Truman had written a newspaper article stating that the "probing tactics" of the Chinese Communists in the Taiwan Straits were "part of a reckless campaign" to determine whether the Soviet Union would support them and whether the United States would "stand up to their use of force to take over Quemoy, Matsu and Formosa." The role of U.S. military forces was "to prevent any mad adventure which could set off a third world war." Until there was absolute assurance that the Communists had abandoned their aim of territorial expansion, he believed that the United States had no other choice "but to meet them and thwart them at every point where it becomes necessary" (*New York Times*, Sept. 14, 1958).

Truman would thank Eisenhower for providing the information and would tell the President that he would regard it as "strictly confidential" (Truman to Eisenhower, Sept. 30, 1958, AWF/N).

866   *EM, AWF, DDE Diaries Series*

To Richard King Mellon   *September 27, 1958*

Dear Dick: You must have had your fill of automobiling yesterday, particularly since you were consistently retracing the same route.[1]

I did not have the time personally to congratulate all of the individuals who did so much to make the ceremonies a real success. I should like, if you have a chance, for you to convey to each an expression of my admiration for their efforts. Moreover, I should have enjoyed an opportunity with you to browse around the restored Fort and to acquire thereby some of its atmosphere. However, I doubt that such a chance will ever arise until after I leave this post and get rid of the entourage that must of necessity follow a President into any public place.

The day was a most enjoyable one. I know that you were rather worried that we might have bad weather, but the slight drizzle actually imposed very little inconvenience on the numbers of people that gathered there.

It was a real privilege to visit your home and to meet there some of your friends.[2]

Finally, I thank you for interesting yourself in the political matter that Hugh Scott believes could be so helpful.[3]

With warm regard, *Sincerely*

[1] The preceding day Eisenhower had attended the bicentennial celebration of Fort Ligonier, the historic British-built fort in Fort Ligonier, Pennsylvania (see no. 751). In his remarks the President had praised the restoration and defended modern overseas military bases. Like the Ligonier settlers, he said, "this nation and our allies are maintaining forts in distant lands." "We have but one purpose," Eisenhower continued, "to defend freedom" and to build "a fortress of freedom to which all mankind can repair" (see *Public Papers of the Presidents: Eisenhower, 1958*, pp. 707–8, and *New York Times*, Sept. 27, 1958).

[2] The President had visited Mellon's 30,000-acre estate in Huntland Downs, near Ligonier. His thank-you letter to Mrs. Mellon of this same date is in AWF/D.

[3] While in Ligonier Eisenhower and Mellon had discussed current political events. Mellon had agreed to raise campaign funds for the Senate primary campaign of Pennsylvania Republican Congressman Hugh Doggett Scott, Jr. (see no. 880). Scott (LL.B. University of Virginia 1922) was currently general counsel for the Republican National Committee and a member of the Republican Policy Committee. He had served in the Army during World War I and in the Navy during World War II. He would be elected to the Senate on November 4 (see *Congressional Quarterly Almanac*, vol. XIV, *1958*, p. 744, and *New York Times*, Nov. 5, 6, 1958).

867   *EM, AWF, Dulles-Herter Series*

To John Foster Dulles   *September 29, 1958*

Memorandum for the Secretary of State: Two or three different individuals have suggested to me the potential value of a bipartisan conference in unifying public opinion in the Formosa problem. One man advises me that both John McCormack and Styles Bridges, for example, have felt that such a meeting would be useful.[1]

In the instances where I have so far replied, I have been fairly discouraging, but I should like your opinion on the matter.[2]

[1] We have been unable to identify these individuals. For background on Democratic Representative M⟨C⟩ormack see Galambos and van Ee, *The Middle Way*, no. 1314; on Republican Senator Bridges, ranking member of the Foreign Relations Committee, nos. 23 and 669. For background on the Formosa problem see no. 838.

[2] At a meeting on this same day Dulles would tell Eisenhower that he was "not very enthusiastic about such a meeting." He thought that the "present highly charged political atmosphere" would make it difficult for Democrats to state publicly that they supported the Administration (Dulles, Memorandum of Conversation, Sept. 29, 1958, Dulles Papers, White House Memoranda Series).

868   *EM, WHCF,*
                                         Official File 149-B-2 Lead & Zinc

To Robert Gordon Menzies   *September 29, 1958*

Dear Prime Minister:[1] I have given careful consideration to the strong representations of the Australian Government through your Ambassador concerning the recent import quotas on lead and zinc.[2] From the beginning of our common study of this whole problem I have tried to avoid any solution that would bear too heavily upon any of our valued friends.[3]

The cause of the current industry crisis is world overproduction of lead and zinc. No one country is responsible for this. The imbalance between production and consumption became so acute in 1958 that the United States mining industry reduced its production by about 25%. In addition, the domestic industry, in an attempt to stabilize the market, accumulated very large inventories. Imports nevertheless continued at very high levels. The result was a steady decline in price.

It was to avoid chaotic conditions in the world industry that my Government and yours made strenuous efforts to agree with other lead and zinc exporting nations on a course of action for restoring order and stability in the industry throughout the world. These consultations, while promising, revealed that there was no early prospect of obtaining unanimous agreement to deal with the emergency. It was only then that I reluctantly decided that prompt action by the United States was necessary.

There is apparently some feeling on the part of the Australians that the quota is designed to transfer the burden of readjustment to other countries. This is not so. According to our estimates, the quota represents an equitable approach to the burdens of readjustment upon both domestic and foreign producers.

I recognize that the base period of the last five years happens to operate with particular severity against the Australian economy.[4]

This is a matter of concern to me. My Government stands willing to discuss with your Government and other interested Governments possible alternative arrangements. In this connection, I am hopeful that the multilateral discussions, which we expect to continue, will result in agreement of all on a formula for equitably sharing the burden of readjustment and at the same time lay the basis for enduring stability in the world industry. If, contrary to our expectations, it should not be possible promptly to reach a multilateral agreement, the United States also stands ready to review with Australia and other interested Governments on a bilateral basis, the most equitable way of dealing with the problem.

I appreciate very much your Government's cooperation in endeavoring to work out this problem on an orderly basis and look forward to a continuance of that cooperation in the future consistent with our intimate relations generally.[5]

With warm personal regard, *Sincerely*

[1] For background on Menzies, prime minister of Australia since December 1949, see Galambos and van Ee, *The Middle Way*, no. 1825. Secretary Dulles cabled the text of this letter to Canberra for delivery to Menzies on this same day (AWF/I: Australia).

[2] On the problems affecting the lead and zinc industry and Eisenhower's decision to impose import quotas see nos. 774 and 859. Dulles had told Eisenhower that the quotas would curtail Australian exports by 50 percent, and that the decision had become a major political issue. Since elections were imminent, Dulles suggested that they "do or say something" that would help Menzies (Memorandum of Conversation, Sept. 23, 1958, Dulles Papers, White House Memoranda Series; see also Telephone conversations, Dulles and Beale, Sept. 23, 1958; and Dulles and Nixon, Sept. 25, 1958, Dulles Papers, Telephone Conversations). State Department officials drafted this letter, which Eisenhower approved after making several verbal and handwritten emendations (Memorandum of Conversation, Sept. 29, 1958, *ibid.*; Mann to Areeda and Hauge to Goodpaster, Sept. 29, 1958, same file as document).

[3] Eisenhower added this sentence to the State Department draft.

[4] The new quotas were based on the average annual imports during the five years from 1953–1957; Australian production of lead and zinc had increased in the 1956–1957 period.

[5] Eisenhower's letter was a "most timely" help in explaining to members of Parliament and the Australian people the quota decision, Menzies would write. He supported multilateral talks but accepted Eisenhower's offer to review the decision through bilateral discussions (Menzies to Eisenhower, Oct. 20, 1958, AWF/I: Australia).

Participants at an international meeting on lead and zinc, held in Geneva in November, would recommend the formation of a lead and zinc study group. That group would hold its first meeting in January 1960 (State, *Foreign Relations, 1958–1960*, vol. IV, *Foreign Economic Policy*, pp. 185–88). For developments see no. 959.

To Arthur Frank Burns   *September 29, 1958*

Dear Arthur: I agree with every word I read in your letter of the twenty-sixth.[1]

Because of your statistical as well as philosophical understanding of the matter, I wonder whether you could quickly prepare for me three or four applicable paragraphs that could be used in every important statement or speech that I may be called upon to make both during this campaign and afterward.[2]

Personally I have tried to make the matter of governmental expenditures the main issue of this campaign.[3] To my dismay not too many Republicans have wholeheartedly agreed with me. Seemingly the disease of Congressional spending is not taken very seriously by candidates for the Congress.

I enclose a copy of a memorandum just sent me by Ezra Benson—incidentally written the same day as yours. He and I had just had a long talk about the matter, and he merely wanted to put the gist of the conversation on the written record.[4]

With warm regard, *As ever*

[1] Burns had discussed his concern over increased federal expenditures, which he believed presented an even greater danger than a budget deficit. While not underestimating the importance of the deficit, he believed that "... if the deficit now in sight had arisen mainly from a tax reduction for business and individuals rather than, as is largely the case, from an expansion of spending in every direction, I would feel more confident about our country's future. For, as you so well know, once the level of government spending has been raised all around, it is very difficult to bring it down again" (AWF/A).

[2] See no. 886.

[3] See no. 850.

[4] Secretary of Agriculture Benson had written that "The threat of inflationary impacts to our economy is again causing major concern," and that the Administration "should fight to keep Federal spending within bounds" (Benson to Eisenhower, Sept. 26, 1958, AWF/A). Benson had suggested that Eisenhower discuss the subject in the Economic Message, the State of the Union message and "other public statements."

870   *EM, AWF, DDE Diaries Series*
To Richard Milhous Nixon   *September 29, 1958*

Dear Dick: As you know, I have had a number of inquiries from California with regard to the use of my name on billboards as an opponent of right to work legislation in California.[1] I understand that your name was also used in this way.

In view of the fact that you are going to be in California on Tuesday, it occurred to me that it might be an appropriate time again to set the record straight as to the position I have consistently taken on the right to work proposals which are on the ballot in various states.[2]

I have repeatedly stated that in my judgment the right to work was an issue to be determined by the several states and not by Federal statute. I have never expressed any opinion as to how this issue should be settled, believing, as I do, that that should be decided by the citizens of each state. Any statement indicating or implying that I have done so misrepresents the facts.[3]

With warm regard, *As ever*

[1] A group opposed to the passage of California's right-to-work initiative (see no. 829) had placed advertisements on hundreds of billboards around the state. Under the statement "These leaders say 'no' on right to work," they had listed both Eisenhower and Vice-President Nixon, along with Chief Justice Earl Warren and former Illinois Governor Adlai E. Stevenson. On September 23 Eisenhower had written Senator William F. Knowland, a vigorous advocate of a right-to-work law for California, denying that he had expressed any opinion on the wisdom of such state laws (AWF/D). Knowland had released Eisenhower's letter to the press on this same day (Anderson, "The 1958 Election in California," p. 291; *New York Times*, Sept. 30, 1958).

[2] In California on September 30, Nixon, following Eisenhower's lead, would refuse to take a stand on the state's right-to-work initiative (*New York Times*, Oct. 1, 1958).

[3] For background on Eisenhower's position on this issue see Galambos and van Ee, *The Middle Way*, nos. 397, 604, 621, 1197, and 1234. On October 1, 1958, Eisenhower would say: "I have never urged any State to vote for a so-called right-to-work law— for the simple reason that I believe it's the State's business, and I'm not going to get into it" (*Public Papers of the Presidents: Eisenhower, 1958*, p. 714). For developments see no. 905.

871

871   *EM, AWF, Administration Series,*
                                                        McElroy Corr.

To Donald Aubrey Quarles   *September 29, 1958*

Dear Don: I have heard of one or two instances where young men just starting in the service have contracted polio.[1]

Why would it not be a good idea to require every individual first entering the service to take three shots of Salk vaccine? There may be some medical or other reason for failing to do so, but I don't know what it could be.[2]

With warm regard, *As ever*

[1] On September 27 Eisenhower had met Justin W. Dart, whose son, First Lieutenant Peter W Dart (USAF, ret.), had contracted polio in 1957. For background see no. 251.
[2] With his October 7 reply Quarles would include a report on poliomyelitis cases in the services in 1958. That same day the President and Quarles would discuss the matter (Goodpaster, Memorandum of Conversation, Oct. 8, 1958, all in AWF/D). For developments see no. 888.

872

EM, AWF,
International Series: Greece

To Paul I, King of the Helenes
Confidential

September 30, 1958

Dear King Paul: I want you to know that I have given most careful study to your recent message expressing concern regarding the repercussions which may follow the application of the British plan for Cyprus.[1]

The United States is gravely disturbed by the imminent dangers posed by the failure to reach a mutually satisfactory settlement of the Cyprus dispute. We have considerable sympathy and understanding for the difficult position in which Greece finds itself. I know you understand that since we are not a direct party to the controversy and are a friend of all concerned, we face real limitations on our ability to intervene in this matter. Nevertheless, we have been working quietly and urgently in an effort to find ways to reconcile the apparent British intention to proceed with initial steps to implement their plan with Greek objections to the plan.[2] We will continue these efforts. It remains our fervent hope that all of those concerned with the dispute will seek a solution in the spirit of the alliance which binds us together.

From personal experience I know how staunchly you believe in the North Atlantic Alliance and the need to maintain Greece's ties with the West. I am sure that you are distressed, as I am, to see how the Cyprus dispute is undermining the unity of NATO and hampering the effective cooperation of allies whose full energies are needed against the common threat. I have been particularly disturbed by the implication in recent public and private statements of Greek Government officials that Greece might be led to risk its basic ties with the West in order to protest what might be considered an unacceptable interim settlement of the Cyprus problem.[3]

I hope most earnestly, Your Majesty, that in pursuing its Cyprus policy Greece will measure its immediate objectives respecting Cyprus against its bonds of interest and interdependence with the other nations of the West. I know that you and I would not want to see endangered a basis of our common strength which, after all, offers the best hope for serving the long-term interests of the Cypriot people, as of the people of the entire free world.[4]

With warm regard, *Sincerely*

[1] For background on the conflict between Greece and Turkey over Cyprus, the British plan for the island, and the objections of both Greece and Turkey to the British proposals see nos. 744 and 745. The threat of civil war between the Greek and Turkish communities on Cyprus during the summer months had prompted NATO Secretary General Paul Henri Spaak to advocate further discussions. Believing that a final solution was not possible at that time, he wanted the parties to work toward a provisional solution that would both increase Cypriot self-government and safeguard the Turkish minority.

At the same time, British Prime Minister Macmillan, after consultations with government officials in Greece, Turkey, and Cyprus, had proposed modifications in the British plan to make it more acceptable to the Greeks without alienating the Turks. The new plan eliminated the concept of dual nationality and the provision that representatives of the two governments should sit on the governor's council. The modifications called for a less intrusive form of Turkish representation in the government of Cyprus and provided for the possibility of separate municipal councils that would deal with local affairs. Although the Turkish government had accepted the British proposals, the Greek government had rejected them (State, *Foreign Relations, 1958–1960*, vol. X, pt. 1, *Eastern Europe Region; Soviet Union; Cyprus*, pp. 642–96; see also Royal Institute of International Affairs, *Documents on International Affairs 1958*, ed. King, pp. 383–85; Macmillan, *Riding the Storm*, pp. 674–87; and John Reddaway, *Burdened with Cyprus: The British Connection* [London, 1986], pp. 111–14).

In his September 20 letter King Paul had told Eisenhower that the British plan would complicate the problem and would have "dangerous repercussions not only on the internal conditions but also on the international relations of Greece." He had asked that Eisenhower exercise his influence with the British (State, *Foreign Relations, 1958–1960*, vol. X, pt. 1, *Eastern Europe Region; Soviet Union; Cyprus*, pp. 703–4).

[2] In a further attempt to avert a crisis Spaak had presented to the North Atlantic Council a new series of proposals, including a postponement of the British plan and further negotiations among representatives from the United Kingdom, Greece, Turkey, and Cyprus. The basis for the negotiations would be the creation of separate assemblies for the Greek and Turkish Cypriots, a single unified assembly to deal with local concerns, and the appointment of the heads of the two communities as advisors to the British governor. The Greeks had accepted Spaak's proposals; the Turks had rejected them. The British had endorsed the conference but refused to postpone their plan (*ibid.*, pp. 700–8; see also Royal Institute of International Affairs, *Documents on International Affairs 1958*, ed. King, pp. 388–92).

[3] After receiving King Paul's letter, Dulles had told Eisenhower that the situation was "very bad" and that if the British initiated their plan on October 1 as planned, the Greeks might "walk out on NATO." State Department officials had talked to the British about a postponement, Dulles said, but they were caught between Greece and Turkey. Eisenhower thought the British should know that King Paul had appealed to him and that there was another reason to delay putting the British plan into effect: "the old saying—don't make any mistakes in a hurry. Once it's done, it's done" (Telephone conversations, Eisenhower and Dulles, Sept. 22, 1958, Dulles Papers, Telephone Conversations; see also Dulles to Eisenhower, Sept. 29, 1958, AWF/I: Greece; *New York Times*, Sept. 26, 1958; and Dulles, Memorandum of Conversation, Sept. 29, 1958, Dulles Papers, White House Memoranda Series).

[4] For developments see no. 874.

To ISIDOR SCHWANER RAVDIN   *September 30, 1958*

Dear Rav: Many thanks for your note.[1] After six years, almost, in this office, I have finally come to accept the fact that each day, usually each hour, will bring its own crisis. Unfortunately for me, all the little problems get solved on their way up—and the major (and sometimes unsoluble) ones land on my desk. But I have learned to live, as best I can, with the situation.

The tragedy of the Sherman Adams' case has been heartbreaking for him and for all of us.[2]

With warm regard to you and Betty, *As ever*

[1] Ravdin had written on September 26 (same file as document) to express sympathy for the President, who recently had been concerned with the Formosa crisis (see no. 844) and the ongoing school desegregation troubles in Little Rock, Arkansas (see no. 833).

[2] On Sherman Adams's resignation and the events that precipitated it see no. 862. Ravdin said he had gotten to know Adams in 1956 while attending the President following his ileotransverse colostomy (see Galambos and van Ee, *The Middle Way*, no. 1912). Adams was "dedicated to you and your work," Ravdin wrote. He said that he "could never believe" Adams would do anything dishonest.

To HAROLD MACMILLAN   *October 1, 1958*
Cable. Secret

Dear Harold: Thank you for your message about Cyprus which Harold Caccia gave to me on September twenty-fourth. I am grateful to you for giving me your thoughts on the way you intend to proceed on this difficult matter.[1]

Much has happened since your letter arrived. Just after receiving it, the news came of Mr. Spaak's trip to Athens and his proposal for a conference.[2] In fact I have delayed replying to your letter until we could have some better idea of what might come of that proposal. Foster has been in close touch with Selwyn and with Harold Caccia on these new developments and we have appreciated their receptiveness to suggestions we have made from time to time.[3] I have made clear to the Greeks that they need a sense of proportion in this matter and should not sacrifice their ancient heritage of democracy, and their new bonds in NATO.[4]

At the moment there seems a chance that a basis for further discussions between your Government and Greece and Turkey can be found. We most assuredly hope that this much can be accomplished and have stated in the North Atlantic Council our willingness to help in whatever way may be appropriate.[5]

With warm regard, *As ever*

[1] For background on the Cyprus situation see no. 872. Macmillan had told Eisenhower that before a final solution to the problem was possible, "violence in Cyprus must cease and all concerned must have breathing space." The British had made many concessions to the Greek point of view, he said, and they intended to implement their plan "step by step and quietly." "The only hope is that in due course they will acquiesce" (Macmillan to Eisenhower, Sept. 24, 1958, AWF/I: Macmillan).

[2] In a memorandum that accompanied the State Department's draft of this letter, Secretary Dulles had told Eisenhower that Macmillan's letter probably had been prompted by information he had received through Dulles that Eisenhower wanted the British to postpone their plan for Cyprus. The British, however, had remained determined to implement their plan on October 1, regardless of Spaak's proposal. "It seems to me," Dulles had told Eisenhower, "that we have no alternative at present but to recognize this intention to proceed and at the same time to utilize every opportunity to get the parties to sit down and talk this out among themselves" (Dulles to Eisenhower, Sept. 30, 1958, *ibid.*; see also Royal Ministry of Foreign Affairs, *The Cyprus Question: Discussion at the North Atlantic Treaty Organization* [Athens, 1958], pp. 3–11).

[3] Dulles had suggested to both Foreign Secretary Lloyd and Ambassador Caccia that the British accept Spaak's plan in principle, even though they could not accept the recommendation to suspend their plan (State, *Foreign Relations, 1958–1960*, vol. X, pt. 1, *Eastern Europe Region; Soviet Union; Cyprus*, pp. 704, 706–8, 711).

[4] For Eisenhower's meeting with the Greek ambassador see no. 872.

[5] For developments see no. 912.

875   *EM, AWF, Administration Series*

TO ROBERT CUTLER   *October 1, 1958*
Personal

Dear Bobby: Today is the date you are due back at the Old Colony, so in a sense this note is both a welcome to your desk and an acknowledgment of your letters and cards from Europe.[1]

I agree with everything you said about Sherman, and it is most discouraging that so many of our friends want only to criticize him, never to try to understand the mesh of circumstances that surrounded him—and, even more important, the inestimable value of his services to the public. The pilloring that was his lot was a sorry display for supposedly civilized, sophisticated and educated human beings. The months since you left have been particularly difficult for everyone, but of course pure hell for him.[2]

Jerry's appointment is being greeted with much praise, which of course is not unexpected. Bryce will do well in his new post. And Gabe left yesterday to become a banker, a la Cutler.[3]

I am glad the trip was beneficial to you and I hope you can get the trouble with your eyes and sleeping under control. Also I hope that one of these days you will come wandering into the White House; it will be good to see you.[4]

With warm personal regard, *As ever*

[1] Eisenhower's former Special Assistant for National Security Affairs had been traveling throughout Europe since July. Following his retirement, Cutler had resumed responsibilities as chairman of the board of Old Colony Trust Company in Boston (see no. 833).

[2] For background on the attacks that led to the resignation of the Assistant to the President Sherman Adams see no. 753. In a letter of September 26 Cutler had described Adams's service as "stout, sound, [and] devoted." Cutler said he had "shame and disregard" for the Republicans who had accused Adams in the "best Dark-Ages style" (AWF/A).

[3] Eisenhower had selected Major General Wilton B. Persons to replace Adams. Bryce N. Harlow, currently Persons's special assistant, would become Deputy Assistant to the President for Congressional Affairs (*New York Times*, Sept. 28, 1958). White House Special Assistant Hauge had resigned to become finance chairman of the Manufacturers Hanover Trust Company (see no. 769).

[4] Cutler had said he felt better and his stamina had returned. He also said he would undergo tests for his eyes and a sleep disorder. The President would next meet with Cutler at the White House on December 16.

876   *EM, AWF, Administration Series*

To WILLIAM PIERCE ROGERS   *October 1, 1958*

Dear Bill: Thank you for your comprehensive letter answering my questions concerning the United Givers Fund.[1] I shall be interested in the figure that finally develops as to the ratio of overhead and administrative expense to actual program expenditures—I, too, am astonished that such a percentage is not available.[2]

With warm regard, *As ever*

[1] Eisenhower had appointed Attorney General Rogers as chairman of the Government Unit of the 1958 United Givers Fund Campaign (UGF). (For background see *Public Papers of the Presidents: Eisenhower, 1958*, p. 472.) At the September 26 Cabinet meeting Eisenhower had asked whether the existence of federal disaster relief programs discouraged individual contributions (Cabinet meeting minutes, AWF/D). On September 29 (AWF/A) Rogers had reported that the Red Cross and the federal government each spent approximately $45 million for disaster relief during FY 1956–FY 1958. According to the national director of the American Red Cross, Rogers wrote,

the federal disaster relief programs had no appreciable effect on the annual Red Cross drives, either as part of UGF or separately. But the federal aid did depress public response when the Red Cross conducted special drives following major disasters. Rogers recommended that the Red Cross stress the fact that federal disaster relief programs and the Red Cross did not overlap, and that only the Red Cross provided direct grants-in-aid to private disaster victims.

The President had established the UGF in 1956 to unite the more than one hundred agencies of the local Community Chests, all of the American Red Cross local chapters, the USO-USO Camp Shows and certain national health agencies. The UGF supported the work of local agencies serving nearly 500,000 people in Washington, Maryland and Virginia (see *Public Papers of the Presidents: Eisenhower, 1956*, pp. 593–94).

[2] Rogers said no breakdown was readily available. He would recommend that the information be compiled on a comparative basis for all the charitable organizations that participate in the UGF drives. There is no further correspondence on this subject in AWF.

877   *EM, AWF, Dulles-Herter Series*

[To John Foster Dulles]   *[October 1, 1958]*

If they should come to Washington—let us make it informal. I could have dinner but no return one by Queen.[1]

[1] Eisenhower had penned this note in the margin of a memorandum to him from Dulles (Oct. 1, 1958). The Secretary of State had raised the question of inviting Queen Elizabeth II and her husband Prince Philip to visit the United States following their visit to Canada to attend the opening of the St. Lawrence Seaway. Dulles also had asked for authorization to discuss with the British the possibility of the Queen's touring the middle and western states. Dulles added that if Eisenhower wanted the British monarchs to visit Washington, D.C., he would propose it to the Ambassador.

On June 26, 1959, Queen Elizabeth II and President Eisenhower would attend the formal dedication of the St. Lawrence Seaway at St. Lambert, Quebec—the point where the Seaway begins to make its long course to the Great Lakes. Following the ceremonies the President would host a luncheon aboard the royal yacht *Britannia* (Ann Whitman memorandum, June 26, 1958, AWF/AWD, and *New York Times*, June 27, 1958). For background on the St. Lawrence Seaway, which opened the upper St. Lawrence River and the Great Lakes to Atlantic shipping, see Galambos and van Ee, *The Middle Way*, no. 114.

To Theodore Francis Green   *October 2, 1958*

Dear Senator Green: I acknowledge your letter of September twenty-ninth with reference to the situation in the Far East.[1] I note that you are concerned that the United States might become involved in hostilities in defense of Quemoy and Matsu; that it does not appear to you that Quemoy is vital to the defense of Formosa or the United States; that in such hostilities we would be without allies, and, finally, that military involvement in the defense of Quemoy would not command that support of the American people essential to successful military action.

Let me take up these points in order:

1. Neither you nor any other American need feel that the United States will be involved in military hostilities merely in defense of Quemoy or Matsu. I am quite aware of the fact that the Joint Resolution of Congress (January 29, 1955), which authorized the President to employ the armed forces of the United States in the Formosa area, authorized the securing and protection of such positions as Quemoy and Matsu only if the President judges that to be required or appropriate in assuring the defense of Formosa and the Pescadores.[2]

I shall scrupulously observe that limitation contained in the Congressional authority granted me.

2. The Congressional Resolution had, of course, not merely negative but positive implications. I shall also observe these. I note that it does not appear to you that Quemoy is vital to the defense of Formosa or the United States. But the test which the Congress established was whether or not the defense of these positions was judged by the President to be required or appropriate in assuring the defense of Formosa. The Congressional Resolution conferring that responsibility on the President was adopted by almost unanimous vote of both Houses of the Congress. Since then the people of the United States reelected me to be that President. I shall, as President and Commander-in-Chief of the Armed Forces of the United States, exercise my lawful authority and judgment in discharging the responsibility thus laid upon me.[3]

I welcome the opinions and counsel of others. But in the last analysis such opinions cannot legally replace my own.

The Chinese and Soviet Communist leaders assert, and have reason to believe, that if they can take Quemoy and Matsu by armed assault that will open the way for them to take Formosa and the Pescadores and, as they put it, "expel" the United States from the West Pacific and cause its Fleet to leave international waters and "go home."

I cannot dismiss these boastings as mere bluff. Certainly there is always the possibility that it may in certain contingencies, after taking account of all relevant facts, become necessary or appropriate for the defense of Formosa and the Pescadores also to take measures to secure and protect the related positions of Quemoy and Matsu.

I am striving to the best of my ability to avoid hostilities; to achieve a cease-fire, and a reasonable adjustment of the situation. You, I think, know my deep dedication to peace. It is second only to my dedication to the safety of the United States and its honorable discharge of obligations to its allies and to world order which have been assumed by constitutional process. We must not forget that the whole Formosa Straits situation is intimately connected with the security of the United States and the free world.[4]

3. You say that in the event of hostilities we would be without allies "in fact or in heart." Of course, no nation other than the Republic of China has a treaty alliance with us in relation to the Formosa area. That is a well known fact—known to the Congress when it adopted the Formosa Joint Resolution and known to the Senate when it approved of our Treaty of Mutual Security with the Republic of China.[5] But if you mean that the United States action in standing firm against armed Communist assault would not have the approval of our allies, then I believe that you are misinformed. Not only do I believe that our friends and allies would support the United States if hostilities should tragically, and against our will,[6] be forced upon us, I believe that most of them would be appalled if the United States were spinelessly to retreat before the threat of Sino-Soviet armed aggression.

4. Finally, you state that even if the United States should become engaged in hostilities, there would not be "that support of the American people essential to successful military action."

With respect to those islands, I have often pointed out that the only way the United States could become involved in hostilities would be because of its firm stand against Communist attempts to gain their declared aims by force. I have also often said that firmness in supporting principle makes war less, rather than more, likely of occurrence.[7]

I feel certain, beyond the shadow of a doubt, that if the United States became engaged in hostilities on account of the evil and aggressive assaults of the forces of Communism, the American people would unite as one to assure the success and triumph of our effort.

I deeply deplore the effect upon hostile forces of a statement that if we became engaged in battle, the United States would be defeated because of disunity at home. If that were believed, it would embolden our enemies and make almost inevitable the conflict which,

I am sure, we both seek to avoid provided it can be avoided consistently with the honor and security of our country.

Though in this letter I have explained the facts and the principles that guide the government in dealing with the critical Formosa Straits situation, I cannot close without saying that our whole effort is now, and has always been, the preservation of a peace with honor and with justice. After all, this is the basic aspiration of all Americans, indeed of all peoples.

Inasmuch as there have been public reports on the essence of your letter, I feel I should make this reply public.[8]

With great respect and best wishes. *Sincerely*

[1] For background on the ninety-one-year-old senator, Chairman of the Foreign Relations Committee, see Galambos and van Ee, *The Middle Way*, nos. 806 and 2090; on the situation in the Formosa Straits see no. 838. Green's letter is in the same file as the document. Arguing that Congress should be called back into session to deal with the emergency, he expressed his fear of "military involvement at the wrong time" and "in the wrong place." He also told Eisenhower that his decision to send the letter had involved "a great deal of soul-searching."

Eisenhower met with Dulles for an hour earlier on this same day to review the State Department draft of this letter (see Dulles, Memorandum of Conversation, Oct. 2, 1958, Dulles Papers, White House Memoranda Series; Ann Whitman memorandum, Oct. 2, 1958, AWF/AWD; and Bernau to Dulles, Oct. 2, 1958, Dulles Papers, Telephone Conversations; see also Nelson to Macomber, Oct. 1, 1958, same file as document. Two drafts, with Eisenhower's handwritten emendations, are in AWF/D-H). Vice-President Nixon would later tell Dulles that he thought that former Secretary of State Dean Acheson had written Green's letter. Dulles, however, thought the author was *New York Times* writer James Reston, who, he said, was "unhappy" because he was "not running" the State Department (Telephone conversation, Oct. 7, 1958, Dulles Papers, Telephone Conversations).

[2] For background on the Joint Resolution see Galambos and van Ee, *The Middle Way*, no. 1265.

[3] Eisenhower added the preceding eight words to the State Department draft.

[4] The President added the concluding sentence of this paragraph.

[5] On the Mutual Security Treaty, signed in 1954, see *ibid.*

[6] Eisenhower added the preceding five words.

[7] The President added this paragraph. Eisenhower also deleted what would have been the first sentence of the following paragraph: "It indeed shocks me that you should hold, express and circulate the sentiment that the United States should abandon principle in favor of immediate expediency." The deletion may have resulted from the urging of White House staff members; see Ann Whitman memorandum, Oct. 3, 1958, AWF/AWD.

[8] For discussions regarding the publication of this letter see Dulles, Memorandum of Conversation, Oct. 2, 1958, Dulles Papers, White House Memoranda Series. The White House would release this letter to the press on October 5 (*Public Papers of the Presidents: Eisenhower, 1958*, pp. 723–25). For developments see no. 883.

To Ralph Emerson McGill   *October 3, 1958*

Dear Ralph: Shortly before we left Newport, Jim Hagerty showed me your letter of the sixteenth and I asked for the privilege of replying to it. Since that time, as you know, I have had more than the usual number of things on my plate and, of course, one of the principal points of concern has been the series of maneuvers in the integration issue.[1]

It is quite possible that your statement that the schools must be closed for a period before there is hope of acceptance of the decision is a correct one.[2] I tend to believe that the students themselves will eventually resolve the issue, merely by their desire to have the educational processes resumed, despite the objections they may have to the conditions under which it may proceed. Incidentally, it is curious how the extra-curricular activities of school life—the football team, the band, etc.—seem to become more important levers in urging the reopening of the schools than does educational opportunity. The children will likely be helpful in bringing pressure upon parents, school boards, and local authorities, for the reopening of the schools.

I, too, am heartened by the shrinking perimeter of the area where prejudices of this kind run so deep.[3] This is a difficult period for all of us, but there must, somewhere, be the common sense and the good will on the part of all to bring about a solution.[4]

With warm regard, *As ever*

[1] McGill, editor of the *Atlanta Constitution,* had written White House Press Secretary Hagerty on September 16, 1958, about the Supreme Court decision (Sept. 12) to reject the Little Rock school board's appeal for a delay in the racial integration of Central High School (for background see no. 840; for Eisenhower's response to the announcement see *Public Papers of the Presidents: Eisenhower, 1958,* p. 701; see also *New York Times,* Sept. 13, 1958). McGill had written that the Court's action was "enormously helpful in that it restores the image of inevitability of the court's decision. This has been considerably blurred by the declaration of Southern governors and senators and White Citizens Council groups that the court had acted unconstitutionally and, therefore, what they ordered was illegal and not binding" (see no. 427; see also Burk, *The Eisenhower Administration and Black Civil Rights,* pp. 191–206).

[2] Arkansas Governor Faubus had immediately responded to the Supreme Court's September 12 decision by closing all four high schools in Little Rock and by signing into law measures that gave him sweeping discretionary power over the state's educational system, including the right to close schools. Virginia's governor had also closed three schools in Charlottesville and Front Royal (see *New York Times,* Sept. 13, 18, 1958). McGill had written that he and others in the Deep South had "known all along that schools would have to be closed before there could be any hope of acceptance of the decision." He was sure that Eisenhower and Attorney General Rogers understood that while such a step was "tragic and painful," there was "no other way out of it, and any appeasement of it would be disastrous in the long run." In a let-

ter to the chairman of a Charlottesville, Virginia, committee dedicated to reopening the closed schools, Eisenhower had deplored the school closings and warned that the racial issue could have "disastrous" consequences for the children involved and for the country (see Rolston to Eisenhower, Sept. 17, and Eisenhower to Rolston, Sept. 24, 1958; see also *New York Times*, Sept. 26, 1958, and *Public Papers of the Presidents: Eisenhower, 1958*, pp. 705–6).

[3] McGill had written that the "number of states offering total resistance dwindled to five: Virginia, Alabama, Mississippi, South Carolina and Georgia." He had excluded Arkansas, he said, because "a number of cities there are managing to go ahead with desegregation." All correspondence is in the same file as the document.

[4] For developments see no. 889.

880 *EM, WHCF, Official File 138-A-9*

To Richard King Mellon *October 6, 1958*
Personal

Dear Dick: In my letter the other day I touched lightly on the subject that we discussed at length during the time we had in Ligonier together—the current political campaign.[1] More and more I am becoming convinced that the real issue in this political campaign is whether or not we can defeat the fiscal irresponsibility that is typical of the ADA-CIO school of thinking.[2] It is characteristic of such people to insist upon higher and higher Federal expenditures, regardless of the size of deficits and the country's increasing inability to manage its debt economically and effectively. I deeply believe that moderate government is the only thing that can stop the United States from sliding more and more toward mortgaging the future. Unless stopped, this will bring financial difficulties that would be bound to bring about profound changes in the procedures of our government, possibly even in its form.[3]

I can sum up my belief in what every man and woman of integrity should do in the simple statement that only by getting into politics up to our necks can we reverse these unfortunate trends. If the people of the country do not take their political responsibilities seriously, they are, in my opinion, going to find that the system of free enterprise that has brought our country to its height will be badly hurt. I know that the Gulf Oil Company has made a good effort to encourage workers at the precinct level, and I congratulate you and your associates on taking the much-needed initiative in this area.[4] I would like to see more and more companies adopt your techniques. (As a matter of fact, I am having a dinner at the White House tonight to express my views in person to some of my business friends whom I have not had a chance to see of late).[5]

Incidentally, I have heard that Joe Pew is among the Republicans who are seemingly apathetic about this year's campaign.[6] Is there anything you can do to get him on the ball?

I started this letter merely to tell you how gratified I was by your phone call to Tom Stephens saying that money for the specific project we discussed had been raised and that you felt you might even exceed the needed amount.[7] I am more than grateful for your help.[8]

With warm regard, *As ever*

[1] Eisenhower's letter of September 27 is no. 866.

[2] See no. 826.

[3] See, for example, no. 784.

[4] In a letter to employees, shareholders, and gasoline dealers, dated September 9, 1958, and published in the Gulf Oil Corporation in-house newsletter, a senior vice-president had said: "If we are to survive, labor's political power must now be opposed by matching force, and there is no place in the United States where such a force can be generated except among corporations that make up American business." He added that Gulf would now supply employees with information on the views, attendance and voting records of senators and congressman. All people affiliated with Gulf were urged to work actively on behalf of those candidates deemed worthy of support. Gulf along with all other American corporations, was involved "up to its ears" in politics, and "must start swimming or drown." The letter received widespread publicity in the *New York Herald Tribune* and in *Fortune* (October 1958) magazine.

[5] That evening the President would host an off-the-record stag dinner at the White House. The twenty-five person guest list would include the presidents of Boeing Airplane Company; Owens-Corning Fiberglas Corporation; Cluett, Peabody & Company, Inc.; Rexall Drug Company; Ford Motor Company; Richfield Oil Corporation; Sears, Roebuck & Company; International Business Machines Corporation; and United Air Lines; and the chairmen of U.S. Steel Corporation; General Electric Company; Firestone Tire and Rubber Company; National Steel Corporation; Cities Service Companies; Republic Steel Corporation; and the Coca-Cola Company.

[6] Joseph Newton Pew, Jr. (M.E. Cornell 1908) had been with the Sun Oil Company since 1908, and had served as its chairman since 1947.

[7] Mellon had financed a television advertisement by Harold Stassen on behalf of Hugh Scott, Pennsylvania Republican senatorial candidate (see Ann Whitman memorandum, Sept. 26, 1958, AWF/AWD).

[8] Mellon would respond on October 9, 1958. While he was in "complete agreement" with Eisenhower's views concerning the danger to the economy posed by "the ADA-CIO school," he was skeptical about Gulf's activities. "I am heartily in favor of corporate officers and employees as good citizens playing their part in political campaigns," he wrote, "but I believe it is dangerous for the corporations as such to enter such campaigns. This may not only be illegal, but could boomerang seriously on our system and on good labor relationships." The President would quote Mellon's comments in a letter to Cliff Roberts (Oct. 14, 1958). All correspondence is in the same file as the document.

To Benjamin Franklin Fairless   *October 6, 1958*
Personal

Dear Ben: I feel badly that, in the confusion at Ligonier, I did not recognize Arnold Palmer as the 1958 winner of the Masters. I have written him a note of explanation.[1]

Your statement that you are working hard in your area to overcome the apathy that exists in Republican ranks gratifies and encourages me.[2] As you may have seen, I tried in my press conference Wednesday to give a general pep talk on the subject. Today I am having two meetings to try to express my views, one with legislative leaders and one with some of my business friends with whom I have not yet had a chance to communicate.[3] I feel so strongly about the seeming drift in this country toward fiscal irresponsibility, with all its resulting evils, and toward Federal control of more and more phases in the life of every individual, that I think all businessmen like yourself, and indeed all the hardworking men and women of integrity throughout the country, whose livelihoods depend upon the existence of our free enterprise system, ought to think very seriously of their political duties. "Get into politics or get kicked out of free business"—unfortunately it seems to me just as simple as that.

I did not mean to make a small speech, but at the same time I feel strongly that a statement such as I have suggested above is just about the core of the situation. At any rate, many thanks for your help—and please keep on working just as hard as you can![4]

With warm regard, *As ever*

---

[1] On the President's trip to Ligonier, Pennsylvania, see no. 866. Twenty-nine-year-old golfer Arnold Daniel Palmer had attended Wake Forest College and had won the U.S. Amateur Golf Tournament in 1954. He had turned professional later that year. He had won the 1958 Masters Tournament (the first of four Masters victories) with a four-day total score of 284. Former U.S. Steel President Fairless, who had introduced him to the President during the ceremonies at Fort Ligonier on September 26, had described him as "a fine young man" who was "very anxious to play a round of golf with you at the Augusta National anytime you are available" (Fairless to Eisenhower, Sept. 30, same file as document). On October 2 Eisenhower had written Palmer to apologize for his "lack of reaction" and to extend his belated but warm congratulations on his victory. He added that he would "very much like" to play golf with Palmer but feared that he "would be more than embarrassed" due to the poor quality of his recent rounds (WHCF/PPF 1829).
[2] Fairless had told Eisenhower, who had urged him to generate support for the Republican cause (see no. 864), that he was "fully aware of the political situation" and was "busily engaged in doing everything" he could to help. He noted that he was sponsoring a luncheon for Vice-President Richard Nixon in Pittsburgh on October 10.

[3] See the preceding document and no. 905 for Eisenhower's meeting with business leaders. On the President's meeting with legislative leaders see nos. 884 and 885.

[4] Pennsylvania Republicans would not fare well in the November elections. Although they would elect Hugh D. Scott to the Senate (see no. 897), they would also lose three seats (and control of their state's congressional delegation) in the House of Representatives. In addition, the Democrats would defeat the Republican candidate for governor (see no. 594) and would gain control of the lower house of the state legislature (*New York Times*, Nov. 6, 1958).

882   *EM, AWF, DDE Diaries Series*

To George Magoffin Humphrey   *October 6, 1958*

Dear George: As regard the first point in your letter, there is no possibility that I can come to Ohio during this campaign, and Mrs. Whitman tells me she has already written Mr. Lowe to so inform him.[1]

The only definite thing I can say about my hoped-for trip to Cedar Point is that the period of the 9th to the 11th is definitely out since I am committed to a speech in Seattle on the 10th (the Colombo Nations meeting). We shall have to see later if we can work out some other period.[2]

As to your suggestion that we try Thomasville early in December, I have always gone to Augusta some time during late November or early December (really it is the most satisfactory time of the year to be there) and had planned, everything being equal, to do so again this year.[3] This of course means that I have to watch out not to be too much away from the White House or there will be the usual uproar in the newspapers.[4] On top of all this—Mamie is trying to bring her mother back to Washington.[5] Just what will happen and how this may disarrange my schedule, I do not know.

So for the time being, let's leave everything in abeyance; perhaps after the election we can come out of the woods and take a better look at my calender.

With warm regard, *As ever*

P.S. It is just possible that on the way out to Seattle I might work something out. I will let you know as soon as possible.[6]

[1] The President was scheduled to campaign for Republicans in the upcoming midterm elections in Iowa, Kansas, Colorado, California, Illinois, Pennsylvania, and West Virginia (see nos. 898 and 909). We have been unable to identify Lowe.

[2] In November 1954 Eisenhower had enjoyed duck hunting as Humphrey's guest at the Cedar Point Club at Maumee Bay, on Lake Erie, twenty miles from Toledo, Ohio (see Galambos and van Ee, *The Middle Way*, no. 1144). On November 8 the President would fly to Tacoma, Washington, to stay with his brother Edgar until the morning of November 10 (see no. 903). The Consultative Committee of the Colombo Plan

for Cooperative Economic Development in Southeast Asia would meet for the first time in the United States in Seattle, Washington, November 10–13. Eisenhower would formally open the conference by addressing cabinet-level delegations of eighteen countries and three colonies (see no. 900; *Public Papers of the Presidents: Eisenhower, 1958*, pp. 839–47; and *New York Times*, Nov. 11, 1958).

[3] For background on Eisenhower's midwinter vacations at Humphrey's Milestone Plantation in Thomasville, Georgia, see no. 7. For developments see no. 892.

[4] On the press's criticism of the President's recreational activities see, for example, nos. 97 and 657 in these volumes, and Galambos and van Ee, *The Middle Way*, no. 439. See also no. 104.

[5] On Mrs. Eisenhower's mother's failing health see nos. 612 and 1297.

[6] Later this evening Humphrey would attend Eisenhower's stag dinner at the White House. For developments see no. 892.

883   *EW, AWF, Dulles-Herter Series*

To John Foster Dulles   *October 7, 1958*
Personal and confidential

Memorandum for the Secretary of State: You will recall that from Newport I telephoned you concerning an idea that had to do with the offshore islands in the Formosa Straits.[1] My thought was that Chiang might be sold on the proposition that he would be in a better position to realize his purpose of retaining a capability for return to the mainland in the event of internal disorder, if he should acquire from the United States a strong amphibious lift and simultaneously remove all or nearly all his garrison from the offshore islands. Of course this would have to be a plan voluntarily adopted by him, during a period when there was no hostile action. Otherwise he would be acting under duress and this would be, of course, unacceptable.

I mentioned the same idea to George Yeh when he called on me recently.[2] The Ambassador seemed to be receptive to the idea but, we agreed, it would be necessary to have a cease fire so that the Nationalists would not seem to be retreating under fire.

Now it occurs to me that the current cease fire might give an opportunity during which this idea could be skillfully presented to Chiang, preferably by one of his own people—possibly Ambassador Yeh.[3]

As I suggested to you, this would restore a great mobility and flexibility to Chiang's force. It would remove the danger of getting involved in a severe battle under unfavorable conditions near the Chinese coastline. It would much improve Chiang's opportunity for intervention on the mainland if and when such a situation should arise. Furthermore, it would certainly give him and ourselves a better position before world opinion. Consequently our defensive alliance would be the stronger because of a unified public opinion at home.

Incidentally, I believe that we have a sufficient amount of unused amphibious equipment, including some escort vessels, that the transfer to Chiang of a number of them would have no harmful effects on our own position. Of course nothing formal can be suggested, but I do think it is the kind of thing that might appeal to Chiang, and if it did, it would offer great advantages to both of us.

I have no reason, naturally, for believing that Chiang would now be more receptive to this idea than he has been to similar ones suggested to him during recent years. However, it is possible that he may feel that conditions are changed and that if he had an amphibious capability that could lift in one load fifteen or twenty thousand troops, that he could sell both himself and his people on the proposition that by this action he would have increased his strength and his position in the area.[4]

[1] For background see nos. 838 and 844; see also State, *Foreign Relations, 1958–1960*, vol. XIX, *China*, pp. 143–328; and NSC meeting minutes, September 18, 25, October 3, 1958, AWF/NSC. Eisenhower had been vacationing in Newport from August 29 until September 23. During this period the Chinese Communists had continued to shell the islands of Quemoy and Matsu, making the movement of supplies to the garrisons difficult and at times impossible. At the same time, negotiations in Warsaw between the American and the Chinese ambassadors to Poland had made no progress toward a solution. Defense Secretary McElroy had told the President that the Joint Chiefs of Staff believed that "from the standpoint of military considerations alone, the islands should be vacated." Eisenhower agreed that it was "a military debit to hold them," but an evacuation, he said, could only occur after negotiations (Goodpaster, Memorandum of Conference, Sept. 15, 1958, AWF/D).

Eisenhower's plan to trade withdrawal for the provision to Chiang of amphibious capabilities, which White House naval aide Evan P. Aurand had first suggested to him, was based upon Chiang Kai-shek's statement that he must remain mobile if he ever hoped to reoccupy the mainland. Eisenhower proposed giving Chiang amphibious ships and reconditioned destroyers; such equipment would confer greater mobility than simply holding the offshore islands. Any training the United States provided, the President told Dulles, would be less expensive than maintaining the Seventh Fleet in the area. Eisenhower had also advised Dulles that he was worried that they were "doing nothing to convert Chiang to flexibility" and suggested "dangling" before him the capacity to lift the garrison (Telephone conversations, Sept. 16, 22, 1958, Dulles Papers, Telephone Conversations).

[2] Eisenhower had met with the Chinese ambassador on September 30 (see Ann Whitman memorandum, Sept. 30, 1958, AWF/AWD).

[3] On the preceding day the Chinese Communists had announced that they would suspend bombardment of the islands for one week and would allow the resupply of the Nationalist garrison on the condition that no American ships would come within the twelve-mile international limit (State, *Foreign Relations, 1958–1960*, vol. XIX, *China*, pp. 329–34; State, *American Foreign Policy, Current Documents, 1958*, pp. 1172–73; see also Herter to Drumright, Oct. 5, 1958, State, *Foreign Relations, 1958–1960*, vol. XIX, *China*, Microfiche Supplement, no. 186; and Christensen, *Useful Adversaries*, pp. 197–98).

[4] On the following day reports from the U.S. Taiwan Defense Command would indicate that supplies were reaching the islands without problems and that the morale of the Nationalist troops was high. Dulles would tell other State Department officials that the cease-fire had presented opportunities to change the status quo in the direction of demilitarization of the islands. He would inform Ambassador Yeh that the initiative lay with Chiang Kai-shek and that he would be willing to travel to Taipei and speak with him directly regarding a new policy (State, *Foreign Relations, 1958–1960*, vol. XIX, *China*, pp. 348–61). For developments see no. 907.

884

To Neil Hosler McElroy   *October 7, 1958*
Personal

Dear Neil: Yesterday I had two political meetings, one of Republican Congressional leaders and the other of prominent businessmen.[1] In both meetings reports were made that our side is suffering because of incorrect but unrefuted partisan charges of inexcusable failures in the Defense Department. Several of the Senators present voiced the conviction that unless you could be available in the late days of the campaign to get the record at least partially corrected, in the next session we would be much weakened in our efforts to develop and maintain an efficient and well-balanced defense.[2]

These leaders, and also the businessmen, were aware of the American Legion speech that you made and thought that it was well done.[3] But they report that at least two opposition and prominent Senators are going throughout the country, with the special mission of charging neglect, incompetence and so on in the Defense Department.[4]

I shall suggest to the Republican National Chairman that he might utilize Secretary Brucker, and possibly Douglas and Gates.[5] But none of these, of course, has the prestige and public relations value that you do.

I realize that you and I thought that your American Legion speech would keep the situation on an even keel. Now it seems that the Congressional leaders who have been our great Defense supporters, as well as the businessmen, are fearful of the consequences of your inability to appear in the campaign.

It may not be possible for you to shorten or curtail your trip without extreme embarrassment to yourself or to our relations with others. However, I suggest that if you should [find] it practical to reduce the duration of your trip sufficiently to allow several public appearances before the election, it would strengthen the morale of our side and would certainly not lessen the respect of the other.[6]

In the public appearances for which I am scheduled, I shall of course take the opportunity to try to reassure our people on this matter, but naturally I cannot make the national defense establishment the single subject of any address while what we apparently need is repeated presentations on this one vitally important subject.

Would you give me your thoughts on this subject?

With warm regard, *As ever*

[1] On Eisenhower's dinner with Republican business leaders see no. 880. On that same day, the President had also hosted a luncheon for Republican congressional leaders, including Senators Leverett Saltonstall, Andrew F. Schoeppel, Wallace F. Bennett, Everett M. Dirksen, and Prescott Bush, and Congressmen Joseph W. Martin, Jr., Leo E. Allen, Leslie C. Arends, Charles A. Halleck, and Richard M. Simpson.

[2] The President had written a similar letter to Treasury Secretary Anderson (see the following document, no. 885). On the election campaign see no. 842.

[3] In a speech to the fortieth annual convention of the American Legion, the Defense Secretary had said that the United States was ahead of the Soviet Union in over-all military power. Although he had conceded that Russia was ahead of the United States in the development of an intercontinental ballistic missile, he believed the United States was "at the point where the spending of more tax dollars would at this time be an unwarranted risk of your money." McElroy warned that "if the United States continued to 'rack up huge deficits,' the foundations of prosperity would be eroded" (*New York Times*, Sept. 3, 1958).

[4] Eisenhower would discuss the matter with Deputy Defense Secretary Quarles, who told the President that he and all the service secretaries stood ready to help. Eisenhower believed it was "extremely important that someone get out and refute some of the statements" that were being made. The President named Senators Stuart Symington of Missouri and John F. Kennedy of Massachusetts as the source of some of the attacks (Goodpaster, Memorandum of Conference, Oct. 8, 1958, AWF/D). In September Kennedy had charged that despite Republican claims that they were "the party of peace," American troops were in Lebanon, the American Navy patrolled the Taiwan Straits and the United States had "teetered consistently on the brink of foreign wars no American wants or could even explain" (*New York Times*, Sept. 11, 1958). Symington had charged that the United States was guilty of a "lack of any real production effort in our long-range missile plans and programs . . ." (*New York Times*, Sept. 1, 1958).

[5] Eisenhower was referring to Army Secretary Wilber M. Brucker, Navy Secretary Thomas S. Gates, Jr., and Secretary of the Air Force, James H. Douglas, Jr.

[6] McElroy would not return early from his trip. On October 9 the Defense Secretary would write the President stating his reluctance to return to Washington (AWF/A). "I find that my trip out here is regarded by foreign officials at all levels as one of extraordinary importance because of its coinciding with the tension in the Taiwan area," he would say. Citing meetings with top leaders in Japan and Korea, dinners with heads of governments and special arrangements planned for his entire itinerary, McElroy asked Eisenhower to "understand the degree to which a cancellation of my trip would be upsetting to our relationships with free world governments."

McElroy would also warn the President that there could be "deleterious" political fallout from a premature return. On October 9 Eisenhower would send a message to the Defense Secretary in Seoul, Korea, stating: "I understand the situation as described in your message. Please carry on with your trip" (AWF/A).

TO ROBERT BERNERD ANDERSON   *October 7, 1958*
Cable. Personal

Dear Bob:[1] Yesterday I had two political meetings, one of which was with Republican leaders of the House and Senate and the other with a large group of business executives, most of whom you know well.[2]

In both groups there was a strong recommendation advanced that you come home as soon as your duties there will permit to make a number of public appearances for the purpose of explaining clearly and carefully the fiscal situation, including its causes, effects, and programs to improve it.[3]

This cable is just to request that if you can foresee a return date that will give you an opportunity for such public appearances, that you so inform Chairman Alcorn and allow him, in cooperation with your Under Secretary, to set up several such appearances for you.

If, of course, you cannot reach here in time, there is nothing to be done. But I do assure you that both the political leaders and the business community are greatly concerned that your authoritative voice in this matter is not being heard to refute some of the partisan statements and charges that are, of course, made only for political purposes.[4]

I do hope that you are finding the meeting interesting and fruitful and, of course, warm personal regard to yourself. *As ever*

[1] On October 3 Treasury Secretary Anderson had traveled to New Delhi, India, to attend the week-long annual meeting of the International Monetary Fund and the International Bank for Reconstruction and Development (the World Bank Group). Anderson served as U.S. governor of both institutions. For background on Eisenhower's authorization to propose expansion of the Bank and IMF see no. 831; see also *New York Times*, Oct. 4, 11, 12, 1958.

[2] The President had given a luncheon for political leaders and had hosted an off-the-record stag dinner for businessmen at the White House. For the names of the attendees see the President's daily appointments, and Ann Whitman memorandum, Oct. 6, 1958, AWF/AWD; see also Whitman's diary entry, Oct. 6, 1958, *ibid.*

[3] On the economic recession, which had resulted in a federal budget deficit, see nos. 784 and 897. On Eisenhower's frustration regarding statements about GOP hopelessness (see nos. 842 and 864). The President sent a similar letter to Secretary of Defense McElroy (see the preceding document).

[4] Anderson would reply (Oct. 9, AWF/A) that he had consulted with State Department officials and they decided that cancellation at this late date would be "badly misinterpreted" and perhaps "more damaging" than the benefits rendered if he made appearances in the United States. He was scheduled to leave New Delhi on October 12 to visit with Foreign Ministers in Bombay, Madras, Colombo, Bangkok, Hong Kong, Taipei, and Tokyo. Both of his Under Secretaries of State, he wrote, had arranged to be available to address fiscal matters in the next weeks. Anderson would return to Washington on November 1, and he would meet with the President at the

White House on November 3 (see Anderson's itinerary in AWF/A). For developments see no. 917.

886   *EM, AWF, Administration Series*

To Arthur Frank Burns   *October 7, 1958*

Dear Arthur: Many thanks for your paragraphs on the economy and related subjects. All of your ideas I endorse, and I am grateful to you for setting them down for me so succinctly.[1]

I have only one comment. I am convinced it is the union leaders, rather than the rank and file of union membership, that tend toward non-cooperation with management. Of course we have said this many times.[2]

Finally, I particularly like items #6 and #7.[3]

With gratitude and, as always, warm personal regard, *As ever*

[1] Burns had written on October 1 (AWF/A) in response to Eisenhower's September 29 request for suggestions for "three or four" paragraphs he could use in election speeches on the economy (see no. 869).
[2] Burns had written: "Private business must do everything in their power to increase productivity, eliminate waste, and reduce prices instead of raising them. These efforts, however, will prove of little avail unless trade unions cooperate with management." Eisenhower had handwritten "leaders" after "trade unions" on Burns's letter.
[3] In item #6, Burns had suggested that the government could not expect businesses and trade unions to follow "a policy of moderation" unless it set an example itself. The government, he argued, should keep both the money supply and federal expenditures from growing at an excessive rate. Item #7 had attacked Congress for going "far beyond what was essential" in appropriations for expenditures.

887   *Dulles Papers,*
                                            White House Memoranda Series

To John Foster Dulles   *October 9, 1958*

Foster:[1] If invited (and we deem wise to comply) to send a representative to Pope's funeral my present thought is as follows:[2]

Provided, only a *one* day stay in Rome is expected or required, <u>you</u> could be the most effective representative.

If only 2 or 3 days required—Mitchell might be best. If longer, McCone.[3]

[1] Eisenhower had handwritten this memorandum and given it to Secretary Dulles at the Cabinet meeting on this same day (see Note, Oct. 10, 1958, Dulles Papers, White House Memoranda Series; see also Telephone conversation, Dulles and Persons, Oct. 8, 1958, *ibid.*).

[2] Pope Pius XII had died of a stroke on the preceding evening at the Papal retreat at Castel Gandolfo. He had suffered a similar stroke two days earlier.

[3] In a subsequent meeting with Eisenhower, Dulles would agree to attend the principal ceremony and would ask Labor Secretary James P. Mitchell and former U.S. Ambassador to Italy Clare Booth Luce to accompany him. Mitchell would decline because of prior engagements, but Atomic Energy Commission Chairman John A. McCone would accept the assignment (Ann Whitman memorandum, Oct. 9, 1958, AWF/AWD; see also Telephone conversations, Dulles and Eisenhower, Murphy, Mitchell, and Luce, Oct. 9, 1958, Dulles Papers, Telephone Conversations). Eisenhower's three representatives would leave on October 17 and attend the solemn requiem mass in St. Peter's Basilica three days later. Dulles would then go on to Taipei for consultations with President Chiang (see no. 907). McCone would return to the United States immediately, and Luce would remain in Rome for several days. On October 28 Angelo Giuseppe Roncalli would become Pope John XXIII (*New York Times*, Oct. 9, 14, 16, 29; see also Dulles, Memorandum of Conversation, Oct. 24, 1958, Dulles Papers, White House Memoranda Series).

888
                                           EM, WHCF,
President's Personal File 1834

To Justin Whitlock Dart   *October 9, 1958*

Dear Justin: Since I know you are vitally concerned lest other fine young men in the Air Force contract polio, as did your son, I want you to know that I followed up on our recent conversation.[1] I am told while it is current practice to inoculate all young men in the Air Force when they enter the service, it is not mandatory. Further, there seems to be some difference of opinion among the experts on the certainty of the protection afforded by the Salk vaccine. As a result of my request, the Defense Department is taking another look at the problem to see if uniform mandatory practices should be adopted.[2]

I hope that your son continues to improve. Please give him my warm good wishes.[3]

With warm personal regard, *Sincerely*

[1] Following Eisenhower's September 27 meeting with Dart, the President had queried Acting Secretary of Defense Quarles regarding immunization against poliomyelitis (see no. 871).

[2] On November 12 Quarles would report that the Department of Defense had decided to administer the complete Salk series to all new personnel entering the military service as well as all military personnel under 40 years of age (same file as document). Eisenhower would thank Quarles on November 18 (AWF/A; McElroy Corr.).

[3] Notifying Dart of the Defense Department decision, the President would say he shared Dart's "personal regret" that "medical science was too late to prevent the attack of polio" that ruined the younger Dart's hopes for an Air Force career. Dart's "prodding," however, would prevent similar misfortunes in the future (Eisenhower to Dart, Nov. 17, 1958, same file as document).

On July 22, 1959, Peter Dart would report on his improving condition to Eisenhower and the President in reply (Sept. 28) would say that he admired Dart's courage and strength (*ibid.*).

889   *EM, WHCF, Official File 142-A-5*

To A. C. MILLER   *October 10, 1958*

Dear Mr. Miller: Thank you for your letter of October second.[1]

We must hope that all Americans, public officials and private citizens alike, will soon come to recognize their responsibility of providing equality of educational opportunity to all students in the nation's public schools, regardless of race.[2] When this equality is denied and some schools are officially closed, numbers of young people are being deprived, even though temporarily, of normal schooling.[3] Unless there is real progress in correcting this situation, both the affected students and the nation will suffer.

Again let me express my appreciation of the support of the Christian Life Commission. With best wishes, *Sincerely*

[1] Miller was executive secretary of the Christian Life Commission of the Southern Baptist Convention, in Nashville, Tennessee. He had written on October 2 (same file as document) in support of the President's September 26 letter to the Committee for Public Education at Charlottesville, Virginia (see no. 879). "We agree heartily with you and there are large numbers of our constituency who support you in the views you have expressed," Miller had said. Eisenhower heavily edited the draft of this letter (AWF/D).

[2] The draft of this sentence had read, "It is evident that all Americans, public officials and private citizens alike, must recognize their duty of complying with the laws of the highest court in the land." Eisenhower had also deleted a sentence that read, "In this vital area of school desegregation, then, there can be no equivocation of responsibility for compliance."

[3] This sentence had originally read, "The greatest losers in this process appear to be some young people who are now being deprived, even though temporarily, of their normal schooling." In addition, Eisenhower had deleted the following: "I would hope that progress in this area may soon resume its movement forward."

To Iskander Mirza   *October 11, 1958*
Cable. Secret

Dear Mr. President: Thank you for your personal message regarding recent developments in your country, and for your assurance that Pakistan will honor its commitments and remain loyal to the free world.[1]

It is always a matter of regret to me, as it must be to you, when a government feels it necessary to resort to extraordinary political measures to avert a national catastrophe. I was therefore gratified by your statement that martial law will remain in effect for the shortest period possible. I understand it is your intention to devise a new constitution and to submit it to a popular referendum.

I can well understand how much deep and anxious thought must have preceded your decision to assume the heavy responsibilities which now rest upon your shoulders. I hardly need emphasize the bonds of friendship and common interest which unite our two peoples. I wish you every success in the momentous tasks of furthering the welfare of the Pakistan people and of re-establishing constitutional government in Pakistan.[2] *Sincerely*

---

[1] Political unrest and dissatisfaction with the government had increased in Pakistan during the summer months. On October 4 President Mirza had informed U.S. Ambassador James M. Langley of his plans; three days later he had declared martial law throughout the country, appointing General Ayub Khan as chief martial law administrator. He also annulled the constitution, dismissed the government of his prime minister, dissolved the national and provisional assemblies, and abolished all political parties. Mirza said that he had watched "with deepest anxiety" the corruption in the government and "the shameful exploitation" of the Pakistani people. Such activities, he said, had led "to a dictatorship of the lowest order," and elections scheduled for February 1959 would not improve the chaotic situation (State, *Foreign Relations, 1958–1960*, vol. XV, *South and Southeast Asia*, pp. 664–73; *New York Times*, Oct. 8, 9, 1958). Mirza had told Eisenhower that the constitution was unworkable under the present conditions and that martial law would be in effect for the shortest possible time. He had asked for Eisenhower's "sympathy and cooperation in the difficult period ahead" (Mirza to Eisenhower, Oct. 8, 1958, AWF/I: Pakistan). In his memorandum accompanying the State Department draft of this letter, Secretary Dulles had told Eisenhower that the reply was worded "to encourage the new regime not to rely indefinitely on authoritarian measures" as a means to maintain stability. After Eisenhower had approved the draft, it was cabled to Ambassador Langley for delivery to the Pakistani president (Dulles to Eisenhower, Oct. 10, 1958, *ibid.*).

[2] According to Langley, Mirza was pleased with Eisenhower's letter and indicated that he might release the text. State Department officials, however, would request that the text not be publicized (State, *Foreign Relations, 1958–1960*, vol. XV, *South and Southeast Asia*, p. 674). CIA Director Allen Dulles would tell the National Security Council that the takeover had proceeded calmly. The situation, he said, was typical of the difficulties involved in making democracy work in underdeveloped countries (NSC meeting minutes, Oct. 17, 1958, AWF/NSC). For developments see no. 1388.

To JOHN HAY WHITNEY   *October 13, 1958*

Dear Jock: Of course I understand the reason why you could not disrupt the reorganization of one of your companies. I understand,
though I have not been told directly, that temporary plans have been
made which make an immediate opening unnecessary for the individual in question.[1]

At any rate, your willingness to help is just another in a long list
of indebtednesses I owe to you.

I hope Betsey is feeling better.[2] Give her my affectionate regard
and to you, all the best as always. *As ever*

---

[1] After Eisenhower had asked Whitney to find a job for a person whom we have been
unable to identify, Whitney had written to apologize for his inability to find a "suitable opening" (Oct. 9, 1958, AWF/A). Whitney explained that the Great Northern
Paper Company recently had completed an extensive reorganization that had
brought many young people into key positions. "It was felt that the introduction of
a person of stature would do real harm to the morale of the new set-up, and to try
to do so on a purely non-functioning basis would be insulting and impossible," he
wrote. Whitney assured Eisenhower that he and his friends would continue to work
on the problem.

[2] On Mrs. Whitney's health see no. 825.

To GEORGE MAGOFFIN HUMPHREY   *October 13, 1958*

Dear George: There are, of course, two fund raising jobs to be done—
the short and long-range one. Your report as to the money raised
in Ohio is encouraging.[1]

Of course I understand about your trip to Brazil, and we will see
how things look about Cedar Point and Thomasville a little later.[2]
Meantime, I am concentrating, in what time I can manage away from
official duties, on the chores involved in the trip to the coast.[3] More
and more things that won't take "but a minute" seem alarmingly to
be creeping into the schedule.

With warm regard, *As ever*

---

[1] Humphrey had attended a stag dinner at the White House on October 6. To
Humphrey's mind the real problem for Republicans was putting into effect a fund-
raising "program of immediate and drastic action" to "produce results right now, not
for the long-term future." Humphrey reported that an additional $50,000 had been

collected in Ohio and he suggested that if similar donations would be collected in Massachusetts, Connecticut, New York, New Jersey, Pennsylvania, Illinois, California, Oklahoma, and Texas, "we'd be well on our way to solvency," with funding enough for whatever had to be done before the November 4 election. On the 1958 midterm elections and other GOP fund-raising efforts see nos. 880 and 926.

[2] Humphrey had invited Eisenhower to a duck hunt at the Cedar Point Club near Toledo, Ohio (see no. 882). The President would join Humphrey on November 7 and 8 (*New York Times*, Nov. 8, 1958).

Humphrey had also invited Eisenhower to spend the early part of December at his Milestone Plantation in Thomasville, Georgia. For several years the Eisenhowers had visited Humphrey in February, but Humphrey said he might be in Brazil in February 1959. As it turned out, the Eisenhowers would visit Humphrey's Milestone Plantation in February (see no. 1069). Meanwhile, they would vacation in Augusta, Georgia, from November 21 to December 2 (see nos. 949 and 953, and *New York Times*, Nov. 21–Dec. 3, 1958).

[3] On the President's campaign tour of the West see no. 898.

893   *EM, WHCF, Official File 102-I-2*

TO HELEN ROGERS REID   *October 14, 1958*

Dear Helen: While I appreciate your courtesy in offering your resignation as a member of the President's Committee on Government Contracts, I hope very much you will reconsider and stay on the Committee. I know that you are devoted to the furtherance of the Committee's objectives and I am told that you are one of its most effective and interested members. It would be difficult to find someone else of your knowledge and reputation, and I trust that you will agree to withdraw your suggestion.[1]

I am sure you are pleased that the negotiations with Jock were finally concluded; I know he will do everything possible to retain the Herald Tribune's fine standing in the newspaper world.[2]

With warm personal regard, *Sincerely*

[1] Mrs. Reid had written on October 8. She explained that Eisenhower had appointed her to the Committee on Government Contracts in 1953, when she was chairman of the board of the *New York Herald Tribune*. As she no longer held the post (see n. 2 below), she felt she should offer to resign. For background on the President's Committee on Government Contracts, established in August 1953 to supervise federal fair employment-policy practices in the performance of government contracts, see Galambos and van Ee, *The Middle Way*, nos. 382 and 385.

On October 13 Rocco C. Siciliano, Assistant to the President for Personnel Management since September 1957 (for background see *ibid.*, no. 360), had reported that Mrs. Reid contributed substantially to the committee and her activities were highly regarded (Siciliano to Whitman; see also memorandum, Whitman to Ferne, n.d.). On October 21 Mrs. Reid would thank Eisenhower for his letter and would agree to continue as a member of the committee.

² On British Ambassador Whitney's recent acquisition of the *New York Herald Tribune* see no. 825. Mrs. Reid said she was pleased with the new association with Whitney. The editorial philosophy of the paper, as well as its standards, remained unchanged, Mrs. Reid wrote, and this would encourage a "healthy competition" in New York City.
    All correspondence is in the same file as the document.

894 *EM, AWF, DDE Diaries Series*

To Richard Milhous Nixon *October 15, 1958*

Dear Dick: In my press conference this morning a question was posed to me asking whether or not I approved certain statements you were alleged to have made about foreign policy.¹ Just before the conference began I learned that some words from the Secretary of State had been taken as disapproval of something you had said and that he, Dulles, had thereupon disavowed any intention of disagreeing with your stand.²

For my part I merely said that as a matter of basic principle the theory of bipartisanship in foreign affairs had to be pursued for the good of all Americans. However, I pointed out that I did not object to others questioning and criticizing detailed operations in the foreign field and that if they did make such criticism that people on our side would reply. I think no explanation is necessary in order to assure you of my confidence in your judgment and loyalty to the Party and to the Administration.

Incidentally I have just now had an opportunity to read the talks Miss Woods sent over just before you left; I think they are excellent.³

I have had reports concerning your campaign efforts, and I am under the impression that you have been most successful in awakening our people to the grave issues in this political campaign and the need for supporting Republicanism enthusiastically.

If there exists in your mind any possible misunderstanding, please call me on the telephone at your convenience. I shall be available this evening only from six to seven-thirty Washington time, but I shall be here all day tomorrow, in case you should call.⁴

With warm regard, and appreciation of your strenuous and effective efforts, *As ever*

¹ In a speech in Chicago at the beginning of his third election campaign tour Vice-President Nixon had accused the Democrats of retaining the "same defensive, defeatist, fuzzy-headed" foreign policy that former Secretary of State Dean Acheson had formulated. Nixon was responding to a statement made by the Democratic National Committee's foreign policy advisory council that had challenged the Republicans to defend Eisenhower's record. "In a nutshell," he had told the audience, "the

Acheson foreign policy resulted in war and the Eisenhower-Dulles policy resulted in peace" (*New York Times*, Oct. 14, 1958). When asked about Nixon's statement, Eisenhower had said that he subscribed to the theory that foreign policy should not be part of partisan debate. "I realize," however, "that when someone makes a charge, another individual is going to reply. I deplore that" (*Public Papers of the Presidents: Eisenhower, 1958*, pp. 740–41).

[2] Secretary Dulles had said that he hoped that the leaders of both political parties would "calm down" and refrain from interjecting current topical aspects of foreign policy into the election campaign (*U.S. Department of State Bulletin* 39, no. 1010 [November 3, 1958], 681–88). After Dulles learned of Nixon's concern that he and the President had not been supportive, he had subsequently defended the Vice-President in a statement intended to clarify his remarks. Dulles said that he had intended his criticism for the Democratic National Committee, and he supported Nixon for his answer to the committee's challenge. "I would, however, have preferred it if the Democratic Advisory Committee had not issued its highly partisan political challenge, so that no reply would have been required" (Dulles Statement, Oct. 15, 1958, Dulles Papers, Telephone Conversations; see also Telephone conversations, Dulles and Hagerty, Oct. 15, 1958; and Dulles and Nixon, Sept. 29, 1958, Dulles Papers, Telephone Conversations). Dulles had admitted to Press Secretary Hagerty that he had caused the problem at his press conference, and he claimed that Eisenhower's statement had perpetuated it. The President had not had time to read Dulles's explanatory statement carefully before he had made his remarks to the press, Hagerty said (Telephone conversations, Dulles and Hagerty, Oct. 15, 16, 1958; Dulles and Macomber, Oct. 15, 1958; and Dulles and Persons, Oct. 16, 1958).

[3] Rose Mary Woods was Nixon's personal secretary.

[4] For developments see the following document.

895   *EM, AWF, Administration Series*

To Richard Milhous Nixon   *October 16, 1958*
Telegram

I have now read Foster Dulles' interpretative statement of yesterday morning. I think this should clear the atmosphere, particularly in pointing out that there is no real difference between the two of you.[1]

For my part I want to point out the following. Both political parties have taken a common stand for a number of years on the essential foundations of a foreign policy. Both of us are dedicated to peace, to the renunciation of force except for defense, to the principles of the United Nations Charter, to opposing Communist expansion, to promoting the defensive and economic strength of the free world through cooperative action, including mutual aid and technical assistance.

While in my view these, with rare exceptions, should not and do not lend themselves to political argument, the matter of administrative operation of foreign policy—whether or not agreed goals are in fact realized—has time and again been challenged both by ourselves in the past and very recently by some of our political opponents. As Foster pointed out, these need to be answered whenever they occur. Questions and criticism have involved Lebanon, our relationship with Nationalist China, the defense of Quemoy and Matsu, etc.[2] These actions, when criticized, should be supported by our side. No one can do this more effectively than you.

At times it is of course difficult to distinguish between policy and administrative operations. However, the generalization I have made is, I believe, a good one.

All the best to you.

[1] For background on the Vice-President's statements regarding U.S. foreign policy and Secretary Dulles's responses, see the preceding document.
[2] For background on these issues see nos. 770, 838, and 883.

896   *EM, WHCF, Official File 69*

TO PAUL DUDLEY WHITE   *October 16, 1958*

Dear Dr. White: Thank you for taking the time to write to me about the Red Cross and your faith in it.[1]

During my period in this position, I have had occasion to come in contact with some of the members of the Board of Governors of the Red Cross. As you know, there are fifty of them. Those whom I have met are, without exception, men of broad vision, deeply interested in humanitarian principles, and most of them appear to be sympathetic to the activity you describe: The promotion of peace by assisting peoples in the less fortunate countries.

I am certain that the Red Cross can be a real factor in the development of better understanding in the world. Just three months ago I met with 23 Junior Red Cross members who were about to leave for Europe to attend European Red Cross Study Centers. I was impressed by their intelligence, their humility, and their dedication, and I understand from General Gruenther that the reactions to their visits in Europe were favorable.[2]

I happen to know that one of the prime reasons why General Gruenther accepted the invitation of the Board of Governors to be President of the Red Cross was because he felt the Red Cross could make a real contribution toward the promotion of peace. As President of the Red Cross he has traveled extensively, not only in the United States but also abroad. I am confident that he is laboring constantly to achieve the objectives that you have in mind.[3]

I understand that the proposal of Mr. Hobbs and Mr. Buxton will be considered by the Board of Governors of the American Red Cross at its meeting on October 25, 26 and 27. I have taken the liberty, therefore, of sending to General Gruenther a copy of your letter and of my reply so that they will be available when the matter is considered by the Board ten days from now.[4]

With warm personal regard, *Sincerely*

[1] On October 6 White, a Boston cardiologist, had written Eisenhower regarding a forthcoming petition asking Congress to add a clause to the American Red Cross Charter that would authorize the organization to engage in activities to prevent war. The Red Cross and its trained personnel, White lamented, had to content itself to limited and local operations in "these tense and dangerous times." White thought that the organization's experience in past wars could be useful in supplementing health programs and educating people in underdeveloped countries. White said that if Eisenhower, as Honorary President of the Red Cross, would approve expansion of the missions, the Board of Governors might accept the idea. Eisenhower would receive the petition, signed by White and more than 150 other prominent Americans, on October 9 (*New York Times*, Oct. 10, 1958).

[2] Eisenhower had met with the Junior Red Cross delegates on June 23. His remarks to them are in *Public Papers of the Presidents: Eisenhower, 1958*, pp. 493–94. The young-sters would return from their two-month course of study in Europe on August 25 (*New York Times*, Aug. 26, 1958).

[3] Gruenther had become president of the American Red Cross in January 1957 (for background see Galambos and van Ee, *The Middle Way*, nos. 1832 and 1837). On Gruenther's current inspection tour of Red Cross activities at U.S. military bases in Europe and Morocco see no. 855.

[4] Conrad Hobbs, a retired Boston wool merchant, was active in the United World Federalists. Frank W. Buxton, former editor of *The Boston Herald*, had won a Pulitzer Prize in 1924. He also had represented U.S. interests on an Anglo-American Committee of Inquiry on the problems of Jews in Europe and Palestine in 1945.

White also had written (Oct. 6) to Gruenther. Gruenther had replied to White on October 15. On the following day Gruenther sent a copy of both letters to Presidential Secretary Ann Whitman. "Confidentially," Gruenther wrote Whitman, "Brother Hobbs is off his rocker...." Gruenther also said that White was uninformed regarding Red Cross activities. On October 22 White would send Eisenhower a copy of his thank-you letter to Gruenther. The cardiologist would admit that he had not known of the international dimension of the Red Cross and would recommend that Red Cross activities be made known to the public. On the Red Cross Board of Governors' meeting see *New York Times*, Oct. 26, 31, 1958. Congress would not revise the charter. All correspondence is in the same file as the document.

897   *EM, WHCF, Official File 138-A-9*

To Eric Harlow Heckett   *October 18, 1958*

Dear Eric: As I am on my way to the West Coast on a political trip, I have just realized that I have not had, as I had hoped, an opportunity to talk to you about what I consider to be the vital and basic issues for which Republicans are fighting in 1958.[1] Because I am so convinced of the necessity that the Republican programs, in which we both deeply believe, are maintained and furthered, I send you this note to ask your help in the final weeks that are left to us.

Here then—as briefly as possible—are the reasons I hope the voters of America—Republican, Independent and discerning Democrats—will assure that the 86th Congress is solidly Republican in character. In the first place I stand squarely on the record of this Administration. It is a good record. It reflects a growing America—prosperous and at peace. America must and can stay prosperous and at peace.

Secondly, if we do not have a Congress that is guided by the basic principles in which we believe, the bright promise of this nation's future will be dimmed or will disappear. This I say because of the signs of fiscal irresponsibility I see in the ranks of the radical opposition; I know, as you know, that a mounting Federal budget, with increasing Federal deficits and the inevitable cheapened dollar, means more trouble for the household budget, and is immediately translated into less food, less clothing, poorer housing and less security for the future of the individual family.[2]

Another seriously damaging result of reckless Federal spending is its accelerating effect upon the wage-price spiral. When demagogues seek votes, they like to spend. Useless procurement is, of course, inflationary.

Another bad feature of governmental procurement is its volume, which is so vast as to defy careful supervision. The alleged need of an item, as well as its urgency, often tend to push up prices and, in the defense area especially, procurement officers tend to negotiate contracts that in effect subsidize inefficiency and extravagance.

I think that most of us see, as the two principal causes of inflation in this country, badly unbalanced Federal budgets and the ever mounting wage-price spiral.[3]

Thirdly, I believe strongly, as I have so often stated, that government should do for the people only what they cannot well do for themselves.[4] The Federal government can and should always be ready to extend a helping and guiding hand, no matter what major problem may confront the American people, but it should not ever attempt to provide the complete solution for any problem that properly belongs to individual localities or states. I do not want my grandchildren to become wards of a welfare state; I want them to be sturdy and self-reliant, with as much—if not more—initiative and opportunity as we of our generation have had. I want them to stand squarely on their own feet, not to depend upon a centralized government in Washington to take care of them.

And finally, I must not fail to mention the matter of racketeering in certain important sections of the labor movement. I see little hope of straightening out this problem, highlighted by the McClellan Committee investigations, unless the political complexion of the Congress is changed.[5] Probably you know of my efforts last session to get legal weapons enacted that would give a remedy and probably you also know of the weird parliamentary maneuvering that took place to defeat my recommendations and to substitute a pallid, ineffective bill in its place.[6] Here indeed is a good cause, in itself warranting an all out effort for a Republican Congress.

There are many other issues in this campaign; I cannot touch on them all in this letter, which is already much too long. But if you believe as I do, I hope you urge your friends and associates, by every means by which you can reach them to vote Republican on November fourth. The opposition has been working hard and has made our job difficult. But with your help, and with the help of people of integrity and a deep love of and desire to preserve our way of life, we will have the kind of Congress we need.

I send you herewith a list of items that, even though it is abbreviated, will bring to your mind a few of the accomplishments of the past five and one-half years.[7] I want to be even prouder of the record of this Administration on January 21, 1961. So, I think we need to ring bells, use the telephone, write letters—in short, give ourselves during the next three weeks the job of electing a Republican Congress and Governorships.[8]

With warm regard, *Sincerely*

[1] On Eisenhower's campaign trip see the following document.

[2] See nos. 784 and 869.

[3] See no. 806.

[4] Eisenhower was quoting Abraham Lincoln; see Galambos and van Ee, *The Middle Way*, no. 1861.

[5] For background see no. 536. John Little McClellan, Democratic Senator from Arkansas since 1942, was Chairman of the Senate Select Committee on Improper Activities in the Labor or Management Field. In 1958 the Committee had continued to investigate labor racketeering, union violence and corruption. On the Committee's hearings on the Teamsters' Union, the Carpenters' Unions, labor racketeering in the Chicago restaurant industry, and the Detroit linen industries see *Congressional Quarterly Almanac*, vol. XIV, *1958*, pp. 674–81.

[6] In response to the President's request in his January 23 labor message to Congress and to the McClellan Committee's revelations, the Senate had introduced legislation requiring unions to report their organizational structure and financial operations to members and to the Secretary of Labor; barring bribes and embezzlement in labor-management relations and the handling of union money; requiring periodic secret-ballot union elections; limiting trusteeship powers of international unions over locals; providing criminal penalties for union misconduct; and giving the Secretary of Labor power to investigate the reports and to subpoena witnesses and records.

Although the Senate had passed the measure on June 17, political maneuvering in the House of Representatives had led to the bill's defeat on August 18 (see Lee, *Eisenhower & Landrum-Griffin*, pp. 74–79, and *Congressional Quarterly Almanac*, vol.

XIV, *1958*, pp. 191–99). Congress had, however, passed S. 2888, the Welfare and Pension Plans Disclosure Act, which sought to reduce pension plan abuses through the publication of financial information (*ibid.*, pp. 200–204). Eisenhower had signed the bill on August 29 because it had established a precedent of federal responsibility, but he had condemned the act for doing little else: "The Congress has failed to respond effectively to the pleas for action in this field, and I am sure that the public is as disappointed with it as I am" (*Public Papers of the Presidents: Eisenhower, 1958*, pp. 663–64).

[7] In his list of accomplishments Eisenhower had included: "the Korean War stopped; largest tax cut of all time; the Defense Department reorganized; satellites launched; standards of living raised to highest ever; highest employment ever; social security coverage expanded; unemployment insurance expanded; statehood for Alaska; the St. Lawrence Seaway; a new agency for outer space; inflation braked; positive effort to return power to the States; economic controls removed; new interstate super highways; a new aviation agency; federal employees reduced by over a quarter of a million; atoms for peace." Eisenhower sent identical letters to many of his friends. See, for example, the one sent on this same day to hotel executive Conrad N. Hilton, and Hilton's October 27 reply.

[8] Heckett would respond (Nov. 4) that he had written to the divisions of his company, Harsco Corporation, requesting that they send letters to all the employees in their divisions. He enclosed a letter sent out by Harrisburg Steel Company as an example. Heckett had also added to the Harsco yearly report a letter urging support in the upcoming election for candidates who supported labor reform. Eisenhower would write again (Nov. 6): "While the results throughout the country—and this is the greatest understatement of the year—were no cause for elation on the part of the Republicans, I am sure that you take the same satisfaction as I do that Pennsylvania chose to send Hugh Scott to the Senate." On the election see no. 928; on Scott see no. 866. All correspondence is in the same file as the document.

898   *EM, AWF, Name Series*

To Edgar Newton Eisenhower   *October 18, 1958*

Dear Ed: While visiting the Abilene Cemetery this morning, I was struck by the fact that there is no way of showing the exact limits of our family plot.[1] As you know, it was purchased jointly by Uncle Chris and Dad. In it now are buried our parents and Uncle Chris and Aunt Amanda, and on the far side of the family stone is Beulah Musser, who was a first cousin of ours.[2] I think it would be a nice thing to put a solidly built, iron picket fence (two to two and a half feet high) around it. I asked Florence to contact the Cemetery Association to see whether they would have any objection to the erection of such a fence.[3]

Assuming that the Association has no such objection, and that you, Earl and Milton would agree, my next step would be to find in the Abilene area a firm that could manufacture and install the fence.

Looking at the plot casually, I believe that its dimensions are something like twenty feet square, possibly a little more. But before going ahead, of course, I would get an estimate, although I cannot believe that the cost would be more than something on order of two to three hundred dollars. I would be quite willing to bear the expense individually, if you approve of the idea.

I am sending this note from Denver so that it will not slip my mind. I hope that you will reply to the White House (I shall be back there next Thursday).[4]

With affectionate regard to Lucy and all the best to yourself, *Devotedly*

[1] The President had visited his boyhood home while campaigning in the West for the upcoming midterm elections (see no. 906).

[2] Christian O. Musser was married to Hannah Amanda Eisenhower, who was the sister of David J. Eisenhower, the President's father. Beulah was Musser's daughter.

[3] Eisenhower had visited with Florence Musser Etherington, another daughter of the Mussers, while in Abilene. For developments see no. 911.

[4] The President would send identical letters to his brothers Milton and Earl. Edgar and Milton would reply favorably to the idea and both expressed the desire to pay a share of the expenses (see Edgar E. to Eisenhower, Oct. 21, and Milton E. to Eisenhower, Oct. 23, all in AWF/N; Earl Eisenhower's reply is not in AWF). On July 13, 1959, Eisenhower would send Earl a photograph and a description of the completed project. In his cover letter the President would say that he had not yet been billed.

899 *EM, WHCF, President's Personal File 223*

To Harry Darby
October 18, 1958

Dear Harry:[1] I always love to come to Kansas, but it is a dreadful thing to be such a slave to schedule as I am these days.[2] My time was all too short everywhere—at my old home, at the Museum, at the cocktail party that was given in my honor, and in the brief interval I had to chat with you and Edith.[3] From past experience I know that you had a great deal to do with the behind-the-scenes arrangements that enabled me to crowd as much as I did into a few hours, and I am, as always, grateful to you.

Particularly, I want once again to thank you for your help with the Eisenhower Library. It is extremely difficult for me to put into words just how heartwarming it is to know that you, and many of my friends, are willing to devote so much time and energy to the project; I simply know it would be impossible of achievement without your help.[4]

So—my deepest thanks to you and, as always, my warm regard to you and Edith. *As ever*

[1] Former U.S. Senator Darby, an industrialist and farmer-stockman of Kansas City, Kansas, had been the Republican National Committeeman from Kansas since 1940. During 1952 he also had led the movement in Kansas to draft Eisenhower for the Republican presidential nomination (for background see *Eisenhower Papers*, vols. X–XIII).

[2] On October 17 the President had visited his boyhood home while campaigning for the upcoming midterm elections (see no. 902 and *New York Times*, Oct. 18, 1958). On October 27 Darby would reply that the people of Kansas experienced a "tremendous thrill" when the Eisenhowers returned (same file as document).

[3] The Eisenhower Foundation had dedicated the Eisenhower Museum in Abilene on November 11, 1954. The museum contained memorabilia Eisenhower had acquired over the course of his career (see Galambos and van Ee, *The Middle Way*, no. 760). Darby's wife was the former Edith Marie Cubbison.

[4] On October 13, 1959, Eisenhower would attend the groundbreaking ceremonies of the Eisenhower Presidential Library in Abilene (*New York Times*, Oct. 14, 1959). The following day the President would thank Darby for undertaking "much of the financing" of the ceremonies. In a thank-you letter (Oct. 15) Darby would say Eisenhower's presence "made the occasion a tremendous success!" Darby would thank the President again on October 18 (*ibid.*). Ceremonies dedicating the Dwight David Eisenhower Presidential Library would take place on May 1, 1962 (see Galambos and van Ee, *The Middle Way*, no. 760, and *New York Times*, May 1, 2, 1962).

900   *EM, AWF, Administration Series*

To Charles Douglas Jackson   *October 19, 1958*

Dear C. D.: This is the first moment I have had to acknowledge, with my grateful thanks, your draft of possible material for use on foreign policy in the speeches between now and the end of the campaign.[1] Frankly I have not yet had a chance to study the document, since I have literally been on the go since it arrived and what time I have had away from seeing people has gone into preparation of the Los Angeles talk.[2] But after the Chicago business, I shall settle down to the next effort, and I shall then give your material the attention I know it deserves.[3]

Don't worry about not being able to take on the Colombo Plan Meeting talk. I suspected that would be the case and I have already asked the State Department to come up with as finished a draft as [soon as] they possibly could.[4]

As to your note of the seventh regarding Foster and the Rule of Law, I talked to him and gave him Harry Luce's speech to read. Enclosed is a copy of a note I had from him on the matter, showing that I gained no ground at all.[5]

With warm regard, *As ever*

[1] Eisenhower had asked Jackson to help draft a foreign policy speech for delivery sometime during the election campaign (see no. 848).

[2] The Los Angeles speech, in which Eisenhower would emphasize the accomplishments of his Administration in both the foreign and the domestic fields, is in *Public Papers of the Presidents: Eisenhower, 1958*, pp. 757–65.

[3] In the afternoon on October 22 Eisenhower would participate in a panel discussion sponsored by the National Republican Committee in Chicago. That evening he would deliver a radio and television address at the "Fight to Win" Dinner Rally in the stockyard arena. Following this talk, he would speak briefly to a gathering of the National Safety Council (see *ibid.*, pp. 780–94).

[4] For background see no. 882. Eisenhower had told Secretary Dulles that he would plan to attend the conference provided that he had "an appropriate address to make." Dulles had suggested the general topic of the development of the less developed nations, a subject, he said, the President knew well (Dulles, Memorandum of Conversation, Oct. 2, 1958, Dulles Papers, White House Memoranda Series). Eisenhower would tell Dulles that although he approved the speech draft "generally," a tight federal budget and credit position would not allow him to "give exaggerated hopes that there would be large increases in foreign aid" (Dulles, Memorandum of Conversation, Nov. 4, 1958, Dulles Papers, White House Memoranda Series).

For other discussions between Eisenhower and Dulles regarding the speech, which was not completed until shortly before delivery, see Telephone conversations, Eisenhower and Dulles, Oct. 27, 30, Nov. 8, 9, 1958, Dulles Papers, Telephone Conversations). On November 10 the President would describe to delegates from eighteen countries and three colonies his program for expansion of trade and aid to the countries of South and Southeast Asia through private American investments (see *Public Papers of the Presidents: Eisenhower, 1958*, pp. 839–47; and Colombo Plan Scope Paper, AWF/Misc: Colombo Plan; see also State, *Foreign Relations, 1958–1960*, vol. IV, *Foreign Economic Policy*, p. 439). Dulles would tell Eisenhower that his "friendly presence" at the opening of the conference was "deeply appreciated" and would assure that the meeting would be "highly regarded throughout all of free Asia" (Dulles to Eisenhower, Nov. 11, 1958, AWF/D-H; see also no. 949).

[5] For background see no. 803. Jackson had enclosed a copy of a speech Henry Luce had made before the Missouri Bar Association on the Rule of Law in Foreign Policy. Jackson had told Eisenhower that although the subject was receiving widespread international interest, no one had assumed a position of leadership. "Both Harry and I have tried to persuade Foster that he is the ideal person to assume that position, and thereby crown his Secretary of Stateship on a high position note," Jackson had written, but they had not succeeded. "If you think well of the idea, maybe you can persuade him to take it on" (Jackson to Eisenhower, Oct. 7, 1958, AWF/A). We have been unable to locate Dulles's note to Eisenhower. For developments see no. 1182.

901

EM, AWF, International Series:
de Gaulle

To Charles André Joseph Marie de Gaulle

Secret *October 20, 1958*

Dear General de Gaulle: I have given considerable thought to the views expressed in your letter of September seventeenth. You have posed serious questions which require earnest thinking and careful study.[1]

The central problem you raise—the organization of the free world's defense—is very much on my mind also. I agree that we should constantly seek means for making that organization more effective.

We are, I believe, in full agreement that the threat we face is global and that our policies should be adapted to deal with the world-wide nature of the threat. Although recognizing that more needs to be done, we believe that our policies have to an extent already been adapted to this end. It is in recognition of the need to deal with the world-wide threat that the United States has joined with its allies in establishing elements of strength throughout the world. The United States and France are closely associated in certain of these groupings, such as NATO and SEATO. The United States has also associated itself with many other countries, in both multilateral and bilateral arrangements, all directed toward the same general purpose. We have also sought to give recognition to the fact that the threat is more than military through our economic, financial, and technical assistance programs designed to aid nations throughout the world to resist subversion.

As for the Atlantic Alliance itself, I believe there has been a significant evolution in NATO over the past two years. Consultation in NATO has in fact been extended well beyond the confines of the European area. We, for example, have sought to use the NATO Council to inform or consult with our allies on the threat facing the Free World in the Far East and the Middle East. We have also sought to use the Council to develop common policies toward the Soviet bloc. We feel that this "habit of consultation" among the NATO nations must be still further broadened but that this cannot be forced. I do not believe that we can afford to lose any of this developing intimacy among all the members of NATO and the closer bonds it forges.

As for the means for dealing with the problem which you propose, our present procedures for organizing the defense of the Free World clearly require the willing cooperation of many other nations, both within and outside NATO. We cannot afford to adopt any system which would give to our other allies, or other free world countries, the impression that basic decisions affecting their own vital interests are being made without their participation.[2] As regards NATO itself, I must in all frankness say that I see very serious problems, both within and outside NATO, in any effort to amend the North Atlantic Treaty so as to extend its coverage beyond the areas presently covered.

All this having been said, I must add that I recognize that a community association to live must constantly evolve and find means to make itself more useful in the face of changing conditions. I am quite prepared to explore this aspect of the matter in appropriate ways.[3]

With best personal wishes, *Sincerely*

---

[1] De Gaulle had written Eisenhower that recent events in the Middle East and in the Formosa Straits had confirmed his belief that the North Atlantic Treaty Organization could no longer provide security to the free world or to France. "The sharing of the risks involved" by NATO countries was not "matched by indispensable cooperation on decisions taken and on responsibilities." The Atlantic Alliance had been designed to provide security for only the North Atlantic area, but political or strategic realities called for global defenses. He recommended that the United States, Great Britain, and France form a tripartite organization that would make joint decisions on political questions affecting world security and make strategic plans regarding the deployment of nuclear weapons. Such a step would allow the organization of other theaters of operations, including such areas as the Arctic, the Atlantic, the Pacific, and the Indian Ocean. De Gaulle told Eisenhower that he had sent the same memorandum to British Prime Minister Macmillan and had asked that representatives of the three countries meet in Washington to discuss his proposals (AWF/I: de Gaulle).

At Secretary Dulles's recommendation, Eisenhower had sent the French president an interim reply, stressing the importance of the issues he had raised and promising a more detailed response after careful study (Dulles to Eisenhower, Sept. 25, Oct. 1, 1958, *ibid.*; and Eisenhower to de Gaulle, Oct. 2, 1958, *ibid.*; see also State, *Foreign Relations, 1958–1960*, vol. VII, pt. 2, *Western Europe*, pp. 81–88).

[2] After learning of de Gaulle's proposal, Italian President Amintore Fanfani had informed Eisenhower through his ambassador of his strong reaction to the French proposal, which, he said, would reduce NATO to nothing. Eisenhower had assured the Italians that the United States had not changed its policies and had never considered creating a "special circle" within NATO. He suggested that "the best course to follow was to sit quietly and not exaggerate the situation" (*ibid.*, pp. 88–89; see also Dulles, Memorandum of Conversation, Oct. 2, 1958, Dulles Papers, White House Memoranda Series). For the reaction of Prime Minister Macmillan, German Chancellor Adenauer, and NATO Secretary General Spaak, see State, *Foreign Relations, 1958–1960*, vol. VII, pt. 2, *Western Europe*, pp. 90–99; and Macmillan, *Riding the Storm*, pp. 452–54).

Dulles had told Eisenhower that a meeting in Washington with the British and French might be necessary. The President had agreed, but only if such a meeting were held at a relatively low level. He also told Dulles that the German and Italian governments should be notified in advance that the meeting was for the purpose of discussing the plan and not the beginning of implementation (Dulles, Memorandum of Conversation, Oct. 13, 1958, Dulles Papers, White House Memoranda Series). In a subsequent conversation Dulles had told Eisenhower that he was beginning to doubt the wisdom of having the talks. Eisenhower had responded: "I agree we should not do this 3 power business *unless* we *have* to" (State, *Foreign Relations, 1958–1960*, vol. VII, pt. 2, *Western Europe*, p. 100; see also Telephone conversation, Eisenhower and Dulles, Oct. 16, 1958, Dulles Papers, Telephone Conversations).

[3] Ambassador Hervé Alphand would tell Dulles that while France did not want to extend the geographic responsibility of NATO, it wanted effective consultations on military strategy among the three nations. The two men agreed that tripartite talks could be justified to the other NATO members as a way to organize the free world more effectively. Representatives from the three countries would meet twice in Washington in December (State, *Foreign Relations, 1958–1960*, vol. VII, pt. 2, *Western Europe*,

pp. 113–21, 128–44; see also Telephone conversation, Dulles and Murphy, Nov. 8, 1958, Dulles Papers, Telephone Conversations). For developments see no. 974.

902   *EM, WHCF,*
President's Personal File 351

TO KATHERINE CARPENTER BERMINGHAM   *October 20, 1958*

Dear "K":[1] Perhaps you know that the other day Mamie and I stopped overnight in Abilene where, of course, as the first order of business we visited my old home.[2] We heard over and over again from the people in charge there how gratified they were (a feeling that is magnified in me) that Ed had taken the initiative (and I suspect supplied most of the necessary financing) in having the underpinning of the house reinforced with steel. I don't believe I ever expressed to him adequately my gratitude for his action, and this note is merely to tell you of my lasting appreciation for that, and for the many other things he did for me over so many years.[3]

Incidentally, the house looks fine and, thanks to Ed, will resist the wear and tear of time and tourists that would otherwise be inevitable.

I am terribly sorry that Mamie and I didn't have a chance to see you at the Brown Palace, since I understand you and the boys also were on the eighth floor.[4] Between hours working on my forthcoming speeches, visiting Min, and seeing a few of the many Denver projects in which I am interested, my time was all too crowded for comfort.[5] Bob tells me you were looking well; I am glad.[6]

With affectionate regard, *As ever*

[1] "K" was the widow of Edward J. Bermingham, who had died on July 13 (see no. 426). On Eisenhower's relationship with Bermingham, whom the President met in 1948 while president of Columbia University, see *Eisenhower Papers,* vols. X–XVII.

[2] On October 17–18 Eisenhower had visited his boyhood home in Abilene while on a campaign tour (see no. 906). He wrote this letter en route to Los Angeles.

[3] The Berminghams had contributed substantially to the restoration of Eisenhower's boyhood home. The dedication and unveiling ceremonies had taken place in November 1956 (see Galambos and van Ee, *The Middle Way,* no. 2132). On the house, located at the Eisenhower Center and open to the public since 1947, see Galambos, *Chief of Staff,* no. 1602, and *Eisenhower Papers,* vols. X–XVII.

[4] After leaving Abilene the Eisenhowers visited Mrs. Eisenhower's home in Denver, Colorado. On November 3 (same file as document) Mrs. Bermingham would thank Eisenhower for his "thoughtful" letter. She said she hoped the house looked like home as the President remembered it. She added that she had had a "lovely" visit with the First Lady, who would remain in Denver until October 21.

[5] The President would campaign in Cedar Rapids, Los Angeles, San Francisco, and

Chicago (see *New York Times,* Oct. 18, 19, 20, 21, 22, 25, 26, 1958; for developments see no. 882). Min was the First Lady's mother, Elivera Carlson Doud. On the Denver real estate investments see no. 764.

[6] White House aide Robert L. Schulz had accompanied the President on his campaign trip.

903   *EM, AWF, Name Series*

To Edgar Newton Eisenhower   *October 23, 1958*

Dear Ed: This afternoon Mrs. Whitman phoned you to tell you that I might be able to spend the day with you on the ninth. She said that you might have some embarrassment if I should stay at your house on Saturday night, coming directly there from McChord Field. The Secret Service tells me that while they would have to put a telephone in my room and one outside the house, they have already made the survey of your place and there would be very little preliminary work necessary.

I can, of course, easily go to the hotel in Seattle and then come down to Tacoma early in the morning. All you have to do is to let me know what you think would be preferable.[1]

There just came to my desk a newspaper account of a speech you made up in Washington. I cannot tell you how encouraged I am to find my brothers supporting middle-of-the-road Republican philosophy.[2] There is always a danger that in condemning the other side, we may overstate our case. Or, as the State Department would say, we make statements that can be "counterproductive."

I think it is fair to charge the radical wing of the Democratic Party—the self-styled liberals—with reckless spending, fiscal irresponsibility both in policy and in practice, with centralization of power in the Federal government, and a persistent effort to meddle more and more in the lives of our citizens, communities and states.

This is, of course, the kind of a road that if followed forever will lead toward socialism, but I rather think there are few people in this United States that would deliberately want a socialistic government.[3]

I start again next Monday to make a couple of political speeches and then the following day one non-political talk. I may have one other appearance before Election Day, and I must say it is wearisome.[4]

Give my love to Lucy—I hope to see you soon. *As ever*

P.S.: Of course if the trip eventuates, I assume that two or three telephone conversations will be necessary to straighten out details. Mrs. Whitman will normally be the one to call you.[5]

[1] Eisenhower was planning to fly to Tacoma on his way to Seattle to speak at a conference of the Colombo Plan nations. For background on the speech and conference see no. 882; for developments see no. 949.

[2] On October 9 Edgar Eisenhower had spoken at a GOP rally in Spokane, Washington, for a Republican senatorial candidate (*New York Times*, Oct. 10, 1958, and *The Spokesman-Review*, Oct. 10, 1958). Earl Eisenhower had made a similar speech in Chicago on October 8 (see the following document).

[3] Edgar had charged the Democratic Congress with establishing programs that took the country "down the road to socialism."

[4] The President would campaign for the upcoming midterm elections in West Virginia, Pennsylvania, and Maryland. He would also travel to New York City to attend the National Football Foundation dinner (see *New York Times*, Oct. 28, Nov. 1, 1958). For developments on the November 4 elections see no. 926.

[5] As it turned out, the President would spend November 8–9 at his brother's home. Edgar would say he "enjoyed" the "opportunity to visit . . . without a lot of people interfering . . ." (see Edgar E. to Eisenhower, Nov. 12, 1958, and Whitman to Edgar E., Nov. 18, 1958, both in AWF/N, and *New York Times*, Nov. 6, 9, 10, 1958).

904   *EM, AWF, Name Series*

To Earl Dewey Eisenhower   *October 23, 1958*

Dear Earl: It was nice to see you and Kathryn the other day. I think we had an opportunity for a longer talk than I have had with you since I became President.[1]

Yesterday afternoon there came to my desk a newspaper account of a speech you had made. I am delighted to have my brothers support Republican policy.[2] The only thing I would ask is that you do not *overstate* the case, particularly in the foreign field. What I mean by this is that I do not believe that it was Democratic failure that allowed the European satellite countries to come under the domination of the Soviets. The fact was that the Soviet Armies were in the region as a result of World War II and simply held their positions by force.

By and large, the responsible leaders of the Democratic Party always try to help me in most matters of foreign policy—I should truly like to see this particular thing on a bipartisan basis. When we talk abroad we should talk as one voice.[3]

But in other fields, especially our economic philosophies, the two parties are very different. Possibly I should say that Republican philosophy differs in observance and practice from that observed and practiced by the extreme wing of the Democratic Party.

Keep up the good work.[4]

With affectionate regard to Kathryn, and all the best to yourself. *As ever*

[1] The Eisenhowers had had lunch with Earl and his wife the preceding day in Chicago, the last stop on the President's western campaign tour. In addition to the lunch Eisenhower attended a coffee hour, was photographed, met with Republican finance committeemen, and addressed supporters at a dinner at the Stockyards (see *New York Times,* Oct. 22, 23, 1958, and Ann Whitman memorandum, Oct. 13–Nov. 2, AWF/AWD). On the tour see no. 902.

[2] On October 9 the *Chicago Daily Tribune* had reported Earl's speech, which he had delivered on October 8. In his talk, the first in a series, he had called for support of Republican candidates and had defended the Republican foreign policy record. Eisenhower's older brother Edgar had made a similar speech on October 9 (see the preceding document).

[3] Earl had praised Republicans for the success in Korea, Lebanon, and China and had charged the Democrats with abandoning one-third of the world to Communists. "It was not the Republican foreign policy which enabled Russia to seize Poland 19 years ago. It was Democrat foreign policy. It was that same Democrat foreign policy which led to the Russian swallowing of Hungary, Czechoslovakia, Romania, Lithuania, Estonia, Latvia, and East Germany."

[4] For developments on the November 4 election see no. 926.

905   *EM, WHCF, Official File 124*

To William M. Allen   *[October 23, 1958]*

Dear Mr. Allen:[1] Thank you very much for your thoughtful letter. I enjoyed the chance to visit with you and the others, and I appreciate your writing me as you did.[2]

First, let me say I am glad to note your comment that you intend to devote more time and effort along the lines of our discussion. You and I—all of us—are very busy, and I am sure we have a full-time job getting our own chores done. Yet, our separate responsibilities have a way of overlapping too. So I welcomed the chance to exhort men like yourself to greater effort in the cause of good government. And I welcome your own thoughts about the problems we in government have to deal with.

I agree that some of the most serious of these problems are in the area of labor-management affairs. We need restraint and responsibility in wage and price policies. Decisions on prices and wages, particularly in key industries, have an important bearing on the value of the dollars in the pockets of each American. I shall continue to speak out on this subject, as I have in the past.[3] There is need also to curb power which has been abused. In the past, the people have enacted laws, in the public interest, to restrict such powers. This must be done again. The recommendations I made to Congress last January were designed to protect the public and union members from the kind of abuses which have been so highly publicized. However, as you know, these recommendations were not approved.[4]

Next January I shall again make recommendations for appropriate federal legislation. Among these recommendations will be one I have made before, that the area of State responsibility in labor matters be clearly defined. In that connection, you should know I have opposed any change in Section 14(b) of the Taft-Hartley Act, the provision permitting each State to decide whether it shall adopt a right-to-work law. I believe this is the type of decision the individual States, rather than the Federal government should make. In keeping with that view, I have refrained from expressing any opinion of my own as to which decision I thought the voters of a particular State ought to make on the question.[5]

In closing, let me add one further comment. I know you and others are working hard on this right-to-work issue in the state of Washington, I hope that in so doing, you will also find time and energy for other issues—and candidates—which I am sure you consider important too. The range of Republican accomplishments is indeed broad, and I know we both agree that aggressive support of all who espouse the Republican cause represents the best hope of preserving the freedoms so dear to all of us.[6]

With warm regard, *Sincerely*

---

[1] Allen (A.B. Montana State University 1922; LL.B. Harvard 1925) had been president of the Boeing Airplane Company since 1945. Before assuming this post he had been a member of Boeing's board of directors and had practiced law as a partner in a Seattle, Washington, legal firm. In 1958 he had campaigned vigorously for a right-to-work initiative in Washington (see no. 870).

[2] On October 6 Allen had attended a stag dinner at the White House, where Eisenhower had urged a number of friends and business leaders to take more active roles in the 1958 election campaigns (see no. 880). Two days later Allen had written the President to thank him for his hospitality, to argue for a strong presidential stand on the right-to-work issue, and to assure him that he had resolved to devote himself "in a proper degree to the public good." On October 15 Ann Whitman had acknowledged receipt of Allen's letter and had said that Eisenhower, then campaigning on the West Coast, wanted to reply "in some detail" after he returned to Washington. Former Associate Special Counsel Edward A. McCabe, who had become Administrative Assistant to the President on September 10, drafted this reply and sent it to Republican National Committee Chairman Meade Alcorn, Council of Economic Advisors Chairman Raymond Saulnier, and Secretary of Labor James Mitchell for approval. Alcorn replied that he thought that it was "a mighty good letter" even though he suspected that Allen would "think, even though he may not say so, that the specific point of his letter has been avoided—and with considerable adroitness and skill" (Alcorn to McCabe, Oct. 22, 1958).

[3] Allen had written Eisenhower about his concern over the great amount of power that had been concentrated in the hands of a few labor leaders. This power, which he thought was in part responsible for the inflationary cycle that was driving up wages and prices, had resulted from the practice of forcing new employees to join unions—a defining characteristic of the union shop system. Allen urged Eisen-

hower to endorse state right-to-work laws in order to eliminate such compulsory unionism, and he argued that such advocacy would ultimately "develop support for the Republican party that it is not now receiving" and would "solidify the position of those citizens who are dedicated to the principles upon which the nation was constituted."

[4] On the McClellan hearings and the fate of the Eisenhower Administration's labor legislation see no. 897.

[5] See no. 829 for background on the Taft-Hartley Act; see also Galambos and van Ee, *The Middle Way*, no. 431. See no. 870 in these volumes for Eisenhower's position on right-to-work laws.

[6] Commenting on Allen's letter in a note to Eisenhower dated October 15, Meade Alcorn had observed that the Boeing president's position was "typical." Allen, "like so many others," seemed to be "so engrossed in the 'right-to-work' cause that he overlooks the urgency of supporting our Party which has other equally important causes requiring aggressive, thoughtful support." Secretary Mitchell, in a separate note to the President on the same day, said that the right-to-work issue had harmed Washington Republicans in the 1956 elections and recommended that Eisenhower continue to remain silent on the wisdom of enacting such state laws. Mitchell also predicted, accurately, that the voters of Washington would defeat the right-to-work referendum in the November election. (See Hugh H. Bone, "The 1958 Election in Washington," *Western Political Quarterly*, vol. XII, no. 1, pt. 2 [March, 1959], 355, 358–61.) All papers are in the same file as the document.

906   *EM, AWF, Name Series*

TO ELIZABETH HAZLETT   *October 23, 1958*

Dear Ibby: Your note about my birthday anniversary, together with the letter Swede had struggled so valiantly to write me the latter part of August, reached me this morning on the last leg of my West Coast jaunt.[1] I am, of course, grateful for your felicitations and good wishes.

I have, of course, gotten regular reports on Swede.[2] His courage I have always admired, and I know he faces this battle with his flags flying.

You might tell Swede, if possible, that when I was in Abilene everyone asked about him. The town looks much the same. I saw Maud Hurd briefly; as you probably know she is not at all well but she is as keen and alert as ever. Charlie Case is unchanged by the years and as great a fan of Swede's as ever.[3]

If there is anything I can do for you, please do not fail to let me know. I would like to see you (although I don't know how or when), but from the medical reports I have had, I don't believe I should try to see Swede. He understands, I am sure, that he is constantly in my thoughts and prayers.[4]

With warm regard, *Affectionately*

[1] Ibby was the wife of Eisenhower's long-time friend Swede Hazlett. In her greeting of October 14 Mrs. Hazlett said that while organizing the papers on her husband's desk she had found a letter he had attempted to write to Eisenhower on August 25 (both in AWF/N). Captain Hazlett had been ill for some time and in March had had a lung removed (for background see no. 622).

True to form, Hazlett had discussed many subjects in his letter. Following some personal news (he referred to himself as "a virtual shutin"), Hazlett complimented the President for completing "a most successful year" for which he was only "beginning to receive due credit." "You have had a hostile Congress eating out of your hand and have put across almost your entire program," he wrote. The defense reorganization plan had interested him from the beginning, he said, because "it made sense, without in the least disturbing our sacred traditions." He called the landings in Lebanon "unavoidable." Those columnists who criticized Eisenhower were "far from wise, or even fair." In conclusion, Hazlett said he prayed daily that the President's vacation would not be "forcibly interrupted by the louse in Arkansas. . . ." For background on these subjects see nos. 826, 802, 753, 808, and 833, respectively.

[2] Hazlett said that Eisenhower's "private intelligence system continues so good that I've no doubt you know more about me than I know of myself." On the President's interest in receiving reports on his friend's health see no. 622.

[3] On October 17 Eisenhower had visited his boyhood home while campaigning for the upcoming midterm elections (see *New York Times*, Oct. 18–25, 1958; see also no. 882). Maude Rogers Hurd was one of the President's oldest friends from Abilene (see Galambos and van Ee, *The Middle Way*, no. 2093). Charles Augustine Case, a former officer of the Eisenhower Foundation, was another of Eisenhower's childhood friends (see Galambos, *NATO and the Campaign of 1952*, no. 683).

[4] For developments see no. 920.

907   *EM, AWF, International Series:*
                                                    Formosa (China)

To Chiang Kai-shek   *October 24, 1958*
Confidential

Dear Mr. President: Secretary Dulles has just returned and told me of his consultations with you and your associates at Taipei. I am fully satisfied with the results.[1] When many outsiders are seeking to distort our respective views to create mischief and division between us, there is no substitute for face-to-face high level talks.[2]

I wholly endorse the communique.[3] It sets forth our solidarity in the face of Chinese Communist armed attacks. Also, I consider it important that your Government should have declared that its success in restoring freedom to the Mainland Chinese depends principally upon the minds and hearts of the Chinese people, and not the use by your Government of force. This free-world principle, not accepted by the Communists, sets us apart from them and morally above them. Your enunciation of that principle will, I am confident, be welcomed throughout the free world.

Secretary Dulles reported your message to me expressing your determination to cooperate with our considered views, arrived at after consultation with you. This is an important declaration which I welcome. We shall try not to abuse the trust and confidence that it signifies. We seek to have consultation on all significant matters of joint concern. No doubt at times there are unintended inadequacies. But I can assure you that it is our purpose never to take any important new position, or to ask anything of your Government, unless we have previously had an opportunity to consider fully your point of view.

I know that these are difficult days, with the Chinese Communists keeping an atmosphere of uncertainty and mixing force with illusory promises.[4] I have no doubt that our two countries will stand together, resolute and firm, in the face of these tactics and that we shall cause them to fail. I am grateful that we have in you so experienced, wise and reliable a leader of Free China.[5] *Sincerely*

[1] For background see no. 883. Soon after the Chinese Communists had announced a further suspension of their shelling of the offshore islands, Chiang had requested a meeting with Secretary Dulles to discuss new policies to cope with this change in tactics (State, *Foreign Relations, 1958–1960*, vol. XIX, *China*, pp. 379–81; see also Cumming to Goodpaster, Oct. 12, 1958, State, *Foreign Relations, 1958–1960*, vol. XIX, *China*, Microfiche Supplement no. 216; and Telephone conversation, Dulles and Goodpaster, Oct. 12, 1958, Dulles Papers, Telephone Conversations). Eisenhower, after discussing the military situation with JCS Chairman Twining, had agreed that a meeting would indicate "positive action." Dulles, however, did not expect that discussions with Chiang would alter the Chinese leader's attitude toward defending the islands. Any change would come about only gradually, he said, and of Chiang's own volition (Dulles, Memorandum of Conversation, Oct. 14, 1958, Dulles Papers, White House Memoranda Series).

In his meeting with Eisenhower to discuss his trip and the draft of this letter, Dulles had told the President that Chiang had agreed to reduce his forces on the islands when the Communists suspended their attacks. He was much more reluctant, however, to abandon the use of force to liberate the mainland (Dulles, Memorandum of Conversation, Oct. 24, 1958, Dulles Papers, White House Memoranda Series; on Dulles's three meetings with Chiang see State, *Foreign Relations, 1958–1960*, vol. XIX, *China*, pp. 382–88, 408–9, 413–19, 421–26, 430–33, 438–40; and NSC meeting minutes, Oct. 31, 1958, AWF/NSC).

[2] Eisenhower had added the word "outsiders" and changed "each other's views" to "our respective views" in this sentence (see Draft 2 in Dulles Papers, White House Memoranda Series; Dulles's public statement with Eisenhower's changes is in *ibid.*).

[3] The communiqué, including the statement renouncing force, is in State, *Foreign Relations, 1958–1960*, vol. XIX, *China*, pp. 442–43; see also *ibid.*, pp. 440–41.

[4] The Chinese Communists, maintaining that a U.S. destroyer had entered territorial waters off the mainland, had resumed shelling the islands shortly before the talks began. Dulles later told the President that the sporadic attacks were probably not part of an attempt to take the islands by force but were intended "to create and perpetuate a state of uncertainty which is bad for moral[e]" (Dulles to Eisenhower, Oct. 21, 1958, AWF/D-H; see also Telephone conversations, Dulles and Eisenhower, Cumming, Herter, and Robertson, Oct. 20, 1958, Dulles Papers, Telephone Conversations; on Dulles's trip see no. 887).

[5] The State Department cabled the text of this letter to the American embassy in

Taipei for delivery to Chiang (Oct. 24, 1958, AWF/I: Formosa [China]). On the following day the Chinese Communists would announce that they would limit their bombardment to even-numbered days, a statement Dulles would call "rather fantastic" (State, *Foreign Relations, 1958–1960*, vol. XIX, *China*, p. 451; see also Telephone conversation, Dulles and Goodpaster, Oct. 24, 1958, Dulles Papers, Telephone Conversations; and Eisenhower, *Waging Peace*, pp. 303–4). For developments see no. 929.

908   *EM, WHCF, Official File 138-A-9*

To Thomas Edmund Dewey   *October 24, 1958*

Dear Tom: Thank you very much for your complimentary wire.[1]

The older I grow the more difficult it is for me to understand why businessmen, workers and professional people—and Republicans in general—need any inspiration or needling in order to see on which side their own bread is buttered. I think the six year record of the Administration, while far from faultless, is not only good but it is such a contrast to what Republicans experienced under Democratic Administrations, and what they would again experience under those circumstances, that you would think each would have a flag flying on his house, signs and billboards filled with slogans and encouraging wisecracks, and that each would be looking for his Finance Chairman so as to make certain of victory in the election. But, of course, as you have long ago discovered, that is not the way things work.[2]

I am scheduled for at least two more talks of a political nature and another in New York that is supposed to be non-political.[3] In the meantime I know you are slugging away for the Rockefeller-Keating slate.[4]

Give my warm greetings to Frances and of course all the best to yourself, *As ever*

[1] Dewey had complimented the President (Oct. 21) on the campaign speeches he had delivered in Iowa and California. Praising the Republican record, Eisenhower had said that the Administration had provided progressive, efficient, and honest government and had given the country an expanding economy and a strong, modern defense. A few more days of this, Dewey said, and the entire nation would follow Eisenhower's lead on November 4. For background on Eisenhower's scheduled campaign trips see no. 898 and the following document; on his speeches see *Public Papers of the Presidents: Eisenhower, 1958*, pp. 752–56, 757–79, and *New York Times*, Oct. 18, 19, 21, 22, 26, 1958.

[2] On Eisenhower's growing concern over apathy within the Republican party see, for example, no. 880. Dewey would share the President's discouragement about the "lackluster attitude" of party members. Whatever the outcome, Dewey wrote on October 28, Eisenhower should feel comfortable knowing he had offered "blazing fine political leadership."

[3] On October 23 Eisenhower had returned from Chicago, where he participated in a radio and newsreel panel discussion sponsored by the Republican National Committee. He had also delivered a radio and television address to Republican precinct workers. By month's end he also would travel to Pennsylvania, West Virginia, New York, and Maryland (see *Public Papers of the Presidents: Eisenhower, 1958*, pp. 780–94, 797–808, 809–15, 819–26, and *New York Times*, Oct. 23, 28, 29, Nov. 1, 1958).

[4] For background on Rockefeller's August 25 nomination as the Republican candidate for Governor of New York see no. 830. Congressman Kenneth Barnard Keating (LL.B. Harvard 1923) had represented New York's thirty-eighth congressional district for six successive terms. He had won the Republican nomination for the U.S. Senate on August 26 (*New York Times*, Aug. 27, Oct. 17, Nov. 5, 6, 1958).

On the eve of the election (Nov. 3) Eisenhower would tell Dewey that he had the satisfaction of knowing that he and Dewey had done all that each of them could do. The President also said he hoped New York would provide the brightest spot in the picture when the returns came in. For developments see no. 964. All correspondence is in the same file as the document.

909   *EM, AWF, International Series:*
Churchill

To Winston Spencer Churchill   *October 24, 1958*

Dear Winston: Your letter of the seventeenth was forwarded to me on the West Coast, where I was engaged in a "political" tour.[1] It was a strenuous and hectic affair, and this is the very first moment I have had to reply.

I am glad you were pleased with the reception accorded your paintings both in Washington and on the tour the exhibit made of major American cities. As I wrote you, the show proved to be the artistic hit of the season in every city in which it was shown.[2]

As I also said in my letter of April thirtieth, I was, and still am, hopeful that you still might come over to America for a visit that would delight me and the American people greatly.[3] I had thought we might together select the one painting that you so kindly want me to have. But if I am to be denied that pleasure at this time, I cling to the selection I originally made—that is, the scene of the Urika River and the Atlas Mountains. I shall be interested in your reaction to my choice![4]

I was delighted to read in the paper the other day an account of your visit to the theatre where Sarah is in a play. By that I judge that you are feeling stronger; I do hope so.[5]

With affectionate regard to you and Clemmie in which Mamie joins, *As ever*

[1] Churchill's letter is in AWF/I: Churchill. Eisenhower had been campaigning for November's midterm elections (see no. 882).
[2] Churchill said he was glad that the exhibition of his works "went off so well." He added that it gained for him "a world-wide reputation as a painter." For background on the exhibit see no. 222; on Eisenhower's letters regarding the reviews see nos. 568 and 668.
[3] Due to failing health Churchill had been forced to postpone his visit to the United States. Eisenhower's April 30 letter to him is no. 668. Churchill would reply (November 1958) that he would like to visit Eisenhower in May 1959. For developments see no. 1023.
[4] Churchill had offered Eisenhower any painting in the exhibit (see no. 222). The former prime minister would reply that he was "delighted" that the President had selected the *Ourika River and Atlas Mountains* scene. For developments see no. 1174.
[5] Churchill's second daughter, Sarah, was a forty-four-year-old actress who had worked in the United States. Following her husband's suicide in August 1957, she returned to England to work in a local repertory company. Churchill would say that he took "great pleasure" in Sarah's theater work (Churchill to Eisenhower, November, 1958, AWF/I: Churchill, and *New York Times*, Aug. 19, 22, 1957, Oct. 16, 1958).

910   *EM, AWF, Administration Series*

To Ezra Taft Benson   *October 25, 1958*

Dear Ezra: Many thanks for your report on the political situations you have found in Indiana and Arizona. When I called your office, I was told you were in Wisconsin today. I can only tell you once again how grateful I am for your energetic efforts.[1]

I shall see you Sunday night, but meantime I wanted to send you this little note to tell you how encouraged I am by your report.[2]

With warm regard, *As ever*

[1] The Secretary of Agriculture's letter to Eisenhower, dated October 23, is in AWF/A. Campaigning in Indiana, Benson had found that Republican candidates and their supporters knew that they were "in a fight this year" and thought that this knowledge would motivate them "to win us more victories than some of the so-called experts are predicting." In Arizona he had delivered "some very good endorsements" for Barry Goldwater and had encountered a large number of Democrats who enthusiastically supported the Republican Senator's reelection drive. He accurately predicted that Republicans would capture two of the four congressional districts that he visited, and that Goldwater would also defeat his Democratic opponent. His prediction that the Republicans would win the contested Indiana Senate seat was, however, mistaken. See *New York Times*, November 6, 1958. Presidential Secretary Ann Whitman may have drafted this letter for delivery by telegraph to Benson.
[2] On October 26 Benson would attend a private concert given by the Mormon Tabernacle Choir in the White House (Benson, *Cross Fire*, pp. 412–13). For developments in the political campaign see no. 913.

To Florence Musser Etherington   *October 25, 1958*

Dear Florence: My brothers are quite pleased with the idea of building an appropriate wrought iron fence around the cemetery plot.[1] Personally I have been thinking of something of the order of two feet high—or somewhere in that neighborhood.

You will remember that you were going to contact the Cemetery Association to determine whether or not they would have any objection to the building of such a fence.[2] It might make slightly more difficult normal maintenance operations; of this I am not sure. But it seems to me that any difficulty of this kind in cutting grass might be minimized should the bottom of the fence be raised some three or four inches off the ground so that some instrument like a sickle or shears could be used along the fence line itself.[3] Another thing that I think would be nice to have is a diagram of the exact size of the plot. I know that Beulah lies just behind your parents, but I am not sure that the comparable section just behind the graves where my father and mother lie belongs in the family plot.[4]

Another question I should like to ask is whether or not "perpetual care" was arranged for at the time of the purchase of the lot. If not, I should like to know if that kind of service is provided by the Cemetery Association, what arrangements have to be made?[5]

If there is any other information you think I should have, I would be very appreciative of your sending it to me.

It was nice to see you, even if only for a few seconds. I must say that both you and Ray looked to be in splendid health.[6] *Devotedly*

P.S. Just as I left the hotel to return to Salina I heard that George had called the previous evening to see me.[7] Actually I had gone to bed very early and was sound asleep so, of course, the staff did not awaken me. Give him my warm greetings when you see him.

---

[1] On October 18 Eisenhower had written his brothers regarding the construction of the fence around the family plot in Abilene Cemetery (see no. 898).

[2] Eisenhower had first discussed this idea with his cousin Florence when he visited his boyhood home October 17–18 (see nos. 898 and 906).

Mrs. Etherington had written to Eisenhower on October 24. Although she knew members of the board "very well," she wrote, she had been advised to have "definite plans before presenting the subject to the association." In a later (undated) reply she would report that permission for the fence had been granted. On November 5 Eisenhower would say he would be in touch with her regarding the plans (all in AWF/N).

[3] As it turned out, the fence would be thirty-one inches high with a two-inch finial, and it would be raised six inches off the ground (Darby to Whitman, Nov. 14, 1958, AWF/N, Etherington Corr.).

[4] The lot measured twenty-six feet long on the west side, fifteen and one-half feet

long on the east side, and twenty-four feet long on the north and south sides. The center of the lot was between Mrs. Etherington's mother's grave and the President's father's (for background on the lot and the family members buried there see no. 898).

[5] The cemetery staff mowed the grass, Mrs. Etherington reported, and she raked the leaves and debris that gathered under the trees. There were "always many bouquets of fresh flowers," and she thought the Eisenhower brothers already had established a perpetual care fund. (In the memorandum granting permission for the fence, the secretary of the Abilene Cemetery Association would note that provision had been made for perpetual care of the entire lot [AWF/N, Etherington Corr.]).

On May 13, 1959, the President would send Earl Eisenhower photographs of the fenced lot (AWF/N; see also no. 898).

[6] Ray was Mrs. Etherington's husband.

[7] The Etheringtons' married son, George, was in the realty and construction business in Salina, Kansas.

912   *EM, AWF, International Series:*
                                                              Macmillan

To Harold Macmillan   *October 31, 1958*
Cable. Secret

Dear Harold: Thank you for your message of October twenty-seventh about the setback to the effort to get a conference about Cyprus under way.[1]

I can readily understand your disappointment at the sudden decision of the Greek Government not to participate in a conference, especially in light of the long and painstaking discussions in the North Atlantic Council and the considerable efforts at compromise which your Government has made in the course of these discussions. We too were greatly disappointed by the Greek Government's decision, and we have made our disappointment known to the Greeks.[2]

We share your belief that there is probably little advantage to be gained in pressing the Greeks further at this time to attend a conference, and we also share your hope that a conference may yet be possible. In spite of our disappointment with the Greeks, we believe that it is very important to keep open the door to further NATO talks on Cyprus. To this end we hope that it will be possible to avoid any action by NATO which could create the impression that NATO is opposed to Greece on this issue. Within recent weeks, we have noticed a healthier and less suspicious attitude on the part of the Greek Government toward the idea of NATO consultation with regard to Cyprus. This new attitude should, in our opinion, be encouraged, since it holds forth the possibility of eventual further productive talks under the aegis of NATO.[3]

I admire your refusal to be disheartened by recent Cyprus developments and your determination to continue to work toward a settlement of this vastly difficult problem. For our part, we always shall be ready to help whenever and however we appropriately can.[4]

With warm regard, *As ever*

[1] For background on the Cyprus situation see no. 872. At the October 6 meeting of the North Atlantic Council the British and Turkish representatives had agreed to confer on the issue. The Greek representative had announced that his country would participate if the agenda included the determination of the final status of Cyprus. Council members then decided, subject to the approval of their governments, to sponsor a conference attended by representatives of the three governments and at least one other NATO power as a neutral observer. After a close vote, however, the Greek cabinet had rejected the proposal (State, *Foreign Relations, 1958–1960*, vol. X, pt. 1, *Eastern Europe Region; Soviet Union; Cyprus*, pp. 719–33; see also Royal Ministry of Foreign Affairs, *The Cyprus Question*, pp. 19–35)

Macmillan had told Eisenhower that the Greeks had been "very weak" about Cyprus and were influenced by the opposition of Archbishop Makarios to the conference. The British felt that "the right course was to let the Greeks simmer for a period. In their hearts," he said, "most of the Greek Government realizes that their attitude is indefensible; if we run after them now it will only consolidate them; but if we do nothing, their self-doubting will take effect" (AWF/I: Macmillan; see also Dulles to Eisenhower, Oct. 30, 1958, AWF/D-H; Macmillan, *Riding the Storm*, pp. 687–88; and Reddaway, *Burdened with Cyprus*, pp. 114–19).

[2] Assistant Secretary of State William Rountree had expressed the attitude of the United States to the Greek ambassador in a meeting four days earlier (State, *Foreign Relations, 1958–1960*, vol. X, pt. 1, *Eastern Europe Region; Soviet Union; Cyprus*, p. 734).

[3] Greek government officials had told the American ambassador in Athens that the Greek attitude toward NATO was much improved in recent weeks. They hoped that the United States would use its influence to prevent the NATO communiqué from blaming Greece for the breakdown of negotiations (*ibid.*, pp. 731–32).

[4] For developments see no. 1054.

VI

Setbacks

NOVEMBER 1958 TO FEBRUARY 1959

14

A "dreary election result"

To CHARLES S. JONES   *November 1, 1958*
Telegram

Dear Charlie: Many thanks for your message of last evening.[1] You are a man not only of decision but of action. Republican accomplishments of the past few days are little short of miraculous. Had we all started a few weeks earlier we could have steam rollered those people.[2] In any event and at the very least we have the satisfying knowledge that we really got into harness and even if we do not secure all the results that we want on November fourth, we have got a good running start for the next campaign. I am more than grateful for all that you have done. Love to Jenny and all the best to yourself.[3] *As ever*

[1] For background on Richfield Oil Company President Jones's activities in connection with the 1958 election campaign see nos. 826, 829, and 842. Jones had helped organize a successful fund-raising luncheon that Eisenhower attended on October 20 during his campaign trip to Los Angeles (Ann Whitman memorandum, [Nov. 2, 1958], AWF/AWD). We have been unable to locate any record of his message in AWF. Presidential Secretary Ann Whitman sent this note to Rodney Rood, Jones's assistant at Richfield Oil, with a request that Rood relay it "to the elusive Mr. Jones— wherever he may be."

[2] Late in October Republicans, led by Eisenhower and Vice-President Richard Nixon, had staged a vigorous last-minute effort to prevent a predicted Democratic victory in the November elections. For reports of speeches, rallies, and other activities see *Public Papers of the Presidents: Eisenhower, 1958*, pp. 786–94, 797 815, 819–26, and *New York Times*, October 30, 31, 1958.

[3] Eisenhower's greeting was to Jones's wife, Genevieve. For developments see nos. 919 and 932.

To JUSTIN WHITLOCK DART   *November 1, 1958*

Dear Justin: I am of course highly gratified that even in retrospect you feel that my Los Angeles trip was successful, particularly from the point of view of the finance luncheon.[1] After the sound and fury of November fourth die away, I shall see what can be done about your suggestions. During the last month I have met with the finance people of both Chicago and New York, but I have never approached them with the specifics of your plan.[2]

The trouble will be, of course, that everyone is going to be tired of politicking and will resist what is obviously the necessity of starting now to work for 1960.

The first sentence of your final paragraph reflects my feeling, as well you know.[3] But if I can, through renewed efforts, leave office in 1961 with a revitalized Republican Party I am perfectly willing to devote whatever energies I have to the task.[4]

Once again my thanks to you, and, as always, my warm regard, *As ever*

[1] For background on the President's campaign trip to Los Angeles and his involvement with the California gubernatorial election see nos. 826, 900, 902, and the preceding document. In September Eisenhower had convinced Rexall Drugs President Dart to assume responsibility for raising funds for William Knowland's gubernatorial campaign. In turn, Dart had persuaded the President to meet privately with California business leaders at a luncheon on October 20, during his trip to the West Coast (Ann Whitman memorandums, Sept. 27 and [Nov. 2], 1958, AWF/AWD; see also Dart to Eisenhower, Oct. 7, 1958, AWF/A, and no. 880). On October 27 Dart had written Eisenhower (AWF/A) that his efforts had generated a "magnificent response" and had made "a tremendous start . . . in the direction of awakening our sleeping giants."

[2] On Eisenhower's conferences with Republican finance leaders, meetings which Dart had advocated as a means of pushing the party toward "solvency and virility," see Ann Whitman memorandums, October 6 and [November 2], AWF/AWD. Dart had given Eisenhower a copy of an undated "Long Range Plan for the Preservation of Personal Freedom and a Free Economy"; a copy is in AWF/A, Dart Corr. It was premised on the assumptions that the "free economic climate" in the United States was "being destroyed by a Labor Monopoly," and that excessive labor costs were endangering economic security; the plan urged business leaders to convince "the workers of America that they may become pawns and slaves of Labor Leaders." Dart recommended that business heads personally establish an annual subscription program to solicit contributions from their associates and employees. The fund-raising quotas for each company were to be based on a percentage of corporate profits.

[3] Dart had written: "I am sure you are saying to yourself that certainly this log jam could be broken by somebody other than yourself." He had added: "You may be right but I surely don't know who it is."

[4] On November 4—election day—Dart would send a telegram to Eisenhower saying that "All funds necessary to cover Knowland's campaign are on hand or committed." He would give partial credit to the President for this accomplishment and, in anticipation of a Republican defeat, would add that he was sure that Eisenhower would "provide the fire to get everybody off the bloody carpet tomorrow morning determined that this tragedy will not happen again in 1960" (AWF/A). For developments see no. 926.

915   *EM, AWF, Name Series*

To CLIFFORD ROBERTS   *November 1, 1958*
Telegram

Dear Cliff: Before another moment passes I want to express my deep gratitude for all you have done in the last few weeks for the cause in which we both deeply believe.[1] I know you have almost single-handedly raised the funds that made the national telecasts possible.[2] Whatever their impact and whatever the results on November fourth, I have the satisfaction, as I hope you have, of knowing no effort has been spared. Also, I truly believe we have right now a good running start for the next campaign.

Thank you for everything, most particularly for your friendship.[3] *With warm regard*

[1] For background on the role played by Eisenhower's friend Roberts in the 1958 elections see nos. 829 and 842; see also papers in AWF/N, Roberts Corr.

[2] Eisenhower had delivered nationally televised speeches on October 22, 27, and 31; in addition, he had participated in a televised panel discussion, sponsored by the Republican National Committee, with a group of Republican women in San Francisco, California, on October 21. See *New York Times*, October 22, 28, and November 1, 1958; see also *Public Papers of the Presidents, Eisenhower, 1958*, pp. 705–74, 780–94, 802–8, 819–26.

[3] Roberts would reply (Nov. 3, AWF/N) that he had "mixed emotions" about Eisenhower's telegram; while he was "proud" to have received it, he felt guilty that he had not already written to thank the President for having made "those three truly great speeches." He also suggested that they should meet to discuss ways to make the Republican party stronger. For developments see nos. 926, 945, and 963.

916
$\qquad$ *EM, AWF, International Series:*
Macmillan

To Harold Macmillan *November 3, 1958*
Cable. Confidential

Dear Harold: Now that the missions of the British forces in Jordan and the American forces in Lebanon have come to a close, I think that your country and mine can take deep satisfaction in the successful accomplishment of undertakings of wide and historic significance.[1]

Without firing a shot in anger, and in close and friendly collaboration with the local authorities, our forces have achieved what they were sent to Lebanon and Jordan to do, at the request of the respective Governments. They have preserved the independence of these two small countries against aggressive subversive forces directed from outside. Our action has proved to the world, and especially to the smaller nations, that we stand by our pledges and that we have the courage to carry out our solemn undertakings, regardless of the threats made against us. No matter what political developments may in the future take place in Lebanon or Jordan, the effect of our actions will remain valid. I consider this development of the highest significance to the Free World. If we had not acted as we did, the determination of the smaller nations to stand firm against the forces of aggression would have been gravely undermined, with all this would have meant for the positions of the United States and the United Kingdom.

We can also take special satisfaction in the complete understanding and splendid cooperation which was evident between our two governments in these undertakings. Both of us are, of course, dedicated to promoting the health and vigor of this spirit, but it is good to feel that in a difficult situation it was effectively applied.[2]

I wanted to let you know what a source of high personal gratification all this has been to me.[3]

With warm regard, *As ever*

[1] For background see nos. 770 and 776. Although the political situation in Lebanon remained unstable after the election of General Fuad Chehab as president in August, the State Department had announced on October 8 that "barring unforseen developments" all American forces would be withdrawn by the end of October. The withdrawal on October 25 was uneventful. All British troops were gone from Jordan by November 2 (State, *Foreign Relations, 1958–1960*, vol. XI, *Lebanon and Jordan*, pp. 539–44, 549–57, 563–67, 569–71, 573–79, 583–84, 599–602, 615, 622–24; NSC meeting minutes, Sept. 18, 25, Oct. 17, 1958, AWF/NSC; and Little, "His Finest Hour?," pp. 52–54; for Eisenhower's message to the withdrawing troops see *Public Papers of the Presidents: Eisenhower, 1958*, pp. 756–57).

Dulles had suggested that Eisenhower send this message to Macmillan to "express gratification at the outcome of our undertakings" (Dulles to Eisenhower, Oct. 31, 1958, AWF/D-H; the second page of the State Department draft, with Eisenhower's handwritten emendations, is in *ibid.*).

[2] Eisenhower had added the final sentence of this paragraph to the State Department draft.

[3] Macmillan would agree that the action had achieved important results. "Despite hostile criticism at the time we took our difficult decisions in July," he wrote, "I am sure that thinking people all over the world now realize the contribution which our action made to stability. Throughout the operations I was personally greatly fortified by the knowledge that we and the United States were moving in complete harmony of purpose" (Macmillan to Eisenhower, Nov. 7, 1958, PREM 11/2389).

917   *EM, AWF, Administration Series*

To Robert Bernerd Anderson   *November 3, 1958*

Dear Bob: In recent months I have sent out letters to selected friends of mine asking for help in projects of importance to the government.[1] I am now impressed with the necessity of getting the help of businessmen and others in keeping down governmental expenditures and in otherwise combatting inflation.

As you know, I have been busy for some weeks in the political field; I have been doing so much speaking, writing and arguing that I seem a little low, not in ideas, but in persuasiveness.[2]

For this reason and of course because I recognize that our views about governmental expenditures and inflation are so nearly the same, I would like to request you to try your hand at preparing for me a draft of a letter that I might in coming weeks send out to some several hundred of my friends. Here and there I could, of course, vary the exact language but in all cases the intent and analysis would be identical. Possibly it is an imposition to ask you to undertake this, but I was impressed today by some of the statistics that you could bring right out of your head, particularly those relating to our debt and our twelve months of financial operation.[3] To be most effective the letter should be as short as possible—one of mine was far too lengthy and I believe it is better to keep them on the short side.[4]

If you do not feel that you have time to do this, I will undertake the thing myself.

With warm regard, *As ever*

---

[1] See no. 897.

[2] See, for example, nos. 908 and the following document.

[3] Eisenhower had met several times that morning with Secretary Anderson.

[4] Anderson would respond (Nov. 12, AWF/A, Anderson Corr.) in a four-page draft letter on the economy, emphasizing the President's concern with the "high level of government expenditures" and the "avoidance of long-run inflation." Eisenhower would make extensive handwritten changes on the document, including the addition of this sentence: "I believe that the greatest reassurance we could now give to everyone who understands the essentials of this problem is to produce and to live by, a balanced budget." There is no indication that this letter was ever sent, but the President would send his friends a similar letter in February; see no. 1042.

---

918   *EM, WHCF, Official File 101 JJ*

To Marshall Smith Lachner   *November 3, 1958*

Dear Mr. Lachner:[1] Thank you for your message of October thirtieth. I appreciate your comments about my presence at the dinner of the National Football Foundation and Hall of Fame dinner; actually the evening was thoroughly enjoyable for me and a refreshing contrast to some of my political appearances of recent weeks.[2]

Following your suggestions I brought up the matter of my concern that every individual who wants to work has the job opportunity he seeks, and my belief in the bright future of the American economy, again in my Baltimore talk.[3] As you well know, it is practically impossible in any political address, made before an audience, to take any special problem or program and devote to it any particular length of time. This is only possible when one is conducting a very full schedule of speeches and has the opportunity to take each subject in turn. However, I did not fail to give emphasis to the points you raised.

With best wishes and again my thanks for your telegram. *Sincerely*

[1] Lachner (Wharton School of Business, University of Pennsylvania 1936) was president of B. T. Babbitt, Inc., a manufacturer of cleansers and aerosol products.

[2] Lachner had sent a telegram to the President on October 30 to congratulate him on his address to the first Football Hall of Fame Dinner on October 28, 1958 (see *Public Papers of the Presidents: Eisenhower, 1958*, pp. 816–19). He had also complimented the President on his radio and television address in Pittsburgh on October 27 (*ibid.*, pp. 802–8). Lachner had been particularly struck by Eisenhower's pledge that, "So long as there is anyone unemployed, who is able and willing to work, especially those with families to support and bills coming due, our problems are not fully solved." "If this is made the theme of many of your speeches from now on . . . ," Lachner wrote, "I am sure you will be able to swing many voters away from the opposition and back again to the Republicans."

[3] Lachner had urged Eisenhower to emphasize job security and "an ever improving standard of living" in a speech scheduled for Baltimore on October 31 (see *ibid.*, pp. 819–26). The President had spoken of the strength of the economy and had mocked one "gloomdoggler" who had accused the Administration of planning the recession. He had also said that the Administration would help workers and eliminate unemployment by striving to control inflation, providing equality of opportunity and seeking a legislative program that aided economically impaired areas, reformed taxes, and helped "drive racketeers and hoodlums out of the American labor movement." All correspondence is in the same file as the document.

919   *EM, AWF, Administration Series*

To Hugh Meade Alcorn, Jr.   *November 3, 1958*

Dear Meade: I have gone through the report that you sent to me under date of November first.[1] It shows that, at the very least, the Republican apathy that seemed to be so noticeable across the country a few weeks ago has largely disappeared.

There is one remark that appears rather frequently in the State reports you have received. It is, in effect, "The President should have started speaking earlier."[2]

As early as August I let it be known that I was quite ready to make a tour across the country, making a minimum of three formal speeches and at such time as the "pros" felt would be best. Since I know that you keep in close touch with state organizations, I had assumed that the timing was about what the majority preferred.

Actually, of course, I made four full dress political speeches, with a number of informal public appearances, before audiences of varying size and types.[3]

With warm regard, *As ever*

[1] On the eve of the 1958 elections Republican party chairman Alcorn had sent Eisenhower three confidential memorandums containing political status reports from state GOP officials (AWF/A). Alcorn had apparently asked the state leaders to evaluate the impact of the President's recent campaign appearances. For background see no. 915.

[2] Of the thirty-seven reports, only three had expressed regret that Eisenhower had delayed his vigorous election efforts. The Texas state chairman, who thought that the President's speeches had been "terrific," had said that he wished Eisenhower "had started this kind of slugging campaign earlier" (Alcorn to Eisenhower, Oct. 30, 1958, AWF/A).

[3] On Eisenhower's speeches see no. 915. Alcorn would reply (Nov. 3, 1958, AWF/A) that he hoped the President would not "attach undue significance" to the critical comments because "few state leaders are ever completely satisfied with what the leadership in Washington does to help them in their states." He assured Eisenhower that both the timing and the location of his speeches had been carefully planned. Had Eisenhower begun earlier, he wrote, his impact would have been "substantially diminished." For developments see no. 926.

920   *EM, AWF, Name Series*

To Elizabeth Hazlett   *November 3, 1958*

Dear Ibby: This note is simply to say what of course you already know. The prayers and hearts of Mamie and myself are with you today, as they have been in the past; we are thinking of you and all the members of your family with love and devotion.

I can never quite tell you what Swede meant to me. While I am glad for his sake that he suffers no longer, his passing leaves a permanent void in my life.[1] *Affectionately*

[1] On November 2, following a long illness, the President's boyhood friend, Captain Edward Everett Hazlett (USN, ret.) had died. On November 5 Eisenhower would attend the funeral services at Arlington National Cemetery. In her note to the President Mrs. Hazlett would say his presence at Arlington was a "joy" to her family. "Swede was pleased, I know!" she added. She also thanked the President for the numerous floral arrangements he had sent them (Nov. 17, 1958, AWF/N, *New York Times*, Nov. 6, 1958, and Ann Whitman memorandum, Nov. 2, 5, 1958, AWF/AWD). On Hazlett's illness see no. 906; on the flowers see, for example, nos. 41 and 622).

On Eisenhower's friendship with Hazlett see his memoir, *At Ease*, pp. 104–6. In her diary Ann Whitman would note that, "The President used to correspond with him [Hazlett] more frankly than any other individual" (Ann Whitman memorandum, Nov. 5, 1958, AWF/AWD). See also Robert W. Griffith, ed., *Ike's Letters to a Friend, 1941–1958* (Lawrence, Kansas, 1984).

To JOHN MERRILL OLIN   *November 4, 1958*
Personal

Dear John: Thank you for your letter which, along with its enclosures,
I read with great interest.[1]

As you know, a great many people in this country have urged some
kind of modification of our income tax laws, particularly in establishing maximum allowable rates. But the difficulty about extremists, at both ends of the political spectrum, is that they constantly
overstate their case. For example, Mr. Lee's proposal that we completely abolish the income tax! How does he propose to meet the
necessary costs of government, to say nothing of the other costs that
have been saddled on us—some not so necessary![2]

As of today the costs of defense and atomic development, to which
we must add interest on the public debt, total something over 50
billion dollars. Two other items that probably cannot be seriously
diminished, because of the temperament of our people, are veterans' benefits and agricultural payments. Add all these together and
we have something well over 60 billion dollars. This takes no account of the money that must be spent to collect our taxes and handle our financial transactions, to support our Justice Department
and to carry on the diplomatic activities required in today's world.
And think of the sums that go into grants to States!

By no means do I mean to imply that a good many of these functions could not be more economically performed; indeed some
could be abandoned. As you probably know, my personal conviction, often repeated, is that unless we get Federal expenditures under control, we are in for real trouble. For as long as I am in this
office, this matter is going to be the subject on which I shall dwell
without ceasing.

But the real battle is between moderates who believe in sensible
functioning of government and those who want a near socialism—
or, at the other end, those who want to shut their eyes to our obligations today. The "do-nothing" extremists do not pitch in to help
wage the bitter fight that has been going on—much of it behind
the scenes—to keep costs at more reasonable levels. What I mean
to say is that people such as Lee, by their blind and foolish insistence that we abolish income taxes, really do nothing to help defeat
the extremists at the other pole, who want to spend and spend.

Finally, we must remember that the struggle to sustain our way of
life is waged on two fronts. One is the home—the other is foreign.
Militant communism grows more and more threatening. We must
be alert.

There is no need to detail here any of the arguments about mutual assistance. You are well acquainted with the system. It is not a "give-away" program designed in the spirit of altruism. It is merely one effective way of helping to defeat that kind of socialism (Imperialistic Communism) which the nations of the world, unaided, could not successfully withstand.[3]

We cannot win the fight on either of these fronts unless we win it on both. Consequently we must have sense and efficiency as our watchwords, and certainly we must make the American people understand fully what they are up against. We must be strong—but we must stop unnecessary spending.

I mentioned the enclosures you sent with your letter. I send to you one which will give you some inkling of exactly what is going on in Red China.[4] This is the kind of thing that presents a real challenge to freedom and liberty in the world. Incidentally, another report on this same region states that the morale of the Chinese people undergoing this regimentation is very high. They seem to see themselves as fanatical followers of a modern Genghis Khan.[5]

In recent months I have sent letters expressing my concern about particular governmental problems to various of my business friends.[6] Soon I may send a third one asking for their help in minimizing governmental expenditures.[7]

With warm regard, *As ever*

---

[1] Olin had written on October 30 in support of Eisenhower's election appeal on behalf of the Republicans (see no. 897). In addition to having "contributed substantially to the Republican party," Olin wrote, he had also "worked diligently to endeavor . . . to urge all whom I have been able to contact to go to the polls next Tuesday and support your administration by voting the straight Republican ballot." Olin had enclosed the October 1958 issue of the Stevenson, Jordan & Harrison "Monthly Digest of Business Conditions and Probabilities," and a column on income taxes by John O'Donnell from the October 29 *New York Daily News*. Eisenhower would forward Olin's enclosures to former White House adviser, Gabriel Hauge (see no. 928).

[2] Joseph Bracken Lee had served as governor of Utah from 1949–1957, and was national chairman of *For America*. For further background see Galambos and van Ee, *The Middle Way*, no. 643. O'Donnell had reported that Governor Lee was dominating his opponents in the polls due to his leadership of the movement to repeal the Sixteenth Amendment to the Constitution, which granted the Congress the power to collect taxes on income.

[3] See, for example, no. 90.

[4] Eisenhower's enclosure is not in EM.

[5] In February 1958 the Chinese government had launched a "Great Leap Forward" movement, calling for steep increases in the production of steel, coal, and electricity. The production campaign was accompanied by the creation of People's Communes that combined the existing agricultural producers' cooperatives. By November 1958 the movement had created 26,000 communes, comprising 98 percent of the farm population. In the cities, urban communes were organized to parallel the rural development. Initial reports seemed to indicate that the movement was a success, with 1958 production surpassing that of 1957 by 65 percent. (See Immanuel C.

Y. Hsü, *The Rise of Modern China* [New York and Oxford, 1990], pp. 655–60; see also Roderick MacFarquhar, *The Origins of the Cultural Revolution*, 2 vols. [New York, 1974–1983], vol. II, *The Great Leap Forward, 1958–1960* [1983], and State, *Foreign Relations, 1958–1960*, vol. XIX, *China*, pp. 472, 520–23).

[6] See, for example, no. 678.

[7] See nos. 917 and 1042.

922   *EM, AWF, Administration Series*

To NELSON ALDRICH ROCKEFELLER   *November 5, 1958*
Telegram

Dear Nelson: Heartiest congratulations on your outstanding victory. You waged a magnificent and tireless campaign and the result should be a source of great personal gratification to you. Under your leadership the great Empire State will experience an era of real progress. I hope you can manage to get a good rest and that I shall see you soon. Meantime, again my felicitations and warm personal regard.[1]
As ever

[1] On November 4 Rockefeller had been elected governor of New York (*New York Times*, Nov. 5, 1958; see also Ann Whitman memorandum, Nov. 4, 1958, AWF/AWD). On the eve of the election Rockefeller had thanked the President for the privilege of working in the Administration and for the President's encouragement during the campaign (AWF/A). For background see nos. 830 and 843. Rockefeller would again thank Eisenhower for his support in a telegram later on this same day (AWF/A). For developments see no. 965.

923   *EM, AWF, Dulles-Herter Series*

To JOHN FOSTER DULLES   *November 6, 1958*

Dear Foster: C. D. presents in the attached letter and memorandum certain objections that others have advanced against the proposal of refusing to seat in the United Nations the Kadar representatives.[1] These objections are four, with one added on the basis of "getting the vote."[2]

One of them that seems to me to have very little validity is that of "keeping an American window in Hungary."[3] If the Communist government of Hungary wants to kick our Embassy out of the place, they can do it with or without an excuse. Indeed, I should doubt that they would deem it a satisfactory retaliatory gesture should we initiate the proposal C. D. suggests.

In any event, I send to you also a copy of the note I am sending C. D. so that he will understand that this whole matter is under consideration in the State Department.[4]

With warm regard, *As ever*

---

[1] C. D. Jackson's October 30 letter and undated memorandum are in Dulles Papers, White House Memoranda Series. On June 16 Radio Moscow had announced that former Hungarian Premier Imre Nagy and other Hungarian officials had been executed for their participation in the 1956 Hungarian revolt (for background see Galambos and van Ee, *The Middle Way*, no. 2067, and no. 417 in these volumes). State Department officials had then considered the advisability of challenging the credentials of the Hungarian delegation in the United Nations General Assembly (State, *Foreign Relations, 1958–1960*, vol. II, *United Nations and General International Matters*, p. 23, and Memorandum of Conversation, Yarrow and Dulles, Oct. 29, 1958, Dulles Papers, Chronological Series; see also no. 832, and *New York Times*, Oct. 28, Nov. 2, 1958).

Jackson had urged the President to tell the State Department that he was in favor of excluding the Kadar regime from the United Nations. Jackson's memorandum listed the State Department's objections to unseating the Hungarians: 1) reprisal action would confuse the public because the executions had been ordered by Moscow and not Budapest; 2) such action could lead to retaliation by the Hungarian regime, including the closing of the U.S. embassy in Hungary; and 3) closure of the embassy could create a serious situation for Jozsef Cardinal Mindszenty to whom the Americans had granted asylum after the 1956 Hungarian Revolution (State, *Foreign Relations, 1958–1960*, vol. X, pt. 1, *Eastern Europe Region; Soviet Union; Cyprus*, pp. 54–55).

[2] Jackson had said that he believed initially that removal would require a two-thirds vote, but that now he knew only a simple majority was necessary. Even if the United States lost the vote, he wrote, America would still have enhanced its "moral position," leading to favorable repercussions behind the Iron Curtain.

[3] Jackson also had objected to the State Department's suggestion of the need for a "window" through which the United States could observe Hungarian developments and the Hungarian people could take note of the American presence.

[4] Eisenhower's reply to Jackson is the following document.

924

To Charles Douglas Jackson   *November 6, 1958*
Personal

Dear C. D.: Thank you for your letter of the thirtieth and for the accompanying document.[1] I have just talked to Foster on the subject.[2]

He said in effect, "First of all, my heart is exactly with C. D. in this matter. In the Department we have been working very hard to find a formula that would be simple and effective." I gather that he does *not* believe that the question is merely one of denying the Kadar representatives a seat in the UN. It was his impression also that any proposal involving expulsion would require some reference to the Security Council and be subject to the veto.[3]

I realize, of course, that there are technicalities in United Nations procedures that are not too familiar to me and sometimes seem inexplicable. In any event, I have told Foster that your memorandum at least produces a favorable reaction so far as my sentiments and emotions are concerned and have asked him to read it very carefully to see if there is any simple action that he believes to be valid under the United Nations Charter.[4]

Since he is still having this question intensively studied in the Department, I am not certain when I shall hear from him; he might communicate with you directly.[5]

With warm regard, *As ever*

[1] Jackson had expressed his frustration over the State Department's objections to unseating the Hungarian delegation in the United Nations General Assembly (see the preceding document).

[2] See Dulles Papers, Telephone Conversations, Eisenhower and Dulles, November 6, 1958.

[3] The State Department would telegram the American embassy in Great Britain on November 20 that action under Articles 5 and 6 of the U.N. Charter to suspend rights or expel Hungary would be subject to Security Council approval. The certainty of a Soviet veto would render any steps the United States could take as a "futile propaganda maneuver" (State, *Foreign Relations, 1958–1960*, vol. II, *United Nations and General International Matters*, pp. 76–77).

[4] On November 7 Dulles would learn from the Office of the Legal Adviser of the United Nations that the General Assembly was empowered to bar the Hungarian representatives from its committees while permitting them to be seated in the plenary sessions (*ibid.*, pp. 73–74). On November 10 Dulles would tell Eisenhower that the State Department would continue to study the question. It was difficult to devise an effective formula to bar the Kadar representatives given the sensibilities of other members regarding credentials, Dulles said. Eisenhower would say that he wanted to take a positive position even if we lost in the United Nations (Dulles, Memorandum of Conversation, Dulles Papers, White House Memoranda Series).

[5] For developments see no. 960.

925   *EM, AWF, International Series:*
                                                    Churchill

To Winston Spencer Churchill   *November 6, 1958*
Cable

I am delighted to learn that you have been made a Companion of the Order of Liberation of France. No one could deserve this recognition more than you. It is an honor that brings to the minds of all free men your contributions to our common cause during World War II, as well as your great friendship for France, our mutual ally and partner.[1]

With best wishes for your continued health and happiness, and with warm personal regard.[2]

[1] A State Department draft of this cable, showing Eisenhower's handwritten emendations, is in AWF/I: Churchill. On November 4 the American embassy in Paris had telegraphed the Secretary of State regarding Churchill's selection for membership in France's most exclusive order. On this day Premier Charles de Gaulle, who had established the Ordre de la Libération in January 1941, would present the insignia of the order to the British wartime leader. General Eisenhower had received the Croix de la Libération in Paris on June 14, 1945 (see State Department to Eisenhower, Nov. 4, 1958, AWF/I: Churchill; *New York Times*, Nov. 7, 1958; Charles de Gaulle, *The War Memoirs of Charles de Gaulle*, 3 vols [New York, 1955–1960], vol. 1, *The Call to Honor, 1940–1942*, Jonathan Griffin, trans. [New York, 1955], p. 166; Charles de Gaulle, *Lettres, Notes et Carnets, Juin 1940–Juillet 1941* [Librairie Plon, 1980], pp. 167–68, 240; and Chandler and Galambos, *Occupation, 1945*, no. 121).
[2] For developments see no. 938.

926   *EM, AWF, International Series:*
                                                Macmillan

TO HAROLD MACMILLAN   *November 11, 1958*
Personal

Dear Harold: Thank you for your personal note of the seventh.[1] I was, to be sure, disappointed by the overall showing of the Republican Party in our recent elections.[2] Fortunately I have never considered myself an expert politician (I am certain a great many people would emphatically agree that I am not), and I can view the matter at least with some detachment.

One thing bothers me. It is the seeming desire of the people of our country to depend more and more upon government—they do not seem to understand that more governmental assistance inevitably means more governmental control. I have not done well in my efforts to point out the dangers to all of us inherent in these trends particularly for our children and grandchildren.

The faults of the Republican Party are many and have been made obvious. One of them is our readiness to believe the charges that we are hopelessly divided among ourselves. We are called "liberal" Republicans and "conservative" Republicans. Scarcely anyone can give me a definition of either term! But falling for this charge, we weaken ourselves with internal strife.[3] The opposition, though representing the extremes of the political spectrum, can always unite for the election battle.

If I could devote myself exclusively to a political job, I'd like to take on the one of reorganizing and revitalizing the Party. But in my present post I conceive my duty to be somewhat broader than that of a mere politician—even though I profoundly believe in a two-party system, and believe that my Party is much the better of the two for the nation.[4]

Again, my deep appreciation of your thoughtfulness in writing, and, as always, my warm personal regard, *As ever*

[1] Macmillan's letter is in AWF/I: Macmillan. Commenting on the recent elections (for background see no. 919), he had assured Eisenhower that the affection that the British people felt for him was "in no way dependent upon the political fortunes of the Republican Party." Macmillan also recalled that during his earliest years in electoral politics, "when one lost one was apt to say how tiresome and foolish all this business of counting noses was: when one won, of course, one felt convinced of the soundness of public opinion."

[2] The 1958 midterm elections had been a disaster for the GOP. The Democrats had won an additional 13 seats in the Senate and would outnumber the Republicans in the next Congress by a margin of 64 to 34. In the House of Representatives the Democrats had picked up 47 more seats and would dominate their opponents by a total of 283 to 153. (In January 1959 Congress would add two seats in the Senate and one in the House for the newly admitted state of Alaska. All three positions would be filled by Democrats.) The Democrats had also won 26 of the 34 possible gubernatorial elections and would exceed Republicans in this category by a margin of 35 to 14. In California (see nos. 836 and 932), Democrat Edmund Brown had defeated William Knowland in the race for governor, and Republican Governor Goodwin Knight had failed in his bid to succeed Knowland in the U.S. Senate. California voters had also rejected the right-to-work initiative (see no. 905; see also *Congressional Quarterly Almanac*, vol. XIV, *1958*, pp. 713–24; and Anderson, "The 1958 Election in California," pp. 289–92).

[3] For more on divisions within the Republican party see no. 826; for developments see no. 932.

[4] Eisenhower would try to develop plans to revitalize the party; see nos. 962 and 963.

927   *EM, WHCF, Official File 103*

To Clare Eugene Hoffman   *November 12, 1958*

Dear Mr. Hoffman: Thank you for your letter inquiring about comments in my November fifth Press Conference.[1]

I believe, of course, that the public, the Congress, and such auditing units as the General Accounting Office should have all the information Departments and Agencies can properly make available. However, the public interest also demands order and efficiency in the operation of these Departments and Agencies. And in my judgment the public interest is not necessarily served by divulging the advice, suggestions, or recommendations which subordinate employees periodically make to their superiors. In this connection, recommendations of Inspectors General have been a most useful advisory tool in administering the military departments; and historically, recommendations and other advisory matter in such reports have not been released. I think this practice is a correct one, and is in the best interest of the Nation. At the same time, I want to add that the facts are distinct from advice and recommendations in these reports. It is my understanding that all the facts developed in the Inspector General's report to which you refer are being made available at the request of the General Accounting Office. *Sincerely*

[1] Hoffman (LL.B. Northwestern 1895), a Republican congressman from Michigan since 1935, had written on November 12 regarding the hearings held by the House Government and Operations Committee's, Government Information Subcommittee. Eisenhower had been asked about reports that the Air Force and the Defense Department, claiming executive privilege (see Galambos and van Ee, *The Middle Way*, nos. 874 and 879), had withheld information regarding spending from the General Accounting Office. The President had responded that he believed "every investigating committee of the Congress, every auditing office like the GAO, should always have an opportunity to see official records if the security of our country is not involved" (*Public Papers of the Presidents: Eisenhower, 1958*, pp. 837–38). "Did you mean to imply by your comments," Hoffman inquired, "that the complete text of Inspector General reports, including recommendations, be made available to Congress and the General Accounting Office?" See Clark R. Mollenhoff, *The Pentagon: Politics, Profits and Plunder* (New York, 1967), pp. 223–28. White House Administrative Assistant Edward A. McCabe drafted this letter for the President.

928   *EM, WHCF, Official File 115*

To GABRIEL HAUGE   *November 12, 1958*
Personal

Dear Gabe: Thank you very much for your note of the sixth.[1] And now, thank you, too, for the letter-to-the-editor that appeared in the New York Times of yesterday.[2] I can think of no more able or effective voice than yours on behalf of that Administration's fiscal policy. As a matter of fact, I am becoming reconciled, only slightly however, to your departure since I am realizing that as a banker in New York you are not bound by the same restrictions of a member of the Administration and that you will be listened to without some of the bias that might attach to you as a member of my staff.[3] But I emphasize that word "slightly"—since all of us miss you greatly and will for all the time remaining to us here.

I think the editorial in this morning's Tribune sums up about as well as can be the Republican lessons to be learned from the dismal results on the fourth.[4] *If* we start now (and I mean all Republicans) to profit from those lessons, I would face 1960 with confidence. But human nature being what it is (a matter which was displayed only too close to home yesterday)[5] I am not at all sure that Republicans in key places have yet learned that there is no room for disunity in the prospect before us.

With warm regard. *As ever*

[1] Eisenhower had sent Hauge the Stevenson, Jordan & Harrison *Monthly Digest of Business Conditions and Probabilities* and an article from the *New York Daily News* regarding Utah Governor J. Bracken Lee's movement to repeal the Sixteenth Amendment (see no. 921). Lee's program, Hauge said, had as much chance of success "as an attempt by El Salvador to conquer the U.S.A." "Some conservatives think the way to change a situation like taxation in some fundamental respect is to move drastically. They often end up having set back their cause perhaps a decade and having liquidated progress painfully gained over many years." Hauge had characterized the Stevenson, Jordan & Harrison *Digest*, which warned against a "steadily growing demand for government hand-outs, with a continuous drift toward a welfare state," as "very good and to the point." "Here again," he said, "I suppose the trouble is that we are talking to ourselves. The readers of this digest likely agree with it."

[2] Hauge's November 10 letter to the editor of the *New York Times* (Nov. 11, 1958) had defended the President against "partisan attacks" on the Administration's spending record (see *New York Times*, Nov. 7, 1958). Hauge argued that the deterioration in the budget situation was due more to lower receipts resulting from the recession than to increased spending. The largest spending increase was for defense. Increased spending for agriculture as a result of weather conditions was also a factor. Hauge noted that Congress was responsible for authorizing $7.5 billion in "specific appropriation items, authorizations and tax adjustments" beyond the President's recommendations.

[3] On Hauge's resignation see no. 769.

[4] Eisenhower may have been referring to an editorial published in the November 6 *New York Herald Tribune*: "The Lesson for Republicans." The *Tribune* had said that the party could win "only by developing candidates of clearly superlative ability, integrity, warm personality and forward-looking views. The answer to the defeat is rebuild the party on modern Republican principles, give greater meaning to its label, greater appeal to the increasing number of voters who are splitting their tickets and voting for the ablest man." On the 1958 election results see no. 935; see also no. 937.

[5] Eisenhower was probably referring to former Pennsylvania Governor Harold E. Stassen's implied criticism of Vice-President Richard Nixon, an event which in fact had taken place on this same day. See no. 932; see also *New York Times*, Nov. 13, 1958.

To Chiang Kai-shek   *November 14, 1958*
Secret

Dear Mr. President:[1] Thank you very much for your letter of November
fifth. I quite understand your apprehensions concerning the attempts
by the Communists to distort the meaning of the joint communique in order to negate its effect and confuse the world.[2] However, I
assure you that reports we have received from capitals around the
world are most encouraging and indicate that the communique has
met with an almost uniformly favorable response.[3] I think it is now
clear to all that our two governments are truly united in their devotion to peace and freedom and that it is the Communists, by contrast, who are imperiling the peace of the world by seeking to extend
the limits of their oppressive rule through force of arms. Your own
wise decision during the present trying crisis to deny the Communists
any conceivable pretext for extending the scope of their attacks has
been amply rewarded by dramatizing this contrast to the world.

I assume of course that your reference to means and actions in
support of anti-Communist activities on the mainland is to be understood as being within the context of the joint communique and
our other understandings.[4]

I believe that our alliance, contrary to Communist expectations,
has become even stronger and closer in the present difficult situation. I join you in believing that our close cooperation in the cause
of freedom serves to keep alive the hopes of those in your country
and elsewhere who are struggling to regain the freedom of which
they have been so cruelly deprived.[5]

With warm regard, *Sincerely*

---

[1] State Department officials drafted this letter to the Nationalist Chinese leader (see
Herter to Eisenhower, Nov. 13, 1958, AWF/I: Formosa [China]).
[2] For background on the situation in the Taiwan Straits and the communiqué issued
after Secretary Dulles's talks with Chiang see no. 907. On October 25 the Communist Chinese Defense Minister had denounced the meetings and the resulting communiqué as serving the interests of the United States and not those of China, whether
Nationalist or Communist (*New York Times*, Oct. 26, 1958; see also State, *Foreign Relations, 1958–1960*, vol. XIX, *China*, pp. 451–52, 461–62). According to Chiang the
Communists had twisted the real meaning of the declaration "in order to negate its
effect and to confuse the world" (AWF/I: Formosa).
[3] Canadian Prime Minister Diefenbaker had told Dulles that he was "greatly relieved
and enthusiastic" about the outcome of the meetings and felt that the danger of war
had passed. Dulles had also provided the details of his meetings to British Foreign
Secretary Lloyd and had told Chiang that the whole free world was relieved that he
had put the mission of his government on a higher plane (State, *Foreign Relations,
1958–1960*, vol. XIX, *China*, pp. 463, 449–51, 485–86).
[4] Chiang had told the President that his government was "duty bound to aid and sup-

port the anti-Communist activities on the mainland through all possible means and by all possible actions so that the enslaved millions of our compatriots may see freedom again at an early date." Dulles had suggested the addition of this paragraph to Under Secretary Herter (Telephone conversation, Dulles and Herter, Nov. 13, 1958, Dulles Papers, Telephone Conversations).

[5] Although Chiang would avoid further provocative action during the following months, he would not significantly reduce his forces on Quemoy and Matsu. At the same time the Communists, while continuing to threaten Taiwan and the islands, would gradually reduce and eventually cease their attacks. In November 1959, after over a year of negotiations, U.S. and Communist Chinese officials would agree to pursue their policies by peaceful means and to renounce the use of force in the Taiwan area except in self defense (State, *Foreign Relations, 1958–1960*, vol. XIX, *China*, pp. 548–50, 538–39, 621–22).

930   *EM, AWF,*
                                                        Administration Series

To Arthur Sherwood Flemming   *November 15, 1958*
Personal and confidential

Dear Arthur: Thank you for your note. I agree that we must not be reactionary or static in our relations to people. And I think that at an early opportunity, we should have an Executive Cabinet meeting on the subjects you raise.[1]

Now I should like to make a few observations—or pose some questions—concerning your memorandum. In it you mention the possibility of "putting the Administration in a position where it finds it impossible to present to the nation a positive on-going program in many areas that require such progress."[2]

(*a*). Without attempting to identify any of the programs which you have in mind, is it not possible that, in the past, we have gone too fast—that we need a bit of time to catch our breath? Our grants-in-aid programs are constantly decreasing the ratio of State responsibility.[3]

(*b*). Progress, in the sense of bettering the opportunities for 175 million people, is not necessarily hastened by additional expenditures.

(*c*). One of the most necessary things now to do—in my opinion—is to assure our people and, indeed, other peoples, in the soundness of the American dollar. There has been an almost continuous outflow of gold from the United States during 1958. While this does not seem to be due, in any appreciable degree, to speculation against the dollar, it does highlight the importance of our continuing to maintain strong confidence, here and abroad, in the United States dollar.[4]

(*d*). To my mind nothing could provide greater reassurance in this field than could the presentation of a balanced budget.

(*e*). You suggest that part of the budgetary gap could be filled by increased revenues. In special fields I think this would probably be wise. For example, our Post Office Department outgo should be balanced against income.[5] The road program should be financed by increased petroleum tax.[6] I think we should again submit to the Congress the proposal that loans for domestic purposes should never be made at an interest rate lower than the rates the Federal government must pay to obtain the money.[7]

There are other reforms and corrections that unquestionably would be helpful.

On the other hand, is it not possible that any general rise in the tax structure could be counter-productive? While admitting that, as the country grows, a greater cost is required for preserving the nation's security and peace in the world, it is still my conviction that over recent years our ratio of expenditures to the GNP is too great. If we are to maintain a healthy economy under our traditional concepts of free enterprise and the maximum of individual liberty, then it is quite clear that we must *not destroy incentive.* During periods of national emergency, the American people can be expected to make the greatest sacrifices for the good of the country. But I am quite sure that when we look ahead over a period of twenty, thirty or forty years, we must take into account human nature, and the natural resistance to very high tax rates in peacetime. Please note the number of votes Mr. Lee received in Utah on an inconceivable program of "no income taxes."[8]

This letter is not meant to be an answer to your communication. The above is merely to suggest some ideas and possibilities which I would hope you will consider in your own thinking as you look, from the standpoint of your Department, into the future.

With warm regard, *As ever*

---

[1] HEW Secretary Flemming's note is not in AWF. He had warned that freezing the status quo might, in some instances, reflect "a warped sense of values," and had suggested holding an executive session of the Cabinet to explore "the possibility of recommending to the Congress a program that will increase our revenues." The Cabinet would meet in Executive Session on December 16, 1958; there are no minutes of that meeting (see, Cabinet Check-List, Executive Session, Dec. 16, 1958, AWF/Cabinet).

[2] Flemming's November 12 memorandum to the President (AWF/A) argued that the Administration must present to Congress a budget that reflected "fiscal responsibility." Without a change in the present tax structure, however, such a budget would allow no new construction starts; no new programs or expansion of existing programs unless there was an immediate and critical need; and would require program retrenchment in areas of low federal interest and priority, or where the federal government was supporting a disproportionately high share of the total cost.

[3] See no. 961; see also *Congressional Quarterly Almanac*, vol. XIV, *1958*, pp. 326–27.

[4] The gold drain had begun in 1958, when the balance of foreign trade had shifted from surplus to deficit, with exports dropping by nearly twenty percent. Imports had risen sharply at the same time, resulting in a deficit of $3.5 billion in the balance of U.S. international payments. Gold outflows had totaled $1.6 billion in the first half of 1958. Although the rate of outflow diminished in the second half of 1958, American gold reserves would fall by some ten percent for the year (see Saulnier, *Constructive Years*, pp. 120–24; Morgan, *Eisenhower versus 'The Spenders,'* pp. 128–29). For developments see no. 961.

[5] In his 1959 budget message, Eisenhower would ask Congress to enact legislation to put the postal service on a self-supporting basis (see *Public Papers of the Presidents: Eisenhower, 1959*, pp. 81–82).

[6] In 1959 Eisenhower would recommend to Congress a temporary increase in highway fuel taxes to support the highway trust fund (*ibid.*, pp. 80–81).

[7] See no. 961; see also *Congressional Quarterly Almanac*, vol. XV, *1959*, pp. 273–75.

[8] See nos. 921 and 928.

931   *EM, AWF, DDE Diaries Series*

TO EZRA TAFT BENSON   *November 15, 1958*
Personal and confidential

Dear Ezra: As I contemplate the preparation of the next Budget, I grow more and more concerned about our farm program.[1] You and I have rarely, if ever, had any difference of conviction as to the basic principles we should follow in our attempt to establish the proper relationship between the government and agriculture.[2] I think we have made real progress, but the constant increase in the government funds that we must pay out under present programs suggests the need for critical re-examination of the laws as now written and possibly some changes in them.

While I realize that unusually favorable growing conditions played a large part in this year's great increase in farm output, is it not reasonable to expect that the continuing and rapid improvements in farm technology will produce ever larger crops in the future?[3] My feeling is that we should attempt to establish expenditure limits, possibly in several directions. How about establishing a maximum level on loans that could be made to any one individual or any one firm? How about cutting from *any* supports all acreage holdings exceeding a certain size? These might be completely impractical but I think it is nevertheless true that in some instances we have been *making millionaires with Federal subsidies*. Such a plan might result in some undesirable fragmentation of farms—but possibly you can suggest something better to do.[4]

In any event, I should like to have a talk with you at your convenience to see what you have in mind.[5] *As ever*

[1] On the farm program see nos. 358 and 553; see also Galambos and van Ee, *The Middle Way*, nos. 1071 and 1841.

[2] See no. 616.

[3] The 1958 harvest had produced record size crops in wheat, corn, and feed grains, with the increase attributable to good weather and scientific and technological advances. The surplus production had resulted in a record $6 billion in federal farm spending, and for the fiscal year, 1959, an increase of $1.5 billion dollars (see *New York Times*, Sept. 11, 14, 1958).

[4] Eisenhower would ask Congress for changes in the support program in his 1959 special message to Congress on agriculture (see *Public Papers of the Presidents: Eisenhower, 1959*, pp. 146–51). The President would argue that price-support and production-control programs had created the problem of surplus commodities. He would recommend an adjustment in the formula for calculating price supports in an effort to "reconcile the farm program with the facts of modern agriculture, to reduce the incentive for unrealistic production, to move in the direction of easing production controls to permit the growth of commercial markets and to cut the cost of federal programs." For developments see no. 1263.

[5] Eisenhower would meet with Benson for a half-hour on December 3, 1958. See Benson, *Cross Fire*, pp. 428–38.

932   *EM, AWF, Administration Series*

To HAROLD EDWARD STASSEN   *November 15, 1958*
Personal and confidential

Dear Harold: I was disappointed that you did not go along with my counsel that personalities should not be introduced, in terms of competition, while our principal task is to seek recruits for the Republican Party.[1] You spoke much of debating issues and policies, but you will recall that I remarked that any constructive work of that kind would be impeded by introducing personalities, which always stimulate newspaper and other speculation that divisive contests are promptly impending.

Of course I recognize your right to act according to your own convictions, but I do feel that in light of the suggestions I made, you could, at least, have chosen some other spot or time to give your opinions concerning some leading Republicans.

Finally, as I told you, I do not share your unfavorable opinion of the Vice President. I do not believe that he, and what you call the Republican hierarchy, are conspiring to defeat the policies and programs for which I stand. On the contrary, I have found him loyal to me and to the Administration and most helpful throughout these past six years. While I have publicly stated, a number of times, that I shall never attempt to "name" the next Republican candidate, I have likewise said that there are some younger men that I admire and respect, and would support for any political office. Of these the Vice President is certainly one.

I do not write these thoughts in any spirit of criticism or irritation. I merely say, again, that I am disappointed that you did not give any heed to my disagreement to the idea of early introduction of personalities into the Republican political picture. *Sincerely*

P.S. (11/17/58). This morning I noticed a newspaper account with respect to the California situation that is apropos of another conviction you expressed. You said that Nixon and Knowland conspired against Governor Knight. I expressed grave doubts that this was true. The story this morning is that Governor Knight is promising to Nixon the support of California's delegation at the next Republican Convention.[2]

[1] On November 12 former Special Assistant to the President for Disarmament Stassen had met with Eisenhower to discuss the plight of the Republican party after the disastrous elections of 1958 (see no. 926). Although both Eisenhower and Press Secretary James Hagerty had advised Stassen to avoid public discussion of possible Republican presidential nominees, he had spoken to reporters outside the White House and had provided them with a list of GOP hopefuls for 1960: Treasury Secretary (and former Democrat) Robert B. Anderson, Interior Secretary Fred A. Seaton, New York Governor-elect Nelson A. Rockefeller, and U.N. Ambassador Henry Cabot Lodge. The name of Vice-President Richard M. Nixon, whom Stassen had indirectly blamed for the Republicans' troubles, was conspicuous in its absence from the list. The *New York Times* (Nov. 13) characterized Stassen's action as "the opening shot in an expected battle to prevent Mr. Nixon from getting the Republican nomination in 1960" (see Ann Whitman memorandum, Nov. 12, 1958, AWF/AWD, and Ambrose, *Nixon*, vol. I, *The Education of a Politician, 1913–1963*, p. 505).

On November 17 Stassen would send Eisenhower a letter (AWF/A) intended "to supplement and confirm" the ideas that he had outlined at the White House meeting; his letter and the President's would cross each other in the mail. Acknowledging that the President's programs were both effective and popular, he would claim that the conservatives who had entrenched themselves in the Republican hierarchy had dragged the party down to defeat and were working to secure Nixon's nomination. Stassen wrote that although Rockefeller had "the best potential" for winning the 1960 election—an election the Vice-President would surely lose—any of the four men he had listed had "qualities far superior in character, maturity, judgment, and philosophy, than Richard Nixon."

[2] On November 16 the *New York Times* had reported that Goodwin Knight, California's outgoing governor, had predicted that Nixon would have "full control" of the state's delegation to the 1960 Republican National Convention; Eisenhower may have seen a summary or variant of this story on the following day. Stassen would reply (Dec. 15, AWF/A) that Knight was pledging the support of the delegation to Nixon in the hope that the Vice-President would find him a job in the federal government "notwithstanding the fact that Knowland and Nixon together have brought about the ruin of the Republican Party in California." Stassen would also argue that "introducing names as well as issues and policies into the national discussion" was necessary in order to seek recruits for the Republican party, and he would insist that conservative GOP leaders "must be defeated within our Party, not only for the sake of our Party, but much more important, for the sake of our country." Eisenhower would not answer Stassen's letter. See Eisenhower to Stassen, October 4 and November 5, 1958, and Stassen to Eisenhower, October 2, 1958, all in WHCF/OF 138-A-9; *New York Times*, October 6 and November 6, 1958; and Montgomery and Johnson, *One Step from the White House*, pp. 235–38. For developments see nos. 977 and 980.

To Leonard Townsend Gerow   *November 15, 1958*
Personal

Dear Gee: Though your main purpose was to send me, via Mamie, the memorandum by General Hill concerning Monty's book, it was pleasant to have some news of you and Mary Louise.[1] Naturally I am pleased by what General Hill had to say; he does a great deal to set the record straight.

I have one rather "plaintive" comment to make. It refers to General Hill's introduction to his critique. He obviously, like so many others, accepts as fact any newspaper account that attempts to give to any incident a bit more color than it actually deserves. He did so in the story of my alleged acquiescence with Monty when he said that had he been in command, he would have sacked both Lee and Meade. As you know, Monty can never resist a newspaper reporter nor a camera.

At the time of the incident he and I were touring the Gettysburg Battlefield. There had been no conversation whatsoever about the quality of the command; but a whole corps of newspaper people were following us around hoping to get material for a story.

At one location I got a bit tired of Monty raising his voice, knowing well that he was doing it for the benefit of eavesdroppers. I walked over to the car, while he remained on the far side of the group of reporters and photographers. Taking advantage of this golden opportunity to try for something sensational, he called over the heads of the crowd something like this: "Both Lee and Meade should have been sacked." I think he added something about incompetence, and then he called to me, "Don't you agree, Ike?" Frankly I was resentful of his obvious purpose and his lack of good taste in his public familiarity, so I merely replied, "Listen, Monty, I live here. I have nothing to say about the matter. You have to make your own comments."

How any reporter could get out of such a remark an interpretation of acquiescence, I do not know. I can assure you that what I actually intended was a rather abrupt expression of annoyance.[2]

Of course all this is of no importance whatsoever. I merely got started telling you the story because of the very great difference in interpretation which is so frequently noticeable between the actual way an incident happened and its reporting.

Again I say that I am really grateful to General Hill for his effort to get part of World War II's history placed in a little bit better perspective than it is presented, according to those who have seen his book, in Monty's "Memoirs." I personally have not read it and shall not do so.[3]

Give my warm greetings to Mary Louise and of course all the best to yourself. If you ever come this way I would like to have you join me for breakfast or lunch—or come in to see me any other time of day that might be convenient for both of us.

With warm regard, *As ever*

[1] General Gerow (USA, ret.), former commandant of the Army Command and General Staff School, had written to the First Lady on November 9. On the President's friendship with Gerow see Galambos, *Chief of Staff*, no. 1304, and Galambos and van Ee, *The Middle Way*, no. 683. Gerow and his wife, the former Mary Louise Kennedy, and the Eisenhowers lived in the same apartment building in Washington, D.C., for many years (see Chandler and Galambos, *Occupation, 1945*, no. 488). Major General Jim Dan Hill (AUS, ret.), an historian and president of Wisconsin State College, had been Gerow's heavy artillery officer during World War II. Hill had reviewed Field Marshal Montgomery's *Memoirs* prior to the volume's publication in 1958. Gerow said he thought the review would give the Eisenhowers "a good laugh."

[2] In the spring of 1957 Montgomery had toured the Gettysburg battlefield while a guest at Eisenhower's farm (see nos. 145 and 184). Hill had referred to the incident and said that Montgomery, with Eisenhower's help, had disposed of Generals Lee and Meade and now was "publishing his post-mortem on Ike's own role as Supreme Commander, Allied Forces in Europe, in World War II." But, Hill added, Montgomery had not "specifically" said that Eisenhower should have "sacked" himself "in favor of Montgomery." Hill went on to say that Montgomery "*lavished unstinted praise*" upon Eisenhower and considered him "*one of the greatest men of our century—except when his decisions were against Monty!*" Hill's review of the volume appeared in the *Saturday Review*, November 1, 1958, pp. 17–18.

[3] In July 1957 Eisenhower and Montgomery had corresponded regarding the publication of Montgomery's memoirs (see no. 238). The memoirs would prove to be controversial; see, for example, nos. 948 and 970.

934   *EM, AWF, Name Series*

To Walter Robert Tkach   *November 15, 1958*

Memorandum for Colonel Tkach: I discussed your investment problem with James Lemon of Johnston, Lemon and Company. His office is on the ninth floor of the Southern Building. The telephone number is Sterling 3-3135. He would be glad to see you any time you want to come and see him, but I suspect it would be better to call and make a date in advance of your visit.[1]

I give below a gist of his conversation.

(1) For the small investor who makes his savings periodically, he believes that the investment trust offers possibly the best way to do it.

(2) Apparently there are companies of different standing in this field, but there is a local one that he thinks is one of the very

best. It is called the "Washington Mutual Investors Fund." The investment can be started with as little as $30 and with increases made at irregular intervals. He inferred, however, that a regular spacing of payments is desirable and the only limitation seems to be that no sum less than $30 can be invested at any one time.

(3) Dividends are reinvested by the Fund as they are accumulated, and this reinvestment is without payment of commission costs. In this way the income is, in effect, compounded.

(4) A yearly report is made to the investor as to the amount of his dividend earnings during the year. This is to enable him to include this amount in his income tax return.

Jim Lemon is one of my very good friends. In my opinion he is not only an honest and skillful operator in the securities market, but I know that he is friendly and helpful. As long as you have this problem in mind, I would urge that you go to see him.

[1] Dr. Tkach was the assistant physician to the President's personal physician, Howard Snyder. James Hanson Lemon (B.S. Princeton 1925) was an investment banker and director of the Washington Mutual Investors Fund. Eisenhower frequently played golf with Lemon at Burning Tree Country Club.

935   *EM, AWF, DDE Diaries Series*

To Hugh Meade Alcorn, Jr.   *November 17, 1958*

Dear Meade: On the day after election, I announced my intention to wage an all-out campaign for sane, sensible government with sound fiscal policies.[1] At the same time, you and I agreed that we must mobilize the Republican Party solidly in support of the basic programs that we believe will keep this country in a strong position both economically and in its political relationship to other countries.

Amidst preoccupations with governmental responsibilities, it is difficult for me to give a great deal of attention to the party problems of obtaining a unified and enthusiastic support for these fundamental purposes. I should be most appreciative if you could drop in occasionally—at intervals of no longer than two weeks—to give me a verbal account of your efforts.[2]

With warm regard, *As ever*

[1] For background on the 1958 elections see no. 926. At his November 5 news conference Eisenhower had bemoaned the fact that the voters had chosen candidates that he "would class among the spenders." He added: "And I promise this: for the next 2 years, the Lord sparing me, I am going to fight this as hard as I know how" *(Public Papers of the Presidents: Eisenhower, 1958,* p. 828). On Republican National Com-

mittee Chairman Alcorn's role in the campaign and his reports to the President see nos. 836 and 919.

[2] Eisenhower would meet with Alcorn on twelve occasions before Alcorn resigned in April (see no. 1125 and President's daily appointments). For developments see nos. 945, 962, 963, and 982.

936   *EM, AWF, DDE Diaries Series*

To Arthur I. Appleton   *November 17, 1958*
Personal and confidential

Dear Mr. Appleton:[1] While I appreciate the kind thought behind your request that I do not reply to your letter, I want to make one observation concerning a statement it contains. This is the quotation to which I refer: ". . . I believe that the Republican party could have taken a little longer to put its policies into effect. As a specific example, I feel that we should have taken the pressure off a little sooner after the brakes were applied to credit."[2]

We must remember that credit brakes are applied or relaxed by the independent Federal Reserve Board. Not always does the Board respond to Administration urging. One reason is that when a situation is fluid or, let us say, indefinite, there are a number of varying opinions held by the members of the Federal Reserve Board and, indeed, by the Boards of the branch banks.[3]

So far as my personal convictions were concerned, at the time of which you speak I was on the side of prompt easing of credit. It took some little time, in spite of the fact that I personally believe (though this is a belief only) that Bill Martin felt the same.[4]

With best wishes, *Sincerely*

[1] We have been unable to identify Appleton.
[2] Eisenhower had written Appleton on November 4, 1958 (WHCF/OF 138-A-9), that he had been told of Appleton's "consistent and generous financial support to the Republican Party despite some differences of opinion" he had with the Administration. "For this reason, I more than ever appreciate your moral and financial backing. When men of good faith, who have differences of opinion, can express their views frankly and openly, and then join forces again to get a job done, I have no concern for the future long term strength of our Republican Party," the President had said. Appleton, who was from Chicago, had responded on November 13, 1958 (*ibid.*), saying that he had been "misquoted," and that he concurred with the Administration's objectives on inflation, credit, and farm subsidies. His major disagreement was "one of timing."
[3] On the Administration's differences with the Federal Reserve Board see, for example, Galambos and van Ee, *The Middle Way*, nos. 2005 and 2006. On the recession see nos. 598 and 615.
[4] See no. 673.

To John Hay Whitney   *November 18, 1958*

Dear Jock: It was good to hear from you again.[1]

Nelson's victory in New York did much to cushion the overall disappointment that the election produced. There were a few bright spots elsewhere, of course. And if the Republicans cannot learn one of the lessons of Nelson Rockefeller and John Lindsay and Mark Hatfield—which is that we must have personable candidates—nothing any of us can do can possibly produce victory in 1960.[2] If the lesson sticks, I am hopeful. At any rate I am going to try, despite the governmental pressures that are with me every day of the year, to try to keep myself informed, better than I have been able to do before, of the activities of the Republican National Committee.[3]

Incidentally, I thought the Tribune editorial, spelling out a blueprint of steps the Republican Party must take, was one of the best in the flood of such pieces that has appeared in print since November fourth.[4]

I am glad that you and Betsey will have a good rest in Thomasville. I cannot predict when I may get there.[5]

I shall read about the Vice President's trip to England with great interest, although with the realization that you will be even busier than usual because of his visit.[6]

Give my love to Betsey and, as always, the best to yourself. *As ever*

---

[1] Whitney had written November 13 that he hoped Eisenhower was not unduly distressed by the November 4 election results (AWF/A). For background on the Democratic landslide, see no. 935.

[2] Whitney had said that the victories in New York lightened "the sting" of the Republican defeat (on Rockefeller's election see no. 922). Whitney had described John Vliet Lindsay (LL.B. Yale 1944), the newly-elected congressman from New York's seventeenth district, as a "progressive attractive candidate." Lindsay, who had not cooperated with the Republican political organization during his campaign, was expected to vote with the liberal wing of the party. Oregon's Secretary of State Mark Odom Hatfield (B.A. Willamette 1943, M.A. Stanford 1948), who had also minimized his ties with the Republican party during his campaign, had been elected governor of Oregon (*New York Times*, Nov. 4, 5, 9, 1958; see also nos. 963 and 964). For Eisenhower's views on the need to bring young Republicans into political positions see no. 932.

[3] See no. 935.

[4] A *New York Herald Tribune* editorial entitled, "How to Rebuild the Republican Party," which appeared on November 13, had emphasized lessons to be learned from the recent defeat. Among the steps needed were: advancing outstanding candidates and solid, progressive programs; reorganizing the party machinery to attract youth, intellectuals, and union members; researching the problems facing the nation, states and cities; and getting out among the people to explain the party's programs. On Whitney's recent acquisition of the *New York Herald Tribune* see no. 825.

[5] Whitney said he and his wife would spend January at their Greenwood Plantation

in Thomasville, Georgia. As it turned out, the Eisenhowers would vacation in Thomasville in February (see no. 1069).
[6] See no. 966.

938 EM, AWF, International Series:
EM, AWF, International Series:
Churchill

To Winston Spencer Churchill   *November 18, 1958*

Dear Winston: Mamie and I are delighted that you are contemplating a visit to the United States in May. That month is usually a good one here in Washington: it is warm, yet the oppressive heat that sometimes develops later in the summer is absent. At the present time my calendar is almost completely free, and I suggest you set a time that would be convenient for you.[1] I hope that Clemmie will find it possible to come with you, but at any event we shall be counting on seeing you then.[2]

Details of your visit can be arranged later and as you desire. If you want your stay at the White House to be completely quiet, we shall be only too happy; if you would like us to have in a few of your good friends that can be easily arranged.

As to the painting: I think "mine" should be included, by all means, in the showing at the Royal Academy. (Incidentally, congratulations on having a solo exhibition there!) You can send it along to me when the show closes or, if you prefer, bring it when you come over.[3]

Let me say once again that you should feel perfectly free to tell me exactly what you would like to do during your visit here; certainly, if you wish, you can almost entirely avoid any public appearances.[4]

With warm regard, *As ever*

[1] Churchill had written that if it were "convenient" he would like to come to the United States in the early summer (see Churchill to Eisenhower, November [n.d.] 1958, AWF/I: Churchill; see also Hall to Eisenhower, November 11, 1958, and Eisenhower to Hall, November 18, 1958, both in AWF/N). Health problems had forced cancellation of the Churchills' visit to the United States earlier in 1958 (see nos. 668 and 750).
[2] On December 31 Churchill would suggest May 4 as a date for his visit. He added that Lady Churchill, who had been suffering recurrent influenza, felt the "journey would be too much for her" (see no. 568).
[3] In 1957 Churchill had put thirty of his paintings on exhibit in several U.S. cities. He had offered the President any painting in the selection, and Eisenhower had chosen "The Ourika River and the Atlas Mountains" (see nos. 86, 222 and 909). In March

1208

London's Royal Academy would exhibit sixty-one of Churchill's paintings, including those exhibited in the United States (Churchill to Eisenhower, Nov. [n.d.] 1958, AWF/I:Churchill, and *New York Times*, Mar. 11, 13, 16, Aug. 4, 1959; see also Eisenhower to Hall, Nov. 18, 1958, AWF/N).

[4] For developments see no. 1023.

939   *EM, WHCF, Official File 124*

To Barry Morris Goldwater   *November 19, 1958*

Dear Barry: I was happy to have the opportunity to talk to you on a number of our political and economic problems of the days ahead. Of course it was good also to be able to congratulate you personally on your recent victory in Arizona.[1]

I have spoken to the Attorney General about the television matter you mentioned; he has promised to give you a ring. From the short conversation I had with him I would judge that the whole question of "immunity" is involved.[2]

Later I talked to Jim Mitchell. He is carefully reading your memorandum and is hopeful of having a chance to talk to you before Sunday.[3]

With personal regard, *Sincerely*

[1] Goldwater, who on November 4 had won reelection to the Senate (see no. 910), had thanked Eisenhower for a congratulatory telegram and had requested a meeting with him (Eisenhower to Goldwater, Nov. 5 and 6, 1958, same file as document). Dismayed by the national Democratic victory (see no. 926), Goldwater was eager to discuss his "thoughts on where the Republican Party can strengthen itself and the means by which this can be accomplished." At an off-the-record meeting at the White House (Nov. 19) the two men talked about the outcome of the elections, Goldwater's Arizona campaign, party organization, and the legislative program for 1959 (McCabe, Memorandum for Ann Whitman, Nov. 21, 1958, AWF/D). After their meeting Eisenhower dictated this note to Presidential Secretary Ann Whitman, who sent it by messenger to Goldwater.

[2] Goldwater had urged the President to investigate possible abuses by members of Congress who had obtained broadcast licenses for radio or television stations in which they had a financial interest. Eisenhower had met with Attorney General William Rogers shortly after his conversation with Goldwater (see Rogers to Eisenhower, Dec. 10, 1958, AWF/A). The immunity mentioned by the President was probably the congressional immunity from arrest "in all cases except treason, felony and breach of the peace" (U.S. Constitution, Art. I, Sec. 6).

[3] Goldwater's memorandum, which is not in AWF, dealt with labor legislation (see no. 897). In his November 5 letter he had told Eisenhower that he was drafting his own labor bill, one that was "not an anti-labor or union-busting measure." The President both telephoned and met with Secretary of Labor James Mitchell on this same morning (Ann Whitman memorandum, Nov. 19, 1958, AWF/AWD; Telephone conversation, Eisenhower and Mitchell, Nov. 19, 1958, AWF/D). For developments see no. 945, 962, and 997.

To Emmet John Hughes   *November 20, 1958*
Personal

Dear Emmet: For a long time I have been pondering the possible value of an attempt to center greater attention in our country, and so far as possible in the free world, on the predominant influence of spiritual values in our lives, and to do this in some rather well organized way so as to get maximum effect.

One rather nebulous idea I have is to bring my purpose, in advance of any personal effort on my part, to the attention of heads of government or of state in all other free countries and to ask their support, each in his own way and his own words. So far I have not even thought of the proper locale, forum or place for a talk by me.

I do not believe that any such effort should be couched specifically in the terms of a freedom-communist struggle. Rather I believe it should be an effort of an affirmative kind because of a conviction that we have been woefully neglecting the field in which the democracies and, indeed, all civilizations based upon a religious faith, should be particularly strong. We have been tending too much toward the material. We have too much thought of bombs and machines and gadgets as the arsenal of our national and cultural strength.

Yet in the realm of their respect for spiritual values, all nations which are either philosophically or politically related to our own have a combined potential strength that is indestructible.

The great problem is to get people—our own people and our friends—to understand these things and to think on them objectively and with a sense of inspiration and uplift. This will require, as I said before, organization as well as the most persuasive and earnest presentation of the case that every leader in his own field could command.

Not long ago I brought this matter, in a long conversation, to the Secretary of State. He volunteered to have some of his staff develop a document which might help clarify my hazy thinking. A copy of the resultant memorandum is attached. Incidentally, it should be treated on a confidential basis, *not* to be circulated.[1]

I would like to request you to read this letter and the memorandum and then for yourself decide whether you think there is sufficient merit in the idea to warrant an effort of the kind I allude to, as well as a personal effort on your part that would [involve?] real time and work. In the event that you do, I think that the next step would be either for you to prepare a first rough draft for me to read or some day at your convenience to come to Washington to talk to me further.[2]

As you well know, there is no slack period in the President's year.

But the late fall and the early winter, to include the first half of February, are the days that are busiest of all. This is one reason why I do not feel it possible to undertake any serious work on the matter myself. Hence my request to you.

I should say that this is one thing that, if tackled at all, must command a great enthusiasm on behalf of the workmen, or it would be useless to start. By this I mean that if you feel any slightest doubt as to the value of the purpose that I have so haltingly described, then please just return the memorandum and let me know that you would rather not undertake anything of this kind. I assure you that I would thoroughly understand any such conclusion because I really cannot clearly see at this time exactly the kind of message I would like to give, or how and where to say it. The only thing I am completely sure of, in my own mind, is that I am confident that sometime, somewhere and by someone the effort *must be made*.[3]

With warm regard, *As ever*

---

[1] The President had discussed emphasizing spiritual values with Secretary Dulles on October 24. On November 17 Dulles had sent a State Department memorandum on the subject to Eisenhower. The following day the President told Dulles that although the paper was excellent, finding a forum could be difficult (Dulles to Eisenhower, Nov. 17, 1958, AWF/D-H; Dulles, Memorandum of Conversation, Nov. 18, 1958, Dulles Papers, White House Memoranda Series; see also Dulles to Barnes, Nov. 19, 1958, Dulles Papers, Chronological Series). We have been unable to locate either Dulles's letter or his memorandum, dated November 3.

On November 18 Dulles had reviewed the basic foreign policies of the Administration in the face of changing world conditions in an address to the World Order Study Conference of the National Council of Churches of Christ in America. Dulles urged the conference to make an "indispensable contribution to the spiritual redemption of our nation" (U.S. Department of State, *American Foreign Policy; Current Documents, 1958*, pp. 57–68, and *New York Times*, Nov. 19, 1958). See also Galambos and van Ee, *The Middle Way*, no. 1030.

[2] Hughes would reply on December 2 (AWF/A) that Eisenhower's letter had stirred his interest "profoundly" and that he shared Eisenhower's feeling that the major issues could not be addressed simply by "rhetoric and exhortation." There was a need to include other governments in asserting "supreme values and purposes," he wrote. The President would discuss the matter further with Hughes on December 10 (Telephone conversation, Dec. 1, 1958, AWF/A, Hughes Corr.).

[3] For developments see no. 971.

---

941   *EM, AWF, Dulles-Herter Series*

TO JOHN FOSTER DULLES   *November 20, 1958*

Dear Foster: The outgoing President of Mexico has certainly done his best to be our good friend. I should like to send a special message to him, one that he could receive even before our Inaugural delegation reaches Mexico City.[1]

While I would like to think of some nice personal present, I think possibly a warm letter would be quite sufficient and possibly even more significant to him.

Within a few minutes I am going to leave for Augusta, but I shall make sure that Secretary Herter knows of my desire and that he will have a draft to send down to me at Augusta immediately after your arrival back in your office.[2] In other words, I should like you to see it before it comes to me so that I would have nothing but editorial changes to make, if that.[3]

As usual I will be at the end of a telephone where you can always get me in a matter of minutes. *As ever*

[1] On December 1, at the conclusion of a six-year term, President of the United Mexican States Adolfo Ruiz Cortines would relinquish his office to Minister of Labor Adolfo López Mateos. Eisenhower's December 1 letter extending his greetings and felicitations to the incoming president is in AWF/D (see also *New York Times*, Dec. 1, 2, 1958). For background on López Mateos see no. 1061.

On the discussions regarding the delegation to attend the inauguration see Dulles Papers, October 24, 30, 1958, White House Memoranda Series; and Dulles Papers, Telephone Conversations, Dulles and Rubottom, November 10, and Dulles and Herter, November 12, 1958.

[2] On the Eisenhowers' Thanksgiving vacation in Augusta see no. 892. Dulles was vacationing at his Duck Island retreat in Lake Ontario. He would return on November 24 (*New York Times*, Nov. 20, 25, 1958; see also Eleanor Lansing Dulles, *John Foster Dulles: The Last Year* [New York, 1963], pp. 209–11).

[3] We have been unable to find a draft in AWF, but on November 25 Eisenhower would express appreciation for the relationship between the two countries and the two leaders. The American people, he would add, had been gratified by the improved well-being of the Mexican people (Eisenhower to Ruiz Cortines, AWF/I: Cortines). On November 30 Dulles would consult with the President in Augusta before departing that afternoon for Mexico City for the inauguration. That evening Dulles and others in the American delegation would confer with López Mateos and Ruiz Cortines at the former president's home (see State, *Foreign Relations, 1958–1960*, vol. V, *American Republics*, pp. 852–58, and Dulles, Memorandum of Conversation, Nov. 30, 1958, Dulles Papers, Chronological Series). On December 5 Ruiz Cortines would thank the President for his letter and for the personal greetings conveyed to him through Dulles (AWF/I: Cortines).

942   EM, WHCF,
                                                    President's Personal File 517

To Stanley Hoflund High   *November 20, 1958*

Dear Stanley: This noon I left Washington for Augusta, taking George Champion with me aboard the COLUMBINE.[1] He gave me my first news of your illness but, fortunately, tells me that in recent weeks you have been feeling much better. I do hope that your progress is steady and sure.

I have missed you and wondered why I did not hear from you. A campaign such as the recent one—even a disastrous campaign—inevitably recalls the 1952 experience, when you were such a stalwart and valuable assistant. As a matter of fact I stayed one night in the same suite at the Blackstone, and recalled vividly those days of the Convention. I might add that while I may be politically more knowledgeable than I was then (a fact which would be disputed by some of my colleagues), such awareness as I have acquired the hard way in the last six years didn't help a bit when the results were in on November fourth![2]

I shall charge George with keeping me informed about you. Please don't bother to acknowledge this, but know that Mamie and I think of you often and that we join in best wishes for your complete recovery.[3]

With warm regard to Mrs. High and all the best to yourself,[4] *As ever*

---

[1] The Eisenhowers would vacation in Augusta, Georgia, through December 2 (see no. 892). Champion (B.S. Dartmouth College 1926), president of Chase Manhattan Bank since 1957, had joined the Chase National Bank of New York in 1933; it merged with the Bank of Manhattan in 1955. Champion was a member and director of the Blind Brook Club in New York and a member of the Augusta National Golf Club.
[2] The President had campaigned for the recent midterm election in Cedar Rapids, Los Angeles, San Francisco, and Chicago (see no. 906). High had served as a speechwriter on Eisenhower's 1952 campaign staff. On October 22 Eisenhower had stayed at the Blackstone Hotel in Chicago, his headquarters during the 1952 Republican National Convention (see Galambos, *NATO and the Campaign of 1952*, esp. nos. 974 and 992, and *New York Times*, Oct. 22, 23, 1958). On the election results see nos. 880 and 926.
[3] High would reply on November 25 (same file as document) that Eisenhower's letter had given him a "wonderful lift." He had returned to work, he wrote, and was looking forward to increased productivity. He added that he was a "proud and unreconstructed Eisenhower Republican" and the election results caused him "great concern."
[4] High's wife was the former Dorothy Brown Cutler.

---

943   *EM, AWF, Dulles-Herter Series*

To John Foster Dulles   *November 21, 1958*

Dear Foster: Paul Hoffman came to see me after a recent visit with Nehru.[1] He feels that Nehru, as the leader of the largest uncommitted nation, might be particularly effective in persuading the world, including the Communists, that something constructive simply must come out of the Geneva negotiations.[2]

Further than this, Paul thought that a word of encouragement from me to Nehru might be helpful. I have tried my hand at a draft, copy of which is attached. I should think that the idea itself is not too bad provided we can be sure that we are stating it correctly.[3]

If you do think favorably of the idea, would you please let me have your comments or suggestions promptly?[4] *As ever*

---

[1] Hoffman had met with Eisenhower on November 18 (see Ann Whitman memorandum, Nov. 18, 1958, AWF/AWD).

[2] For background on the technical test suspension talks see nos. 822 and 824. After the negotiators had reported in their communiqué that detection was feasible, the United States had called for a conference on the cessation of nuclear tests, the creation of an international control system, and the drafting of a test ban treaty. This conference, which had begun on October 31, had deadlocked immediately over the Soviet Union's demands for an immediate end to all nuclear weapons tests. The United States and Great Britain had wanted to establish an inspection system first. Negotiations were also complicated by the detection of two Soviet tests soon after the conference had begun (State, *Foreign Relations, 1958–1960*, vol. III, *National Security Policy; Arms Control and Disarmament*, pp. 660–65; 675–67; Hewlett and Holl, *Atoms for Peace and War*, pp. 546–51; Divine, *Blowing on the Wind*, pp. 237–40, 243–45; and Eisenhower, *Waging Peace*, pp. 476–79).

Dulles had told Eisenhower that the American national security bureaucracy wanted to emphasize that disagreements with the Soviets were based on their insistence on the interdependence of test suspension and effective controls, and not primarily on specific agenda items. He also told the President that if negotiations were to break down, the United States would "force" the Soviets to walk out. In that eventuality, the United States and Great Britain could stay in Geneva to work out a formula for the resumption of limited testing (Dulles to Eisenhower, Nov. 16, 1958, AWF/D-H; see also Harlow, Memorandum for the Record, Nov. 18, 1958, AWF/D; and Dulles, Memorandum of Conversation, Nov. 18, 1958, Dulles Papers, White House Memoranda Series).

The Surprise Attack Conference, which was taking place at the same time, had also stalled over procedural disagreements. The United States wanted to confine the discussions to the technical aspects of the problem while the Soviets wanted the conference linked to the abolition of nuclear weapons and the liquidation of military bases on foreign soil (for background on this conference see nos. 521 and 665; see also Dulles, Memorandum of Conversation, Oct. 8, 1958, Dulles Papers, Chronological Series; and State, *Foreign Relations, 1958–1960*, vol. III, *National Security Policy; Arms Control and Disarmament*, pp. 666–69, 674–75, 677–82; see also Jeremi Suri, "America's Search for a Technological Solution to the Arms Race: The Surprise Attack Conference of 1958 and a Challenge for 'Eisenhower Revisionists,'" *Diplomatic History* 21, no. 3 [1997], 417–51).

[3] Three drafts of the letter to Nehru, two including Eisenhower's handwritten emendations, are in AWF/D-H.

[4] Dulles would suggest a redraft of the Nehru letter making "somewhat less clear" the implication that Nehru had a role to play in the outcome of the Geneva talks. "The reason I do this is that so long as we hold to the interdependence of cessation of testing and progress in other aspects of disarmament, Nehru will be against us" (Dulles to Eisenhower, Nov. 25, 1958, AWF/D-H). Dulles would later tell Eisenhower that the Soviet Union had made some movement toward the U.S. position on a control system but had insisted on separating test suspension from other disarmament

issues. The British were pressing the United States to reconsider its stand, Dulles said, in order to move the negotiations forward.

Eisenhower told Dulles that he was willing "to consider the matter with all concerned and recalled that he personally had previously been disposed to contemplate abandoning insistence on a link between test suspension and other measures of disarmament" (Dulles, Memorandum of Conversation, Nov. 30, 1958, Dulles Papers, White House Memoranda Series; see also Telephone conversation, Dulles and McElroy, Nov. 26, 1958, Dulles Papers, Telephone Conversations; and Macmillan, *Riding the Storm*, pp. 567–69). For the letter to the Indian prime minister and the changes to Eisenhower's original draft see no. 952; for developments regarding the Geneva conference on test suspension see no. 992.

944   *EM, WHCF, Official File 116*

To JOHN COWLES   *November 24, 1958*
Personal

Dear John: Many thanks for your note of the twentieth.[1] Paul Hoffman talked to me in particular of his conviction that Prime Minister Nehru, as the leader of the largest uncommitted nation, might be particularly effective in persuading the world, including the Communists, that something constructive simply must come out of the Geneva negotiations.[2]

Your article pointing up what you see as our many errors in foreign policy in the Far East area practically bewilders me.[3] How, for example, we could have "given the impression that our principal concerns were not peace and freedom and a better life for the poverty stricken Asians, but the waging of war on Russia and Mainland China" is beyond my comprehension. It seems to me that everyone in the Administration, including myself has, at every possible opportunity, stressed our desire to raise the living standards of all peoples. We are loyal supporters of the principles of the United Nations Charter. Time and time again we have demonstrated our faithful adherence to the principle that all nations, including our own, should renounce force in the settlement of disputes.

I am equally concerned (not that this is the first time I have read such a statement) that we are considered a war-mongering nation. I agree that this erroneous impression is far too prevalent, but sometimes I think that "none is so blind as he who will not see."[4]

With warm regard, *Sincerely*

---

[1] Cowles, president of the *Minneapolis Star and Tribune*, had written Eisenhower about his recent visit with India's Prime Minister Nehru. He had also enclosed an article he had written on U.S. policies in South and Southeast Asia.
[2] See the preceding document.

[3] American influence in Asia had deteriorated, Cowles had written, with only five remaining nations that could be considered "functioning democracies." He believed that much U.S. aid had gone to military rather than economic purposes and that the United States had overemphasized Asian military alliances "of dubious value" instead of a more proper emphasis on peace, freedom, and economic development ("Military Pacts Little Help to Asia," *Minneapolis Morning Tribune*, Nov. 19, 1958).

[4] Cowles would reply that although Eisenhower personally had often voiced his concern for peace and freedom, Communist propaganda had emphasized the bellicose statements made by American military personnel. "I do not believe our military men should be permitted to make extreme, belligerent statements on international political matters," Cowles wrote. "I think American policy should be stated solely by you and your state department civilian appointments" (Cowles to Eisenhower, Nov. 29, 1958). All papers are in the same file as the document.

945   *EM, WHCF, Official File 138-C*

To Robert Earl McConnell   *November 25, 1958*

Dear Bob: To the important subject first—of course I am having trouble with my golf. I cannot remember when I have not. But this time the difficulty seems to be in putting. I simply cannot get even the simplest and easiest putts to fall. For once the other departments of my so-called game are comparatively good—for me. But so it goes.[1]

I agree completely that, despite our best efforts, we have failed to "sell" the Republican Party as we should have, and as the Administration accomplishments, in my opinion, merit. We obviously do need a competent study and professional advice, in which statement I am sure Meade Alcorn would endorse. I have had, off and on, many conversations over the last six years with Sig Larmon on this very problem, and he has been most helpful. But perhaps none of us has devoted as much time and effort and concentration as we should have done to this one very important problem.[2]

Incidentally, in an effort myself to think of some label that would divest the Republican Party from some of the tired misconceptions that it still carries, I came up with the "Party of justice for all the people." That isn't quite catchy or short enough, but it does indicate what I think should be our basic "selling" effort.[3]

Cliff has gone off to New York, but when he returns I suspect we shall have another session on politics and on remedies for the unfortunate turn of events of November fourth.[4] I am grateful for your thoughts, and, as I said in the beginning, I am in complete agreement. I shall also talk to Meade Alcorn when I return to Washington.

With warm regard, *As ever*

[1] McConnell, a retired mining engineer, was mayor of the town of Jupiter Island in Hobe Sound, Florida. During World War I he had served as a lieutenant in the Naval reserves; during World War II he had served as a consultant with the Treasury Department and as a deputy in the Civil Affairs Division of the War Department. McConnell had written on November 24 (same file as document) that he was glad that Eisenhower would enjoy golfing during a ten-day vacation at Augusta, Georgia (on the Eisenhowers' Thanksgiving vacation see no. 892).

[2] The recent Republican defeat, McConnell had written, could be traced to lack of knowledge and appreciation of what voters think and want of government. McConnell had recommended that Republican National Committee Chairman Alcorn enlist the help of academics to develop an effective means of marketing itself to present an appealing image to the average voter. For advice on ways to sell the GOP, McConnell had suggested Sigurd S. Larmon, a New York advertising executive and a member of the U.S. Advisory Committee on Information.

[3] Eisenhower had made a similar statement regarding Republican party objectives at a dinner in Chicago on January 20 (see no. 554).

[4] Cliff Roberts had accompanied the President to Augusta and, after a brief absence, would return to Augusta on November 30. Eisenhower's record of their conversation is no. 962.

946   *EM, AWF, DDE Diaries Series*

To Erwin J. Lampe and   *November 26, 1958*
Deborah Fredericks Fort

Dear Mr. Lampe and Mrs. Fort: Thank you very much for your letter of November tenth.[1] I know that you, and the Citizens for Eisenhower Nixon of Southern California, did everything possible in the difficult political situation that confronted you this year. I assure all of you that I am deeply grateful for your efforts. While I share your disappointment in the overall results, I am sure your efforts contributed greatly to the return to Washington of the incumbent Republican Congressmen from your area.[2]

I have given a great deal of thought to your offer to be helpful. For the time being I believe it would be best if you could keep the Citizens' organization in Southern California in what I would call a "caretaker status." If I may, I suggest also that you would, for the next months at least, suggest to your people that they work with the regular Republican Party in an effort to reinvigorate and rebuild it.[3] At the same time, as I said before, I think it important that at least the nucleus of your organization, as well as all such organizations throughout the country, be kept intact.

Incidentally, I have heard from my personal friends in California of the splendid leadership the two of you gave to the effort; this note brings to you both my personal and warm thanks.[4]

With best wishes, *Sincerely*

[1] Lampe and Fort were Chairman and Co-Chairman, respectively, of the Southern California branch of the Citizens for Eisenhower-Nixon. They had written Eisenhower to express their dismay at the results of the recent midterm election in California (see nos. 829, 926, and 932); they had also offered to "help in rebuilding" (WHCF/PPF 49-B-15). Lampe (B.S. University of Iowa 1922), an accountant and tax lawyer, had previously served as treasurer of the group; we have been unable to identify further Mrs. Fort. For background on the Citizens organizations, which sought to win independent and Democratic support for Republican programs and candidates, see no. 278.

[2] Republicans had controlled the state's congressional delegation by a margin of seventeen to thirteen. But when the new Congress convened in January, the Democrats would have sixteen of the thirty seats. In the only Southern California district lost by the Republicans, the incumbent had not been a candidate for reelection (see *Congressional Quarterly Almanac*, vol. XIV, *1958*, pp. 716, 719–23; and Anderson, "The 1958 Election in California," pp. 278–79).

[3] This note is a greatly reduced version of an earlier letter (Nov. 24, AWF/D) that Eisenhower drafted but chose not to send. The earlier version termed the election results "a blessing in disguise" and expressed the hope that the Citizens should "not only be kept alive, but strengthened, during the two year period before the next campaign." Eisenhower suggested that since the Citizens had shown by their actions that they wanted "to support *personalities* in whom they trust," they should therefore "work among themselves and with the regular Republican organization in an effort to interest and build up into local prominence attractive, young candidates with sensible and progressive philosophies." He urged the Citizens to make extensive use of television in order to introduce these political novices to the electorate: "I think the television camera provides, in most cases, an accurate portrait of character, and the American people are relying more and more—and rightly so—upon their own estimates of the kind of people they want to elect to office."

Eisenhower thought, however, that it would be a mistake to limit attention to potential candidates for office: "While interest is undoubtedly easy to focus on personalities, I think we would all do better, for the time being, to concentrate on *issues*." He was certain that the Citizens shared his fundamental beliefs. The Republican party, Eisenhower wrote, had "a real interest in the welfare of all Americans—not of any special interest, be it business or labor or whatever." He urged the Citizens to participate in a restructuring process that would help create a "solid—and broad— grass roots base" that would lead to "the type of progressive organization that we must have" (see Eisenhower, *Waging Peace*, pp. 382–83; see also Rood to Whitman, Nov. 26, 1958, WHCF/PPF 49-B-15).

[4] For developments see no. 962.

947   *EM, AWF, Name Series*

To Milton Stover Eisenhower   *November 26, 1958*

Dear Milton: I have read your document carefully and find it both informative and interesting.[1]

So far as I am concerned, I see nothing objectionable in it. (I am attaching a memorandum of minor comments.)[2] As I suggested, however, by telephone (through Mrs. Whitman) that I must reserve final agreement on a satisfactory confirmation by the Secretaries of State and Treasury. I repeat that this is not because of anything in it that I think unwise or objectionable; it is merely that in certain instances I have not done the study that would qualify me to make an objective judgment.

Naturally I recognize your right, without reservation, to express your own convictions about these matters, but I am hopeful that in order to achieve the maximum benefit from the result that we can achieve concurrence among those most interested.[3]

With warm regard, *As ever*

[1] For background on Milton Eisenhower's fact-finding trip to Panama, Honduras, Costa Rica, Nicaragua, Puerto Rico, El Salvador, and Guatemala see no. 516; see also State, *Foreign Relations, 1958–1960*, vol. V, *American Republics*, pp. 249–64; *U.S. Department of State Bulletin* 39, no. 1000 [August 25, 1958], 309–10; and Eisenhower, *The Wine is Bitter*, pp. 208–23. In his report Milton had referred to his ten-nation visit to South America in 1953 (see Galambos and van Ee, *The Middle Way*, no. 259), reaffirming with "a note of urgency" his previous recommendation that "the nations of Latin America and the United States re-examine their attitudes and policies toward one another and constantly seek to strengthen their economic, political, and cultural relations, to their mutual benefit."

In his 1958 report Milton urged the need for the United States to take a leadership role with the Organization of American States in developing understanding between peoples and governments; to expand USIA activities in the area; to establish an Inter-American Bank, funded in large part by the United States; to improve technical cooperation programs; and to develop a common market for Latin America. He also reported that during his travels he had often heard the charge that the United States supported Latin American dictators. Although he believed this attitude to be a "serious misunderstanding," he recommended that the United States "refrain from granting special recognition" to Latin American dictators and constantly reaffirm the principles of democracy (AWF/M: AP; see also *U.S. Department of State Bulletin* 40, no. 1021 [January 19, 1959], 89–105).

[2] Eisenhower's memorandum, suggesting some additions and deletions in wording and asking for some clarifications, is in AWF/N. On the recommendation to establish a technical cooperation program to be supervised by the U.S. ambassador to each country and coordinated by the Assistant Secretary of State for Inter-American Affairs, Eisenhower said that he was not qualified to comment. "It is one that I think should especially be studied by the State Department." Eisenhower also questioned the use of the word "special" in Milton's recommendation regarding U.S. policy toward dictators, but the wording would remain the same in the final report.

[3] Milton would tell Eisenhower that he would be willing to come to Washington to discuss any serious questions government officials might have about the report (Milton Eisenhower to Whitman, Dec. 10, 1958, AWF/N). For developments see no. 968.

To Henry Ludmer   *November 26, 1958*
Personal

Dear Professor Ludmer: Thank you for reminding me of the publications of the Military Intelligence Division of the War Department,
and for telling me the specific ones you believe might be helpful in
the current situation have been declassified.[1]

As you probably know, I have taken no part in the flurry over the
claims made by Field Marshal Montgomery in his "Memoirs." I am
nonetheless gratified by your kindness in writing me, particularly
since you have obviously informed yourself concerning the phases
of the Western European operation, on which the Field Marshal has
passed on such extraordinary judgments.[2]

With best wishes, *Sincerely*

[1] Ludmer (Ph.D. Czechoslovakia Technological School of Commerce 1939) taught
economics and public finance at Roosevelt University in Chicago, Illinois. He had
been an intelligence specialist in the U.S. Army during World War II and had contributed to such War Department Military Intelligence Division publications as "Order of Battle of the German Army," "The German Replacement Army," and "Military Headquarters and Installations in Germany." His letter of November 18 is in
WHCF/PPF 1-C-3.

[2] For background on the publication of Montgomery's *Memoirs* see no. 238. Ludmer
considered the book to be inaccurate because it was contradicted by the U.S. Military Intelligence Division's publications. The British War Office and British military
intelligence units, including Montgomery's, had approved the publications, Ludmer
said. High-ranking officers of the German Wehrmacht had also verified the accuracy
of the volumes.

Ludmer went on to suggest that the declassified publications should be used to
prove to the public that a direct thrust toward Berlin would not have shortened the
war; that Eisenhower's aggressive course of action was "the only sensible strategy of
the Allies"; and that Montgomery's "cocky over-confidence was partly responsible"
for the loss of thousands of Americans killed or hurt in the Battle of the Bulge.

For more on the controversy over Montgomery's memoirs see, for example, no.
970.

To James Frederick Gault   *November 26, 1958*

Dear Jimmy: First of all, let me tell you personally how sorry I was
that I could not arrange that golf game we talked about before your
departure for England.[1] As you know, I was on the verge of a trip to
the West Coast, and the speech that I had to give before the

Colombo Pact Nations didn't go at all well in preparation; consequently, I had to spend far more time than I had anticipated on it before leaving Washington.[2] I trust your visit to Canada and the United States was successful, and I shall look forward to seeing you the next time you are over here.

Now a really important question. Someone asked me to identify a regimental insignia picked up on the battlefield in France. It is about two and a half inches by two inches—has a coat-of-arms surrounded by a wreath about the size of a dollar—bears a crown on the top of the wreath—and contains the words "Argyll and Sutherland." I think it must be a regimental insignia of the Argylls, but I wonder whether you could not only confirm this but give me anything more about it.[3]

I hope the ceremonies at St. Paul's Cathedral go well; I can imagine you have been very busy in connection with the preparations.[4]

Mamie and I are down here in Augusta (which of course you remember) for about ten days.[5] The weather, until today, has been ideal, a term I cannot possibly use to describe the state of my present golf game.

With warm regard, *As ever*

[1] On October 16 Gault had lunched with the President and in the evening had attended a black-tie stag dinner at the White House with many wartime friends (see no. 823). As it turned out, Eisenhower and Gault would next play golf on September 6, 1959, in Maybole, Scotland (see no. 1305).

[2] The Colombo Plan Consultative Committee had met in Seattle, Washington, November 10–13. On the preparation of the speech see no. 900; and Ann Whitman memorandum, Nov. 10, 1958, AWF/AWD).

[3] After consulting an expert in regimental history, Gault would reply (Dec. 18, WHCF/PPF 71) that the insignia was probably some form of the Argyll insignia. The full title of this regiment, he wrote, is the Argyll and Sutherland Highlanders (Princess Louise's). As the Highland regiments have various forms of insignia for different parts of Highland dress, he said, we cannot accurately identify the insignia from the description. He offered to send more details if he were furnished the insignia or a photograph. For developments see no. 996.

[4] Gault would reply that the dedication of the American Memorial Chapel in St. Paul's Cathedral in London, was "impressive and inspiring." The chapel, built with British contributions, was dedicated to more than 28,000 Americans who gave their lives during World War II while stationed in Britain, en route to Britain, or permanently based in Britain (*New York Times*, Nov. 27, 1958).

[5] On the Eisenhowers' Thanksgiving vacation in Augusta see no. 892. Gault had been the President's guest at Augusta in December 1956 (see Galambos and van Ee, *The Middle Way*, no. 2165).

To Mrs. Percy R. Patterson   *November 26, 1958*

Dear Mrs. Patterson: You will understand that the volume of White House mail is so great that when a letter requires an answer by a technical division of the government, the reply is prepared and signed by the individual responsible for that particular department. The letter sent to you by Mr. McElvain was handled in that fashion.[1]

From the correspondence you sent to me, I assume that the unfavorable reply that you received from Congressman Auchincloss in August of this year contained the detailed reasons why it was not possible to approve your request for Federal assistance.[2]

Deeply sympathetic, as I am, with the disastrous family situation that you describe, I am still, as a government official, limited in the discharge of my responsibilities by the laws that apply to particular cases. I assume from the letter you have from the Social Security Administration that the laws do not permit the kind of Federal assistance that you believe justice demands. I know that every impulse and desire of the Social Security people is to give to American citizens, and particularly our older groups who find themselves in distressing circumstances, every possible assistance that the laws permit. Since I am certain of this attitude, I cannot possibly give you any definite promise for the help you now request from Federal resources. But I shall again make inquiry of the technical experts whether there is any factor in your case that has been overlooked.[3]

Needless to say, I do most earnestly hope that something can be done to alleviate the serious situation in which you and your husband find yourselves.[4] *Sincerely*

---

[1] Mrs. Patterson, of Belmar, New Jersey, had sent Eisenhower a copy of the November 21 letter she had received from Joseph E. McElvain, Chairman of the Office of Appeals Council of the Social Security Administration (same file as document). Mrs. Patterson had written across the bottom of the copy: "Please note, Mr. President. Have at least 7 of this sort of a reply. We just want justice and fairness and human consideration." Her cover letter is not in EM. McElvain had informed Mrs. Patterson that the letter she had sent to the President (Oct. 31) had been referred to his office for reply, and that her husband's claim for disability under the Social Security Act had been carefully reviewed and disallowed. Presidential Secretary Ann Whitman noted that McElvain's "bureaucratic language" had "irritated" Eisenhower (Ann Whitman memorandum, Nov. 26, 1958, AWF/AWD).

[2] McElvain had reported that the Patterson claim had been resolved over a year ago and the details were "fully explained" in an August 20, 1958, letter to Republican Congressman from New Jersey James Coats Auchincloss (A.B. Yale 1908).

[3] After reviewing the Patterson case, Department of Health Education and Welfare Secretary Flemming would report that nothing more could be done. Eisenhower would direct him to inform Mrs. Patterson in what Ann Whitman called a "non-

bureaucratic way!" (Flemming to Whitman, Dec. 15, 1958 and Whitman to Flemming, Dec. 10, 1958, same file as document).

[4] On November 30 Mrs. Patterson would thank the President for giving her a "ray of
hope to cling to" (*ibid.*). See also the following document.

To Mrs. Percy R. Patterson   *November 26, 1958*
Personal and confidential

Dear Mrs. Patterson: I was particularly touched by the observation in
your recent letter to me that while I was so fortunate as to have my
grandchildren with me for Thanksgiving dinner, you cannot invite
yours. Consequently I hope that you will accept from me, as my own
acknowledgment of the personal good fortune that makes my own
Thanksgiving a very satisfying one, the enclosed present which I
trust you will use to have your family with you for a reunion dinner,
even though it will be impossible for you to have this before Thanksgiving Day. I assure you that on my part this little gesture is nothing more than a feeling of obligation for a fellow human in distress.[1]

With best wishes, *Sincerely*

P.S. I request that you tell no other person about the contents of
this note—even members of your family.

[1] For background on Mrs. Patterson's letter and her financial difficulties see the preceding document. The Eisenhower family was in Augusta, Georgia, for the Thanksgiving holiday. The President would give $50 to Ann Whitman, who wrote a personal
check in that amount to Mrs. Patterson (Ann Whitman memorandum, Nov. 26, 1958,
AWF/AWD). Mrs. Patterson's November 30 thank-you note is in WHCF/OF 156-C.

To Jawaharlal Nehru   *November 27, 1958*
Confidential

Dear Prime Minister: Paul Hoffman, who has just returned to this
country, gave me an account of the interesting conversation he recently had with you.[1] He was profoundly impressed by your clear
dedication to the cause of a just and lasting peace.

Universally you are recognized as one of the most powerful influences for peace and conciliation in the world.[2] I believe that because

you are a world leader for peace in your individual capacity, as well as a representative of the largest of the neutral nations, your influence is particularly valuable in stemming the global drift toward cynicism, mutual suspicion, materialistic opportunism and, finally, disaster.

For my part, I shall without ceasing continue the attempt to convince the world, including the Soviets and Red China, of our non-aggressive, peaceful intent. I ask nothing more from them than the right, which I am equally ready to accord to them, for each side to satisfy itself that the other is sincere in its peaceful protestations.

A case in point is the seeming impasse that has been encountered in the progress of negotiations at Geneva on the techniques of preventing surprise attack and developing an acceptable plan for the cessation of nuclear tests. These negotiations, I feel, must not break down.

Quite naturally we, on our side, believe we have been eminently reasonable and conciliatory in our attitude. But our conviction in this regard does not necessarily mean that our people's sincerity, so obvious here, is accepted by all peoples elsewhere.

This note is inspired not only by Mr. Hoffman's recent report to me of his visit with you, but by my lively recollection of the friendly and, to me, profitable conversations that we had in 1956, as well as by the profound feeling I have that there is no greater task lying before any political leader today than that of helping to relieve the tensions that plague mankind.[3]

With assurances of my deep respect and continued warm regard,
Sincerely

[1] For background on Nehru and the Geneva talks on disarmament and atomic testing see no. 943. The State Department would cable the text of this message to New Delhi for delivery to Nehru on this same day (AWF/I: Nehru).

[2] At this point in the original draft Eisenhower had included the sentence: "The importance of your position is all the more emphasized because India is one of the uncommitted nations." Secretary Dulles had eliminated this sentence to minimize the implication that Nehru had a role to play in the outcome of the Geneva talks.

[3] On the Indian leader's December 1956 visit to Washington and Gettysburg see Galambos and van Ee, *The Middle Way*, no. 2139. The people of India, in their "more limited way," were working for peace and the lessening of world tensions, Nehru would reply. Some step toward disarmament was "urgently needed," and "nuclear tests should be ended." He said he would take advantage of any opportunity to be of service but hesitated to intervene unless convinced that such action would be helpful (Nehru to Eisenhower, Dec. 3, 1958, AWF/I: Nehru). For developments in Geneva see no. 992.

To Charles H. Gibboney *November 27, 1958*

Dear Dr. Gibboney: Noting that the Reid Memorial Presbyterian Church is in the midst of its "pledge" campaign, Mrs. Eisenhower and I are delighted to make a donation to the Church shortly after the beginning of the New Year.[1]

You will understand, of course, that our major church activities and support involve primarily our church in Washington. Secondarily we are concerned with similar activities in Gettysburg, Pennsylvania, and Denver, Colorado.[2] I give this as a short explanation of the relatively modest size of our gift.

Our pledge is $200. I would appreciate it if no publicity is given to the gift.

I believe we shall have to defer seeing the tablet that has been placed under the Redemption Window until another time. The Secretary of State is stopping in Augusta on his way to Mexico City on Sunday morning, and his visit comes at the time when church services are held.[3]

With warm regard, *Sincerely*

P.S. It is possible that my son and daughter-in-law will be able to attend services Sunday, but even that is not definite.

[1] The Eisenhowers attended services at Reid Memorial while they vacationed in Augusta, Georgia.
[2] The First Family also attended services at the National Presbyterian Church in Washington, D.C., at the Presbyterian Church of Gettysburg, and at Corona Presbyterian Church in Denver. For background on Eisenhower's decision to join the Presbyterian church see Galambos and van Ee, *The Middle Way,* no. 13.
[3] The President would meet with John Foster Dulles at 10:30 A.M. on November 30. On Dulles's trip to Mexico see no. 941.

To Helen Maurer Nielsen *December 2, 1958*

Dear Helen: Mamie and I have been greatly concerned since we learned of your attack, but a note from Aks says that the doctors are completely satisfied with your progress. I am relieved—and delighted.[1]

If there was any one lesson I discovered from my similar experience of over three years ago, it was the value of patience (a difficult matter, as well you know, for a man of my temperament). At any rate, please don't rush the matter of convalescence.[2]

You know so much about my own illness that it seems a little ridiculous to offer you any "advice." But I cannot resist one thing. If your doctors request, as mine did, that you rest for an hour or so in the middle of each day, I do hope you will do so, without deviation. As a matter of clinical observation, I find that—while this is the one concession I make nowadays to my own illness—I really look forward to an hour or so of quiet, if not actually of sleep. And if you make it a matter of routine, you don't find it at all onerous.[3]

Needless to say, Mamie and I have been thinking of you constantly, and join in the most sincere good wishes for your speedy and complete recovery (all of which I hope Aks reported to you after my phone call).[4]

With affectionate regard, *As ever*

[1] Mrs. Nielsen had suffered a heart attack on November 24. Her husband Aksel had written of her progress on November 28 (WHCF/PPF 1-JJ-1). See also Nielsen to Whitman, December 2, 1958, AWF/N, Nielsen Corr.

[2] While vacationing in Denver, Eisenhower had suffered a coronary thrombosis on September 24, 1955 (see Galambos and van Ee, *The Middle Way*, no. 1595).

[3] On the President's immediate reaction to his physicians's advice to take a midday rest see *ibid.*, nos. 1710 and 1853.

[4] Eisenhower had telephoned Nielsen on November 25 (Telephone conversation, AWF/AWD). See the following document.

955 *EM, AWF, Name Series*

To Aksel Nielsen *December 2, 1958*

Dear Aks: It was good to learn from your letter of the twenty-eighth that Helen is making all the progress that the doctors can expect.[1] Please tell her that while I had long recognized she was a very VIP, I hadn't realized that the power of a woman would bring about such a disastrous stock market decline. But apparently word reached New York that she was on the mend—and all is now well.[2]

Thanks for the information on curing meat. I shall see if we can't profit from it.[3]

I understand you will be in Washington on the tenth; as always I look forward to seeing you.[4]

With warm regard, *As ever*

[1] Nielsen's letter is in WHCF/PPF 1-JJ1. On Helen Nielsen's heart attack see the preceding document.

[2] Nielsen said his wife had commented that her coronary might differ from Eisenhower's, but "both caused a serious setback to the market." On November 24 the shares listed on the New York Stock Exchange suffered their most severe loss since

the trading day following the President's heart attack of September 24, 1955. The decline in 1958 was temporary, however, as prices had begun to rise on November 26 and had continued to do so (*New York Times*, Nov. 25, 26, 27, 28, Dec. 2, 1958).
[3] The President probably had asked Nielsen for the information at an off-the-record meeting on November 17. Eisenhower had asked for similar advice from Nielsen earlier this year (see no. 636). Nielsen said he had checked with a local packing company and had learned that beef should be hung for three weeks at a temperature from 33 to 36 degrees, with humidity no higher than 40 percent. He went on to list the different cuts of meat that would result from dressing the carcasses, and included a specific example of profits that would be realized through this method.
[4] See Nielsen to Whitman, December 2, 1958, AWF/N, Nielsen Corr.

956   *EM, AWF, Name Series*

To Aksel Nielsen   *December 3, 1958*

Dear Aks: I have gone over the information you gave me about curing beef and I should like to ask one further question.[1] It concerns the length of the curing time.

In the two carcasses I cured in my curing room I allowed one to remain 35 days and the other 39 days, with the temperature from around 34 to 36 degrees. I had no way of controlling the humidity, but I could of course get an accurate instrument to determine average humidity. My question then is in two parts:

(*a*). Is there any damaging effect of curing for longer than three weeks that is recommended?[2]

(*b*). Is the effect of excess humidity to slow down the curing process or to speed it up?[3]

Finally, I should add another question, which is: what other adverse effects from excess humidity are to be anticipated?[4]

With warm regard, *As ever*

[1] See the preceding document.
[2] Nielsen had recommended keeping the humidity slightly under 40 percent (Nov. 28, 1958, WHCF/PPF 1-JJ-1).
[3] Nielsen would reply on December 11 (AWF/N) that any damage would depend upon how soon the meat was put in a cooler from 32 to 34 degrees with humidity at 40 percent. Placing the carcass in a cooler within 48 hours after butchering would prevent bacteria from growing, Nielsen wrote. If the bacteria had begun to grow, he said, you cannot cure the meat longer than three weeks.
[4] Excess humidity speeded up the curing process, Nielsen reported. He added that if the humidity was higher than 40 percent, bacteria would enter the open end of the beef, which would then become "a little slimey rather than dry," and would begin to mold. See also Nevins to Whitman, December 6, 1958, AWF/Gettysburg. Eisenhower would thank Nielsen on December 15 (AWF/N).

To Clifford Roberts   *December 4, 1958*

Dear Cliff: You and I were talking lately about the relative advantages of tax free municipal and normal commercial bonds for the investor.[1] It seems to me that these advantages will vary greatly according to the top tax bracket of the prospective investor.

A specific opinion I would like is on something like this. Take an individual whose top bracket is from thirty to forty percent; would you believe it would be better because of yield and lack of risk to buy a good commercial bond rather than to go into tax exempts?

I assure you I am not looking for a long analysis and detailed study. I simply want your shot gun opinion based on the general outline of my question.[2]

I hope that you and Bill reached New York without any difficulty the other evening.[3] Both weather and cancelled schedules seemed to be a little against you that night, but since I heard nothing from either of you I assumed that everything went okay.

Incidentally, the household seemed very quiet and even a little forlorn with all the children back home in Alexandria! *As ever*

[1] Roberts had joined the President and First Lady and their son and his family in Augusta, Georgia, for the Thanksgiving holiday (see no. 892).
[2] For more on Eisenhower's financial investments see no. 934. Roberts's reply is not in EM.
[3] On the afternoon of December 2 William E. Robinson and Roberts had accompanied Eisenhower aboard the *Columbine* from Augusta to Washington, D.C.

To Neil Herman Jacoby   *December 5, 1958*

Dear Dr. Jacoby: Thank you very much for your interesting letter of the twenty-sixth.[1]

The governmental individuals who, with me, are most interested in the Federal activities that affect our fiscal situation are the Secretary of the Treasury, Bob Anderson, Dr. Saulnier, the Director of the Bureau of the Budget, Mr. Stans, and the Chairman of the independent Federal Reserve Board, Mr. Martin. At intervals we meet to discuss these matters.

I think I am safe in saying that all of us would agree with that part of your letter beginning "The real threat to a resumption of price inflation. . .". Certainly we agree that the real culprit in producing the kind of inflation we have had in recent years is the push of costs, particularly wage costs, on prices. But likewise we believe that large Federal deficits help this process along and it is clear that they give rise to apprehension abroad as well as at home concerning the Federal Government's willingness and capacity to do its part in containing inflationary pressures. And, as you know, deficits do raise very troublesome problems in the management of our debt during the next twelve months.[2]

Another observation that seems important at the moment is this: Each of the five recommendations you outline requires law.[3] Frankly, I am skeptical of inducing the Congress, with its present composition, to do anything really constructive along the lines you suggest. I shall, of course, in both my State of the Union Message and in the Economic Report urgently support these principles, which thoughtful people recognize as being sound.

In a situation in which we cannot anticipate the enactment of laws that will be intelligently directed toward a solution of this whole problem, we believe it is especially important that the Administration do its full share in the area of government in which it has a special responsibility, namely in developing the budget, to avoid unnecessary upward pressures. My opinion that the necessary laws will not be promptly forthcoming does not in any way diminish my determination to do the very best I can on this matter for the next two years.[4]

I hope you will not mind my sending a copy of your letter to associates who will be especially interested in your views.

With warm personal regard and renewed thanks for your earlier services to the Administration, as well as my thanks for reporting to me Dr. Allen's diagnosis of my "appearance." Should you see him, remember me to him kindly.[5] *Sincerely*

---

[1] Neil Herman Jacoby (Ph.D. University of Chicago 1938) had served as dean of the Graduate School of Business Administration at the University of California, Los Angeles, since 1948. His letter of November 26, 1958, is in the same file as the document.

[2] Jacoby had argued that the impending budget deficit did not represent a real threat of inflation because inflation was "not likely to be caused by an excessive demand for goods and services by government or private households and businesses." Rather, the real threat would come from the "push of rising *costs*, resulting from 'administered' prices and wage rates." See no. 961.

[3] Jacoby had recommended action along five fronts to counter inflationary pressures: more flexible monetary and tax policies; extension of the antitrust laws to labor unions and other exempt activities; reduced barriers to international trade; gradual withdrawal of federal farm supports and stockpiling programs; and reform of the federal tax structure to encourage replacement of obsolete plant and machinery. Even though an unbalanced federal budget might be blamed for any resumption of inflation, Eisenhower would "do a great service to our country" by pointing out the "real culprit" was the "undisciplined power of labor unions and other factors that impede competition in the economy."

[4] For developments see no. 1040.

[5] Raymond Bernard Allen (M.D. 1928, Ph.D. 1934, University of Minnesota) had served as chancellor of the University of California at Los Angeles since 1952. He had met with Eisenhower on November 17 to discuss the People-to-People program. Jacoby had quoted Allen as having said that the President looked "like a man under 60" and appeared in "better physical condition than at any time he has seen you in recent years."

959   *EM, WHCF, Official File 116-J*

To Lamar Fleming, Jr.   *December 5, 1958*

Personal

Dear Mr. Fleming: Thank you for your letter of November nineteenth calling my attention to the increasingly critical attitude toward the United States which members of your firm have observed developing in Latin America in recent months.[1] Few firms have a wider background of experience in that area than Anderson, Clayton and Company, and for that reason its analysis of the situation there is particularly valuable. From other sources I have had similar reports, though somewhat less specific than yours.[2]

From the many public statements that I have made on the general subject of multi-lateral trade, it is obvious that I have no disagreement with the observations you make about the United States and its political and economic opportunities and responsibilities internationally.[3] There is, however, one added consideration that, though obvious, is too often overlooked.

Ours is a government based upon the popular will. In any problem involving ourselves and other countries, the public too often loses sight of our own best interests from the national viewpoint. We know that a minority interest, even though it may not be particularly important in itself, can sometimes successfully combine with others to produce a popular opinion that compels unwise governmental action. Sometimes these can be successfully opposed—in most cases a disapproval of the Tariff Commission's findings can be sustained unless, of course, there should develop an overwhelming Congressional sentiment to the contrary.

It was the use of this Presidential authority to disapprove Tariff Commission findings that incited the sternest opposition to renewal of the Trade Act.[4]

You know of the long and bitter struggle that we had to keep the Reciprocal Trade legislation on the books. This was finally accomplished—but at some cost in compromise.

In our relations with other nations we have tried to avoid the imposition of legalistic and formal obstacles to trade even where the domestic pressures for unilateral restrictions by tariff have been very great. Congressional action in response to this pressure has often been attempted; on occasion an Administrative compromise has appeared almost mandatory in order to avoid crippling legislation. Such solutions, when they must be developed, have at least the virtue of fluidity in that they are not crystallized into law. Moreover, when, for example, restrictions were imposed on lead and zinc, I submitted a personal explanation of the incident and the reasons for our decision to the heads of the affected states. I assure you that we have searched, in these cases, for some better solution.[5]

My brother is shortly to issue a report on his trip to Central America.[6] In it he makes some specific recommendations with regard to this entire problem. Admittedly his suggestions cannot solve all the problems, but they may be at least partially helpful in getting other countries to understand why we have no alternative to certain decisions. At any rate I shall send you a copy of the report as soon as it is made available.

Again my thanks for your letter; I shall, of course, see that Foster Dulles has a copy of your analysis of the situation.[7]

With warm regard, *Sincerely*

[1] Lamar Fleming was chairman of the board of Anderson, Clayton and Company, a processor of consumer and institutional foods, oilseed products, and animal and poultry feeds with subsidiaries in several Central and South American countries. Eisenhower had selected Fleming as a member of the Commission on Foreign Economic Policy (Randall Commission) in May 1953 (see Galambos and van Ee, *The Middle Way*, no. 170). Fleming had written about a growing Latin American trend toward "hostile nationalism," which had caused his company to exercise greater caution in the expansion of its operations. Actions taken by the U.S. government in exporting surplus commodities abroad and the import quotas imposed on oil, lead, and zinc had contributed to the problem, Fleming had written. The extreme left in the Latin American countries had exploited these actions for anti-U.S. propaganda purposes (Fleming to Eisenhower, Nov. 19, 1958, same file as document; on the lead and zinc issue see no. 859; see also State, *Foreign Relations, 1958–1960*, vol. IV, *Foreign Economic Policy*, pp. 182–90).

[2] Eisenhower may have been referring in part to recent discussions with his brother Milton regarding the final report on Milton's trip to several Latin American countries (see no. 947).

[3] On Eisenhower's trade philosophy see, for example, his special message to Congress on the Reciprocal Trade Agreements program in January 1958 and his speech before the Canadian Houses of Parliament in July (*Public Papers of the Presidents: Eisenhower, 1958*, pp. 132–35, 529–36; see also no. 786).

[4] For background see no. 753.

[5] For Eisenhower's letters to Mexican President Ruiz Cortines and Canadian Prime Minister Diefenbaker see no. 859.

[6] See no. 968.

[7] Fleming would write Eisenhower that he had never doubted the President's commitment to a liberal trade policy and that only "some element of compromise" could

produce action advantageous to the total national interest (Fleming to Eisenhower, Dec. 26, 1958, same file as document). For developments see no. 1170.

960

To Charles Douglas Jackson   *December 6, 1958*
Personal and confidential

Dear C. D.: I have lived quite constantly with this Kadar problem ever since you reminded me of its existence. Frankly, my *own* position is not completely in accord with yours.[1]

My feeling is that we should express disapproval—and find means of making this expression positive and public. However, I believe it unwise to submit and sponsor, on an all-out basis, a resolution of rejection. Frankly, I have great difficulty in differentiating between the Soviet and Hungarian delegations insofar as their acceptability is concerned. While I realize that the technical position of the two delegations is different, yet in principle it seems to me that a proposal to refuse to seat a delegation is very little different from a resolution for expulsion.[2]

This morning I again had a talk with Chris Herter on the matter.[3] (By the time this letter reaches you, you will know that Foster is temporarily in the hospital).[4] I expressed views to Chris about like those in this letter; I made it clear that I was not rigid in this attitude. I am simply giving my conclusions, based upon all of the conflicting considerations that apply to problems such as this in this kind of world.[5]

With warm regard, *As ever*

[1] Although Eisenhower had once agreed with Jackson regarding the unseating of the Kadar regime in the U.N. General Assembly, he had later changed his mind (for background see nos. 923 and 924).

[2] On November 20 the State Department had urged the British to join the United States in rejecting Hungarian credentials; it had argued that such an action was the only effective sanction available to the United Nations. In a November 26 memorandum British Foreign Secretary Lloyd had questioned the authority of a simple majority to decide the matter. While action of this sort would satisfy and encourage the Hungarian people, Lloyd preferred condemnation of both the Soviet Union and Hungary's Kadar regime, and he favored continuing the policy of leaving the question of Hungarian credentials in suspense (State, *Foreign Relations, 1958–1960*, vol. II, *United Nations and General International Matters*, pp. 76–77).

On November 30 Dulles had described the British position to the President. The Secretary of State suggested that the United States introduce a resolution to expel the Hungarian delegation on the ground of "flagrant and persistent violation of UN resolutions." He argued, however, that the United States should "avoid full engagement" of its prestige and should not actively seek support of other delegations; the project, he thought, was "almost certain of failure." The President had agreed with Dulles, and directed that "at such time as a resolution is introduced to accept these credentials, we then declare our opposition and introduce a resolution for rejection" (Dulles, Memorandum of Conversation, Nov. 30, 1959, Dulles Papers, White House Memoranda Series, and State, *Foreign Relations, 1958–1960*, vol. II, *United Nations and General International Matters*, pp. 78–80; see also Telephone conversation, Dulles and Lodge, Nov. 26, 1958, Dulles Papers, Telephone Conversations).

[3] Earlier on this same day Eisenhower had also discussed the Hungarian issue at a breakfast meeting with Ambassador Lodge, who had spoken with Secretary Dulles the day before (State, *Foreign Relations, 1958–1960*, vol. II, *United Nations and General International Matters*, pp. 85–86).

[4] On December 5 Dulles had entered Walter Reed Army Hospital with an initial diagnosis of diverticulitis (*New York Times*, Dec. 9, 1958; see also Dulles, Memorandum of Conversation, Nov. 8, 10, Dulles Papers, White House Memoranda Series). For developments see no. 1167.

[5] On December 12 the United Nations General Assembly would adopt a resolution on the situation in Hungary. The resolution, cosponsored by the United States and 36 other countries, denounced the execution of Imre Nagy and other Hungarian officials; condemned the continued defiance of U.N. General Assembly resolutions on Hungary; exhorted Soviet and Hungarian authorities to respect Hungarian rights; and declared that the United Nations would continue to examine the situation (State, *Foreign Relations, 1958–1960*, vol. II, *United Nations and General International Matters*, pp. 91–92). For developments see no. 1234.

As a result of the decision to forgo an all-out campaign to expel the Hungarians, Jackson would tender his resignation from the board of Radio Free Europe (Dulles to Jackson, Jan. 8, 1958, Dulles Papers, Chronological Series, and Jackson to Dulles, and Jackson to Whitman, Dec. 9, 1958, both in AWF/A, Jackson Corr.)

961   *EM, AWF, DDE Diaries Series*

MEMORANDUM   *December 6, 1958*

Memorandum for the record: Budgetary struggles and the outlook for refinancing: Recently I have had several talks with the Secretary of the Treasury and the Chairman of the Council of Economic Advisers, Dr. Saulnier, on these subjects. Possibly I have recorded elsewhere some of our projected difficulties in refinancing as outlined and detailed to me by Bob Anderson, the Secretary of the Treasury.[1] Unquestionably these problems are serious, the principal factors being as follows:

In the year 1959 we have to refinance more than 50 billion dollars of bond issues, each of which is more than one year term. In addition to this, we have to roll over four times during the year something on the order of 26 billion dollars worth of short term papers.[2] Beyond this we must find 12 billion dollars of new money because of the '59 deficit.[3] Still above this, we must get the additional money in November and December that will represent the difference between receipts and expenditures during that low point of the year.

Finally, whatever projected deficit there will be in the '60 budget will be overhanging the market.

In view of the fact that we are already spending more than 8 billion a year for interest alone, without any amortization, the scope of this problem and the rates of interest that we have to pay are, to say, the least, serious.

On the other hand, Saulnier takes a very much more optimistic view than Anderson does with regard to the gravity of this problem. Whereas Anderson believes that, unless we have a balanced budget we are going to have very bad effects in foreign banking circles because of a diminishing faith in the dollar, Saulnier believes that there is very little danger of this at the moment. Moreover, he is not particularly concerned about the accelerated outward movement of gold.[4] He believes that as corporation earnings go up—and he believes that the rate of increase is going to be higher than most people feel—that corporations will have to find use for their money. Many of them will be purchasing notes and short term securities, and this will greatly strengthen the bond market and tend to minimize our interest costs.[5]

On the other hand, Saulnier does not by any manner of means minimize the seriousness of the situation that will develop if, in addition to the obvious obstacles, we should have a disappointing performance of the economy insofar as its next twelve months recovery is concerned.

In any event, both agree that a balanced budget would have the most salutary effect on our fiscal situation that could be imagined.[6]

[1] For background see nos. 793 and 930. See also Ann Whitman memorandum, November 17, 18, AWF/AWD.

[2] Eisenhower was concerned about the growing competition within the economy for available funds. In 1959, forty-two percent of the total marketable Treasury securities, with a cumulative value of $80 billion, would become due within one year. With a legally fixed interest rate ceiling of 4¼ percent, long-term Treasury securities were at a serious disadvantage relative to higher rate short-term notes. The Treasury Department had not offered a long-term bond since June 1958 because of a "generally unsettled market atmosphere growing out of the substantial decline in prices of all types of bonds in the market during the late summer and early fall" (Anderson to Eisenhower, Jan. 9, 1958, AWF/A; see also Anderson to Eisenhower, Nov. 7, 18, 1958, AWF/A). Increased reliance on short-term debt produced inflationary pressures on the economy which the Administration also opposed (see Morgan, *Eisenhower Versus 'The Spenders,'* p. 129; *Congressional Quarterly Almanac*, vol. XV, *1959*, p. 273). In 1959 the President would ask Congress for legislation raising the ceiling on long-term federal debt interest rates.

[3] On the deficit see no. 784.

[4] See no. 930.

[5] See Saulnier, *Constructive Years*, pp. 119–24.

[6] For developments see no. 976 and 1040.

Memorandum for the Record   *December 6, 1958*
Confidential

A few days ago in Augusta I had a long talk with Cliff Roberts about the political situation.[1] The general tenor of that conversation was very similar to one that I held later with the Vice President, reported below.[2] The only point on which Cliff Roberts had a positive conviction, that is not shared by Dick Nixon and me, (and certainly not by the principal members of the White House Staff) is that Meade Alcorn should be removed as Chairman of the Republican National Committee. He also believes an effort should be made to substitute for him Chuck Percy of Chicago.[3]

I agree without reservation that Chuck Percy is a very unusual and capable young man and in my opinion would, if we could induce him to take this post, make an extraordinarily effective Chairman. Further than this I did not concur with Cliff's conclusion, for reasons that appear in the following paragraph.

Meade Alcorn has been the best Chairman of the Republican National Committee that I have known. His intelligence, energy, imagination and dedication are exemplary. Cliff, while not well acquainted with Mr. Alcorn, had no reason, he said, to differ with this evaluation. Cliff's big point is that Meade Alcorn is not a "real figure" in the national scene. He says that Alcorn cannot be effective for the simple reason that people do not pay attention to him. Moreover, Cliff feels that the terrible drubbing that the Republican Party took in the recent election is bound to be laid largely to Alcorn's door, even if the allegation is unjust and really represents nothing more than the effort of others to alibi their own inefficiencies. He concludes that since Alcorn's name is connected with failure and since he has not succeeded in establishing himself as a real influence in the Party, we should let him go.

My final remark was that I never thought it wise to fire anybody unless I knew *that I had a better person to take over.* In addition, I again repeated the list of Alcorn's good qualities and I pointed out to Cliff that in four attempts to get what he or anyone else would consider a "big" man, (in the sense that he was regarded nationally as an influential figure) I had not been successful. Honesty, courage, intelligence and incessant work, after all, can be of more importance than reputation.[4]

---

[1] Eisenhower had vacationed at the Augusta National Golf Club from November 20 until December 2 (see nos. 945 and 957). While there he had met with Roberts several times. A draft of this memorandum, bearing Eisenhower's handwritten emendations, is in AWF/N: Political Committee—1959.

[2] As originally dictated, both this and the following document had formed a single memorandum; Eisenhower separated the two parts after he revised his draft.
[3] On Alcorn's role in the campaign and his reports to the President see nos. 836, 919, and 935; on the outcome of the midterm elections see no. 926. In March Eisenhower had included Bell & Howell Company President Charles Percy in a list of the younger Republicans who should lead the party in the future (see no. 590).
[4] Alcorn would resign in April 1959; see no. 1125. For developments see the following document and no. 982.

963   *EM, AWF, DDE Diaries Series*

MEMORANDUM FOR THE RECORD   *December 6, 1958*
Confidential

The Vice President and I agreed that we should try to get a broadly based committee to analyze Republican difficulties and failures and to work out the finest possible plan we could develop for their correction.[1] We further agreed that time is of the essence because we have to do a lot of rebuilding.

I shall attempt, below, to lay out an outline of the steps we thought should be tried and some of the problems that we think must be met and solved.

1. The committee should be organized as soon as possible. On it there should be the Vice President, Alcorn, Justin Dart, and a number of others who could possibly include Summerfield, Chuck Percy, and at the very least one of the individuals who was in the original committee in 1951-52 to support my original nomination and election. Such a person could be Lodge, Clay, Paul Hoffman or Dewey.[2] (We discussed briefly the desirability of getting at least one Senator and one member of the House to serve on the Committee, but I believe we left the matter open).

Two men that I would like to see brought in and very closely questioned—possibly one or both could be members of the committee—are Congressman-elect Lindsay from New York City and Governor-elect Hatfield of Oregon. Both of them ran beautiful races almost on their own and both were successful.[3]

There ought also possibly be at least one well known businessman and another individual from the university world.

In the shake down I believe there should not be over nine members and possibly this might be too many.

A necessary recording staff could be provided by Meade Alcorn.

(With respect to favoring such a committee, a later talk with

Alcorn developed that he was thinking along these same lines and indeed he has already talked with the Vice President about doing something of the kind suggested above).[4]

2. We should make a survey of exactly what happened on November fourth in the various areas and why. We believe that the pollsters as well as reports from county and state chairmen and others should be examined. The analysis of this report should be undertaken by someone selected by the committee, who is experienced in research of this kind.

3. The next step for the committee would be to work out procedures by which:

    a. An organization can be built up from the grass roots. This organization's effort should emphasize youth, vigor and progress so that as it develops upward there will be elected as county and state chairmen the finest young leaders that we can find. The same effect will finally be noted in the type of our national committeemen, but in this case elections can be held once only every four years.

    b. We can develop a sturdy, broadly based and hardworking finance group which would bring in necessary revenue on a continuing monthly basis.

4. We should decide upon the form of the top organization. Here we mean not only the possible reorganization of the National Committee as such, but a careful examination of the need or lack of need for the so-called Congressional and Senatorial Committees as now organized and supported. It is reported to me that the Congressional Committee is particularly costly, its maintenance expense being something over $64,000 a month. This not only raises the question of getting our money's worth out of these two Committees, but it raises a far more serious question of a single versus a tri-headed political effort.

The National Chairman is of course the alter ego on Party matters of the President. This means that the proclamations and policies and plans of the National Committee must, under the President's leadership, provide the guide lines for Party effort, always, of course, within the limits laid down by the National Platform. If the heads of the Congressional or Senatorial Committees take a different political line and urge a different doctrine, then not only is our effort weakened, but we have the curious spectacle of the National Committee of supporting with very large sums of money a Committee which is preaching something that the President, the Administration and the National Chairman disapprove. This sort of thing happened in some instances in the last campaign.

Incidentally, to point up the importance of this problem we

should note that the amount of donations made to the Congressional Committee by the National Committee in the years '56 and '58 were respectively $1,600,000 and $400,000. I have no idea how the money was used, but I was importuned to help raise money, and did so.[5]

Relating further to the question of top organization, there could be a voluntary advisory committee to the National Chairman to be made up of businessmen, and, if the Congressional and Senatorial Committees were either eliminated or drastically reduced, another could be made up of a combined group of Senators and Congressmen—possibly six in number.

5. Throughout the organization from top to bottom there must be useful and dedicated voluntary workers; in addition we must have, according to the need, the necessary paid workers.

6. With this kind of an organization developed we must have, in addition to a clear understanding of our problems and policies and programs, the finest possible candidates. Again these people—men and women—should be young and vigorous and intelligent. If the preliminary organizational steps are properly accomplished, the result in terms of good candidates will be almost automatic. However, nothing can be taken for granted and we believe that it would be a good move to have in the National Committee two or three "travelling salesmen" who are clear headed people looking out for this type of candidate and able to get the local people to carry out the necessary measures.

There were, of course, a number of other related subjects discussed between the Vice President and myself.[6] A later conversation with Meade Alcorn was almost identical.

Alcorn is, at this moment, December sixth, in San Francisco or Hawaii. He will be back in a few days and he and the Vice President will start this work at once.

* * * * *

There was nothing significant in my conversation with Bill Knowland, except to note that he talked more objectively and sensibly after his defeat than he did before.[7]

---

[1] Richard Nixon had met with Eisenhower on November 5, the day after the midterm elections (see no. 926).

[2] For background on Rexall Drugs President Dart's fund raising during the 1958 election campaign see no. 914. On the campaign efforts of Republican National Committee Chairman Alcorn and the suggestion that Bell & Howell Company President Charles Percy might replace him, see the preceding document. Postmaster General Arthur Summerfield had served as chairman of the Republican National Commit-

tee during Eisenhower's 1952 campaign. For background on the 1952 campaign positions held by General Lucius Clay, U.S. Ambassador to the United Nations Henry Cabot Lodge, former Studebaker head Paul Hoffman, and former New York Governor Thomas Dewey, see Galambos, *NATO and the Campaign of 1952*, no. 740, n. 3.

[3] On the election victories of John Lindsay and Mark Hatfield see no. 937.

[4] Alcorn had met with Eisenhower on December 5.

[5] At this point in his original draft Eisenhower had said, "We have never had an accounting of these expenditures" (for details on the campaign expenditures of the Republican National Committee and the House and Senate Republican campaign committees see *Congressional Quarterly Almanac*, vol. XIV, *1958*, p. 747).

On the Republican Congressional Campaign Committee's lack of support for the Administration's positions see no. 406. In November the President had told House Minority Leader Joseph Martin that the House and Senate Republican campaign committees should be merged. Martin had disagreed, and the two groups would remain separate (Harlow, Memorandum for Record, Nov. 19, 1958, AWF/D). In January, however, Martin would fail in his attempt to win reelection as Minority Leader. See Eisenhower, *Waging Peace*, p. 384; Hughes, *Ordeal of Power*, pp. 276–77; and Joseph William Martin, Jr., *My First Fifty Years in Politics*, as told to Robert J. Donovan (New York, 1960), pp. 3–19; see also Anderson to Whitman, December 18, 1958, AWF/D, and no. 998.

[6] Eisenhower deleted the following sentence from his earlier draft of this memorandum: "There is no need to carry this list further."

[7] For background on Senator William Knowland's unsuccessful campaign to become governor of California see no. 932. He had met with the President on December 4. For developments see no. 982.

964   *EM, AWF, Administration Series:*
Adams Papers

To Sherman Adams   *December 8, 1958*

Dear Sherm: Recently in Augusta I ran into a couple of friends who had had contact with you during the last month or so; one of them saw you briefly at luncheon at a New York club.[1] He observed that you ate lunch hurriedly and seemed as busy as ever.

As you know, we are in the throes of budgeting, preparing the "State of the Union" message, planning for a meeting of the Republican legislative leaders (the Democrats refused this year) and at the same time, so far as I am personally concerned, Meade Alcorn is laying out for me a series of January chores that are completely political.[2]

Referring again to friends who have seen you or heard about you, one of them—I think Slats Slater—told me that through Sidney Weinberg you had given some consideration to two or three commercial positions, but that you had declined to accept any of them. I had a chance also to talk to Doug Black, who told me he had had some conversations with you.[3]

In spite of whatever may be your principal preoccupation at the moment, I suppose that skiing will have a major part in your life for the next several months. I know nothing about the New Hampshire snow crop at the moment, but if there is any there at all I am quite sure you will find it.

Nelson Rockefeller dropped in to see me Saturday evening; he seems to be attacking his job not only enthusiastically but very intelligently. His victory, together with that of Keating, Hatfield and one or two others, has provided a bright spot in an otherwise dreary election result.[4]

So far as I know, you have not honored our fair city with your presence recently, but whenever you do come down, please drop in to see me.[5]

My warm greetings to Rachel and, of course, the very best to yourself. *As ever*

[1] Several friends had visited the Eisenhowers while they vacationed in Augusta, Georgia, over the Thanksgiving holiday (see, for example, no. 957). The friend who had seen Adams was probably Ellis D. Slater, who reported that he thought Adams was writing a book (see n. 3 below). For background on Adams's resignation as the Assistant to the President see no. 753.

[2] On the struggles with the economy and the budget see no. 961. On the State of the Union Address see no. 1003. On Eisenhower's plan to revitalize the GOP and his assessment of Republican National Committee Chairman Alcorn see no. 962.

[3] Slater had visited Eisenhower at the White House on December 6 and 7 (Slater, *The Ike I Knew*, pp. 185–87). Adams would reply on December 12 (AWF/A) that in October he had spoken to Weinberg, vice-chairman of the Commerce Department's Business Advisory Council, but had not received any "commercial offer." Douglas Black was president and director of Doubleday & Company. Adams would confirm that he was writing a "good constructive story" of his experiences. His memoir, *Firsthand Report*, would be published in 1961.

[4] On Rockefeller's election see the following document. On Keating see no. 908. On Governor-elect Hatfield of Oregon see no. 963. On the midterm election results see nos. 880 and 926. Adams would not "comment" on the election, he wrote, but he repeated his offer to assist the President in any unofficial tasks.

[5] On February 2, 1960, Adams would attend an off-the-record meeting with the President at the White House.

965 *EM, AWF,*
Administration Series

To Nelson Aldrich Rockefeller *December 8, 1958*

Dear Nelson: I was delighted to have the opportunity for a personal chat with you Saturday evening, before we got into the business of your Committee. For almost six years you have been Chairman of my informal Committee on Government Organization and, as a result, it is almost a shock for me to consider your resignation from the post.[1] Naturally I recognize the necessity—but I still regret it.

I will shortly reply to your letter and I shall, of course,—but sorrowfully—accept your resignation, according to our understanding, as of December thirty-first.[2]

As I told you, I am highly gratified by your success in the recent election. It encourages me to believe that people have decided that "moderate government" when properly explained by a personable, intelligent candidate is still a goal of the majority of Americans. To say that I wish you every possible success in your conduct of your critically important post and that I will be watching the result with the keenest interest is understatement.[3]

Please convey my warm greetings to your charming bride and remember me kindly to the other members of your family.

All the best, *As ever*

[1] Rockefeller, who had been elected governor of New York on November 4, had visited the President at the White House on December 6 before meeting with the other members of the committee (see the preceding document as well as no. 922, and Ann Whitman memorandum, Dec. 6, 1958, AWF/AWD). He had brought with him an informal letter of resignation, dated December 4 (WHCF/OF 103-A-2).

[2] On December 22 Rockefeller would submit a formal resignation and a report on the activities of his committee. The letter, the report, and Eisenhower's December 29 reply are in *ibid*. On December 30 the press would print the text of Rockefeller's letter and the President's formal reply (*New York Times*, Dec. 30; see also Kimball to Rockefeller, Dec. 22, 1958).

[3] Eisenhower had said that Rockefeller's election had cushioned the "overall disappointment" of the election (see no. 937). On January 1 Eisenhower would send Rockefeller best wishes in undertaking his duties as governor. Rockefeller would thank the President on January 6 (both in AWF/A).

966   *EM, AWF, Administration Series*

To John Hay Whitney   *December 9, 1958*

Dear Jock: I neglected to cable you after receiving your fine message about the dinner attended by The Queen.[1] I am sorry that I overlooked the matter for the moment, but I do hope that you will find an opportunity through Selwyn Lloyd or through Harold Macmillan to assure her of the appreciation that Mamie and I felt for the gracious message in which she joined.[2]

Your glowing reports on the success of the Nixon trip paralleled others that I have received. I regret that he and Pat could not have had more time to travel about Europe so that many in other countries could understand that the young, progressive men and women in the Republican Party comprise a force and an ideal that will yet be felt throughout the free world, to its benefit.[3]

My very best to you and Betsey, and particularly my gratitude for the magnificent way in which you handled all the details of Dick's and Pat's visit. *As ever*

[1] Ambassador Whitney's message is not in EM. On November 27 Vice-President Nixon had entertained Queen Elizabeth II at a Thanksgiving dinner in the U.S. embassy residence in London. Nixon had traveled to London to attend the dedication ceremonies of the American Memorial Chapel at St. Paul's Cathedral (see nos. 937, 949, and *New York Times*, Nov. 25, 26, 28, 29, 30, 1958).

[2] These were the British Foreign Secretary and British Prime Minister, respectively. See Eisenhower to Nixon, November 28, 1958, AWF/A.

[3] For background on Eisenhower's efforts to promote younger Republicans see no. 590.

967
EM, AWF, International Series:
Brazil

To Juscelino Kubitschek de Oliveira
Cable
December 10, 1958

Excellency: I fully agree with Your Excellency's view, as expressed in your message which was delivered by Ambassador Peixoto on December 8, 1958, that it would be of the highest convenience if the termination of the current meeting of the Special Committee could coincide with a reiteration by the United States Government of its support for the principles of "Operation Pan America".[1] I have therefore instructed the United States Delegate to deliver, at the closing meeting of the Committee, the following message from me:[2]

"I extend my congratulations to the 'Special Committee to Study the Formulation of New Measures for Economic Cooperation' for its perseverance and diligence in carrying out the tasks assigned to it last September by the Foreign Ministers of the American Republics.

My personal interest in what has come to be known as 'Operation Pan America' began when President Kubitschek of Brazil wrote to me on May 28 of this year.[3] The Secretary of State thereafter formally expressed the willingness of my Government to cooperate in finding ways of making inter-American economic cooperation more effective. This remains the policy of the United States Government, and I assure you that the United States will lend its warmhearted cooperation to 'Operation Pan America'.

I am informed that the Special Committee has now completed its general review of the problem of underdeveloped countries and has decided to constitute a working group which, during the time the Special Committee is in recess, will address itself to specific concrete measures that can be taken to promote, by cooperative effort, a greater degree of economic development. I am confident that this work will go forward in the same spirit of mutual understanding and cooperation that has always characterized inter-American relations and that meaningful and constructive measures will be devised to achieve our common objective.

The economic development of Latin America is of vital importance to the strength and well-being of the whole of the free world. I hope that the working group will make rapid progress so that the Special Committee may soon resume its meeting here in Washington. As Americans I am sure that we all share a confidence in the future of this hemisphere and that we are determined to press forward with the concrete measures necessary to make inter-American cooperation in the economic field as fruitful as it has been in the political field."

I am confident that this message will serve to re-emphasize to the public the continuing support of the United States Government for the economic development of the Americas, which Your Excellency has so dramatically called to the hemisphere's attention through 'Operation Pan America'.[4]

I renew to Your Excellency the assurances of my personal esteem and highest consideration.

[1] For background on President Kubitschek's initiative to strengthen Pan-Americanism see nos. 729 and 730; see also State, *Foreign Relations, 1958–1960*, vol. V, *American Republics*, pp. 685–89. During Secretary Dulles's official visit to Brazil in August 1958, Kubitschek had proposed the formation of a special committee to study the problems of underdevelopment in the American states. The committee, known as the Committee of 21, had begun its meetings in Washington on November 17 and was scheduled to recess on December 12 (*ibid.*, pp. 691–706; and *New York Times*, Nov. 17, 26, Dec. 6, 9, 13. For the joint communiqué on Operation Pan America, issued after Dulles's meetings with Brazilian officials, see *U.S. Department of State Bulletin* 39, no. 1000 [August 25, 1958], 301-2).

Kubitschek had told Eisenhower that because of the meetings, people knew that Operation Pan America was not designed to solve immediate political problems but to seriously review the "essential and grave" problems of cooperation among the American nations and other free world countries. A statement by Eisenhower supporting "really effective measures to overcome underdevelopment," he said, would have "profound repercussions" throughout Latin America (Kubitschek to Eisenhower, Dec. 7, 1958, AWF/I: Brazil; for Acting Secretary Herter's recommendations and draft of this letter see Herter to Eisenhower, Dec. 9, 1958, *ibid.*).

[2] The U.S. delegate was Thomas Clifton Mann, Assistant Secretary of State for Economic Affairs.

[3] See no. 730.

[4] In November 1959 Eisenhower would establish the National Advisory Committee for Inter-American Affairs to advise the Secretary of State on U.S. relations with Latin America (State, *Foreign Relations, 1958–1960*, vol. V, *American Republics*, pp. 266–67). For President Kubitschek's letter regarding this decision and Eisenhower's response see Kubitschek to Eisenhower, November 18, 1958; Eisenhower to Kubitschek, November 28, 1958; and Dillon to Eisenhower, November 26, 1958, all in AWF/I: Brazil. For further developments in U.S.-Latin American affairs see no. 1170.

968

EM, AWF,
Administration Series

To Christian Archibald Herter

December 10, 1958

Dear Chris: Enclosed is a copy of Milton's report on his visit to Central America, which he has already gone over with Roy Rubottom.[1] I am wondering, however, if you could ask Doug Dillon to give it a final clearance from State's point of view, since I don't want to ask you to take this on yourself in view of all the additional chores you have at this time.[2]

Milton is anxious to release it as soon as possible since it is already overdue. If you do turn it over to Doug, would you ask him to give me—or Milton—any suggestions or comments he might have?[3]

With warm regard, *As ever*

[1] On the report see no. 947. Rubottom, who was Assistant Secretary of State for Inter-American Affairs, had accompanied Milton Eisenhower on his trip. Eisenhower had sent a similar message on this same day to Treasury Secretary Anderson, asking him to review the report (AWF/A).

[2] Douglas Dillon was Under Secretary of State for Economic Affairs. Secretary Dulles had entered the Walter Reed Army Hospital on December 5 and was under observation for what his doctors were then describing as an inflammatory condition of the lower colon.

[3] Milton Eisenhower would submit the final report, as modified by State and Treasury Department officials, to Eisenhower on December 29. The State Department was "anxious to have it released," Milton would write, so that the material would be available prior to an upcoming meeting to discuss the charter for an inter-American development bank (Milton Eisenhower to Eisenhower, Dec. 29, 1958, AWF/N; see also *New York Times*, Dec. 9, 1958).

An informal committee to study the recommendations in the report would meet with Milton Eisenhower on January 15 (State, *Foreign Relations, 1958–1960*, vol. V, *American Republics*, pp. 265–66; on the establishment of the National Advisory Committee on Inter-American Affairs see the preceding document). For more on U.S. policies in Latin America see no. 1170.

To Thomas Jefferson Davis   *December 10, 1958*
Personal

Dear Tommy: The subject matter of your recent letter is something that I have been thinking about for a long time.[1] I think a bit of background history may help to clarify the matter for you.

The original plan for giving some additional compensation to the active forces was based on two principal considerations. The first of these was the need for a general and permanent pay raise to meet the increased cost of living since the most recent prior pay adjustment. This pay rise was calculated at six percent.

This, it was thought, was just and fair to all.

But there was another problem. It concerned technicians in the Armed Services. We found that with new military equipment, which requires an average of one year of special and very costly training in the enlisted grades, we were losing these trained men to industry, after they had rendered only about ten months of useful service. They left the services because of the high civilian pay for mechanics, machinists, electronic and radio engineers and so on. Consequently the purpose was to give to such personnel, while on active duty, a rate of pay that would provide reasonable inducement for a good percentage to make a career in the Armed Forces.

Likewise, we found that in certain grades of the commissioned ranks resignations were far too high, particularly among the younger trained men who had only a few years of active service after graduation. It was felt that we had to do something to halt this rate of attrition.

The next necessary step in planning came about as it became clear that if special inducements—meaning sizeable pay increases—were offered on behalf of these particular groups, then we were going to have morale and other types of problems resulting from the resentment of people who had not been assigned to technical duty or who were for other reasons excluded from special treatment.

This meant then that the special pay inducements granted in order to avoid undesirable and expensive attrition, would have to be expanded into a general pay system that would be fair, in general, to all people on active duty.

But I repeat that the basic purpose was to keep *more men and officers on active duty.* Early retirement was something that we hoped to discourage, not only among officers but among enlisted men.

It was for this reason that the plan limited the general and permanent increase to six percent. This included personnel already retired. I am not sure whether it was the Congress or the Defense Department that was principally responsible for the final formula that was crystallized into law.

Since the enactment of the law, a number of protests have been submitted by retired officers to the government. General Paul, who is President of the Retired Officers Association, came to see me, with two or three others, only a month or so ago.[2] We are again studying the whole matter on an urgent basis. While I am under the impression that during most of our history retired pay has always borne a definite relationship to active duty pay of the same period, I have been informed that there have been some exceptions to this rule.

I think I do not have to assure you that I want to do what is right and just for all, including the active services, retired personnel and the entire citizenry. I shall be more than glad to inform you of any developments that may come out of the studies that I have referred to.[3]

It is good to know that you and Nina are well and happy.[4] Please give her affectionate greetings from me, and, of course, to you I send warm and lasting regard. *As ever*

---

[1] Brigadier General Davis (USA, ret.) had known the President since the 1930s, when they both were stationed in the Philippines. During World War II he had served as Eisenhower's Adjutant General in Europe and North Africa. In 1946, after thirty-one years of active duty, Davis had been forced to retire because of a heart ailment (for background see *Eisenhower Papers*, vols. I–XIII).

Davis had written on December 3 regarding the military pay raise bill (P.L. 422) signed into law on May 20. As passed, Davis noted, the legislation created a discrepancy between the pension received by those who retired prior to enactment (June 1), because they were not included in the dollar-pay readjustment provided in the new law, and those who would retire subsequently (see *Congressional Record*, vol. 104, *1958*, p. 15675; *Congressional Quarterly Almanac*, vol. XIV, *1958*, pp. 235–36; and *U.S. Statutes at Large*, vol. 72, pt. 1 [1958], pp. 122–32).

On July 31 a bill to equalize the pay of retired members of the uniformed services (S. 4207) had been introduced in the Senate, referred to the Committee on Armed Services and then sent to the Department of Defense for recommendation. Congress had adjourned before the Defense Department made its report, and it was thought that a bill similar to S. 4207 would be introduced in the Senate when the Eighty-sixth Congress reconvened. Davis had asked Eisenhower to make his position known before the measure would be reconsidered.

[2] Willard S. Paul and a representative of the Retired Officers' Association had met with Eisenhower on November 12. They asked the President to support efforts to establish a single pay scale for merit and service. Eisenhower agreed to listen to future presentations "with an open mind" (see Ann Whitman memorandum, Nov. 12, 1958, AWF/AWD; Houser to Paul, Oct. 17, 1958, AWF/D; and Harlow, Memorandum for the Record, Nov. 17, 1958, *ibid.*).

[3] On January 8, 1959, the chairman of the Retired Officers' Association committee on retired pay would urge retired generals and admirals to cooperate in the "rectification of this error in national policy" (Bolte to all Retired General and Flag Officers, same file as document). On January 14, S. 269, a bill to equalize the pay of retired members of the uniformed services, would be introduced in Congress (see *Congressional Record*, vol. 105, *1959*, pp. 610, 790, and *Congressional Quarterly Almanac*,

vol. XV, *1959*, p. 515). At the legislative leaders meeting on January 20 the President would mention the correspondence he had received from retired persons protesting the changes in retired pay. Eisenhower would say that in light of these comments he felt that a review was necessary and that he might "swing around" to support the requests of the retired officers because it might cost less in the long run (Legislative Leadership Meeting, Jan. 20, 1959; see also Harlow to Stans, Jan. 20, 1959, both in AWF/D). For developments see no. 1230.

[4] Davis's wife was the former Nina Eristova-Shervashitze.

970
EM, WHCF, Confidential File:
Montgomery Memoirs

To Frederick Arthur Montague Browning
Personal and confidential   *December 10, 1958*

Dear Boy: Thank you for your note.[1] I most deeply appreciate your statement that British officers continue to feel toward the great Allied organization of which we were all a part in the European campaign the same loyalty as they then did. Of course I am personally touched by your references to me as the Commander of that splendid force.[2]

All of us know that it is easy to criticize after the event; in fact there is always a great inducement to criticize the past, especially if the critic feels a need for bolstering or gilding his own reputation. That distortion or misstatement of fact is used in the attempt is no real deterrent to such ambitions.

In any event, I have never spoken a public word either in defense of my own past military decisions, or in argument with any critic of them. I feel that the venture in which we were so fully engrossed in those days was largely successful because of the splendid spirit of comradeship that was engendered throughout the command. To belittle others, either seniors or juniors, is to my mind to belittle by some measure the operation itself and the people who sacrificed so much in it. I will have nothing to do with such and if ever any meaning of this kind has been or may be found in any word or action of mine, then it is certainly unintentional.[3]

Enough of this. Please do not fail to convey my warm greetings to any of my old friends that you may happen to meet. Oddly enough, although I do not regularly correspond with them these days, still as the years go by I think that today I feel closer to the individuals of the Allied Forces of World War II than even when we were all together.

Won't you also extend my personal greetings to your lovely bride and, of course, all the best to yourself?[4] *As ever*

[1] At the start of World War II Browning was Chief of the British Airborne Corps. In 1944 he became deputy commander of the First Allied Airborne Army (Chandler, *War Years*, nos. 503, 1826). He had written on November 24 (same file as document). See also no. 823.

[2] Although Field Marshal Montgomery's memoirs had "stirred up quite a lot of excitement over this side," Browning wrote, Montgomery's criticism of Eisenhower did not change "by one degree the devotion and loyalty we British Generals feel for you as our leader in those great days."

On Eisenhower's reaction to the publication of Montgomery's *Memoirs* see nos. 933 and 1012; see also nos. 948 and 1104. Eisenhower had corresponded with Montgomery regarding the manuscript in July 1957 (see no. 238).

[3] Eisenhower had, however, given Ann Whitman his private opinion of Montgomery's wartime performance (Ann Whitman memorandums, Nov. 21, 23, 1958, AWF/AWD). The President had characterized Montgomery as "timid and uncertain, rather than the bold hero he tries to make himself out to be." For developments see no. 989.

[4] Browning's wife was the author Dame Daphne du Maurier.

971   *EM, AWF, Administration Series*

To Emmet John Hughes   *December 12, 1958*
Personal

Dear Emmet: I have been continuing to ponder the subject of our recent conversation. While my prior letter gives a fair description of what I have in mind, as I told you, I am very anxious to follow up the initial attempt I have described with a program of deeds and action—if we can possibly do so.[1]

Right now I find that I have been invited to address an Assembly of the World's Religions, to be held in Dallas, Texas, on April nineteenth, under the auspices of the Dallas Council on World Affairs. I add this piece of information as indicating that the timing of such an address would be appropriate to the initial effort I have in mind, if made, and would give ample time also to seek a cooperative effort from other governments.[2]

I shall have no opportunity to discuss this whole thing in detail with Foster until after he has returned from Europe. He will probably not reach Washington until right after the first of the year.[3]

It was good to see you again and, as always, I am grateful for your readiness to come down and talk over with me subjects of common interest.[4]

With warm regard, *As ever*

[1] On December 10 Eisenhower and Hughes had discussed focusing on spiritual values in the free world as a step toward world peace (see Eisenhower's earlier letter to Hughes, no. 940; see also Hughes, *Ordeal of Power*, pp. 277–82).

[2] See the following document.

[3] Dulles was in France attending the annual North Atlantic Council meeting (see no. 974). In a Christmas and birthday letter to Hughes, Eisenhower would add that he had not yet talked with Dulles (Dec. 22, 1958, AWF/A).

[4] In a five-page reply (Dec. 22, AWF/A), Hughes would emphasize the need for a creative initiative that would not conflict with the realities of foreign policy. He also reinforced Eisenhower's view that he should orient his effort more toward the hope of peace than toward the threat of war. Hughes suggested that a few months were needed to "weigh and cross-examine proposals" for action and urged the President to consider traveling abroad as part of an overall program (see Hagerty to Eisenhower, Dec. 9, 1958, AWF/N). On January 28, 1959, (AWF/A) the President would write that he had "read and re-read—and in between times pondered" Hughes's letter and asked if they could pursue the subject in a conversation. For developments see the following document.

972   *EM, AWF, Dulles-Herter Series*

To John Foster Dulles   *December 12, 1958*

Memorandum for the Secretary of State: With respect to your memorandum of December 11th about a possible address on April nineteenth before an Assembly of the World's Religions, to be held in Dallas, I refer only to the next to last paragraph of the memorandum, concerning the information you received from Secretary Anderson. On this there is some slight misunderstanding. I did not express my readiness to make the address; I merely promised to take it under advisement.[1]

Consequently I have no commitment that places any compulsion on me whatsoever. My decision will be made after a complete discussion with you—and after we have together reached some appropriate conclusions.[2]

[1] Dulles had written that Treasury Secretary Anderson had said Eisenhower was willing to accept the invitation. Dulles told the President that it would be a suitable occasion to speak about the predominant influence of spiritual values in the lives of people in the free world (AWF/D-H). For background on Eisenhower's interest in the importance of such a talk see the preceding document and no. 940.

[2] On January 8 Eisenhower and Dulles would discuss "at great length and without conclusion" the possibility of Eisenhower taking an intensive world-wide goodwill tour during his last months in office. One week later the two men would decide that the President should not attend the assembly and should avoid speaking "on a religious theme in view of the delicacy of seeming to mix religion with politics" (Dulles, Memorandums of Conversation, Jan. 8, 15, 1959, Dulles Papers, White House Memoranda Series).

On September 9, 1959, however, Eisenhower would address a delegation of 100 members of the National Council of Churches at the White House. The following day, in a radio and television speech, Eisenhower would describe any national system characterized by "godless" atheism as an "enemy" (*New York Times*, Sept. 10, 1959).

To George Venable Allen   *December 16, 1958*

Dear George: I am sorry if my observation the other day at NSC concerning my convictions as to the proper functions of the Voice of America and other facilities, clandestinely supported by our government, caused you to feel a necessity for giving me a rather detailed written report.[1]

You and I have so long agreed on the best practices and procedures for getting over our messages to the world that I by no means meant to criticize the policies you are following. On the contrary I have more than once remarked to others—and I thought to you— on my satisfaction with the progress you are making in raising the prestige and particularly the credibility of the VOA messages.

To make sure that the "Report of Action" on the recent NSC meeting makes this clear, I have directed it to be amended to express my satisfaction on the progress being made under your leadership.[2]

With warm regard, *As ever*

[1] An Operations Coordinating Board report to the NSC had indicated that Nasser exerted a strong appeal in Libya with a corresponding lack of support for the pro-Western policies of the Libyan government. Eisenhower, who professed himself "very tired of the matter," told the council members that when the United States wanted to broadcast propaganda to the Libyans, it should use only "indigenous media with our support but not with our hand showing." He had urged this concept on every USIA director, he said, and it was "exasperating" to have this kind of report. The VOA should give facts and news, not entertainment or propaganda broadcasts (NSC meeting minutes, Dec. 11, 1958, AWF/NSC).

The USIA was working with other U.S. agencies to improve the internal communications capabilities in several Middle Eastern and Asian countries, Allen had written. The agency was providing its expertise to build indigenous information programs, but these programs could only be launched in countries where governments wanted such aid. The Voice of America was not engaged in any programming that was "purely for entertainment," Allen said. Only the programming for the Arab nations carried large amounts of popular music mixed in with news and commentary in order to compete with the Voice of Cairo (Allen to Eisenhower, Dec. 12, 1958, AWF/A, Allen Corr.).

[2] The NSC meeting minutes stated that the President had "expressed his gratification that important progress has been made toward achieving this aim" (AWF/NSC).

To John Foster Dulles   *December 16, 1958*
Cable. Top secret

Dear Foster: I have had your two reports and I hasten to assure you that I fully understand your feeling of frustration after your two long conferences yesterday afternoon.[1] It does seem that our friend should cease insisting upon attempting to control the whole world, of course with partners, even before he has gotten France itself in good order.

New Subject. A message from Harold clears up the matter about the special aircraft and I agree with his suggestion that you make no effort to take it up with Selwyn Lloyd.[2] He feels that the two of you will have enough on your plate just now without adding that particular subject to it.

Thank you for keeping me informed.[3] All the best to yourself. *As ever*

[1] Secretary Dulles was in Paris for the ministerial meeting of the North Atlantic Council. On the preceding afternoon he had met first with General Norstad, Supreme Allied Commander in Europe, who had told him of the "obstructive tactics" he had encountered from the French. Dulles then described for Eisenhower his own "most unsatisfactory" meeting with President de Gaulle. De Gaulle, although "entirely correct and cordial personally," was irritated because the United States had not voted against a resolution for Algerian independence in the United Nations and had not supported the French in the attempt to keep the African nation of Guinea out of the United Nations. De Gaulle's primary concern was NATO, however, and he had repeated his desire to establish a tripartite organization that would determine global policy (see no. 901). He made it clear, Dulles said, "that France was not interested in cooperating with NATO on infrastructure, atomic stockpiles, IRBM's and the like when the whole show was being run by the US." Dulles had told de Gaulle that the United States, Great Britain, and France could exchange views on an informal basis but a formal organization like the one he had proposed was not possible. Dulles had found that the French president, who was "quite solid" on the Berlin question (see no. 983), had no intention of taking "a separate line on Berlin out of resentment" (Dulles to Eisenhower, Dec. 15, 1958, AWF/D-H; see also Dulles to Eisenhower, Dec. 14, 1958, *ibid.*; and State, *Foreign Relations, 1958–1960*, vol. VII, pt. 1, *Western European Integration and Security; Canada*, pp. 377–78). Dulles would later tell Eisenhower that he and British Foreign Secretary Lloyd both thought the French president wanted NATO "scrapped and a fresh start . . . made under triumvirate auspices." Dulles did not believe that de Gaulle's advisers shared his "rather extreme views" (Dulles to Eisenhower, Dec. 16, 18, 1958, AWF/D-H).
[2] We have been unable to locate Macmillan's message.
[3] For developments see no. 981.

975   *EM, AWF, Administration Series, Herter Corr.*

To Walter Hoving   *December 16, 1958*

Dear Walter:[1] Of course I don't know either whether the report is true about the alleged refusal of the State Department to allow the Egyptian government to purchase textbooks—but I shall inquire. And I do very much appreciate your bringing a matter like this to my attention.[2]

With warm regard, *As ever*

[1] Hoving (Ph.B. Brown University 1920), former president of several New York department stores, was chairman of the board of Tiffany and Company (see Galambos and van Ee, *The Middle Way*, no. 2025).

[2] Hoving had told Eisenhower that he had learned from friends that Egyptian universities were not able to purchase medical and scientific textbooks printed in English from American publishers. "For some reason or another," he wrote, "the State Department is not permitting this purchase on the grounds that it might be an act which would 'aid and abet Nasser.'" He also understood that Russian was one of the languages being taught in schools and that more and more textbooks were being written in Russian (Hoving to Eisenhower, Dec. 11, 1958, AWF/D-H).

Eisenhower would send a copy of Hoving's letter to Acting Secretary Herter, asking "as a matter of curiosity" whether the allegations were correct (Dec. 16, 1958, *ibid.*). Herter reported that there were "no United States restrictions whatsoever on the sale of books published in the United States to persons or institutions in the United Arab Republic (Egypt or Syria)." Currency problems, however, were a limiting factor since dollars were in short supply in these countries.

Herter thought that Hoving's informant might have confused the normal sale of textbooks with the special arrangements made with several countries under the Informational Media Guaranty program—a plan that made dollars available to U.S. publishers in exchange for local currencies they received from the sale of their books. Although an IMG agreement had been signed with Egypt in 1955, it had not been implemented because at that time the country had sufficient dollar funds. The Suez crisis and the resulting deterioration of U.S.-Egyptian relations had further delayed the program. Although the limited IMG funds had been allocated for the 1959 fiscal year, the State Department was giving "careful consideration" to including the UAR in the program for 1960.

Regarding the introduction of the Russian language into Egyptian schools, Herter said that according to the U.S. Ambassador instruction in Russian was only available in the Higher Institute of Languages. Even though the Soviet Union was encouraging the use of Russian in other schools, he did not believe that it was supplanting other languages, primarily English and French (Herter to Eisenhower, Dec. 19, 1958, AWF/D-H).

976   *EM, AWF, Administration Series*

To Gabriel Hauge   *December 17, 1958*

Dear Gabe: I need not tell you how much I value your opinion on all governmental matters, and particularly on the subject of the Federal budget. We are going through our usual pangs in connection with the 1960 budget, but I am bearing much in mind your cautions.[1] The matter of a balanced versus an unbalanced budget is not yet settled, but I did not want to wait longer before thanking you for writing me so fully your views.[2]

And I appreciate, too, the telephone call that you made to Ann this morning: certainly that merger is an interesting development[3] (and one that concerns me in a sense in a personal way since the grandchildren's accounts are at one of the companies involved).

With warm regard, and the hope that all the Hauges have a wonderful Christmas, *As ever*

[1] See nos. 958 and 961.
[2] Hauge had written on December 12, 1958 (AWF/A), with his thoughts on the FY 1960 budget. While he believed that the early achievement of a balanced budget should be a high priority, he cautioned that eliminating a budget deficit of $12 billion in one fiscal year was "a very considerable fiscal step." It need not be a "deleterious" step, however, if certain mistakes were avoided. Taxes should not be raised; the country needed lower, not higher taxes. He also cautioned that inflating "revenue estimates to an unrealistic point, or even to the outer limit of the range of possibilities to make the budget balance would . . . disturb rather than build confidence." Hauge recommended that the budget should be balanced through expenditure reductions "*provided* the informed public does not regard it as an artificial proposal." If, under these conditions, "restoring the balance takes two years, such a proposal could be sold as a reasonable and attainable goal both here and abroad. Direction may well be as important as speed in this case."
[3] Hauge had reported to Ann Whitman on the proposed merger of J. P. Morgan & Company and the Guaranty Trust Company of New York (see no. 1028, and *New York Times*, Apr. 25, 1959).

977   *EM, AWF, DDE Diaries Series*

"FOOTNOTE TO HISTORY"   *December 17, 1958*

Governor Stassen has several times informed me that it was only by his prompt and decisive action that he swung the Minnesota delegation to me in 1952 and thereby achieved nomination on the first ballot.[1]

The other day, about December 10, 1958, Senator Thye called me on the telephone to say goodbye.[2] (He was defeated in the last Senatorial campaign). He started off the conversation with words about like these: "Since the moment that I made advance arrangements for and did swing the Minnesota delegation to your side in 1952, thereby achieving your nomination on the first ballot . . . ". Several times I have heard refuted by others Governor Stassen's claim that he took the initiative in this matter and accomplished it. Senator Thye's testimony in the matter is of a very direct and personal character.[3]

[1] Eisenhower may have dictated this recollection after reading a memorandum prepared by General Lucius Clay and former Attorney General Herbert Brownell; see no. 980. Clay and Brownell had been attempting to assist former Assistant to the President Sherman Adams, who was then in the process of writing his memoirs. They had minimized the role played by Harold Stassen, former Governor of Minnesota and Special Assistant to the President for Disarmament, in securing the 1952 Re-

publican presidential nomination for Eisenhower. Clay and Brownell, who had been working for Eisenhower in that year, had stated that Eisenhower had never been under any obligation to give Stassen a job in his Administration. Furthermore, they said, Stassen had tried to prevent the Minnesota delegation from switching its votes to Eisenhower even after it had become apparent that he was going to win the nomination (Memorandum, n.d., AWF/A, Clay Corr.). For background see Galambos, *NATO and the Campaign of 1952*, nos. 408, 409, and 545.

[2] Edward Thye served as U.S. Senator from Minnesota from January 3, 1947, until January 3, 1959. He had called the President on December 10 (Telephone Conversations, AWF/D).

[3] At the end of the roll call for the first ballot during the 1952 Republican convention, Eisenhower was still nine votes short of the number needed to secure the nomination. Thye, the chairman of the Minnesota delegation, had then switched the votes from his state that had been cast for Stassen to Eisenhower, assuring him a first-ballot nomination. See John Robert Greene, *The Crusade: The Presidential Election of 1952* (Lanham, Md., 1985), pp. 114–15; Herbert S. Parmet, *Eisenhower and the American Crusades* (New York, 1972), pp. 98–100; and Eisenhower, *Mandate for Change*, pp. 43–44.

978   *EM, AWF, Name Series*

To Edgar Newton Eisenhower   *December 17, 1958*

Dear Ed: By no means did I mean to interfere in your program for your birthday celebration. I merely thought that the dinner could be more conveniently served here for all of us than it could be at the hotel.[1]

I talked to Bill Rogers about your friend Bantz. He is enthusiastic about him but of course any decision must wait on the necessary investigations. I assume from what Bill said that they have already been started.[2]

Merry Christmas to Lucy and to you, and, of course, to Janis and Bill and the children.

With warm regard, *As ever*

[1] Edgar would celebrate his seventieth birthday on January 19. He had written on December 15 that he felt "like a beggar" when he learned that Eisenhower had suggested the celebration should be moved from the Statler Hotel to the White House. "I guess my brand of humor is difficult for some people to understand," Edgar would reply on December 26. He understood the President's "problem of trying to get away from . . . prison," he wrote, and was "perfectly agreeable" to spending the evening of the nineteenth at the White House (both in AWF/N; see also Telephone conversation, Eisenhower and Mrs. Eisenhower, Dec. 11, 1958, AWF/D). For developments see no. 987.

[2] In his letter of the fifteenth Edgar recommended that the President consider appointing William B. Bantz, a Spokane lawyer, to fill the vacancy in the Federal District Court for Eastern Washington. Bantz, appointed United States Attorney for

Washington's Eastern District by Eisenhower in 1953, had resigned his position in July to run for Senator; he had not been successful. In October Edgar Eisenhower had spoken on behalf of Bantz at a dinner in Spokane (see no. 903, and *New York Times*, July 20, 26, Oct. 10, 1958). According to Edgar, Bantz was "young, vigorous, intelligent, courageous and experienced." For developments see no. 1097.

979   *EM, WHCF, Official File 3-C-12*

To Neil Hosler McElroy   *December 18, 1958*

Dear Neil: In regard to your letter of December eighth, with which you transmitted a copy of the Air Force comments on the recommendation of the Board of Visitors to the Air Force Academy, I would offer the following informal observations which are not to be interpreted as final decisions:

a. I would not approve the idea of incorporating a flying program in the curriculum of the Air Academy, as set forth in the first recommendation. My own conviction is that the need for a thorough education of the cadet, both physically and intellectually, would rule out the feasibility of including flight training in the curriculum.[1]

b. In connection with the second recommendation of the Board of Visitors, I understand from the Bureau of the Budget that no request is before them for airfield construction at the Air Academy in the FY 1960 budget. Frankly, I see no need for an airfield to be built especially for the Air Academy, particularly since Ent Air Force Base is located nearby. In the absence of persuasive argument to the contrary, I would oppose such construction.[2]

In the event your view is different on these matters, I will be glad to talk them over with you at your convenience.[3] *Sincerely*

[1] McElroy had attached Air Force Secretary James H. Douglas's memorandum commenting on the Board of Visitors' report to the Air Force Academy for 1958. Douglas said the superintendent of the Air Force Academy had been looking into a flying program for cadets. United States Air Force Headquarters was reviewing the study. Major John S. D. Eisenhower drafted this letter for the President (see Eisenhower to Stans, Dec. 17, 1958, and Carey to Eisenhower, Dec. 18, 1958).

[2] The board had recommended that a portion of an airfield complex be included in the FY 1960 military construction program. Ent Air Force Base also was located in Colorado Springs, Colorado.

The Board of Visitors had also recommended that cadets be allowed to use rifles in parades and ceremonies and be required to serve as officers for terms of four years following graduation or the beginning of pilot training.

[3] We have been unable to find any further correspondence on this subject in EM. All papers are in the same file as the document.

To Lucius Du Bignon Clay   *December 18, 1958*

Dear Lucius: I read the memorandum that you and Herb Brownell jointly prepared as a reply to some of Sherm Adams' questions concerning our activities in the Commodore in late 1952. By and large I agree without qualification with your answers. A few specific comments might add something to the story, so far as my memory gives any value to the following.[1]

I had never met George Humphrey before he came to my suite in the Commodore. You, personally, were the one to tell me that in your opinion he would be the finest Secretary of the Treasury we could get.[2]

One of the controlling factors in the selection of McKay involved the matter of geography.[3] It had become customary that the Secretary of the Interior should be appointed from an area west of the Mississippi (Ickes was an exception).[4] Moreover, it was a delicate matter to pick the particular state from which the man should come, one reason being the perennial struggle over water rights between California on the one hand and several of the upper river states on the other.

At the time the Hell's Canyon controversy was a bitter one and we felt that about the only states that we could consider were first Oregon or Nebraska, and secondly, the state of Washington or possibly the Dakotas.[5] Since we wanted a man who had a record of political and business accomplishment, we fixed on ex-Governor McKay.

I had known Oveta Hobby quite well and I think all of us felt that she would be natural, provided she would accept.[6]

So far as Governor Stassen was concerned I thought, at that time, that he could be a real asset to the Administration. This I believed because of his capacity for work, his interest in the youth of the country, and his enlightened view of America's necessity for leadership internationally. I think all of us recognized that he could easily be a bit of a stormy petrel but we decided to try it.[7]

I shall send a copy of this to Herb. Moreover, if you should think that anything I have said would be helpful to Sherman, I would of course be glad if you should send this letter on to him but with the understanding, of course, that I am not to be personally quoted.

I think of you often but it seems we never have time for a visit. Would it be convenient for you to have breakfast with me on Tuesday or Wednesday of this coming week? Alternatively I wonder if you and Marjorie could come down for a family dinner—just the four of us with possibly some grandkids thrown in—on Tuesday evening, the 23rd. I have to go to the annual Christmas Tree lighting that afternoon, but I should certainly be home by 5:30. If the two of you could reach here around that hour we could have a nice chat and you could either spend the night here or take your plane back, as you choose.

I realize that this is short notice to suggest either of the alternatives I have just described, but if you could come I would like it very much.[8] In any event, Merry Christmas and a happy holiday season to you both.

With warm regard, *As ever*

[1] The memorandum mentioned by Eisenhower is in AWF/A, Clay Corr. Clay, Eisenhower's old friend and political adviser, was chairman of the board and chief executive officer of Continental Can Company. Former Attorney General Herbert Brownell had returned to private practice in November 1957 (see no. 22). Sherman Adams, who had resigned his post as the Assistant to the President in September, was apparently in the early stages of writing his memoir, *Firsthand Report* (see no. 753). In the fall of 1952 President-elect Eisenhower had asked Clay and Brownell to advise him on Cabinet appointments; Adams had assisted them. For background on the President's selections see Galambos, *NATO and the Campaign of 1952*, no. 1020; Galambos and van Ee, *The Middle Way*, no. 23; Ambrose, *Eisenhower*, vol. II, *The President*, pp. 20–24; and Eisenhower, *Mandate for Change*, pp. 83–87, 89–92. On Brownell's role in the process see his memoir, *Advising Ike*, pp. 132–36; for Adams's account see *Firsthand Report*, pp. 45–46.

[2] Although Adams had thought that the President had Humphrey in mind for Secretary of the Treasury in November of 1952, Clay and Brownell said that Humphrey's was only one of several names recommended for the position. Clay had discussed the post with Humphrey late in 1952 at a Business Advisory Council meeting.

[3] Even though Adams had said that he remembered the circumstances regarding Douglas McKay's nomination, Clay and Brownell attempted to set the record straight. The Interior Secretary position, they wrote, had been offered first to the governor of Washington, who had declined it. The committee then selected outgoing Oregon Republican Governor McKay. McKay had served in both world wars, had been mayor of Salem, Oregon, and had served as a state senator. For further background see Galambos, *NATO and the Campaign of 1952*, no. 995, and Galambos and van Ee, *The Middle Way*, no. 1886.

[4] The late Harold Le Clair Ickes, a Pennsylvanian, had served as Secretary of the Interior in the Cabinets of Presidents Roosevelt and Truman (for background see Galambos, *Chief of Staff*, no. 1742, and Galambos, *Columbia University*, no. 40).

[5] Hell's Canyon extended for forty miles along the Snake River on the Idaho-Oregon border. In March 1952 a House Subcommittee on Irrigation and Reclamation had opened hearings on a bill to authorize construction of Hell's Canyon Dam as the initial phase of the Snake River reclamation project. The dam had become a campaign issue when Democratic presidential nominee Adlai Stevenson, who favored the project, criticized the Eisenhower supporters who opposed it as a further step in federal control (see *Congressional Quarterly Almanac*, vol. VIII, *1952*, p. 345, and *New York Times*, June 15, 23, Oct. 16, 1952).

[6] Adams suggested that Eisenhower had hoped to find a woman of proven ability for a Cabinet post and had known of Oveta Culp Hobby's accomplishments. Brownell and Clay agreed with this recollection and added that Eisenhower had no specific woman or position in mind. The informal committee had recommended Hobby, a Texan who had directed the Women's Army Corps during World War II. Eisenhower appointed her director of the Federal Security Agency, and after he created the Department of Health, Education and Welfare, Hobby became its first secretary. For

background on Hobby see Chandler, *War Years*, no. 1090, and Galambos, *NATO and the Campaign of 1952*, no. 1020; see also Galambos and van Ee, *The Middle Way*, nos. 1513, 1801, and 2096).

[7] Clay and Brownell had remembered that Stassen had been one of several persons suggested for the position of Administrator of the Foreign Operations Authority. On Eisenhower's views of Stassen and on Stassen's loss in the 1958 Pennsylvania gubernatorial campaign see nos. 594 and 977.

[8] On December 23 at 5:15 P.M., the President would light the national Christmas tree after delivering his annual Christmas message to the nation. The Eisenhowers would entertain General and Mrs. Clay at the White House for dinner at 5:30 P.M.

981   *EM, AWF, Dulles-Herter Series*

To John Foster Dulles   *December 19, 1958*

Dear Foster: I realize the difficulties you encountered at the NATO Conference and I congratulate you both on your patience and the persuasive powers that resulted in, to quote your own words, a "creditable" communique.[1]

Most importantly I hope you are not too tired by the trip to Jamaica and that you will get the rest and sunshine you so richly deserve.[2]

Please give my best to Clarence and Mrs. Dillon.[3] To you all my good wishes for a Merry Christmas, and my special and affectionate regard to Janet and yourself. *As ever*

[1] For background on the NATO ministerial meeting see no. 974. Dulles had told Eisenhower that the last three hours of the conference had been devoted to "the usual linguistic battle" over the communiqué, which he called "creditable although not spectacular" (Dulles to Eisenhower, Dec. 18, 1958, AWF/D-H; for the text of the communiqué see *U.S. Department of State Bulletin* 40, no. 1019 [January 5, 1959], 3–4).

[2] Dulles had spent a week in the hospital prior to the meetings (see no. 968). He had cabled Eisenhower from Paris that he was "holding out reasonably well," although his friends in the Western delegation reportedly were concerned about his health (Dulles to Eisenhower, Dec. 14, 1958, AWF/D-H; and *New York Times*, Dec. 15, 1958).

[3] Dulles had flown directly from Paris to Montego Bay, Jamaica. There he stayed at the home of Clarence Dillon, father of C. Douglas Dillon, Under Secretary of State for Economic Affairs (see Dulles to Eisenhower, Dec. 18, 1958, AWF/D-H). Dillon's wife was the former Anne McE. Douglass.

To Clifford Roberts   *December 19, 1958*
Personal

Dear Cliff: This is by way of giving you a little outside, disinterested, evidence on Meade Alcorn and his capabilities.[1]

In the early part of this week Meade held a two day budget meeting with the main figures in his Finance Committee. As you can see from the time needed, this is a detailed performance. Every contemplated program must be explained and justified because only in this way can the budgetary proposals be approved. I am sending you a list of the businessmen who attended.[2] (I have checked the ones I think you know).

After this meeting Charlie Hook came in to the White House on some other business and gave a report about as follows:

> "The entire Committee was impressed by the energy, imagination, good sense and dedication of our Chairman, Meade Alcorn. They found him not only completely informed as to the details of his budgetary requirements, but on top of this, he was able to lay before them programs that they felt were vitally necessary in revitalizing the hierarchy of the Party and in getting us started on the long road back to a majority position. Charlie particularly approved the recommendations of Meade designed to correct organizational defects, particularly at the top, and the programs for getting this organizational effort all the way down to the grass roots."

This report was made to me through General Persons, but I think it very accurately reflects Charlie Hook's opinion and, according to him, the feeling of the entire committee.[3]

*   *   *   *   *

I just this minute received your letter of the sixteenth commenting on the memorandum I sent you. Dick and I have found that everyone seems to have his own individualistic ideas as to what is the most important thing for the Republican Party now to do.[4] Because of this I have asked a few Party stalwarts—together with a couple of professional pollsters—to come in to see me in the first week of January. There will be an all day meeting on this subject and I am sure that one of the results will be to recommend the establishment of some kind of outside committee to investigate past difficulties and defects and to help develop and design a forward-looking program.[5]

The membership of the committee would, I hope, be such as to represent every view and would certainly reflect a high degree of dedication and devotion.

Financing is something that I had not thought of until I received your letter, but I suspect this preliminary meeting will have to deal with that subject also. If Charlie can properly help out with some of the money he has left, I think that would be a very desirable thing to do.[6]

After Cabinet meeting I shall hand your memorandum to Dick Nixon so that he may read it.[7]

With warm regard—and Merry Christmas! *As ever*

[1] On dissatisfaction with Republican National Committee Chairman Alcorn in the aftermath of the 1958 midterm elections see no. 962.

[2] The list is not in AWF.

[3] For background on past president of the National Association of Manufacturers Charles Ruffin Hook see Galambos and van Ee, *The Middle Way*, nos. 666 and 1180. Assistant to the President Wilton Persons and Alcorn had met with Eisenhower on December 15. Alcorn's proposals, as outlined in two confidential memorandums (Dec. 15, AWF/A), were aimed at producing "a militant, enlightened Republicanism 365 days a year." He wanted to appoint "an impartial committee to study Party organization at the National level (National Committee, Senatorial Committee and Congressional Committee)" but admitted that merging the three groups or redefining their responsibilities was "probably not, as a practical matter, attainable." He also proposed a number of small-group evaluation sessions, regional conferences, and inspection teams whose task it would be to strengthen and improve the party at the state, regional, and local levels.

In an effort to bring new blood into the GOP, Alcorn advocated that each state and national party official should appoint as an alternate a person under thirty-five years of age and that more attention should be paid "to the college and university group and the before-voting-age group." He specifically wanted "to enlist the interest and support of the nation's teachers and professors of political science and government." This group, he noted, had been "extensively used by and attracted to the opposition and neglected by us."

[4] After reading Eisenhower's December 6 memorandum (no. 963), Roberts had urged the President to minimize Alcorn's role in the process of reassessing and rebuilding the Republican party (Roberts to Eisenhower, Dec. 16, 1958, AWF/N). The proposed study group, Roberts thought, "should be completely free to discuss the mistakes of the present National Committee." He also argued that the group's head should be "a high calibre, strong man" who was also "a real leader," and he suggested that Bell & Howell Company President "Chuck Percy or someone like him" be chosen (see Eisenhower to Roberts, Dec. 10, and Roberts to Eisenhower, Dec. 17, 1958, *ibid.*). The President had met with Vice-President Richard Nixon on December 18.

[5] Eisenhower would meet with twelve Republican political figures on the afternoon of January 5; among those attending were Nixon, Alcorn, Percy, GOP fund-raiser Justin Dart, and public opinion research executive Claude Everett Robinson (see Galambos, *NATO and the Campaign of 1952*, no. 920). Concluding that the President's personal popularity had not resulted in gains for his party, they discussed the composition and agenda of a possible study group. With Eisenhower's approval the Republican National Committee would establish a Committee on Program and Progress, chaired by Percy, in February 1959 (Ann Whitman memorandums, Jan. 5, 13, 17, AWF/AWD; Alcorn to Eisenhower, Mar. 13, 1958, and Republican National Committee news releases, Feb. 25, Mar. 13, 1959, AWF/A, Alcorn Corr.; and Eisenhower, *Waging Peace*, p. 382).

[6] Roberts had suggested that Richfield Oil Company President Charles S. Jones (see

no. 826) could provide $30,000 in funds left over from the California political campaign to pay for the proposed study committee's staff salaries and expenses. Fearing the exertion of undue influence by Alcorn, Roberts had opposed use of Republican National Committee funds for this purpose.
[7] For developments see nos. 1025 and 1360.

983   *EM, AWF,*
                                                              Administration Series

To Christian Archibald Herter   *December 24, 1958*
Secret

Dear Chris.[1] I have read the draft of your proposed reply to the Soviet note of November 27th.[2]

I have one question only. It involves the sentence on page four reading "The Government of the United States will continue to hold the Soviet Government directly responsible under existing agreements."

I assume that there are other responsibilities under various phases of these agreements which have not been properly fulfilled by the Soviets. What we are now talking about is the Soviet agreement to respect our rights in Berlin, both in the occupancy of that city and Western Power access to it.

It would seem to me that the sentence should either be a bit modified or alternatively, it could be eliminated because the attitude of the United States is implicit in the context.

Otherwise, I repeat that I think the draft is excellent.[3] *Sincerely*

---

[1] Herter was Acting Secretary of State while Secretary Dulles was on vacation (see no. 981).

[2] For background on the troublesome issue of Western access rights to the occupied city of Berlin see Chandler and Galambos, *Occupation, 1945,* nos. 157, 468; and Galambos, *Columbia University,* no. 183. Throughout 1958 the movement of people and material between the Federal Republic of Germany and West Berlin had proceeded with only minimal interference by the Soviets and East Germans. On November 10, however, Soviet Premier Nikita Khrushchev had alleged that the Western Allies had violated the Berlin agreements and, therefore, had forfeited their legal right to remain in that city. The time had come, he said, for the powers that had signed the agreements to give up the occupation of Berlin, and he proposed to turn over to the German Democratic Republic all the functions it still exercised there (U.S. Department of State, *Documents on Germany, 1944–1985* [Washington, D.C., 1985], pp. 542–46; State, *Foreign Relations, 1958–1960,* vol. VIII, *Berlin Crisis 1958–1959* [1993], pp. 36–40, 46–85; see also Herter to Eisenhower, and Status Report on Berlin, Nov. 13, 1958, *ibid.*). Eisenhower told Dulles after Khrushchev's speech that the situation "was basically untenable," but that "we were where we were and had to stand firm" (Dulles, Memorandum of Conversation, Nov. 18, 1958, AWF/D-H; for the President's account

of the decisions regarding Germany and Berlin after World War II see Eisenhower, *Waging Peace*, pp. 329–31, 334–36).

On November 27 the Soviet Union had expanded on Khrushchev's pronouncement with a twenty-eight page note proposing that West Berlin become a demilitarized free city with its own government—a status that would be guaranteed by the four occupying powers. Because of the time necessary to establish guidelines for the new city, the Soviet Union pledged not to introduce any changes to the existing system of access to and from West Berlin for six months. If Berlin had not become a free city by that time, the Soviet Union threatened to transfer all of its responsibilities to the German Democratic Republic, which the United States had refused to recognize (State, *Documents on Germany, 1945–1985*, pp. 552–59). The State Department immediately released a statement, approved by Eisenhower, maintaining the U.S. commitment to the security of West Berlin and the determination to reject any agreement that would abandon the West German people (*U.S. Department of State Bulletin* 39, no. 1021 [January 19, 1959], 81–89; State, *Foreign Relations, 1958–1960*, vol. VIII, *Berlin Crisis 1958–1959*, pp. 86–134; and Telephone conversation, Eisenhower and Dulles, Nov. 27, 1958, Dulles Papers, Telephone Conversations; see also Thompson to Dulles, Dec. 3, 1958, AWF/D-H; William Burr, "Avoiding the Slippery Slope: The Eisenhower Administration and the Berlin Crisis, November 1958–January 1959," *Diplomatic History* 18, no. 2 [1994], pp. 177–96; and John S. D. Eisenhower, *Strictly Personal*, pp. 211–18. Two drafts of the statement are in Dulles Papers, Telephone Conversations; see also Dulles, Memorandum of Conversation, Nov. 30, 1958, Dulles Papers, White House Memoranda Series).

The foreign ministers of the United States, Great Britain, France, and West Germany had met to formulate a coordinated reply. The approved draft, which Herter had sent to Eisenhower, reminded the Soviet Union of its obligations under the Berlin agreements as well as the summit agreement in 1955, which recognized a common responsibility for the settlement of the German question. The United States would not accept the unilateral denunciation of the accords, the substitution of East German authority in providing free access to West Berlin, or the proposal for a free city. There could be no discussions of these questions "under menace or ultimatum" (State, *Foreign Relations, 1958–1960*, vol. VIII, *Berlin Crisis 1958–1959*, pp. 190–219, 224; State, *Documents on Germany, 1944–1985*, pp. 573–76; on the British reply see Macmillan, *Riding the Storm*, pp. 571–81; on the NATO meetings see no. 974; and Dulles to Eisenhower, Dec. 16, 1958, AWF/D-H; and "Synopsis of State and Intelligence Material Reported to the President," Dec. 16, 1958, AWF/D).

[3] In the final version, delivered to the Soviet foreign ministry on December 31, this sentence would read: "The government of the United States will continue to hold the Soviet Government directly responsible for the discharge of its obligations undertaken with respect to Berlin under existing agreements" (*U.S. Department of State Bulletin* 40, no. 1021 [January 19, 1959], 79–81). For developments see no. 1039.

984   *EM, AWF, DDE Diaries Series*

To Clifford Roberts   *December 24, 1958*
Telegram

Dear Cliff: When I realized over the telephone last evening that you were growing a bit coy, I went back to my guests and gave them as my considered judgment that something very unusual and very pleasant had happened to you.[1] Actually I should have expressed my opinion in much more glowing terms. Anyway, Mamie and I send to you and your lovely bride our warmest felicitations and our wish that you may have a long and happy life together. (Incidentally and for your eyes alone, could you get a pink pass for a bit of bridge this weekend. Don't answer.)[2] Finally our very best Christmas wishes go to you both.

[1] Roberts had called the President (Telephone calls, Dec. 23, 1958, AWF/D) to announce his marriage to his second wife, Letitia. The Eisenhowers were dining with General and Mrs. Clay at the White House on the evening of December 23.
[2] The Eisenhowers would spend December 26–January 3 at their Gettysburg farm, but Roberts would not join them.

985   *EM, AWF, International Series: Rhee*

To Syngman Rhee   *December 25, 1958*
Cable. Secret

Dear Mr. President: The recent developments in the Korean National Assembly prompt me to write directly to you to express my personal concern.[1] I understand that action to revise the National Security Law was taken in order to provide a more effective legal basis to deal with Communist infiltration, espionage and subversion efforts in the Republic of Korea. This is an objective with which we, of course, strongly agree. The manner in which this law was adopted by the National Assembly, however, greatly troubles me.

The Republic of Korea and you, Mr. President, enjoy the high esteem of the American people. We have made common cause with you during tragic times of trial and we have sought to contribute to the reconstruction and development of your country ever since then. We intend to continue this course to the extent we are able. It is because of our relationship that it grieves and disturbs me to read the reports which have appeared lately of the incidents which attended the consideration and passage of this bill. Regrettably, the manner in which the law has just been passed, with Democratic Party Assemblymen confined outside the Assembly hall, will raise serious doubts in the minds of the allies and friends of the Republic of Korea as to the merits of the law, regardless of its true value or the real necessity for the law. To the extent such doubts are raised we are handicapped in our efforts to muster the strong support we desire for Korea in the United Nations and elsewhere. The image which Korean actions create abroad necessarily affects our ability in this regard.

This development is now attracting the attention of the press and public of the United States.[2] It would be my hope that in implementing the law the Republic of Korea Government will demonstrate that it will be used, as it was announced it was intended, to deal effectively with the Communist threat of subversion and that the apprehensions that have been voiced as to the prospects of the continued growth of the democratic and representative government in the Republic of Korea will have been without foundation.

I have written you in this way, Mr. President, as a friend of Korea and trust that you will receive my comments in this spirit.[3] *Sincerely*

[1] On November 18 the Liberal party government of President Rhee had submitted to the National Assembly a revision of the 1948 National Security Law dealing with subversive activity. While the new law provided more legal safeguards for suspects, it made it a crime to report or spread falsehoods or distorted news. Denouncing the measure as an end to freedom of the press, the opposition Democratic party had pledged an all-out fight against the measure. On the preceding day guards had forcibly ejected opposition members from the assembly hall, reportedly injuring several in the process. Then, after barring American embassy observers from the deliberations, Liberal party members had unanimously passed the law (State, *Foreign Relations, 1958–1960*, vol. XVIII, *Japan; Korea*, pp. 508–22; see also *ibid.*, Microfiche Supplement, nos. 656, 682, 686, 688–89, 692–93).

Acting Secretary of State Robert Murphy had told Eisenhower that the opposition and the press were convinced that the government would use the law to suppress its political opponents and ensure its success in the 1960 Korean presidential elections. After Eisenhower approved the State Department draft of this letter, it was transmitted by priority telegram to the U.S. ambassador in Seoul, who would deliver it immediately to President Rhee (Murphy to Eisenhower, Dec. 24, 1958, AWF/I: Korea; see also Parsons to Dowling, Dec. 27, 1958, State, *Foreign Relations, 1958–1960*, vol. XVIII, *Japan; Korea*, Microfiche Supplement, no. 701).

[2] See *New York Times*, December 25, 1958.

[3] Rhee would write Eisenhower that opposition members had been excluded from the deliberations because they "had attempted to disrupt normal proceedings." He assured the President that the new law would be applied in a way that would enhance democracy in Korea (State, *Foreign Relations, 1958–1960*, vol. XVIII, *Japan; Korea*, pp. 523–25, 526–28). Eisenhower would accept Secretary Dulles's recommendation that he not reply to Rhee's letter (Dulles to Eisenhower, Jan. 27, 1958, AWF/I: Rhee).

986   *EM, AWF, Name Series*

TO WILLIAM EDWARD ROBINSON   *December 29, 1958*
Telegram

Dear Bill: Let me urge you to prolong your Florida visit beyond the one or two days that you are counting on and get some good rest in the sun. You work too hard and don't forget the old saying that

that kind of thing will make you a dull boy. You can't afford that when you have George as a partner.[1]

Mamie and I have never had a happier weekend.[2] We felt it was a real lark. She and David are loud in your praises as the prognosticator, and, incidentally, the weekend was helped out a lot by the provision of caviar that we had a result of your thoughtfulness.

I have just heard that the plane reservation did not work out.[3] I am sorry. *As ever*

[1] Robinson would reply on this same day that he probably would take Eisenhower's advice and remain in Florida. He had the flu, he wrote, and the medicine he took for it was getting him "down a bit" (AWF/N; see also the longhand note Robinson to Eisenhower, n.d., AWF/N). George E. Allen was a member of the group who played bridge with the President.

[2] The Eisenhowers and their son John and his family were spending December 26–January 3 in Gettysburg (see no. 984). Robinson had visited on December 28.

[3] We have been unable to find any information concerning Robinson's airplane reservations.

---

987   *EM, AWF, Name Series*

To Earl Dewey Eisenhower   *December 30, 1958*

Dear Earl: I am afraid I was not too explicit about my invitation to you and Kathryn to stay at the White House when you come to Washington to help Edgar celebrate his 70th birthday. Mamie and I would love to have you stay at the White House from whatever time you arrive, up to and including the evening of the nineteenth.[1] We have, however, a large formal dinner for the President of Argentina on the twentieth and the house will be full.[2]

Incidentally, if you and Kathryn would like to attend such a formal affair, I wish you would let me know. It's a white tie occasion, and when I asked Edgar about it, he refused enthusiastically. However, if you and Kathryn have any interest, just let me know and the Social Secretary will make all the arrangements.[3]

Incidentally, I have asked Edgar and Lucy to stay at the White House time and again and they have always refused; they prefer the greater freedom of a hotel such as the Statler.

In other words, just tell us what you want to do and we will proceed accordingly.[4]

With all the best to the two of you for a fine New Year, and affectionate regard, *As ever*

[1] For background see no. 978. On December 23 Earl had written that he and his wife would stay at the White House unless the President had other guests.

[2] Arturo Frondizi, the first Argentine President to visit the United States while in office, would be a guest at the White House January 20–22 (*New York Times*, Jan. 22, 23, 24, 1959).

[3] In his January 6 reply Earl would decline the invitation to the reception, adding that no one attended "a white tie affair except under duress."

[4] Earl would say he had decided to stay at the Statler, even though he doubted that he would be able to "stand Ed for three days." All correspondence is in AWF/N.

The Eisenhower brothers and their families would celebrate Edgar's birthday at the White House the evening of January 19 (*New York Times*, Jan. 20, 1959).

988   *EM, AWF, Name Series*

To MAY NOVY IRVIN   *December 31, 1958*

Dear Mrs. Irvin: I have by no means forgotten your extraordinary suggestion that you present to me your late husband's library.[1] I well understand from your description that it is a most unusual one. You indicated that there was a reason for considering the matter on an urgent basis because of the fact that you plan to leave your present home and therefore must dispose of the library.

As I told you when we had the opportunity for our very brief chat on Christmas afternoon, I anticipate that in a few years I shall have an adequate and, indeed, an admirable place in which it would be possible to maintain this collection. Should anything occur to prevent the completion of the "Eisenhower Library" in the State of Kansas, I would of course have to make, at that time, arrangements for the transfer of the documents to another suitable repository, because I realize that the collection you describe could not be properly housed in a private home. Moreover, I should add that I know of no reason to suppose that the "Eisenhower Library" will not be completed as planned.[2]

In the meantime I think that it should not be too difficult for me to find a proper place for storage either in the White House itself or in a place that would be equally suitable. Possibilities in this line would depend, I should think, upon the size of the library and the manner of packing the different volumes.[3]

It occurs to me that if you should want to pursue your suggestion further, I could ask my Aide to come to New York to see you and to get some idea of what might be involved. If you should like him to visit you for such a purpose, you might drop me a note—and later I could have him telephone to you to arrange details.[4]

Personally I feel highly complimented that you should want me to have something that meant so much to your late husband and which would have a real value for the public and posterity. In any event, whatever you believe should be done, I am quite sure that a discussion with my Aide, Colonel Schulz, would be helpful in clarifying the plan. Further, if you should decide that it would be wiser to send the library to someone other than myself, please be certain that I will not only understand but promptly concur. I feel that the important thing is that you yourself may be completely satisfied with whatever action you may take.[5]

This note is dictated in the closing hours of 1958. As you know, Mamie and I are in Gettysburg, and this morning we were joined by all of the grandchildren. We are going to have a small celebration tonight in honor of Susie's seventh birthday, and, of course, of the New Year.[6]

With best wishes to you for the best possible New Year and, again, my gratitude for your more than kind suggestion. *Sincerely*

[1] Mrs. Irvin was the wife of Effingham Townsend Irvin, a stockbroker and former commodore of the New York Yacht Club. Her husband had died in November. Since she began corresponding with the First Lady in 1956, Mrs. Irvin had given cards and gifts to the Eisenhowers and had attended state dinners at the White House. On December 15 she had sent to the President several books, papers and photographs from her late husband's collection. Eisenhower's December 20 thank-you letter, and a list of the items are in AWF/N; see also Gift cards, Irvin, Dec. 15, 1958, WHCF/Gift File. Another version of this letter, apparently not sent, is in AWF/D.

[2] The Eisenhower Foundation had dedicated the Eisenhower Museum in Abilene in 1954. On October 13, 1959, Eisenhower would attend the groundbreaking ceremonies for the Dwight David Eisenhower Presidential Library in Abilene. The library would officially open in May 1962 (see no. 899).

[3] On July 2, 1959, Mrs. Irvin would send another shipment of nine books directly to the White House (Gift cards, Irvin, July 2, 1959, WHCF/Gift File).

[4] Schulz had initiated the process of cataloguing Eisenhower's books (between 3,500 and 4,000 in number) at the Gettysburg farm (Galambos and van Ee, *The Middle Way*, no. 1437).

[5] In October 1959 Mrs. Irvin would ship ten crates containing more than 1,000 volumes directly to the Eisenhower Library in Abilene, Kansas. Most of the books are shelved in the presidential office in the library. The collection includes leather-bound sets of works by Rudyard Kipling, Charles Dickens, Edgar Allen Poe, Victor Hugo, Alexander Dumas, and William Shakespeare (Correspondence, Pankratz, May 18, 1998, EP).

[6] On the birth of the Eisenhowers' third grandchild, Susan Elaine, see Galambos, *NATO and the Campaign of 1952*, no. 594.

15

"Debate is
the breath of life"

To Lucius Du Bignon Clay, Jr.   *January 1, 1959*
Personal and confidential

Dear Lucius: At the bottom of this letter you will see a list of names
of individuals to whom I am addressing communications, all of them
identical with this one.[1]

Undoubtedly each of us has from time to time had a feeling of
bewilderment, to say nothing of resentment, at some of the things
he has read during the past thirteen years about the European
phase of World War II. Many of the books and articles published
on the subject have been hopelessly prejudiced, largely undocu-
mented and, in many cases, contain distortions or mis-statements of
fact.[2]

For some time I have been wondering whether it would not be a
most interesting exercise if the group of people that I have named
below could meet together for a period of something like a week
and develop an agreed document concerning incidents which are a
part of their individual or collective experiences.

I would personally like very much to have such a group as my
guests for the time we might need. I have a place in mind, located
not too far from Washington, where we could be completely free to
do as we please. There would be some opportunity for recreation.
Our cover story would be that we are merely a group of veterans
from the Mediterranean and European Theatres who have planned
their own personal reunion at this particular moment.[3]

Of course each of us would realize that a great deal of individual
preparation would be necessary before such a project could be undertaken with the slightest prospect of success. This would require
time. For myself a date something like mid-October of this year
would appear to be convenient and would afford an opportunity for
the necessary preparation.

I think that none would have to bring along any great number of
documents, but of course diaries, a few official orders, and possibly
copies of wartime correspondence might be useful.

The thought I am expressing is, at this moment, nothing more
than a hazy idea. But on the personal side I would think such a meeting would promise a considerable enjoyment because of the opportunity to renew old associations and friendships, and we might
even produce something of value.

I pose a number of questions:[4]

    1. Do you like the idea?
    2. Could and would you plan to be present?

3. Do you think of any individual who should clearly be included, other than those named below?

(I had thought of asking a number of others, but for one reason or another have not included them, and I would not like to enlarge the group markedly unless there was general agreement that some individual's presence would be helpful.

For example, I had thought of: Kirk of the American Navy, so as to have naval representation.[5] However, rarely is the Navy history brought into question. I thought also of Andrew Cunningham, but I understand he is not well.[6] Others might be: Boy Browning, because of his experience with the airborne troops; Simpson, who commanded the 9th U.S. Army, which unit served intermittently with both the British and American Army groups; General Koenig of the French Army (while most of us would be interested principally in British-American operations, Koenig's information of the French situation, particularly at the time of D-Day, should be valuable.)[7] Of course I would have included Alexander, but he, too, is not well. Should I ask General Crerar of Canada?)[8]

4. Would the time seem suitable to you?

5. Do you have any other suggestions?

Of course we would have to have a small staff to prepare something on the order of an agenda, to research the documents, and for dictation; I believe I could produce an adequate group of staff people. In addition, we could have recording machinery available that would be helpful.

One other point intrigues me. I think there has never been a time in history when a group of veterans, representing different nationalities and types of activity and branches of service, has attempted out of the memories and records to produce a group report on the basic planning and events of an important campaign.

Incidentally, I must regretfully say that the place I have in mind would not be large enough to include wives. During the period of this particular exercise (I'd think of seven to ten days) we would have to be on a stag basis. Nevertheless if the meeting should come off, I would want to plan for a dinner in Washington where all wives would be welcome, and of course I would hope that during the period of the men's "retreat" the ladies could find some way of amusing themselves.

In any event, and even though the majority may think I have gone a bit off the beam in dreaming up such an idea, this letter at least gives me a chance again to say "Happy New Year" and warm regard. *As ever*

P.S. It would be a great help to me if each individual named would give me an early reply. It is possible that the idea might be generally approved but that a particular individual might not find it too convenient to make the trip. In this case, we might want to secure an alternate.[9]

[1] Although the list is missing from this file in AWF, a list of names for this same purpose, dated, June 8, 1959, may be found in AWF/N: War Reunion. A draft of this letter showing Eisenhower's extensive handwritten emendations is in *ibid.* (see no. 1197).

[2] On the recent publication of Field Marshal Montgomery's controversial memoirs see nos. 933, 948, and 970.

[3] Eisenhower was referring to Camp David, the presidential retreat in Maryland's Catoctin Mountains (see Telephone conversations, Eisenhower and Aurand, Jan. 1, and Eisenhower and Smith, Jan. 2, 1959, both in AWF/D).

[4] In his draft of this letter Eisenhower had originally written: "Since I am so uncertain in my mind, I submit the following questions:"

[5] Admiral Alan Goodrich Kirk had been Chief of Staff of American Naval Forces in Europe during World War II. Following his retirement in 1946 he had served as U.S. representative on the United Nations Special Committee on the Balkans, American Ambassador to Belgium and Minister to Luxembourg (Chandler, *War Years,* no. 1739 and Galambos, *Columbia University,* no. 18).

[6] Andrew Cunningham had served as Britain's First Sea Lord and Chief of Naval Staff during the war.

[7] Frederick Arthur Montague ("Boy") Browning had been deputy commander of the First Allied Airborne Army during World War II. General William Hood Simpson had commanded the Ninth Army from 1944 to 1946, when he assumed command of the Second Army. He had retired in 1946 following a heart attack (see Galambos and van Ee, *The Middle Way,* no. 683). General Marie-Pierre Joseph Koenig had commanded the French Forces of the Interior during World War II. He had been French Commander in Chief in Germany from 1945 to 1949, and in 1954–1955 he had served as French Defense Minister (for background see *Eisenhower Papers,* vols. I–XVIII).

[8] Field Marshal Harold Alexander had been Supreme Allied Commander of the Mediterranean theater in 1944–1945. Henry Duncan Graham Crerar had assumed command of the Canadian First Army in January 1944. Since his retirement in 1946 he had served on the boards of directors of the Guarantee Company of North America and Cockshutt Farm Equipment, Ltd. (see *Eisenhower Papers,* vols. I–IX). In his earlier draft the President had included the name of British Admiral Bertram Home Ramsay, who had commanded Allied naval forces during Eisenhower's campaign in Northwest Europe. Ramsay, however, had been killed in an airplane crash in 1945; see Chandler, *War Years,* nos. 1475 and 2234.

[9] Eisenhower probably did not send this letter. There is no reply in EM. For developments see no. 991.

990   *EM, WHCF, Official File 102-R*

To Arthur Vivian Watkins   *January 2, 1959*

Dear Arthur: I am complimented by the kind things you say in your letter of December twenty-third; I am even more gratified that you had the confidence in my own feeling of friendship and respect for your character and capabilities that you could, without embarrassment, request consideration for Federal appointment.[1]

Frankly, I should very much like to see an individual of your standing on the Court of Claims. The real obstacle to such an appointment is the matter of age. Not only have I observed over the past six years the policy of avoiding the appointment of any individual to the Federal bench after he has attained the age of 62, but we have on the books a law that allows the retirement of judges at the age of 70. It seems quite inconsistent to appoint someone who has already attained that age.[2]

I cannot tell you how much I regret to have to reply in this fashion. It is possible that there may occur some other type of vacancy in which the matter of age would not be a stumbling block, but which would at the same time be a challenge to your demonstrated qualities. I shall instruct General Persons to watch for such possibilities and if any occur, to contact you promptly.[3]

I should like to say again that in the next session of the Congress I will miss you and the support that I always counted on from you when any serious question was up for discussion. Needless to say, my best wishes for the health and happiness of yourself and your family are with you always.

With warm regard, *Sincerely*

[1] Watkins, Republican Senator from Utah since 1947, had been defeated in his bid for reelection in November 1958. In his December 23 letter (same file as document), he wrote of his "great pride in having been a part of the Republican Team" during the Eisenhower Administration, and thanked the President for "the many courtesies" and "the cooperation and great help you have given my state and the region in which it is located." He had asked for an appointment to the U.S. Court of Claims.
[2] Watkins, born on December 18, 1886, had just turned seventy-two. See also nos. 593 and 638.
[3] Eisenhower would appoint Watkins to the Indian Claims Commission on August 15, 1959.

991   *EM, AWF, Name Series*

To Walter Bedell Smith   *January 3, 1959*
Personal

Dear Bedell: I am enthusiastic about the proposition that Strong puts forward.[1]

In the meantime, as I contemplate more seriously some of the obstacles that would be encountered in the scheme I discussed with you on the telephone, I have lost some of my own eagerness for it.[2] For one thing, in order to cover the period from the year 1942 until the end of '45, I think we would probably have to have more people present than I first contemplated. In addition, more time might be consumed to do anything intelligible than I had originally thought (that is, I had been considering something on the order of seven to ten days).

There is one variant that I did not mention to you that we might consider and that is to get over here all the British officers that we considered necessary, together with two or three of the more critical ones in the American group, and then to ask others of the Americans to come up from Washington for a day at a time. That would be the only way, as I see it, we could handle as many as we would want to hear.

As far as the time element goes, we might be able to conquer it by having a clear agreement on fundamentals and arranging for a good staff to do the editing and make a final report to each of us. To guide the staff procedures we should probably have to have a little executive committee—for example, you, Spaatz and Strong or Jock Whiteley.[3] The three of you could communicate with each other in order to give the necessary guidance for the staff in the editing of the conversations.

Finally, I rather think that if I make the proposal at all I shall make the primary purpose that of an enjoyable reunion, and I would make the recording of reminiscences a secondary purpose. In any event, I rather think I will want to wait until Strong comes over here before I make any further move. (Of course I want to see him, and hope that the two of you will come in together). Certainly it appears that you and he and I seem to be thinking along the same lines.[4]

With warm regard, *As ever*

[1] Major General Sir Kenneth William Dobson Strong was Director of the Joint Intelligence Bureau, in the British Ministry of Defence. During World War II Strong served as SHAEF's intelligence officer and later as director of British Foreign Office and defense intelligence bureaus (for background see Chandler, *War Years*, no. 831; and Galambos, *NATO and the Campaign of 1952*, no. 449). Strong had written Smith (Oct. 27, 1958, AWF/N) that the recent publication of Montgomery's memoirs had prompted him to set the record straight in a "dispassionate" manner. For background on Montgomery's controversial volume and Eisenhower's reaction to it see nos. 933 and 1012.

[2] The President had telephoned Smith on January 2 about his plans to gather his wartime colleagues together in order to compose an agreed-upon document regarding events during the European phase of World War II (Telephone conversation, Eisenhower and Smith, Jan. 2, 1959, AWF/D; and Ann Whitman memorandum, Jan. 3, 1959, AWF/AWD). For background on the idea see no. 989.

[3] General Carl Andrew Spaatz had commanded the American air forces in Europe during World War II. General Sir John Francis Martin ("Jock") Whiteley had been SHAEF Assistant G-3 at the end of World War II. Following the war he had served

as commandant of the National Defense College and Canadian Army Staff College, Canada, and as Deputy C.I.G.S. He was chairman of the British Joint Services Mission in Washington and was the United Kingdom representative on the Standing Group of the Military Committee of NATO from 1953–1956, when he retired.
[4] Strong said he might be in the United States in January or February. As it turned out, Strong would not visit the President until December 1960. On January 15 Eisenhower and Smith would hold an off-the-record meeting at the White House. For developments on the reunion see no. 1194.

992

EM, AWF, International Series:
Macmillan

To Harold Macmillan   *January 3, 1959*
Cable. Secret

Dear Harold: Thank you very much for your cable and for the expression of your views.[1] This is a matter to which my associates and I have been giving consideration over a period of many weeks, but up to this moment have thought it wiser to insist upon the interdependency of the two subjects. We are immediately starting an intensive review of the whole matter and you will hear from me within, say, a week. I hope this will be satisfactory.[2] *As ever*

[1] For background on the Geneva disarmament negotiations and the linkage between atomic testing and disarmament see no. 943. Macmillan had long been convinced that the United States and Great Britain should eliminate the condition that the two issues be connected before progress in either could be made. The link was "a vague formula," he wrote Eisenhower, "impossible to define precisely." Eliminating the linkage would prevent the Soviets from blaming the United States and Great Britain for lack of progress in the talks. If the Russians were to agree to a test suspension treaty, Macmillan reasoned, they would eventually have to accept a proper control system to enforce it (Macmillan to Eisenhower, Jan. 1, 1959, PREM 11/[2860]).
[2] Eisenhower had sent a draft of this letter to Under Secretary Herter, asking that it be sent by cable immediately unless Herter found something he wanted to bring to Eisenhower's attention. "In the meantime," he wrote, "please arrange for a reexamination of our position. As you know, I have felt for a long time that we were possibly being too rigid and in so doing, were hurting ourselves a bit" (Eisenhower to Herter, Jan. 3, 1959, AWF/D-H). For developments see no. 1004.

993   EM, AWF, Administration Series

To Gabriel Hauge   *January 5, 1959*

Dear Gabe: I just have your note and I realize that you do have a bit of a problem to solve.[1]

Foster has a date to meet Mr. Mikoyan this noon and I believe it is tentatively planned that I am to receive him at least for a short visit, possibly tomorrow.[2] If I could give you a substantive answer after we have had some opportunity to make a guess as to his serious purpose in coming to the United States, I think it would be more to the point than I can now say. My shooting-from-the-hip answer, which I was about to dictate, could well be wide of the mark that I would set up after a little better knowledge.

Incidentally, Foster is just back from Jamaica and I hear that he has got a virus. However, the doctors are hopeful that it is a very light case and I trust he will be able to talk to Mr. Mikoyan today, as planned.[3]

In spite of the temptation to give you, out of my own great personal wisdom, an immediate reaction to your question, I will let the matter wait until my charming (! acw) secretary brings it back to my attention.[4] *As ever*

[1] Secretary Dulles had told the National Security Council in December that the Soviet Union had requested permission for Deputy Premier Anastas Ivanovich Mikoyan to visit the United States as a guest of the Soviet ambassador. Dulles believed that the real purpose of the visit was to assess American public opinion regarding Berlin and other international issues (NSC meeting minutes, [Dec. 18, 1958], AWF/NSC; see also State, *Foreign Relations, 1958–1960*, vol. X, pt. 1, *Eastern Europe Region; Soviet Union; Cyprus*, pp. 207–9; and Herter to Eisenhower, Jan. 2, 1959, AWF/I: Russia Mikoyan Visit).

Hauge, former Presidential Assistant for Economic Affairs, had written Eisenhower about an address he was to make on January 14 before the Economic Club in New York. The club had invited Mikoyan to be the guest of honor and to speak briefly at the end of the program. Hauge had asked Eisenhower for guidance. Should he ignore or capitalize on the Soviet official's attendance? "Had he not been present," Hauge wrote, "I would simply have gone ahead with my discussion of economic and fiscal policy pitched to a plea that the thousand businessmen in the audience go down the line for your budget lock, stock and barrel" (Hauge to Eisenhower, Jan. 2, 1959, AWF/A).

[2] For Dulles's two-hour meeting with Mikoyan on this day and Eisenhower's meeting on January 17 see the following document.

[3] On Dulles's Jamaica vacation see no. 981.

[4] For developments see the following document. Ann C. Whitman was Eisenhower's secretary.

994   *EM, AWF, DDE Diaries Series*

To Gabriel Hauge   *January 5, 1959*
Personal

Dear Gabe: It turns out that I am not to see Mr. Mikoyan until after he has completed his tour about the country, possibly the 19th or

20th of January. However, Foster had a two hour meeting with the gentleman today and as a result of that meeting, I had a short, secondhand, report.[1]

Mr. Mikoyan seemed very serious and had no hesitation whatsoever in opening up for conversation every conceivable subject that affects the relationship between our two countries. As I understand it, there was no debate or meeting of minds on any subject; it was rather a listing of the items in which Mr. Mikoyan had great interest.[2]

The Secretary did make one remark that would have appeared in the note that I started writing to you this morning, but which I postponed until I learned more about the Russian's attitude. The Secretary said that he saw no reason or any particular advantage in "lionizing" Mr. Mikoyan.

Now to get back to your specific question: On the assumption that he is here for serious purposes, the foremost of which is to learn something about our industries, our people—their aspirations and their way of life, and assuming further that your purpose is not either to glorify him or to ignore him, I would suggest an introductory line that would reflect the sincerity and honesty of your own presentation. By this I mean that you might in the very introductory part of your talk express interest in his visit and the hope that he has through his stay here gotten a better appreciation of American life. You might then point out that since you are addressing a body whose primary interest is economics, you invite his particular attention to the basic difference between our economy and that of the Soviets. This difference is that, as opposed to the Communist system, our economy is owned by our people as *individuals*. This means that each is free to seek work of his own selection in any location he pleases and is then free to change from one job to another whenever he so desires.

This places upon every member of society a responsibility for *self-*discipline. For example, if the workers of any factory would insist upon such wage standards as would spell bankruptcy for the company, then those workers would be damaging their own best interests. In the same fashion, the business man must be satisfied, in a competitive enterprise, with reasonable profits or he will price himself out of the market and will go bankrupt.

We then see that the great distinction is that the American system presents a responsibility for self-discipline on both business and the worker, but in other economies the government imposes discipline upon both producer and worker.

Now I do not think the explanation should be as laborious as what I have here outlined. I am merely trying in this note to suggest the desirability of using a sentence or two that will let Mr. Mikoyan know that you, the speaker, are well aware of the basic differences in these two economies. This you do of course under the guise of informing him merely because otherwise, in his own later talk, he might pretend ignorance of this fundamental difference.

I am sorry this note has to be so long and roundabout; I have no time to make it shorter. I have to dash off to, of all things, a political meeting.[3] I feel that you react with pity in your heart to this statement.

With warm regard, *As ever*

P.S.: A thought that occurs to me: someone has pointed out that capital is the difference between what we produce and what we consume. If the state holds consumption to minimum levels, it is easy to see that the results in accumulation of capital are far greater than in any state where one of the primary purposes of production is to raise the levels of individual consumption.

This was just an added thought as a possibly simple way of pointing up the difference of which I speak. Of course as an economist you can think of a thousand ways—occasionally a more ignorant person has to find a simpler illustration!

[1] For background on Deputy Premier Anastas Mikoyan's visit to the United States see the preceding document. Dulles had reported on his January 5 meeting by telephone to Ann Whitman (see Dulles Papers, Telephone Conversations). For memorandums of the meeting see State, *Foreign Relations, 1958–1960*, vol. X, pt. 1, *Eastern Europe Region; Soviet Union; Cyprus*, pp. 210–13; and State, *Foreign Relations, 1958–1960*, vol. VIII, *Berlin Crisis 1958 1959*, pp. 233 39; see also Stassen to Eisenhower, Jan. 7, 1959, AWF/A; and Dulles, Memorandum of Conversation, Jan. 8, 1959, Dulles Papers, White House Memoranda Series.

Eisenhower's January 17 meeting with the Soviet official would center primarily on the German problem (see Memorandum of Conversation, Jan. 17, 1959, AWF/I: Russia Mikoyan Visit; see also Eisenhower to Dulles, Jan. 16, 1959, *ibid.*; and Eisenhower, *Waging Peace*, pp. 339–40).

[2] See the preceding document.

[3] On this same day Eisenhower would meet with Vice-President Nixon and other Republican leaders in an effort to reshape and reorient the party in the wake of the 1958 mid-term elections; see no. 982. Hauge would use the President's ideas in an extemporaneous introduction to his speech on January 14. The *New York Times* would characterize his remarks as "a review of rosy American economic prospects for the future" (Hauge to Whitney, Jan. 14, 1959, AWF/A, Hauge Corr.; *New York Times*, Jan. 15, 1959).

995   *EM, AWF, DDE Diaries Series*

To Willard Stewart Paul   *January 6, 1959*

Dear Stewart: The first part of your letter assumes a more unequivocal acceptance than I actually intended of your invitation for April 4, 1959. You will recall that after we talked about dates, we began to discuss the actual purpose of the Convocation and specifically the stage of development of your proposal for establishing an "Institute of Peace."[1] Since this proposal has apparently gone no further than the expression of a hope or eventual purpose, I tried to convey the thought that the timing of an appearance of my part was not good. I am quite clear in my own mind that the proposal you make must have a unique, as well as a very practical character, if it is to receive any great support.

What I have in mind is this. When I was in New York I was one of the Trustees of the Carnegie Foundation for International Peace.[2] Likewise, I established a Chair in the Historical Division of Columbia University to look into the results and causes of war and, in addition, the question of how a democracy can organize itself to wage war successfully.[3] At Duke University there is a new Institute for the promotion of the "Rule of Law."[4] There are other organisms that have been established with purposes relating to that of preventing war and maintaining a just peace.

By no means do I want to discourage you from doing something worthwhile in this field. However, I pointed out that since you do not have the time yourself to develop the idea beyond the statement of purpose, I believe you must find some man who can do this for you, before there is any possibility of my helping to promote the plan.

I readily concurred with the idea and I was quite ready, as President, to give such support as I could, but it is quite evident that until the matter has been developed further than merely a statement of purpose, any effort on my part would be futile.

As I recall, we left the matter on the basis that you and one of your friends would come to my office to discuss this subject a bit further. Until we can do so, the matter of my participation in any ceremony should be left in abeyance.[5]

It was indeed nice to have a talk with you and particularly to meet your charming bride. *As ever*

---

[1] General Paul had thanked the President for accepting an invitation to speak at the Gettysburg College Founder's Day Convocation (Jan. 3, 1959, WHCF/PPF 22-C Gettysburg College). At a White House meeting on November 17 Eisenhower had suggested to Paul that they discuss the subject at his Gettysburg farm. General Paul and his wife, the former Louella Musselman Arnold, had visited the Eisenhowers at their farm on December 30 (see Memorandum for the Record, Nov. 17, 1958, AWF/D; and the Chronology).

[2] For background on Eisenhower's association with the Carnegie Endowment for International Peace, an organization founded in 1910 to abolish war, see Galambos, *Columbia University*, no. 63.

[3] While president of Columbia University Eisenhower had established the Institute of War and Peace Studies (*ibid.*, no. 1056).

[4] On the Rule of Law for Peace Center at Duke University, and on the Administration's efforts to develop a coordinating Presidential Commission on Rule of Law for

Peace see nos. 777, 803, and 900. See also Gene M. Lyons and Louis Morton, *Schools for Strategy: Education and Research in National Security Affairs* (New York, 1965), pp. 91, 170, 272. For developments see no. 1182.

[5] Paul would agree that he was not ready to launch a peace center or Civil War institute. Instead he would ask the President to talk about current issues. On January 14 Eisenhower would agree to speak and would ask about the circumstances under which he would address the convocation. He would also say he could not commit to a definite date. Paul would reply that Eisenhower would be the only speaker and that the topic would be the importance of liberal arts in a technically specialized world. Secretary to the President Thomas E. Stephens later would tell Paul that the President would make a short, off-the-cuff speech at the convocation on April 4, but by no means would he be the major speaker (Paul to Eisenhower, Jan. 12, 1959; Eisenhower to Paul, Jan. 14, 1959; Stephens to Paul, Jan. 26, 1959, all in WHCF/PPF 22-C Gettysburg College).

In his talk, entitled "The Importance of Understanding," Eisenhower would urge Americans to recognize the significance of foreign aid to U.S. security (*Public Papers of the Presidents: Eisenhower, 1959*, pp. 309–17; *New York Times*, Apr. 5, 1959; and Ann Whitman memorandum, Apr. 2, 3, 4, 1959, AWF/AWD).

996   *EM, WHCF,*
                                                         President's Personal File 71

To James Frederick Gault   *January 6, 1959*

Dear Jimmy: Many thanks for the information on the Argyll and Sutherland Highlanders insignia. The friend who inquired about it says you have more than answered all of her curiosity about it, and she doesn't want to bother you further. She sends along her "sincere appreciation of your effort" to which I add my own.[1]

From the reports we received here, the ceremonies at St. Paul's went off beautifully.[2] I am, of course, delighted that the Vice President and Mrs. Nixon made such a good impression on people of your country.[3]

I have just returned from ten days (half work, half relaxation) in Gettysburg; now we settle down to a tough period during which the majority of my messages to the Congress go up to the Hill. There is, of course, endless work in the preparation of any such message, since inevitably the Administration's position represents a compromise between the views held by members of the Cabinet and, of course, by me.[4]

With best wishes for the finest of New Years, and warm personal regard, *As ever*

[1] For background on the insignia see no. 949. See also Eisenhower to Mrs. Grace Harwood Schoo, Dec. 27, 1958, and Schoo to Eisenhower, n.d., both in same file as document.

² For background on the dedication of the American Memorial Chapel in St. Paul's Cathedral in London see no. 949.

³ On the Nixons' trip to the United Kingdom see no. 966.

⁴ In addition to the annual message to the Congress on the State of the Union (Jan. 9), the annual budget message to the Congress for Fiscal Year 1960 (Jan. 19), and the annual message presenting the economic report to the Congress (Jan. 20), Eisenhower would transmit the first Annual Report Under the National Aeronautics and Space Act on February 2. He would send special messages to the Congress on the subjects of labor-management relations (Jan. 28); agriculture (Jan. 29); civil rights (Feb. 5); and an increase in the resources of the International Bank for Reconstruction and Development (World Bank) and the International Monetary Fund (Feb. 12). For the text of the messages see *Public Papers of the Presidents: Eisenhower, 1959:* on the State of the Union Address see no. 1003.

997   *EM, WHCF, President's Personal File 606*

TO PHILIP YOUNG   *January 7, 1959*

Dear Phil: With your letter and a little prompting, Howard produced the cheese. I thought some of employing your second suggestion, but a few well directed inquiries located it. As always, Mamie and I are grateful for your thought of us.¹

Of course I enjoyed greatly your report of the Christmas party at the Embassy. I can only hope that the bell ringers proved to be a little more receptive to training than the White House group did a couple of years ago; at any rate I trust that the result was not too off key.²

All your other news was interesting, including your promotion of the tradition of American thanksgiving.³

Here I am in the last throes of the State of the Union Message; by the time you receive this note, the effort, fortunately, will be over. It is an almost impossible and completely frustrating task to assemble a talk that meets with the approval of all the principal members of the Administration, and which will—and this is, of course the important thing—be backed up by every Cabinet member and subordinates.⁴ This year we have two widely divergent views among Cabinet members as to what I should say about labor; we have the proponents and the opponents of the balanced budget; and we have, of course, a wide divergence of views as to what our civil rights program should be. I shall be glad when the Friday hurdle is over.⁵

Mamie joins me in all the best to you and Faith for a good New Year (and less inside and outside fog) and in warm regard.⁶ *As ever*

¹ In his December 23 letter (same file as document) Ambassador to the Netherlands Young had told the President that he had sent him a Herkimer County cheese in care of Eisenhower's physician, Howard Snyder. Young suggested that if Snyder didn't de-

liver the cheese, Eisenhower call him and inquire: "Since when have I been forbid-den to eat cheese?" Alternatively, Eisenhower might "ask Edgar Hoover to check up very quietly to see if Howard actually received them in the first place. Or, thirdly, just say to Mamie, 'Well, we didn't like cheese anyway!'"

[2] For an account of bell ringing at the White House see Morrow, *Black Man in the White House*, pp. 112–13.

[3] Young's description of Thanksgiving Day activities in the Netherlands is in his December 24, 1958, letter to Eisenhower (same file as document).

[4] On concerns over the support given by members of the Executive Branch in testimony before congressional appropriation hearings see Cabinet meeting minutes, December 19, 1958, AWF/Cabinet, and Cabinet Paper 58/44/1, December 16, 1958, AWF/Cabinet.

[5] See Ann Whitman memorandum, January 7, 1959, AWF/AWD. For developments see nos. 999 and 1003. Eisenhower would deliver the State of the Union Address on January 9. The President would call for renewed efforts to enact federal labor legislation to "protect the public interest and to insure the rights and economic freedoms of millions of American workers" (for developments see no. 1291). He would promise to submit a balanced budget for 1960, "a realistic budget with wholly attainable objectives" (see no. 1040). Eisenhower would condemn the closing of schools to prevent integration, saying: "The image of America abroad is not improved when school children, through closing of some of our schools and through no fault of their own, are deprived of their opportunity for an education." See no. 1048.

[6] Young had written that the weather was so bad it was the first time he had ever worked in a government office "where the fog is continuously thicker on the outside than it is on the inside...."

998   *EM, WHCF, Official File 99*

To Charles Abraham Halleck   *January 7, 1959*

Dear Charlie: The report that I was asleep when you, along with Mr. McCormack, called me at 1:32 today to say that the House was in session, was not correct.[1] At that moment I was sweating hard over the State of the Union Message with which I hope to overwhelm all of you on Friday.[2]

I appreciate your courtesy in calling me and assure you that your message was transmitted to me promptly.

With warm personal regard, *Sincerely*

[1] On the evening of January 6 Eisenhower had congratulated Indiana Congressman Halleck on his election as House Minority Leader. Democrats unanimously reelected Massachusetts Representative John W. McCormack as House Majority Leader. The first session of the Eighty-sixth Congress had convened at noon (see *Congressional Quarterly Almanac*, vol. XV, *1959*, pp. 24–25; *New York Times*, Jan. 7, 1959; Ann Whitman memorandum, Jan. 6, 1959, AWF/AWD; and Telephone Conversation, Eisenhower and Halleck, AWF/D). Eisenhower also sent this letter to McCormack (Jan. 7, same file as document).

[2] On the State of the Union message see no. 1003.

To Arthur Sherwood Flemming   *January 7, 1959*

Dear Arthur: To illustrate an idea about the establishment of National Goals in the State of the Union Message, I have made quite a pitch for schools and teachers. While I do not follow your recommendations exactly, I think the idea of personal concern is so emphatically stated that you will not be too disappointed.[1]

With warm regard, *As ever*

[1] On January 3, 1958, Eisenhower had sent a memorandum to each Cabinet member requesting comments on the draft State of the Union Address (see Cabinet Paper 59-89, Jan. 3, 1959, AWF/Cabinet). Flemming had responded with suggestions for the President in two memoranda (both dated Jan. 5, in AWF/A), calling for the insertion of two paragraphs on education and welfare. Flemming had argued for a fiscally responsible program of federal aid to education featuring assistance for poorer school districts and funding for construction. He undoubtedly discussed the issue further during his meeting with the President on January 6.

Eisenhower would incorporate Flemming's ideas into a suggestion made by Chicago businessman Charles Percy for the establishment of a Commission on National Goals to seek the moral, educational and material betterment of the United States (Ann Whitman memorandum, Jan. 5, 1959, AWF/AWD; see also no. 982). In the State of the Union Address the President would call for the establishment of a Committee comprising educators and representatives of labor, management, finance, and the professions to make "the necessary appraisal of the potentials of our future." The need for a "National Goal," he said, was especially apparent in the field of education, where a lack of national standards had led to wide divergence in the quality of facilities, teacher salaries, and teacher competence. For developments see no. 1059.

1000   *EM, WHCF, Official File 102-I*

To Neil Hosler McElroy   *January 8, 1959*

Memorandum for the Secretary of Defense: The changes taking place in Defense procurement as new weapons are adopted and old are curtailed are such that careful, top-level Defense attention to the matter is indicated—since in many cases contracts for sizeable projects will be terminated while contracts for new projects are being initiated, with major impact on particular communities and particular firms.[1]

In addition to strict supervision of contracting procedures and relationships, there is need for consideration, in cancelling or initiating programs, of such questions as the dispersion of productive capacity, and economies to be found in utilizing efficient, going organizations. For example, in many companies the management resources and facilities that exist were developed at great expense to the government and have great future value to the government. In addition, major program changes can affect the whole pattern of geographic dispersion of the production base.

The implications of decisions in this field are of such importance that, in my opinion, major changes should be made in the procurement program of the Defense Department only with the approval of the Secretary or Deputy Secretary of Defense.

[1] Eisenhower had directed General Goodpaster to draft this memorandum before a meeting with Defense Secretary McElroy and Deputy Defense Secretary Donald Quarles on January 8. He told the Defense Department leaders of the need for guarding against "improprieties on the part of contracting officers which might besmirch the entire Administration." The President also recalled that as Army Chief of Staff "he used to employ Inspector Generals to check contracts and contract procedures." McElroy said that he welcomed the President's memo and noted that the issue had been very much on his mind (Goodpaster, Memorandum of Conference, Jan. 9, 1959, AWF/D).

Eisenhower's concern would presage an investigation by the House Armed Services subcommittee, which would begin in June 1959, on the influence of the "munitions lobby" on the awarding of defense contracts. The subcommittee investigation would be inspired by remarks the President would make at a news conference on June 3, 1959, when he would say that "political and financial considerations" had influenced defense plans and that "something besides the strict military needs of this country" might be affecting defense decisions (see *Public Papers of the Presidents: Eisenhower, 1959*, pp. 431–32; and *Congressional Quarterly Almanac*, vol. XV, *1959*, pp. 727–30).

1001   *EM, AWF, International Series:*
De Gaulle

To Charles André Joseph Marie De Gaulle

January 8, 1959

Dear General de Gaulle:[1] At this historic moment I deem it a privilege and honor to extend to you greetings and congratulations upon your inauguration as the first President of the Fifth French Republic.[2]

France has a special place in the hearts of the American people. Moreover, you yourself have come to symbolize for us not only French valor and resolution in the face of adversity but also a dynamic and youthful France determined to go forward with renewed vigor and faith. For these reasons the American people join me in saluting the beginning of the Fifth Republic with great hope and confidence. We send to you and to the noble people you have the honor to lead a special message of friendship and of good wishes for your own future and that of the French nation.

The traditional friendship between our two peoples and our two Governments is firmly established in our foreign relations. I believe, however, that this is a most fitting occasion for us to rededicate ourselves to strengthening these ties and to build an ever more intimate and understanding partnership.[3]

Please accept, Mr. President, my best wishes and the assurances of my highest esteem. *Sincerely*

[1] The State Department draft of this message with Eisenhower's handwritten emendations is in AWF/I: de Gaulle. The message was sent by cable to the American embassy in Paris three days earlier for delivery to the French President on January 8—his inauguration day (see Calhoun to Goodpaster, Jan. 2, 1959, *ibid.*).
[2] For background see no. 722. This paragraph had originally stated that it had given the President "very real pleasure" to extend his congratulations; Eisenhower had inserted the words shown above.
[3] For developments in U.S.-French relations see no. 1106.

1002   *EM, AWF, Name Series*

To Aksel Nielsen   *January 8, 1959*

Dear Aksel: It was so difficult to imagine you in a hospital bed that it was with an unusual sense of relief that I learned that you were again a free man. I disagree with your disdain of the "take it easier" program that the doctors prescribe.[1]

I believe that if you will reach home at least forty-five minutes before luncheon, go immediately to bed and refuse to read any letters, memoranda or books, that you will be astonished how much the practice will finally mean to you. The effort to make your mind a blank—to refuse to think—is not an easy one. But a measure of success can finally be attained. As a consequence you will be astonished to find that in a rest period such as that, you will frequently fall asleep and have a good nap of a quarter or half hour.[2]

After all, you are no longer a fledgling.

May I remind you also that most men have the habit of ignoring the doctors' advice after their first bout of illness. As a matter of fact, each of us regards such a thing as not only an accident, but really a dirty trick. The second experience has a more sobering effect. The point is to try to prevent that second one.

Free advice is always worthless. That we know. So I am trying to avoid a lecture—I merely make a few statements that I earnestly believe are factual. And I might say that if you don't take advantage of this great wisdom, I shall write Helen and enlist her help.

And speaking of wisdom, tomorrow I expound on the State of the Union. The task is an onerous one, particularly since I find such a wide range of disagreement among top Administration officials on the position we should take on the various problems that must be mentioned. I have worked over this talk many long hours, and now—twenty-four hours before delivery—I am still far from satisfied.[3]

But the main purpose of this letter, when I started to dictate it, was to wish you a Happy Birthday, instead of lecturing you on your health and habits.[4] You know, I am sure, that I wish for you the best of everything.

I hope that Helen's progress will be steady and that the balance of 1959 will find you both increasingly in good health and spirits.[5] I shall look forward to seeing you on the twentieth.[6]

In the meantime, my love to Helen, and my felicitations and warm personal regard to yourself, *As ever*

[1] Nielsen had contracted viral pneumonia and had been hospitalized for nine days. He had written Eisenhower that fewer hours at work would make little difference because he would think about business no matter where he was (Jan. 5, AWF/N).
[2] Following his coronary thrombosis in 1955 the President's physicians had advised him to take a midday rest (see Galambos and van Ee, *The Middle Way*, no. 1595). For his immediate reaction to that advice see *ibid.*, nos. 1710 and 1853.
[3] See the following document.
[4] Nielsen was born January 11, 1901.
[5] Helen Nielsen had suffered a heart attack on November 24 (see nos. 954 and 955).
[6] Nielsen's illness had forced him to postpone his visit to Washington until January 20. As it turned out, he would not make the trip; in May the President would see him in Denver (see no. 1168). For developments see no. 1034.

1003   *EM, AWF, DDE Diaries Series*

TO WILTON BURTON PERSONS   *January 9, 1959*
Top secret

Memorandum for General Persons: The following outlines the manner in which the State of the Union Message for 1960 is to be prepared.[1]
1. The contributions and recommendations of the several Departments and Agencies will be in my hands no later than the first of December.
2. Thereafter these submissions will not be changed except under unusual circumstances. Any part of them not accepted or approved by me will be discussed with the government official himself.

3. Before November fifteenth I shall have completed the work of organizing and outlining the subject matter as to basic objectives, sequence and emphasis, working with the White House staff.
4. A working draft will be completed by December tenth. Immediately thereafter each Cabinet officer and the heads of each important agency will receive a copy for his *personal* information.
5. If any changes are recommended in these copies, each will be returned to me no later than December fifteenth.
6. Thereafter no changes will be made except of an editorial nature.
7. This memorandum is for you *only*, except that you will give the schedule to necessarily interested members of your staff. A memorandum will be sent to each Department and Agency involved as to the directions in paragraphs 1,2,4 and 5, immediately after the close of the present Congressional session.

[1] On the preparation of the 1959 State of the Union Address see nos. 997 and 999. Following the resignation of Sherman Adams, Persons had assumed the position of Assistant to the President.

1004   *British Public Record Office,*
PREM 11/[2860]

To Harold Macmillan   *January 12, 1959*
Secret

Dear Harold: I have now had an opportunity to think about your letter on our position in the Geneva nuclear test negotiations and to discuss it with some of my advisors.[1]

We have considered the course of the negotiations to date as well as the points you set forth and we are prepared to drop our insistence that any agreement we may reach with the Russians have in it an explicit requirement that cessation of nuclear tests depend on disarmament progress. I agree with you that to a certain extent this link is an academic one since, as you point out, the central issue is whether we now have an opportunity to get the Russians to accept a real control system. Certainly, if the Russians were to accept the kind of controls which we both believe are necessary, this very fact would mean that one of the principal bars to future progress in disarmament would have been removed. This is a point we might well make in explaining our attitude on this question.

Although, on the basis of the progress to date, it seems to me that the prospects are not bright that the Russians will accept an effective control organization in the current negotiations, I agree that our public position would be much better if we remove as a point of contention the issue of the link to disarmament, which the Russians may use as a screen to evade accepting responsibility for failure in the negotiations or to evade facing up to the control problem.

I believe that we can propose in the negotiations that we accept as a principle that the ban on weapons tests would be indefinite in duration. The arrangement, we believe, should include schedules for the construction and operation of the control system. Withdrawal from or suspension of the treaty would be possible if on annual review it were found that the control system was not being installed on schedule or not being operated properly. If desirable, we will agree to the first annual review being held two years after the treaty enters into force; thereafter, the review automatically would be on an annual basis.

Obstruction or violation of the agreement itself would, of course, be cause for withdrawal.

I believe that it would be unwise to give this change in position any undue publicity by making it the subject of a public announcement at this time. However, I believe that we should in the negotiations exploit our flexibility on this question in every way possible to put pressure on the other side to make concessions.

I have requested Foster to discuss with your people how best to put forward this position in the negotiations.[2] *As ever*

---

[1] For background see no. 992; see also Hewlett and Holl, *Atoms for Peace and War*, pp. 551–52. On this same day Eisenhower had discussed the question of the link between disarmament and the nuclear test ban with State and Defense Department officials. Originally, the United States had sought a test-ban agreement that would be subject to termination on a year-to-year basis if satisfactory progress were not made toward general disarmament. The Soviets had cited this tactic as a reason to end the negotiations and some observers had feared that they had gained a propaganda advantage by placing responsibility on the United States. Eisenhower, who termed a system of controls to be "the real heart of the matter," approved the wording of this message, and it was sent by cable to the American embassy in London for delivery to Macmillan (J. S. D. Eisenhower, Memorandum of Conference, Jan. 19, 1959, AWF/D; see also Ann Whitman memorandum, Jan. 12, 1959, AWF/AWD; and Goodpaster, Memorandum of Conference, Jan. 6, 1959, AWF/D).

[2] For developments see no. 1065.

1005   *EM, AWF, Administration Series*

To Neil Hosler McElroy   *January 12, 1959*

Dear Neil: The meeting of chief public affairs officers of the major Defense Commands provides welcome opportunity to take up with them the new responsibilities arising from last year's defense reorganization, under which these top commanders report directly to the Secretary of Defense and the President.[1]

Stronger supervision and control by the Secretary of Defense over public affairs throughout the Defense establishment have been a major goal in the reorganization plan. Because of their great importance in the effective execution of national defense programs, public affairs activities are today a major command responsibility. I look to the major commanders to insure that public affairs activities throughout all echelons of their commands properly reflect our national aims and objectives.[2]

With my best wishes for a successful conference, *Sincerely*

[1] For background see nos. 630, 631, and 699. The reorganization had distributed operations among ten Assistant Secretaries of Defense (Health and Medical, International Security Affairs, Manpower Personnel and Reserve, Properties and Installations, Supply and Logistics, Atomic Energy, Legislative Affairs, Special Operations, and Public Affairs), as well as a Director of Defense Research and Engineering, and a General Counsel. All reported directly to the Secretary of Defense (see *New York Times*, Jan. 1, 1959; Watson, *Into the Missile Age*, pp. 243–91).

[2] For background on Eisenhower's experience with this problem see Galambos, *Columbia University*, no. 315. A draft charter for the Assistant Secretary for Public Affairs had been drawn up in December 1958. It gave the Secretary responsibility for overall supervision of public information activities in the Defense Department, in line with the President's desire for stronger central control of these activities. However, the final charter, which would be issued on February 27, 1959, would be modified to reflect the Secretary's fears that the changes might jeopardize his relationships with the press and with Congress. Although the final directive would still authorize the Secretary to "communicate directly with the unified and specified commands," it would also state that he was to consult and coordinate "with the military departments and the JCS" (*ibid.*, p. 286).

1006   *EM, AWF, Administration Series,*
                                                    Rogers Corr.

To Charles B. Shuman   *January 13, 1959*
Personal

Dear Mr. Shuman: I thoroughly enjoyed the meeting this morning with the delegation from the American Farm Bureau Federation. Moreover, I was interested in the outline of the legislative plan that you and your associates expect to follow during this session, particularly respecting your efforts to preserve the value of our dollar.[1]

At my first opportunity, I began to read the little pamphlet you handed to me. My attention was caught by the title "The Supreme

Court of the United States." I do not quarrel at all with some of your conclusions and your right to make them, but I am puzzled by this one clause in the second paragraph, ". . . the acquiescence of the Executive Branch in such decisions . . ."[2]

Considering the separation of the three branches of government and the system of checks and balances implicit therein, I am rather curious about your meaning. The oath of the President is to support and defend the Constitution of the United States—not to interpret it. I am afraid we would have chaos if each started giving his own interpretation to the words of the Constitution.[3]

In any event, I have one simple question. Do you have anything to suggest that a President should do, if he should personally disagree with a decision? I remind you that if ever he made such disagreement public, then he would always be under the suspicion that in such cases he would probably not be interested in enforcing the law faithfully, even though his oath requires him to do so.[4]

Again I want to tell you what a pleasure it was to see you this morning.

With best wishes, *Sincerely*

[1] Shuman (M.S. University of Illinois 1929), who had been with the American Farm Bureau since 1945, had been its president since 1954. During his twenty-minute meeting, he had told the President that the Farm Bureau was "stoutly behind him in his efforts to stop inflation, hold down the cost of living, and balance the budget" (Jack Anderson memorandum, Jan. 13, 1959, AWF/A, William P. Rogers Corr.). Farmers were willing to accept cuts in federal farm spending to help reduce expenditures, and they would press for congressional action to clear up the "terrible mess" in the price support program for wheat (see *New York Times*, Jan. 14, 1959).

[2] Shuman had given the President a copy of the resolutions adopted by the Farm Bureau Federation at its most recent convention. One resolution stated: "We are seriously concerned over the present tendency of the Supreme Court to legislate, the acquiescence of the Executive Branch in such decisions, and the tendency of Congress to yield certain of its legislative powers to the Supreme Court. These attitudes destroy the system of checks and balances which is a fundamental concept of the Constitution."

[3] See nos. 234 and 689; see also Galambos and van Ee, *The Middle Way*, no. 1147.

[4] Shuman would respond on both January 29 and February 16, 1959, with an extensive explanation of his beliefs (AWF/A, Rogers Corr.). He decried recent court rulings that tended to reduce state authority to control water resources, and he noted that the Justice Department had opposed congressional efforts to reverse these decisions. He also advocated restrictions on the appellate jurisdiction of the Supreme Court as a means of curbing the judicial branch (see Murphy, *The Constitution in Crisis Times*, pp. 330–33).

To WILLIAM PIERCE ROGERS   *January 13, 1959*

Memorandum for the Attorney General: I again emphasize how important I believe it is to anticipate vacancies in the Courts and make our selections and announcements of appointments before pressures begin to build up in favor of particular individuals. To delay is to make enemies all over the place—and very few friends.[1] Right at this moment I notice people are beginning to write in recommending various individuals for a vacancy in the Court of Claims.[2]

[1] For background see no. 593; for developments see no. 1052.
[2] See no. 990.

1008   *EM, AWF, Dulles-Herter Series*

To JOHN FOSTER DULLES   *January 13, 1959*

Dear Foster: I refer to the State Department's memorandum sent to General Goodpaster on 9 January, and signed by Mr. Calhoun.[1] It is difficult for me to see the reason for the conclusion that an answer to President Ydigoras' personal message to me is unnecessary or undesirable. I personally think that I owe him a message—to fail to answer him would, I believe, be discourtesy and a mistake.

I do agree that I should not get into any argument as to the merits of coffee prices.[2] *As ever*

[1] John A. Calhoun, Director of the Executive Secretariat of the State Department, had sent Goodpaster a telegram from Guatemalan President Miguel Ydígoras Fuentes asking Eisenhower for assistance in improving the country's economy, which had been hurt by falling coffee prices. The Guatemalan government had submitted several applications for loans, Calhoun had written, but the Development Loan Fund had not yet decided on the requests. The State Department had recommended that the American ambassador to Guatemala should acknowledge the telegram. "This would not only avoid the President's having to make reference to the Guatemalan loan application in a message," Calhoun said, "but would also have the effect of indicating to President Ydígoras that it would be preferable not to continue direct correspondence with the President on this subject" (AWF/D-H). For background on U.S. relations with Guatemala see Galambos and van Ee, *The Middle Way*, no. 965 and no. 259 in these volumes.
[2] Dulles would tell Eisenhower that the Development Loan Fund was studying four loan applications totaling $33.5 million; one was in the final stages of consideration (Dulles to Eisenhower, Jan. 15, 1959, AWF/I: Guatemala; see also State, *Foreign Relations, 1958–1960*, vol. V, *American Republics*, Microfiche Supplement, GT-12). In his reply, drafted by State Department officials, Eisenhower would tell Ydígoras that the

loan requests were being studied. "I hope it will be possible soon to inform your Government how, within the limits of our own capabilities and resources, we in the United States can be helpful" (Eisenhower to Ydígoras, Jan. 19, 1959, AWF/I: Guatemala). Although deterioration in the Guatemalan political situation would delay U.S. aid, the Export-Import Bank would grant a $5 million credit to Guatemala's central bank for loans to private industry in December (see State, *Foreign Relations, 1958–1960*, vol. V, *American Republics*, Microfiche Supplement, GT-15, 16; and *New York Times*, May 15, 16, Dec. 5, 1959). For developments see no. 1644.

1009   *EM, AWF, Name Series*

To John Stewart Bragdon   *January 13, 1959*

Memorandum for General Bradgon: As we discussed yesterday, I should like to have as many of our classmates either to a luncheon or dinner some time during February.[1] Examination of my calendar shows that some time along about the 23rd or 24th might be best for me. Since Mrs. Eisenhower will be in Arizona during this particular period, I would have to have the affair, either luncheon or dinner, on a stag basis.[2]

Would you find out for me by inquiry among the Washington group:

(*a*). Would they like to come over to the White House for luncheon or dinner?

(*b*). Which would they prefer?

Do you think it would be all right to send out firm invitations to everybody in the local area—say, Pennsylvania, Maryland, Virginia and the District—and then send a conditional invitation to all other classmates, asking each to attend if they so desire. The number would make little difference so long as I had enough advance information. Of course I would not want to put the matter in such urgent terms that any would feel he would have to express any other reaction except that based upon his own desire and convenience.

If, in your inquiry among the Washington group, there should be any real clearly expressed feeling that wives ought to be present, I would then have to postpone the whole plan because of the increased official activity during the latter stages of the Congressional session, as well as the problem of making fixed commitments very far in advance.

If you would like to talk to me before you make these inquiries, drop in any time. The point is I would simply like to do something of this kind—and my own preference would be for a stag dinner merely because of the time it would give to us for a real get-together.[3]

¹ On January 12 the President and Special Assistant to the President for Public Works Planning Bragdon had attended a monthly luncheon with their West Point classmates in Washington. In her diary, Presidential Secretary Ann Whitman noted that Eisenhower had had a "wonderful time" at the luncheon and was "all wound up" about the prospect of a stag dinner for his classmates (Ann Whitman memoranda, Jan. 12, 1959, AWF/AWD).

² On February 10 the First Lady would travel to the Maine Chance resort in Phoenix; she would return to Washington, after a visit with her mother in Denver, on March 9 (*New York Times*, Jan. 30, Feb. 11, 16, Mar. 4, 10, 1959). For background on Mrs. Eisenhower's earlier visit to the resort see no. 579.

³ Eisenhower and Bragdon would discuss the upcoming reunion on the telephone and would meet at the White House on January 21 (see Ann Whitman memorandum, Jan. 16, 1959, AWF/AWD, and Telephone conversation, Jan. 19, 1959, AWF/D. As it turned out, the President would host an off-the-record stag dinner for forty-one of his classmates on February 23 (Ann Whitman memorandum, Feb. 23, 1959, AWF/AWD).

1010
*EM, WHCF,
President's Personal File 1379*

TO WILLIAM HOWARD LAWRENCE   *January 13, 1959*

Dear Bill: As you assume your duties as President of the National Press Club,¹ I extend to you heartiest congratulations, and venture a word of warning:

Some afternoon when you close your desk upon the burdens of your office to sneak away for an hour of exercise and recreation at Burning Tree, the chances are that your fellow Club members will hold a protest meeting in the lounge. Worse, if you should go away for a couple of days at Pine Valley—or even Augusta—you may be sure that some members will say this proves that your Budget is in balance and that you are false to the established policy of running the Club at a deficit.

But, if you have any respect for your putting stroke, you will go right on playing the game and—despite the outcries from non-golfing members—the Press Club, I am sure, will have a highly successful year under your leadership.

So, my best to you and to your associates as you start your Administration. May you all keep your eyes on the ball, swing easy and hit them far and straight down the middle.²

With best wishes, *Sincerely*

¹ Lawrence, *New York Times* national correspondent since 1948, had been elected in December (Phillips to Hagerty, Dec. 31, 1958, same file as document). Lawrence had begun his newspaper career as a reporter for the *Lincoln Star* in 1932. During World War II he was the *New York Times's* chief correspondent in Moscow and in the Pacific.

² On February 4 Lawrence would thank Eisenhower for this letter. He also would as-

sure the President of his plans to "sneak off" for some golf "—balanced budget or no balanced budget" (*ibid.*).

1011

EM, AWF, Administration Series

TO JOHN HAY WHITNEY   *January 13, 1959*
Telegram

Over the ticker I learn that you are becoming known as the host for a group of law breakers.[1] Their loss of money may help the coffers of Thomas County, but your loss of prestige is bound to have national, possibly international complications. Quel dommage! This reminds me that George Humphrey always carefully provides me with a copy of the game laws.[2] Or can't your guests read?[3]

[1] U.S. Ambassador to Great Britain Whitney had returned to the United States on January 4 for an extended vacation at his Greenwood Plantation in Thomasville, Georgia (see no. 937 and *New York Times,* Jan. 1, 6, 1959). Eisenhower's reference was probably to a reported violation of hunting laws on Whitney's estate (see, for example, Kahn, *Jock,* p. 171).

[2] In February Eisenhower would vacation at Humphrey's Milestone Plantation in Thomasville (see no. 882 and *New York Times,* Feb. 5, 6, 8, 9, 1959). For developments see nos. 1050 and 1057.

[3] On some of the Whitneys' notable guests and on their activities at Greenwood see Kahn, *Jock,* pp. 164–68.

1012

EM, AWF, Name Series

TO LIONEL HASTINGS ISMAY   *January 14, 1959*
Personal and confidential

Dear Pug: I am truly sorry that you have had to fight another battle with pneumonia, but relieved that you are now recovering well, even if slowly. Take care of yourself; I could think of no finer news than to learn that you are feeling truly healthy and vigorous once more.[1]

So far as Monty's book is concerned, my opinion is probably so much lower than yours that I would not like to express it, even in a letter. As a matter of fact, I think that, regardless of how he might have conducted and expressed himself during post war years, he would scarcely stand much chance of going down in history as one of the great British captains.[2] Alexander was much the abler.[3] He was also modest.

I recall the impatience with which we waited for any northern movement of Montgomery's out of the Catania Plain and the long and unnecessary wait before he stepped across the Massena Strait.[4] Do you remember the great promises that he made during the planning for OVERLORD about moving quickly to the southward beyond Caen and Bayeux to get ground fit for airfields, and his postwar assertions that such a movement was never included in the plan? Next consider his preposterous proposal to drive on a single pencil-line thrust straight on to Berlin, and later his failure even to make good his effort for a lodgment across the Rhine, and this after I had promised and given to him everything he requested until that particular operation was completed.[5]

I cannot forget his readiness to belittle associates in those critical moments when the cooperation of all of us was needed.[6] So, I personally believe that, on his record, historians could never be tempted to gild his status too heavily, even if his memoirs had not reflected traits far from admirable.

On the other hand, so far as Brookie is concerned, I think that while he possibly made an error in publishing a diary that reflected the anxious doubts and frustrations of a wartime experience, yet he was always honest, quick and generous. That image of him will never be destroyed in my mind. I believe that just about a year ago I wrote you what he said to me on March twenty-fourth of 1945, just as we had, for the third time, crossed the Rhine. I felt then, and still do, that in those comments was evidence of bigness.[7]

With all my heart I applaud your idea of telling your story without consciously throwing grenades or even bricks.[8] During the years that publishers in this country were trying to get me to write a war memoir (this they started in 1943) the negative argument I always advanced was that I had no intention of trying to make a profit out of criticism of others—their personalities or their judgments. I told the publishers that I would never write anything sensational in the hope that the sale of books would be helped. It was only after two publishers assured me that they would never urge or argue that I do anything more than tell the plain unvarnished truth about the war as I saw it and experienced it that I finally agreed to make the attempt at writing. You can imagine, therefore, my satisfaction when, in the event, the book had a far greater sale in this country than any other book on the war. The publishers actually made a profit out of it, even though they had paid me handsomely.[9]

You have had a long and rich experience that gives assurance that your book will contain much that will be both interesting and helpful. I hope that it will not be too long delayed in its distribution.

With warm greetings to your charming Lady and, of course, all the best to yourself, *As ever*

P.S. Because I have never before, to my knowledge, put on paper or spoken publicly in a disparaging fashion about any other public figure—particularly if he was an old comrade-in-arms—I hope you will understand why I am marking this letter personal and confidential.[10] And, I suppose you know that Winston is planning to come to visit me in Washington, the date of his arrival being May fourth. I cannot tell you how eagerly I am looking forward to seeing him. Indeed, today at a meeting with the press, I had an opportunity to say something about him publicly. While admitting that he and I had had some rather strong differences in ideas and convictions on occasions, I asserted that he was one of the few men that I knew that, in my opinion, was entitled to be considered one of the "greats" of our time; and that my friendship for him would never be shaken.[11]

[1] Ismay had written on January 9 (AWF/N) that he had spent most of the autumn in England hospitalized for pneumonia and that he was recovering slowly in Barbados.

[2] Ismay wrote that he "deplored" the recent publication of Field Marshal Montgomery's memoirs (see nos. 948 and 970). He had hoped Montgomery would be recorded in history as one of the "great British captains of war," but Montgomery had "insured by his own hand" that posterity would never forget his less attractive qualities. Eisenhower recently had pondered getting his wartime colleagues together in order to compose an agreed-upon document regarding events during World War II (see nos. 989 and 991).

[3] Field Marshal Sir Harold Rupert Leofric George Alexander.

[4] Issues involving overall command of ground forces had produced considerable friction between Eisenhower and Montgomery; see Chandler, War Years, vol. IV. The Catania Plain is in Sicily, and the Strait of Messina is the channel between northeastern Sicily and southern Italy. On Eisenhower's recollections of Montgomery's actions during the Sicily campaign (HUSKY) see his memoir Crusade in Europe, pp. 173–92; see also Chandler, War Years, nos. 969 and 1091.

[5] On Montgomery's role during the invasion of Normandy (OVERLORD), the advance on Berlin, and crossing the Rhine see Eisenhower, Crusade in Europe, pp. 266, 305–6, respectively; see also Chandler, War Years, vol. IV.

[6] See David Irving, The War Between the Generals (New York, 1981) for an account of relationships among the Allied leaders.

[7] "Brookie" was Alan Francis Brooke, First Viscount, Baron Alanbrooke of Brookeborough, British field marshal and chief of the Imperial General Staff during World War II. Ismay reported that a second volume of Alanbrooke's memoirs was forthcoming, and in light of the hostile criticism the first had received, he expected improvements. Eisenhower's letter to Ismay about Alanbrooke's diary is no. 550 in these volumes.

[8] For developments see no. 1679.

[9] Eisenhower's memoir had been written and published in 1948 (for background see Galambos, Chief of Staff, nos. 1977 and 2011, and Galambos, Columbia University, nos. 34 and 321).

[10] On Eisenhower's earlier remarks regarding the memoirs see, for example, nos. 933 and 948. For developments see no. 1104.

[11] Ismay said he had seen former British Prime Minister Churchill frequently last summer and commented that although he looked frail and no longer did well in a

crowd, in private conversations he was his old self. For developments see no. 1023. For Eisenhower's remarks at the golden jubilee of the National Press Club see *Public Papers of the Presidents: Eisenhower, 1959*, pp. 18–32.

1013   *EM, AWF,*
                                                             Administration Series

To Cortlandt van Rensselaer Schuyler
                                                              [January 14, 1959]

Dear Cort: I hadn't forgotten your thought that it would be best to have your successor take over sometime this year, and I agree that a date in the summer would probably be most suitable. Needless to say, I appreciate very much your having stayed on during this past year.[1]

We will make plans to get a successor there in good time. I have already spoken to the Secretaries of State and Defense, and to General Twining, about the matter.[2] I have no doubt they will be in touch with General Norstad shortly.[3] The selection is obviously a matter for the most careful thought and decision.[4]

Many thanks for your letter—I am particularly grateful for your offer of further help in future need.[5] All the best to you and Wy.

With warm personal regard, *Sincerely*

[1] Fifty-eight-year-old NATO Chief of Staff Schuyler had written on January 12 (AWF/A) of his desire to retire from the Army and to pursue a new career. Schuyler had held his post for six years and thought that "new enthusiasms, new thinking, and perhaps a younger man" might prove beneficial. Schuyler had first raised the subject of his retirement in January 1958 (see no. 543).

[2] On January 12 Eisenhower, Dulles, McElroy, and Twining had discussed Schuyler as the logical successor to Supreme Allied Commander, Europe, Lauris Norstad, who hoped to retire in January 1961 (John S. D. Eisenhower, Memorandum of Conference, Jan. 13, 1959, AWF/D). During their deliberations the President stated that he wanted a young officer of "recognized brilliance" to work three months under Schuyler before becoming Chief of Staff. Eisenhower thought that same young officer, after serving in the position for perhaps one year, would be capable of replacing Norstad as SACEUR. The President would continue to consider personnel changes in Europe (see John Eisenhower and Andrew Goodpasters' Memorandums of Conference with the President, Feb. 10, 28, Mar. 10, 1959, AWF/D).

[3] According to Schuyler, Norstad had agreed that Schuyler, the elder of the two, should retire first.

[4] As it turned out, Lieutenant General James Edward Moore (USMA 1924), Army Deputy Chief of Staff for military operations, would be appointed as the understudy for Schuyler on April 22. During World War II Moore had served as chief of staff, 35th and 30th Infantry Divisions, XII Corps, 4th Army, 9th Army and 2nd Army. Before assuming his present position he had been commandant of the Army War College. On October 15 Moore would succeed Schuyler, who would retire from the Army on October 31 (*New York Times*, Feb. 19, Apr. 23, Oct. 16, Nov. 8, 1959; see also Memorandum of Conference with the President, Mar. 6, 1959, AWF/D). Norstad would

remain Supreme Allied Commander, Europe, until he retired in 1963. For developments see no. 1495.

[5] Schuyler had offered "to scrap all plans and remain" if the President needed him.

1014   *EM, WHCF, President's Personal File 884*

To Earl Henry Blaik   *January 14, 1959*

Dear Red: It was with feelings considerably stronger than astonishment that I learned last evening of your resignation. I hasten to say that although I clearly recognize that your leaving will be an irreparable loss to present and future Army football teams, to West Point, to the Army and, yes, to the public, yet I heartily approve of your action.[1]

Few people, I am persuaded, understand the intensity of the nervous strain under which a coach must live who has to train teams that are engaged in highly competitive athletics. It is no wonder that as the years inevitably creep up on all of us, the man occupying such a demanding position sometimes looks toward an occupation where concentration is less rigorous, the pace a bit slower, and remuneration a bit better. What I am trying to say is that it is high time you thought of yourself—and you have already given more of yourself for the sake of your deeply felt loyalties than have most people.

There was some speculation in my morning's paper that your decision might be based on differences of opinion in the Army as to whether or not West Point should play in post season bowl games. As for this, I have never even heard the matter discussed by any other West Pointer except in terms of "whatever Blaik feels is best, I am for it." For my part I never even turned on the television or the radio to keep track of a bowl game. My interest is in the contests of the season, but possibly this reaction is somewhat affected by my knowledge that West Point has not played in bowl games.[2]

In any event, along with the gratitude that I have always felt for the dedicated, selfless and brilliant services you have rendered at the Academy, I send you also my very best wishes for an even better record in the commercial world. I am quite certain that many thousands, particularly including the Cadets who have played under your tutelage, would like to join in an expression of these sentiments.[3]

Please remember me warmly to Mrs. Blaik, and to both of you my personal regard and Godspeed. *As ever*

[1] Blaik, who had coached Army's football team since 1941, had announced his decision to retire on January 13 (*New York Times*, Jan. 14, 1959).
[2] The *New York Times* had reported speculation that Blaik was leaving because he

wanted to see his teams play in post-season games, contrary to the Army's current policy (*ibid.*). In a thank-you letter of January 23 (same file as document) Blaik would write that the news reports were only "fabricated conjecture." He admitted, however, that he had "little regard for the judgment of our present Academy leadership."

[3] During his news conference of this same day the President would praise Blaik's self-less dedication (*Public Papers of the Presidents: Eisenhower, 1959*, p. 26, and *New York Times*, Jan. 15, 1959). In February Blaik would become vice-president and a management committee member of Avco Manufacturing Company (*New York Times*, Feb. 3, Apr. 10, 1959). For developments see no. 1717.

1015   *EM, WHCF, Official File 3-K*

TO PRICE MARION DANIEL   *January 14, 1959*

Dear Price: Thank you for your letter concerning the promotion and retirement of Brigadier General William L. Lee.[1] It is, as always, gratifying to learn that a member of the armed forces has conducted himself in such a manner as to merit the keen interest which you in Texas have shown him.

As you may not know, General Lee is an old friend of mine, who voluntarily, and on an "out of hours" basis, gave me flying instruction in the Philippines in 1936–39.[2] My personal regard for him and my gratitude to him have never diminished. I have always regarded him as a fine, upstanding officer.

In regard to his promotion status, I am afraid there is little that can be done. The law specifies that an officer may not be promoted to a permanent grade without the recommendation of a selection board. When I learned that General Lee had not been selected for promotion by a board which met last October, I inquired to ascertain that he had received every consideration. I was assured that he had, but the percentage of those selected had been, of necessity, exceedingly small.

As a personal friend of General Lee, I regret that this forces his retirement in July, but statutory processes prohibit any extension of his active duty.[3]

With warm regard, *Sincerely*

[1] Texas Governor Daniel had written Eisenhower that Lee was "a fine officer and the kind of man we should retain in the service as long as possible" (Dec. 16, same file as document). William Lecel Lee (B.S. Texas Agriculture and Mechanical College 1927) was Commanding Officer of the Amarillo Air Force Base in Texas. He had been commissioned a second lieutenant in the U.S. Army in 1929, and during the 1930s, had organized the Philippine Army Air Corps under General Douglas MacArthur. Two drafts of this letter and related correspondence are in *ibid.* For background on Eisenhower's interest in military retirement benefits see no. 969.

² Eisenhower's account of Lee's patience during his flight training is in *At Ease*, p. 226.

³ Lee would retire August 1. In a letter read at the retirement ceremonies the President would praise Lee for his work with the Air Force and express hope for an enjoyable retirement (*New York Times*, Aug. 2, 1959).

1016
*EM, AWF, Name Series,
Luce Corr.*

To Thomas Sovereign Gates, Jr.   *January 15, 1959*

Dear Mr. Secretary: Herewith is a communication from Henry Luce, who is Chairman, I believe, of a lay committee that is interested in developing a National Presbyterian Church here in the Capital. Personally I support the project as a member of this particular church: I likewise believe strongly that another church edifice built in the city in a cathedral-like pattern would serve not only as another fine symbol for America, but would be of great public interest as an imposing architectural development.[1]

After two years of search and having been thwarted in two or three serious attempts to get a proper site for the development, they have come to the conclusion that the ideal site would be that part of the Naval Observatory area that lies along Massachusetts Avenue. Their proposition is to purchase the necessary part—I think they have in mind something on the order of fifteen to twenty-five acres—at a fair market value as determined by appraisers who would be acceptable to the Navy Department.

I realize that any governmental agency sees little advantage to itself in disposing of property, even at a good price, for the reason that the proceeds normally go into general receipts. However, in this case it might be possible for special legislation to permit the Navy to use the funds for such renovation, rebuilding and extension of accommodations on the reservation as might seem desirable and which otherwise could not easily be financed.[2]

In any event, I am taking no active part in the prosecution of this project and the only request I make of you is that you see Mr. Luce and the presiding pastor, Dr. Elson, who would like to confer with you, Admiral Burke and any others you might choose to include in the group.[3]

If you agree to such a meeting, would you have your secretary get in touch with Dr. Elson (who can easily be reached here in Washington) to arrange an appointment at such time as may be convenient to yourself? Incidentally, I have just learned that Mr. Luce is

1301

going to be in town on Monday afternoon next, if by chance you have any time available then.[4]

With warm regard, *Sincerely*

[1] For background on Eisenhower's interest in the project see no. 281. At a meeting with the President on January 12 Luce and Edward L. R. Elson had asked Eisenhower to arrange an appointment with Secretary of the Navy Gates. On January 14 they had submitted a personal and confidential memorandum to the President outlining their plan to purchase a tract of land on the site of the Naval Observatory in order to erect a church, national headquarters and administrative buildings, school facilities, and an auditorium. See also Elson's letter to the President of the same date (both in AWF/N, Luce Corr.).

[2] Gates would agree with the President's suggestion and would add that legislation of this type could aid both in liquidating government assets of a long-term contingency nature and in modernizing the military establishment (Gates to Eisenhower, Feb. 27, 1959, WHCF/OF 144-B-1-A).

[3] Rear Admiral Arleigh Albert Burke had been Chief of Naval Operations since August 1955. He had served as a combat commander during World War II and later served as commander of the Atlantic destroyer force (for background see Galambos and van Ee, *The Middle Way*, no. 1430).

[4] After meeting with Luce, Gates would conduct a Navy Department feasibility study on selling some Observatory land to the National Presbyterian Church. He would explain that the Observatory performed an essential service in celestial navigation and establishing accurate worldwide time standards. Any large building placed within one thousand feet of the principal instruments would cause interference. The work of the Observatory and its specialized facilities could not be accomplished elsewhere, he said, and moving the installation would be costly. Gates said he had notified Luce and Elson and had offered to explore other possibilities. For developments see no. 1145.

1017   *EM, AWF, DDE Diaries Series*

TO EDWARD THOMAS FOLLIARD   *January 15, 1959*
Personal

Dear Eddie: Many thanks for sending me the photograph that was taken, if I am not mistaken, on Easter Sunday of 1946.[1] You must have had a background briefing to be so conversant with the subject matter of my visit that day with President Truman!

Frankly, I had no idea that more than four people—at the outside—knew about the purpose the President had in mind when he called me to the Williamsburg on the day that picture was taken. Some day—off the record—I will show you a curious little memento of that trip in which you may have some interest, even after all these years.[2]

I greatly enjoyed the Press Club luncheon; I am glad you think the affair went off well.[3]

With warm regard, *Sincerely*

[1] Folliard, a reporter with the *Washington Post and Times Herald* since 1923, had been a war correspondent in Europe during World War II. In 1947 he had been awarded a Pulitzer Prize for distinguished reporting on American national affairs. The photograph Folliard sent, which showed President Truman welcoming U.S. Army Chief of Staff Eisenhower aboard the presidential yacht *Williamsburg*, had appeared in most major newspapers (see, for example, *New York Times*, Apr. 27, 1946).

[2] Eisenhower was referring to the circumstances surrounding the appointment of General George C. Marshall as Secretary of State. For background see Galambos, *Chief of Staff*, nos. 844, 909, and 921; on the memento and for developments, see no. 1177.

[3] On January 14 the President had attended the golden jubilee of the National Press Club (see no. 1012).

1018

EM, AWF,
Administration Series

To Alfred Maximilian Gruenther

January 15, 1959

Dear Al: I have an interesting letter from Pug. He has not been well but seems to be improving.[1] When you have read it, will you please return it to my files?

Last evening, sharply on the minute of half past five, I asked Mrs. Whitman to give you a ring, thinking that our spirits should possibly be stronger. She reported that you were then on your way home, a piece of information that at least delights me to the extent that it shows you are not—on some days—finding it difficult to make a decision to go home before dinner time.

If you happened to see my televised press conference, I am interested in your reaction to one thing only—the reminiscences about the war.[2] *As ever*

[1] General Ismay was recovering from pneumonia. Eisenhower's reply to him is no. 1012.

[2] The preceding day the President had participated in the golden jubilee of the National Press Club (see *ibid.*). The club's president had asked Eisenhower to recall some of his associations with Winston Churchill, Generals Montgomery and de Gaulle, and other allied leaders. Eisenhower remembered Churchill as a man who "clearly deserves the title great." He also praised Generals Bradley, Marshall, and British Air Chief Marshal Portal. He did not discuss Montgomery or de Gaulle. (For Eisenhower's full remarks see *Public Papers of the Presidents: Eisenhower, 1959*, pp. 29–31.) On the recent publication of Montgomery's memoir and the President's reaction see nos. 989 and 1012. On Eisenhower's relationship with newly-elected French President de Gaulle see no. 722. Gruenther would meet the President at the White House later this same evening (Ann Whitman memorandum, Jan. 15, 1959, AWF/AWD).

EM, AWF, Name Series

To Wilton Burton Persons   *January 16, 1959*

Dear Jerry:
                        Regarding: Garfield Kass
For a long time I have been hearing about a Mr. Kass. I think he lives in the District, but he is quite a real estate operator in this particular area and he may possibly live in Virginia. He is reported to me as being a staunch Republican (and one who habitually contributes to the Party), an outstanding man in the community and quite wealthy.[1]

For some months the only man from whom I heard these things was our barber, Steve Martini—who, incidentally, is himself very prosperous as a small businessman.[2]

However, in the last two or three months, I have heard Mr. Kass' name mentioned by a number of other people, always favorably. My impression is that he is about sixty years of age.

I would like for you to have his record checked up, and should any type of temporary or even only honorary position for one of his qualifications, I would like to know whether he would be particularly suitable.[3]

[1] After Eisenhower left office, Kass, a sixty-eight year-old millionaire real estate developer, would serve as an unpaid consultant to the State Department on foreign embassy and office space.
[2] Steve E. Martini was the professional name of Stephen J. Egiziano, who would also serve as barber for Presidents Kennedy, Johnson and Nixon.
[3] There is in AWF no further correspondence relating to Kass, who would not receive any federal appointment during the remainder of Eisenhower's Administration.

1020   *EM, AWF, DDE Diaries Series*

To Robert Bernerd Anderson   *January 17, 1959*

Dear Bob: Many thanks for sending me the first hundred new Lincoln pennies.[1] I am relieved to learn from Mrs. Whitman that you paid for them yourself. I know full well you can afford that large expenditure far better than can the United States Treasury.

I distributed them, as you suggested, to the Republican leaders last night.[2] And I thought some of giving one to Mr. Mikoyan this morning, but decided against such a capitalistic gesture![3]

With warm regard, *As ever*

[1] The Lincoln one-cent coins, a feature of the sesquicentennial Lincoln observance, had gone into circulation ahead of the scheduled February 12 release (*New York Times,* Jan. 25, 1959).
[2] For a list of those who had attended the President's off-the-record meeting see President's daily appointments.
[3] Eisenhower had met with Soviet Deputy Premier Anastas Mikoyan, who had been visiting the United States (see nos. 993 and 994, and Eisenhower to Dulles, Jan. 16, 1959, AWF/I: Russia Mikoyan Visit).

1021   *EM, AWF, Administration Series*

To Justin Whitlock Dart   *January 19, 1959*

Dear Justin: The postscript on your letter of January seventh reminded me that I had meant, immediately after our meeting of January fifth, to write to you.[1] I wanted first of all to thank you personally for coming all the way East for the meeting, and to express my regret that the conversation never got around to your particular—and very vital—field.[2] As so often happens in an informal group of that kind, a very important phase of the whole problem got lost in the broader context of aims, policies, organization and methods. But the tough matter of financing has not been lost from sight—I think we are getting organized to attack all along the front.[3]

 With warm regard, *Sincerely*

[1] For background see nos. 914, 962, and 963. Dart's January 7 letter (AWF/A) thanked the President for the gift of Eisenhower's painting, "Deserted Barn." Dart had handwritten a postscript to his letter: "Left our meeting of the other day feeling very sick!" In an undated memorandum Presidential Secretary Ann Whitman had asked the President if he wanted to discuss Dart's postscript with him. She thought that "some letter from you thanking him for coming and saying something about [the] meeting might be indicated" (AWF/A).
[2] On Eisenhower's January 5 meeting with Dart and other Republican political figures see no. 982.
[3] On January 13 the President had telephoned Bell and Howell President Charles Percy to clarify his desire that Percy take the chairmanship of the proposed Republican committee (and not the bipartisan Committee on National Goals, see no. 999). In a subsequent conversation with White House aides Wilton Persons and Robert Merriam, Eisenhower had threatened to sit out the 1960 elections unless the Republicans formed a planning committee (Ann Whitman memorandum, Jan. 13, 1959, AWF/AWD). In February Republican National Chairman Meade Alcorn would announce the formation of a forty-four member committee charged with drafting a long-range statement of party policy and objectives. Percy would chair the committee (see no. 982; see also *New York Times,* Feb. 26, 1959). For developments see nos. 1025 and 1125.

To Clifford Roberts   *January 19, 1959*

Dear Cliff: Thank you very much for your readiness to continue helping Mamie and me in our efforts to do a bit of investing for our children and grandchildren.[1] John and Barbara are likewise grateful.

Enclosed are two checks for $16,500 each, one made out by Mamie to me and endorsed by me to Reynolds and Company, and the other my personal check drawn to the order of Reynolds and Company. The total sum of $33,000 is to be invested at your discretion according to the following schedule:

John S. D. Eisenhower	$6,000.00
Barbara Thompson Eisenhower	6,000.00
Mary Jean Eisenhower	
(John S. D. Eisenhower, Guardian)	6,000.00
Dwight David Eisenhower, II	
(John S. D. Eisenhower, Guardian)	5,000.00
Barbara Anne Eisenhower,	
(John S. D. Eisenhower, Guardian)	5,000.00
Susan Elaine Eisenhower	
(John S. D. Eisenhower, Guardian)	5,000.00

In the case of the grandchildren, I have put down John's name as guardian because I understand that this practice is quite proper in registering stocks in the name of a minor.

We have already agreed, on the telephone, that it might be wise for you to watch the market for some time before making these investments. But you know also that current income is important to the children because of the heavy educational expenses they incur on behalf of our grandchildren. Any stock that is sound and gives a reasonable return could in some respects be better than one that had greater growth potential.

Should minor opportunities of this kind come to your attention, you might feel it wise to make the purchase on a "now and then" basis rather than to wait completely for what may seem to be a much better time for investments. This is just a thought.

Please remember Mamie and me to your charming bride and, of course, all the best to yourself.[2] *As ever*

---

[1] Eisenhower and Roberts had discussed the arrangement on January 17 (Telephone Conversations, AWF/D; see also Roberts to Eisenhower, Jan. 29, 1959, AWF/M: AP, John Eisenhower Corr.). For background on Roberts's previous investment advice see no. 957.

[2] On Roberts's recent marriage see no. 984. On January 22 the President and Roberts would meet twice (off the record).

To Winston Spencer Churchill   *January 20, 1959*

Thank you for your note from Marrakech. In view of our weather here today—cold, sleet mixed with rain, and a general dismal atmosphere—I cannot fail to be a little envious of the sunshine I trust you are enjoying.[1] Incidentally, the President of the Argentines arrives within the hour, and I am afraid that Washington will not, because of the weather, give him a very warm welcome.[2]

As you suggest, we shall have a bit of time to develop the details of your forthcoming visit, but unless I hear differently from you we are still expecting you to arrive on or about May fourth.[3] For several days you and I should have some fun in making a final decision as to the identity of the General, Admiral or Air Marshal who really did win the War![4]

With affectionate regard to Clemmie and to yourself,[5]

[1] Churchill had written on January 14 (AWF/I: Churchill).
[2] Arturo Frondizi, the Argentine president, would be a guest at the White House until January 22 (see nos. 658 and 987). On the issues discussed during his visit see Dulles, Memorandum of Conversation with the President, January 20, 1959, Dulles Papers, White House Memoranda Series, and Dulles to Eisenhower, January 21, 1959, AWF/D-H.
[3] For background on the former British Prime Minister's upcoming visit to the United States see no. 938. On January 6 Eisenhower had invited Churchill to stay at the White House as long as his schedule permitted (AWF/I: Churchill). The President also said he would arrange for as much or as little social activity as Churchill sought.
[4] Churchill had expressed his wish to stay in Washington for two or three days. The President was reacting to the recent publication of Field Marshal Montgomery's controversial memoir; see no. 1012.
[5] For developments see no. 1174.

To Ezra Taft Benson   *January 21, 1959*
Personal

Dear Ezra: There is no question as to my instinctive agreement with the convictions you express in your note of the nineteenth.[1]

The problem posed is *not* constitutional in character. By this I mean that the Constitution neither forbids nor directs Federal participation in the educational process. However, the Federal government did start the Academy at West Point about 1800 and since then has established several others. Further, in many ways the Federal government has intervened in certain phases of education.[2]

Important factors of the problem, as I see it, are:

(a). There is a national need for a good educational system. This has been recognized from the beginning of our history and, indeed, a number of our early leaders frequently expressed the conviction that a democracy could not succeed *unless* there was an educated citizenry.[3]

(b). Traditionally and properly we have entrusted this function primarily to states and communities. While, as I have pointed out, the Federal government has participated only for special purposes in the educational process, and we have acted mainly on the theory that the education of the child should be a matter for the parent, the locality and the state, yet not all of our states and localities have properly discharged their responsibility respecting schools.

(c). The acceptance by the Federal government of any additional responsibility, previously dispersed to the several states, inevitably brings about some degree of increased Federal authority and a lessening of the power of the localities.

The national need of a good education as a basis for good citizenship is recognized as a "principle." Our belief in avoidance of unnecessary centralization of responsibility and authority is likewise classed as a "principle."

But if the states do not perform efficiently, then these principles seem to collide at this point. Since there is no way of compelling states and communities to fulfill their responsibility in the educational field—if for any reasons they either will not or cannot do so—we produce a problem and political argument centering around these conflicting considerations.

Pondering these things, I feel that the critical factor becomes that of demonstrating need and this I personally believe should be done by making the determination of what states cannot properly do the job rather than what districts cannot do so. But if a clear need, on a state-wide basis, could be established—and this in spite of a reasonable tax effort in such a state—then I would favor sufficient Federal assistance to make up this particular deficit, *and no more.*

The trouble is that the problem is never going to be settled on any such reasonable basis. I do not need to point out or describe the political considerations that are brought to bear.[4]

Only the wisdom of Solomon could really decide how to divide this baby. *As ever*

---

[1] Benson's January 19 letter on federal aid to education is in AWF/A. The Agriculture Secretary had written as a follow-up to the January 16 Cabinet meeting during

which the Secretary of Health, Education and Welfare had argued for federal par
ticipation in school construction (see Cabinet meeting minutes, Jan. 19, 1959, AWF/
Cabinet; see also no. 999). Benson had argued that, contrary to the arguments expressed during the Cabinet meeting, large grants of federal funds to education were
a mistake and "would likely provide a great disservice to our public school system
and tend to stymie initiative on the part of the local people." In the long run, national grants for education would mean "controlled education." See Benson, *Crossfire*, pp. 422–23.

[2] See, for example, nos. 416, 516, and 767; see also Galambos and van Ee, *The Middle Way*, nos. 1314, 1801, and 1910. On West Point see Stephen E. Ambrose, *Duty,
Honor, Country: A History of West Point* (Baltimore, 1966), pp. 1–23; see also Galambos and van Ee, *The Middle Way*, no. 980.

[3] See Rush Welter, *Popular Education and Democratic Thought in America* (New York,
1962), pp. 24–29.

[4] In January the House had introduced legislation calling for direct federal grants to
states for public school construction and teachers' salaries. Although the bill would
be amended in April, to provide for a four-year program with substantially reduced
funding, it would not be cleared for floor action in the 1959 session. In the Senate,
legislation introduced in February would call for an emergency two-year program of
$500 million a year in federal matching grants to the states for school construction
only. The bill contrasted with the Administration's plan, which called for a five-year
program of $600 million in federal-state matching grants for school construction. In
any event, no action would be taken on school construction legislation in 1959 (see
Congressional Quarterly Almanac, vol. XV, *1959*, pp. 300–301.

1025   *EM, AWF, DDE Diaries Series*

To Hugh Meade Alcorn, Jr.   *January 21, 1959*
Telegram

This meeting of our Party's National Committee underlines the continuous nature of our political system.[1] I deeply regret that some
people look upon our Party as a kind of hibernating elephant who
wakes with a mighty trumpet blast at election time and then rest
calmly until the next campaign.[2] Political activity must be a matter
of unremitting effort. It must go on 365 days a year if we are to maintain the vitality that has made our nation great. Only 658 days remain until the next national election. We must make each of them
count. Every day we lose is one we can never get back.

Immediately we must give the millions of Americans who look to
the Republican Party for progressive leadership a clear understanding of our long-range objectives.[3] The publicizing of such Party
guide-lines is sorely needed to make meaningful the value of our
political system to the voter and the Party worker. Only in this way
can we lift creative Republicanism to new heights of national
achievement.

Your meeting this week should be the first step in a continuous work program of the Republican party that will never cease. This demands constant attention to organization, to cooperation at all levels, to assuring that candidates are capable, vigorous, personable and dedicated; that finances are secured on a continuing and satisfactory basis; and that every Republican and every friend of Republicanism keep everlastingly at the job of recruiting for the party.[4]

I look forward to your personal report on the results of this important session and send you, the Republican National Committee, and its staff, my warmest personal regard.

[1] Eisenhower's message to the Republican National Committee meeting would be read by Party Chairman Alcorn on January 22 (see *New York Times*, Jan. 23, 1959).
[2] See nos. 962 and 963.
[3] See no. 1021.
[4] For developments see no. 1125.

1026   *EM, AWF, Ann Whitman Diaries*

MEMORANDUM   *January 21, 1959*
Confidential

Memorandum of conversation with Mrs. Ogden Reid: Mrs. Reid is worried about the fact that Jock Whitney is going to remain in London as Ambassador, rather than coming back home where she would expect him to take editorial charge or direction of the Herald-Tribune.[1] She is of the conviction that Jock has put a fine business man in charge of the financial and business affairs of the paper. His name is Brundage.[2] She is equally sure that there is a vacuum in the editorial direction and that this must be promptly corrected.

She obviously has tremendous faith in Jock himself. But she believes that as a sound business arrangement things would be much improved if Jock could appoint a man who is his alter-ego in the editorial affairs of the paper. She knows a man, now in Jock's organization, named Sam Park, that she believes could do the job well.[3]

She is hopeful that I can bring some conversation with Jock around to the point where Jock himself might recognize this need and move to improve the situation. She is equally anxious that her visit to me be maintained on a secret and off-the-record basis.

Her concern seems to be the paper only—its improvement and usefulness. She thinks that if it were ever known that she made any suggestion, even through a third person, that it might be harmful.[4]

[1] For background see nos. 759 and 893. Reid had met with the President for a half-hour that afternoon.

[2] On December 30, 1958, Ogden R. Reid had announced his resignation as president and editor of the *New York Herald Tribune*, noting that he had fulfilled his agreement to remain at the paper during its transition to its new owner, John Hay Whitney. The board of directors had named Howard Denton Brundage (B.A. Dartmouth 1944) as the new president. Brundage, who had previously been with Morgan Stanley and Company, and the Hanover Bank, had been vice-president and secretary-treasurer of Plymouth Rock Publications, a corporation formed in May 1958 to operate Whitney's publishing interests (*New York Times*, Dec. 31, 1958). Brundage would serve as editor only until July 1959, when he would return to Plymouth Rock Publications (see below).

[3] Samuel Culver Park, Jr. (M.B.A. Harvard 1927) had been a partner with J. H. Whitney and Company since 1946.

[4] In July the *Tribune* would announce the appointment of Robert M. White II (A.B. Washington and Lee University 1938) as president and editor. White had been editor and publisher of the *Mexico* (Mo.) *Ledger*. He was also a director of the American Newspaper Publishers Association and a consultant to the *Chicago Sun-Times* (see *New York Times*, July 14, 1959, and Kahn, *Jock*, pp. 265–69).

1027   *EM, AWF, DDE Diaries Series*

NOTE   *January 22, 1959*

This is state policy; decision belongs to me.[1]

[1] Eisenhower had handwritten this observation at the bottom of a staff note reporting comments by John A. McCone, Chairman of the AEC since July 1958, on atomic reactor development. Eisenhower had discussed this subject with McCone on January 16 (Goodpaster memorandum, Jan. 20, 1959, AWF/D). On January 21, 1959, McCone had stated during a news conference that the high cost of developing reactors to the point where they became competitive with conventional power plants made it necessary "to be selective and move into advanced stages of reactor development only when it is clear that a concept will accomplish a major objective not readily accomplished by any other reactor concept." McCone's comments were interpreted in the press as signaling a major change in the government's program to achieve economical nuclear power in the next decade. See Goodpaster memorandum, February 11, 1959, AWF/D; Hewlett and Holl, *Atoms for Peace and War*, pp. 489–506; and *New York Times*, June 7, 1958, January 22, 1959.

1028   *EM, WHCF, Official File 2-B-1*

To HENRY CLAY ALEXANDER   *January 23, 1959*

Dear Mr. Alexander:[1] Yesterday Harold Boeschenstein and S. D. Bechtel brought to me the report made by you and other members of the Committee on World Economic Practices on a program to counter the mounting Sino-Soviet bloc economic offensive. He also gave me your letter pointing out certain reservations you have about the report.[2]

I have read with great interest both the report and your letter, and I am struck with the amount of thinking that you and the other Committee members have done on this most important subject. Personally I liked the report, although I agree with you that further steps must now be proposed. To that end I have submitted copies of the report to the people in government who are primarily concerned with the problem. I have further asked Clarence Randall to call a meeting of these Administration people in order that they may arrive at an agreed position and make these recommendations to me.[3]

Needless to say, I am more than grateful to you for the hard work that necessarily went into a study of a problem of this magnitude and importance.

May I further add a personal note? I was much interested in the recently announced proposal to merge J. P. Morgan and Company with the Guaranty Trust Company; I trust that it will work out well for all of you.[4]

With warm regard, *Sincerely*

[1] For background on Henry Clay Alexander, chairman of the board of J. P. Morgan and Company, see Galambos and van Ee, *The Middle Way*, no. 731.

[2] For background on Boeschenstein's Committee on World Economic Practices, which had been formed in 1958 to examine courses of action to counteract Soviet and Communist Chinese economic offensives, see State, *Foreign Relations, 1958–1960*, vol. IV, *Foreign Economic Policy*, pp. 14–15, 22–23; see also nos. 137 and 424). Stephen Davison Bechtel, president of the Bechtel Corporation and chairman of the Business Advisory Council of the U.S. Department of Commerce, was also a member of the committee.

The Boeschenstein Committee's report, which emphasized the importance of expanding world trade and encouraging economic interdependence among free nations, had recommended the formation of a business-government partnership that would support worthwhile projects and help develop "a sound expanding Free World economic system." The committee proposed that steps be taken to improve the image of America and that understanding of U.S. institutions and goals was as important as economic assistance: "The behavior and attitude of our people at home and abroad often have greater effect than grants or loans. Actions speak louder than words" (Report of the Committee on World Economic Practices, Jan. 22, 1959, same file as document; see also U.S. Department of State, *American Foreign Policy; Current Documents, 1959* [Washington, D.C., 1963], pp. 1432–49).

Alexander had charged that the report failed to make specific recommendations for improving the Mutual Security Act. He also objected to the report's failure to consider the creation of an International Development Association or U.S. participation in regional banks and lending institutions (Alexander to Boeschenstein, Jan. 20, 1959, same file as document).

[3] Eisenhower had sent copies of the report to the Secretaries of State, Commerce,

and the Treasury, as well as to the Director of the ICA and the chairman of the Council on Foreign Economic Policy. He asked that particular attention be paid to the committee's recommendation for a "centrally directed" economic effort that would provide for more rapid and effective action (Memorandum, Jan. 22, 1959, AWF/A: Committee on World Economic Practices). There is no record of the March 4 meeting of Randall's group (see State, *Foreign Relations, 1958–1960*, vol. IV, *Foreign Economic Policy*, pp. 37–38; see also *ibid.*, pp. 191, 317–18, 325).

[4] In his response Alexander would tell Eisenhower that he hoped that the proposed merger would "work out well and result in the creation of an institution that will be able to serve better the needs of our growing economy than could the two institutions separately" (Feb. 9, 1959, same file as document). The two banks would merge on April 24 (*New York Times*, Apr. 15, 1959).

1029   *EM, AWF, Dulles-Herter Series*

To JOHN FOSTER DULLES   *January 26, 1959*
Secret

Dear Foster: This note refers to your memorandum of your conversation with the French Ambassador. This whole question raises again—this time from the other side—the doubt that I have so frequently expressed that the command structure involving our United States Naval Forces in the Mediterranean is properly devised.[1]

In short, I believe that the United States forces should be primarily assigned to SACEUR in the Mediterranean, but with the proviso that such forces can be used by the United States government for diplomatic and other special missions as required.

The agreement should specify that prior notice would be given to SACEUR.

I have previously spoken to Secretary McElroy about this matter.[2] The receipt of this message from de Gaulle through his Ambassador indicates that we should do some thinking on this business. Possibly you and McElroy, and maybe even some of the other Defense officials, should have a little conference on the subject.[3] *As ever*

[1] For background see no. 974; on Eisenhower's involvement with this issue as Supreme Allied Commander, Europe, see Galambos, *NATO and the Campaign of 1952*, nos. 692 and 694. Ambassador Hervé Alphand had told Dulles that French President de Gaulle did not propose any change to the commitment of French forces to NATO that would affect Western Europe. Alphand did, however, insist that French naval forces in the Mediterranean should be as free to take independent action as "the U.S. Mediterranean forces, notably the Sixth Fleet" (Dulles to Eisenhower, Jan. 23, 1959, AWF/D-H; Dulles's conversation with Alphand is in State, *Foreign Relations, 1958–1960*, vol. VII, pt. 2, *Western Europe*, pp. 164–66).

[2] No record of this conversation has been found (see State, *Foreign Relations, 1958–1960*, vol. VII, pt. 1, *Western European Integration and Security; Canada*, p. 409).

³ Dulles would tell Eisenhower that he agreed the matter merited "immediate consideration," that State and Defense Department officials were beginning talks, and that he would soon give him "a firm recommendation" (Dulles to Eisenhower, Feb. 3, 1959, WHO/OSS: Subject [State, State Dept.]). On March 3 Assistant Staff Secretary John S. D. Eisenhower would meet with military officials to clarify the peacetime assignment of NATO forces to SACEUR. Technically U.S. and U.K. naval forces remained under national command in peacetime except for short periods of time during training exercises when they were placed under the command of SACEUR.

Although a 1954 change in the assignment of forces to SACEUR had placed peacetime restrictions on the Mediterranean forces of France, Italy, and Greece that were not placed on American and British forces, a subsequent resolution had effectively nullified that arrangement. Under the new resolution, a government could withdraw units committed to NATO in order to meet an emergency elsewhere after informing the appropriate military authorities and the North Atlantic Council. According to John Eisenhower's memorandum the French fleet, for all practical purposes, was as much under national control as were the American and British fleets, and de Gaulle, "as a matter of French pride, [was] belaboring a technicality" (State, *Foreign Relations, 1958–1960*, vol. VII, pt. 1, *Western European Integration and Security; Canada*, pp. 413–15). For developments see no. 1102.

1030   *EM, AWF, Dulles-Herter Series*

To John Foster Dulles   *January 26, 1959*

Dear Foster: This is fine. I made one or two notations that may be of some value. If not, please ignore.¹

Here are a couple of thoughts that you might want to insert where I have marked (a) on page seventeen. I give them to you very roughly, simply as an indication of what I have in mind.

> "The basis of our policy was first announced in 1947. That policy is based, first of all, on our hope of achieving a just peace and firmness in opposing aggression. Ever since that time the American people and their successive governments have stood by these basic purposes steadfastly and firmly in spite of every kind of provocation.
>
> "I assure you that we are as alert and vigilant in seeking every reasonable avenue to achieving a better understanding with those who are hostile to us as we are alert and vigilant in maintaining the kind of strength that will convince any other nation of the folly of aggression against us."²

With warm regard, *As ever*

¹ On this same day Secretary Dulles had asked Eisenhower to look over the draft of a statement he was to make before the House Foreign Affairs Committee. He had told the President that the statement took into account the visit of Soviet First Deputy Chairman Anastas Mikoyan and was similar to the one he had made earlier to the

Senate Foreign Relations Committee (Dulles, Memorandum of Conversation, Jan. 26, 1959, Dulles Papers, White House Memoranda Series. On the Mikoyan visit see no. 993; on Dulles's January 14 remarks to the Senate committee see *U.S. Department of State Bulletin* 40, no. 1023 [February 2, 1959], 151–55).

[2] Dulles would include these paragraphs, with minor changes, in his statement before the House committee on January 28. He would blame the Soviets for the cold war and characterize their proposals for ending it "not remedies but drugs which would numb us to the real danger which will then become greater than ever" (Dulles to Eisenhower, and Statement, Jan. 28, 1959, AWF/D-H; see also *U.S. Department of State Bulletin* 40, no. 1025 [February 16, 1959], 219–22).

1031   *EM, AWF, DDE Diaries Series*

To Douglas MacArthur   *[January 26, 1959]*

My heartfelt congratulations to you as so many of your friends meet to honor you and to celebrate your 79th anniversary. My best wishes for your continued success, health, and happiness.[1]

Your old friend and assistant[2]

[1] Later this same day the President's telegram would be read at a birthday party given for General MacArthur by former staff officers at the Waldorf-Astoria Hotel in New York (*New York Times*, Jan. 27, 1959).

[2] On his handwritten draft of this message Eisenhower had started to write the word "subordinate" but had crossed it out and substituted "assistant."

MacArthur would thank Eisenhower in a wire of this same date (AWF/D).

1032   *EM, AWF, Administration Series: Nixon Corr.*

Diary   *January 27, 1959*

The Vice President, in talking to me last evening mentioned the fact that he had met a number of very fine foreign service officers in the numerous countries he had visited in the past several years.[1] However, from that the Vice President went on to state that an astonishing number of them have no obvious dedication to America and to its service—in fact in some instances they are far more vocal in their criticism of our country than were many of the foreigners that Pat and Dick met.

He thought that this was possibly due to the fact that most of these men had been appointed to the career service during the New Deal years and consequently they felt no loyalty to the present government. Nevertheless, he felt that the matter was somewhat deeper than this, thinking that the tendency represented sort of an expatriate attitude toward his native country.

As an example of the kind of thing, he mentioned a statement made in many forms but with a similar general meaning to the effect "I hope I never have to go back to the United States."

His wife, Pat, who is very sensitive to these things, was more emphatic than Dick in expressions of belief that there was a very great deal of this kind of feeling and thinking in the foreign service.[2]

[1] Eisenhower had given a dinner for Vice-President Nixon and members of the Cabinet. On Nixon's foreign visits see Galambos and van Ee, *The Middle Way*, nos. 608, 1325; and nos. 132 and 711 in these volumes.
[2] According to an addendum by Ann Whitman, after dictating these words, Eisenhower had said: "and the trouble is I don't know what to do about it."

1033   *Prime Minister's Office Records,*
PREM 11/2874

TO HAROLD MACMILLAN   *January 27, 1959*
Cable. Top secret

Dear Harold:[1] Respecting your note, I am sure you have correctly assumed I knew nothing about the Greers Dam turbine contract until the decision affecting it had been effected.[2]

The reason given to me for the decision was that in this country we are getting woefully short of companies that have the kind of heavy machinery that must be used in the production of this large equipment. Our defense mobilization people believe that we should have for safety's sake three or four widely separated facilities where this kind of work can be done. It was this conviction of theirs that led to a decision that national security considerations required the awarding of the contract to the American firm.[3]

So far as I know there is no feasible method by which the decision could be set aside and the matter reviewed. However, on the chance that there is any remaining possibility in this regard, I am having the whole record of the case re-examined. Should there be any change in the situation as I now understand it, I shall inform you promptly.[4]

I regret that my response must be so negative, but at this moment I see no alternative.

With warm regard. *As ever*

[1] The State Department sent the text of this message to the American embassy in London, which then forwarded it to the British Prime Minister.

[2] Macmillan had written Eisenhower regarding the U.S. decision to reject a British bid to supply two turbines for the Greer's Ferry Dam project in Arkansas. "I expect you are as much worried about . . . the contract as I am," Macmillan wrote. He was particularly concerned about the injury "that so small a thing can do to the cause that you and I have so much at heart of Anglo-American cooperation and understanding and the liberalism and interdependence with which your name will always be associated" (Macmillan to Eisenhower, Jan. 27, 1959, same file as document). Before writing to Eisenhower, Macmillan had asked British Ambassador Harold Caccia about the contract: "If lobbying or graft results in a declaration that British equipment is not dependable, and therefore threatens a national emergency, I do not see much future for the high principles which I and the President have called into being about interdependence" (Macmillan to Caccia, Jan. 18, 1959, *ibid.*).

[3] Secretary Dulles would tell the British that no precedent had been established by the decision, and that it did not mean that all future bids by British firms would be rejected on national security grounds (Dulles to Lloyd, Feb. 3, 1959; see also Lloyd to Dulles, Jan. 27, 1959; both in the same file as this document; and Telephone conversation, Dulles and Mann, Jan. 27, 1959, Dulles Papers, Telephone Conversations).

[4] Macmillan would write Eisenhower that although he understood the difficulties of dealing with one particular case, the incident had had "a very sad effect" in Britain. He had learned, however, that the Tennessee Valley Authority had awarded a 500,000-kilowatt turbo-generator contract to C. A. Parsons and Company of Newcastle-upon-Tyne. "This is just the sort of development I hoped for," Macmillan said (Macmillan to Eisenhower, Feb. 10, 1959; and Bishop to Macmillan, Feb. 10, 1959, both in the same file as this document; see also *New York Times*, Feb. 7, 11, 14, 1959).

1034 EM, AWF, Name Series

To Aksel Nielsen

January 27, 1959

Dear Aks: This morning Bill Nicholson was in my office and during the course of the conversation he said (referring to you) "No matter what time of day I call him on the phone, he is always in his office."[1] If this is even approximately true, I cannot tell you how distressing it is to me.[2]

The hardest lesson that any man ever has to learn—but one that he must learn some time in his life unless he puts it off until it is too late—is that he should always work within limits that are logically established by his age and his normal habits of exercise. To run reasonably well for a lifetime is far better than to run very fast for part of a lifetime and then either to stop completely or spend the rest of your life between a rocking chair and an occasional shuffle around the block.

Of course I realize that advice that costs nothing is valued by the recipient at exactly that amount. But at least I have a good deal of experience that gives me a little bit of a platform from which to speak.

I *know* that you need a regular, definite, daily period of complete rest. The habit is easy to form and within a few days is not too irksome. Your best friends—and I certainly hope that you may count me among these—would, if they had listened to doctors as long as I have been compelled to listen, agree completely in the devout hope that you would establish this custom. I am sure that you have no reluctance about following any dietary regulations that your doctor has laid out for you, but I am equally certain that unless you discipline yourself you are going to continue to work too hard and too long every day.[3]

I shall not, of course, nag you on this matter, even though I did send you one prior letter respecting it.[4] This one is simply to assure you that I feel very deeply and earnestly about it—hereafter I will not play the doctor further.

Give my love to Helen and my earnest hope that she is improving steadily and surely.[5]

With all the best to yourself, *As ever*

[1] William F. Nicholson (B.S. Dartmouth 1922) was mayor of Denver and a member of the Cherry Hills Country Club. The former Colorado state senator had served as a colonel in the United States Army Air Force during World War II. On Eisenhower's meeting with Nicholson see Memorandum for the Record, January 28, 1959, AWF/D.
[2] In December Nielsen had been hospitalized for viral pneumonia (see no. 1002).
[3] Following his coronary thrombosis in 1955 the President's physicians had advised him to take a midday rest (see Galambos and van Ee, *The Middle Way*, nos. 1595, 1710, and 1853).
[4] The letter is no. 1002 in these volumes.
[5] On Mrs. Nielsen's health see nos. 954 and 955. Nielsen would reply that he appreciated Eisenhower's concern: "I hope you don't quit reminding me what I should and should not be doing, but really I am trying to do what is right so far as taking care of myself is concerned" (Jan. 30, 1959, AWF/N). Nielsen added that when his wife was well enough to travel they would take an extended vacation.

1035   *EM, AWF, DDE Diaries Series*

To Donald H. Glew, Jr.   *January 27, 1959*

Dear Dr. Glew: I was interested in the account of your latest experiences and, indeed, in the little pamphlet about abdominal wounds.[1]

Respecting the Christmas memento I sent to you and your family, "The Deserted Barn," it has a curious background.

As you well know, I have had no instruction in painting. I know nothing whatsoever about technique and in the course in mechanical drawing I pursued at West Point I was such a failure that I ran the risk of discharge.

Actually, my great interest is colors. They intrigue me and I try to indulge my bent in this direction by applying myself to attempt in oils a representation of any scene or person I can think of. Frankly, I don't even know how to mix colors decently. Sometimes it is a real effort to achieve the approximate color and value I seek.[2]

So far as my latest reproduction is concerned, I started it merely as an imaginative sketch. I wanted to see whether I could, from memory, project the straight lines to their approximately correct vanishing points—and do so without the aid of any model or drawing. In order to make the exercise of some interest to myself, I wanted also to represent desolation or hopelessness if this could be done in a structure. The other items of the composition were put in there merely incidentally, so I might judge my success in achieving the effect of relative distance and of color.

Once I had finished with this particular exercise, I was on the point of throwing it away when other members of the family asked me not to do so. Later I found that they had decided a reproduction would make a nice Christmas memento, but in the meantime I had given the painting away to a friend.[3] So we had to get it back—and that is the way the project got underway despite all the imperfections I could easily see in the thing. After 1961 I am going to start taking lessons.

With warm greetings to your family and personal regard to yourself, *Sincerely*

[1] Major Glew, a member of the United States Army Medical Corps, had been a resident surgeon on the surgical staff at Walter Reed Army Hospital while Eisenhower was recuperating from his ileotransverse colostomy in June 1956 (see Galambos and van Ee, *The Middle Way*, no. 1894). In November, after receiving certification by the American Board of Surgery, Glew had become Chief of Surgery at the United States Army Hospital at the Aberdeen Proving Ground in Maryland. He had written the President on January 17 (WHCF/PPF 1-A-7) to thank him for his Christmas gift, a reproduction of an Eisenhower painting that Glew praised as "an effort worthy of a professional." The pamphlet to which Eisenhower refers is not in EM.
[2] Glew thought that Eisenhower's use of colors was "outstanding."
[3] We have been unable to determine the identity of the friend to whom Eisenhower gave his painting (see *New York Times*, Dec. 23, 1958).

1036

EM, WHCF, Confidential File: Russia

TO ARTHUR HAYS SULZBERGER
Personal and confidential

January 28, 1959

Dear Arthur: Two articles on this morning's editorial page of the TIMES appeal to me very much. I am writing to tell you how greatly

I applaud the main editorial entitled "Soviet Challenge and Western Response."[1] Later I shall send a note to Cy on his column concerning Pope John's move for a greater unity in religious organizations.[2]

Cy well recognizes the great difficulties in the implementation of Pope John's suggestion. These may be insuperable. But I am persuaded that if all religious organizations could direct their attention to one main point, namely that of insisting upon the supremacy of spiritual values and thus demonstrating clear kinship among themselves, there would develop a more unified and stronger purpose among free peoples to yield no single inch or advantage to atheistic communism.

The main editorial has summed up, it seems to me, succinctly and in clear language, the world situation, how it came to this point and what might be done about it.

Until I read the editorial I had not realized that our persistent efforts to reach the Soviets with some kind of proposal that might finally develop into a self-enforcing treaty might be understood as a failure to view the problem as a whole. I think this has possibly come about because of rebuffs that have left us with a feeling that the only avenue to progress was to find some point on which some slight penetration could be effected and agreement be reached and enforced. In any event, your article has set me to pondering whether or not I have been looking at these matters in proper perspective.

I send this note as a personal and confidential one only to express appreciation of two articles that I found both thought-provoking and clearly and lucidly presented.[3]

With warm regard, *As ever*

[1] The lead editorial had reviewed the peace proposals made by the Western powers since World War II and the latest Soviet initiative—the Berlin ultimatum presented to the Western powers on November 27, 1958 (see no. 983). More than the fate of the two million people of Berlin was at stake, the editorial stated; peace itself was involved. Having failed to state their case effectively or to present a detailed plan, the Western powers needed to mobilize the moral forces of the world behind a proposal attractive enough to persuade the Soviets that they had more to gain than to lose by accepting it. Western statesmen had frequently proposed the essential elements of such a plan, but "in such a tentative, cursory and piecemeal manner as to fall short of the impact they should have." A move toward real peace could not start with negotiations over Berlin alone—the Berlin problem was part of the German problem, which in turn was part of the total European problem. The military balance of power could not change to the detriment of either side, the editorial argued. The boundaries of NATO defenses should remain the same; missile bases should be prohibited on German soil; and the military forces of both East and West on German soil should be reduced. Such a comprehensive settlement would win the support of all men of goodwill (*New York Times*, Jan. 28, 1959).

[2] Eisenhower's letter to Cyrus Leo Sulzberger, the newspaper's chief foreign correspondent, is no. 1039.

[3] Arthur Sulzberger, publisher and chairman of the board of the *New York Times*,

would tell Eisenhower that the editorial had been prompted by the recent visit of Deputy Soviet Premier Anastas Mikoyan to the United States (see no. 993). He also told the President that he would like to share the letter with the editor "and the man who did the most work on the piece itself" (Sulzberger to Eisenhower, Jan. 30, 1959, same file as document).

1037   *EM, AWF, DDE Diaries Series*

To W. B. HAMILTON, JR.   *January 28, 1959*

Dear Mr. Hamilton: Thank you so much for your letter concerning my recent appearance at the National Press Club. I enjoyed the informality of the "press conference" and I am delighted that you feel it came through effectively.[1]

You do not give me enough specifics to allow me to form a clear conviction on the matter of the auto accident. However, if you were the very young boy who was struck by a form of taxi that we called a "jitney" somewhere close to 1216 McCullough Avenue, then you can be sure I am the officer who picked you up and carried you across the street to a house that I think was your home.

If this is the accident to which you refer, I can assure you that my memory of the matter is still very clear.[2]

With best wishes, *Sincerely*

[1] Hamilton owned Big Three Welding Equipment Company and San Antonio Oxygen Company in Texas. He had written on January 15 that he hoped all who saw or heard Eisenhower would share the "deep satisfaction" he felt (WHCF/PPF 47 National Press Club). The President had spoken at the National Press Club on January 14 (see no. 1012).

[2] Hamilton, who had briefly reminded Eisenhower of the assistance he had rendered after the mishap, had written: "This incident has probably been long forgotten by you, but I shall ever be in your debt." While stationed at Fort Sam Houston, Texas, Lieutenant Eisenhower had met and courted the First Lady, whose family was spending the winter in a house on McCullough Avenue in San Antonio (see Susan Eisenhower, *Mrs. Ike*, p. 35).

1038   *EM, AWF, International Series:*
                                                        Iran

To MOHAMMED REZA PAHLAVI   *January 30, 1959*
Cable. Secret

Your Majesty, The direct contact which Your Majesty and I have maintained over the past years on matters of mutual interest has always been a source of gratification to me.[1] It is in the context of these friendly exchanges that I now address Your Majesty with respect to certain reports I have received. I have in mind information to the effect that your Government is considering the conclusion of a new treaty with the Soviet Union. While we have no confirmation of this and no knowledge of the precise terms of any proposed treaty, I believe that in view of the possible far-reaching implications of the matter I should let you know of my concern.[2]

The most troublesome aspect of these reports is the implication, as we see it, for the future security of your country. It is my profound conviction that the principal objective of the Soviet Union in Iran remains unchanged and that that objective is inconsistent with Iran's independence and integrity and with the security and stability of Your Majesty's regime. History demonstrates that the Soviet Union has repeatedly used non-aggression and "friendship" pacts to lull prospective victims and make them less alert to their danger. I refer, for example, to Latvia, Lithuania, Esthonia,[3] Finland, Poland and the Nationalist Government of China. The Soviet Union has recently manipulated its economic relations with Finland and Yugoslavia in attempts to interfere in their internal affairs.[4] In a major policy speech January 27, Premier Khrushchev spoke in support of the Communist Party in the United Arab Republic and that Party's opposition to that Government's policies, and sharply attacked the United Arab Republic as "reactionary" because the government has adopted certain domestic measures to combat the internal communist threat.[5]

I realize, of course, that Your Majesty has had long experience in dealing with Soviet pressures and threats, as well as with Soviet blandishments. From our many past contacts I know that you are aware that a Soviet objective is to separate Iran from its friends and allies and, as one means of achieving this, to destroy the collective security arrangements among Iran, Turkey, and Pakistan, supported by the United Kingdom and the United States.[6] Indeed, during his recent visit here Soviet Deputy Prime Minister Mikoyan made no secret of this.[7] I feel certain that the Soviet Union still desires to create a situation in which its subversive efforts in Iran will be given a much better chance of success than now exists because of the firm policies of, and precautions exercised by, Your Majesty and your Government. It would suit Soviet purposes to achieve a situation in which it appeared that Iran's devotion to the principle of collective security and Iran's cooperation with other members of the Free World had been weakened.

I know, of course, that Your Majesty must do what you consider to be in the best interests of your country. In making your decisions, you have always wisely considered possible internal and external reactions. Almost regardless of the actual terms of any new treaty with the Soviet Union, the impact on your friends would be unhappy.

I understand that you are gravely preoccupied with the increasing pressures that have been placed on Iran by the Soviet Union and other countries. I am entirely sympathetic with you in this concern. My letter to you of July 19, 1958, was clear evidence of my country's desire to strengthen Iran's security position.[8] Indeed, the whole history of Iranian-American relations is marked by examples of United States determination to help Iran in the preservation of its independence and integrity. We are no less determined to continue this policy.

It is inevitable that differences should arise between the best of friends, and Iran and the United States are no exceptions. Such differences as we have had, however, have never related to fundamental principles or to basic objectives. One difference has arisen over our respective estimates of the size of the military program that should be maintained, and could be supported, without grave jeopardy to the Iranian economy. It has been reported to me that you are also concerned with the role of your country in the Baghdad Pact and that you have some concern regarding the content of the bilateral agreements being negotiated pursuant to the London Declaration of July 1958.[9] I do not want to burden you with a recitation of our position in these matters, but I do want to emphasize that our continued strong determination to support Iran's independence and integrity has not in the past depended upon, and need not in the future depend upon, any particular provision of formal agreements between us. The consistent role of the United States in supporting its friends, and particularly Iran, is clear.

I recall with great pleasure the frank and cordial conversations we had when you visited Washington last summer, and I also recall your impressive grasp of world affairs and your appreciation of the nature of the threat, not only to your country, but to all free nations.[10] I am confident that you would not knowingly take a step which would imperil your country's security and possibly weaken Iran's relations with its proven friends, and that we can continue to work together to accomplish our common aims in a spirit of frankness and mutual confidence. Certainly you can be assured of our continuing support for Iran.

I have asked Ambassador Wailes to discuss this matter with Your Majesty and to transmit to me as soon as possible Your Majesty's response.[11]

With warm personal regard, *Sincerely*

---

[1] See, for example, Galambos and van Ee, *The Middle Way*, no. 2133 and no. 779 in these volumes.

² CIA Director Allen Dulles had told the National Security Council that Iran had felt "let down" by the United States and was considering a fifty-year non-aggression pact with the Soviet Union. On this same day Eisenhower had told Secretary Dulles that the situation was "disturbing" and that the Shah was "engaging in blackmail." Both men agreed that they would "not play that way" (Telephone conversations, Eisenhower and Dulles, Jan. 30, 1959; and Dulles and Rountree, Jan. 29, 1959, State, *Foreign Relations, 1958–1960*, vol. XII, *Near East Region; Iraq; Iran; Arabian Peninsula*, pp. 626–27; see also NSC meeting minutes, Nov. 13, 1958, Jan. 22, 1959, AWF/NSC; and Synopsis of State and Intelligence Material, Jan. 20, 30, 1959, AWF/D. On U.S. policy toward Iran and State Department contacts with the U.S. ambassador regarding the proposed treaty see State, *Foreign Relations, 1958–1960*, vol. XII, *Near East Region; Iraq; Iran; Arabian Peninsula*, pp. 605–15; 622–24). State Department officials drafted this letter and, after receiving Eisenhower's approval, had sent it by cable to the American embassy in Tehran for delivery to the Shah.

³ Estonia.

⁴ The Soviet Union had shown increasing displeasure with the government of Finland, which was dominated by socialists. Soviet officials had delayed trade talks and had informed three large Finnish metal manufacturers that regardless of contracts, Soviet exports would be curtailed. They had also recently withdrawn their ambassador without appointing a successor, and in December the ruling coalition had collapsed (State, *Foreign Relations, 1958–1960*, vol. X, pt. 2, *Eastern Europe; Finland; Greece; Turkey*, pp. 515–26; see also *New York Times*, Oct. 13, Nov. 23, Dec. 5, 1958).

Yugoslavia had long been the target of Soviet attacks on revisionist attempts to liberalize Marxist doctrine. Recent trade talks between the two countries had collapsed, and the Soviets were demanding increased shipments of raw materials while at the same time accepting fewer Yugoslavian industrial products (*New York Times*, Jan. 18, 23, 1959; see also *Foreign Relations, 1958–1960*, vol. X, pt. 2, *Eastern Europe; Finland; Greece; Turkey*, p. 366).

⁵ Khrushchev had spoken before 1,200 delegates to the twenty-first congress of the Soviet Communist Party (State, *Foreign Relations, 1958–1960*, vol. X, pt. 1, *Eastern Europe Region; Soviet Union; Cyprus*, pp. 258–60; and *New York Times*, Jan. 28, 1959).

⁶ This alliance was the Baghdad Pact; for background see Galambos and van Ee, *The Middle Way*, no. 1681; see also State, *Foreign Relations, 1958–1960*, vol. XII, *Near East Region; Iraq; Iran; Arabian Peninsula*, pp. 120–21.

⁷ On the Mikoyan visit see no. 993.

⁸ See no. 779.

⁹ The London Declaration, formulated and signed at the July meeting of the Baghdad Pact Ministerial Council, provided for multilateral agreements to preserve the security of the Baghdad Pact countries, and Secretary Dulles had told Eisenhower that the United States had been negotiating these with Iran, Pakistan, and Turkey. He also told the President that these countries had expressed concern that U.S. support for the pact had begun to wane (State, *Foreign Relations, 1958–1960*, vol. XII, *Near East Region; Iraq; Iran; Arabian Peninsula*, pp. 111–14, 126, 173, 614, 623; NSC meeting minutes, Aug. 1, 1958, AWF/NSC; see also Dulles to Eisenhower, Jan. 21, 1959, AWF/D-H; and no. 791 in these volumes. For the text of the declaration see State, *American Foreign Policy; Current Documents, 1958*, pp. 894–95).

¹⁰ The Shah had begun an unofficial three-day visit to the United States on June 30 (see State, *Foreign Relations, 1958–1960*, vol. XII, *Near East Region; Iraq; Iran; Arabian Peninsula*, pp. 562–75).

¹¹ U.S. Ambassador Edward T. Wailes would inform the State Department that he had delivered Eisenhower's letter to the Shah on January 31. The Iranian leader was grateful for U.S. aid, Wailes reported, but complained that the amount did not enable Iran to progress in either the economic or military areas. He was, therefore, negotiating a non-aggression pact with the Soviet Union to provide additional security.

The negotiators were far apart, however, and Wailes thought the Shah would welcome a breakdown in the talks (*ibid.*, pp. 029–32). The Shah would later reassure Eisenhower that Iran intended to remain in the Baghdad Pact and would maintain relations with the West. Talks with the Soviet Union had collapsed, he would write, and the Soviet delegation had left "in a huff" for Moscow (Pahlavi to Eisenhower, Feb. 11, 1959, AWF/I: Iran).

Acting Secretary Herter would inform Eisenhower on February 23 that negotiations to formulate the bilateral agreements between the United States and Turkey, Pakistan, and Iran had concluded. Despite Soviet threats against Iran, he expected the agreements to be signed in Ankara within the week (*ibid.*). The pacts would in fact be signed on March 5. For more on Iranian affairs see no. 1391.

1039   *EM, WHCF, Official File 144*

To Cyrus Leo Sulzberger   *January 31, 1959*
Personal

Dear Cy: Your column in the TIMES on Thursday morning of last week interested me greatly. It concerned, of course, Pope John's suggestion to convene an Oecumenical Council.[1]

I personally support the idea because I believe that much good can come out of it provided that the objective is simple, clear-cut, and one that can achieve unanimous approval.

There is no need to dwell here upon the obvious difficulties that would be encountered in an attempt merely to convene a council of all faiths. But assuming the convening of such a great body of religious leaders, I believe that if all factions could direct their attention to a single main point—namely that of insisting upon the supremacy of spiritual values and thus demonstrating clear kinship among themselves—there would develop a more unified and stronger purpose among free peoples to yield no single inch or advantage to atheistic communism.[2]

My fear would be that zealots would introduce so many questions and argumentative subjects into a convocation of such a kind that most of the discussion would revolve around relatively unimportant points. On the other hand, the need, in my opinion, is for recognition of the ascendency of spiritual values and a ringing declaration that it is because of their importance that free men always stand ready, individually and collectively, to defend them, support them and advance them. Such a declaration, I believe, would do much to alert us to the threat posed by Communist imperialism, and to unite us better in the search for peace.

Most of this I wrote to Arthur, but I also wanted to tell you personally how much your column appealed to me.

Here in Washington things go on much the same, though the problems that occupy every twenty-four hours change. At the moment, of course, Berlin occupies most of our attention on the international scene—and the fight on the budget is shaping up as the predominant topic as far as domestic matters are concerned.[3]

Al and I are, of course, undisputed bridge champions whenever we get an opportunity to play.[4] That opportunity doesn't come too often, primarily because he seems constantly to be on the speech-making trail.

With warm regard to you and Marina, and congratulations on an excellent article.[5] *Sincerely*

[1] For background see no. 1036. Sulzberger, chief foreign correspondent for the *New York Times*, had written about Pope John XXIII's desire for unity with other Christian communities and his call for an end to the spiritual conflict that existed, particularly between the Roman and the Greek Orthodox churches. "Even a slight success would have much political importance," Sulzberger had written. "For if all those who believe in divinity can in any way be drawn together, communism will suffer a serious setback" (*New York Times*, Jan. 28, 1958).

[2] For more of Eisenhower's thoughts on spiritual values see no. 971.

[3] On the tensions regarding Berlin see no. 983; on the budget see no. 1040.

[4] The reference is to Eisenhower's close friend and bridge partner Alfred M. Gruenther.

[5] Sulzberger's wife was the former Marina Tatiana Lada. Sulzberger would profess himself "flattered" by Eisenhower's letter. "I was sure you would support the Pope's idea," he would write. "I can only hope that the groundwork for his proposed conference is laid with such expert preparation that it will stand a real chance of success" (Sulzberger to Eisenhower, Feb. 10, 1958, same file as document).

1040   *EM, WHCF, Official File 115-E*

TO ROBERT DOUGLAS STUART   *January 31, 1959*

Dear Douglas: Thank you very much for your note. I am delighted that you are apparently once again feeling quite like yourself and that you were able to get away for a little quail shooting in Alabama (even if the results were not up to expectations).[1]

Your support of the program of the Administration to balance the Budget is highly gratifying. I agree with you completely that it is difficult to dramatize the dangers of inflation and while I am willing to resort to television in an effort to talk to the people of the country as a whole, I find that it is very hard, even using that media, to get much coverage or interest.[2] For instance, the day the Budget Message went up to the Congress I did a short, approximately three minute talk, recorded for use on the news programs. I am told it was not used to any great degree; I can assume only that the net works felt the public would not be interested. At any rate, the proposal to use the television is constantly before me, and I probably shall make one or two talks during the forthcoming and inevitable battle on the Hill.[3]

Incidentally, I suppose you saw the recent Gallup Poll on the subject (just in case you did not, I am enclosing a clipping). While I do not have complete faith in polls, it indicates an awareness on the part of the public that is encouraging. [4]

When you make that visit to Washington by all means give my office a ring; if at all possible I should like very much to see you.[5]

Again my thanks for your letter, and warm personal regard. *Sincerely*

[1] Former Quaker Oats Company President Stuart had resigned as U.S. Ambassador to Canada in April 1956 (for background see Galambos, *NATO and the Campaign of 1952*, no. 908, and Galambos and van Ee, *The Middle Way*, no. 1662). His January 28, 1959, letter (same file as document) described his recent vacation with Eisenhower friends Lucius and Marjorie Clay and Kathrine Bermingham.

[2] While Stuart believed that Eisenhower's news conferences were helpful in delivering his message, it was "exceedingly difficult to dramatize the dangers of inflation through the printed word." "Our citizens have complete confidence in you," he wrote, "so I suggest in all humility that the only effective way of presenting the grave dangers of inflation to the people of our country is through a series of television programs—reverting, if you will, to the technique that President Roosevelt used in his Fireside Chats. I had no love for President Roosevelt but I am convinced that the Fireside Chats had a tremendous impact on the people (*ibid.*)". See also no. 958.

[3] For background see nos. 976 and 961. Eisenhower had presented his budget message to Congress on January 19 (*Public Papers of the Presidents: Eisenhower, 1959*, pp. 36–113). Concerned about continued inflation and the outflow of gold, the President had called for expenditures of about $77 billion. Since receipts were estimated to be $77.1 billion, a surplus of $70 million was forecast. These figures were based upon continued improvement in the economy, congressional action to reduce expenditures and an increase in certain rates and excise taxes (see *Congressional Quarterly Almanac*, vol. XV, *1959*, pp. 644–48; see also Morgan, *Eisenhower Versus 'The Spenders,'* pp. 127–51). For developments see no. 1042.

[4] Eisenhower had enclosed a clipping from the January 31, 1959 *Washington Post and Times Herald* reporting the results of a January 30 Gallup poll on the budget. Fifty-six percent of Gallup's sample believed that if the budget was unbalanced, prices would rise, and fifty-eight percent believed that an unbalanced budget would lead to a decrease in the value of the dollar (see George H. Gallup, *The Gallup Poll: Public Opinion 1935–1971*, 3 vols. [New York, 1972], vol. III, *1959–1971*, pp. 1588–89).

[5] The Ambassador would not visit with the President at the White House.

To JOHN HENRY RAY   *February 2, 1959*

Dear John: Thank you for your letter to Bryce Harlow concerning the quotation from Lincoln that I have used so often and that, to me, represents the finest statement that has yet been made as to the proper role of the government in the lives of our citizens. I did know that the exact statement had been found in "fragments" published after Lincoln's death.[1]

You make an interesting point that Lincoln made no distinction between federal and state government—or, for that matter—local government.[2] In our efforts to get the communities and states to assume more responsibility, we are, of course, trying to return to the control of the leaders in those communities the affairs of the people.[3] Despite the complexity of our society, the local and state governments are a part of the life of the average citizen that the far-off Federal government can never hope to achieve.

Again my appreciation of your interest, and warm regard, *Sincerely*

[1] On January 20 White House aide Bryce Harlow had forwarded to the President a letter he had received from New York Republican Congressman John Ray (LL.B. Harvard 1911). A member of Congress since 1953, Ray had been associated with the American Telephone and Telegraph Company from 1923–1951. Ray had found the source for the statement made by Lincoln on the purposes of government, frequently cited by Eisenhower, in two "fragments" published in the *Complete Works of Abraham Lincoln*, edited by John G. Nicolay and John Hay, 12 vols. (c. 1905): "The legitimate object of government is to do for a community of people whatever they need to have done, but cannot do at all, or cannot so well do, for themselves, in their separate and individual capacities" (see Galambos and van Ee, *The Middle Way*, no. 1861; see also Larson, *The President Nobody Knew*, pp. 125–27).

[2] Ray had also included a portion of a speech made by Lincoln to the House of Representatives on June 20, 1848. Lincoln had suggested that the federal government be responsible for larger projects and the states the smaller ones, "and thus, working in a meeting direction, discreetly, but steadily and firmly, what is made unequal in one place may be equalized in another, extravagance avoided, and the whole country put on that career of prosperity which shall correspond with its extent of territory, its natural resources, and the intelligence and the enterprise of its people." The other fragments, Ray noted, made no distinction between the federal and the state governments. Harlow had recommended that the President should reply: "If he should send a little note to Ray, Ray's joy would know no bounds" (Harlow to Whitman, June 20, 1959, same file as document).

[3] In his January 9 State of the Union Address, the President had called for increased federal spending on health programs, science and education, the development of water resources, urban renewal and federal highways. At the same time he observed: "The major responsibility for development in these fields rests in the localities, even though the Federal Government will continue to do its proper part in meeting the genuine needs of a burgeoning population" (*Public Papers of the Presidents: Eisenhower, 1959*, p. 10).

To William Edward Robinson   *February 3, 1959*

Dear Bill: I know that you are as much concerned as I am about the
potential danger of future inflation and of the damaging effects of
deficit spending by the Federal government, particularly in a period
of rising prosperity. Moreover, all of us are aware that security costs
are most burdensome, but must remain so during the foreseeable
future. But if we can keep Federal spending within the aggregate
given in the balanced budget that I sent to the Congress, we will do
much to sustain the integrity and purchasing power of our dollar,
so necessary to the steady and sound expansion of our economy.[1]

I realize that inflation is not caused solely by Federal deficit spending, but such deficits are one of the inciting causes. Moreover, it is
one that people can help defeat by seeing that appropriations are
kept to sensible levels.[2]

In the development of the budget we first provided adequately
for the unequivocally necessary programs, such as the nation's security and interest on the debt. Other programs, highly desirable
and, at certain levels at least, necessary, were provided for according to their degree of indispensability. Appropriations for most of
these programs have been steadily increasing during recent years,
some of them markedly. In many programs it is not only possible
but reasonable to diminish the rate of increase of these appropriations, while in others real savings can be made without damage to
the United States.

For example, the budget now before the Congress provides for
the continued support of such programs as housing,[3] depressed area
development[4] and improvement of air fields.[5] Recommended appropriations for these activities reflect the good of the entire nation
rather than only the special interests of particular groups. I am informed that the Congress is moving *rapidly*[6] toward the passage of
bills in the three fields I have just mentioned. Unfortunately it seems
apparent that these bills will fix far higher appropriation levels than
I believe justified. If passed, they will unbalance the budget before
we are well started in the session.

I am enclosing some abbreviated fact sheets so that you can compare my budgetary recommendations with the possible expenditures
to be authorized by Congress.[7]

Already the headquarters of major organizations are committed
to help toward influencing the Congress to keep spending no higher
than the recommended levels. I sincerely hope that you will, *as speedily as possible*, help in every way that you think proper.[8] I assure you
that I shall do everything within my power to this end.

With warm regard, *Sincerely*

P.S. One other program which I did not mention, but which on no account must be reduced, is that dealing with our mutual security. It is vital to our nation's welfare and the free world's military, moral and economic strength.[9]

[1] Eisenhower had sent an identical letter to several of his friends, including Gabriel Hauge, Richard Mellon, and Charles S. Jones (see correspondence in WHCF/OF 107-B). On the budget message see no. 1040.

[2] See no. 976.

[3] In his budget message to Congress, Eisenhower had recommended that states and cities assume a gradually increasing share of urban renewal costs. His request would trigger a major congressional fight over housing legislation (*Public Papers of the Presidents: Eisenhower, 1959*, pp. 82–86; *Congressional Quarterly Almanac*, vol. XV, *1959*, pp. 245–56). For developments see no. 1224.

[4] For background see Galambos and van Ee, *The Middle Way*, no. 1579. The 1959 budget had called for area redevelopment legislation that would place the major responsibility on local citizens, authorize loans to places where unemployment had been above the national average for two or more years; authorize grants for technical assistance to these stricken areas and to those dependent upon a single industry or situated in rural low-income areas; and give responsibility for overseeing these programs to the Department of Commerce, which could call upon the assistance of other federal agencies.

The congressional bill would far exceed the Administration's requests for an area redevelopment program. The Area Redevelopment Act of 1959, in its final form, would establish an Area Redevelopment Administration to identify areas of need; authorize borrowing of $200 million from the Treasury to set up two revolving loan funds for industrial and rural redevelopment; allow the borrowing of an additional $100 million for the construction and improvement of public facilities; and authorize appropriations of an additional $89.5 million for other specified loans and grants (*Congressional Quarterly Almanac*, vol. XV, *1959*, pp. 221–24).

[5] Eisenhower's budget message had called for "an orderly withdrawal" from a program in effect since 1946, which had authorized the federal government to pay half the cost of building airports. Congress's airport construction bill—calling for a $575 million, five-year program designed to prepare the nation's airports for the new jet aircraft—had followed the same formula as the airport bill of 1958 that Eisenhower had pocket-vetoed (*Public Papers of the Presidents: Eisenhower, 1959*, pp. 78–79; *Congressional Quarterly Almanac*, vol. XV, *1959*, pp. 225–28). For developments see no. 1114.

[6] Eisenhower had underscored by hand both this term and the words "as speedily as possible."

[7] The President had included with his letter four fact sheets (WHCF/OF 107-B). The first outlined the U.S. budget for fiscal year 1960; the second detailed the Administration's proposals for aid to airports; the third contrasted the Administration's proposals for area assistance with the bill in the Senate; and the fourth compared the differences between the Administration's proposals for housing and urban renewal with the provisions in the Senate bill. The fact sheets pointed out that the congressional price tag for the airport bill was roughly 450 million dollars higher than the Administration's proposal and that the Senate Housing Bill would authorize expenditures of almost $3 billion, as compared to the Administration's $1.65 billion price tag.

[8] Robinson would reply on February 9, 1959 (AWF/N). He promised to "get in touch with some of my old friends among the newspaper editors, columnists, and televi-

sion and radio commentators in the hope of getting them to see the grave danger of an unbalanced budget as a spur to inflation." For other responses to Eisenhower's appeal for support on the budget see the correspondence in WHCF/OF 107-B. For developments see no. 1087.

[9] For background on the mutual security program see nos. 753 and 782. On March 13, 1959, Eisenhower would deliver a special message to Congress detailing his request for the 1960 Mutual Security Program (see *Public Papers of the Presidents: Eisenhower, 1959*, pp. 255–72). Calling mutual security "essential to our survival and important to our prosperity," the President outlined a program that essentially followed the same pattern as that of the Mutual Security Act of 1958. In July Congress would authorize $3,556,200,000 ($373,795,000 less than the President requested; see *Congressional Quarterly Almanac*, vol. XV, *1959*, pp. 178–94). For developments see no. 1150.

1043   *EM, AWF, Dulles-Herter Series*

To John Foster Dulles   *February 3, 1959*
Memorandum

Attention: The Under Secretary of State for Economic Affairs: I send you herewith the Determination under Section 451(a) of the Mutual Security Act of 1954, as requested by your memorandum of January 30, 1959.[1] I assume, of course, that this matter was completely staffed, but I send along two items that I think may have some bearing on it. It is possible that you may not have seen both.

The first is a clipping from the New York Times today.[2] The second is a notation found in the Central Intelligence Bulletin under date 3 February 1959. It is the final item on page one and deals with Communist shipments to Indonesia.[3]

[1] Under Secretary of State C. Douglas Dillon had requested that Eisenhower authorize, under the relevant provisions of the Mutual Security Act of 1954, up to $15 million from funds available in 1959 to furnish military assistance to Indonesia. The funds would augment a similar determination for $7 million in aid that Eisenhower had authorized in August 1958. Dillon added that the military assistance program in Indonesia had produced a "favorable impact," had helped stem Communist advances, and was clearly important to the security of the United States (Dillon to Eisenhower, Jan. 30, 1959, WHCF/CF: Mutual Security and Assistance; see also Dulles to Eisenhower, Feb. 3, 1959, *ibid.*; and State, *Foreign Relations, 1958–1960*, vol. XVII, *Indonesia*, pp. 316–18. For background on Indonesia's political situation see no. 662; see also NSC meeting minutes, Jan. 29, 1959, AWF/NSC; and State, *Foreign Relations, 1958–1960*, vol. XVII, *Indonesia*, pp. 334–44).

Eisenhower asked that the State Department notify the following parties about this action: the Senate Committee on Foreign Relations; the Speaker of the House of Representatives; the Secretary of Defense; and the Director of the Bureau of the Budget (Eisenhower to Dulles, Feb. 3, 1959, WHCF/CF: Mutual Security and Assistance).

[2] The *New York Times* article had recounted the impatience felt by Indonesian officials because the United States had failed to respond to their two-month-old request for military assistance. The article speculated that further delays could force the Indonesian government to buy the equipment elsewhere. An Indonesian army officer was also quoted as saying that after the arms arrived in Indonesia they would then be used against a rebellion in Sumatra and the Celebes—the same rebellion that had been covertly supported by the United States (*New York Times*, Feb. 3, 1959).

[3] The highly classified Central Intelligence Agency bulletin (WHCF/CF Mutual Security and Assistance) had noted that the Sino-Soviet bloc had recently transferred four piston-engine light bombers to the Indonesian government. This shipment was part of a larger aid package that had provided the Indonesians with fifty-five jet fighters and twenty to thirty twin-jet bombers. Indonesian President Sukarno would express his gratitude to Eisenhower for the American assistance, but he emphasized that as much as military and economic aid meant to Indonesia, political support meant even more (State, *Foreign Relations, 1958–1960*, vol. XVII, *Indonesia*, p. 350).

European allies of the United States, particularly Great Britain and West Germany, would also provide military assistance to Indonesia, ending any further significant requests from Jakarta for Soviet aid (Kahin and Kahin, *Subversion as Foreign Policy*, pp. 205–9). For developments in U.S.-Indonesian relations see no. 1763.

1044

EM, WHCF,
President's Personal File 308-B

To James Paul Mitchell

February 3, 1959

Dear Jim: My only quarrel with the dramatic list of "failures" of Abraham Lincoln is that he did serve, during that period, for one term in the Congress.[1] Perhaps that is not exactly a success! And perhaps also the Republican Party can find a parallel and a hope somewhere in the record.[2]

Incidentally, I understand that you made a very effective appearance on one of the television programs yesterday.[3] Congratulations—and thanks.

With warm regard, *Sincerely*

[1] Labor Secretary Mitchell had written on January 31, 1959 (same file as document), enclosing a brief story about "a businessman, who, whenever someone comes to his office bemoaning his misfortune in business, love, or life in general, takes him aside and invites him to study a framed, hand-lettered sign hanging on the wall. It reads: Failed in business, '31; Defeated for legislature, '32; Failed in business again, '33; Sweetheart died, '35; Suffered nervous breakdown, '36; Defeated for Congress, '43; Defeated for Senate, '55; Defeated for Vice President, '56; Defeated for Senate, '58; Elected President of the United States, '60. And the name beneath this record of misfortune, crowned by final success? Abraham Lincoln." Mitchell had suggested that this story might "have some significance in the present dilemma of the Republican Party."

Eisenhower was referring to the fact that Lincoln had been elected as Representative from the Seventh Congressional District of Illinois on August 3, 1846. Running

as a Whig, he had defeated his Democratic opponent by a large majority (David Herbert Donald, *Lincoln* [New York, 1995], pp. 114–15).
² See no. 1025.
³ Mitchell had spoken on "Face the Nation" on CBS on Sunday, February 1. He had defended the Eisenhower Administration's guided missile programs (see nos. 457 and 1051), and had stated that he would accept the nomination for Vice-President if offered by the Republican party (*New York Times*, Feb. 2, 1959).

1045   *EM, AWF, Dulles-Herter Series*

To John Foster Dulles   *February 5, 1959*
Personal

Memorandum for the Secretary of State:
    Note: To be held until after he returns from Europe[1]
I have had several conversations with the head of the Immigration Service who believes that we are making a mistake in our failure to attempt to extend the provisions of Public Law 414 to areas other than Canada and Bermuda.[2] I believe a case that is currently under consideration is that of the Bahamas. Eventually, of course, General Swing believes that waivers of non-immigrant visas should be extended to the countries of Western Europe.

General Swing admits that he has had serious differences of opinion with the State Department, but he believes the matter should be reconsidered. He says that Congressman Walters, J. Edgar Hoover and Clarence Randall, as well as the Hoover Commission and the Wright report all support his conclusion that we are not operating very efficiently in this respect.[3]

At some future time, at your convenience, I should like to talk to you about the matter.[4]

¹ On Secretary Dulles's trip to London, Paris, and Bonn see no. 1057.
² For background on General Joseph M. Swing, appointed commissioner of the Immigration and Naturalization Service in May 1954, see Galambos and van Ee, *The Middle Way*, no. 571; see also *ibid.*, no. 819. Eisenhower is referring to the Immigration and Nationality Act of 1952 (see Galambos and van Ee, *The Middle Way*, no. 101; and *U.S. Statutes at Large*, vol. 66 [1952], pp. 163, 169, 189, 191–96). Swing had proposed that pre-flight inspections, conducted in the countries of origin by the INS, should replace the issuance of non-immigrant visas.
³ These were Democratic Congressman from Pennsylvania Francis Eugene Walter, FBI Director Hoover, and Chairman of the Council on Foreign Economic Policy Randall. For background on the Hoover Commission see nos. 157 and 846. For background on Loyd Wright, Los Angeles lawyer and chairman of the International Bar Association, see Galambos and van Ee, *The Middle Way*, no. 920. In 1957 Wright had headed the Commission on Government Security, which had recommended, as had the Hoover Commission, that the 1952 act be amended to transfer authority for the

issuance of most visas from the Department of State to the Department of Justice (*Report of the Commission on Government Security* [Washington, D.C., 1957], pp. 519–25, 550–61, 566–67, 572–78, 602, 604).

On May 12, 1958, Eisenhower had sent Congress a report prepared by Randall that recommended the liberalization of restrictions to international travel and proposed giving the State Department and the Immigration and Naturalization Service the authority to waive U.S. visa requirements (U.S. Congress, House, *International Travel: A Report on the Barriers to International Travel and Ways and Means of Promoting and Developing, Encouraging, and Facilitating Such Travel,* A Message from the President of the United States, 85th Cong., 2d sess., *Miscellaneous House Documents,* House Doc. 381, Fiche 4, no. 12142, 46, nn. 348, 372, 381, 449 [Washington, D.C., 1958]; *U.S. Department of State Bulletin* 39, no. 988 [June 2, 1958], 922; and *New York Times,* May 13, 1958).

[4] On this same day Eisenhower had asked Budget Director Maurice Stans about the visa issue (Eisenhower to Stans, Feb. 5, 1959, AWF/D). Stans would reply that the Budget Bureau had already undertaken a preliminary study of non-immigrant visa waivers and pre-flight inspections. He had also sent the INS proposal to waive visa requirements for Cuba, Mexico, and the Bahamas to the State Department and to the Central Intelligence Agency for comments (Stans to Eisenhower, Feb. 17, 1959, AWF/A).

Eisenhower, who said he had a "keen personal interest" in the problem, would meet with Deputy Under Secretary of State for Administration Loy Henderson and Under Secretary C. Douglas Dillon. Eisenhower would tell them that General Swing believed that the lower echelons of the State Department had resisted his ideas for a new screening policy for immigrants. Although Henderson would say that he did not believe that pre-flight inspections would provide screenings comparable to current procedures, he said that he would be "quite happy to abide by any decision the President might reach" (J. S. D. Eisenhower, Memorandum of Conference, Feb. 14, 1959, AWF/D; see also Greene, Memorandum of Conversation, Feb. 9, 1959, Dulles Papers, White House Memoranda Series; and Ann Whitman memorandum, Feb. 14, 1959, AWF/AWD).

Although the issue would not be settled during Eisenhower's presidency, changes in federal regulations would result in liberalized restrictions on non-immigrant aliens in 1959 (see U.S. Department of State, *Federal Register of Rules and Regulations,* Title 22, pt. 41, 1959, pp. 1901, 8548, 11080–83; see also *Congressional Quarterly Almanac,* vol. XVI, *1960,* pp. 304–5).

1046   *EM, AWF, Name Series*

To Edgar Newton Eisenhower   *February 7, 1959*

Dear Ed: Thank you for sending me the piece by Raymond Moley.[1] I was much interested in it, and I do not for a minute think he exaggerates the difficulties ahead in the battle for the balanced budget and against inflationary measures. Witness the Congressional actions of the last week, for example.[2]

You mention Mr. Moley's association with President Roosevelt.[3] I am not sure that you realize that in 1952 he was helpful and active in my campaign; he has not always agreed with me since that time but I am glad that on the present primary domestic issue we do see eye to eye.

It was wonderful to have you in Washington; you must have another birthday party soon so we can work up another family celebration.[4]

With love to Lucy, and all the best to yourself, *As ever*

[1] The President's brother had written on February 3, 1959 (AWF/N) to forward a newspaper article by Moley, a contributing editor with *Newsweek* since 1937. In an article entitled "Ike and His Final Struggle" Moley had argued that by selecting a balanced budget and inflation as his primary issues with Congress, the President had chosen a battlefield where the odds were "fearfully" against him. While inflation was universally opposed in the abstract, in day-to-day affairs "the essence of it is favored by innumerable somebodies." Moreover, the psychological nature of inflation—which could spawn fears concerning the value of money and could lead to capital flight—would prevent the President from pointing out inflation's perils as a means of summoning public support: "The President must induce caution without exciting fear. That is a formidable task."

[2] The previous week the Senate Banking Committee had approved an omnibus housing bill appropriating approximately $1 billion more than the President had requested (see no. 1042; *New York Times*, Feb. 3, 1959).

[3] Edgar had written that Moley, Assistant Secretary of State in 1933, had been "a member of the Roosevelt 'brain trust,' [but] he very quickly left that position for Newsweek."

[4] The Eisenhowers had hosted a 70th birthday celebration for Edgar on January 19, 1959. The family dinner had included Milton Eisenhower, Mr. and Mrs. Earl Eisenhower, Major and Mrs. John Eisenhower, as well as the honoree and his wife. See also no. 978.

1047   *EM, AWF, Name Series*

To William Edward Robinson   *February 9, 1959*

Dear Bill: This morning I started, among my staff members, an inquiry as to the situation in New York State that had so aroused your ire toward the new Governor.[1] The facts, as I understand them, are somewhat as follows:

(*a*). When Dewey left the Governor's chair, there was in the Treasury a small surplus, as well as one or two contingency funds.[2]

(*b*). During the four years of Harriman's regime, these surpluses were expended and a considerable deficit incurred.[3]

(*c*). Throughout his political campaign last fall, Rockefeller insisted that he must eliminate that deficit and thereafter the state government should live within its means.[4]

(*d*). It seems that the programs which have caused this deficit over the past four years have been in vogue for a considerable time. In other words, no one knows whether or not they could now be eliminated.[5]

(*e*). It is for this reason that Rockefeller's emphasis was placed upon raising more revenue rather than reducing expenditures.

Whether or not this is a true picture of the situation and the developments I do not know. At the very least it is somewhat different from the impression you have from your conversations in New York.

I hope you and Barry made New York safely and without too much discomfort or delay. As always, it was a great pleasure to be with you—especially in the relaxed atmosphere at Milestone.[6] I have, however, one piece of bad news to report: I gained six pounds in four days! Now I have just one more problem in life—I have either to get rid of that excess immediately or some alterations have to take place in my wardrobe.

With warm regard,[7] *As ever*

---

[1] In a February 9 letter to Eisenhower (see no. 1042), Coca-Cola President Robinson had reported that the editor of the *New York Daily News* had told him that the paper had received more mail concerning New York Governor Rockefeller's spending and tax program than about any other political matter in the history of the newspaper. Ninety-five percent of the mail was in opposition to Rockefeller's programs. Most of the public's irritation was in response to Rockefeller's recent request that the state legislature approve a record rise in state taxes, including personal income taxes, the cigarette tax, and the estate tax (*New York Times*, Feb. 3, 1959). Robinson said he had "predicted this development weeks ago." On Rockefeller's election see no. 922.

[2] Thomas Edmund Dewey had served as New York's governor from 1943 to 1955; for background see no. 908; see also Richard Norton Smith, *Thomas E. Dewey and His Times* (New York, 1982), pp. 609–20.

[3] William Averell Harriman had served as New York governor from 1955 until 1958. On his term as governor see Rudy Abramson, *Spanning the Century: The Life of W. Averell Harriman 1891–1986* (New York, 1992), pp. 516–69.

[4] See nos. 922 and 965; see also Reich, *The Life of Nelson A. Rockefeller*, pp. 684–769.

[5] In a state-wide television address following his budget requests to the legislature, Rockefeller had explained that while he had done "everything possible" to hold down expenditures and cut departmental requests, the expenditures required in this budget were "largely the direct results of laws enacted and administrative decisions made months and years ago." He noted that over the past four years the state's expenditure had increased about 50 percent, while state revenues had increased only about 33 percent (*New York Times*, Feb. 3, 1959).

[6] Eisenhower had vacationed at George Humphrey's Milestone Plantation from February 4–9. Robinson and Barry Leithead had also been guests (see nos. 1049 and 1050).

[7] Robinson would reply on February 10 (AWF/N): "I have known Nelson for a long while and I like him personally. I contributed to his campaign for the nomination as well as his campaign for election." Nonetheless, Robinson was irate at Rockefeller's failure to follow Eisenhower's lead in balancing his budget by holding down expenditures and not by raising taxes. "I thought that Nelson, immediately after his inauguration, should have declared he was going to seek new legislation to cut out ex-

cessive and wasteful expenditures, and attempt to balance the budget through frugality. He could have made the statement that, If this failed, he might have to get
additional taxes." For developments see no. 1061.

1048   *EM, WHCF,*
                                                               Official File 102-B-3

To ROBERT WINSHIP WOODRUFF   *February 9, 1959*

Dear Bob: This morning I read a copy of a talk made by the Attorney General.[1] I send it along to you because I think it will give you
a better idea than the newspapers can of what he is trying to get at.

Incidentally, I had a talk with him about your feeling that one section of the proposed bill might be construed so as to legalize interference with the right of free speech.[2] He vigorously asserts that
the language is so carefully drawn as to eliminate any such possibility. In fact, he was so sure of this that I asked him to telephone
to you to explain the matter more accurately than I could.[3]

It was wonderful to see you.[4] Give my love to Nell and all the best,
of course, to yourself. *As ever*

[1] Attorney General William Rogers had addressed members of the Fordham University Law Alumni Association on February 7 (see Eisenhower to Rogers, Feb. 9,
1959, AWF/D; *New York Times*, Feb. 8, 1959). He had expressed confidence in the
"ability of Southern states and communities to work out their school desegregation
problems peacefully" and urged every community "to develop for itself a program
best suited to its own needs without waiting for lawsuits and court decrees."
[2] Eisenhower may have been referring to the Administration's proposed civil rights
legislation, which had been submitted to Congress on February 5. The seven-point
program included an anti-mob bill; an anti-bombing bill; a bill giving the Justice Department the right to inspect voting records; a bill extending the life of the Civil
Rights Commission; a bill providing a temporary program of financial and technical
aid to state and local agencies to assist them in school desegregation; and a bill giving to the President's Committee on Government Contracts statutory authority to
eliminate discrimination in private employment. The possible threat to freedom of
expression came in connection with measures intended to prevent threats of violence
and obstruction of court orders in school desegregation cases (see *Congressional Quarterly Almanac*, vol. XV, *1959*, pp. 291–94; *Public Papers of the Presidents: Eisenhower, 1959*,
pp. 164–67; and *New York Times*, Feb. 6, 1959). For developments see no. 1078.
[3] Rogers would call Woodruff on February 10 (see Woodruff to Eisenhower, Feb. 10,
1959, same file as document).
[4] On Eisenhower's Georgia vacation see nos. 1049 and 1050.

To George Edward Allen   *February 9, 1959*

Dear George: So far I have received no reports on your reduction program. I assume that by this time you are down to something about two hundred and twenty. This reflects, of course, my confidence in your sturdiness of purpose and intensity of effort.[1]

All the above is my prelude to a dismaying fact that I discovered this morning when I mounted my scales—the first time since leaving here last Wednesday morning.[2] They balanced at one hundred and seventy-nine, a clear gain of five pounds in four days. Sausage, hot cakes, ham, lobster, caviar and broiled-in-butter quail were even more delectable than in the past. This I now regret.

Mrs. Whitman learned this afternoon through Reynolds that you liked the ham.[3] I am delighted. So far we have not used one of the hams, but we have had a piece of a shoulder, and both the children and ourselves found this very good indeed. I think the bacon is not quite up to the ham, but it is still very good.

It was most fortunate that Mamie did not go with me to Milestone. We had a rough trip going down and had to use an alternate field where the field equipment was better suited for landing. The rain and wind were so heavy that we had to circle the field for some forty minutes before finally reaching the runway, and even then we went in under a ceiling that was about as low as anything I have ever encountered, at least in a big plane.[4]

Following that we had three days of fairly good shooting, but only on one of these could I have been called a "hot shot."

Incidentally, all my talk about having to come back Sunday night was based on a misconception that I picked up somewhere that I had two speeches on Tuesday of this week. This morning I found that I had my dates mixed and the talks are, instead, on Wednesday.[5] Even so it is probably just as well that I came home since the weather in Thomasville turned bad yesterday and I suspect has been similar to what we have had here today—in other words, dark, rainy, damp and coldish.

Give my love to Mary and, of course, all the best to yourself. *As ever*

---

[1] Allen had been among the group of old friends who joined the President for a stag weekend at Camp David January 23–25 (New *York Times,* Jan. 24, 25, 26, 1959). For background on Eisenhower's efforts to have Allen lose weight see Galambos and van Ee, The *Middle Way,* nos. 953 and 1846. For developments see no. 1053.

[2] On the President's vacation at Milestone Plantation in Thomasville, Georgia (Feb. 4–9), see the following document.

[3] Reynolds probably worked for the Allens. On January 31 Eisenhower had made

arrangements to send the ham (see Ann Whitman memorandum, Jan. 31, 1959, AWF/AWD; see also no. 1057).

[4] According to Presidential Secretary Ann Whitman's notations the flight to Thomasville had been "awful, and quite bumpy." The pilot, who had been forced to land at an Air Force base sixty-five miles away from Thomasville, missed the runway with one wheel. They returned, she wrote, in another "blinding rainstorm" (Ann Whitman memorandum, Feb. 4, 9, 1959, AWF/AWD).

[5] On the afternoon of February 11 Eisenhower would address the National Rural Electric Cooperative Association. In the evening he would speak briefly at the National Lincoln Day Sesquicentennial Dinner. For his remarks to both groups see *Public Papers of the Presidents: Eisenhower, 1959*, pp. 178–83; see also Ann Whitman memorandum, February 9, 11, 1959, AWF/AWD.

1050   *EM, AWF, DDE Diaries Series*

To George Magoffin Humphrey   *February 9, 1959*

Dear George: The best evidence that I had a restful and beneficial few days at Milestone is my bulging waistline; I find to my dismay that I gained six pounds in four days.[1] The problem of getting back into my clothes is just an additional one that I must now take on—possibly it will help take my mind off some of the others that are even more disagreeable.

Every time I think of that Friday evening when you had to dash out suddenly to the scene of Pam's accident, I am reminded again to thank the Good Lord for her miraculous escape. Though, on Sunday, she said that she was discovering bruises that on Friday evening she did not know were there, so far as looks were concerned she was still her charming and cheerful self.

I am sending a note to Mrs. Hasty to thank her for the camellias because I am afraid that in Mamie's rush of packing, she may have no time for correspondence.[2] I think they are as beautiful as any I have ever seen and I am deeply grateful for her thoughtfulness.

I do hope that Murphy's box camera pictures of Inaugural Day and me come out well.[3] I am anxious to have a couple.

Give my greetings to Brownie, Murphy, Inaugural Day, and all the latter's associates in the barn.[4]

The trip back was uneventful. It was quite cloudy and we flew at seventeen thousand feet, but we had no such experience as we did last Wednesday. Landing was normal and we arrived back at the White House about 6:45.[5]

Thanks again for a wonderful time. Visits to Milestone are always an event to remember with the keenest of pleasure.[6]

Give my love to Pam and, of course, all the best to yourself. *As ever*

[1] The President had visited former Budget Director Humphrey's Milestone Plantation in Thomasville, Georgia, February 4–8 (see the preceding document and *New York Times*, Feb. 5, 6, 8, 9, 1959).

[2] Mr. and Mrs. Gordon Hasty probably worked for the Humphreys. Eisenhower's letter to Mrs. Hasty (Feb. 9) is in AWF/D. On the First Lady's vacation at the Maine Chance resort in Phoenix see no. 1009.

[3] Murphy also probably worked for Humphrey. Inaugural Day was undoubtedly an animal living on Humphrey's farm.

[4] Brownie probably worked for Humphrey as well.

[5] On the flight to Thomasville see the preceding document. On the return flight to Washington see Ann Whitman memorandum, February 9, 1959, AWF/AWD.

[6] On Eisenhower's midwinter trips to Humphrey's plantation see nos. 131 and 578.

1051   *EM, WHCF, Official File 102-G*

To Robert J. Biggs   *February 10, 1959*
Personal

Dear Mr. Biggs: I was much moved by your recent letter to me, and can well appreciate from it the serious thought and reflection you are giving to problems affecting our country.[1] The points you raised (some not entirely clear to me) included three that especially impressed me. Some of them clearly have significance to our free society and form of government.

I refer to your comments that normal confidence and feeling of security can be easily shaken in these times; your implied request that I undertake to stabilize the spirit of our population, and your conviction that if the government and its leaders know the nation's goals and missions and state the way they should be achieved, those leaders could be sure of the backing of our people.[2]

Concerning these comments I have several observations.

I think it is undeniably true that the activities of our government have tended to become much more complex, impersonal and remote from the individual, with consequent loss in simplicity, direct human contact and clear guidance by higher authority I believe you to be urging. In good part this situation is inherent in life in the mid-twentieth century—in a highly developed economy and a highly complex society such as our own. The complexity is reflected in the need to qualify (to "hedge" is the term you use) many of our policies, which means simply to give careful thought to the possibility that what we do in one field may have unacceptable impact in another.[3] To reduce complexity I believe it essential to keep governmental activities as close as possible to the people concerned. I have frequently stressed the need for these functions to be performed at local and state level rather than at the Federal.[4] Incidentally, I assure you that I have tried always to avoid creating any doubt in anyone's mind as to my own goals and convictions. If I have failed in this respect, it has been purely an error of an expression and not one of purpose.

Another part of the difficulty undoubtedly comes from the high degree of confusion and uncertainty on major national problems that seems to exist today. As you know, for four years our government has been a divided government, with the Administration confronted by a Congress controlled by the opposition—and the two working, if not in opposition, at least at cross purposes much of the time. An example is the sparring that seems to go on constantly over our defense situation—and specifically over our missile position. It is difficult indeed to maintain a reasoned and accurately informed understanding of our defense situation on the part of our citizenry when many prominent officials, possessing no standing or expertness except as they themselves claim it, attempt to further their own ideas or interests by resort to statements more distinguished by stridency than by accuracy.[5]

Even if this division in the government did not exist, I doubt that citizens like yourself could ever, under our democratic system, be provided with the universal degree of certainty, the confidence in their understanding of our problems, and the clear guidance from higher authority that you believe needed. Such unity is not only logical but indeed indispensable in a successful military organization, but in a democracy debate is the breath of life.[6] This is to me what Lincoln meant by government "of the people, by the people, and for the people."

The mental stress and burden which this form of government imposes has been particularly well recognized in a little book about which I have spoken on several occasions. It is "The True Believer," by Eric Hoffer; you might find it of interest. In it, he points out that dictatorial systems make one contribution to their people which leads them to tend to support such systems—freedom from the necessity of informing themselves and making up their own minds concerning these tremendous complex and difficult questions.[7]

But while this responsibility is a taxing one to a free people it is their great strength as well—from millions of individual free minds come new ideas, new adjustments to emerging problems, and tremendous vigor, vitality and progress.

One of my own major aims and efforts has been to assist in every way open to me in giving our people a better understanding of the great issues that face our country today—some of them indeed issues of life and death. Through being better informed, they can best gain greater assurance regarding our nation's situation and participate in establishing policies and programs which they think to be sound and right. The quest for certainty is at best, however, a long and arduous one. While complete success will always elude us, still it is a quest which is vital to self-government and to our way of life as free men.

May I end by saying how stimulating I found your letter and the thoughts it evoked, and how much I admire your fortitude in pondering these problems despite your deep personal adversity. My best wishes are with you in your grave illness. *Sincerely*

[1] Biggs, a 44-year-old World War II veteran who had served in the Army from July 1942 to November 1945, had written on November 8, 1958 (same file as document). He had been employed as a road and safety supervisor for a trucking concern in Washington State and had previously been a bank trust officer. He had been hospitalized since December with a diagnosis of inoperable pancreatic cancer. Presidential Secretary Ann Whitman had asked General Goodpaster if this letter appealed to him as "something the President should answer (and that you would *like* to draft?)."

[2] Biggs had written that contemporary American feelings of insecurity "manifest themselves in the guise of a recession, etc." Eisenhower, he said, had an unprecedented opportunity to remedy the situation by making "well thought out direct statements to the public to assure them that government does not operate without them and in consideration of them."

[3] Biggs had said that he "felt from your recent speeches the feeling of hedging and a little uncertainty. We wait for someone to speak for us and back him completely if the statement is made in truth."

[4] See, for example, no. 1041.

[5] In January 1959 perceived disparities in guided missile capabilities between the United States and the Soviet Union—the so-called "missile gap"—had rekindled a controversy (for background see no. 396). Surveying U.S. missile program progress, the *New York Times* had described what Administration critics saw as a growing gap in missile production. At a National Press Club luncheon on January 14 Eisenhower had conceded that it would be "a little stupid" to deny the Russian lead in certain phases of missile development. But, he emphasized, it was "absolutely fatuous and futile" to try to compare United States progress against that of the Soviet Union on an item-by-item basis (*Public Papers of the Presidents: Eisenhower, 1959*, pp. 25–26). On January 17 Senate majority leader Lyndon Johnson had announced an investigation to "straighten out the confusion" over the nation's defenses. Other Senators called for the quick adoption of more extensive airborne defenses and the purchase of additional first-generation ICBMs. The Air Force took the opportunity to pressure the Administration to support its program for the creation of twenty-nine Atlas and Titan missile squadrons. See *New York Times*, January 12, 15, 18, 31; Watson, *Into the Missile Age*, pp. 314–19; Glennan, *The Birth of NASA*, p. 23; and Levine, *The Missile and Space Race*, pp. 86–88. For developments see no. 1100.

[6] Biggs had written that Americans needed "more of the attitude of a commanding officer who knows the goal and the mission and states, without evasion, the way it is to be done."

[7] See Eric Hoffer, *The True Believer: Thoughts on the Nature of Mass Movements* (New York, 1951). Hoffer's frustrated, isolated and insecure "true believer" was a person who found meaning in his life by joining a movement. Hoffer had written, "Of what avail is freedom to choose if the self be ineffectual? We join a mass movement to escape individual responsibility, or in the words of the ardent young Nazi, 'to be free from freedom'" (p. 30). Unhappy with his life and social setting, a true believer was

prepared to make great sacrifices in a collective effort to rebuild society to his lik
ing (James T. Baker, *Eric Hoffer* [Boston, 1982], pp. 22–25). Eisenhower had read
Hoffer's book in 1952 and had given copies to his friends. In 1956 *Look* magazine
had run a feature on Hoffer, calling him "Ike's Favorite Author."

1052   *EM, AWF, Administration Series*

To William Pierce Rogers   *February 10, 1959*
Personal and confidential

Dear Bill: From my viewpoint there are a few disturbing flaws in the
procedures that we are using in selecting individuals for appointment to the Federal judiciary.[1] The situation could well be due entirely to a possible failure of mine to make sufficiently clear the policies that I believe applicable.

Primarily, of course, I depend upon the Attorney General to assist me in this work and, indeed, to take the initiative in mobilizing
pertinent facts upon which I can base a decision. Your findings, involving such factors as character, experience, and ability, are of necessity practically conclusive. But the White House has a very direct
interest in other considerations, an interest that must often express
itself long before the time has arrived for a final decision.

Too often the White House, by which I mean my two principal assistants as well as myself, is uninformed as to vacancies, prospective
vacancies, and possible candidates for some judicial position until it
is far too late to have any flexibility in choice. It is more than embarrassing to find, for example, that I have approved a man's name
for appointment, and later to discover that a number of highly respected citizens and political associates were vigorously sponsoring
another individual, but without full White House knowledge of
the situation. Lately I was confronted with a statement from an old
friend and acquaintance that some four years ago I had promised a
future appointment to an individual and that I had later forgotten
the matter and approved the appointment of another.[2]

I expect my staff to give me timely information provided by you
and by outside individuals as to pertinent facts in these cases so that
I may have adequate freedom of choice before any appointment, direct or indirect, has been made on my behalf. In turn my staff will
keep you informed as to facts presented directly to the White House
by others.

It is the responsibility of the Attorney General, of course, to present for consideration only men of the highest professional standing and unimpeachable character. (Incidentally, if occasionally you

find a man highly qualified for appointment who does not exactly meet some of the criteria I have personally established you are, of course, at liberty to include his name in the group for consideration. Such criteria are established as general guides, but this does not mean that in a special case one or more could not be violated).

To keep abreast of developments in this kind of case, I request that you follow the simple procedure below outlined:

> (1). Either personally, or by *confidential* memorandum sent to me (through either General Persons or Mr. Morgan) you will please, at the earliest practicable moment, notify me of what vacancies are expected to occur or have actually occurred.

> (2). In the same or a later *confidential* memorandum to me, list the names of the individuals who have been recommended to you and those who are being considered by your office, together with the names of principal sponsors, particularly where these include the Governors, Senators, or members of the Congress from any given state.

> > (Note: If either item 1 or 2 is carried out through personal conversation between you and me, please leave with me a short memorandum of pertinent facts).

> (3). When you believe that the accumulated information warrants a decision, please confer with me as soon as convenient in order that I can personally discuss with you the matter and give final approval.

> (4). Thereafter the final papers should be processed as promptly as practicable.

In the past I have always tried to keep these matters almost wholly on a verbal basis, particularly because of the importance of avoiding leakage while the process of selection goes on. However, I have found that not only is my memory far from infallible, but it is also important that in certain considerations applying to the appointing process I need the counsel and advice of my own principal staff officers.

Incidentally, I believe that in both the Attorney General's office and in the White House the fewest possible persons should have any knowledge of the work involved in selecting nominees. So far as possible the matter should be kept on an "eyes only" basis.[3]

With warm regard, *As ever*

---

[1] For background see nos. 990 and 1007.

[2] Eisenhower's letter was prompted by a meeting he had on February 10, 1959, with Republican Senators John Sherman Cooper and Thruston B. Morton from Kentucky. Presidential Secretary Ann Whitman recorded that the Senators were upset "because a judge is to be appointed from that area, and the one they recommended was NOT to get the appointment" (Ann Whitman memorandum, Feb. 10, 12, 1959, AWF/AWD; see also Galambos and van Ee, *The Middle Way*, nos. 1254 and 1337). The ap-

pointed judge may have been Paul Charles Weick of Ohio, who would be confirmed in September to the United States Court of Appeals for the Sixth Circuit (Ohio, Michigan, Kentucky, and Tennessee); see *New York Times*, September 9, 10, 1959.

[3] Eisenhower would meet with the Attorney General to discuss this letter on February 12. The President would not give the letter to Rogers during the meeting, but would have it sent to his office later for comments. Eisenhower would also ask Rogers to keep the letter on an "Eyes only basis" (Eisenhower to Rogers, Feb. 12, 1959, AWF/A); see also Ann Whitman memorandum, February 12, 1959, AWF/AWD. For further examples of presidential involvement in judicial appointments see Ann Whitman memorandum, February 4, 1958, AWF/AWD; and Telephone Call, January 28, 1959, AWF/D.

1053   *EM, AWF, Administration Series*

To George Edward Allen   *February 11, 1959*

Dear George: If you could show me any way to make the journey between your particular paradise and Washington, D.C., in less than three hours, I would be delighted to accept your invitation.[1] Even for you I fear that such a feat is impossible. However, I do send you my congratulations on losing eight pounds, which measure, I hope, is down from the fairly respectable 236 with which you left here, rather than the top level of 242![2]

If you are doing that well regularly, it is my advice that you stay right there and continue to play golf for the next three months.

Incidentally, if you want any more ham—or a shoulder and some bacon—please send me word and I will have it in the mail.[3]

Please convey my adoring admiration to that angel who has found it possible to live with so much of you for so long.

With all the best, *As ever*

P.S. If Sid is there remember me to him kindly.[4]

[1] This letter may have been misdated. On February 13 Allen would wire Presidential Secretary Ann Whitman to invite the President to his home in LaQuinta, California, where there were "eight golf courses within ten miles" (AWF/A).

[2] On Eisenhower's efforts to reduce the girth of Allen see no. 1049. Allen would report that he was dieting "religiously."

[3] The President had sent a ham to Allen in late January (see no. 1049).

[4] The reference was to Fort Worth oil magnate Sidney Williams Richardson.

To Harold Macmillan   *February 12, 1959*
Cable. Confidential

Dear Harold: Press reports indicate that Turkey and Greece have settled their differences over Cyprus in a spirit of friendliness and conciliation.[1] I realize that this cannot be finalized until you have approved, but if and when you do, I should like to send both Menderes
and Karamanlis a congratulatory telegram. My idea is to point out
to each that the solution of the problem in this fashion cannot fail
to be beneficial to the strength and vigor of the whole NATO alliance. Can you let me know whether this matter has been sufficiently finalized that you believe a congratulatory message from me
would be in order?

Of course I am saying nothing here about the hard work you have
done for so many months to bring this matter to some kind of a decent solution. I cannot tell whether or not it is completely satisfactory to you, but I have so assumed because of your frequent statements to me that "Anything Turkey and Greece will mutually agree
on will be acceptable to us so long as our own requirements are
met."[2] *As ever*

[1] For background see no. 912. After a December debate in the United Nations General Assembly regarding the Cyprus issue, the foreign ministers of Greece and Turkey
had begun direct discussions. At the conclusion of these talks both governments
agreed to further meetings with Prime Ministers Constantine Karamanlis and Adnan
Menderes. These negotiations, which had begun in Zurich on February 6, resulted
in an accord on the future of the island and a partial, draft constitution for an independent Cyprus republic. An ethnic Greek Cypriot president and an ethnic Turkish Cypriot vice-president would preside over the new republic. There would be a
single legislative chamber with proportionate representation of the Greek and Turkish communities. The vice-president would have veto power over any policies that
would affect the security of Turkey and the position of the Turkish Cypriot minority. Final discussions on the proposed agreement were to begin in London on February 17 (State, *Foreign Relations, 1958–1960*, vol. X, pt. 1, *Eastern Europe Region; Soviet Union; Cyprus*, pp. 749–70; *New York Times*, Feb. 11, 12, 1959; see also Macmillan,
Riding the Storm, pp. 692–94; and Reddaway, *Burdened with Cyprus*, pp. 120–27).
[2] Macmillan hoped that the London talks would lead to a final agreement. "I think
in fact that we are nearly home," he would write Eisenhower, "although I still find it
hard to believe." He would ask the President to delay messages of congratulations to
anyone until he had written again (Macmillan to Eisenhower, Feb. 13, 1959, PREM
11/2629). For developments see no. 1064.

To Sam Houston Jones   *February 12, 1959*

Dear Sam: Thank you for your letter. As probably you know, Emma Michie called my office on the same subject, and suggested that you and she—or some other group of interested people—come to Washington to discuss with me the closing of Fort Polk.[1]

I am sure you will understand the necessity for the action by the Defense Department if I give you a little bit of the background of the matter. As you know, the Defense Department is emphasizing the introduction of more advanced, more powerful weapons throughout the Armed Forces, with consequent savings in manpower and consequent consolidation of many units. These weapons, although tremendously powerful, are also extremely costly, and their costs are increasing. It has therefore become necessary to close some of the Army's installations, where this action is made possible by these savings and consolidations.[2]

The operation of posts and camps is one of the Army's major expenses. I do not need to tell you that to keep a large post open for relatively few troops becomes an uneconomical business.

The closing of installations has serious effect, of course, on the surrounding communities wherever they are located. This was particularly recognized in the case of Fort Polk (and I might add parenthetically that because of my knowledge of the Fort Polk area I feel personally very concerned). Nevertheless, the interest of the nation as a whole dictated that the Army consolidate at other stations. The decision to close Fort Polk was not an easy one and was made only after a thorough study of what action would be best in the interest of our national security.[3]

As to the "commitments" that were allegedly made by the Defense Department, because of which the local authorities made substantial expenditures, I believe you refer to the designation of Fort Polk as a permanent installation contingent upon securing the necessary maneuver rights. This was done on October 27, 1955.[4] But such designations can be made only in regard to the foreseeable, at the time, future. This was recognized at that time by the incorporation of a provision in each agreement with the individual land owners for automatic termination in the event Fort Polk was inactivated.

The Army has acknowledged and is most appreciative of the fine community support in the areas surrounding Fort Polk. I regret, as do I know both Secretary McElroy and Secretary Brucker, the necessity of closing Fort Polk in the interest of applying available resources to the ever-increasing costs of missiles and other adjuncts of modern military preparedness. But the decision has been made by the Department of Defense and I cannot ask them to reconsider the matter.

If you and Emma—or any one else—wish to come to Washington to see the Defense people, I am certain an appointment can be arranged (and, if I am in town, I shall be glad to see you briefly if I can fit it into my schedule). But I do not want in the slightest to encourage you to think that the decision can be reversed.

It is always distressing to me to know that a community will suffer because of the closing of a Defense Department installation; again I say that such difficult decisions are necessary, in times like these, because of the changing world in which we live.

With deep regret that my reply cannot be more favorable, and warm personal regard,[5] *Sincerely*

---

[1] For background on Jones, an attorney and former Louisiana governor, and Emma Calvert Michie, a past president of the Louisiana Hotel Association, see Galambos, *Chief of Staff*, no. 1420. Jones had written on February 6 protesting the closing of Fort Polk, which was scheduled to be shut down at the end of the fiscal year because of a proposed reduction in the strength of the Army's ground forces. Jones's letter to the President and other documents outlining the history of Fort Polk are in the same file as the document. Eisenhower had sent a similar letter to Louisiana Governor Earl Kemp Long on January 22 in response to his protest against the Fort's closing. See also Jones to Michie, February 6, 1959, *ibid.*

[2] See no. 630.

[3] See no. 1000.

[4] Jones had described to the President the promise made by the Defense Department in 1955 to make the Fort a permanent installation, and the "substantial expenditures" made on the basis of this commitment. Camp Polk had been created in 1941 in the area of Western Louisiana that had served in 1939 and 1940 as the site of the largest maneuvers ever held by the United States Army. Eisenhower had met Jones and Michie during the 1940 maneuvers. Closed at the end of World War II, the camp was reopened in 1950 to provide a training ground for units fighting in Korea, but had again closed in June 1954. In 1955 the Army entered into negotiations with Louisiana to provide an area in which to conduct atomic-warfare maneuvers. The Army had agreed to reopen Fort Polk on a permanent basis if Louisiana could provide a maneuver area of approximately 7,000,000 acres without cost to the Government.

[5] Jones would reply on Feb. 19 (same file as document) that although he was "disappointed" that the news was not better, he understood "the bigger overall problem" and knew that Eisenhower was acting "in the national interest." "I hope time will bring some utilization of the facilities at Polk, possibly for industrial purposes of some kind." Fort Polk would reopen in 1961.

To Ezra Taft Benson   *February 13, 1959*
Personal

Dear Ezra: Thank you for your comment on the REA speech.[1] I do
not particularly enjoy being cast in the role of debating with a pip-
squeak whose job is little more than that of a lobbyist.[2] However, he
does seem to be a very successful one, since I see from the paper
that the convention rejected my recommendation by a unanimous
vote.[3] *As ever*

[1] Agriculture Secretary Benson had written (Feb. 12, AWF/A) that he thought the
President's February 11 speech was "excellent." On that day the President had addressed the 17th annual meeting of the National Rural Electric Cooperative Association (*Public Papers of the Presidents: Eisenhower, 1959*, pp. 178–81; for background see
Galambos and van Ee, *The Middle Way*, no. 1303). Eisenhower, who had been reluctant to speak to an audience that he considered hostile, had used the occasion to
advocate a balanced budget and fiscal conservatism (see no. 1042; see also Ann Whitman memorandum, Feb. 11, 1959, AWF/AWD).
[2] The President was probably referring to Clyde Taylor Ellis, general manager of the
Rural Electrification Administration (REA) since 1943. Ellis, who had been admitted to the Arkansas Bar in 1933 and had also served as a member of Congress from
1939 until 1943, was an outspoken critic of the Administration's REA policies. In
June 1958 he had accused the Administration of engineering a plan to destroy the
REA (*New York Times*, June 6, 1958).
[3] Eisenhower may have been referring to his call for changes in programs such as
REA in which borrowers were provided loans at artificially low rates of interest. The
President had recommended that Congress authorize the Treasury to set these rates
at a level that would recover the cost of the money loaned. Benson had enclosed an
editorial from the February 7 *Deseret News*. For more on the Administration's struggles with REA legislation see *Congressional Quarterly Almanac*, vol. XV, *1959*, p. 314;
see also Benson, *Crossfire*, pp. 447–52.

To John Hay Whitney   *February 13, 1959*

Dear Jock: Thank you for your note of the seventh. Foster's performance on the last trip was brilliant all the way around, and the more
amazing because of the tremendous physical odds under which he
was laboring. At the moment I am dictating this note, he is undergoing the operation for hernia at Walter Reed.[1]

We missed you at Thomasville.[2] Bill Robinson and Barry Leithead
stayed with us at Milestone, and Bob Woodruff came over a couple
of times to join us.[3] After a bad flight down (we had to land, even-

tually, at Valdosta instead of Moultrie where the field had more complete equipment for instrument landing), we had three days of comparatively good weather.[4] The shooting was fair, and I did not exactly distinguish myself. Altogether it was, however, a relaxing, quiet few days that I much enjoyed.

Mamie is presently in San Antonio, on her way to Phoenix.[5] And next week I go to Acapulco for two days, after which I hope—the weather cooperating—to stop at Augusta for a weekend of golf.[6]

These are minor matters, but I did want to acknowledge your note. Today my overriding concern is for Foster, of course. I know you are anxious too.[7]

With warm regard, *As ever*

[1] Whitney's letter is in AWF/A. He had praised Secretary of State Dulles on his recent discussions with heads of state in London, Paris, and Bonn regarding the Western position on the future of Germany (Memorandum of Conversation, Jan. 26, 1959, Dulles Papers, White House Memorandum Series; Telephone conversation, Eisenhower and Dulles, Jan. 30, 1959, Dulles Papers, Telephone Conversations; Dulles to Eisenhower, Feb. 4, 1959, AWF/D-H; *New York Times*, Feb. 7, 10, 1959; on the situation in Berlin see no. 1062). Dulles had entered Walter Reed Army Hospital on February 10. Although the hernia operation would be successful, tests made after the surgery showed a recurrence of abdominal cancer (Statement by the President, Feb. 14, 1959, AWF/D-H, and *New York Times*, Feb. 10, 22, 1959).
[2] On Eisenhower's vacation at former Budget Director Humphrey's Milestone Plantation in Thomasville, Georgia, see no. 1050.
[3] Coca-Cola Director Robert W. Woodruff owned Ichuaway, a 47,000-acre plantation, near Albany, Georgia (for background see Galambos, *Columbia University*, no. 656).
[4] On the flight see no. 1049.
[5] On the First Lady's vacation see no. 1009.
[6] On February 19 and 20 Eisenhower would go to Acapulco, Mexico, to make an informal call upon Mexican President López Mateos (see nos. 1062 and 1063, and *New York Times*, Jan. 29, Feb. 17, 22, 1959). As it turned out, the weather in Georgia would alter the President's plans (*New York Times*, Feb. 22, 1959; see also no. 1059).
[7] For developments see no. 1069.

1058   *EM, WHCF, Official File 114*

To Harold Boeschenstein   *February 15, 1959*

Dear Beck: In reading over the memorandum that Mr. Allyn sent to you, there remain one or two questions unanswered in my mind:[1]
    1. In deploring a recent reduction in the rate of capital expenditures (which, I agree, was unfortunate), it appears that the year 1957 was taken as a norm. It is my impression that 1957 was our *best* year—but without looking up the statistical charts, I cannot be certain of this point. In trying to make ac-

curate comparisons it seems to me that we are too prone to think of the economic cycle as coinciding with each circuit of the earth around the sun.

Since free enterprise is bound to cause certain ups and downs, I think that we should look constantly at the *general curve of increase* rather than at detailed dips and rises, even though these may be at the moment very significant.[2]

2. In the next to last paragraph of page two the question of capital expenditures is discussed in terms of stimulation. It seems to me that this effort will lose some of its value unless such capital expenditures allow us to produce goods that will, in competition with others, increase our foreign markets. I do not mean to say that the domestic market is by any manner of means saturated. But our present and potential productivity—both in industrial and agricultural activity—seems to indicate that the products of our industry cannot be fully utilized except as we *can sell goods profitably in the foreign market.*[3]

The entire memorandum is interesting, but these particular two points seem to me to need a bit more explanation.

I do not mean to ask you for a long reply, but if you should indicate a general agreement with the points I make, please let me know and I will have some of our people make a somewhat more exhaustive analysis for my benefit.[4]

With warm regard, *As ever*

---

[1] Stanley Charles ("Chick") Allyn (A.B. University of Wisconsin 1913) was chairman of the board of the National Cash Register Company and had been a member of the Committee on World Trade Practices. He had sent his memorandum (WHCF/OF 114) to Owens-Corning Fiberglas Corporation President Boeschenstein and to other committee members on January 21, 1959, not "with any thought of changing or altering" the committee report upon which it commented, but "simply to help crystallize my own thinking on the subject." For more on the report of the committee see *New York Times*, March 3, 1959.

[2] Allyn believed that the United States could strengthen the free enterprise system and effectively combat the Soviet economic offensive by increasing capital expenditures. "In 1957 we spent $37 billion on capital goods. In 1958 we spent about $30 billion, or seventeen percent less than in 1957. In 1959, according to preliminary surveys of private capital expenditures, we again will spend about $30 billion." While these levels of expenditures were "tremendous," they were not enough to sustain growth. On the rate of capital expenditure between 1954 and 1958 see Bert G. Hickman, *Growth and Stability of the Postwar Economy* [Washington, D.C., 1960], pp. 121–56.

[3] Allyn believed that the United States government should stimulate capital investment by private industry. "A stimulation of capital expenditures, either by announced expansion objectives or by various incentives such as a reinstitution of accelerated amortization, would accomplish two major things; it would stimulate our economic growth and indirectly that of our friends and allies, and it would be a major factor in the economic fight with Russia. For, without strength and momentum in the American economy, all our efforts abroad will be to no avail."

4 Boeschenstein would submit Eisenhower's questions to Allyn, and would later send the President a copy of Allyn's response (Allyn to Boeschenstein, Feb. 26, 1959). Allyn recognized that 1957 did represent a high rate of capital investment, but said that the 1958 and projected 1959 capital expenditures of private industry were at about the same level as they were in the early 1950s. The stagnation in capital expenditures had caused a lack of growth in the gross national product, which in constant 1958 dollars had declined from $2,633 per capita in 1955 to $2,514 in 1958. Allyn believed there was a direct relationship between capital expenditures, the general price level, and the ability to compete in foreign markets. He pointed to "those companies trading in the foreign markets that have benefited from improved productivity by installing new capital equipment." They have, he said, "been able to raise the wages of their workers, hold their prices steady, and retain their foreign markets in the face of steadily mounting competition from West European and Japanese industries."

On March 10, 1959, the President would thank Allyn for "the time you took to expand your ideas so fully for me." Eisenhower would also thank Boeschenstein on that same date (all correspondence is in same file as document). See also no. 1060.

1059   *EM, AWF, Name Series*

To George Champion   *February 16, 1959*
Personal and confidential

Dear George: I was somewhat dismayed to get your opinion of Dr. Conant, relayed to me by Mrs. Whitman. I know that over the years he has been a controversial figure, but during my years of association with him, first when we were both Presidents of Colleges and later during his service as High Commissioner (after that as Ambassador) to West Germany, I found him a highly intelligent person and a positive character. Some of his books on educational needs, particularly in the secondary field, have interested me very much.[1]

Since receiving your message I have inquired among others who have known him well. While all seem to agree that some of his views are original, unorthodox and even startling, the impression I get is that he is well respected. I was not able to obtain any opinion as to your belief that he may be an agnostic. I have never heard him express his opinion, one way or another, as to his attitude toward religion.[2]

The reason that I am trying to explain this matter a bit is that long before I learned of your opinion—and I do assure you that I value your opinions highly—I had invited Dr. Conant to come to my office to talk about a project I have in mind. I am expecting him to come in this afternoon.[3]

Incidentally, I do know that in the course of his lectures on education, he is doing a pretty good job in awakening his audiences, largely made up of educators, as to the meaning of the Berlin crisis and the great need we have to understand the Communist menace and the methods they use to achieve their ends.[4]

I am very hopeful of spending the 21st, 22nd and 23rd at Augusta. As yet I cannot say that this effort will be successful, but if we should both be there, we might talk a little more on this subject.[5]

Of course you know that I am deeply appreciative of your courtesy in sending me your views and even more so for the frankness with which you express them.

With warm regard, *As ever*

[1] James Bryant Conant had served as president of Harvard from 1933–1953. In 1953 Eisenhower had appointed him U.S. High Commissioner for West Germany. After serving as U.S. Ambassador to Germany from 1955 to 1957, Conant had returned to the United States and, pursuing an earlier interest in public education, had conducted studies of junior high and high schools. Among Conant's books on educational policy were *Education and Liberty* (1953) and *The American High School Today* (1959). For background see Galambos and van Ee, *The Middle Way*, no. 51; see also James B. Conant, *My Several Lives: Memoirs of a Social Inventor* (New York, 1970). There is no record in AWF of Chase Manhattan Bank President Champion's communication with Presidential Secretary Ann Whitman.

[2] Conant considered himself a Unitarian (*ibid.*, p. 10; see also James G. Hershberg, *James B. Conant: Harvard to Hiroshima and the Making of the Nuclear Age* [New York, 1993], p. 13).

[3] For background on the establishment of a National Goals Committee see no. 999. Eisenhower would meet with Conant on February 16 from 2:34 P.M.–3:40 P.M. In June the President would name former Chairman of the Council of Economic Advisers Arthur Burns and president of General Dynamics Frank Pace, Jr., as Cochairmen of the National Goals Committee (*New York Times*, June 16, 1959); for developments see no. 1185.

[4] On Berlin see no. 983.

[5] Eisenhower would not go to Augusta (see no. 1061).

1060   *EM, AWF, DDE Diaries Series*

[MEMORANDUM]   *February 16, 1959*

Someone told me it takes about $15,000 of investment in capital goods to produce one job in industry. Since we have an average addition of 700,000 per year to our labor force, it would appear that we have to invest some $10 to $11 billion dollars each year for these recruits.[1]

I do not know the amount of money we have to put in for replacement or renovation of equipment already installed. In addition to investments for these two purposes, we must of course provide for increase in productivity per man in the entire labor force.

Over the last years our average investment in new plants and equipment has been about $28,500,000,000 annually. It would appear that a figure something on the order of $32 or $33 billion dollars—always of course increasing a little bit each year—would be about our safe minimum.

[1] For background see no. 1058. See also Hickman, *Growth and Stability of the Postwar Economy*, pp. 121–56, 184–96.

1061
EM, AWF,
Administration Series

To Nelson Aldrich Rockefeller
Personal

February 17, 1959

Dear Nelson: The immediate cause of this note is that I am off tomorrow for a quick trip to Mexico to call informally upon President Lopez Mateos. Knowing your deep and continuing interest in Latin American affairs, I thought you might like to know also that Milton has agreed to make the trip with me.[1]

You seem to have quickly become a controversial figure in the financial thinking of New York State. In three instances at least, you and I have had certain similarities in our political positions. We each inherited a sorry fiscal condition in government. Both of us have tried to operate by the doctrine that government must live within its means. Finally neither of us was under any illusion that an Executive position in politics is any bed of roses.[2]

Some visitors to this office have been quick to criticize your effort to raise more revenue for New York State. They have justified their complaints by saying that it would have been easy enough to have reduced some of the services for which the State is now paying. I have not had the opportunity to read the details of your entire budgetary message and so I do not know how much emphasis you placed upon the possibility of making significant reductions.[3]

Knowing so little about it I have not tried to argue too much with these people, contenting myself merely by saying, "Nevertheless I believe that we must, at all echelons of government, live within our means."[4]

[1] See no. 1062.
[2] See no. 1047.
[3] On March 9 Rockefeller would telephone Presidential Secretary Ann Whitman to tell her that he had prepared a long letter to the President about his budget problems. He had decided against sending it, however, since he thought the budget matter would

be settled soon. Eisenhower would later tell Rockefeller that in budget matters it was not only a question of how much capital was extracted from the economy, or by what means, but also how the money was to be most equitably distributed. Should the government cut funding from things that were in themselves desirable but could be deferred, or should it continue to do these things to promote the welfare of the people and the economy? The President commiserated with Rockefeller, noting that those who tried to extract money were never very popular. Rockefeller would tell Eisenhower that he would send him a digest of the long letter he had been preparing and would call him to let him know the outcome. Eisenhower's final words to the New York governor were: "Keep swinging!" (Telephone Calls, Mar. 9, 1959, AWF/D; see also Ann Whitman memorandum, Mar. 9, 1959, *ibid.*). For developments see no. 1105.

[4] Ann Whitman had typed at the bottom of this letter the following note: "Second page of this letter temporarily lost." Eisenhower's original letter to Rockefeller is in the Rockefeller Archive Center. The second page reads: "Finally, my warm greetings to your lovely bride and, as always, the very best to yourself. Sincerely,".

1062

EM, AWF,
Dulles-Herter Series

To CHRISTIAN ARCHIBALD HERTER
Secret

February 19, 1959

Draft of message for the Acting Secretary of State: One of the subjects that commanded a considerable attention at our afternoon's talk was that of our subsidy action respecting cotton.[1] The discussion was in a very friendly tone, but it was obvious that the Mexican group was disappointed as to the action itself as well as what they considered the abruptness with which it was announced. Apparently the State Department had little or no chance to provide timely notice so that the Mexican government might prepare the Mexican cotton growing industry for the bad news. If it did have the opportunity, it nevertheless seems that the government here was astonished as well as surprised.

I told President Lopez Mateos that I assumed that the action of the Secretary of Agriculture was taken in compliance with law. While I still think this is probably true, I could make no explanation of why we had, in this instance, failed to prepare the way for a development that has very serious consequences on their major crop.

I promised the President that our State Department would meet with the Secretary of Agriculture to ask a few questions:

(*a*). Has the decision in this matter become final?

(*b*). Was the action taken one of administrative judgment or of compliance with law?

(*c*). If the answers to the first two are in the affirmative, did we do everything we could to explain the matter to the Mexican government?

There were other questions raised, but this is one to which I should like to have an answer some time during the day of the 20th, if practicable, because it is possible I might do something to ease hurt feelings.

During all my talks here I have assured the President of our firm purpose to consult with them before taking any action that involved our common interest. I am, of course, quite certain that the Department has been doing this right along, but it is possible that there has been some slip up somewhere along the line.[2]

New subject. The following is for Secretary Dulles: During the many trips that you have taken during the past six years on behalf of American interests, you have unfailingly kept me informed by cable of the developments of your talks and efforts. For once I am able to turn the tables.[3] My first report is that I found the new President to be a dynamic, friendly and very informal individual. He is firm in his assurances that he wants to earn and hold the friendship of the United States. And he is certain in his own mind that if we can act in close cooperation concerning our common problems, that certainly his country will benefit and in some measure our own.

He asked me to assure you of his earnest wishes for your early recovery, saying that not only the United States but the world needs you.

The members of his Cabinet who were with us for the afternoon meeting were likewise friendly, intelligent and, it seemed to me, very well informed.[4] They expressed a hope of pushing forward with us on the construction of the additional dam on the Rio Grande, but seemed to throw cold water on the idea of an international recreational area in the Big Ben because they said constitutional considerations would prevent them from participating in this.[5]

Ambassador Hill continues to enjoy the high esteem and admiration of all and, of course, Rubottom and my brother Milton were most helpful in the conversations.[6]

The following again for the Acting Secretary. Senator Johnson had mentioned to me the subjects of the dam on the Rio Grande River and the proposed international recreational area. If Senator Johnson returns to Washington before I do, it will be quite appropriate for you to inform him as to my comments on these two matters as contained in this cable.[7]

[1] Eisenhower had arrived in Acapulco, Mexico, on this day for informal talks with newly-elected president Adolfo López Mateos (see Dulles, Memorandum of Conversation, Jan. 26, 1959, Dulles Papers, White House Memoranda Series; see also Telephone conversations, Eisenhower and Dulles, and Hagerty and Dulles, Jan. 27, 1959, Dulles Papers, Telephone Conversations; and State, *Foreign Relations, 1958–1960*, vol. V, *American Republics*, pp. 860–61). On February 4 the Department of Agriculture had announced an increase in the subsidy it would pay on U.S. cotton shipped

abroad. The new subsidy, which would begin on August 1, would allow growers to reduce the price of cotton sold on the world market to between four and five cents below the current price, making U.S. cotton competitive with the prices of other cotton-exporting countries. During a luncheon aboard the Mexican president's yacht Foreign Minister Manuel Tello Baurraud had commented on the recently announced price support program and its effect on the Mexican cotton industry. He expressed regret that no consultations with the Mexican government had taken place before the new program had been announced. Eisenhower admitted that U.S. officials had "blundered" and promised to look into the problem (State, *Foreign Relations, 1958–1960*, vol. V, *American Republics*, pp. 862–64; and *New York Times*, Feb. 5, 1959; see also Paarlberg, *American Farm Policy*, pp. 238, 240–41).

[2] For Herter's response see the following document.

[3] Dulles was recuperating from abdominal surgery and was scheduled to undergo his first radiation treatment for the recurrence of cancer (see Dulles to Eisenhower, Feb. 20, 1959, AWF/D-H; see also Eleanor Lansing Dulles, *The Last Year*, pp. 227–28).

[4] Accompanying President López Mateos were Foreign Minister Tello, Ambassador to the United States Antonio Carrillo Flores, and former Secretary of the Treasury Ramón Beteta.

[5] A joint statement, issued immediately before Eisenhower's departure the following evening, would deal with the collaboration on the Diablo Dam, to be built 100 miles north and west of the Falcon Dam, which Eisenhower had helped dedicate in 1953 (see *U.S. Department of State Bulletin* 40, no. 1028 [March 9, 1959], 331–32; see also Galambos and van Ee, *The Middle Way*, no. 214). Earlier discussions between Mexico and the United States regarding the development of an international park in the Big Bend area of southwest Texas along the Rio Grande River, had broken off in the late 1940s (see State, *Foreign Relations, 1958–1960*, vol. V, *American Republics*, p. 871; see also no. 1080; and John R. Jameson, *Big Bend National Park: The Formative Years* [El Paso, 1980], pp. 1–32).

[6] For background on Robert C. Hill, who had become U.S. Ambassador to Mexico in July 1957, see Galambos and van Ee, *The Middle Way*, no. 1325. Roy R. Rubottom, Jr., was Assistant Secretary of State for Inter-American Affairs.

[7] Eisenhower would write Texas Senator Lyndon B. Johnson regarding these issues; see no. 1080.

1063   *EM, AWF, Dulles-Herter Series*

To CHRISTIAN ARCHIBALD HERTER   *February 20, 1959*
Secret

To the Acting Secretary of State: In view of the contents of your telegram, I shall not even hint to President Lopez Mateos of its existence. In my view the mention of the caution that Mexican and other world exporters should observe restraint in selling cotton would in itself start a speculative movement that could not fail to be damaging.[1]

Pending my return to Washington, please inform the Agriculture Department that under no circumstances are any new actions to be publicly suggested until I can give specific approval in each case.

At the earliest convenient moment, I want to have a joint meeting with State Department and Agriculture officials to make an exhaustive analysis of this matter.[2]

For the Secretary of State. Please tell the Secretary of State that our conversations today have proceeded with a continuation of the same spirit of friendliness as they did yesterday. The suggested communique is, from my view, as always at least three times as long as it should be, but the Mexicans clearly see some local advantage to be gained by lengthy discussion. However, I think nothing will be harmed in any way.[3]

I saw your son last evening and was able to tell him that your morale was tiptop.[4]

I thank the Good Lord for the news that you tolerated very satisfactorily your first radiation treatment.[5] *With affectionate regard*

[1] For background see the preceding document. Herter had cabled Eisenhower that he should tell Mexican President López Mateos that the United States shared with Mexico the desire to maintain cotton prices at the highest level consistent with the law. He also told the President that State Department officials would discuss the problem with Mexican embassy personnel in Washington in order to find a solution. Secrecy regarding the consultations was essential, Herter added, because of the impact on the cotton market and the "possible advantage to speculators." Answering the three questions Eisenhower had posed in his message on the preceding day, Herter had said that the decision announced by Agriculture Secretary Benson was final; it involved both compliance with the law and administrative judgment; and no prior clearance with the Mexican government had occurred. "We agree there should have been" (Herter to Eisenhower, Feb. 20, 1959, AWF/D-H).

[2] We have found no record of a meeting with Eisenhower, however, a March 2 statement would indicate that the International Cotton Advisory Committee would discuss the cotton export policies of various countries in an effort to solve the problems they were experiencing (Mar. 2, 1959, AWF/AWD). For developments see no. 1094.

[3] On the day's discussions see State, *Foreign Relations, 1958–1960*, vol. V, *American Republics*, pp. 866–70; on the communiqué see *U.S. Department of State Bulletin* 40, no. 1028 [March 9, 1959], 331–32.

[4] Secretary Dulles's older son John Watson Foster Dulles was a mining engineer in Mexico City.

[5] See the preceding document. Dulles had received the treatment on this same day.

1064   *EM, AWF, DDE Diaries Series*

To Harold Macmillan   *February 20, 1959*

Dear Harold: It is possible that poor communications between Acapulco and Washington could have created a slight misunderstanding. If it did, I trust that no damage resulted.[1]

Last evening I had a message notifying me of the Cyprus solution and with the added notation that the "ban is now off." This I took to mean that your telegram telling me that I might send congratu latory messages had already arrived. However, it was actually noon today before I had your very welcome communication. If, therefore, I was a few hours early with my messages I am sorry, and I assure you that it was not intentional.[2]

Again I express to you my congratulations and rejoice with you that your patience, skill and understanding, which have had so much to do with this successful outcome, have been thus rewarded.

Last evening I saw Anthony Eden at dinner. He appeared in good condition and assured me that he felt much better than for a long time. I understand that he is returning to Britain the latter part of this month.[3]

With warm regard, *As ever*

[1] Eisenhower had arrived in Acapulco on the preceding day for talks with newly-elected Mexican President Adolfo López Mateos (see no. 1061; State, *Foreign Relations, 1958–1960*, vol. V, *American Republics*, pp. 861–70; and Eisenhower, *Waging Peace*, p. 344).

[2] For background on the Cyprus settlement and Macmillan's request for a delay in sending congratulations to the Greek and Turkish prime ministers see no. 1054. On February 19 Macmillan had notified Eisenhower that he and the Greek and Turkish leaders had initialed the agreements for what he hoped was a final settlement of the Cyprus problem. The agreements provided for British control of military base areas in a way that would ensure their effective use, Macmillan said. The arrangement would be guaranteed by international treaties among the three governments and the new Cyprus republic. He told Eisenhower that "the moment has now come" to send the President's congratulatory messages (Macmillan to Eisenhower, Feb. 19, 1959, PREM 11/2629; see also Eisenhower to Macmillan, Feb. 19, 1959, AWF/I: Macmillan; Eisenhower to Karamanlis, Feb. 19, 1959, and Karamanlis to Eisenhower, Mar. 19, 1959, AWF/I: Greece; Eisenhower to Menderes, Feb. 19, 1959, AWF/I: Turkey; State, *Foreign Relations, 1958–1960*, vol. X, pt. 1, *Eastern Europe Region; Soviet Union; Cyprus*, pp. 768–71; and Macmillan, *Riding the Storm*, pp. 695–98).

[3] Former British Prime Minister Eden was vacationing in Mexico and writing his memoirs. For developments in Cyprus see no. 1584.

1065

EM, AWF,
Dulles-Herter Series

To Christian Archibald Herter
Secret

February 21, 1959

Memorandum for the Acting Secretary of State: I attach a copy of a message I have just received from Harold Macmillan. Since he is now in Moscow, I am uncertain as to whether or not he expects an answer, particularly in view of the closing sentence of his message.[1]

The message seems to be ambiguous. Mr. Macmillan speaks of his readiness to accept something less than "perfect control." Both Fos-

1359

ter and I have already indicated that we do not press for an elabo-
ration of the mechanics of an inspectional system so that we could
be sure that any nuclear explosion, no matter how small its size nor
where exploded, could be detected. But we are insistent that such
stations as are agreed upon be allowed to function without interference from the government in whose territory the stations are set
up. In any agreement to which we would be a party, we cannot coun-
tenance a veto either in the establishment of the detection system
or in the carrying out of procedures and examinations authorized
by the agreed plan.[2]

We have already agreed that the cessation of tests need not be
connected with any feature of disarmament, but we must be quite
clear that our arrangements must operate so effectively that they
give to each side the assurance that the inspections will be freely
and honestly carried out and in accordance with the agreed plan.[3]

If you believe that we should send anything to Macmillan while
he is still in Moscow, please let me know.[4]

[1] For background on the Geneva Conference on nuclear testing see no. 1004. Prime
Minister Macmillan had left for Moscow on the preceding day (see Macmillan, *Riding the Storm*, pp. 582–86, 590–92). He had written Eisenhower about his concern
that the conference would end without producing an agreement. Even though disadvantages and risks were involved, Macmillan wrote, an agreement might result in
a reduction in tension, a deterrence to the spread of nuclear weapons to other countries, and "a pilot scheme" for agreements in other fields. Willing to accept "something less than perfect control," he felt that if they could create a system that featured a "significant degree of risk to a potential violator that he cannot get away
undetected . . . then we shall have done enough to justify our accepting the disadvantages and risks involved." He did not, however, accept the Soviet idea of a veto
power over the operations of a control system, particularly regarding the dispatch of
inspection teams. Macmillan concluded: "I have no doubt this Conference will be
mentioned while I am in Moscow. You can rely on me to press Khrushchev hard
about the veto" (Macmillan to Eisenhower, Feb. 20, 1959, PREM/11 [2860]).
[2] For discussions among State and Defense Department officials and members of the
Atomic Energy Commission regarding the veto proposal see State, *Foreign Relations,
1958–1960*, vol. III, *National Security Policy; Arms Control and Disarmament*, pp. 692–709.
[3] On the linkage of limits on testing with disarmament see no. 1004.
[4] For developments see no. 1071.

1066   *EM, WHCF, Official File 225*

To Bernard Mannes Baruch   *February 21, 1958*
Personal

Dear Bernie: Thank you very much for your memorandum. I agree
with all six observations that you make.[1]

Likewise, I believe that the Soviets must recognize the truth of the things you have been trying to impress upon them. But they like to fish in troubled waters; they think that it is to their advantage to promote fear, suspicion and anxiety in the world, believing that in this fashion they will progress continuously toward their objective of world revolution.

I assume you have heard mention of the book, "What We Should Know About Communism", by Mr. and Mrs. Overstreet. All in all it is very interesting, and here and there it makes some points about Communism which had never before specifically occurred to me. Their chapters about the Communist party in the United States tend to grow somewhat tedious. The others are most readable.[2]

Thank you very much for your courtesy in passing your thoughts on to me; I shall of course share your memorandum with the State Department.

With warm regard and best wishes for your continued health and happiness, *As ever*

[1] Baruch had told Eisenhower that he had written because of the pending crisis over Berlin and Secretary Dulles's illness. Over the years he had tried to impress several thoughts upon Russian officials "in a diplomatic and friendly manner." These included: 1) the world would not know peace or security until the German question was settled; 2) only international controls would solve the problem of atomic energy; 3) Russian threats and procrastination would force the United States to give the bomb to the Germans, whose use of the weapon the Americans would then be unable to control; 4) China threatened the Soviet Union more than the United States; 5) the Russian people eventually would want to know why relations with the United States were not closer; 6) Russia was trying to promote world communism more than improving the living standards of its people (Baruch to Eisenhower, Feb. 16, 1959, same file as document).

[2] See Harry A. and Bonaro W. Overstreet, *What We Must Know About Communism* (New York, 1958). The second section of the book was titled "The Party in Our Midst."

1067   *EM, WHCF, Official File 107-B*

To Donald Prescott Loker   *February 21, 1959*
Personal

Dear Mr. Loker: Charlie Jones was good enough to forward to me your letter of the thirteenth. I am more than grateful for your willingness to be helpful in the present "battle" to preserve the fiscal integrity of the American dollar.[1]

I agree wholly that there has been an unfortunate, a deplorable, change in the philosophy by which many of the people in this country now seem to live. I don't think it is entirely advancing age that makes me convinced that some of the old-fashioned characteristics such as thrift, hard work, and self-reliance were responsible for the greatness of our nation today.[2] Recently someone showed me a quotation from a current book which, I am afraid, more or less sums up the way some of our citizens feel.[3] At the risk of making this letter entirely too long, I shall quote to you a few sentences.

"After all his years of being on relief, or
getting Unemployment Compensation and Aid to
Dependent Children and things like that, Pop
didn't think of himself as The Public. He
figured he was just about part of the government
on account of he worked with it so close.
The government helped Pop, and Pop done his
best to keep the government busy and happy,
and they was both dependent on each other."

For six years I have been preaching—to me it seems with endless repetition on this subject; I shall continue to do—and I am glad to have allies such as yourself in the job of awakening the people of America to the dangers inherent in such a philosophy.

At any rate, I did want you to know of my deep gratitude.
With best wishes, *Sincerely*

[1] For background see no. 1042. Loker (B.A. Harvard 1925), vice-president of Star-Kist Foods, had served as an adviser to General MacArthur on the rehabilitation of Japanese fisheries from 1947 to 1948. Richfield Oil Company President Jones had written Loker on February 11 in support of the Administration's efforts on behalf of a balanced budget. Loker had responded on February 13: "Certainly something has to be done to deter the devaluation of the dollar or the entire economic structure of our country will be in grave danger." On February 19 Jones had forwarded the letter to Ann Whitman with a request that since Loker was "such a dedicated friend of the President," the President send him a thank-you note.

[2] Loker had said that Eisenhower was "fighting a large group wanting more and more government financing which inevitably leads to more and more government control, but the underlying cause is the unfortunate and pitiful change in the philosophy of thinking of a tremendous number of people in our country. Such unfortunate thinking is based on the belief that the government owes everyone a living, resulting in a lack of interest in personal sacrifice and in hard and constant work and represents a departure from the basic concepts of frugality and personal saving." All correspondence is in the same file as the document.

[3] Eisenhower was referring to *Pioneer Go Home* by Richard Pitts Powell (New York, 1959).

To Adolfo López Mateos   *February 21, 1959*
Confidential

Dear President López Mateos: As my first act after reaching Washington I must thank you once again for the warm hospitality shown to me and to my party by you, as well as by your associates in the Mexican government and the citizens of Acapulco.[1] It was a great privilege and distinct honor to meet you and a valued opportunity to exchange with you views on matters of interest to both our countries.

The appropriate parts of this government will continue with me to give earnest study to the specific problems to which you adverted and I assure you we constantly seek methods by which cooperation between us can be improved.[2]

Needless to say, I am delighted that you find it possible to accept my invitation to visit the United States, the details to be worked out by our diplomatic officials. I suggest that you and I promptly make a simultaneous announcement in Mexico City and in Washington that you have accepted the invitation in principle for a visit some time this spring, with the exact time to be fixed later. Such a simple statement would eliminate any undesirable speculation and would provide timely information to the people in each country. If you agree to this suggestion, I propose that each of us make such a short announcement on Wednesday morning, February twenty-fifth, at 9:30 Mexico City time.[3]

Finally I want to assure you that I highly value your thoughtfulness in presenting to me and Mrs. Eisenhower gifts and mementos characteristic of Mexican culture and history. The members of my party share my feeling of gratitude and appreciation.

I shall be looking forward to seeing you again during the spring.[4]
Your friend

---

[1] For background on Eisenhower's two-day goodwill trip to Mexico see no. 1062.

[2] On the issue of cotton subsidies see no. 1063. For discussions regarding coffee prices, construction of the Diablo Dam, and the migrant labor problem see State, *Foreign Relations, 1958–1960,* vol. V, *American Republics,* pp. 862–70.

[3] Both men agreed to a visit sometime during the second half of April. State Department officials would inform the White House on April 15 that the Mexican president wished to postpone his visit until the fall. The press release announcing the change in plans was issued the following day (*ibid.,* p. 872; and *U.S. Department of State Bulletin* 40, no. 1036 [May 4, 1959], 637). López Mateos would arrive for a four-day state visit on October 9.

[4] For developments see no. 1170.

To John Hay Whitney   *February 21, 1959*
Personal and confidential

Dear Jock: Thank you very much for your handwritten note. I found
that I could read it without trouble and this news, from what you
say, may astonish you considerably.[1]

You are quite right in all the assumptions you make respecting
my present concern and difficulties involved in the unfortunate illness of Foster. Sad as I feel for him and his family, I am even more
saddened by the loss that the country will experience when the time
comes that it can no longer have the benefit of his wisdom, courage
and tireless energy.[2]

As of now, I tend to agree with your comments about personalities. So far as Chris is concerned, the obvious fear would be that his
crippling arthritis might so damage his usefulness as to cast doubt
on the wisdom of his holding the number one spot. As far as his
head and heart are concerned, I rate him in the top rank. Respecting his physical difficulties, you might be interested to know
that he made a point of seeing me off when I started on my trip to
Mexico Wednesday afternoon, and was out at the field again this
morning when I reached here at eight o'clock. If his physical difficulty is not a *progressive* one, I rather feel he could carry on.[3]

Cabot, of course, is experienced and would have to be considered.
But he already occupies a position of extreme importance and delicacy.[4]

Of course if daily prayers will do any good, we will be able to keep
Foster with us for a long time. But cases of this kind are most tricky
and unpredictable. I shall try to keep you in touch with his progress
because I know you are deeply interested.

We had a very fine day with Gordon and Gene. In the early morning the dogs had considerable trouble. A rather severe wet spell had
just ended and apparently the birds were scattered out considerably
looking for food. As a consequence they were going up wild. Later
in the morning, however, the conditions got better and we had some
very splendid shooting. It was the only one of the three days where
I shot well. On the third day on one of George's tracts, I was simply too tired to get on the ball.[5] As a matter of fact, as early in the
day as I could I got in the wagon and watched the others shoot.

As usual Mr. Kamerick (I am not sure the spelling is correct)
arranged a splendid luncheon which we enjoyed out in the field.[6]
Barry Leithead and Bill Robinson went along with us and Barry tried
shooting for a while. Bill told me something I had not previously
known—that he has a cataract on his right eye which some day will

have to be removed. Nevertheless he is interested in seeing whether John Olin could fix him up a gun with an offset so that he could use his left eye; and Barry Leithead tells me he is starting instructions right away in shot gun shooting. (Incidentally I could personally use that kind of instruction to very great advantage).

Give my love to Betsey and, of course, all the best to yourself. *As ever*

P.S. Write to me whenever the spirit moves you, and if anything occurs where I feel I should like to talk things over with you at some length, I shall let you know promptly.[7]

[1] Whitney's letter of February 15 is in AWF/A. He had thought the President might wish to destroy it because its subject was so sensitive that he had written it by hand. "I do not have easily read handwriting," he said. "I hope Mrs. Whitman can transcribe my scrawl."

[2] Secretary of State Dulles had abdominal cancer (for background see no. 1057).

[3] Whitney had suggested that Eisenhower consider Under Secretary of State Christian A. Herter as the logical replacement for Dulles. Whitney was "much impressed" by Herter, he said, although Herter's physical appearance was a "drawback." For developments see nos. 1139 and 1167.

The President had paid an informal call upon Mexican President López Mateos on February 19 and 20 (see nos. 1062 and 1063).

[4] Whitney's second choice for Secretary of State, U.N. representative Henry Cabot Lodge, had "the experience and the stature."

[5] Gordon Simmons and his nephew, Gene Simmons, were dog trainers on Whitney's Greenwood Plantation in Thomasville, Georgia. While vacationing at George Humphrey's Milestone Plantation in Thomasville, Eisenhower and his friends had hunted ducks, quail and doves at Whitney's nearby Greenwood (see no. 1050).

[6] Ed Komarek was Whitney's estate manager.

[7] Eisenhower would next meet with Whitney at the White House on March 19; see also no. 1183.

1070   *EM, AWF, Name Series*

TO AKSEL NIELSEN   *February 21, 1959*

Dear Aks: Thank you very much for your nice letter of the eighteenth. It gave me the information I wanted, except for one thing. The names you use are a bit baffling. I of course connect the Turnpike Land Company certificates and the certificate #20 in the B-A-W with the Broomfield project.[1] From there on I am lost.

All that I need is a key such as

Wynetka Investment Co equals ?

Middlefield Development Company equals ?

Lake View Investment Co. equals ?

Dutch Creek Investment Co. equals ?[2]

Just as your letter came in I was talking on the phone to Mamie. She gave me a ring as soon as she knew I had landed in Washington.[3] I asked her about the package in the safety deposit box marked for her and she replied she knew nothing whatsoever about it. However she is talking to Schulz this morning and I suppose later she will send you a note directly or have Schulz do so. Otherwise you might have to act blindly in an emergency.[4]

George is still in California—the lucky dog.[5] I wonder whether you ever have the same feeling that occasionally touches me. It is that for just *once* in my life I would like to do nothing, comfortably, lazily and completely, until I actually felt that I wanted to go to work. I know, of course, that I could not stand any such condition permanently, but it would be most interesting to find out how long I could.[6]

In any event, thanks for your note and, of course, all the best to yourself. *As ever*

P.S. My love to Helen.

[1] Nielsen had been overseeing the President's real estate investments near Denver (for background see no. 309). He had reported that he had endorsed the B-A-W stock certificate and placed it in a safe deposit box in the Bank of Denver (see also Nielsen to Eisenhower, Feb. 16, 1959). On the Turnpike Land Company see Galambos and van Ee, *The Middle Way*, no. 1686; on the Broomfield project see no. 309 in these volumes.

[2] Nielsen would reply (Feb. 24) that the various stocks issued by the Wynetka, Middlefield, Lake View and Dutch Creek Companies were connected with land development enterprises near the Columbine Country Club (see Galambos and van Ee, *The Middle Way*, no. 1686). The land was purchased and divided into four pieces; part of each piece was given to each of the four companies. The Middlefield Development Company was a "normal income proposition," he wrote, and the others would produce capital gains as they were sold.

[3] On the President's informal visit to Mexico see nos. 1062 and 1063.

[4] Nielsen had listed several items, including a sealed package, that belonged to Mrs. Eisenhower and had been placed in a safe deposit box. Presidential aide Robert L. Schulz would telephone Nielsen on February 24 to request that Nielsen send the package to him (Nielsen to Eisenhower, Feb. 24, 1959).

[5] For background on the real estate investment program Nielsen had developed for Eisenhower and George Allen see Galambos and van Ee, *The Middle Way*, no. 1252. On Allen's visit to La Quinta, California, see no. 1053.

[6] Agreeing with the President, Nielsen would write that he too would be "anxious to get back in the harness" after any period of illness.

All correspondence is in AWF/N.

To Harold Macmillan   February 23, 1959
Secret

Dear Harold: While I accept and appreciate your statement that you
have gone to Moscow to talk rather than to negotiate, I still believe
that I should reply briefly to your cabled message of February 20th.[1]
I agree with the points you make about the importance of the negotiations in Geneva and the advantages which would come to us
from a sound agreement. I agree also that construction of a perfect
system, capable of detecting explosions of every type or location, is
impossible in practice. However, I am firmly convinced that it would
be folly for us to relax our position respecting the right of mutual
and effective inspection. Certainly we cannot tolerate vetoes over
any part of an agreed inspectional process.[2]

I concur that an agreement with the USSR on nuclear testing will
establish a precedent for controls in other fields. This point concerns me very much. It reinforces the need to continue to press the
USSR for a satisfactory agreement on fundamentals before moving
to other issues. The important points are the methods by which the
right of inspection is provided for. We must be careful that the
staffing pattern of the control posts is not such as to interfere with
the integrity of the collection and transmission of data. We must be
sure that the voting procedures do not legalize obstruction of the
operations of the control system. I am sure that you will agree with
me that on these points we must be absolutely firm.

Our concern about your proposal for setting an annual upper
limit on inspections is that it would get us into negotiations on numbers without agreement on the basic elements of inspection and control.[3] Further, there would be an ever-increasing pressure on us,
once we accepted the upper limits principle, to go lower and lower
until there would no longer be an acceptable level of deterrence.
Therefore, I believe we should contemplate no proposals of this type
until and unless the important points I have described above are satisfactorily settled.

Thank you very much for your short note dispatched after you
had your first talk with your friends.[4]

With warm personal regard, *As ever*

---

[1] For Macmillan's message and his Moscow visit see no. 1065.
[2] In a discussion with Acting Secretary Herter on this same day, Eisenhower had "extensively modified" the State Department draft of this letter "to concentrate very directly upon the question of the veto ... the breaking point in the negotiations"
(Goodpaster, Memorandum of Conference, Feb. 24, 1959, AWF/D).

[3] Macmillan had suggested that since neither the United States nor Great Britain would be physically able to inspect every unidentified event, the parties should establish an annual upper inspection limit. When the British had first made the proposal at earlier meetings with U.S. officials in Washington, the United States contingent had expressed reservations about such a concession to the Soviets. "I regard it as just the opposite," Macmillan had written, "because its purpose is, while protecting all our essential requirements, to nail them down on the veto, and make their position in asking for a veto still more untenable" (Macmillan to Eisenhower, Feb. 20, 1959, PREM 11/2860).

[4] Macmillan had written on the preceding day that he had had a number of conversations with Soviet Premier Khrushchev, with Foreign Minister Andrei Gromyko and First Deputy Anastas Mikoyan in attendance. The talks had been during or after meals, Macmillan said, "with [the] normal accompaniment of vodka, caviare and so on" and had been friendly and courteous. "I am still not without hope that we may probe into their minds a bit, and get some information which may be useful to all of us" (Macmillan to Eisenhower, Feb. 22, 1959, AWF/I: Macmillan).

In his reply to this message Macmillan would tell Eisenhower that he saw the force of his argument against setting an annual upper limit on inspections, but he did "still earnestly believe that this may be the best way round the difficulty." Macmillan had proposed his idea "in an extremely tentative non-committal fashion" to Khrushchev before he had received Eisenhower's message. Khrushchev, Macmillan would report, "seemed to like the idea and said it sounded like a sincere attempt to avoid securing advantage to either side. He clearly understood that there was no room for a veto in the idea" (Macmillan to Eisenhower, Feb. 24, 1959, *ibid.*). For developments see no. 1095.

1072   *EM, AWF, Name Series*

To DANIEL CHARLES GAINEY   *February 23, 1959*
Personal and confidential

Dear Dan: Respecting the message you phoned Mrs. Whitman, I assure you that I deeply appreciate your thoughtfulness, as well as your obvious concern about the current State Department situation.[1] I am quite sure that you share my profound hope that before long Foster can be restored sufficiently in strength and health that he will feel fully capable of carrying on—at least for a considerable time—his accustomed duties.

Because we are such good friends, I want to give you my very frank and personal views—*not* to be communicated to anyone else.

I think that the people you have been talking to about the State Department problem have not thought about it very deeply.

In the first instance, I do not believe that any one of your informants could have a truly clear idea of the inestimable value of international experience to any one charged with the responsibility for heading up the State Department. For this particular post Mr.

Dulles has been studying for an entire lifetime. It was always his ambition to follow in the footsteps of his grandfather and of his uncle.[2] But he and I have by no means failed to look squarely in the face the potential effects of a continuance of the physical difficulty he first experienced more than two years ago.[3] We have, therefore, patiently put together a team of high officials in the State Department that in my opinion (and in Foster's) *know* more about the world situation, including the risks implicit in it, than anyone else. Admittedly there is no figure in America, in or out of government, who so stands out, in comparison with any other, as does Foster Dulles. This applies to his knowledge, his understanding, his moral courage, his negotiating ability, and his firmness.

Nevertheless he has, for some years, been training and educating subordinates so that, even though we might not be able to find an ideal State Department head, I could nevertheless have a strong, knowledgeable, loyal team to assist me in *my* constitutional duty of conducting the foreign relations of the United States. So I cannot share the feeling of "abhorrence" of some of your informants about the possibility of entrusting the State Department to any individual that Foster himself has selected, trained and trusted.[4]

With warm regard, *Sincerely*

[1] Eisenhower's friend Gainey had told Ann Whitman that a large number of people "abhorred" the prospect of either Christian A. Herter or C. Douglas Dillon replacing Secretary of State John Foster Dulles. Neither, said Gainey, was "well trained" (Ann Whitman memorandum, Feb. 23, 1959, AWF/AWD).

[2] John Watson Foster, secretary of state under President Benjamin Harrison, and Robert Lansing, secretary of state under President Woodrow Wilson.

[3] On Dulles's earlier surgery for cancer see Galambos and van Ee, *The Middle Way*, no. 2134.

[4] "Mr. Dulles is a truly great servant," Gainey would respond. "Since both of you think as you do, I am reassured. A few words from *you* on television if and when a change must be made would enhance public acceptance, for all have great confidence in you" (Gainey to Eisenhower, Mar. 2, 1959, AWF/N).

1073   *EM, AWF,*
                                                        Administration Series

To Lewis Lichtenstein Strauss   *February 23, 1959*
Personal and confidential

Dear Lewis: I am writing a short note to Frank Stanton to express the satisfaction I feel in the suggestions he has made about informing the public better as to the implications of the budget problem.[1]

Since you are the individual to whom he addressed his letter, I wonder whether you could undertake to pass along to him some suggestions about getting the programs into operation. While undoubtedly CBS experts know the best techniques to be used, it seems to me that you might be helpful with regard to the important points of personalities, subjects, timing and format. Also, I should think that there should be considered related subjects that will necessarily be discussed or at least mentioned in the context of budgetary considerations.

As to timing, I would think that the first program should be done very soon, and that others could follow along in some agreed order and at agreed intervals.[2]

To suggest a few of the personalities who might appear effectively on such programs, I might mention

> The Vice President
> Secretary of Commerce Strauss[3]
> Secretary of the Treasury Anderson
> Secretary of Labor Mitchell
> Senator Byrd
> Senator Dirksen
> Congressman Halleck
> A like-minded Democratic Congressman
> Director of the Bureau of the Budget Stans
> Arthur F. Burns
> American representatives from business, the professions and labor who could make a real contribution.

A much smaller group could possibly work with you and Dr. Stanton in deciding on methods. I would suggest yourself, Dr. Stanton, Bob Anderson, Jim Hagerty and, of course, any experts from the television business that Dr. Stanton might want to suggest.

As for my own participation, I would be willing to do anything that we, together, agreed was wise and effective.

In view of Dr. Stanton's suggestion, I believe we should make promptly some preliminary decisions so that at the very least he will understand our great interest in his ideas. I would be prepared to talk to you about the matter any time you see fit.[4]

With warm regard, *As ever*

---

[1] Columbia Broadcasting System President Frank Nicholas Stanton had written Commerce Secretary Lewis Strauss on February 13 (AWF/A, Strauss Corr.). Concerned about the need for broad public support for the President's budget program, Stanton had noted that he had scheduled four special one-hour network television programs on inflation (for background see no. 1042). Stanton wrote: "We hope to persuade the most articulate people we can find to ventilate this subject thoroughly before our cameras. It seems to me that this might be one way to attract public attention to this important problem."

In his February 23 letter (AWF/A, Strauss Corr.), Eisenhower would assure Stanton that he was ready to do his part "in the vital campaign of informing all our people; just exactly how I could be most effective and persuasive is, of course, something that will require a consensus of our best thinking."

[2] Although Stanton had told Strauss that he was reluctant to suggest timing, he was certain that "in the final analysis, there is no substitute for the President taking his case directly to the people."

[3] Eisenhower had appointed Strauss interim Commerce Secretary on October 24, 1958 (see *New York Times*, Oct. 25, 1958, and Jan. 18, 1959). For developments see no. 1134.

[4] The President would discuss the broadcasts in a meeting with Strauss on February 27 (see Ann Whitman memorandum, Feb. 27, 1959, AWF/AWD). For developments see no. 1109.

1074   *EM, AWF, International Series:*
                                                         Macmillan

To Harold Macmillan   *February 24, 1959*
Secret

Dear Harold: Thank you very much for the message giving your impressions after forty-eight hours in Moscow. I have no doubt that the conclusions presented in your first paragraph are quite accurate.[1]

We are of course aware of Khrushchev's apparent rigidity with respect to the Soviet attitude toward Berlin and Germany. This morning, February twenty-fourth, we received cabled extracts from the statement that he made today in Moscow that are seemingly even more belligerent and unyielding than those he has made in the past.[2]

Presumably the conversations which you and he are carrying on should be producing a better atmosphere in which the West and the East can negotiate. By Khrushchev's own words he has no apparent interest in such a development. For example, he is quoted this morning as saying that, if the West should attempt to maintain contact with Berlin either by ground or by air, such an attempt would be considered a "threat of war."

To attempt to draw any conclusion as to his basic purpose in such statements would be nothing more than an exercise in speculation. However, it seems that he is intensifying his efforts to create division within the Western group and thus to weaken our resolution. In effect he is saying, "We are destroying the Western rights in Germany and in Berlin, and if you make any attempt to defend those rights you are guilty of aggression and warlike acts."

Tomorrow morning I shall probably have some searching questions put to me by the press respecting the latest statement of Khrushchev, and the rigidity of the line he is taking. I shall say as little as possible, particularly during the duration of your visit. However, I believe I should reiterate that the West is a unit in its determination to defend its rights and to carry out its responsibilities respecting Berlin, and that, while we are completely ready to negotiate where there is any possible negotiable ground, we are not going to be divided or defeated by threats.[3]

With warm regard, *As ever*

[1] Prime Minister Macmillan had left London on February 20 for a ten-day visit to Russia (see Macmillan, *Riding the Storm*, pp. 592–605; see also no. 1071). After talking informally with Khrushchev, Macmillan said he thought that in spite of their new power and wealth the Russians were "still obsessed with a sense of insecurity." "Like a poor man who has suddenly made a fortune they feel uneasy in their new situation and they are resentful and nervous of their neighbors" (Macmillan to Eisenhower, Feb. 23, 1959, AWF/I: Macmillan).

[2] After Khrushchev's November 27 note announcing his plan to turn Berlin into a free city and the U.S. response (see no. 983), the Soviet Union had called for a conference to draft a final peace treaty with Germany. At a meeting on January 29 Eisenhower and State and Defense Department officials had agreed to a plan that included a refusal to acquiesce in the substitution of East German officials for the Soviets in Berlin; military preparations in advance of the May 27 deadline just serious enough to be detected by the Soviets without creating public alarm; and a call for a foreign ministers' meeting with the Soviet Union in the middle of April. A note reviewing the Berlin crisis and calling for the conference had been delivered to the Soviet foreign minister on February 16 (State, *Foreign Relations, 1958–1960*, vol. VIII, *Berlin Crisis 1958–1959*, pp. 246–49, 265, 299–306, 371–72; John S. D. Eisenhower, Memorandum of Conference, Jan. 29, 1959, AWF/D; Eisenhower, *Waging Peace*, pp. 340–42; John S. D. Eisenhower, *Strictly Personal*, pp. 218–21; and Burr, *Avoiding the Slippery Slope*, pp. 200–203).

In a two-hour speech earlier this same day Khrushchev had denounced the Western position on Berlin, rejected the proposal for a foreign ministers' meeting, and asked for a summit meeting to negotiate the dispute (State, *Foreign Relations, 1958–1960*, vol. VIII, *Berlin Crisis 1958–1959*, p. 387; *New York Times*, Feb. 25, 1959; see also Macmillan, *Riding the Storm*, pp. 605–6). The speech had prompted the composition of the following paragraph, later deleted, in an earlier draft of this letter:

> Moreover, at the very moment he is insisting that a Foreign Ministers meeting is out and that there should be a Heads of Government meeting, he tells you, as the Head of a major Western Government, that the Soviet position on these vital questions permits no room for maneuver. In effect he is saying that even a Heads of Government meeting would be completely useless except as it would give opportunity for a combined surrender by the West to the East.

(See State, *Foreign Relations, 1958–1960*, vol. VIII, *Berlin Crisis 1958–1959*, p. 387.) In a telephone conversation regarding the draft, Eisenhower had agreed with Herter that the paragraph should be eliminated because they were not certain of Khrushchev's actual words. Eisenhower said that his intent was to let Macmillan know how much he appreciated being kept informed and to make observations on the situation so Macmillan would "not be feeling lost and alone" (Telephone conversation, Eisenhower and Herter, Feb. 14, 1959, Herter Papers, Telephone Conversations; see also Whitman to Herter, Feb. 14, 1959, AWF/I: Macmillan).

[3] For Eisenhower's news-conference comments see *Public Papers of the Presidents: Eisen-*

been "very cool" since Khrushchev's speech. Their subsequent conversations had disappointed the Soviet leader since Macmillan would not respond to Khrushchev's pleas to advance some fresh proposals for Germany and Berlin (see Macmillan to Eisenhower, Feb. 26, 1959, PREM 11/2690). For developments see no. 1079.

1075   *EM, AWF,*
Dulles-Herter Series

To Christian Archibald Herter   *February 24, 1959*

Memorandum for the Acting Secretary of State: Governor Price Daniel, in a recent message to me, suggested that since two friendly nations are undertaking the Diablo Dam project, the name of the project should be changed to "Dos Amigos." I think this would be a good idea.[1]

While we would necessarily have to coordinate with the Mexican government, I am quite sure that the matter is not of a kind that would lend itself to official action. If the State Department thinks well of this idea, could we not, by informal diplomatic exchange, agree that on March first we would both state that we were going to use this name hereafter.

This is not an earth-shaking affair, but if we could do this, it might have some real significance on the relationships of our two countries.

At your convenience I should like to hear from you about it.[2]

[1] For background on the Diablo Dam project see no. 1062. Daniel was governor of Texas.

[2] The suggestion was "excellent," Herter would answer. The dam had no officially adopted name, and he agreed to ask the commissioner of the International Boundary and Water Commission to propose the name "Dos Amigos" to the Mexican commissioner (Herter to Eisenhower, Feb. 26, 1959, AWF/D-H; see also Telephone conversations, Eisenhower and Herter, Feb. 27, 28, 1959, Herter Papers, Telephone Conversations).

Eisenhower and Mexican President López Mateos would later agree on the name "Amistad," meaning friendship. In August 1960 Eisenhower would sign the appropriation bill authorizing funds for the dam's construction, and in a joint declaration in Ciudad Acuña the following October, the two men would state that construction of the dam would begin as soon as possible (*Public Papers of the Presidents: Eisenhower, 1960–61*, pp. 83, 721, 796, 797–98, 995; see also *Congressional Quarterly Almanac*, vol. XVI, *1960*, pp. 388–90).

To Harold Macmillan   *February 25, 1959*
Secret

Dear Harold: We have become so accustomed to the rudeness of the
people in the Kremlin that I suppose that Khrushchev's speech of
yesterday, made at a time when you were a guest in his country,
should give us little reason for astonishment.[1] Nevertheless this latest instance of deliberately bad deportment seems to me an affront
to the whole free world.

In my prior messages to you I have not meant to imply that we
are lacking in a readiness to be flexible in the effort to negotiate a
reasonable agreement at Geneva.[2] I think the West has proved that
readiness by the concessions already made. With respect to our objection about limiting inspection by fixing a maximum number of
trips permitted to teams, my only point was that I have always been
somewhat fearful of getting into the numbers racket.

One thought that occurred to us here is that on this matter of
trips there might be proposed some commitment that useless or unnecessarily repetitive trips would not be countenanced. Since the
group decision would be controlling, this matter would be no more
subject to veto than would a group decision to make an inspection.
In other words, one member could not, on his own, compel a trip
to a suspected incident.

This is, of course, no more than just thinking aloud. I put it down
merely to indicate our interest in the search for anything that is
workable and in which we can have confidence, but at the same time
that should answer any legitimate fears of the Soviets that the whole
inspectional process could be turned into a wholesale seeking for
military intelligence.[3]

I know that you are working hard and earnestly in a very difficult
situation. I think of you every day. At the very least the impressions
you bring back will be fresh and even if, because of the intransigence of the Soviets, you accomplish nothing of greater importance
than this, I feel that the trip will prove to be worthwhile.[4]

With warm personal regard, *As ever*

[1] See no. 1074.
[2] On the Geneva negotiations and the issue of inspection visits see no. 1071.
[3] Eisenhower had discussed the issues of detection and inspection with his science
advisor James R. Killian, Jr., and with General Goodpaster on this same day (Goodpaster, Memorandum of Conference, Feb. 25, 1959, AWF/D).
[4] For developments see no. 1084.

To Freeman F. Gosden   *February 25, 1959*
Personal

Dear Freeman: Since you were, after all, one of the initial instigators of the idea of my going to Mexico for a brief visit with Lopez Mateos, I thought at the very least you deserve a personal report.[1]

The entire trip was, on the whole I think, beneficial. My impression of the new President was, I imagine, much like yours. I found him intelligent, friendly, and eager to work toward better relationships for the good of the people of both our countries. He was kindness itself and so much was done to assure my comfort that it was slightly embarrassing. For instance, I heard stories of palm trees being planted at night to line the highway—and, the most incredible of all, that the pebbles that lined the walk outside my suite were washed with loving care every morning.

I enjoyed the trip; the setting could not have been lovelier, and the only difficulty, from my point of view, was that of the necessity to speak through an interpreter and, I must add, always to speak as the Head of State whose every word may come back to haunt me at some future time. He is to pay a return visit to the States some time later in the year, probably this spring.[2]

And so, Mr. Ambassador, you see the results of the seed you planted some two months ago!

With affectionate regard to Jane and, as always, the best to yourself,[3] *As ever*

[1] Gosden had been a member of the U.S. delegation to the inauguration of Mexican President Adolfo López Mateos in November (see no. 941).
[2] López Mateos would pay a four-day state visit to the United States in October (see no. 1068).
[3] Gosden, who had been in the hospital for a series of tests, would tell Eisenhower that his letter had given him "a terrific lift" (Gosden to Eisenhower, Mar. 6, 1959, same file as document).

1078   *EM, AWF, Name Series*

To Ralph Emerson McGill   *February 26, 1959*
Personal and confidential

Dear Ralph: I was truly interested in your letter of the twenty-third.[1] I agree with your observations about the Southern Senatorial group, except that I place Olin Johnston, Thurmond and Eastland in a special group.[2] These three, it seems to me, reflect a viewpoint that is not only extreme but rigid. They seem so entrenched in their prejudices and racial antagonisms that they never show so much as a glimmer of a readiness to see the other side of the problem.

I was particularly interested by your evaluation of Senator Talmadge.[3] With the equipment he has, it would be a pity if he allows it to be dissipated by a too great anxiety to be "right"—to pick the expression out of your letter.[4]

It occurs to me that, in these times, there are great opportunities for our abler Southern Senators and Congressmen to rise to real heights of statesmanship. With the party machine normally in pretty good order and confronted by no active, virile and growing opposition party, most of them can be fairly well assured of re-nominations and therefore need not worry too much about their political careers. Many people consider that Holland, Stennis, Fulbright and Talmadge have real ability.[5] If they should choose to use that ability with the single thought of promoting the *national* good, as their own study of the facts might reveal the nation's good, they could become outstanding figures on the national scene, and in history.

At least four others of the so-called Southern group are committed to partisan political ambitions, beyond redemption.

For the two Virginia Senators I have a very great liking, and, in many ways, great respect.[6] I think their attitudes toward race are far more flexible than are those of some of the others, even though they have felt forced to take leadership in intransigence. While they sometimes put revenues above obvious national need, it is such a great relief, these days, to find conservatives in spending that I cannot fault them seriously in this particular regard.

Political developments have given to the Democrats a great majority in both the Senate and the House.[7] I rather suspect that for the political leadership in these two Houses this is not an unmixed blessing because the Democrat Party is *not*, by any stretch of the imagination, unified insofar as adherence to common economic convictions and political aims makes a party. The Northern and Southern Democrats have a marriage of convenience and though there is a great deal of family fighting and even, in the election years, talk of a divorce, the matter goes no further than that when the prize of committee chairmanships remains so glittering and tempting.

As you know, the reason that I so earnestly support moderation in the race question is because I believe two things. The first of these is that until America has achieved reality in the concept of individual dignity and equality before the law, we will not have become completely worthy of our limitless opportunities. The second thing is that I believe that coercive law is, by itself, powerless to bring about complete compliance with its own terms when in any extensive region the great mass of public opinion is in bitter opposition. This generalization was true under the carpet-bagging government of the South, under the Prohibition Amendment and the Volstead Act,[8] and it is still largely true within the four states you name in the deep South.

But this second fact does not excuse us from using every kind of legitimate influence to bring about enlightenment through education, persuasion, leadership and, indeed, example. Of course, we cannot overlook the need for law, where law is clearly necessary and useful. Stated in another way, neither government—at any level—nor we, as individuals, can neglect our clear responsibilities and duties if we are to progress steadily, even if slowly, toward realization of what we like to call the American dream.

The legislative program I have placed before the Congress is a modest, but I believe, effective, one. Its enactment should be accomplished quickly. One of the finest results that I would anticipate would be a wider acceptance of the philosophy of progress through moderation. This might inspire extremists on both sides to gravitate a bit more toward the center line, which is the only path along which progress in great human affairs can be achieved.[9]

This letter is long but, as you see, your communication found me in much the same mood as you apparently were.

With warm regard, *Sincerely*

[1] *Atlanta Constitution* editor McGill had written on February 23 (AWF/N) regarding ongoing problems with desegregation in the South (for background see no. 879). At the end of January 1959, Georgia Senator Herman Eugene Talmadge and seven other Southern Senators had proposed a constitutional amendment giving states exclusive power to decide whether school systems should be integrated (*New York Times*, Jan. 28, 1959). McGill told Eisenhower that he need not be "too concerned about the confusing, often contradictory, actions of the senators from at least four states; namely Georgia, Mississippi, Alabama and South Carolina. Possibly Arkansas and Louisiana should be included, although not with the same emphasis."

[2] Eisenhower was referring to Democratic Senators Olin Dewitt Johnston, J. Strom Thurmond of South Carolina, and James Oliver Eastland of Mississippi.

[3] McGill had written that Talmadge had become, to Georgians, "THE Senator." McGill described Talmadge as "a very able, shrewd and hard-working man," who was "likable and has an unusually attractive personality when he wishes to make it so. He is dogmatic and usually speaks with what has been described as 'an air of finality.' Privately he knows the facts of life."

[4] McGill had contrasted Georgian Senator Richard B. Russell, who was "almost frantically trying to be 'right' on the racial question so as to have no opposition in the summer primary of 1960," with Talmadge, who had "about four and a half years before he must be 'right.'" Talmadge, therefore, could "take a most statesmanlike position and can assume one attitude in the Congress and another in his native state without any seeming contradiction to the people."

[5] Eisenhower was referring to Democratic Senators Spessard L. Holland of Florida, John Cornelius Stennis of Mississippi, and James William Fulbright of Arkansas.

[6] The Senators from Virginia were Harry Flood Byrd and A. Willis Robertson, both Democrats.
[7] See no. 926.
[8] The Volstead Act was enacted in 1919 to enforce the Eighteenth Amendment, which prohibited the manufacture and sale of alcoholic beverages.
[9] In addition to Eisenhower's February 5 request for a seven-point civil rights program (see no. 1048), the Senate was also considering legislation introduced by Senate majority leader Lyndon Johnson. The Johnson bill contained an anti-bombing provision, extended the life of the Civil Rights Commission, granted subpoena powers to the Justice Department when investigating voting rights cases, and established a Federal Community Relations Service to assist in the conciliation of segregation and integration disputes (see *Congressional Quarterly Almanac*, vol. XV, *1959*, pp. 291–94).

1079   *EM, AWF, Administration Series:*
                                                            Berlin Paper

MEMORANDUM FOR THE FILES   *February 27, 1959*
Top secret

I have directed the Acting Secretary of State to confer with Gordon Gray with a view of calling together a special meeting of the statutory members of the National Security Council and including the Acting Secretary of State and the Attorney General. The meeting will not be listed as a formal one of the Security Council.[1]

The purpose will be to review all of the measures and actions we propose to take in the event that the Soviets actually go through, on May 27th, with their threat to leave East Germany and decline thereafter to take any responsibility with respect to Berlin.

These steps have been fairly well thought out, but we must review them to see that our thinking is up-to-date with respect to them.[2] Moreover, and even more important, we need to go a step further and consider what action might be required in an emergency, in the event that during any period of excess tension either before or after the specified date there were brought about unexpected developments either through miscalculation or muddling.

It seems to me that a number of questions ought to be examined specifically, such as:

(*a*) What measures should we take to keep Congressional leaders informed of developments in the situation?

(*b*) What would be our logical reaction to any unforeseen crisis brought about by a Soviet statement that could take the form of an ultimatum.

(*c*) How could we be sure of the necessary support from Congress even though we might suddenly face a critical emergency and would be under a compulsion to act quickly so as to avoid any unnecessary damage to ourselves.

(d) How can we preserve, throughout, the necessary secrecy?

(e) Should we be taking any specific steps to warn the American people and the West of the potential gravity of the situation, but at the same time not unnecessarily alarming them?

(f) How do we keep coordination with our NATO allies, and more particularly, Britain, Germany and France?

In such a meeting innumerable other questions will arise. The big thing is that we do not neglect any point that deserves attention.

This paper will be kept in the secret files and must, for the moment, be known only to General Goodpaster and Major Eisenhower. Both of them will be required to read it, but will not have a copy of it.

General Goodpaster is charged with keeping in touch with Mr. Gray to determine when such a meeting could be held. Any questions that Mr. Gray has respecting time, personnel to be present, and subjects to be discussed should be brought to my attention.[3]

[1] For background on the Soviet proposals regarding Berlin see no. 1074; on Eisenhower's conversation with Acting Secretary Herter on this same day see Telephone conversation, Eisenhower and Herter, Feb. 27, 1959, Herter Papers, Telephone Conversations.

[2] On U.S. military contingency planning see Burr, "Avoiding the Slippery Slope," pp. 193, 199–200.

[3] Herter, Attorney General William P. Rogers, and the statutory members of the NSC would meet with Eisenhower immediately following the regular National Security Council meeting on March 5. The discussion involved the use of East German personnel to control access to Berlin and the possibility of referring the issue to the United Nations. West Germany, supported by the United States, had always recognized only Soviet control of access routes and feared that the substitution of East German for Soviet officials would be tantamount to recognition of the Communist regime by the West. The British, however, were reluctant to risk war over such a minor matter as East Germany's insistence on the right to stamp papers for convoys traveling to Berlin. Discussing the threat of a possible second Berlin blockade, Eisenhower said that the prospect "left him rather cold," because the city could be "choked off" within two weeks. The problem, the President told those assembled, "was how not to get hysterical." After a discussion of British Prime Minister Macmillan's forthcoming visit (see no. 1091) and the need to inform congressional leaders of the situation, Eisenhower agreed to meet with the minority and majority leaders of the House and Senate on the following day. He also approved a recommendation from General Lauris Norstad that the United States should maintain U.S. Army strength in Europe. When Eisenhower asked about plans to retain access rights to Berlin, Secretary Herter said that "we planned to keep moving until the other side shoots at us" (State, *Foreign Relations, 1958–1960*, vol. VIII, *Berlin Crisis 1958–1959*, pp. 419–25; see also John S. D. Eisenhower, *Strictly Personal*, pp. 222–23; on the meeting with congressional leaders see Eisenhower, *Waging Peace*, pp. 347–49; and John S. D. Eisenhower, Memorandum of Conference, Mar. 6, 1959, AWF/D). For developments see no. 1106; see also Goodpaster, Memorandum of Conference, May 15, 1959, AWF/D.

To Lyndon Baines Johnson   *February 27, 1959*
Personal

Dear Lyndon: Referring again to your letter of February seventeenth telling of your meeting with President Lopez Mateos last November, I find that my own impression of the new President confirms your favorable report.[1] Even though such visits as yours and mine can contribute importantly to good relations between this country and our southern neighbor, there is nothing which can take the place of effective day-to-day representation of U.S. interests by our Ambassador and his country team.[2]

President Lopez Mateos conveyed to me a sense of vigor and dynamism. Yet he seemed to be holding a tight rein on himself, and I can understand that he might still be feeling his way along, notwithstanding his long experience in public office. He is burdened by serious economic problems, almost none of which he is capable of solving within his own country because of the complexities of today's international trade. It would be helpful to our relations with Mexico, as well as in our own interest, to consult closely with Mexico on a number of our common problems.

I share with you the firm belief that we should develop the closest relationship with Mexico and that, in doing so, we shall be strengthening our relations with Latin America. President Lopez Mateos seems to recognize the historic role which Mexico can play in the hemisphere. I impressed upon him the need to maintain a favorable climate for investment, both foreign and domestic. He expressed agreement with me on this point.

I raised the question of the development of the Big Bend area as an international park.[3] He said that Mexico's studies of fifteen or sixteen years ago had indicated that a constitutional amendment would be required if they were to participate in this project, thus posing a delicate problem. We shall pursue this matter, nevertheless, through diplomatic channels, to see whether Mexico cannot be persuaded to take the steps necessary to join us in the park.

The President made no mention of the financial discussions which have been carried on by the officials of our governments for the last month or two. He did express appreciation for the cooperation which we have extended to Mexico in this broad sector in the past.[4]

As you will have learned by the time you receive this letter, I am looking forward to a return visit by President Lopez Mateos some time later in the spring. This will give us additional opportunity to develop the close personal ties which contribute so much to the building of good relations with our neighbors.[5]

With warm regard, *Sincerely*

[1] López Mateos was "a vital personality, seasoned in public life, vigorous in spirit and gifted with intellectual capacity and perceptiveness," Johnson had written. López Mateos's aim was to raise the living standards of the Mexican people through economic reform, placing Mexico in the lead among Latin American nations. Johnson's letter and the State Department draft of this response, with Eisenhower's handwritten emendations, are in the same file as this document; see also Calhoun to Goodpaster, Feb. 26, 1959, *ibid.*; and State, *Foreign Relations, 1958–1960*, vol. V, *American Republics*, pp. 847–52. For more on Eisenhower's Mexican visit see no. 1062.

[2] Robert C. Hill, former Under Secretary of State for Mutual Security Affairs and Assistant Secretary of State for Congressional Relations, had become U.S. Ambassador to Mexico in July 1957. The original State Department draft had included the following sentence, later deleted by Eisenhower: "My own impression of Ambassador Robert Hill and those of his staff who accompanied him to Acapulco confirms your favorable report."

[3] On the Big Bend area see no. 1062.

[4] López Mateos believed that Mexico had proven its government's stability, Johnson reported. "Hence, he seems to see it as desirable that foreign capital should be content with smaller profit spread over a longer period of years, rather than withdrawing profit rapidly as in less stable countries." For financial discussions between officials of the two countries see State, *Foreign Relations, 1958–1960*, vol. V, *American Republics*, pp. 847–49.

[5] The visit would be postponed until the fall (see no. 1068). For developments in Mexican-American relations see no. 1163.

1081

EM, WHCF,
Official File 124-A-1

TO FOSTER FURCOLO

February 27, 1959

Dear Governor Furcolo: I have your letter in which you request that I appoint a Commission to investigate the unemployment situation.[1]

My associates and I all have a profound and most sympathetic concern for those who are out of work. It was because of this that last year I recommended that Congress enact temporary legislation to provide supplementary unemployment compensation to those who had exhausted their benefits under the State law.[2] Our laws at present provide for a statutory body—the Federal Council on Employment Security consisting of representatives of employees, employers, and the public—to make the kinds of studies and recommendations you have in mind.[3] This Council considered the whole problem last fall, and its members have come up with differing recommendations that reflect virtually every point of view. All of these are presently under study within the Administration. Under these circumstances, I do not believe the appointment of another group to go over the same ground would be helpful.

I was glad to have your views on this question,[4] *Sincerely*

[1] Governor of Massachusetts since 1957, Furcolo (LL.B. Yale 1936) had also served as Democratic Congressman from Massachusetts from 1949–1951. He had written on February 12, 1959, regarding his concerns over "the current unemployment crisis," and the 142,000 jobless residents of his state. Since the 1957–1958 recession, U.S. unemployment figures for January and February 1959 had shown little recovery, matching the November 1958 level of over 6 percent. (On the recession see nos. 598 and 677.)

[2] For background on the Temporary Unemployment Compensation Act of 1958, which provided federal funds to states for the extension of unemployment benefits up to a maximum of fifty percent see *Congressional Quarterly Almanac*, vol. XIV, *1958*, pp. 153–56. See also nos. 598 and 633. Furcolo was concerned because the law was scheduled to end benefits on April 1, 1959. He expected more than 11,000 people would be dropped from the list of those receiving assistance in Massachusetts.

[3] The Federal Advisory Council on Employment Security, comprising representatives of labor, management, and the general public, was charged with advising the Secretary of Labor on unemployment compensation programs.

[4] General Goodpaster had sent Furcolo's letter to the Secretary of Labor for preparation of a draft reply, which had been completed on February 24. White House aide Gerald Morgan had also prepared a response to the Massachusetts governor. Eisenhower had incorporated portions of each draft in his letter (both drafts are in the same file as document).

On March 4, Furcolo would again request Eisenhower to extend the Temporary Unemployment Compensation Act beyond its April 1 deadline. Responding on March 14, Eisenhower would say that the program "was proposed and enacted as a temporary undertaking to meet an emergency need at a time when many state legislatures were not in session." Since most state legislatures were then in session, the President was reluctant to take "action that would invite the transformation of this temporary program into a permanent Federal program not in keeping with the long standing responsibilities of the states over the twenty-year history of the unemployment insurance program." On March 25, however, Congress would vote to extend the limit for collecting unemployment insurance by an additional three months (Furcolo to Eisenhower, Mar. 4, 1959, and Eisenhower to Furcolo, Mar. 14, 1959, *ibid.*; see also *Congressional Quarterly Almanac*, vol. XV, *1959*, pp. 219–21). For developments on the economy see no. 1204.

1082   *EM, WHCF, Official File 101-B-1*

To Richard King Mellon   *February 27, 1959*

Dear Dick: I owe you an apology which I hasten to make.

There has not been the slightest doubt in my mind, since our conversation on the point at Ligonier, as to the exact relationship between you and Paul Mellon. I can give no other explanation for my lapse in referring to him in my note of February seventeenth as your brother,

other than to say that in the press of work my tongue responded to a subconscious memory—back to the period when I had been under the impression that your relationship was that of brothers.[1]

The above is obviously more of an excuse than a reason. But at least I want to assure you that I know better than I spoke.

Please remember me kindly to your charming bride and, of course, warmest regard to yourself. *As ever*

[1] On September 26, 1958, the President had participated in the bicentennial celebration of Fort Ligonier, an historic landmark near Pittsburgh, Pennsylvania (see no. 866). Eisenhower had asked Richard Mellon if he thought his "brother Paul and his wife" would enjoy a State Dinner at the White House.

Richard Mellon had replied on February 24 that although he and Paul were first cousins, they were more like brothers because of shared interests in various corporations. Mellon also said that he was sure that the Paul Mellons would be pleased to accept an invitation to the White House. All correspondence is in the same file as the document. Mr. and Mrs. Paul Mellon would attend a White House dinner for the president of Ireland on March 17 (see President's daily appointments).

1083   *EM, WHCF, Official File 101-J*

To Bernard Mannes Baruch   *February 28, 1959*

Dear Bernie: I remember the statement to which you refer.[1] Arthur Krock was in the group and spoke to me later. He approved very heartily of what I had said.[2]

Later my remarks were taken out of context and distorted to imply that I was at heart a socialist; that I wanted to destroy free enterprise. Actually the statement was brought up again in its distorted form five years later, in the political campaign of '52. I merely laughed at people who were trying to make something of the matter, although I did time and again repeat what I had actually said.

I particularly like the last thing in your letter where you say that "When the politicians get through with any of us and they have tried to please everybody, we generally find ourselves in a mess."[3]

With warm personal regard, *As ever*

[1] Baruch had reminded Eisenhower of his remarks at a dinner on December 5, 1947, at the 1925 F Street Club in Washington. After dinner informal conversation had turned to the problem of inflation, and Eisenhower had said that industrialists should make some personal sacrifices in order to help keep costs down and stop inflation.
[2] On December 6, 1947, General Eisenhower had written to Krock, who was head of the *New York Times* Washington bureau (see Galambos, *Chief of Staff*, no. 1926).
[3] Baruch had been one of the President's informal political advisers for many years. In January 1946 he had warned Eisenhower to "Beware of the Politicos" (*ibid.*, no. 630).